WRITING THE WORLD

Reading and Writing
about Issues of the Day

WRITING
THE WORLD

READING AND WRITING ABOUT ISSUES OF THE DAY

CHARLES R. COOPER
SUSAN PECK MACDONALD

BEDFORD/ST. MARTIN'S

Boston ◆ New York

For Bedford/St. Martin's

Executive Editor: Marilyn Moller
Development Editors: John Elliott, Mark Gallaher, Talvi Laev, and Judith Voss
Senior Production Editor: Michael Weber
Senior Production Supervisor: Cheryl Mamaril
Marketing Manager: Brian Wheel
Art Director: Lucy Krikorian
Text and Cover Design: Anna George
Cover Art: Karl Petzke
Composition: Stratford Publishing Services, Inc.
Printing and Binding: R.R. Donnelley & Sons Company

President: Charles H. Christensen
Editorial Director: Joan E. Feinberg
Editor in Chief: Nancy Perry
Director of Editing, Design, and Production: Marcia Cohen
Managing Editor: Erica T. Appel

Library of Congress Catalog Card Number: 99-65525

Manufactured in the United States of America.

5   4   3   2   1   0
f   e   d   c   b   a

For information, write: Bedford/St. Martin's, 75 Arlington Street, Boston, MA 02116   (617-399-4000)

ISBN: 0-312-11159-2

Acknowledgments

Text

Elijah Anderson. "The Code of the Streets." Originally in *The Atlantic Monthly* 273. No. 5 (May 1994). Copyright © 1994 by Elijah Anderson. Reprinted with the permission of the author and W. W. Norton & Company, Inc.

Elizabeth Bird. "For Enquiring Minds." From *For Enquiring Minds: A Cultural Study of Supermarket Tabloids* by S. Elizabeth Bird, 1992, pp. 204–209. Reprinted by permission of The University of Tennessee Press.

(Acknowledgments and copyrights are continued at the back of the book on pages 738–41, which constitute an extension of the copyright page. It is a violation of the law to reproduce these selections by any means whatsoever without the written permission of the copyright holder.)

Preface

Writing the World is a new reader and writing guide that will prepare students to join the conversations about some important issues of the day. It offers seventy-seven current, provocative readings that will engage students' interest, along with extensive writing guidance to help them enter the conversations about these issues themselves—to write the world, if you will. Reading the texts on these pages and writing their own essays in familiar public and academic genres, students will begin to practice the essential strategies of informed, reasoned civic literacy.

This book grew out of a first-year core course on American culture at the University of California at San Diego. This course called upon students to confront important social and political issues, and we saw that writing enabled them to grapple with issues deeply. We discovered that with direction and support, students could speak and write authoritatively about complex issues. We found in particular that they did their best thinking and learning when we offered them not one way of thinking about an issue but several ways. When we respected their experience and intelligence, they nearly always wrote well beyond anything they had attempted before. They welcomed our attempts to bring together the worlds of their experience with the worlds of social conflict, political posssibilities, and civic life. With confidence, they became readers and writers of the world.

Writing the World aims to meet two large goals:

- to offer lively, challenging readings on some important issues of the day
- to provide reading and writing instruction that will enable students to enter the conversations about these issues, helping them understand the various viewpoints and then to articulate views of their own

Compelling Readings on Important Issues of the Day

By offering provocative, real-world readings about several complex issues—campus speech regulations, violence among young men, and tabloid TV, to name a few—we hope to get students thinking about some important matters of the day.

Seventy-Seven Widely Varied, Highly Engaging Readings.   Information comes to us in many forms and genres, and students must learn to comprehend, draw from, and produce different types of texts themselves. Readings in this book represent many genres—newspaper and magazine articles, cartoons, personal narratives, court cases, even campus speech regulations. From Mari Matsuda's speech arguing for campus speech regulations to Todd Gitlin's magazine article challenging the widely held view that TV violence causes violent behavior among young men to William Julius Wilson's assessment of the effects of poverty from his book *When Work Disappears*, these are readings that should engage students.

A Balance of Opinions and Perspectives.   Readings reflect many varied opinions and perspectives. Research suggests that students are most likely to take interest in unfamiliar issues when they are presented with a range of viewpoints. We believe as well that students are most likely to rethink or at least complicate their own views when they find them both represented and challenged—and when they must argue against other views as well as in support of their own. Readings in this book present many varied opinions and perspectives, reflecting real public conversations about real issues.

A Look at Race, Class, and Gender in Meaningful Contexts.   We consider issues of diversity in the context of other issues, rather than as isolated topics. Instead of considering these issues in chapters on "race" or "class" or "gender," we put them in more meaningful contexts—looking at the possible causes of violence among young men, for instance, or at the way men and women communicate in relationships.

Extensive, Class-tested Writing Instruction

To prepare students to understand the issues and then to put forth ideas of their own, we provide practice in close reading and guides to writing, helping students make the important move from reading to writing.

Each Chapter Focuses on One Issue and Teaches One Kind of Discourse for Writing about That Issue.   Chapter 2, for example, teaches students to *report information* by explaining what advice self-help books give about communicating in relationships. The kind of writing taught in this book poses challenges very much like those that all college and professional writers face when they must write on assigned topics. Students are usually required to address clear questions, to be aware of particular arguments and counterarguments, or to synthesize material from multiple sources. We believe the first-year writing course is the place for students to begin confronting such challenges. *Writing the World* thus invites them to move from reading to writing in different ways for different purposes, incrementally constructing meaning from the readings, both to understand an issue and write about it.

We believe that the clear expectations created by question-centered assignments not only resemble the sort of expectations common to many academic and professional writing situations but also enable students to write with authority and purpose. Our own experience with loosely defined essay topics (e.g., family, gender, the environment, popular culture), is that students may never articulate a clear question and, as a result, all too often flounder in their writing. By beginning with a clear purpose and focus, they are better able to choose wisely from the diverse sources we offer them for each assignment. Since each of our questions calls up a genre, we give students the theoretical advantage more experienced writers enjoy when a clearly defined purpose and audience helps them shape their writing.

Question-centered assignments, together with the carefully chosen readings, offer students sufficient material and focus to enter deeply into the assignment: considering competing accounts, discovering what they themselves would say, and choosing supporting material that suits their own purposes.

Reading and Writing Activities Help Students Progress to Writing an Essay.   Students using this book need not be experts, at home with an issue from the first reading or able to choose a stance immediately. We have designed each chapter to help them *progress*—from knowing relatively little about an issue to having a lot to say and even being able to choose from various rhetorical options. This progress is supported by the sequence of readings as well as by the reading and writing tasks in the "writer's notebook" feature.

These activities help students understand challenging issues gradually, from writing a few sentences or making a list, to rereading part of a reading, to writing briefly about their own firsthand observations. Most important, the writer's notebook tasks are designed to help students understand the issue at hand and prepare to articulate their own ideas in a guided conceptual and rhetorical framework. Typical writer's notebook tasks ask students to use an argument in one reading to interpret an incident in another, or to summarize one key part of an argument and explain its importance to the whole argument. As such, they provide practice in key reading strategies like summarizing, listing, and applying one text to another. (Appendix 1 provides instruction in the strategies of close reading and critical thinking: previewing, annotating, outlining, summarizing, synthesizing, and evaluating an argument.)

Writing Guides Lead Students through the Steps of Composing an Essay.
This book offers students comprehensive support planning, drafting, and
revising, helping them consider the rhetorical situation, the particular issue
and genre, and the available materials.

The "Writer's Guide" in the second half of each chapter takes students step
by step, helping them select materials, prepare a prospectus, organize their
drafts (considering genre features), and revise.

Each chapter also offers a section on sentence strategies that are especially
useful for that chapter's assignments—ways to use lists when reporting (Chapter 2), for instance, or to use conjunctive adverbs for indicating causal relationships (Chapter 3).

Attention to the Use of Personal Experience.   Each writing assignment presents opportunities for students to draw on their own personal experience—and
provides guidance for doing so appropriately. Observing men and women in
conversation (Chapter 2), recalling an incident in which their own civil rights
were violated (Chapter 4), or interviewing their parents about their work histories (Chapter 7), students will connect the issues in this book to their own
lives—and, most important, see how they can use their own experience as support for their writing.

Guidance Working with Sources.   Since students will rely on published
sources for ideas and for support in their arguments, they must cite sources. We
teach two ways to cite sources: informal and formal. We offer informal citation—naming the author and source in the sentences of the essay—because it is
widely practiced in newspapers, magazines, and trade books and also because it
permits teachers, if they wish, to wait until the third or fourth essay to introduce
students to the formal citation styles of the Modern Language Association or
American Psychological Association (both covered in Appendix 2).

And if students want to find more sources on an issue than those found in
this book, they can consult the section at the end of each chapter on gathering
current information. More than a list of sources, this section offers specific
Library of Congress subject headings and World Wide Web sites—as well as
specific strategies for locating other useful sources.

Additional Writing Projects Offer More Ways of Writing about an Issue.
Each chapter includes several additional writing projects, enabling students to
write about that chapter's topic in several other genres. The chapter on tabloid
TV, for instance, includes a project analyzing a different television genre,
whereas the chapter on hate speech offers assignments reporting on the
debate or proposing a solution. Each chapter includes an assignment that
invites students to write an essay based on their own personal experience.

The readings and instructional materials in *Writing the World* have been taught
and class-tested at twenty colleges and universities across the United States.

We have seen how our own students learned to think about important issues, to understand and question arguments from many perspectives, and (most important of all) to offer well-reasoned arguments of their own. We hope that this book will help many more students to do the same—to add their voices, to offer their opinions, to write their worlds.

Acknowledgments

We gratefully acknowledge the assistance of many people. We thank the many teachers who reviewed the many drafts: Linda Adler-Kassner, University of Minnesota; Bonne August, Kingsborough Community College, CUNY; Richard Batteiger, Oklahoma State University; Susan N. Bernstein, Shippensburg University; Richard Boyd, San Diego State University; Richard Bullock, Wright State University; Don Bushman, University of North Carolina at Wilmington; Cheryl Clark, Miami-Dade Community College–Wolfson Campus; Lynda Corbin, San Diego Mesa College; Robert Corrigan, Baltimore City Community College; Linda Daigle, Houston Community College; Steve Dilks, University of North Dakota; Diane Dowdey, Sam Houston State University; Rhonda Eakins, Indian Hills Community College; Hugh English, Rutgers University; Gail Gordon, Hunter College; Susan Green, University of Oklahoma; Paul Heilker, Virginia Tech; Will Hochman, University of Southern Colorado; Sue Ellen Holbrook, Southern Connecticut State University; Marsha Lee Holmes, Western Carolina University; Pam Kennedy-Cross, Stockton College; Margaret Lindgren, University of Cincinnati; Erik Lunde, Michigan State University; Michael Mackey, Community College of Denver; Nancy McKoski, University of Kentucky; Mark Miller, Pikes Peak Community College; Robert Mundhenk, Northampton Community College; Marshall Myers, Eastern Kentucky University; Scott Odom, Loyola Marymount University; Carole Clark Papper, Ball State University; William Powell, Lane Community College; Daniel Royer, Grand Valley State University; Stephen Ruffus, Salt Lake Community College; John Ruszkiewicz, University of Texas at Austin; Julie Segedy, Chabot College; Brad Siebert, Washburn University of Topeka; Phillip Sipiora, University of South Florida; Carolyn Smith, University of Florida; David Sonstroem, University of Connecticut; Sheryl Stevenson, University of Akron; Frank Walters, Auburn University; Alison Warriner, California State University, Hayward; Irwin Weiser, Purdue University; Lizabeth Wilson; Rosemary Winslow, The Catholic University of America; Linda Woodson, University of Texas at San Antonio; and Dede Yow, Kennesaw State University.

We thank the teachers who class-tested early versions of some of the chapters: Mary Ellen Alea, University of Wisconsin–Eau Claire; Lori Amy, University of Florida; Eva Bednarowicz, University of Illinois, Chicago; Bonnie Brinkman, Long Beach City College; David Chevalier, Weber State University; Jennifer Courtney, University of Illinois, Urbana; John Hagerty, University of California at Santa Barbara; Johnny Johnston, California State University, Long Beach; Richard Joines, University of Florida; Amy Joyce, University of

Illinois, Chicago; Barbara McCleary, Central Connecticut State University; Elizabeth Rhoades, University of Akron; Mark Roberts, California Polytechnic State University; Linda Schuppener, Kirkwood Community College; Cary Ser, Miami-Dade Community College; Wendy Smith, San Diego State University; Martha Thomas, University of South Carolina–Columbia; Alison Warriner, California State University, Hayward; and George Yatchisin, University of California at Santa Barbara.

We are grateful to those instructors who responded to a survey about the assignments in this book: Laura J. Adamson, Stephen F. Austin State University; Mary Ellen Alea, University of Wisconsin–Eau Claire; Paul Beauvais, The University of Findlay; Marvin A. Bell, Kirkwood Community College; Todd W. Berseley, California State University, Northridge; Bruce Boeckel, Northwestern College; Hansel Burley, McLennan Community College; David V. Chevalier, Weber State University; Michael S. Connell, Kirkwood Community College; Helen Dale; Susan Farrell, College of Charleston; Roger G. Fink, University of Southern California; Ann Forrester, Community College of Philadelphia; Pauline Harding, Hawkeye Community College; Marie C. Hennedy, Providence College; Kathleen M. Herndon, Weber State University; Michael Hriciti, Westmoreland County Community College; Carol A. Jensen, Barstow College; Johnny Johnston, California State University, Long Beach; Martin Lara, Coconino County Community College; Martin McKoski, University of Akron; Richard A. Milum, Ohio State University–Lima; Barbara McCleary, Central Connecticut State University; Mary Natal, Coconino Community College; Jeanne Purdy, University of Minnesota, Morris; Donald Rhoads, Elizabethtown College; Fredric Rissover, St. Louis Community College; Chris Roberts, Clark State Community College; Susan Roberts, University of Connecticut, Hartford; Ottilia Scherschel, Chapman University; Kriston Sites, Indiana University; Roberta Silverman, California State University, Dominguez Hills; Lane Stiles, University of Minnesota; Deborah Vause, The College of West Virginia; Gwendolyn Hope Wilkinson, University of Texas at San Antonio; Dr. Charles Wukasch, Austin Community College and the University of Texas at San Antonio.

Charles Cooper thanks in particular the faculty and graduate-student teaching assistants in the Dimensions of Culture Program at Marshall College, University of California at San Diego for continuing his own education in American history and culture. He also thanks students in his writing courses at UCSD and the University of Nevada, Reno, for their enthusiasm for the assignments in this book and their many ideas for improving them. He dedicates this book to his three children: Vince, who composes music and plays guitar professionally; Laura, who makes art in various media, designs gardens, and teaches at the Art Center College of Design in Pasadena; and Susanna, who writes editorials and occasional feature articles as associate editor at the Sacramento *Bee*.

Susan Peck MacDonald thanks her former students and colleagues at the University of California at San Diego and Irvine for their many stimulating insights into current thinking in the humanities and social sciences. She also thanks her former English 100 students at Irvine Valley College, who tried out early versions of these chapters, and her students at California State University, Long Beach, who are using the final version as this book goes to press. Finally, she would like to thank her two sons, Josh and Geoff, who have kept her in touch with the way young people today think, read, and compute.

Charles R. Cooper
Susan Peck MacDonald

Contents

4   EVALUATING CIVIC STANCES   223
Conservatism? Liberalism? Libertarianism?

A LOOK AHEAD: Evaluating a Civic Stance   224

READINGS   225

7   SPECULATING ABOUT THE FUTURE   533
What Does a Restructured Economy Mean for Your Generation?

WRITING THE WORLD

Reading and Writing
about Issues of the Day

1

INTRODUCTION

■ ■ ■

Writing the World aims to help you join in some of the important current conversations of the day. You will find here readings on several important issues in the United States, readings reflecting a wide variety of perspectives—conservative, liberal, libertarian, and more. In each chapter, you will have the opportunity to write about one issue—and to do so with conviction, clarity, and a well-informed sense of what is at issue.

What does it mean to "write the world"? It means entering the conversation, finding out what others think, figuring out what you think, and gaining a deeper understanding of the world you live in. One of the best ways of coming to terms with important issues is by writing about them. As you work your way through this book, you will find brief writing assignments as well as full-length essay assignments, all of which will get you thinking about issues and entering ongoing debates. The challenges you meet in reading and writing about each issue will prepare you for the writing you will do in all your college courses—and also for the conversations you will have as a citizen of the world.

Writing the World invites you to take part in public discussions about each of the following issues:

- what self-help books say about communicating in relationships
- whether it is constitutional—or even feasible—to try to regulate offensive speech
- why so many young men commit violence
- how tabloid TV represents social life in America
- which civic stance seems preferable to you

- how new features of today's economy—the widening income gap between rich and poor, the increase in two-earner families, lower pay and reduced benefits—will affect you and your generation

The cover of this book features an image of coffee cups, symbols of conversations with friends as well as of solitary moments of reflection or work. Discussing issues of the day over a cup of coffee or tea or something else has a long tradition, from the cafés in Paris and Vienna to the teahouses in Samarkand to the coffeehouses in San Francisco to the coffee machine in every office and dorm. As companions to our daily conversations and work, coffee cups symbolize the many ways we interact with others as we think and read and talk—and write.

HOW THIS BOOK WORKS

Each chapter of *Writing the World* has two main parts: readings, which introduce an important issue, and a "Writer's Guide," designed to help you plan and write an essay about that issue.

Readings

The readings introduce and discuss an issue and can serve as sources for your own writing about that issue. Each reading includes a note about the author(s) and other background information.

A Writer's Notebook

Interspersed with the readings are suggestions to help you understand a reading more fully, reread key parts of it critically, evaluate it, connect one reading to another, bring your own experience to bear on an issue, or react in some other way. Working on these "writer's notebook" tasks will further your understanding of each issue and develop useful material for the essay you yourself will write about it later.

The Writer's Guides

Each chapter includes a guide that can help you plan, draft, and revise an essay, and then reflect on what you have learned.

Each guide opens with detailed advice about *planning* your essay: establishing your purpose, considering your readers, selecting material from the readings or the work you did in your writer's notebook, trying out a tentative essay plan by drafting a prospectus, organizing the essay, and developing your argument.

Then come guidelines for *evaluating and revising* an essay draft, your own or someone else's, and *editing and proofreading*.

Of special note are illustrations of two or three kinds of sentences especially useful for this kind of essay writing to keep readers on track, integrate source materials smoothly into an essay, and achieve other goals.

Each Writer's Guide ends with a section on ways of reflecting on what you have learned. Research on learning shows that if you reflect on challenging tasks once you complete them, you will remember longer what you have learned and make better use of your learning in later completing similar tasks. This section gives guidelines for you to reflect on the subject and kind of writing you have just worked on, as well as to review what you learned, how your ideas may have changed, and what problems you have solved in constructing your essay.

At the end of each chapter is a section to help you find *very recent or current information* to update or supplement the readings in the chapter.

Additional Writing Projects

Each chapter closes with several additional writing projects on the chapter's subject. These additional projects allow you to use the same readings but to do different kinds of writing—personal narratives, arguments, reports—from the main assignment of the chapter.

Helpful Appendices

Finally, two appendices offer further help. Appendix 1 illustrates six strategies for reading critically: *previewing, annotating, outlining, summarizing, synthesizing,* and *evaluating.* Some writer's notebook tasks require one or another of these strategies, so consult Appendix 1 to find out how to proceed.

Appendix 2 offers step-by-step help researching issues—from deciding what types of sources you need to searching for and evaluating sources to documenting sources using MLA style or APA style.

Clearly, it is no small task to write the world. It means paying real attention to important issues, taking the time to learn about them, thinking hard about what *you* think about them (and why). One of the best ways to figure out what you think—and to say what you think—is by writing. Here's where this book can help. So get yourself a cup of coffee (or tea or soda or water—your choice), and sharpen a few pencils or start up your computer. This book will challenge you, and help you, to write the world.

What Do Self-Help Books

Say about Communicating?

2

REPORTING INFORMATION

The complaint most often voiced by women about the men with whom they are intimate is "He doesn't talk to me"—and the second most frequent is "He doesn't listen to me."

> –DEBORAH TANNEN, " 'Put Down That Paper
> and Talk to Me!' Rapport-Talk
> and Report-Talk"

Women get burned not only when they unknowingly invade a man's introspective time but also when they misinterpret his expressions.

> –JOHN GRAY, "Men Are from Mars,
> Women Are from Venus"

All the important communication tools can be reduced to five basic skills. They are free, non-fattening, and legal.

> –SUSAN PAGE, "Essential Traits
> of Couples Who Thrive"

If you are worried about the future of your marriage you have plenty of company. . . . Two out of every three new couples are headed for divorce—unless something changes.

> –JOHN GOTTMAN, "The Two Marriages:
> His and Hers"

$\mathbf{I}$f you have ever felt that a spouse or a romantic partner was not really listening to you—or not completely understanding you—you are not alone. Millions of people are concerned about communication in close relationships, and particularly communication between men and women. Countless jokes and sitcom plots center on men wondering "What do women want?" and women feeling mystified by men, and comic strips routinely offer examples of people failing to understand each other. But the spate of recent best-sellers such as John Gray's *Men Are from Mars, Women Are from Venus* and Deborah Tannen's *You Just Don't Understand* suggest that many of us today want to get beyond the jokes to discover why communication can be so difficult. Many of these "self-help" books are intended to help married couples communicate better, but the enormous popularity of books on relationships in general suggests that people outside of marriages—those who are divorced, dating, hoping for a long-term relationship, or merely trying to get along with colleagues—care about improving their communication skills.

A LOOK AHEAD: REPORTING ON ADVICE   This chapter includes an essay assignment asking you to report on some of the advice given in current self-help books about how to improve communication in personal relationships. This kind of report is a common and important kind of writing. As a student you will often be called on to read a variety of reports about a topic and then summarize the information contained in them. Such reports are also important beyond the university. A city planner or an environmental planner, for instance, might write a report that summarizes research in order to provide information for decision makers. A technical writer might write a report for an agricultural magazine, while a sports writer might report on a recent increase in head injuries during football games. In all such reports, the writer's goal is to convey information in a clear and straightforward way for readers looking for information.

In this essay, you will need to concentrate on the valuable—though deceptively complex—skill of reporting accurately. You need not speculate about *why* gender differences occur, take sides with either men or women, or find fault with any particular communication style.[1] Instead, your task is to *report* what various researchers and counselors claim to have learned about effective communication.

To report on others' research or conclusions, you may have to complete some of the following tasks:

- classify and organize the information
- define key terms and use them consistently
- clarify information readers may not already be familiar with

---

[1] The term *sex* is generally used to refer to one's biological maleness or femaleness; *gender*, on the other hand, generally refers to behavioral or cultural attributes that may change over time and from place to place. Just as men's and women's clothes have changed in the past hundred years, so have their ways of talking. Possible differences in the ways men and women communicate are considered *gender* differences.

- summarize accurately what each writer has to say on the topic
- attribute ideas to their authors
- note, though perhaps only briefly, significant criticism of ideas you report on

At the end of each set of readings are some suggestions for keeping a writer's notebook. They are designed to help you organize important information in each report so that you will be better able to decide how to use the information in your own report. You might want to look ahead to these writer's notebook tasks before you begin reading.

COMMUNICATING IN RELATIONSHIPS

The readings in this chapter report on advice from linguists[2] and psychologists about how to talk and listen in ways that strengthen personal relationships. These particular readings concentrate on couples—usually married couples—but the same talking and listening skills are important to all relationships. We convey our feelings through talk, expressing affection, stating interest, arguing opinions, taking care of our daily business, strengthening social ties, pursuing personal goals. We make assumptions about other people's feelings partly by listening to and interpreting the ways they talk. Sometimes we *mis*understand others because of how they talk or how we listen. In other words, talking and listening matter deeply.

"PUT DOWN THAT PAPER AND TALK TO ME!" RAPPORT-TALK AND REPORT-TALK

Deborah Tannen

Deborah Tannen is a linguistics professor at Georgetown University, known for several best-selling books about language and communication. These include You Just Don't Understand: Women and Men in Conversation *(1991), from which this reading comes,* Gender and Discourse *(1994),* Talking from 9 to 5: Women and Men in the Workplace *(1995), and* The Argument Culture: Moving from Debate to Dialogue *(1998).*

Tannen's work on language fits into a strand of research that has its roots in the 1970s, when a group of researchers began to study the actual back-and-forth exchanges that occur when people talk to one another. These researchers found that ordinary conversation is full of elaborate, unspoken rules. They began to describe talk as performing the work *of getting along with others, accomplishing tasks, gaining others' cooperation, conveying information, or even creating an image of one's self. Around the same time, a second group of researchers—influenced by the rise of feminism—turned to conversation analysis as a way of examining whether women talk differently from men.*

Debates have since developed over whether men and women actually do talk differently and, if so, what causes these differences. Tannen believes that men and

---

[2]*Linguists* are researchers who study human speech and language, including structure, sound, meaning, patterns of communication, and the cultural place of language in human behavior.

women talk differently because they are raised in something like two different cultures: a male culture from which young men learn to speak like men and a female culture in which young women learn to speak like women. Not everyone accepts Tannen's theories, but the general public has shown great interest in what she has to say.

As you read, pay attention to what Tannen means by "rapport-talk" and "report-talk"—where each occurs, who characteristically uses each type of talk, and how, according to Tannen, the two kinds of talk lead to miscommunication.

I was sitting in a suburban living room, speaking to a women's group that had invited men to join them for the occasion of my talk about communication between women and men. During the discussion, one man was particularly talkative, full of lengthy comments and explanations. When I made the observation that women often complain that their husbands don't talk to them enough, this man volunteered that he heartily agreed. He gestured toward his wife, who had sat silently beside him on the couch throughout the evening, and said, "She's the talker in our family."

Everyone in the room burst into laughter. The man looked puzzled and hurt. "It's true," he explained. "When I come home from work, I usually have nothing to say, but she never runs out. If it weren't for her, we'd spend the whole evening in silence." Another woman expressed a similar paradox about her husband: "When we go out, he's the life of the party. If I happen to be in another room, I can always hear his voice above the others. But when we're home, he doesn't have that much to say. I do most of the talking."

Who talks more, women or men? According to the stereotype, women talk too much. Linguist Jennifer Coates notes some proverbs:

A woman's tongue wags like a lamb's tail.
Foxes are all tail and women are all tongue.
The North Sea will sooner be found wanting in water than a woman be at
    a loss for a word.

Throughout history, women have been punished for talking too much or in the wrong way. Linguist Connie Eble lists a variety of physical punishments used in Colonial America: Women were strapped to ducking stools and held underwater until they nearly drowned, put into the stocks with signs pinned to them, gagged, and silenced by a cleft stick applied to their tongues.

Though such institutionalized corporal punishments have given way to informal, often psychological ones, modern stereotypes are not much different from those expressed in the old proverbs. Women are believed to talk too much. Yet study after study finds that it is men who talk more—at meetings, in mixed-group discussions, and in classrooms where girls or young women sit next to boys or young men. For example, communications researchers Barbara and Gene Eakins tape-recorded and studied seven university faculty meetings.

They found that, with one exception, men spoke more often and, without exception, spoke for a longer time. The men's turns ranged from 10.66 to 17.07 seconds, while the women's turns ranged from 3 to 10 seconds. In other words, the women's longest turns were still shorter than the men's shortest turns.

When a public lecture is followed by questions from the floor, or a talk show host opens the phones, the first voice to be heard asking a question is almost always a man's. And when they ask questions or offer comments from the audience, men tend to talk longer. Linguist Marjorie Swacker recorded question-and-answer sessions at academic conferences. Women were highly visible as speakers at the conferences studied; they presented 40.7 percent of the papers at the conferences studied and made up 42 percent of the audiences. But when it came to volunteering and being called on to ask questions, women contributed only 27.4 percent. Furthermore, the women's questions, on the average, took less than half as much time as the men's. (The mean was 23.1 seconds for women, 52.7 for men.) This happened, Swacker shows, because men (but not women) tended to preface their questions with statements, ask more than one question, and follow up the speaker's answer with another question or comment....

RAPPORT-TALK AND REPORT-TALK

Who talks more, then, women or men? The seemingly contradictory evidence is reconciled by the difference between what I call *public* and *private speaking*. More men feel comfortable doing "public speaking," while more women feel comfortable doing "private" speaking. Another way of capturing these differences is by using the terms *report-talk* and *rapport-talk*.

For most women, the language of conversation is primarily a language of rapport: a way of establishing connections and negotiating relationships. Emphasis is placed on displaying similarities and matching experiences. From childhood, girls criticize peers who try to stand out or appear better than others. People feel their closest connections at home, or in settings where they *feel* at home—with one or a few people they feel close to and comfortable with—in other words, during private speaking. But even the most public situations can be approached like private speaking.

For most men, talk is primarily a means to preserve independence and negotiate and maintain status in a hierarchical° social order. This is done by exhibiting knowledge and skill, and by holding center stage through verbal performance such as storytelling, joking, or imparting information. From childhood, men learn to use talking as a way to get and keep attention. So they are more comfortable speaking in larger groups made up of people they know less well—in the broadest sense, "public speaking." But even the most private situations can be approached like public speaking, more like giving a report than establishing rapport.

°**hierarchical:** A social order in which some people have higher rank or greater importance than others.

PRIVATE SPEAKING: THE WORDY WOMAN AND THE MUTE MAN

What is the source of the stereotype that women talk a lot? Dale Spender suggests that most people feel instinctively (if not consciously) that women, like children, should be seen and not heard, so any amount of talk from them seems like too much. Studies have shown that if women and men talk equally in a group, people think the women talked more. So there is truth to Spender's view. But another explanation is that men think women talk a lot because they hear women talking in situations where men would not: on the telephone; or in social situations with friends, when they are not discussing topics that men find inherently interesting; or, like the couple at the women's group, at home alone—in other words, in private speaking.

Home is the setting for an American icon° that features the silent man and 10 the talkative woman. And this icon, which grows out of the different goals and habits I have been describing, explains why the complaint most often voiced by women about the men with whom they are intimate is "He doesn't talk to me"—and the second most frequent is "He doesn't listen to me."

A woman who wrote to Ann Landers is typical:

> My husband never speaks to me when he comes home from work. When I ask, "How did everything go today?" he says, "Rough..." or "It's a jungle out there." (We live in Jersey and he works in New York City.)
>
> It's a different story when we have guests or go visiting. Paul is the gabbiest guy in the crowd—a real spellbinder. He comes up with the most interesting stories. People hang on every word. I think to myself, "Why doesn't he ever tell *me* these things?"
>
> This has been going on for 38 years. Paul started to go quiet on me after 10 years of marriage. I could never figure out why. Can you solve the mystery?
>
> —THE INVISIBLE WOMAN

Ann Landers suggests that the husband may not want to talk because he is tired when he comes home from work. Yet women who work come home tired too, and they are nonetheless eager to tell their partners or friends everything that happened to them during the day and what these fleeting, daily dramas made them think and feel.

Sources as lofty as studies conducted by psychologists, as down to earth as letters written to advice columnists, and as sophisticated as movies and plays come up with the same insight: Men's silence at home is a disappointment to women. Again and again, women complain, "He seems to have everything to say to everyone else, and nothing to say to me."...

If individual people or particular relationships were to blame, there wouldn't be so many different people having the same problems. The real problem is conversational style. Women and men have different ways of talking. Even with the

---

°**icon:** Symbol.

best intentions, trying to settle the problem through talk can only make things worse if it is ways of talking that are causing trouble in the first place.

BEST FRIENDS

Once again, the seeds of women's and men's styles are sown in the ways they learn to use language while growing up. In our culture, most people, but especially women, look to their closest relationships as havens in a hostile world. The center of a little girl's social life is her best friend. Girls' friendships are made and maintained by telling secrets. For grown women too, the essence of friendship is talk, telling each other what they're thinking and feeling, and what happened that day: who was at the bus stop, who called, what they said, how that made them feel. When asked who their best friends are, most women name other women they talk to regularly. When asked the same question, most men will say it's their wives. After that, many men name other men with whom they do things such as play tennis or baseball (but never just sit and talk) or a chum from high school whom they haven't spoken to in a year. . . .

Men and women often have very different ideas of what's important—and at 15 what point "important" topics should be raised. A woman told me, with lingering incredulity, of a conversation with her boyfriend. Knowing he had seen his friend Oliver, she asked, "What's new with Oliver?" He replied, "Nothing." But later in the conversation it came out that Oliver and his girlfriend had decided to get married. "That's nothing?" the woman gasped in frustration and disbelief.

For men, "Nothing" may be a ritual response at the start of a conversation. A college woman missed her brother but rarely called him because she found it difficult to get talk going. A typical conversation began with her asking, "What's up with you?" and his replying, "Nothing." Hearing his "Nothing" as meaning "There is nothing personal I want to talk about," she supplied talk by filling him in on her news and eventually hung up in frustration. But when she thought back, she remembered that later in the conversation he had mumbled, "Christie and I got into another fight." This came so late and so low that she didn't pick up on it. And he was probably equally frustrated that she didn't.

Many men honestly do not know what women want, and women honestly do not know why men find what they want so hard to comprehend and deliver.

"TALK TO ME!"

Women's dissatisfaction with men's silence at home is captured in the stock cartoon setting of a breakfast table at which a husband and wife are sitting: He's reading a newspaper; she's glaring at the back of the newspaper. In a Dagwood strip, Blondie complains, "Every morning all he sees is the newspaper! I'll bet you don't even know I'm here!" Dagwood reassures her, "Of course I know you're here. You're my wonderful wife and I love you very much." With this, he unseeingly pats the paw of the family dog, which the wife has put in her place before leaving the room. The cartoon strip shows that Blondie is justified in feeling like the woman who wrote to Ann Landers: invisible.

Another cartoon shows a husband opening a newspaper and asking his wife, "Is there anything you would like to say to me before I begin reading the news-paper?" The reader knows that there isn't — but that as soon as he begins read-ing the paper, she will think of something. The cartoon highlights the difference in what women and men think talk is for: To him, talk is for informa-tion. So when his wife interrupts his reading, it must be to inform him of some-thing that he needs to know. This being the case, she might as well tell him what she thinks he needs to know before he starts reading. But to her, talk is for interaction. Telling things is a way to show involvement, and listening is a way to show interest and caring. It is not an odd coincidence that she always thinks of things to tell him when he is reading. She feels the need for verbal interac-tion most keenly when he is (unaccountably, from her point of view) buried in the newspaper instead of talking to her.

Yet another cartoon shows a wedding cake that has, on top, in place of the 20 plastic statues of bride and groom in tuxedo and gown, a breakfast scene in which an unshaven husband reads a newspaper across the table from his dis-gruntled wife. The cartoon reflects the enormous gulf between the romantic expectations of marriage represented by the plastic couple in traditional wed-ding costume, and the often disappointing reality represented by the two sides of the newspaper at the breakfast table — the front, which he is reading, and the back, at which she is glaring.

These cartoons, and many others on the same theme, are funny because people recognize their own experience in them. What's not funny is that many women are deeply hurt when men don't talk to them at home, and many men are deeply frustrated by feeling they have disappointed their partners, without understanding how they failed or how else they could have behaved.

Some men are further frustrated because, as one put it, "When in the world am I supposed to read the morning paper?" If many women are incredulous that many men do not exchange personal information with their friends, this man is incredulous that many women do not bother to read the morning paper. To him, reading the paper is an essential part of his morning ritual, and his whole day is awry if he doesn't get to read it. In his words, reading the news-paper in the morning is as important to him as putting on makeup in the morn-ing is to many women he knows. Yet many women, he observed, either don't subscribe to a paper or don't read it until they get home in the evening. "I find this very puzzling," he said. "I can't tell you how often I have picked up a woman's morning newspaper from her front door in the evening and handed it to her when she opened the door for me."

To this man (and I am sure many others), a woman who objects to his read-ing the morning paper is trying to keep him from doing something essential and harmless. It's a violation of his independence—his freedom of action. But when a woman who expects her partner to talk to her is disappointed that he doesn't, she perceives his behavior as a failure of intimacy: He's keeping things from her; he's lost interest in her; he's pulling away. A woman I will call Rebecca, who is generally quite happily married, told me that this is the one source of serious dissatisfaction with her husband, Stuart. Her term for his taciturnity is *stinginess of spirit*. She tells him what she is thinking, and he listens silently. She asks him what he is thinking, and he takes a long time to answer, "I don't know." In frustration she challenges, "Is there nothing on your mind?"

For Rebecca, who is accustomed to expressing her fleeting thoughts and opinions as they come to her, *saying* nothing means *thinking* nothing. But Stuart does not assume that his passing thoughts are worthy of utterance. He is not in the habit of uttering his fleeting ruminations, so just as Rebecca "naturally" speaks her thoughts, he "naturally" dismisses his as soon as they occur to him. Speaking them would give them more weight and significance than he feels they merit. All her life she has had practice in verbalizing her thoughts and feelings in private conversations with people she is close to; all his life he has had practice in dismissing his and keeping them to himself.

What to Do with Doubts

In the above example, Rebecca was not talking about any particular kind of thoughts or feelings, just whatever Stuart might have had in mind. But the matter of giving voice to thoughts and feelings becomes particularly significant in the case of negative feelings or doubts about a relationship. This difference was highlighted for me when a fifty-year-old divorced man told me about his experiences in forming new relationships with women. On this matter, he was clear: "I do not value my fleeting thoughts, and I do not value the fleeting thoughts of others." He felt that the relationship he was currently in had been endangered, even permanently weakened, by the woman's practice of tossing out her passing thoughts, because, early in their courtship, many of her thoughts were fears about their relationship. Not surprisingly, since they did not yet know each other well, she worried about whether she could trust him, whether their relationship would destroy her independence, whether this relationship was really right for her. He felt she should have kept these fears and doubts to herself and waited to see how things turned out.

As it happens, things turned out well. The woman decided that the relationship was right for her, she could trust him, and she did not have to give up her independence. But he felt, at the time that he told me of this, that he had still not recovered from the wear and tear of coping with her earlier doubts. As he put it, he was still dizzy from having been bounced around like a yo-yo tied to the string of her stream of consciousness.

In contrast, this man admitted, he himself goes to the other extreme: He never expresses his fears and misgivings about their relationship at all. If he's unhappy but doesn't say anything about it, his unhappiness expresses itself in a kind of distancing coldness. This response is just what women fear most, and just the reason they prefer to express dissatisfactions and doubts—as an antidote to the isolation and distance that would result from keeping them to themselves.

The different perspectives on expressing or concealing dissatisfactions and doubts may reflect a difference in men's and women's awareness of the power of their words to affect others. In repeatedly telling him what she feared about their relationship, this woman spoke as though she assumed he was invulnerable and could not be hurt by what she said; perhaps she was underestimating the power of her words to affect him. For his part, when he refrains from expressing negative thoughts or feelings, he seems to be overestimating the power of his words to hurt her, when, ironically, she is more likely to be hurt by his silence than his words.

These women and men are talking in ways they learned as children and reinforced as young adults and then adults, in their same-gender friendships. For girls, talk is the glue that holds relationships together. Boys' relationships are held together primarily by activities: doing things together, or talking about activities such as sports or, later, politics. The forums in which men are most inclined to talk are those in which they feel the need to impress, in situations where their status is in question.

MAKING ADJUSTMENTS

Such impasses will perhaps never be settled to the complete satisfaction of both 30 parties, but understanding the differing views can help detoxify the situation, and both can make adjustments. Realizing that men and women have different assumptions about the place of talk in relationships, a woman can observe a man's desire to read the morning paper at the breakfast table without interpreting it as a rejection of her or a failure of their relationship. And a man can understand a woman's desire for talk without interpreting it as an unreasonable demand or a manipulative attempt to prevent him from doing what he wants to do.

A woman who had heard my interpretations of these differences between women and men told me how these insights helped her. Early in a promising relationship, a man spent the night at her apartment. It was a weeknight, and they both had to go to work the next day, so she was delighted when he made the rash and romantic suggestion that they have breakfast together and report late for work. She happily prepared breakfast, looking forward to the scene shaped in her mind: They would sit facing each other across her small table, look into each other's eyes, and say how much they liked each other and how happy they were about their growing friendship. It was against the backdrop of this heady expectation that she confronted an entirely different scene: As she placed on the table an array of lovingly prepared eggs, toast, and coffee, the man sat across her small table—and opened the newspaper in front of his face. If suggesting they have breakfast together had seemed like an invitation to get closer, in her view (or obstructing her view) the newspaper was now erected as a paper-thin but nonetheless impenetrable barrier between them.

Had she known nothing of the gender differences I discuss, she would simply have felt hurt and dismissed this man as yet another clunker. She would have concluded that, having enjoyed the night with her, he was now availing himself of her further services as a short-order cook. Instead, she realized that, unlike her, he did not feel the need for talk to reinforce their intimacy. The companionability of her presence was all he needed, and that did not mean that he didn't cherish her presence. By the same token, had he understood the essential role played by talk in women's definition of intimacy, he could have put off reading the paper—and avoided putting her off.

THE COMFORT OF HOME

For everyone, home is a place to be offstage. But the comfort of home can have opposite and incompatible meanings for women and men. For many men, the comfort of home means freedom from having to prove themselves and impress through verbal display. At last, they are in a situation where talk is not required. They are free to remain silent. But for women, home is a place where they are free to talk, and where they feel the greatest need for talk, with those they are closest to. For them, the comfort of home means the freedom to talk without worrying about how their talk will be judged.

MEN ARE FROM MARS, WOMEN ARE FROM VENUS

John Gray

John Gray's 1992 book Men Are from Mars, Women Are from Venus *has sold more than six million copies and has been translated into forty different languages. Following this success, Gray published* Mars and Venus in the Bedroom *(1995);* Mars and Venus Together Forever *(1996);* Men, Women and Relationships: Mars and Venus in Love *(1996);* Mars and Venus on a Date *(1997); and* Mars and Venus Starting Over *(1998). Unlike Deborah Tannen, who has a doctorate in linguistics and began her research in an academic setting, John Gray began his career as an assistant to transcendental meditation leader Maharishi Mahesh Yogi, then became an inspirational speaker and writer on relationships. The success of his books has led to guest appearances on* Oprah, Good Morning America, *and* Larry King Live, *and he now writes a syndicated newspaper column, "Ask John Gray." Mars and Venus books, music, workshops, and more are available at the John Gray Store and on his Web site <http://marsvenus.com>.*

Clearly, Gray's metaphorical use of the planets Mars and Venus to discuss how men and women can better understand each other has met with enormous popular interest. You need not take seriously the notion that men and women literally speak different languages, as the title of this reading suggests; you might just think of his Mars and Venus metaphor as a way of thinking about misunderstandings. But behind the metaphor lies a concept much like Tannen's: that men and women are different either in some essential way or at least in some way that is strongly embedded in contemporary culture. Like Tannen, he has been criticized for oversimplifying the issue and reinforcing stereotypes, yet at the same time millions of people (from many different cultures) have apparently found that Gray's descriptions conform to their own experience.

As you read, then, note the nature and the details of these "different languages" that Gray claims that men and women speak.

To fully express their feelings, women assume poetic license and use various superlatives, metaphors, and generalizations. Men mistakenly take these expressions literally. Because they misunderstand the intended meaning, they commonly react in an unsupportive manner. In the following chart ten complaints easily misinterpreted are listed, as well as how a man might respond unsupportively.

TEN COMMON COMPLAINTS THAT ARE EASILY MISINTERPRETED

Women say things like this	*Men respond like this*
"We never go out."	"That's not true. We went out last week."
"Everyone ignores me."	"I'm sure some people notice you."
"I am so tired, I can't do anything."	"That's ridiculous. You are not helpless."
"I want to forget everything."	"If you don't like your job, then quit."
"The house is always a mess."	"It's not always a mess."
"No one listens to me anymore."	"But I am listening to you right now."
"Nothing is working."	"Are you saying it is my fault?"
"You don't love me anymore."	"Of course I do. That's why I'm here."
"We are always in a hurry."	"We are not. Friday we were relaxed."
"I want more romance."	"Are you saying I am not romantic?"

You can see how a "literal" translation of a woman's words could easily mislead a man who is used to using speech as a means of conveying only facts and information. We can also see how a man's responses might lead to an argument. Unclear and unloving communication is the biggest problem in relationships. The number one complaint women have in relationships is: "I don't feel heard." Even this complaint is misunderstood and misinterpreted! . . .

WHEN VENUSIANS TALK

The following section contains various excerpts from the lost *Venusian/Martian Phrase Dictionary*. Each of the ten complaints listed above is translated so that a man can understand [its] real and intended meaning. Each translation also contains a hint of how she wants him to respond.

You see, when a Venusian is upset she not only uses generalities, and so   5
forth, but also is asking for a particular kind of support. She doesn't directly ask for that support because on Venus everyone knew that dramatic language implied a particular request.

In each of the translations this hidden request for support is revealed. If a man listening to a woman can recognize the implied request and respond accordingly, she will feel truly heard and loved.

The Venusian/Martian Phrase Dictionary

"We never go out" translated into Martian means "I feel like going out and doing something together. We always have such a fun time, and I love being with you. What do you think? Would you take me out to dinner? It has been a few days since we went out."

Without this translation, when a woman says "We never go out" a man may hear "You are not doing your job. What a disappointment you have turned out to be. We never do anything together anymore because you are lazy, unromantic, and just boring."

"Everyone ignores me" translated into Martian means "Today, I am feeling ignored and unacknowledged. I feel as though nobody sees me. Of course I'm sure some people see me, but they don't seem to care about me. I suppose I am also disappointed that you have been so busy lately. I really do appreciate how hard you are working and sometimes I start to feel like I am not important to you. I am afraid your work is more important than me. Would you give me a hug and tell me how special I am to you?"

Without this translation, when a woman says "Everyone ignores me" a man   10
may hear "I am so unhappy. I just can't get the attention I need. Everything is completely hopeless. Even you don't notice me, and you are the person who is

supposed to love me. You should be ashamed. You are so unloving. I would never ignore you this way."

"I am so tired, I can't do anything" translated into Martian means "I have been doing so much today. I really need a rest before I can do anything more. I am so lucky to have your support. Would you give me a hug and reassure me that I am doing a good job and that I deserve a rest?"

Without this translation, when a woman says "I am so tired, I can't do anything" a man may hear "I do everything and you do nothing. You should do more. I can't do it all. I feel so hopeless. I want a 'real man' to live with. Picking you was a big mistake."

"I want to forget everything" translated into Martian means "I want you to know that I love my work and my life but today I am so overwhelmed. I would love to do something really nurturing for myself before I have to be responsible again. Would you ask me 'What's the matter?' and then listen with empathy without offering any solutions? I just want to feel you understanding the pressures I feel. It would make me feel so much better. It helps me to relax. Tomorrow I will get back to being responsible and handling things."

Without this translation, when a woman says "I want to forget everything" a man may hear "I have to do so much that I don't want to do. I am so unhappy with you and our relationship. I want a better partner who can make my life more fulfilling. You are doing a terrible job."

"This house is always a mess" translated into Martian means "Today I feel like relaxing, but the house is so messy. I am frustrated and I need a rest. I hope you don't expect me to clean it all up. Would you agree with me that it is a mess and then offer to help clean up part of it?"   15

Without this translation, when a woman says "This house is always a mess" a man may hear "This house is a mess because of you. I do everything possible to clean it up, and before I have finished, you have messed it up again. You are a lazy slob and I don't want to live with you unless you change. Clean up or clear out!"

"No one listens to me anymore" translated into Martian means "I am afraid I am boring to you. I am afraid you are no longer interested in me. I seem to be very sensitive today. Would you give me some special attention? I would love it. I've had a hard day and feel as though no one wants to hear what I have to say.

"Would you listen to me and continue to ask me supportive questions such as: 'What happened today? What else happened? How did you feel? What did you want? How else do you feel?' Also support me by saying caring, acknowledging, and reassuring statements such as: 'Tell me more' or 'That's right' or 'I know what you mean' or 'I understand.' Or just listen, and occasionally when I pause make one of these reassuring sounds: 'oh,' 'humph,' 'uh-huh,' and 'hmmm.'" (*Note:* Martians had never heard of these sounds before arriving on Venus.)

Without this translation, when a woman says "No one listens to me anymore" he may hear "I give you my attention but you don't listen to me. You used to. You have become a very boring person to be with. I want someone exciting and interesting and you are definitely not that person. You have disappointed me. You are selfish, uncaring, and bad."

"Nothing is working" translated into Martian means "Today I am so overwhelmed *and* I am so grateful that I can share my feelings with you. It helps me so much to feel better. Today it seems like nothing I do works. I know that this is not true, but I sure feel that way when I get so overwhelmed by all the things I still have to do. Would you give me a hug and tell me that I am doing a great job? It would sure feel good."

Without this translation, when a woman says "Nothing is working" a man 20 may hear "You never do anything right. I can't trust you. If I hadn't listened to you I wouldn't be in this mess. Another man would have fixed things, but you made them worse."

"You don't love me anymore" translated into Martian means "Today I am feeling as though you don't love me. I am afraid I have pushed you away. I know you really do love me, you do so much for me. Today I am just feeling a little insecure. Would you reassure me of your love and tell me those three magic words, I love you? When you do that it feels so good."

Without this translation, when a woman says "You don't love me anymore" a man may hear "I have given you the best years of my life, and you have given me nothing. You used me. You are selfish and cold. You do what you want to do, for you and only you. You do not care about anybody. I was a fool for loving you. Now I have nothing."

"We are always in a hurry" translated into Martian means "I feel so rushed today. I don't like rushing. I wish our life was not so hurried. I know it is nobody's fault and I certainly don't blame you. I know you are doing your best to get us there on time and I really appreciate how much you care.

"Would you empathize with me and say something like, 'It *is* hard always rushing around'? I don't always like rushing either.'"

Without this translation, when a woman says "We are always in a hurry" a man may hear "You are so irresponsible. You wait until the last minute to do everything. I can never be happy when I am with you. We are always rushing to avoid being late. You ruin things every time I am with you. I am so much happier when I am not around you."

"I want more romance" translated into Martian means "Sweetheart, you have been 25 working so hard lately. Let's take some time out for ourselves. I love it when we can relax and be alone without the kids around and no work pressures. You are so romantic. Would you surprise me with flowers sometime soon and take me out on a date? I love being romanced."

Without this translation, when a woman says "I want more romance" a man may hear "You don't satisfy me anymore. I am not turned on to you. Your romantic skills are definitely inadequate. You have never really fulfilled me. I wish you were more like other men I have been with."

After using this dictionary for a few years, a man doesn't need to pick it up each time he feels blamed or criticized. He begins to understand the way women think and feel. He learns that these kinds of dramatic phrases are not to be taken literally. They are just the way women express feeling more fully: That's the way it was done on Venus and people from Mars need to remember that! . . .

Understanding the Cave

Women have a lot to learn about men before their relationships can be really ful-filling. They need to learn that when a man is upset or stressed he will automat-ically stop talking and go to his "cave" to work things out. They need to learn that no one is allowed in that cave, not even the man's best friends. This was the way it was on Mars. Women should not become scared that they have done something terribly wrong. They need gradually to learn that if you just let men go into their caves, after a while they will come out and everything will be fine.

This lesson is difficult for women because on Venus one of the golden rules was never to abandon a friend when she was upset. It just doesn't seem loving to abandon her favorite Martian when he is upset. Because she cares for him, a woman wants to come into his cave and offer him help.

In addition, she often mistakenly assumes that if she could ask him lots of 30 questions about how he is feeling and be a good listener, then he would feel better. This only upsets Martians more. She instinctively wants to support him in the way that she would want to be supported. Her intentions are good, but the outcome is counterproductive.

Both men and women need to stop offering the method of caring they would prefer and start to learn the different ways their partners think, feel, and react.

Why Men Go into Their Caves

Men go into their caves or become quiet for a variety of reasons.

1. He needs to think about a problem and find a practical solution to the problem.
2. He doesn't have an answer to a question or a problem. Men were never taught to say "Gee, I don't have an answer. I need to go into my cave and find one." Other men assume he is doing just that when he becomes quiet.
3. He has become upset or stressed. At such times he needs to be alone to cool off 35 and find his control again. He doesn't want to do or say anything he might regret.

4. He needs to find himself. This fourth reason becomes very important when men are in love. At times they begin to lose and forget themselves. They can feel that too much intimacy robs them of their power. They need to regulate how close they get. Whenever they get too close so as to lose themselves, alarm bells go off and they are on their way into the cave. As a result they are rejuvenated and find their loving and powerful self again.

Why Women Talk

Women talk for a variety of reasons. Sometimes women talk for the same reasons that men stop talking. These are four common reasons that women talk:

1. To convey or gather information. (This is generally the only reason a man talks.)
2. To explore and discover what it is she wants to say. (He stops talking to figure out inside what he wants to say. She talks to think out loud.)
3. To feel better and more centered when she is upset. (He stops talking when he is 40 upset. In his cave he has a chance to cool off.)
4. To create intimacy. Through sharing her inner feelings she is able to know her loving self. (A Martian stops talking to find himself again. Too much intimacy, he fears, will rob him of himself.)

Without this vital understanding of our differences and needs it is easy to see why couples struggle so much in relationships....

WHEN MARTIANS DO TALK

Women get burned not only when they unknowingly invade a man's introspective time but also when they misinterpret his expressions, which are generally warnings that he is either in his cave or on his way to the cave. When asked "What's the matter?" a Martian will say something brief like "It's nothing" or "I am OK."

These brief signals are generally the only way a Venusian knows to give him space to work out his feelings alone. Instead of saying "I am upset and I need some time to be alone," men just become quiet.

In the following chart six commonly expressed abbreviated warning signals 45 are listed as well as how a woman might unknowingly respond in an intrusive and unsupportive manner:

SIX COMMON ABBREVIATED WARNING SIGNALS

When a woman asks "What's the matter?"

A man says	*A woman may respond*
"I'm OK" or "It's OK."	"I know something's wrong. What is it?"
"I'm fine" or "It's fine."	"But you seem upset. Let's talk."

"It's nothing."	"I want to help. I know something is bothering you. What is it?"
"It's all right" or "I'm all right."	"Are you sure? I am happy to help you."
"It's no big deal."	"But something is upsetting you. I think we should talk."
"It's no problem."	"But it is a problem. I could help."

When a man makes one of the above abbreviated comments he generally wants silent acceptance or space. At times like this, to avoid misinterpretation and unnecessary panic, the Venusians consulted their *Martian/Venusian Phrase Dictionary*. Without this assistance, women misinterpret these abbreviated expressions.

Women need to know that when a man says "I am OK" it is an abbreviated version of what he really means, which is "I am OK because I can deal with this alone. I do not need any help. Please support me by not worrying about me. Trust that I can deal with it all by myself."

Without this translation, when he is upset and says "I am OK" it sounds to her as if he is denying his feelings or problems. She then attempts to help him by asking questions or talking about what she thinks the problem is. She does not know that he is speaking an abbreviated language. The following are excerpts from their phrase dictionary.

The Martian/Venusian Phrase Dictionary

"I'm OK" translated into Venusian means "I am OK, I can deal with my upset. I don't need any help, thank you." 50

Without this translation, when he says "I am OK" she may hear "I am not upset because I do not care" or she may hear "I am not willing to share with you my upset feelings. I do not trust you to be there for me."

"I'm fine" translated into Venusian means "I am fine because I am successfully dealing with my upset or problem. I don't need any help. If I do I will ask."

Without this translation, when he says "I am fine" she may hear "I don't care about what has happened. This problem is not important to me. Even if it upsets you, I don't care."

"It's nothing" translated into Venusian means "Nothing is bothering me that I cannot handle alone. Please don't ask any more questions about it."

Without this translation, when he says "Nothing is bothering me" she may 55 hear "I don't know what is bothering me. I need you to ask me questions to assist me in discovering what is happening." At this point she proceeds to anger him by asking questions when he really wants to be left alone.

"It's all right" translated into Venusian means "This is a problem but you are not to blame. I can resolve this within myself if you don't interrupt my process by asking more questions or offering suggestions. Just act like it didn't happen and I can process it within myself more effectively."

Without this translation, when he says "It's all right" she may hear "This is the way it is supposed to be. Nothing needs to be changed. You can abuse me and I can abuse you" or she hears "It's all right this time, but remember it is your fault. You can do this once but don't do it again or else."

"It's no big deal" translated into Venusian means "It is no big deal because I can make things work again. Please don't dwell on this problem or talk more about it. That makes me more upset. I accept responsibility for solving this problem. It makes me happy to solve it."

Without this translation, when he says "It's no big deal" she may hear "You are making a big deal out of nothing. What concerns you is not important. Don't overreact."

"It's no problem" translated into Venusian means "I have no problem doing this or solving this problem. It is my pleasure to offer this gift to you."   60

Without this translation, when he says "It's no problem" she may hear "This is not a problem. Why are you making it a problem or asking for help?" She then mistakenly explains to him why it is a problem.

Using this *Martian/Venusian Phrase Dictionary* can assist women in understanding what men really mean when they abbreviate what they are saying. Sometimes what he is really saying is the opposite of what she hears....

When a man goes into his cave he is generally wounded or stressed and is trying to solve his problem alone. To give him the support that a woman would want is counterproductive. There are basically six ways to support him when he goes into his cave. (Giving him this support will also shorten the time he needs to spend alone.)

How to Support a Man in His Cave

1. Don't disapprove of his need for withdrawing.
2. Don't try to help him solve his problem by offering solutions.
3. Don't try to nurture him by asking questions about his feelings.
4. Don't sit next to the door of the cave and wait for him to come out.
5. Don't worry about him or feel sorry for him.
6. Do something that makes you happy.

If you need to "talk," write him a letter to be read later when he is out, and if   65
you need to be nurtured, talk to a friend. Don't make him the sole source of your fulfillment.

A man wants his favorite Venusian to trust that *he* can handle what is bothering him. To be trusted that he can handle his problems is very important to his honor, pride, and self-esteem.

Not worrying about him is difficult for her. Worrying for others is one way women express their love and caring. It is a way of showing love. For a woman, being happy when the person you love is upset just doesn't seem right. He certainly doesn't want her to be happy *because* he is upset, but he does want her to be happy. He wants her to be happy so that he has one less problem to worry about. In addition he wants her to be happy because it helps him to feel loved by her. When a woman is happy and free from worry, it is easier for him to come out.

Ironically men show their love by not worrying. A man questions "How can you worry about someone whom you admire and trust?" Men commonly support one another by saying phrases such as "Don't worry, you can handle it" or "That's their problem, not yours" or "I'm sure it will work out." Men support one another by not worrying or minimizing their troubles.

It took me years to understand that my wife actually wanted me to worry for her when she was upset. Without this awareness of our different needs, I would minimize the importance of her concerns. This only made her more upset.

When a man goes into his cave he is generally trying to solve a problem. If 70 his mate is happy or *not* needy at this time, then he has one less problem to solve before coming out. Knowing that she is happy with him also gives him more strength to deal with his problem while in the cave.

ESSENTIAL TRAITS OF COUPLES WHO THRIVE

Susan Page

Susan Page has a master's degree in divinity and has worked as a campus minister, has directed women's programs at the University of California at Berkeley, and has run a domestic-violence-prevention agency. In 1980 such work led her to begin conducting relationship workshops. She has since published such books as If I'm So Wonderful, Why Am I Still Single? *(1988) and* How One of You Can Bring the Two of You Together *(1997). This reading from* The 8 Essential Traits of Couples Who Thrive *(1994) suggests that good communication is an "essential trait."*

Much of her material comes from her workshop discussions and in-depth interviews with thirty-two happily married couples, as well as from her own personal experience with two marriages, one divorce, and six years as a single.

As you read, pay attention to her explanation of five basic skills that can enable most couples to communicate successfully.

The quality of communication in a relationship is a decisive factor in whether it is able to thrive. A few simple principles, thoroughly understood and regularly practiced, can turn failing relationships around, and send already thriving relationships into the stratosphere. They are essential skills for friendship, for intimacy, for parenting, for any business or service that wants to offer customer satisfaction, for supervision and management, and for negotiating, whether it be an agreement between two people or a treaty between two nations. Virtually every relationship can be improved by the use of these simple principles and will be weaker without them.

Yet there is still widespread resistance to learning and using them.

The happy couples I interviewed almost universally reported that their communication is good; in fact, they usually mentioned their "good communication" early and with pride and pleasure. But as I questioned them in more depth, I discovered that, in many cases, they didn't think about or even necessarily know communication "rules." What they meant when they said they had good communication was one or more of the following: They had relatively few communication impasses; they were able to talk easily about difficult subjects; they felt they understood each other; they withheld very little from each other; and they could rely on their ability to resolve conflicts.

Those are the goals couples want to achieve when they learn communication "rules." Couples who have an abundance of goodwill may not be aware of the rules or skills they use in order to achieve good communication; they may simply be using them naturally. But I also spoke with many thriving couples who had learned specific communication skills from books, workshops, marriage counselors, or even magazine articles, and who had used them to great advantage.

All the important communication tools can be reduced to five basic skills. 5
They are free, non-fattening, and legal. They can provide you with immense personal satisfaction. Your skills can be a generous gift to others. If you learn and use them, you will be able to give more to the people you love. You will achieve more of what you want in life, and you will be capable of achieving great riches in your human relationships.

They are:

1. Make "I" statements, not "You" statements
2. Listen
3. Understand and accept the differences between men and women
4. Ask for what you want
5. Affirm others. . . .

1. MAKE "I" STATEMENTS, NOT "YOU" STATEMENTS

When you are angry with someone or you feel very hurt by that person, your natural tendency is to say something like what Beth says in this hypothetical scene:

> BETH: You never pay any attention to me, and then you spent all that time with Sarah at the party. How do you think that made me feel? You just don't think about what you do. You're so thoughtless sometimes. Do you love me or not?

These are "you" statements. They blame, accuse, and criticize the person you are angry with. Beth's partner has virtually no alternative but to feel blamed, accused, and criticized. It is extremely unlikely that he will agree that he is thoughtless and never pays any attention to Beth. His natural reaction will be to defend himself:

> ROBERT: What do you mean? That conversation with Sarah was nothing. I spend lots of time with you.

Then he is also quite likely to make some of his own "you" statements.

> You are so sensitive. You're ridiculous. You react to the tiniest thing.

This scene would be completely different if Beth had used "I" statements. An "I" statement is a report about how you feel or how you experienced something. It says nothing about the other person.

> BETH: Robert, I'd like to talk with you about something. I feel hurt—and a little bit scared—about the amount of time you spent with Sarah at the party. I know it may be irrational, but I've been feeling kind of distant from you anyway lately. It just seems like we haven't had that much time together.

Now Beth has given Robert some information about herself. Her statement is much more likely to elicit concern and caring from Robert than defensiveness—especially if this is a relationship where there is goodwill—because Beth is talking about a problem *she* is having.

> ROBERT: Gee, Sweetheart. I had no idea you were feeling that way. I'm so sorry. Let's talk about it.

This simple device, making an "I" statement when you are upset, can make a staggering difference in a relationship. It can actually transform what might otherwise be a fight into a constructive and even very close, warm conversation. Most people use "you" statements spontaneously when they are emotionally charged. But as soon as you catch yourself doing it, stop. Shift gears, and make an accurate "I" statement. Simply let the other person know how you feel.

Listen to the difference:

You spend too much money on clothes! You aren't thinking about the big picture!

vs.

I feel very anxious when you spend that much money on clothes. I feel like there is a big iron vise in my stomach.

You always interrupt me!

vs.

I feel like I don't get to finish what I want to say.

You forgot to bring home milk *again?*

vs.

I'm feeling really annoyed right now.

Using "I" statements, together with the second skill we will discuss, listening and reflecting back what you heard, a couple should be able to work through virtually any anger, hurt, or difficult feelings they have without fighting. . . .

2. LISTEN

When we hear about the need for "good communication skills," we usually 15 think about talking—expressing ourselves more clearly, saying things in the right way, getting our message across. In fact, however, 98 percent of good communication is listening. . . .

Listening means putting yourself in the other person's shoes. It means trying to understand a different point of view before you try to make yourself understood. It means empathizing—that is, identifying with or vicariously experiencing—the feelings, thoughts, or attitudes of another person. That's all. It couldn't be simpler.

Contrary to the belief of some, listening is not a highly refined skill that is reserved for deep, intimate conversations or delicate negotiations. Rather, it is a simple habit, that, unless you are living alone on a desert island, you will have numerous opportunities to use every day.

Let's look first at some extremely common situations in which listening is called for. First we will hear a typical *nonlistening* response. Later, we will see what an effective listening response would be.

STORE CLERK: Gee, we seem to be out of that.

CUSTOMER: No, you can't be! I called this morning, and I just drove twenty-five miles to come pick one up! I need it tonight.

STORE CLERK: I've been here all day, and no one told me you called. We missed a delivery last week, so we are out of a few other items too. We'll be getting more in next week.

The clerk immediately becomes defensive. She tries to get the customer to understand her point of view by explaining what happened. She sees only her own position. She is seeking not to understand but to be understood. Her message is, "It's not *my* fault, don't bother *me*, this isn't *my* problem."

If the store clerk had been listening, and had put herself in the customer's 20 shoes and empathized, she would have said, "Oh, how frustrating for you! You need it tonight? I am so sorry we are out! I don't blame you for being upset." Then, of course, she could see whether she might actually help the customer by calling another store or looking in the warehouse or suggesting a close substitute. But first, she would be conveying that she understood the woman's frustration, and she would be validating it. Her understanding and validation would probably allow the woman to stop venting her fury and move on to finding a solution....

> WIFE (to husband who had just arrived home with the news that the bakery was out of the fruit tart she had specifically ordered—and a carrot cake): I'm so angry. That tart is my dad's favorite, and I really wanted to surprise him with it. I just can't believe this. I ordered it three days ago and was very specific.
>
> HUSBAND: Oh, Honey, this carrot cake is good. Nobody will know you had planned the tart. Really, it doesn't matter. Carrot cake is fine.

He was trying to be helpful, but he didn't listen. He stayed in his own shoes. It didn't matter to *him*. Carrot cake was fine with *him*.

I actually witnessed this scene. What happened next was predictable. The wife felt all the more irritated by her husband's remarks. "But my dad loves that tart and I was counting on surprising him. How could that bakery do this!"

The husband saw that he wasn't going to convince his wife of his point of view, so he turned and took the carrot cake out to the kitchen. No connection. No good feelings. No chance for warmth and kindness to pass between the two.

The man could have made any number of remarks that would have made his 25 wife feel heard and understood. He could have said, "I knew you'd be disappointed," or "I'm so sorry, Honey, it *is* infuriating."

As we can see from these examples, there are always two steps to listening. The first is to hear what the other person is saying, experiencing, and feeling. The second is to convey to the person that you have heard and that you understand.

Perhaps the most important and at the same time the most difficult time to listen is when someone else is upset with you, especially someone who has *not* learned effective communication. The natural human tendency is to become defensive in this situation. Let's see what happens when the upset person has *not* learned to make "I" statements:

> "You are always late!"
> "I am not!"

"How can you back out on me? You promised!"
"How could I know the boss would need me this weekend?"

"This is the third weekend you haven't fixed the broken window!"
"I've had too much else to do!"

How different these simple interactions would have been if the accused had empathized first—had first heard and then conveyed back to the accuser, in effect, "I understand your feelings."

"You're always late!"
"I know it upsets you when I'm late. I'm sure it must be exasperating."

"How can you back out on me? You promised!"
"I know you're disappointed. I'm sorry. I don't blame you for being angry with me."

"This is the third weekend you haven't fixed the broken window!"
"I'm sorry. I'd be annoyed too if I were in your shoes."

One of the common excuses people give for resisting the use of listening skills is that reflecting back what a person has said sounds fake and feels silly. But as is apparent from these examples, it is entirely possible to convey that you have understood someone without using formulas or simply repeating the same sentence back to the person. It is important to reflect back what you have heard, not by rote, but with your heart. If you are listening deeply, and if you truly care, then what you reflect back to the person who is speaking will not be mechanical....

Listening to someone doesn't mean you can't also talk. It simply means that you listen *first*—and convey to the other person that you have heard and understood and taken in what he or she said. Then you can give your side of the story. And of course, if you have listened well, your remarks are much more likely to be on target.

If you want a relationship that truly thrives, there is no more important skill for you to master than listening. Listening is the foundation of affirmation and verbal intimacy, of conflict resolution, of negotiating, and of being happy together day in and day out.

Is It True That Happy Couples Never Fight?

Most of the happy couples I interviewed rarely fight. Many of them told me about major blowups they have had, but fighting is not a way of life for these people. For the most part, they resolve their conflicts and differences without fighting, making each other "wrong," hurting each other, putting each other down, or "winning" over the other.

People argue when they feel they are not being heard.

When two parties in a conflict are willing and able to listen to each other and to understand each other's point of view, they can negotiate peacefully. If they are angry or hurt, they may need to express their emotions for a few minutes in a way that is not rational or reasonable. But unless they are simply mean-spirited, they will soon regain a spirit of goodwill and make an effort to resolve the conflict.

Here are some simple, effective guidelines for peaceful conflict resolution. 35

1. Don't let yourself respond defensively. If you feel defensive, simply say, "I feel defensive, and I don't want to respond when I feel this way." Then wait. Talk a little more, or let your partner talk. See if the defensive feelings subside.

   If you feel you have put your partner on the defensive because of something you have said, say, "I'm sorry I put you on the defensive."
2. If your partner wants to talk about something that is disturbing for either of you, curb your desire to respond. Sit quietly and listen. If your partner pauses, say, "Tell me more." Let him or her know that you are there and that you are truly listening.
3. When you do respond, state your partner's position as clearly as you can. If you don't understand, or you don't agree, or you can't imagine why your partner holds this position, ask why. Search for the reasons behind what your partner wants. Try to understand fully before you respond with your own point of view.
4. Take turns talking and listening. 40

Perhaps the single most important guideline for resolving conflicts without fighting is this one: Remember that your goal is to find a resolution that works for both of you, not to "win."

Often people who do fight and argue a great deal place a lot of importance on being right. They may not be aware of this, but deep inside, they believe that in order to feel good about themselves, or in order for other people to feel good about them, they have to be right and prove to others that they are right. These people would rather be right than have friends; they would rather be right than be happy; they would rather be right than be respected or liked. Couples who thrive and who have little conflict in their lives can let go of being right. They can move away from a position if they see it is getting them negative results. They can give in without feeling humiliated.

Remember, there is a very big difference between disagreeing with a person and judging a person. "I disagree with you" is a very different statement from "You are wrong" (implying you are a bad person for having that point of view)....

A second important principle in peaceful conflict resolution is to avoid blame. When you find yourself blaming the other person for anything, ask yourself, what is my role in this conflict?

One couple I interviewed said their main ongoing problem was that he felt 45 she bought too many books. He thought people should use libraries and that owning books was stupid. They take up space, collect dust, and usually get read only once — if that. But she loved books and loved to write in the margins, lend them to friends, and keep them around for reference. They couldn't get any resolution until he realized that he was blaming her, and that he might have to look to himself to resolve the conflict. When he began to look at his own role, he saw that pestering her about her books was just as offensive to her as owning books was offensive to him. *He* was the source of the conflict, not she. She was just being herself. If he could change and simply relax and let go of his criticism, there would be no conflict. He did make the change, and it was an enormous relief to them both. He resolved this conflict by giving up his blame and looking at his own role in the conflict. . . .

3. UNDERSTAND AND ACCEPT THE DIFFERENCES
BETWEEN MEN AND WOMEN

For a decade or so around the seventies, we were excited about our newfound freedom from strict gender roles. Men and women aren't all that different; women can be professionals, men can change diapers. Unisex° fashions were the rage. We were intent upon eliminating gender distinctions. But we soon realized that while our roles can be interchanged, our psyches cannot. Men and women are very different.

Joe Tanenbaum, Anne Wilson Schaef, Lillian Rubin, Deborah Tannen, John Gray, and others have shed much light on male/female differences. Their work is a great gift. We now recognize that men and women belong to different subcultures, and that, even though the other sex's behavior is different from ours, it is not wrong. If we judge it as "bad," we are simply being myopic — and old-fashioned. Because we can now anticipate how the other sex will behave and recognize it as normal behavior, we can give up railing against it and instead accept each other and change our expectations.

We have at last realized that there are valid historical and psychological reasons for most of the dramatic differences between men and women. If we understand our differences, we can get along. We can honor and celebrate our separate subcultures and still continue to work for social, political, and economic equality. And we can even broaden our own range of behaviors by learning from each other. Different is good, not bad. Our only problem was expecting that we would be exactly like each other. Now that we know we are different, we can give up that expectation, and focus on learning how to get along with a different subculture. We can stop impugning each other's motives and recognize that we are both trying to achieve the same goals. We simply use different language and different behavior to get there.

° Unisex: The same for either sex.

This monumental shift in consciousness from "equal means identical" to *"vive la différence!"* is as significant an advance in our culture as the Sexual Revolution was in the sixties. Let's look here at its implications for communication.

The F/PS Rule

From Deborah Tannen's important work we have learned that men often use 50 conversation to solve problems and make decisions, while women often use conversation to work ideas through, to express feelings, to feel their connection with each other, and to establish rapport and intimacy. Conversationally speaking, women are feelings sharers (F), and men are problem solvers (PS).

If a man and [a] woman don't know each other's styles, their conversation can be terribly frustrating. For example:

SHE: I am so tired of that stupid job. Just listen to what a customer did to me today!

HE: Honey, I keep telling you to ask for a transfer.

Before we had this magic key—women-are-rapport-builders-and-feeling-sharers; men-are-problem-solvers—the above exchange could have sent this couple to a counselor in despair:

SHE: He won't listen to me. He just cuts me off. He knows I can't ask for another transfer so soon. He doesn't care about me or how I feel. He never wants to talk about anything. I just wanted to tell someone about this stupid customer to get it off my chest, but instead, he just puts me down. And he always thinks he knows more than I do. He makes me so mad. I just don't feel close any more.

HE: I don't know what she wants! I do care about her. I was trying to be helpful. I don't see any reason why she can't ask for a transfer. I don't understand why she gets so angry. She's hysterical. She'll go on and on about one scene at the store. She won't listen to me.

The impasse in this scenario is caused by the couple's ignorance of the F/PS Rule. They both had goodwill and were both doing what they did best. She was doing a fine job of sharing her feelings and of trying to connect with him. He was doing a great job of trying to help her by solving her problem. Because they didn't have the simple key of the F/PS Rule, they even misjudged each other's motives. They couldn't see through their disparate approaches to their goodwill.

So how can knowledge of the F/PS Rule help? What might they have done—and what can you do—to make use of the F/PS Rule in your daily life?

The answer is so simple it can be applied instantly, and with very little prac- 55 tice: Simply label the type of conversation you want to have, and ask the other person to join you. For just because men have a tendency to solve problems and women have a tendency to share feelings doesn't mean that each isn't capable of the other mode. Here's how the above conversation could have proceeded.

Assume that this couple have already discussed the F/PS Rule and understand both types of conversations.

> SHE: I am so tired of that stupid job. Just listen to what a customer did to me today!
>
> HE: I keep telling you to ask for a transfer.
>
> SHE: You know, Honey, I'd like to have a feelings conversation right now, okay? I just need to get this thing off my chest. Could I tell you about it?
>
> HE: Of course. Thanks for the clue. Why don't you tell me about it?
>
> *(She relates the incident. He empathizes. When she seems finished, he continues.)*
>
> HE: That was an awful situation. But it seems to me you handled it really well. Would you be willing to have a little problem-solving conversation now? Because I do feel some frustration that these situations continue to come up. I'd like to talk about some ways you might be able to change the situation.
>
> SHE: Sure. I appreciate your concern. I think I could talk about some ideas now. *or*
> SHE: Truthfully, I'm too exhausted to do that right now. I promise I'll talk about it some time in the next several days. How about Sunday morning. Would that be okay?

Labeling a conversation "feelings-oriented" or "problem solving"—as soon as you realize the two of you may be in different modes—is a magic tool. Of course I'm assuming that there is goodwill present on both sides. No one is suggesting that men are wrong to be solution-oriented or that women are wrong to be feelings-oriented, or that one of these modes is better than the other. You are honoring the validity and importance of both styles but agreeing to use one or the other of them for the time being.

I have noticed other differences in conversational styles between men and women as well. In my workshops, both men and women have found it very useful to anticipate these strong tendencies:

Women give—and want to hear—lots of details; men give broad outlines and get straight to the point.

Women talk about people, about feelings, and about personal issues; men talk about "topics" like politics, sports, work, movies, and so on.

Women want to be liked and included by others; men want to be respected 60 and admired by others.

Men are subliminally aware of their "status" in a conversation, and try to engineer things so that they can be "one-up" rather than "one-down." Women, on the other hand, are more tuned in to whether or not they are being "liked," and are quite willing to sacrifice status if they feel they are being well received. . . .

Awareness is the key. By recognizing what our respective subcultures have taught us to want, we can make choices for ourselves, and we can evaluate the other sex's behavior in an entirely different light.

For example, imagine this scene at a cocktail party. A man and [a] woman strike up a conversation. They get to talking about politics. She offers an opinion. He agrees and goes on to elaborate at some length. She eggs him on by asking a couple of questions. He is delighted at this and explains himself at even greater length. They end warmly, smiling and saying how nice it is to find kindred spirits.

Later, she says to a friend, "He's very bright, but he's too impressed with his own importance." Meantime, he says to a friend, "She's really nice, but she's not too knowledgeable."

He was interested in getting her to respect him. He succeeded. But being not well liked by her was an unsought side effect. 65

She was interested in being liked by him. She succeeded. But losing his respect was an unsought side effect for her.

But look at how an awareness of these patterns can alter them. If both of these people take the trouble to think back on their conversation in the light of their knowledge about the usual habits of men and women, she may realize, "I need to speak up more. I had a lot to say too, but I just let him go on. That was silly. I was doing my passive woman number." He may realize, "I should have asked her what she thinks. After all, she brought up the subject. I didn't have to impress her. Why did I dominate the conversation so?"

MEN need to be aware that women like to share and talk things through in a non-solution-oriented way. Actually, this is their way of getting to a solution sometimes. But their main reason for talking this way is to build a connection with you. Relax. Listen. Ask questions. Acknowledge her feelings. Focus on experiencing the connection between you. Respect your partner for her ability to build this connection. And remember that by listening and refraining from solving her problem, you are giving her exactly the kind of closeness she craves with you. But also, don't feel you have to adjust your identity to communicate satisfactorily. When you have reached your limits for this sort of interacting, let her know—in a completely nonjudgmental way. She is not asking that you become an expert at this kind of talking. She is only asking that you shift to her mode for a while and refrain from problem solving.

When the woman you love is troubled, depressed, or upset about something, what she needs most from you is not a solution to her immediate problem. Rather, she needs to know you love her even when she can't love herself. Hold her. Let her talk, complain, or cry. Tell her that you love her, and that you understand. And when she's excited about something, let her tell you about it. Be interested. Pay attention. Tell her how happy you are for her.

Also, men, you need to know that you may have a natural tendency to try to impress others and win their admiration. But a woman cares more about liking you than admiring you. Admiration creates distance between the admirer and the admired, yet what she wants more than anything is closeness. If you want her to feel good about you, and if you want to please her, get in the habit of 70 asking her questions. Show that you are interested in her. She will love you for this, and loving you is what she wants to do. Ironically, of course, she will respect you more, too.

Learn to ask your wife questions—about her work, her friends, her opinions. This is a gift to her, and it will do wonders for your relationship.

WOMEN need to be aware that men like to help and proffer support by making suggestions, giving advice, and offering solutions. They do this to help and support you. They have no intention of cutting you off or putting you down. Be grateful and appreciative of their help. If you want to talk more open-mindedly for a while, ask for this, out loud and nonjudgmentally, but be willing to shift to the problem-solving mode also. Let yourself be assisted in this way. Feel the support they are offering. Contribute your own solutions and suggestions. Shift into the problem-solving mode yourself for a while, and work to make the conversation as useful to yourself as possible.

When you have established that the two of you are having a feelings discussion, and you are talking about your feelings but he is not talking about his, try simply asking, "How do you feel about such and such?" It could be that it just didn't occur to your partner to think about or mention how he feels.

Also, women, you need to be aware that you have a natural tendency to try to please others and win their affection. A man wants to like you, but even more, he wants to respect you. Don't play down your expertise, talents, and skills in order to let a man show his off. Always strive for equality in a conversation. Just because a man doesn't ask for your opinion or your stories, don't assume he isn't interested. Take responsibility for equalizing conversations with men. Show that you have a head on your shoulders. He will respect you for this, and respecting you is what he wants to do. Ironically, of course, he will like you more, too.

BOTH SEXES must be aware of the difference between problem-solving con- 75 versations and feeling/rapport-building conversations. Label the type of conversation you want to have, and get the agreement of the other party before proceeding. In all your conversation, work for a balance between talking and listening. Show you are interested in the other party by asking questions. . . .

4. ASK FOR WHAT YOU WANT

Even couples who thrive have trouble sometimes asking for what they want in their relationship. From happy couples I heard as many anecdotes about problems in this area as in any other. Most of these stories were about times when the couples had eventually overcome their obstacles and had been able to ask for what they wanted. Couples who are not thriving often go for years without ever telling each other what they want.

Why is it so difficult?

Basically, because we are afraid that asking for what we want will cause conflict or discomfort of one kind or another. "The other person won't want to give what I want and will get mad," we tell ourselves. "I don't know what will happen if I ask." "My mate will feel criticized." "I'll never get what I want anyway." "What I want is probably stupid; I should just learn to live without it." "I've asked before and it doesn't do any good." "It just never seems like the right moment to ask." "My mate should know what I want and need. I shouldn't have to ask." "It spoils it to have to ask; what I want is for my mate to see what I want and give it spontaneously." "I'll just be nice and not bother my mate with my wish."

If you hear yourself saying or thinking one of these excuses for not asking for what you want, then tell yourself, "This is not a good enough excuse. If my partner is not giving me something I want, this is my responsibility. My partner cannot read my mind. I might even have to ask more than once. That's okay. If I want my needs satisfied, I must find a way to ask!"

Asking for what you want in your relationship is crucial for several reasons. 80 First, if you don't ask, the consequences can be terrible. Anything you want and are not requesting becomes a secret, because now one person knows something the other person isn't privy to. It becomes a little wall between you. Worse, the person who is withholding will inevitably begin to resent not getting what he or she wants. Then the resentment becomes an additional wall, an additional distancing device. As one man told me, "She was resenting me, and I had not the least clue what she was resenting."

On the other hand, if you can bring yourself to ask for what you want, something in your relationship will shift. It is true that you do not exactly know what will happen when you ask. But you can be sure that whatever happens will move the two of you forward. Even if your asking creates a conflict, it is almost certainly something that needed to come out in the open and that can now be resolved. As long as you withhold, nothing can happen.

Kathryn and Max had been going together for more than a year when the events she relates occurred.

> We were having dinner at quite a nice restaurant. At the end, I offered to pay, but Max, as usual, brushed off my offer and swept up the bill.
>
> This time, I stopped him. I said, "Would you just ask me why I want to pay for my own dinner?" The question startled him a bit, and he slowed down. He sensed I was trying to get his serious attention. He asked me. Then I thanked him, and I told him what I had been longing to say for some time, that I believed so fervently in equality that I felt like a hypocrite letting him pay, that even though I knew he was paying for me in a spirit of generosity, it made me feel like he didn't respect me as an equal. I explained, I just liked the *feel* of paying my own way. It was a pleasure for me. It made me feel professional and independent, and it was an important symbol for me of my feminism. He was stunned to hear all this. He had no idea how I felt. But he understood right away, and he had no problem switching. He thanked me for telling him, and couldn't understand why I hadn't told him sooner. After his sweet reaction, I couldn't understand either! It had seemed so difficult to me. Actually, I know why it seemed difficult. It's because when I tried to

pay with other men in the past, they didn't listen. They called my ideas silly, or put me down as a huffy feminist or whatever. In my head, I knew Max wouldn't do that. He is a feminist himself. But it was still very hard emotionally to ask.

I don't know how I got the idea to ask him to ask me why I wanted to pay. It just came to me in that second. But it worked. It gave me the opening I needed to ask finally for what I wanted....

Sometimes we fail to ask for what we want because it doesn't occur to us to get specific. Wendell and Elizabeth have been married for twenty-seven years, and only four years ago solved one of their thorniest problems.

ELIZABETH: We always seemed to fight about occasions—birthdays and the like. Wendell would forget them, and I'd feel awful about it. Once after an incident like this I was talking with a friend who said, "Have you ever told him exactly what you want?" So I went home and told him, "I need three presents a year—birthday, anniversary, and Christmas—and a card on Valentine's Day." Wendell loved it. He said, "That I can do!" It has been great ever since....

Common wisdom says that you should never expect your partner to change. But I have always felt that this is true in some circumstances but not others. It is inappropriate—to say nothing of futile—to ask your partner to change basic personality characteristics. But if your partner is capable of the change you want, and if it would make an enormous difference to you, ask! Even though you may be requesting something that will require great effort on the part of your spouse, you may be doing both of you a favor in the end.

Whether you are asking your partner to sweep the porch, to spend more quality intimate time with you, or to try to become a more thoughtful person, a few simple guidelines and principles will make success much more likely. 85

1. *Figure out exactly what you want to ask for.* Sometimes this is the hardest part. If you have only a vague sense that something isn't right, that you are unhappy or dissatisfied in some way, you can try one of several strategies for determining exactly what you want. Talk with a friend to see if you can clarify your thoughts. Or, talk with your partner. If you do this, set up the conversation to make it as nonthreatening for your partner as possible. You might say, "Would you be willing just to talk something over with me? I'm not asking for anything, I just want to see if I can become clearer about it."

The one rule that is critical is, If you feel emotional about something, talk about it. If something is gnawing away at you, if you feel angry or "charged up," bring it up and discuss it. Don't feel that you have to have your specific request all worked out in advance. You can't know ahead of time what will result from your discussion; that's all the more reason to discuss it. Unfortunately, the issues you feel strongest about are likely to be the hardest to bring up. They make you feel vulnerable, out of control. You fear the issue will cause a fight. When it comes time to talk about it, you may minimize it or even temporarily forget it.

Kathryn's strong feeling about not wanting Max to pay for her dinner is an example. She had held the feelings for several months. But she always talked herself out of saying anything. Kathryn told me,

> I never wanted to spoil our good times with each other. And I was afraid Max would be angry or hurt or insulted or feel criticized. I would convince myself that the whole thing was silly. I know what finally pushed it to the surface enough for me to bring it up: I talked with a friend about it. That just clarified the issue for me. It gave me a chance to see that I really did have feelings about it. But I was so reluctant to bring it up. I didn't know what would happen.

You can never work through a problem and get to a resolution if you don't have the courage to bring it up and discuss it. And you *will* work it through if you do have the courage to bring it up. Couples who thrive talk to each other about what is troubling them. If they feel emotionally charged up about something, they talk about it!

2. *Pave the way for your request.* Before you begin, tell your partner that you are not criticizing him or her, that you are simply stating a preference.

We all have a tendency to hear requests as criticisms. For example, one partner may say, "I'd really like to eat dinner at six rather than seven or seven-thirty. Would that be okay?" But the other partner may hear, "You are late with dinner. You can't get it together." . . .

. . . If something you say causes your partner to feel defensive, you can say, "Wait a second. I really didn't mean to make you feel defensive. I'm sorry I put it that way. Let's just talk about it." You are giving your partner a chance to shift. In the same way, if you notice yourself starting to feel defensive, the best thing in the world to say is, "I'm feeling defensive." This lets your partner know that something he or she has said felt critical to you. It stops any fighting or bickering before it begins. And it gives you a chance to shift off the defensive stance and to open yourself up to listening to your partner in a nondefensive way. . . .

3. *Time your request appropriately.* Try not to ask for a favor when your mate is tired, stressed, or in a bad mood. If you are making a major request, set up a time when you won't be interrupted, and when you can have some time to talk it through.

4. *Be specific.* If you are annoyed that the dishwasher hasn't been emptied, don't say, "I wish you'd be more helpful around here." Say, "Would you be willing to empty the dishwasher sometime this morning?" Rather than, "I'd like you to be more affectionate," say, "I'd like us to have a big hug every morning when I leave for work." . . .

5. *Be brief.* Do not embellish your request with a list of reasons why you 95 think it is a great request. This is extremely unappealing and ineffective: "Honey, I have to shop and pay bills this morning, and I was up so late last night. You don't have to be anywhere for another hour. I'd love to get some help, I mean, do you think maybe you could empty the dishwasher or something?"

6. *Ask in an open-ended, nondemanding way.* Understand that your mate has a right to say no. If you make a reasonable request and you get a negative response, it may be time for you to do some listening. Maybe for some reason your mate doesn't consider your request to be as reasonable as you think it is. Before you argue back, find out.

The phrase "Would you be willing to . . ." is very useful. It subtly communicates that you understand that your mate may not be willing for some reason. It allows you to be specific in a nondemanding way. "Would you be willing to take the kids to school tomorrow morning?" "Would you be willing to pick up some milk on the way home?"

7. *If asking in one way doesn't work, try a new method.* There is a difference between asking for something, and actually communicating your request to your partner. Your partner's background experiences and frame of reference—and your partner's own needs—may be so different from yours that he or she may actually not fully realize what you are asking for. . . .

Couples who thrive have also achieved a balance between asking for changes in their partner and accepting those qualities in their partner that will never change. . . .

5. AFFIRM OTHERS

Everyone needs to be affirmed, complimented, praised, thanked, and acknowl- 100 edged. A study of couples reported in *Psychology Today* found clear evidence that "both men and women deem romance and passion far *less* important than affirmation and warm fuzzies.". . .

Virtually all the thriving couples I spoke with affirm each other in a variety of ways, regularly and consistently. The understanding between couples who thrive goes something like this: "This relationship is rare and valuable. It must be actively cared for. Like a beautiful plant, it will thrive if given water and sunshine and food, and it will wither and die if it is neglected." Couples who thrive feel extremely fortunate to be together, and their entire relationship takes place against a backdrop of their feeling of being blessed. Consistent compliments and affirmations are more the *result* of a flourishing relationship than the cause of one.

On the other hand, compliments can make an extraordinary difference in any relationship. Listen to Margaret's story:

Ross and I were at a very low point in our relationship. He was having a big struggle with his business. He really wanted out but couldn't find a way to get out, and basically he had been depressed for three years. He just wasn't there for me. I remember saying to him at the end of a vacation, "I feel like I've been on this trip alone!" I was committed to him, but I was feeling pretty discouraged.

One night we were hanging around the hot tub. He has a big scar on his leg, and I was thinking, Yuk, what an ugly scar. And suddenly it hit me. I'm looking at everything negative and nothing positive. I've got to turn this around! Right then, I said to him, "Ross, you are such a great father. I really love how much you do with the kids." He looked up at me and smiled, and I just realized, I was probably a drag to be around, too! I started complimenting him on all sorts of things, and every day I told him I loved him. Those words had fallen totally out of our vocabulary! I'll tell you, it was the beginning of a major turnaround. I felt better because I was remembering all the things I love about him, and he started paying a lot more attention to me. Within a month, he had figured out how to split up and sell the company. And we regained the old *joie de vivre* we had when we first met. It was a total turnaround.

Affirming others means more than remembering to toss a few kind words in their direction: in the same way that genuine listening means climbing into the other person's shoes for a moment, affirming another person means thinking about how that person feels, remembering what that person is concerned about, giving your attention fully to him or her. If you compliment a woman on her appearance, at some level you are acknowledging that she went to a lot of trouble to pick out those clothes, find matching earrings, skillfully apply her makeup, and so on. . . .

The most heartfelt compliments are genuine expressions of delight on the part of the giver. When you say, "You look really nice tonight," in the most heartfelt way, what you will be *feeling* is, "You are a pleasure *for me* to look at. I'm really lucky." If you are feeling good yourself about whatever you are commenting on, your partner will feel the most complimented. When Mayer looks at me and asks someone, "Isn't she wonderful?" I know he is enjoying me, and not just trying to be a good husband.

One of the reasons so many of us are stingy with affirmations of others, and 105 have to be reminded how important they are and taught how to give them, is that we have a tendency to be extremely self-involved. We get preoccupied with ourselves. When two people are in love, they become preoccupied with each other. One of the qualities that couples who thrive for many years together have is that they pay a lot of attention to each other.

Since affirming is actually about paying attention to another person, another important method of affirming is mentioning details. Rather than, "That was a great speech," say, "You seemed so relaxed. The joke about the little boy was perfect. I absolutely loved your ending." Be specific.

One of the best affirmations you can give a person is to ask a question that indicates that you remember what is going on in that person's life. Sales people are trained to jot down notes about their customers or clients so that when they see the person a month later they can say, "How did your son do on his science fair project?" or "How did that conversation with your supervisor go?" It's even more important to do this with our friends and lovers. When you see your spouse at the end of the day, unless something noteworthy happened to you that you are bursting to relate, ask him or her a question about something specific you knew was going to occur that day. This simple thoughtfulness can be a wonderful gift....

Everyone thrives on strokes. But John Gray, author of *Men Are from Mars, Women Are from Venus,* points out a subtle difference between the types of strokes that women like and those that men like. Women, he says, like consistency. Every small affirmation counts in a big way for them. The simple spontaneous comment "You look lovely tonight" counts just as much for a woman as what seems to her husband to be a much more major affirmation, like bringing her flowers unexpectedly. While men count saying "I love you" as a 1 on the affirmation scale, and bringing home flowers as a 100, women score both as 100. Little spontaneous acts or words of thoughtfulness mean a great deal to women. According to Gray, women are more oriented toward connection; men, toward accomplishments, so women want to be affirmed for who they are, men, for what they do. This is important information, because it is best to give the kinds of affirmations you know the other person most wants, not the kind you would like to get yourself.

You can easily brighten a woman's life every day with a verbal expression of your love. But men misunderstand this quality in women. The critical point men often fail to see is this: Women like to hear compliments and adoring comments, not because they are afraid that you don't love them anymore, not because they are insecure about their appearance, not because they are worried about your feelings for them. Rather, they want to hear these affirmations because it is a source of pleasure for them. A woman wants, not only to have, but to experience her connection with you. A compliment gives her enormous pleasure. It lets her know, not only that you love her, but that you are aware of your love, that you are thinking about it, that it gives you pleasure to love her.

A man will perk up when you verbally appreciate him for who he is and for the things he does for you. 110

In the end, for everyone, being affirmed is so important that any compliment works wonders. Indeed, a person who is getting no attention at all may pick a fight just as a way to get noticed, because negative attention is better than none. Couples who thrive affirm each other in a variety of ways, spontaneously, and often.

Any couple—whether thriving or hoping to thrive—can make a staggering difference in their relationship if they learn to use the five basic communication skills we have just discussed:

1. Make "I" statements rather than "you" statements, especially when feeling emotionally charged up.
2. Differentiate between "feelings-oriented" and "solution-oriented" conversations.
3. Listen nondefensively and focus on understanding the other person's point of view.
4. Ask for what you want.
5. Affirm each other regularly and often.

If you use these skills enough, they will become habits. But it is important to recognize that in stressful situations, when the skills are most important of all, you will have a tendency to revert to old behavior. Communication skills always require special attention and deliberate thought. Even if you know better, it is easy to become self-involved and forget to affirm your partner; to suppress your true desires and acquiesce to your partner without standing up for what you want; or to become defensive. . . .

Good communication skills should not be reserved for special situations. They can be used all the time and in a wide variety of settings. In your normal, day-to-day routines, you can remember to toss your spouse a kiss, or when listening, to make a simple comment like, "That must have made you angry." Good skills are especially critical when you are trying to resolve a conflict. But they are important all the time. They are the day-to-day substance of a thriving relationship.

THE TWO MARRIAGES: HIS AND HERS

John Gottman

John Gottman is a professor of psychology at the University of Washington. He has spent most of his career as an academic researcher, doing complex, long-term research, often sponsored by grants from the National Institute of Mental Health, for other experts in his field. Recently, however, Gottman's research on the relationships between 2,000 married couples turned up results notable enough to offer to the general public. Consequently, in addition to a 500-page academic study filled with statistics and methodological explanations titled What Predicts Divorce? The Relationship between Marital Processes and Marital Outcomes *(1994), he published a second book half that size written for lay readers titled* Why Marriages Succeed or Fail . . . and How <u>You</u> Can Make Yours Last *(1994). This reading comes from that book.*

Gottman's scientific research methods involve the intense examination of couples' conversations—including their facial expressions, fidgeting, gestures, and heart rates. He and his research team now claim to be able to predict with 94 percent accuracy which couples are heading for divorce. Contrary to much common wisdom, they find that marriages do not fall apart because of money problems, sexual disagreements, or incompatibility; more crucial, they say, is how couples deal with areas of disagreement. Gottman and his team find that a variety of styles can lead to a good marriage just so long as there are five times as many positive as negative moments in couples' communication.

In the following reading, Gottman describes four strategies for positive communication, as well as four missteps that can lead to disaster.

As you read, take note of the four strategies that can improve communication and of how the other four lead to the destruction of relationships.

I believe some conflict and disagreement are crucial for a marriage's long-term success. The idea that conflict is healthy may sound like a cruel joke if you're feeling overwhelmed by the negativity in your relationship. But in a sense a marriage lives and dies by what you might loosely call its arguments, by how well disagreements and grievances are aired. The key is *how* you argue—whether your style escalates tension or leads to a feeling of resolution.

You may assume that learning a healthy disagreement style is a complex, virtually impossible task. Far from it. Although many marriage manuals offer long lists of communication techniques you can follow, I think that most couples (even those in the most miserable marriages) don't really need an intricate, step-by-step program. After all, the same couples who are unable to communicate at home easily do so with their neighbors or at work....

Obviously, the problem isn't a lack of skill. It's that their ability to communicate with their loved one is stymied by the negativity that's enveloping their marriage. It's all too easy to let simple disagreements become knock-down, drag-out fights that leave one or both of you wondering if this marriage can be saved. The real problem is a lack of strategy—in other words, losing sight of when to apply the skills you already have.

In fact, I believe there are only four crucial strategies that you need to utilize in order to break through most of the negativity. If you can put them to use, your marriage is almost certain to improve dramatically—all your natural communication and conflict-resolving abilities will come to the fore. Of course, it won't always be easy to put these essentials to work. It will take courage, strength, and trust to use them when you're feeling hurt, angry, and victimized. The key is not only to understand these strategies intellectually but to use them so often that they become second nature and are available to you *even when you are feeling very upset*—the moments you'll need them most. I call this *overlearning* and it is the one principle you need to adopt for my program to work at all....

I may surprise you by claiming that you ought not to worry so much about 5 solving your marital problems as [about] dealing with the emotions they stir.

In fact, what a couple in one type of stable marriage means by "solving" the problem will be entirely different than what another means.

If problem solving isn't the main goal of my recommendations, then what is? The major goal is to break the cycle of negativity and give whatever natural repair mechanisms you already have in your repertoire a chance to work. There are four key strategies for accomplishing this goal.

In the following pages, I'll explain how to incorporate the four strategies for a lasting healthy marriage into your own relationship. The major goal is to break the cycle of negativity. You'll learn (1) how to *calm yourself* so that flooding doesn't block your communication; (2) how to *speak and listen nondefensively* so that your discussions or disagreements will be more productive; (3) how to *validate each other* as well as your relationship even (or especially) when the going gets tough; (4) how to *overlearn these principles* so that your new skills become almost second nature.

As you read on, you may feel that some of the strategies sound a bit unnatural or alien to you. Don't worry about absorbing them all in one sitting. As with any new endeavor, learning to argue effectively takes practice. I've left you plenty of opportunity to try out your new abilities. Have faith—you'll get there.

For starters, make an agreement with your partner to limit discussions of disagreements to fifteen minutes at a sitting. Set a kitchen timer. If you decide to go for longer at the end of fifteen minutes, add only another fifteen minutes.

STRATEGY #1: CALM DOWN

The first step is learning to calm down. This is a specific remedy for several 10 problems, most related to flooding.° It eases the need to be defensive and to stonewall,° undercuts the physical feelings that sustain distress-maintaining thoughts, and is the antidote to flooding. And because flooding is the trigger for the Distance and Isolation Cascade,° calming down is a preventive measure.

Because flooding is so destructive to a relationship, the first strategy you need to learn is to recognize when you're feeling overwhelmed and then to make a deliberate effort to calm yourself. From the data gathered in our lab we've seen how quickly discussions fall apart as soon as one spouse's heart rate begins to soar. Because physical responses are such an accurate barometer of your ability to communicate at a particular moment, tracking your arousal level during intense conversation will keep your discussions on track as well. Learning to calm down helps prevent unproductive fighting or running away

---

° **flooding:** The feeling of being overwhelmed by one's partner's negativity and one's own emotional upset.   ° **stonewall:** To remove oneself from communication by retreating into silence, at the same time conveying disapproval.   ° **Distance and Isolation Cascade:** Gottman uses this phrase (suggesting a rapid descent down the marital waterfall) for the final and most disastrous result of flooding.

from discussions you need to have. The notion of monitoring your physical responses and calming yourself are direct applications of my insights into couples during marital conflict resolution.

Calming down is the exact physiological opposite of flooding. When you're flooded, you are extremely upset and physiologically aroused. By calming down you take a direct step toward reversing that distress.

Calming down is especially important for men, since as we know, they are more likely to feel physiologically overwhelmed sooner than women during a heated marital exchange. And it takes less intense negativity for men to get physiologically overwhelmed. Also, men are more likely to rehearse destructive, innocent-victim or vengeful thoughts once they feel flooded. But whatever your gender, it's virtually impossible to think straight when your blood is pumping furiously and your heart is racing. For that reason you're likely to fall back on automatic, overlearned behavior once you become flooded. This is why overarousal leads you to say things you later regret, why you may want to run away, why you stonewall, why you may fly off the handle—and why it would be better to take a deep breath and simply soothe yourself.

For all these reasons you should take your pulse every five minutes or so during difficult discussions with your spouse as a way to monitor your physiological reactions, specifically your heart rate. You may think pulse-taking is silly and unnecessary, but most people are actually very poor judges of their own heart rates. A quick check of your pulse will ensure that you're aware of your true arousal level. Taking your pulse is fairly simple—you may already have learned to do it during aerobic exercise or to monitor a heart condition.

Gently press your right index and middle fingers against your right carotid 15 artery, which is two-to-three inches below your earlobe and under your jawbone. You should be able to feel your pulse. To calculate your pulse rate per minute, count the number of pulse beats you feel in fifteen seconds and multiply by four. To determine your average, baseline rate, take your pulse three different times while you're sitting comfortably. Although individual pulse rates vary widely, most women clock in at between 82 and 86 beats per minute while men average between 72 and 76 beats per minute.

Once you know your baseline rate, it's simple to check your arousal level during discussions. If at any time your rate climbs to 10 percent above your resting rate (an increase of about 8 to 10 beats per minute), you know you're overaroused and need to take a break.

This chart can help you assess your pulse rate:

Baseline Heart Rate:_____
10 Percent of Baseline:_____
Sum of the Above:_____ *(Your heart rate during discussions should not exceed this.)*

If, for example, your baseline rate is 80, it's best to take a break if you hit 88. It is absolutely crucial that you take a break if your heart rate goes over 100 BPM.

When your heart is beating that fast, your body is releasing relatively larger quantities of adrenaline than it normally does, triggering a panicky fight-or-flight stress reaction that will make it virtually impossible for you to absorb what your partner is saying.

At first it may feel forced and artificial to request an intermission when your spouse is sounding off about, say, your sloppy showering habits. But if you clarify why you're doing it, and both agree to use this strategy, over time you'll both get used to it. Explain that you're not trying to avoid the discussion. On the contrary, taking a break now will simply allow you to calm down so you'll be better able to hear and understand your partner's point of view.

Call a time-out using whatever method feels most comfortable to you: hold 20 up both hands or simply announce to your mate that it's time to knock off for a bit. This is not unlike the bell that sends two fighters retreating to their corners during a bout—except that your goal when you return is to communicate better, not pummel each other.

How long do you think it will take you to calm down? Many people guess about five minutes. In fact, it takes most people closer to twenty minutes for their physiological responses to return to baseline. As I mentioned, many of us are surprisingly poor judges of our own heart rates. In fact, most people believe they have calmed down completely when their pulse rate is still a good 10 percent above their normal, resting pulse. It is easy to *think* you've settled down when actually you're still riled up. So be sure to take your pulse before returning to the discussion.

There's an important reason you should not return until you're truly calm: a psychological phenomenon called the "Zillmann Transfer of Excitation Effect." Studies show that if you believe you have calmed down but are still physiologically aroused when you reapproach your spouse, you'll be very susceptible to taking on any emotion he or she expresses. In other words, you'll channel your remaining physiological excitation toward duplicating whatever emotion is prevailing at the moment. So if your partner is still angry when you resume your talk, you'll pick up the anger as well, defeating the purpose of your time-out.

What should you do during the recess? Whatever will soothe you. For some people that means simply leaving the room. Others find it helps to hop in the car for a relaxing drive, take a bath, listen to music, call a friend, work, and so on. But whatever your physical location, the real key to calming down is what you tell yourself.

Rewriting Your Inner Script

Too often, people spend a time-out rehearsing all kinds of hurtful or vengeful comments they plan to make when they return. They tend to repeat to themselves distress-maintaining thoughts—those inner scripts of righteous indignation or innocent victimization.... Some typical thoughts along these lines are:

"That really hurt me."
"I can't forgive and forget what he (she) said and did."
"I will not let go of my anger and hurt."
"I'm getting out of this marriage."
"I'm not going to take this anymore."
"I'll show her (him)."
"I'll get even."
"That makes me mad."
"He (She) is *(Fill in the blank with an insult)*."...

For a time-out to be effective you need to make a conscious effort to replace 25 these distress-maintaining thoughts with soothing and validating ones. Try these:

"Calm down. Take some deep breaths."
"No need to take this personally."
"He's (she's) upset right now, but this isn't a personal attack."
"This isn't really about me."
"This is a bad moment, but things aren't always like this."
"I'm upset now, but I love him (her)."
"She (he) has a lot of nice qualities."...

Relaxation Methods

While changing your distressing thoughts is one route to cooling off, another is to simply make yourself physically relaxed (a combination of both approaches can be especially effective)....

Once your pulse rate indicates that you have calmed down physically, approach your spouse and continue your discussion for another fifteen minutes.

Training yourself to take calming breaks when you're at risk of feeling flooded won't solve your marital problems. But it is an essential first step that will keep you receptive to other strategies that can help you dramatically.

STRATEGY #2: SPEAK NONDEFENSIVELY

Listening or speaking without being defensive helps counter several destructive habits. Nondefensive *listening* is especially helpful to ease defensiveness. If you are a nondefensive listener, it will make the cycle of negativity less likely. And a nondefensive attitude also helps defuse flooding and the need to stonewall, particularly for men. But defensiveness is a two-way street; if you start *speaking* nondefensively, you will lessen your partner's need to be defensive....

This will be tough to do at first. After all, listening and speaking without 30 being defensive are not strategies we learn in school, or anywhere else. But couples who work hard at weeding defensiveness out of their interactions find a dramatic rise in their marital satisfaction.

Praise and Admiration: Unseating the Four Horsemen

The single most important tactic for short-circuiting defensive communication is to choose to have a positive mindset about your spouse and to reintroduce praise and admiration into your relationship. If your arguments are marked by defensiveness, it's likely that your marriage is being overrun by all four horsemen.° As the negativity in your relationship swells, the balance of positive to negative feelings and interactions between you and your spouse is thrown off. Depending on your particular personality and circumstances, this negativity will lead you toward being mostly a critic, an abuser, or a stonewaller. But in any case, having and expressing a positive attitude toward your spouse is the most powerful antidote....

Even a little bit of nondefensive listening and validation at the right times can have dramatic effects. Herb was a steady social drinker and his wife Jan complained that his drinking at his social club often left her all alone and lonely. Herb became very defensive and said that he deserved this time with his friends and that his club gave him valuable business contacts. Jan became increasingly more upset and alienated from him as the conversation progressed when suddenly, out of the blue, Herb said, "So what you'd like is if when I got to the club I called you and asked you if you wanted to come down and join me." The atmosphere changed immediately and she said, "Yes, that's it." He said, "Well, I think I can do that. Not every time, but certainly most of the time." A little while later the affection had grown so much that Jan said, "Now I know why I married you.".…

To improve or save your marriage you must remind yourself that your mate's negative qualities do not cancel out all the positives that led you to fall in love. Nor do bad times wipe out all the good times. If your marriage is going through a rocky period it's particularly important to recall specific happy memories you have of your mate. Even force yourself to sit awhile and think about them. For example, you could look through picture albums from past vacations, or reread some old love letters.

The bottom line is that you need to become the architect of your thoughts. It's up to you to decide what your inner script will contain. You can habitually look at what is *not* there in your relationship, at your disappointments, and fill your mind with thoughts of irritation, hurt, and contempt. Or you can do the opposite. For example, you could walk into the kitchen in the morning and fume because your partner did a lousy job of cleaning the counter and left dishes in the sink. Or you could look on the positive side — most of the dishes did get washed and you know your spouse was very tired last night. "We've

---

° **four horsemen:** Using the metaphor of the four horsemen of the apocalypse (in the Bible's Book of Revelations, the precursors of ultimate disaster), Gottman refers throughout his book to four kinds of behavior that can destroy relationships: criticism, contempt, defensiveness, and stonewalling.

been under a lot of pressure lately," you might think. "It's amazing how many things *are* getting done.". . .

If looking on the bright side doesn't come naturally to you, start with small 35 steps. Make a list of your partner's positive qualities—things he or she does to contribute to your life together. Memorize this list and think about how much harder life would be without these positives. When you find yourself following a critical train of thought about your mate, use elements from the list to *interrupt* your thinking. Make a habit of this process and the change can be dramatic. You may want to work on restructuring your habitual thoughts together with your partner. Going through the process as a team can double the benefits.

Of course, there must be a real basis for feeling good about your partner's contributions. In so many marriages, this basis really does exist—yet it's amazing to me how easily the partners lose sight of it. You can all too readily fall into the rut of thinking critically about your marriage and what your mate is *not* doing right.

Once you begin "rethinking" your marriage, don't keep your positive thoughts to yourself. Everyone, including your spouse, responds to genuine praise, thanks, and simple heartfelt compliments on a regular basis. At first, you may need to remind yourself to speak your positive thoughts. Try to give your partner this gift every day, especially if you've been fighting a lot lately. I'm not suggesting that you lie about your feelings toward your spouse. You must be genuine. But, as I've said, if you look at your partner's actions objectively you're more than likely to find some things that are worth applauding. Here are the sorts of simple strokes that will go a long way:

"I really appreciated your cooking dinner tonight."
"You really handled that contractor well."
"Thanks for calling the insurance company."
"I just love watching you play with Jason."
"You were a very considerate father tonight."
"I know you've been stressed lately, and I admire the way you've been coping with it all."
"One thing I like about you is your guts. You really stood up to her when she put you down. I admire that."
"You were really funny tonight. I just love your sense of humor."

Don't be surprised if your spouse expresses some cynicism upon hearing your first few compliments. He or she may have become conditioned to expect negativity from you. But if you keep at it, your mate will eventually come to believe that your attitude has changed and will respond by being less defensive. Sooner or later you're likely to be on the receiving end of compliments as well.

As therapists know, it is very difficult for change to occur except in a climate of acceptance. One of the great paradoxes in therapy is that people don't change unless they feel accepted as they are. What people praise and admire tells us what they aspire to be, what they value and respect. Saying what you admire about your mate will make your partner feel accepted. Admiration is the opposite of contempt, possibly the most destructive of the horsemen. But it only works if it is genuine. It has to be real—and it can't just be empty words that are said to get an effect. Seasoning your interactions with genuine praise and admiration will significantly limit your spouse's defensiveness. But the third horseman, defensiveness, is still likely to surface in the heat of an argument. Fortunately, there are ways you can unseat him at such crucial times, whether your spouse is speaking or you are.

When You're the Listener

The key to defusing your spouse's defensiveness is to be a good listener. While 40 your mate has the floor, it is your job to genuinely understand and empathize with the feelings behind the words you hear. I admit that this can be extremely difficult, especially if your spouse is criticizing you or yelling. The trick here is to try very hard not to take what your spouse is saying as a personal attack that demands you defend or counterattack, even if you're hearing a lot of contempt. Think of the intense negativity as simply underlining the strength of his or her feelings so that you will pay serious attention to them.

Recently a man I have never met called me for marital advice. He told me that his wife said they should consider getting a divorce and should think about what to do with the children. His question was whether he should take his wife seriously. I told him that, although I did not know his wife, I would certainly take the statement seriously. He seemed surprised by my advice, probably as surprised as I was by his question. This man had probably been ignoring many less intense signals his wife had been giving him for some time. Finally, with her ultimate escalation—with the unmistakable underlining— he took notice of her feelings.

I can't emphasize this point enough. If an issue has a history of frustrating interaction, the negative feelings will intensify over time. This is an act of both frustration and desperation. Your partner's negativity is a way of emphasizing how strongly your partner feels about the issue. Even if you strongly disagree with the words that go along with your partner's negativity, see them as a way of underlining how strongly your partner feels about the issue—a way to get you to pay attention.

Nondefensive listening doesn't mean you need to agree with your partner. Your mission is to try to understand your partner's feelings—to accept them as legitimate even if you don't share them. If you can send the message, "Gee, I don't see it that way, but I can understand why you might, given your perspective," you will have gone a long way toward repairing the damage of previous negativity. The highest level of nondefensive listening entails empathizing with your partner's emotions and viewpoint. This means putting yourself in your spouse's shoes and truly comprehending his or her feelings from within yourself.

There is a hierarchy of less powerful to very powerful nondefensive listening. Even the mildest form is effective. Just saying, "Uh-huh, go ahead, I'm listening," or "I can see why you'd feel that way," or "It makes sense that you'd feel that way," or even a periodic "Yeah," can communicate that you're trying to understand even if you don't necessarily have the same point of view. Just acknowledging that perhaps two points of view exist, and that both have some validity, is a powerful form of acceptance.

The most powerful form of nondefensive listening is to genuinely feel what 45 your partner is feeling and communicate that empathic response. Again, this empathy has to be real for it to work. You can't pretend to be empathetic. In between these two levels are lots of variations, all of them good.

The following strategies can help improve your ability to listen nondefensively:

Embrace the Anger.   Often, when people express themselves heatedly it's because they think that's the only way to make you listen. Remember that the anger or insult is really for emphasis, a "thwack" to get you to pay attention to what they're saying. If you respond defensively or stonewall to protect yourself from intense emotions, your spouse is likely to increase rather than lessen the emotional volume of his or her words. Thus, defensiveness and withdrawal will destroy any chance you have of really understanding what your partner is trying to say.

Especially for Stonewallers: Back-Channel.   If you tend to stonewall, you are probably trying to defend yourself from feeling attacked by your partner's words. Obviously your withdrawal and the thoughts that accompany it make it impossible for you to be an engaged listener. Many stonewallers present blank faces to their mates, which sends the signal that they are not listening and just upsets their spouse even more. If your mate tends to complain that speaking to you is like talking to a wall, make a conscious effort not to stonewall and to send little signals that show you hear him or her. Psychologists call these signals *back channels:* they include nodding your head occasionally and making brief vocal indications that you understand, such as "uh-huh," "yeah," "oh I see," "um-hmmm." Back channels let your partner know that you haven't tuned out....

Beware of Your Own Body Language.   Although it isn't necessary to agree with what your partner is saying, you shouldn't show signs of disapproval while listening. Avoid at all costs facial expressions that convey mockery or contempt. Don't roll your eyes, purse your lips, or twist them in a sarcastic smile.

There are two other facial expressions that send very strong signals that 50 you're not empathizing at all with your mate. The *domineering listener* look suggests that you're ready to squelch your partner if he or she expresses anything you disagree with. In this stance your head is tilted downward and your frowning eyes are staring straight into your spouse's as if you're trying to control what your spouse is thinking.

A *belligerent* facial expression is equally counterproductive when you're attempting to listen. It is an attempt to provoke your partner. In this stance, you cock your head so that the plane of your face is turned away from your mate and you are leading with your chin. This suggests that you are just itching for a fight. Your arms may be folded across your chest, a further sign that you're blocking any information your partner is sending.

Obviously, these expressions are likely to anger or intimidate your spouse. Either way, they stymie communication. To be a good listener, make sure your facial expression and body language show that you're receptive to what your partner is saying. This will let him or her know that you really are listening and trying hard to understand. . . .

When You're the Speaker

There are times in any relationship when you don't like something your partner has just said. If your marriage has become filled with negativity, your knee-jerk response may be to express your displeasure by criticizing or expressing contempt toward your mate. Unfortunately, this is likely to make your spouse defensive, which just escalates the conflict. Your goal should be to simply *complain* to your spouse rather than make the attack personal. . . .

Before you utter a word, remember that you really do have a choice. Think of your next statement as a fork in the road of your argument. Here is where you decide whether to keep the conversation reasonable by expressing a specific complaint or to head into rocky terrain by criticizing or verbalizing contempt. (If, despite good intentions, you slip and take the rocky road, you can always start over by calling a break.)

Let me clarify . . . the distinctions between a complaint, a criticism, and contempt. 55

- A complaint is *specific,* limited to one situation. It states how you feel. ("I am upset because you didn't take out the garbage tonight.")
- A criticism tends to be global and *includes blaming* your partner. You'll often find the word *always* or *never* in a criticism. ("You never take out the garbage. Now it's overflowed and that's your fault. I can't ever rely on you.")
- Contempt adds insult to the criticism. It is verbal character assassination in which you accuse your spouse of stupidity, incompetence, etc. ("You idiot, why can't you ever remember to take out the garbage?") . . .

If you understand how a complaint differs from criticism or contempt but still have difficulty controlling yourself from being negative during an argument, keep the following general guidelines in mind:

- Remove the blame from your comments.
- Say how *you* feel.

- Don't criticize your partner's personality.
- Don't insult, mock, or use sarcasm.
- Be direct.
- Stick with one situation.
- Don't try to analyze your partner's personality.
- Don't mind-read.

Most of all, try to be as specific as possible when you complain. The more 60
concrete your grievance, the more you'll improve your partner's understanding
of why you're upset. Think of your complaint as a set of directions. We all
know how easy it is to follow instructions that are clear and explicit.... A specific complaint lets your partner know exactly where you are, while vague complaints can be misinterpreted and get you off track.

A good way to keep a complaint specific is to couch it in what I call an "X, Y, Z" statement. Think of this approach as a kind of game in which you fill in the blanks with your particular gripe in mind: "When you did (or didn't do) X in situation Y, I felt Z."

Example: "When you didn't call to tell me you were going to be late (X) for our dinner appointment (Y), I felt frustrated (Z)." Using this X, Y, Z formula will help you avoid insults and character assassination. It allows you to simply state how your partner's behavior affects your feelings and, in turn, your response.

Let's say you're upset about the family finances. It's more constructive to say, "When you bounced several checks (X) and the bank called (Y), I felt embarrassed and angry (Z)," rather than, "You are incredibly irresponsible for bouncing a check. I'm constantly having to pick up after your mistakes and fix everything you screw up."...

Two other manners of speaking that can trigger a defensive response in your spouse are a belligerent and [a] domineering style. Domineering speech lets your spouse know you want him or her to respond only as you see fit. ("When I want your opinion I'll give it to you.") Whether your tone is threatening or patronizing, your message is the same: You've got the floor and you're not giving it up. Certainly not to your partner. You may repeat yourself simply to maintain your "rights" as speaker. Domineering speech may be very slow and deliberate, indicating that you're adamant about your point of view and nothing is going to change it. Or your tone may be condescending, indicating that your partner is a simple child who needs to be shown the right way.

Belligerent talk lets your partner know you're really ready to fight. At the 65
very least, you want to get a rise out of him or her. Phrases like, "Do you have an attitude problem or what?" "What is it *now?*" "Just trying to get on my nerves, is that it?" "What have you got to say for yourself?" "What's your complaint? Speak up!" are signs of this bullying.

If you recognize yourself in the description of belligerent or domineering speaking (or if your spouse recognizes you), you must work especially hard *not* to talk this way during arguments. No matter what justifications you may believe you have for these responses, the reality is that you will never be able to communicate effectively if you subject your mate to blatant or veiled threats.

Training yourself to speak to your spouse in a way that doesn't trigger a negative response will greatly cut down on your mate's defensiveness, which can only improve the communication between you. But it isn't enough. After all, at times when you'll be on the receiving end of a destructive, negative statement or look from your spouse, what do you do then? Most people reflexively become defensive in an attempt to ward off the attack. But as I'm sure you know by now, such phrases usually have the opposite effect, dragging you both further into a quagmire of accusations and hurt feelings.

When you're responding to a less-than-perfect comment from your spouse it's up to you to extricate both of you from a nasty, counterproductive confrontation. To do so, you need to avoid ... defensive responses ... :

- Denying responsibility for a problem
- Making excuses
- Using phrases like "yes, but ..."
- Whining
- Reacting to negative mind reading
- Cross-complaining ...

Instead, try to respond in a way that lets your spouse know you're considering his or her perspective, even if you don't agree with it.

Below are some very defensive exchanges for which I have put more produc- 70 tive alternative statements in parentheses. I hope this will give you an idea about how to rewrite your own conversations. You may want to look over these examples with your spouse:

Example #1

WIFE: You never told me that your father was coming to visit us this weekend.

HUSBAND: I did so! (Alternative: "I thought I told you, but maybe I didn't. Sorry.")

WIFE: You did not! (Alternative: "Well, maybe you did and I didn't register it.")

HUSBAND: I did! (Alternative: "This is ridiculous. I'll take the blame for not telling you. I've been under some stress lately, so it's possible I forgot.")

Example #2

WIFE: You never take me out anymore.

HUSBAND: Baloney. I take you out lots. (Alternative: "Well, if that's the way you feel, then that's awful. Let's do something about it. How about dinner and a movie this Saturday?")

Example #3

WIFE: You never take me out anymore.

HUSBAND: Well, maybe you're right, but didn't you say you'd first have to find another babysitter? (This yes-but is like saying, "Yes, you are right, but you are also wrong." Alternative: "Well, what about asking your sister to babysit this Saturday and taking in dinner and a movie?")

STRATEGY #3: VALIDATION

Letting your spouse know in so many little ways that you understand him or her is one of the most powerful tools for healing your relationship. It is an antidote to several of the horsemen—criticism, contempt, and defensiveness. Instead of attacking or ignoring your partner's point of view, you try to see the problem from your partner's perspective, and show that you think that viewpoint may have some validity.

Validation is especially important for men who tend to respond to their 75 wives' upset by becoming hyperrational.° Rather than acknowledge the emotional content of their wife's words, they try to offer a practical solution to the problem being described. This can be quite well-meaning, but it too often misses the mark. If your wife is being extremely emotional she probably isn't interested in hearing advice. She mostly needs to know that you understand what she's *feeling*.

Validation is simply putting yourself in your partner's shoes and imagining his or her emotional state. It is then a simple matter to let your mate know that you understand those feelings and consider them valid, even if you don't share them. Validation is an amazingly effective technique. It's as if you opened the door to welcome your partner. When your partner feels validated, he or she will feel much more comfortable confiding in you, and much more open to hearing your perspective as well.

Validation is a real art and has many gradations. At the top of the scale is true empathy and understanding. This entails actually feeling a bit of what your partner is experiencing and being able to see the world through your partner's eyes. Expressing this deep empathy will show that you not only understand your partner's view of the world but his or her sense of self. Few things make a person feel more loved and valued. There are some specific ways you can add a high level of validation to your talks.

Take Responsibility.   If your husband says he gets upset when you don't call to let him know you'll be home late from work, try answering with, "Gee, I really made you angry, didn't I?" You are acknowledging that your actions might have provoked your partner's response.

Apologize.   Similarly, a straight-out apology is a very strong form of validation because it lets your partner know you consider his or her gripe valid and worth respecting. To apologize you don't have to always say, "I'm sorry." You can

---

°hyperrational: Extremely rational.

simply say, "I see what you mean. I was wrong." Everyone is wrong from time to time. However, admitting this in an argument can have very powerful results.

Compliment.   Honestly praising your spouse for handling a situation well will 80 go a long way. Especially when there is tension between you, reminding your partner (and yourself!) that you really admire him or her is likely to have a powerful, positive effect on the rest of your conversation.

Doing the Minimum.   At first, you may not be able to muster these high forms of validation. Fortunately, even a relatively minor type of validation, simply listening to and acknowledging your partner's point of view even if you don't share it, can work wonders. This type of validation can be as straightforward as saying, "Yes, I know that upsets you," when your husband says he's concerned about the children's grades. Be careful, however, not to end the sentence by harping on the fact that you don't agree. Do this and you'll cancel out the validation. Right now, your job isn't to argue for your point but to let your partner know you understand his or hers.

To see what an enormous difference a little bit of validation can make, consider the following discussion between Ward and Bridget. Both are unhappy with how things go between them when Ward gets home after a hard day's work.

Bridget's complaint is that Ward's only interest is to be fed dinner. She's exhausted after tending to the kids all day, running errands, etc. Rather than adding to her work load, she wants him to take care of *her* when he gets home — engage in adult conversation, maybe bring her flowers on occasion — or at least express interest in her thoughts or let her know he finds her attractive.

From Ward's perspective, he's exhausted at the end of the day and just wants to unwind. He'd like to relax, have his dinner, be given some peace and quiet, and have his wife express happiness that he's home. Being fed dinner makes him feel taken care of. It's a sign to him of Bridget's affection, that she's glad to see him. It's also the only time that the entire family spends together. He looks forward to this after a long, grueling day.

If Bridget and Ward attempted to discuss this conflict without expressing 85 any validation, here's what their talk would sound like:

BRIDGET: You come home and right away you want supper.

WARD: At the end of a day usually I'm tired and I just want to unwind.

BRIDGET: And I've been home all day with the kids, and I've had it up to here, errands all day, no time for myself, and I look forward to your coming home so I can get a little relief.

WARD: I want to be left alone for a few minutes. I'd appreciate a little peace and quiet when I walk in the door.

BRIDGET: I want someone to take care of *me* for a change. I'd like some adult conversation.

WARD: I'd like a little concern or affection, or a sense that you're glad to see me....

While reading this dialogue you could probably feel the tension increase as Bridget and Ward barreled ahead without recognizing each other's feelings or point of view. Now, here's the same dialogue, with each partner adding a touch of validation—just doing the minimum.

BRIDGET: You come home and right away you want supper.

WARD: I can see how that would feel like just another demand in a long list you've had to deal with all day. Me, at the end of a day, usually I'm tired and I just want to unwind.

BRIDGET: I know that you've had a hard day on your feet with all that tension. And I've been home all day with the kids, and I've had it up to here, errands all day, no time for myself, and I look forward to your coming home so I can get a little relief.

WARD: I've been looking forward to seeing you, too. But to tell you the truth, I want to be left alone for a few minutes. I'd appreciate a little peace and quiet when I walk in the door.

BRIDGET: You need a little breathing room to unwind when you first walk in. And here I'm thinking I want someone to take care of *me* for a change instead of me doing for someone else all day long, and maybe having some adult conversation. Maybe you can do that once you've had a little breathing room, a chance to unwind.

WARD: Yeah, that would be great. I can see why you want someone taking care of you at the end of a day. Those kids can be pretty demanding. We need to provide some relief for each other. I can do that after I've relaxed for a few minutes. I also want a little concern and affection, to know you're glad to see me....

These two conversations are worlds apart in how they leave Bridget and Ward feeling. Yet the only difference between them is a small amount of validation.

If your relationship suffers from a high level of negativity, being able to acknowledge your partner's feelings may be more than you can muster right now. In that case you may find it encouraging to know that even a begrudging acceptance of your spouse's point of view is a form of validating. So even if you can't drum up an enthusiastic tone of voice, it's worth attempting to validate your spouse.

If, no matter how hard you try, you just can't see your partner's point of view, let him or her know that you're trying. You can simply say, "Right now, I'm just taking in what you're saying and attempting to understand how you feel." This at least conveys that you're giving it your best shot. Remember, though, that you can't fake validation. It must be genuine to be effective.

If you need extra motivation to try to empathize with your spouse during tough times, keep in mind that all this psychological and emotional awareness is good for your physical health. Research has clearly demonstrated that when you validate your spouse, you're helping to keep your blood pressure down and your heart rate from skyrocketing. In one study of newlyweds I found that adrenaline secretions decreased during a conversation if a couple were validating and positive toward each other. But couples who were not validating tended to secrete more and more adrenaline as their conversation progressed—and their tension rose.

STRATEGY #4: OVERLEARNING—TRY AND TRY AGAIN

When you've had one successful fight using these techniques, you may think you've mastered the strategies. I'm afraid there's more work involved. In fact, the worst thing you could do is to read this chapter once and never look at it again. It's not enough to have an intellectual understanding of "fighting smart." These lessons have to be practiced *often*. So often, in fact, that they become almost automatic....

You and your spouse have to practice these skills even when you don't necessarily feel like it. That means when you are tired, distracted, happy, sad, driving, watching TV, showering together—under all circumstances and conditions until it becomes a natural, effortless part of your interactions. You have to make it your own, imbue it with your own sense of humor, style, and personality. Then just keep doing it again and again. Keep clocking up the hours using the skill.

The idea is that if you overlearn a communication skill, you'll have access to it when you need it most—during an argument or heated fight when you are physiologically aroused. That's when all of this overlearning will pay off.

If you practice, practice, practice these skills you will have gone a very long way toward improving your marriage. It has been my experience that these four principles—*calming down, communicating nondefensively, validating,* and *overlearning*—are all that most marriages need in order to get back on track. I believe this is even true of marriages that have been almost completely subsumed by negativity. I don't mean to imply that you will see changes overnight, or that transforming your marriage will be easy. But if you are motivated, work hard, and don't let every setback discourage you, over time you will find your marriage a far happier place to be.

A WRITER'S NOTEBOOK

Communicating in Relationships

The following tasks are designed to help you think about the readings and identify and start to work up material you might use in your own essay.

1. *Fill out information worksheets.* Fill out a copy of the information worksheet on page 61 for each of the preceding reports. The rereading and notemaking invited by these worksheets will help you understand the readings and compare

and contrast their conclusions. Later, the worksheet notes will help you plan your essay.

2. *Explain Deborah Tannen's views.* Write a page or so explaining how Tannen would answer the question that she asks in paragraphs 3 and 6: "Who talks more, women or men?" Make sure that you explain the distinctions Tannen develops in paragraphs 3–8.

3. *Consider your own conversations.* As you think about and discuss the readings and plan your essay, consider your own personal conversations in light of Tannen's and John Gray's conclusions. Record your ideas about at least three conversations, more if possible. Focus on opposite-gender conversations in which you are one of two to four participants. (More participants may make it difficult for you to pay attention to and recall the interactions.) For each conversation, write a few sentences about who was involved and where and then explain what was discussed. Describe the conversation you observed in light of the conclusions in one of the readings. You may find that your observations either confirm those conclusions or fail to support them.

4. *Interview long-term couples.* Interview at least two couples who have been together six months or more. They may be parents, relatives, or friends, heterosexual or same sex. After preparing specific interview questions based on generalizations in the readings, ask about their communication habits and styles. For example, you could ask whether they eat breakfast together and talk to each other at that time, or they both read a newspaper in the morning and, if so, whether they discuss it while reading.

5. *React to John Gray's metaphor.* Relate an incident when you either went to your cave, as Gray describes it, or talked in order to air your feelings and gain emotional support. Are you more likely to do one or the other? Speculate about why you react as you do and then comment on whether your experience matches the Mars-versus-Venus analysis Gray offers.

6. *Explain what Susan Page means.* Write a half-page or so explaining what Page means by *defensiveness* and why she thinks it should be avoided.

7. *Explain John Gottman's main point.* Gottman makes the at first seemingly unusual claim that what makes a successful marital relationship is not whether couples argue and disagree, but *how* they do so. Reread paragraphs 10–28. Write a half-page to a page explaining why, in his view, emotional reactions, negativity, and a high pulse rate tend to escalate conflict.

8. *Connect Gottman's ideas with Page's.* Despite some differences in Gottman's and Page's explanations and recommendations, you can probably see common ground between them. Write a page or so focusing on one of Page's five "basic skills" and explain what part of Page's advice about that skill you think Gottman would agree or disagree with.

INFORMATION WORKSHEET

Author and title of reading:

_____

List types of communication that this writer thinks will cause misunderstandings:

_____

_____

_____

_____

_____

_____

List communication skills that this writer thinks will help create understanding and resolve conflicts:

_____

_____

_____

_____

_____

_____

List differences that this writer sees between men's and women's styles of
communication:

_____

_____

_____

_____

_____

_____

CRITICAL RESPONSES

How has the advice given by Deborah Tannen, John Gray, Susan Page, and John Gottman been received? One indication of their reception comes from their sales; all four of these writers have found a wide audience of people willing to pay for their advice. John Gray's book has sold over six million copies, and his and Deborah Tannen's books were on best-seller lists for years. All four writers are sought after as speakers or seminar leaders, and Gottman's advice about communication in marriage has been announced in newspapers across the country. That certainly indicates how much people crave advice about communicating in relationships and perhaps suggests the extent to which some readers have been helped by the advice of Tannen, Gray, Page, or Gottman. Successful communication may be a topic that just will not go away or, in a society with a greatly increased incidence of divorce, a problem so pressing that people will pay to try to solve it.

Some critics, however, have found fault with some of their conclusions, particularly those related to gender differences. Following are several critical reviews, specifically of the work of Tannen and Gray. The first review, by Katha Pollitt, offers a feminist critique of "difference feminism's" belief that men and women are basically different from each other either by their very nature or by virtue of growing up with strikingly different conventions about how to talk and behave. The second review is by a linguist, Senta Troemel-Ploetz, who criticizes some of the linguistic assumptions common to "difference feminism" and raises political questions. Finally comes a *Time* magazine article on John Gray, questioning his work.

ARE WOMEN MORALLY SUPERIOR TO MEN?

Katha Pollitt

Katha Pollitt, an award-winning essayist and columnist for the Nation, *from which this 1992 article is excerpted, has also written for many other influential magazines, among them the* New Yorker, *the* New Republic, *and* Mother Jones. *In addition, she is a poet; her most recent collection is* Antarctic Traveller *(1982).*

In the following essay, Pollitt criticizes Deborah Tannen and others for endorsing "difference feminism" rather than "equality feminism." Difference feminism, Pollitt suggests, is founded in the belief that, while women and men are different, in some respects women are superior to men—for instance, in their empathy and nurturance and their concern for equal, nonhierarchical relationships. Men, by contrast, according to difference feminism, are individualistic and competitive, less interested in relationships than women are, and more interested in autonomy. Pollitt criticizes difference feminists for their essentialism—*their belief that men and women are essentially different rather than different because of an economic and cultural system that discriminates against women.*

As you read, pay attention to why Pollitt is critical of Tannen's and John Gray's belief that there are two cultures, one belonging to women and the other to men.

'RELATIONAL' WOMEN, 'AUTONOMOUS' MEN

In the 1950s, which we think of as the glory days of traditional sex roles, the anthropologist Ashley Montagu argued in "The Natural Superiority of Women" that females had it all over males in every way that counted, including the possession of two X chromosomes that made them stabler, saner and healthier than men, with their X and Y. Montagu's essay, published in *The Saturday Review* and later expanded to a book, is witty and high-spirited and, interestingly, anticipates the current feminist challenge to male-defined categories. (He notes, for example, that while men are stronger than women in the furniture-moving sense, women are stronger than men when faced with extreme physical hardship and tests of endurance; so when we say that men are stronger than women, we are equating strength with what men have.) But the fundamental thrust of Montagu's essay was to confirm traditional gender roles while revising the way we value them: Having proved to his own satisfaction that women could scale the artistic and intellectual heights, he argued that most would (that is, should) refrain, because women's true genius was "humanness," and their real mission was to "humanize" men before men blew up the world. And that, he left no doubt, was a full-time job.

Contemporary proponents of "difference feminism" advance a variation on the same argument, without Montagu's puckish humor. Instead of his whimsical chromosomal explanation, we get the psychoanalytic one proposed by Nancy Chodorow in *The Reproduction of Mothering:* Daughters define themselves by relating to their mothers, the primary love object of all children, and are therefore empathic, relationship-oriented, nonhierarchical and interested in forging consensus; sons must separate from their mothers, and are therefore individualistic, competitive, resistant to connection with others and focused on abstract rules and rights. . . .

Popularizers of Chodorow water down and sentimentalize her thesis. They embrace her proposition that traditional mothering produces "relational" women and "autonomous" men but forget her less congenial argument that it also results in sexual inequality, misogyny° and hostility between mothers and daughters, who, like sons, desire independence but have a much harder time

---

°**misogyny:** Dislike of women.

achieving it. Unlike her followers, Chodorow does not romanticize mothering: "Exclusive single parenting is bad for mother and child alike," she concludes; in a tragic paradox, female "caring," "intimacy" and "nurturance" do not soften but *produce* aggressive, competitive, hypermasculine° men. . . .

. . . Deborah Tannen, in the best-selling *You Just Don't Understand,* claims that men and women grow up with "different cultural backgrounds"—the single-sex world of children's play in which girls cooperate and boys compete—"so talk between men and women is cross-cultural communication.". . . Tannen is quick to attribute blatant rudeness or sexism in male speech to anxiety, helplessness, fear of loss of face—anything, indeed, but rudeness and sexism. . . .

But the biggest problem with Chodorovian accounts of gender difference is 5 that they credit the differences they find to essential, universal features of male and female psychosexual development rather than to the economic and social positions men and women hold, or to the actual power differences between individual men and women. In *The Mismeasure of Woman,* her trenchant and witty attack on contemporary theories of gender differences, Carol Tavris points out that much of what can be said about women applies as well to poor people, who also tend to focus more on family and relationships and less on work and self-advancement; to behave deferentially with those more socially powerful; and to appear to others more emotional and "intuitive" than rational and logical in their thinking. Then, too, there is the question of whether the difference theorists are measuring anything beyond their own willingness to think in stereotypes. If Chodorow is right, relational women and autonomous men should be the norm, but are they? Or is it just that women and men use different language, have different social styles, different explanations for similar behavior? Certainly, it is easy to find in one's own acquaintance, as well as in the world at large, men and women who don't fit the models. Difference feminists like to attribute ruthlessness, coldness and hyperrationality in successful women—Margaret Thatcher° is the standard example—to the fact that men control the networks of power and permit only women like themselves to rise. But I've met plenty of loudmouthed, insensitive, aggressive women who are stay-at-home mothers and secretaries and nurses. And I know plenty of sweet, unambitious men whose main satisfactions lie in their social, domestic and romantic lives, although not all of them would admit this to an inquiring social scientist. . . .

So why [is] Tannen the [toast] of feminist social science, endlessly cited and discussed in academia and out of it too, in gender-sensitivity sessions in the business world and even, following the Anita Hill° testimony, in Congress? The success of the difference theorists proves yet again that social science is one part science and nine parts social. They say what people want to hear: Women

---

°hypermasculine: Extremely masculine.   °**Margaret Thatcher:** Former prime minister of Britain.
°Anita Hill: On the eve of the U.S. Senate confirmation hearings of Clarence Thomas as a justice of the Supreme Court in 1991, Hill accused Thomas, her former employer, of sexual harassment.

really are different, in just the ways we always thought. Women embrace [them] because they offer flattering accounts of traits for which they have historically been castigated. Men like them because, while they urge understanding and respect for "female" values and behaviors, they also let men off the hook: Men have power, wealth and control of social resources because women don't really want them. . . .

MAN'S WORLD, WOMAN'S PLACE

Despite its intellectual flabbiness, difference feminism is deeply appealing to many women. Why? For one thing, it seems to explain some important phenomena: that women—and this is a cross-cultural truth°—commit very little criminal violence compared with men; that women fill the ranks of the so-called caring professions;° that women are much less likely than men to abandon their children. Difference feminists want to give women credit for these good behaviors by raising them from the level of instinct or passivity . . . to the level of moral choice and principled decision. Who can blame women for embracing theories that tell them the sacrifices they make on behalf of domesticity and children are legitimate, moral, even noble? . . . [Difference feminists] offer women a way to argue that their views have equal status with those of men and to resist the customary marginalization° of their voices in public debate. . . .

The vision of women as sharers and carers is tempting in another way too. Despite much media blather about the popularity of the victim position, most people want to believe they act out of free will and choice. The uncomfortable truth that women have all too little of either is a difficult hurdle for feminists. Acknowledging the systematic oppression of women seems to deprive them of existential freedom, to turn them into puppets, slaves and Stepford wives.° Deny it, and you can't make change. By arguing that the traditional qualities, tasks and ways of life of women are as important, valuable and serious as those of men (if not more so), [difference feminists] let women feel that nothing needs to change except the social valuation accorded to what they are already doing. It's a rationale for the status quo,° which is why men like it, and a burst of grateful applause, which is why women like it. Men keep the power, but since power is bad, so much the worse for them.

Another rather curious appeal of difference feminism is that it offers a way for women to define themselves as independent of men. In a culture that sees

---

°**cross-cultural truth:** Something that can be found true in many different cultures. °**caring professions:** Those such as nursing, teaching, day care, or social work that focus on some form of caring for people. °**marginalization:** Being kept out of the center of power or influence. °**Stepford wives:** Novel and film in which women were turned into robot-like, perfect, compliant wives. °**status quo:** The way things are.

women almost entirely in relation to men, this is no small achievement. Sex, for example—the enormous amount of female energy, money and time spent on beauty and fashion and romance, on attracting men and keeping them, on placating male power, strategizing ways around it or making it serve one's own ends—plays a minute role in these theories.... [I]t is always children whom women are described as fostering and sacrificing for, or the community, or even other women—not husbands or lovers. It's as though wives cook dinner only for their kids, leaving the husband to raid the fridge on his own. And no doubt many women, quietly smoldering at their mate's refusal to share domestic labor, persuade themselves that they are serving only their children, or their own preferences, rather than confront the inequality of their marriage....

Difference theorists would like to separate out the aspects of traditional 10 womanhood that they approve of and speak only of those. But the parts they like (caring, nurturing, intimacy) are inseparable from the parts they don't like (economic dependence and the subordination of women within the family). The difference theorists try to get around this by positing a world that contains two cultures—a female world of love and ritual and a male world of getting and spending and killing—which mysteriously share a single planet. That vision is expressed neatly in a recent pop-psychology title, *Men Are from Mars, Women Are from Venus*. It would be truer to say men are from Illinois and women are from Indiana—different, sure, but not in ways that have much ethical consequence.

The ultimate paradox of difference feminism is that it has come to the fore at a moment when the lives of the sexes are becoming less distinct than they ever have been in the West. Look at the decline of single-sex education (researchers may tout the benefits of all-female schools and colleges, but girls overwhelmingly choose coeducation); the growth of female athletics; the virtual abolition of virginity as a requirement for girls; the equalization of college-attendance rates of males and females; the explosion of employment for married women and mothers even of small children; the crossing of workplace gender lines by both females and males; the cultural pressure on men to be warm and nurturant fathers, to do at least some housework, to choose mates who are their equals in education and income potential.

It's fashionable these days to talk about the backlash against equality feminism—I talk this way myself when I'm feeling blue—but equality feminism has scored amazing successes. It has transformed women's expectations in every area of their lives. However, it has not yet transformed society to meet those expectations. The workplace still discriminates. On the home front few men practice egalitarianism, although many preach it; single mothers—and given the high divorce rate, every mother is potentially a single mother—lead incredibly difficult lives.

In this social context, difference feminism is essentially a way for women both to take advantage of equality feminism's success and to accommodate themselves to its limits. It appeals to particular kinds of women—those in the "helping professions" or the home, for example, rather than those who want to be bomber pilots or neurosurgeons or electricians. At the popular level, it encourages women who feel disadvantaged or demeaned by equality to direct their anger against women who have benefited from it by thinking of them as gender traitors and of themselves as suffering for their virtue—thus the hostility of nurses toward female doctors, and of stay-at-home mothers toward employed mothers.

For its academic proponents, the appeal lies elsewhere: Difference feminism is a way to carve out a safe space in the face of academia's resistance to female advancement.... The difference feminists cannot say that the differences between men and women are the result of their relative economic positions because to say that would be to move the whole discussion out of the realm of psychology and feel-good cultural pride and into the realm of a tough political struggle over the distribution of resources and justice and money.

Although it is couched in the language of praise, difference feminism is 15 demeaning to women. It asks that women be admitted into public life and public discourse not because they have a right to be there but because they will improve them. Even if this were true, and not the wishful thinking I believe it to be, why should the task of moral and social transformation be laid on women's doorstep and not on everyone's—or, for that matter, on men's, by the you-broke-it-you-fix-it principle. Peace, the environment, a more humane workplace, economic justice, social support for children—these are issues that affect us all and are everyone's responsibility. By promising to assume that responsibility, difference feminists lay the groundwork for excluding women again, as soon as it becomes clear that the promise cannot be kept.

SELLING THE APOLITICAL

Senta Troemel-Ploetz

Senta Troemel-Ploetz has a Ph.D. in linguistics from the University of Pennsylvania and teaches in Germany. She writes frequently about language issues from a feminist perspective.

In this 1991 article, Troemel-Ploetz criticizes Deborah Tannen for ignoring the likelihood that differences between men's and women's ways of conversing result from differences in power. Troemel-Ploetz is especially critical of Tannen's argument, in You Just Don't Understand: Women and Men in Conversation

(1991), that such differences come from growing up in two different conversational cultures and that they are essentially unchangeable. She describes men as being allowed to use "dominant speech acts" (commands, orders, advice, criticism, and so on) while women instead have to apologize, defend, agree, support, and so on.

As you read, try to understand the reasons Troemel-Ploetz offers in arguing that men's and women's differences in talk involve more than cross-cultural misunderstanding.

This is a dishonest book precisely because of its non-engaged and apolitical stance. It veils and conceals the political analysis to which women have given their energy during the last 30 years, and the changes they have brought about with the help of fair men. It waters down our insights; it equalizes where differences have to be acknowledged; it hardly ever talks about inequity—and never with real concern; it again and again stops short of drawing any political inferences that would suggest that significant changes are needed in the communication and relationships between women and men.

The author shields her readers also from linguistic knowledge. Thus if one would not know, one would never find out that there is an enormous body of feminist literature presenting a critical analysis of the differences in power and access to power between women and men, on all levels, public and private, and in all areas—work, pay, family, sexuality, the professions, the institutions, e.g., medicine, the court system, even academia (where Tannen is located), and even conversational analysis (which is her field).

The main thesis of Tannen's book is that women's and men's conversation *is* (not even *is patterned like*) cross-cultural communication (pp. 18, 42, 47). This is entirely unsupported and unproven. What Tannen claims, that "if adults learn their ways of speaking as children growing up in separate social worlds of peers, then conversation between women and men is cross-cultural communication" (p. 47), simply does not follow. Even if it were true that girls and boys grow up in different linguistic worlds, it would not follow. Girls and boys, women and men (always remaining within the white middle class) live together in shared linguistic worlds, be it in the family, in schoolrooms, in the streets, in colleges, in jobs; they are probably spending more time in mixed-sex contexts than in single-sex contexts, and, above all, they are not victims of constant misunderstandings. On the contrary, they understand each other quite well. They know who is allowed to use dominant speech acts, like commands, orders, explanations, contradiction, doubts, advice, criticism, evaluations, definitions, punishment, attacks, challenges, accusations, reproaches; and who has to apologize, defend, ask for favors, beg, request permission, justify herself, agree, support, adjust, accommodate, and accept someone else's definition of the situation.

By using these speech acts to a large extent asymmetrically,° a conversational reality is being constructed in which men claim more authority and autonomy for themselves, and women become more dependent and non-autonomous. We are acting out our social roles and producing, via our speech acts, a conversational world in which our social reality is reflected and corroborated: men have power, women submit.

Consequently, we find two conversational cultures or two different styles that are not equal. Men, the speakers of the dominant style, have more rights and privileges. They exhibit their privileges and produce them in every conversational situation. Men are used to dominating women; they do it especially in conversations: they set the tone as soon as they enter a conversation, they declare themselves expert for almost any topic, they expect and get attention and support from their female conversational partners, they expect and get space to present their topics and, above all, themselves—their conversational success is being produced by the participants in that conversation. Women are trained to please; they have to please also in conversations, i.e., they will let men dominate and they will do everything not to threaten men: not set the tone, not insist on their own topics or opinions, package opposing views pleasantly, not refuse support, not take more space than men, i.e., let men win conversationally and renounce their own conversational success and satisfaction in the process.

Men also exhibit and produce their conversational rights: the right to dominate, the right to self-presentation or self-aggrandizement at the expense of others, the right to have the floor and to finish one's turn, the right to keep women from talking (by disturbance or interruption), the right to get attention and consideration from women, the right to conversational success. Women, on the other hand, have conversational obligations: they must not disturb men in their dominating and imposing behavior; they must support their topics, wait with their own topics, give men attention, take them seriously at all times, and, above all, listen and help them to their conversational success. By assuming, attributing and reconstructing men's rights and privileges and women's obligations in every conversation, status differences between women and men are being confirmed and produced in most mixed-sex interactions—the social hierarchy remains intact.

Reading through what a German critic called Professor Tannen's "chatter," one searches in vain for concepts like dominance, control, power, politics of gender, sexism, discrimination, and finds two of them mentioned after 200 pages but not explored, borrowed probably from another author. Concepts like feminism° or patriarchy° never occur, being evidently far too radical for the

---

°**asymmetrically:** Not the same on both sides. In this case, men use more dominant and women use more submissive kinds of speech.   °**feminism:** The belief that women should be politically and socially equal to men.   °**patriarchy:** A social order in which men are superior politically and socially to women.

author. Tannen is selling political naïveté, but neither is sociology quite so naïve nor linguistics quite as apolitical as Tannen would have us believe. In both fields women have, long before Tannen started publishing on mixed-sex communication, given political analyses of their data and introduced new concepts from a feminist perspective that suggested a revision of the existing male models. . . .

Significantly, the feminist literature in her own field is not even mentioned by Tannen or, where mentioned en passant, as in the case of Aries, Edelsky, Goodwin, Spender, it is reduced in such a way that its spark is neutralized and its critical impetus watered down so as not to offend anyone or lead him to think. But we do not hear about Lee Jenkins. . ., who first worked on storytelling in a women's group concentrating on women's competence and their high degree of cooperation, in the process doing away with the stereotypes of women's style found in linguistics as elsewhere. We do not hear about new work done on women's discourse, work on women's friendships, women's professional style, emphasizing the competence of women whose style lends itself very well to all kinds of verbal endeavors, from psychotherapy to teaching to management, and whose success is appreciated independently in these fields. . . .

Turning away now from academia and her colleagues, to the women and men who are the subjects of Tannen's *You Just Don't Understand,* it is difficult to believe that they could feel their communication adequately described. The plaintive reproach of the title is obviously a woman's utterance, resigning to not being understood instead of insisting to be understood. This is indicative of what is to come. As a critic wrote: "Tannen's wailing lament about male conversational behavior is bound to frustrate frustrated women even more.". . . Women are being told that men who are unempathic, who do not care about women's feelings or their wishes, who are selfish and self-centered, speak a different language, called a language of report, and are interested in a different goal, namely the solution of problems. This will not comfort the women who think that men should also be able to communicate on an emotional level and who want to educate men to their emotional culture. Are they to give up the idea of a loving heterosexual relationship based on mutual sharing?

Take for instance the woman who had a breast operation and felt she had 10 been cut into and that the seam of the stitches "had changed the contour of her breast" (p. 49). Her husband replies only one sentence to his wife's distress: "You can have plastic surgery to cover up the scar and restore the shape of your breast" (p. 49). Then the following dialogue evolves (p. 50):

> WOMAN: I'm not having any more surgery! I'm sorry you don't like the way it looks.
>
> MAN: I don't care. It doesn't bother me at all.
>
> WOMAN: Then why are you telling me to have plastic surgery?
>
> MAN: Because you were saying *you* were upset about the way it looked.

Note that in this dialogue the man has the last word and the woman afterwards "felt like a heel." We hear a lot about her feelings—e.g., she felt guilty about snapping at him—but we hear nothing about his feelings, only that he was reacting to her complaint by reassuring her that there is something she could do about it. Tannen concludes: "Eve wanted the gift of understanding, but Mark gave her the gift of advice. He was taking the role of problem-solver, whereas she simply wanted confirmation of her feelings" (p. 50). Tannen's analysis ends here.

It is interesting to see who gets their needs fulfilled. The man solved a problem and presented his solution—he did what he needed to do. The woman did not get what she needed in her situation. There is not the slightest suggestion that especially in a difficult situation of that kind the man should perhaps for once not react to his wife with the usual unempathic, unconcerned, cold, problem-solving response. Is this woman to accept that even when she most needs compassion and empathy (a word that does not occur in Tannen's book), she is not going to get it? And should she believe Tannen's explanation that her husband did not *understand* what she wanted?

Many women know that men just do not *want* to be interested in what they need and it often shows most dramatically in situations where a woman is sick or pregnant or becomes disabled or gets old. It is not that men do not understand what women want and, if they only knew, they would generously give it. Neither women nor men are as dumb as Tannen wants us to believe: "Many men honestly do not know what women want, and women honestly do not know why men find what they want so hard to comprehend and deliver" (p. 81). Many men, however, must appreciate Tannen's analysis—they do not have to find out what women want and, above all, they do not have to change. My thesis is that men understand quite well what women want but they give only when it suits them. In many situations they refuse to give and *women cannot make them give.* . . .

. . . The majority of relationships between women and men in our society are fundamentally asymmetrical to the advantage of men. If they were not, we would not need a woman's liberation movement, women's commissions, houses for battered women, legislation for equal opportunity, antidiscrimination laws, family therapy, couple therapy, divorce. We would not even need Tannen's book. . . .

Although women are submitting, annoyed, hurt and losing out in one example after the other, and men are getting their needs fulfilled, Tannen ends up rescuing the men. She explains them to us so we can perceive them as they should be perceived: in their puzzlement, confusion, frustration, while they all get their way.

However, at one point Tannen's explanation stops: men don't talk to their [15] heterosexual partners, Tannen claims, but she does not tell us why. She fails to explain why men who talk all day long, whose business is talk, including talk of a high degree of indirectness, in politics, law, advertising, sales, journalism, on school boards, in academia, cannot say two sentences to their wives at home. Take the man who cannot answer his wife's question "What's new with X?" and says "Nothing" (p. 80). Do you think if his boss asked him the same question about the same X, he would say "nothing"? And if he did indeed, and his boss reacted in anger, would he not know why? As a native speaker he knows that his answer means not only there is nothing new about X but also that it has an indirect message of "I don't care to talk with you now," and is a refusal to enter into further conversation. But how is it that a man, when talking to his female boss, knows more about indirect meaning and indirect speech acts than when he talks with his wife? Because he can afford to. He *has to* supply information to his boss, but at home *his wife has to* work at drawing information out of him and he gives it only when he is good and ready....

Whereas Tannen tries to explain away male insensitivity, many sensitive men have been taking a stand during the last ten years, looking critically at themselves and their colleagues. They have supported feminist lawyers, instituted task forces in one US state after the other to identify discriminatory verbal behavior in the courts; they have worked for change. Ironically, Tannen's understanding of the social and political function of language falls below what sensitive and reasonable men in high positions know, without being linguists. To quote one of them, Robert N. Wilentz, Chief Justice of New Jersey:

> There's no room for gender bias in our system...there's no room for the funny joke and the not-so-funny joke, there's no room for conscious, inadvertent, sophisticated, clumsy, or any other kind of gender bias, and certainly no room for gender bias that affects substantive rights.
>
> There's no room because it hurts and it insults. It hurts female lawyers psychologically and economically, litigants psychologically and economically, and witnesses, jurors, law clerks and judges who are women. It will not be tolerated in any form whatsoever. (The First Year Report of the New Jersey Supreme Court Task Force on *Women in the Courts,* June 1984)

I do not think this man will change his politics to a watered-down stance about men's different style of communication. I hope other self-critical and fair men will also refuse Tannen's thesis, recognizing it for what it aims at: the cementation of patriarchy.

Knowledge gained about discourse in the courtroom or in medical practice can easily be extended to private conversations, for what is going on in this arena is, after all, not that different. The repertoire of speech acts is quite the same; the construction of dominance and superiority is quite similar. The difference is that private talk among lovers or wife and husband *could* be symmetrical. Hierarchy in private relationships is not as formalized as in the court system. Private talk has a chance courtroom interaction, unless there is an enlightened judge, does not have. (How could the attorney who was called a child demand and construct symmetry?)

This is why Tannen's book is so depressing. In one example after the other she is trying to make the man's responses understandable, to explain his ignorance, his disinterest, selfishness or rudeness. She is telling women who have gained insight in the power politics of talk that men and women do not understand each other (without her explanation). She completely misses the point that conversations are constructed, that people don't "fall into differences of their interactional habits" (p. 125) or "find themselves arrayed in an asymmetrical alignment" (p. 125), but that we produce equality or inequality, symmetry or asymmetry in every conversation, only it is usually the more powerful who have the choice to give up some of their privileges and rights, and the less powerful who cannot just demand equality or symmetry and get it.

To tell professional women, who have worked for two decades in rape crisis centers, with domestic violence, in universities and state women's commissions with sexual harassment, defining it on a scale from verbal utterance to date rape or acquaintance rape, to tell women lawyers and doctors who have worked with sexual abuse of girls and baby girls at home by fathers and male relatives, that "the real problem is conversational style" (p. 79), or "misunderstandings arise because the styles are different" (p. 47), or "that men have a different way of showing they care" (p. 298) is more than absurd. These women know that underlying the conversational politics and the body politics is the power politics of female-male relationships where men have social control of women and, if need be, recourse to violence. There are many other manifestations of the power relationship between the sexes, e.g., an analysis of women's and men's economics shows men earn 90 percent of the world income, own 99 percent of the world property, while doing only one-third of the world's work (UN Report of 1980—with the growing poverty of women also in the USA, these figures have probably changed for the worse in the last decade).

I hope Tannen's readers will see through her "explanations," will not be kept [20] at the naïve level of ignorance the author assigns them to. . . .

I hope Tannen's readers will not stay in their place. I hope they will see through the patterns of domination in their exchanges with men. I hope they will see that *their* understanding the masculine style does not help them (p. 123) and that nothing changes if men just *understand* female style without valuing it as more humane and changing their style to become more empathic and caring. I hope they test Tannen's claim of the good intentions in males and insist on symmetry—if they are listening supportively to a man's problem, they should get the same, if they are freely giving information, they should get it just as freely, if they are open, their partner should also open up. I hope they know that the "hope for the future" (p. 148) does not lie in *their* changing their style, but in men being less dominant, and learning from women.

This book trivializes our experience of injustice and of conversational dominance; it disguises power differences; it conceals who has to adjust; it veils differences again and again and equalizes with a leveling mania any distinction in how we experience women and men.

TOWER OF PSYCHOBABBLE

Elizabeth Gleick

Elizabeth Gleick is a senior writer at Time *magazine, in which this 1997 article was published. She has also written for* Vogue *and* People.

You will see from the tone of Gleick's article that she is critical of John Gray's metaphor of Mars and Venus, as well as of his commercialism, although she also concedes that many people find his advice helpful.

As you read, pay attention to Gleick's criticism and consider whether it in any way changes your opinion of Gray's advice.

Pay attention, folks, because there's going to be a quiz later. Here's how to give a woman a compliment: you tell her she looks nice. Or better yet, you say, "You look so nice." Or, "You really look so nice." Or, "You look very, very nice." Got it? But did you need a book to tell you how to mix those adverbs and adjectives so very creatively?

For the millions of devotees of John Gray's *Men Are from Mars, Women Are from Venus*, the answer is apparently yes. This week 300,000 copies of the newest addition to Gray's oeuvre, *Mars and Venus on a Date*, will hit bookstores, and it will tell all sorts of people all sorts of things they already know. Remember that old baseball euphemism from make-out parties in junior high school? Gray, writing as if he invented the metaphor, explains how to get to first base and so on, ending with "sliding into home." More to the point, *Mars and Venus on a Date* will rehash some of the very same anecdotes and concepts — men are like blowtorches, women are like ovens — that can be found in Gray's other six books. Such criticism fazes Gray — a man who must have left his humility on Mars when he fell to Earth — not at all. He announces proudly that the new book took him a grand total of seven weeks to do and that it is "without a doubt in my mind the greatest book I've ever written." Relaxing in the living room of one of two houses he owns in Mill Valley, Calif., Gray sounds awestruck by his own wizardry: "I'm sitting there writing, and these beautiful ideas come out."

The sourdough starter here, the mold from which all other efforts have grown, is the 1992 *Men Are from Mars, Women Are from Venus*, and that, at least, seems to have been a beautiful idea. It has sold a staggering 6 million copies — making it, according to publisher HarperCollins, the best-selling hard-cover nonfiction book ever — and has been published in 38 languages. The book has earned Gray somewhere in the neighborhood of $18 million. And that's not counting the spin-offs. So far Gray has produced *Mars and Venus in the Bedroom, Mars and Venus in Love, Mars and Venus Together Forever.* Ask about future books, and his answer is, frankly, a little scary: *Men Are from Mars, Women Are from Venus, Kids Are from Heaven,* a parenting book due out in 1998; *Daddy's from Mars, Mommy's from Venus; MAFM, WAFV over 50; MAFM, WAFV over 50 Together Forever; MAFM, WAFV over 50 in the Bedroom; Mars and Venus in the Boardroom; Mars and Venus in the Counseling Room; Mars and Venus Single Again.* Why not *Mars and Venus for Dummies*?

In addition to the books, there's an infomercial, sets of audiotapes and video-tapes, weekend seminars, a CD-ROM, Mars and Venus vacations and a one-man show that began with a Broadway appearance last February and will continue at arenas across the country this summer. Gray also has a movie deal with 20th Century Fox and a planned sitcom. His new CD features a Mars and Venus song co-written by that Renaissance man Gray himself and performed as a sort of call and response by his-and-her vocalists. Sample lyrics: Her: "Every time I try to tell you something, you get mad and run off to your cave." Him: "You're so up and down with your emotions."

These works all have a very simple message at their heart: men and women   5 are so different, they might as well come from different planets—and can't we all just get along? But it is a message with enough of a truthful core that it struck a popular nerve at a very particular time: the early '90s, when it again became permissible for people to discuss gender difference. For this, thanks must be given to Georgetown University linguistics professor Deborah Tan-nen's groundbreaking *You Just Don't Understand: Women and Men in Conversa-tion,* which perched on the *New York Times* best-seller list for close to two years before Mars and Venus came out and for two years after. The books could not be more different in many ways; in the back, for instance, where Tannen has placed footnotes, Gray has 800-numbers for ordering his products. But both are about the frustrations of male-female communication—how men hate to ask for directions when driving, say, or how women need to talk to feel closer. Says Tannen: "I suppose if I had wanted to build an empire I would be resent-ful, but I didn't." Gray acknowledges the similarities between his work and Tannen's—up to a point. "I do tend to skim all the best-sellers," he admits. "I've heard criticism that I'm just a watered-down version of Deborah Tannen. [But] I was teaching those ideas before I'd heard of her."

Gray insists that the growth of his empire is merely a response to the outpour-ing of interest in his work—hey, if people want a book for singles, he'll oblige. But though his intentions may be honorable and though any number of people swear by his methods, his sketchy credentials and entrepreneurial energies have some mental-health professionals more than a little concerned. "Couples rela-tionships are incredibly complex," says Anna Beth Benningfield, president-elect of the American Association for Marriage and Family Therapy. "To tell a couple to go read this book and do this one thing and you'll be fine is very misleading."

Gray's latest foray into the for-profit world is his new Mars & Venus Coun-seling Centers, in which therapists pay $2,500 for training in the Mars & Venus "technique," an initial licensing fee of $1,900 for the right to hang out a shingle and use the logo as a Mars & Venus counselor, and then a $300-a-month "royalty" payment. Gray says he has acquired his special love insights after years of counseling couples and hearing anecdotes from his fans at book signings and lectures. But he is not a licensed anything other than driver, to which some mental-health professionals would say, *Caveat emptor.*° Dorothy Cantor, immediate past president of the American Psychological Association, questions the ethics of essentially franchising a form of therapeutic practice. "B. F. Skinner° did not say, 'I discovered behaviorism. Now you can have it only if you pay me for it,'" she points out.

In a sense, it hardly matters what the naysayers think of Gray's work, which may explain why Gray will say things to journalists that others might consider ill-advised. About his limited run on Broadway, during which he performed to savage critics but sellout crowds at New York City's 1,900-seat Gershwin Theater, he says, "I have no preparation before I go onstage, and I don't do any thinking." When asked how he arrived at the Mars and Venus concept, he says it was from seeing the movie *E.T.* For Gray, it is easy to come up with such popular blends of fact and fiction, even when talking about extraterrestrials. In fact, he says, "I've seen a spaceship. I was traveling north on the California coast and I saw a ball of light that was traveling alongside my car, and it shot off in a Z pattern." He adds, "I certainly believe in extraterrestrial life, but I am definitely from Earth."

It is just such guilelessness, or what the Gray acolytes persist in referring to as "sharing," that has helped win Gray an almost cultlike following. Many of the people who work for Gray are true believers who have dropped everything to spread his message of marital harmony. Phoenix businessman Michael Najarian took one of Gray's seminars 10 years ago in Santa Cruz, Calif., when he was fresh from a divorce. "When the student is ready, the teacher appears," he says. "My whole life really changed after that weekend." Najarian, who is now president of Personal Growth Productions, which produces Gray's tapes, acts as a sort of surrogate John Gray, giving the occasional seminar or talking to business groups at $10,000 a pop—Gray charges $35,000—even, a little creepily, using the same mannerisms. Ellen Coren says that when she and her husband took their first workshop with Gray 12 years ago, "it was an incredible experience for both of us." Coren eventually trained to become a therapist and is now clinical director of the counseling centers. Eric Smith, an Orange County, Calif., computer consultant who hopes to become a Mars & Venus "facilitator," which would entitle him to run weekend workshops, says Gray "has a remarkable gift for healing."...

°*Caveat emptor:* Latin for "Let the buyer beware."   °**B. F. Skinner:** Famous psychologist, founder of behaviorism.

Though John Gray is now rich beyond even his dreams, he believes he has 10 won this wealth for a reason — "so that I can understand how money is made and managed" and eventually help redistribute it. For Gray is just getting rolling with his master plan. "I feel it's in me to help negotiate peace in the world," he announces. "I know it will happen one day." And now it's time for that quiz. Where, exactly, is John Gray from?

A WRITER'S NOTEBOOK

Critical Responses

The following tasks are designed to help you think about the readings and identify and start to work up material you might use in your own essay.

1. *Explain Katha Pollitt's point.* In criticizing "difference feminism," Pollitt points out that difference theorists "say what people want to hear" (paragraph 6). Explain why, according to Pollitt, both men and women are attracted to the message of difference feminists.

2. *React to Senta Troemel-Ploetz's views.* In paragraph 9, Troemel-Ploetz faults Deborah Tannen for advising women to be resigned "to not being understood instead of insisting to be understood." In paragraph 10, she provides an example from Tannen to illustrate her point. What do you think of this criticism? Write a page or so telling your reaction, using the example Troemel-Ploetz provides or others of your own choosing from the Tannen reading.

3. *React to Elizabeth Gleick's criticism.* Gleick's criticism of John Gray himself may or may not change your view of the usefulness of his advice. Write a page or so telling how you react to Gleick's criticism of Gray.

At this point you should be ready to write your own report on the advice self-help books offer about communicating in relationships. You should find ample information to draw on in the readings, and, if you have been completing the information worksheets and the tasks suggested in the writer's notebook sections, you already have written quite a lot. In addition, you have years of experience listening and contributing to conversations—with your parents, siblings, neighbors, teachers, friends, romantic partners, and schoolmates. You can now sort, classify, and organize the material you have read—by both the self-help writers and their critics—and report on it in such a way that interested readers will be able to understand the kinds of advice being offered for better communication in relationships and, perhaps, some possible limitations of this advice.

This Writer's Guide will help you

- plan, draft, revise, edit, and proofread an essay reporting on advice in self-help books about communicating in relationships, as well as criticism of that advice

- illustrate your report with supporting details from the readings and your own observations

- construct certain sentences appropriate for reporting information

- work with sources—to gather current information and to cite material that you draw upon

- reflect on what you have learned completing this assignment

PLANNING AND DRAFTING YOUR ESSAY

This section provides guidelines and examples to help you plan and draft a clear report on the advice you have read. It will help you

- understand your readers and your writing situation

- select materials

- prepare a prospectus

- organize your essay

- explain the information clearly

- cite sources

THE WRITING ASSIGNMENT   Write a report explaining some of what these readings say about effective communication in relationships or, more specifically if you wish, between men and women. You need not argue for or against their interpretations or value one style of communication over another. Begin by organizing the information you wish to report in a way that is clear and easy for a reader to follow. You will need to put these writers' ideas into categories, compare and contrast their different ideas, and illustrate the kinds of communication they discuss. Your job is to make your reader's learning as effortless as possible, to sort and stitch together information from these reports coherently so that a reader can readily understand it. If you focus on differences in the way men and women communicate, you will want to acknowledge that some have criticized the advice these writers present or the way they have articulated the problem, so you will want to find a way to indicate that not everyone agrees.

Understanding Your Readers

Assume that you are writing for a magazine or a newspaper that reports on issues of human interest for interested nonexperts, like *Psychology Today,* and that your readers are people who may not have time to read extensively about this subject but are particularly interested in having the results condensed into a readable explanation. Perhaps they are interested in using the lessons derived from these readings to improve their own communication and conflict-management skills. Certainly they are interested in people's behavior and curious about research into that behavior.

Selecting Materials

The readings and the writing tasks in this chapter provide a great deal of material; your task is to sort and arrange the advice offered by some or all of the four writers and perhaps the views of their critics. You might proceed by first deciding how to classify the material you have read and then choosing a plan for organizing the material.

Classifying the Information. A good way to begin is to review the information worksheets and writer's notebook entries you may have already written, this time trying to decide what options you have for arranging the information into classes or categories. Classifying is a key intellectual activity—key to this assignment as well as many other academic and everyday thinking tasks. The readings in this chapter suggest a number of different categories or classifications. John Gray, for instance, divides the world into male (Martians) and female (Venusians) and emphasizes their different communication styles. John Gottman focuses only briefly on gender difference; his main categories are the "four crucial strategies" couples can use to avoid negative conflict.

Keep in mind that similarities among classifications can be obscured by the use of different terms. Susan Page, for instance, lists *affirmation* as one of the five traits of couples who thrive while Gottman considers *validation* as particularly important. But since *affirmation* and *validation* are near synonyms—and Page and Gottman use them in the same ways—they both recommend the same kind of communication skill when they refer to *affirmation* or *validation*.

Organize Your Information. A classification scheme will help you bring together information from the different readings to organize your essay and make it easy for your reader to follow. Two obvious ways to classify the information in these reports are (1) by the types of advice they give or (2) by what they say about men's and women's differences.

These two ways of classifying are observable in the readings: Deborah Tannen and Gray organize their reports around distinctions they find between men's and women's ways of communicating; Page and Gottman, around four or five types of advice. Since the advice they give differs, to some extent, it is clear that even writers who use the same general way of classifying can nevertheless divide their classifications into different subtopics or organize their presentation of their subtopics differently. Whatever organizational strategy you choose, you should include main topic headings followed by subtopic headings under each.

Here's how organizing by types of advice might look in outline form:

Plan 1—Organizing by types of advice
– opening
– advice about understanding one's partner
  [individual subtopics]
– advice about talking to resolve conflicts
  [individual subtopics]
– advice about asking for what you want
  [individual subtopics]
– conclusion

With this plan, you might name your major topic classifications differently or have a different number of subtopic headings under each of the main topics, depending on what you choose from the readings. (Remember that the writers use different terms for similar kinds of advice, so you can organize your report in such a way as to classify together advice that seems similar even when the terms may differ.) Note that in this plan, you are likely to downplay — or even ignore — gender differences except when the reports themselves offer different advice for men and women.

A second plan is to focus specifically on what the writers say — or imply — about gender differences. Claims about gender differences are likely to be controversial, but for report writing, you need only acknowledge that there is a controversy, not personally take a position on it. After pinpointing what assumptions about gender difference you find and what criticisms reviewers have offered, you can simply report on those criticisms.

The two easiest ways to organize advice about gender differences are (1) by advice or (2) by gender. The sample outlines presented here, organized by gender, are also organized in terms of more specific topics.

Plan 2—Organizing by advice about men's and women's differences
– opening
– what writers say men need to do to communicate better
  [individual subtopics]

–what writers say women need to do to communicate better
   [individual subtopics]
–critics' views of this advice
–conclusion

Plan 2 (b)—Organizing by what the readings say about men's and women's dif-ferences
–opening
–how men can be more empathetic
   [individual subtopics]
–how women can make clearer what they need or want
   [individual subtopics]
–critics' views of this advice
–conclusion

You can probably think of several other ways to classify the writers' comments about gender differences. Note that, in both these plans, critics' reaction to the advice is placed after the advice itself. You could instead treat some of the critics' concerns throughout, explaining how they would respond to the advice writers' views of each topic. If you find yourself particularly interested in the critics, you might devote as much attention to their views as to those of the other writers.

Preparing a Prospectus

After you have classified the information and done some planning, your instructor may want you to prepare a prospectus for your essay. Professional writers, engineers, and businesspeople write prospectuses for their projects to try out their ideas and win support for them. For your essay, too, writing a prospectus can help you decide whether you have enough information and whether your plan for classifying information will allow you to write a clear report. You can also show your prospectus to others, who can ask you questions and give advice.

Here are some guidelines for drafting a two- or three-page prospectus. Your responses need not be polished; they can be fragmentary and can contain brief lists or outlines as well as explanations because they reflect your trying out a plan for your draft.

1. *Select an organizational plan.* Select one of the organizational plans presented above or prepare your own plan. Write a few sentences telling briefly why your chosen plan seems best suited for classifying the advice in the reports.

2. *Develop one topic.* Choose *one* topic (or subtopic) in your plan and list which advice from one report you can discuss under that heading.

3. *List how you might use one report.* Choose *one* of the four reports and list how many—and which—of the topics and subtopics in your plan that particular report could be discussed under. (Each reading is likely to have advice relevant to more than one topic or subtopic.)

4. *Identify a useful passage.* Identify *one* passage in *one* reading that you might use as a particularly clear illustration of some part of the advice and write a few sentences telling what it might illustrate and why.

5. *Consider which critics' reactions to use.* If you are focusing your essay on advice, list two or three of the reactions critics have had to the advice offered in these readings. If focusing on gender differences, explain briefly how they react to such claims.

6. *Draft one section.* Select one topic or subtopic heading in your plan and report briefly on the information you will use under it. Review the readings and draft this one section of your report. Write quickly. Your purpose is simply to try out one section of your report—to see whether the plan you have chosen is workable and what more you need to do to make it work.

Organizing Your Essay

Once you have decided on a plan that will be helpful to a reader not already familiar with this research, you are ready to begin deciding which pieces of information fit into the different parts of your plan. Whichever plan you choose, your essay will have two parts: (1) the opening and (2) the report itself. In the first part, you will establish the importance of advice on communicating in relationships and provide readers a context for understanding the advice. In the second part, you will report on the advice itself.

In the second part, you construct a more detailed version of your basic plan. If you choose to organize your information by types of advice, for instance, you might arrange the parts of your essay like this:

Establishing the importance of good communication in relationships
– an engaging opening
– brief information about the research or counseling experiences that led to the advice these authors give
– a forecast revealing your plan for presenting the information

Reporting the information
– advice about understanding one's partner
  [individual subtopics]
– advice about talking to resolve conflicts
  [individual subtopics]
– advice about asking for what you want
  [individual subtopics]
– closing

Such a plan can guide your drafting. Keep in mind that a plan is not a paragraph outline. Some parts may be accomplished in one paragraph, but others may require several paragraphs.

Establishing the Importance.   Before reporting the advice on communicating in relationships to your readers, you need to establish its possible significance for your readers' lives or their families', friends', and coworkers' lives so they will want to read further and understand enough to proceed.

WRITING AN ENGAGING OPENING.   A successful opening draws your readers in and prepares them to understand the new information you will present. There are several ways to do this. You might, for example,

- Relate a personal observation of men and women not understanding each other or speaking at cross-purposes.
- Quote one passage of typical male and female speech from the readings.
- Appeal directly to readers' interests in communicating better with everyone.
- Relate a hypothetical example of miscommunication or of escalating conflict between partners.

You will need only one or two of these strategies, or you may think of other possibilities.

PROVIDING BRIEF INFORMATION ABOUT THE CONTEXT OF THE RESEARCH.   Offer your readers whatever contextual information you think they will need about the research, counseling, or workshops that led to the advice given in the readings. You might include some brief comments about sales of self-help books on communication or about the importance of understanding communication in relationships. You might even hint that not everyone agrees with all of these writers, though you won't be able to explain the disagreement until you have explained the advice itself more fully. If you yourself began this chapter not knowing about this research, you can easily imagine what sort of initial information another reader needs to make sense of the information that will follow. You need not say much about the four writers, but your report will look more authoritative if you offer some of the information about them that you will find immediately preceding each reading.

DEVISING A FORECASTING STATEMENT.   The forecasting statement tells your readers how and in what order you will present the information. It offers a way for them to follow your report more easily and anticipate what is coming. You will not need a thesis statement since you are not taking a position or offering your own argument, but a forecasting statement will help your reader follow along easily as you report on information.

Reporting the Information.   In this section—the longest and most important one—you report the advice itself. Here you will use whichever classification plan you have chosen to arrange your report by *topics*, taking one topic heading at a time and reporting information relevant to that topic before you proceed to the next one. This will be much more effective—and useful for your readers—than simply summarizing first one reading and then the next. Reporting the advice by topic will save your reader from struggling to make specific connections among topics, and you will be practicing a skill valuable in the university and elsewhere: the ability to synthesize information from different sources.

CLOSING EFFECTIVELY. Closing gracefully and effectively requires important choices. You have a number of options:

- Summarize key advice that you have reported on.
- If you began your report by referring to a personal experience, frame your essay by referring back to it.
- Use a particularly telling quote from one of the writers in this chapter to summarize the significance of the advice.
- Mention, briefly, the possible limitations in the advice you have reported on and assert the importance of learning more about differences in the ways people talk with each other.
- Speculate briefly about how understanding differences in communication or using the advice these writers offer may help people avoid misunderstanding and improve their relationships.

Developing Your Report

This section offers strategies for writing the central part of your essay, in which you report the advice the readings' writers are offering.

Orienting the Reader.   To orient your readers as to what is coming, you need a thesis statement announcing what you are going to report on and what categories of advice readers can expect to find. The thesis statement in a report serves a different purpose from the thesis in an argument. In a report, the thesis merely identifies your topic whereas in an argument the thesis asserts your point of view. The thesis you need for this essay should forecast clearly where you are going. For this purpose, you will need key terms: a combination of general words like *language* or *communication* and some of the words that you will use in the topics and subtopics of your classification, words like *empathy, rapport, defensiveness*. If you announce these key terms at the beginning and use them consistently throughout your essay, then your reader is likely to find your report readable.

The following example comes from an essay by Jennifer Price:

> A visit to the self-help section of your local bookstore will show that preventing misunderstandings in communication has become a major publishing industry. There are books on preserving marriage and books on getting a date. What these books have in common is the feeling that men and women need to take steps to communicate better with each other, and these books are full of advice about communicating better. <u>The most common</u>

> advice is that men and women need to understand each
> other's differences, talk in ways that can help resolve
> conflicts, and learn to ask for what they want.

This orienting statement tells what categories Price plans to use for reporting on the advice in the readings and forecasts the path her essay will take.

Here are some further orienting statements. The first is from an essay by Sarah Jacobson:

> Above all, these four writers agree that trouble can be
> avoided and understanding can be achieved if men and women
> avoid blaming and defensiveness.

This is student Brian Lee's statement:

> These four writers would probably not agree about how
> great a difference there is between men's and women's
> communication or where that difference comes from, but
> they seem to agree that men can learn to show more empathy
> and women can ask more directly for what they want.

EXAMPLES FROM THE READINGS. Read the orienting statements by Deborah Tannen (paragraph 6), Susan Page (paragraphs 5–6), and John Gottman (paragraph 1).

Explaining Your Categories. This is the central part of your essay. Remember—your essay should not take a position; instead, you should aim to offer a clear explanation of what advice the four writers in this chapter give. These writers classify what they have to say and then offer their explanations one piece at a time. You need to do the same, except that the categories (or pieces) you choose will come from putting together advice from four different writers.

Here is one paragraph from Jennifer Price's essay explaining part of Page's advice and linking it to Gottman's:

> The most important rule for talking about conflicts is to
> avoid blaming one's partner. Susan Page suggests that the
> best way to avoid blame is to make "I" statements instead
> of "you" statements. By this she means that it is better
> to say something like "I feel like I don't get to finish
> what I want to say" rather than "You always interrupt me"
> (28). The "you" statement, according to Page, will arouse
> resentment or defensiveness, and the conflict may grow
> worse. John Gottman cautions, similarly, against being
> defensive and urges that people both listen and speak
> non-defensively. He even offers a formula "When you did
> (or didn't do) X in situation Y, I felt Z" in order to
> help his readers learn to say "When you bounced several
> checks and the bank called, I felt embarrassed and angry"
> instead of "You are incredibly irresponsible for bouncing

> a check. I'm constantly having to pick up after your
> mistakes and fix everything you screw up" (54). Both Page's
> advice to use "I" statements and Gottman's recipe for
> nondefensive speaking involve the same reference to how
> the speaker feels and avoidance of blaming the listener.

As this student has done, you are likely to need to offer brief examples of speech—either quotations from the examples these writers use or examples of your own—that you think illustrate the advice you are trying to explain.

Now and then, you may need to impose a common language on different pieces of advice or interpret how seemingly different advice is related. In the example above, for instance, Jennifer Price connects Page's and Gottman's advice about defensiveness. But you may need to go even further in interpreting how these writers agree or disagree. Here is how Jim Chen interprets Gottman's apparent disagreement with the other writers on one issue.

> Though these four writers overlap in many ways, John
> Gottman offers one piece of advice that separates him
> from the others. Gottman stresses the importance of
> physiological reactions such as pulse rate and, therefore,
> the importance of calming down. He suggests that people's
> heart rates during discussions should not go over their
> baseline heart rates by more than 10 percent. For men this
> will be 82-86 beats per minute and for women 92-96. When
> the heart beats much higher, it is a sign that a person is
> releasing adrenaline and getting angry. Gottman advises
> couples not to try to solve conflicts when they are in
> this angry state. However, even on this piece of advice
> about calming down, Gottman may be in agreement with the
> others. When John Gray talks about men needing to retreat
> to their caves to be alone and work out their problems, he
> may be thinking along the same lines as Gottman. Gray's
> cave may provide men with a place and time to calm down,
> just as Gottman's "time-out" would do.

EXAMPLES FROM THE READINGS. Notice how the readings' authors

Use actual examples of men and women talking: Tannen (paragraph 11), Page (paragraphs 21, 82–83, and 102), and Gottman (paragraph 32)

Use hypothetical examples to illustrate a difference or to contrast ineffective and effective communication: Gray (paragraphs 2 and 46), Page (paragraphs 7–11, 13, 18, and 27–28), or Gottman (paragraphs 24–25, 37, 71–73, and 85–86)

Draw on personal experience: Tannen (paragraph 15) and Page (paragraph 104)

Interpret examples of conversation: Tannen (paragraphs 15–16)

Refer to media images: Tannen (paragraphs 18–21)

Use examples from friends, clients, or advice seekers: Tannen (paragraphs 11, 23–25, and 31)

Acknowledging Critics' Views.   Reports on subjects that involve controversy—such as differences between men and women—often refer to critics' responses or to points on which not all writers agree. Because you are not taking a position in this report, you do not need to take sides in the controversy about whether gender differences in conversation can be explained in the way Tannen, Gray, and Page suggest. However, your report on their advice will be more complete and more informative if you acknowledge, at least briefly, that not everyone agrees on this subject. You can weave this acknowledgment into your report when you present information that critics might disagree with, or you can state it in a separate section after you have reported on the advice itself.

Here is how Jim Chen refers to Gray's critics. This paragraph follows the one above in which Chen suggests that Gray's cave might serve the same function as Gottman's advice that partners need to calm down when they are disagreeing.

```
Gray's advice that men should be able to retreat to their
caves is open to criticism. His advice suggests to critics
like Senta Troemel-Ploetz that Gray thinks men are special
or, at least, essentially different from women. Because he
assumes men and women are essentially different, Gray
encourages relationships that are "asymmetrical," as
Troemel-Ploetz would say. Gottman, however, does not seem
to imply that men and women are essentially different. He
tells both sexes to calm down, not just one, and he
doesn't assume that men need to be treated specially.
Other critics, like Time magazine's Elizabeth Gleick,
might complain that Gray's theories are not based on
research and that Gray's cave is simply an untested belief
he holds, not something he has done open-minded research
about. So, although Gray and Gottman both offer ways for
men to calm down, many critics might prefer Gottman's
advice to Gray's.
```

EXAMPLES FROM THE READINGS.   For further examples, see Troemel-Ploetz (paragraph 9) and Gleick (paragraph 7).

SENTENCES FOR REPORTING INFORMATION

Once you have your report in good form, you can focus some attention on matters of style. Reporting on information requires care in forming sentences so that they are clear and straightforward, accurately convey the information, and capture its careful distinctions.

Following are some sentence strategies you may find useful for writing this sort of report. You may want to review the material in this section now as a preview of some of the special kinds of thinking and writing with which you will be engaged as you draft and revise your essay. You will find the definitions and examples here most helpful, however, as you revise your essay. At that time, you will want to examine closely the wording of all your sentences and the relationships between them.

Using Verbs Precisely

Note that the choice of verb before the *that* clause allows a writer both to label information as coming from a particular source and to differentiate between what is *suggested, argued,* or merely *said.* In constructing your sentences, consider these common verbs for presenting information:

To indicate neutrality about the ideas presented: *says that, states that, reports that, notes that, finds that*

To indicate particularly well supported findings: *indicates that, finds that, shows that, demonstrates that, concludes that*

To indicate more tentative findings: *suggests that, implies that, believes that, proposes that*

To indicate speculative or theoretical statements: *speculates that, theorizes that, supposes that, conjectures that*

To argue tentatively: *urges that, advises that, claims that*

Using *That* Clauses

One common sentence pattern used by writers to report information includes a *that* clause: "So-and-so suggests that . . ." This kind of sentence enables you to say *who* said *what* without taking a position yourself as to whether the information is correct or not. Here are some examples of *that* clauses from this chapter's readings:

> Barbara and Gene Eakins found *that,* with one exception, men spoke more often and, without exception, spoke for a longer time. (paragraph 4)
> —DEBORAH TANNEN
> " 'Put Down That Paper and Talk to Me!'
> Rapport-Talk and Report-Talk"

> Dale Spender suggests *that* most people feel instinctively (if not consciously) that women, like children, should be seen and not heard [. . .]. (paragraph 9)
> —DEBORAH TANNEN
> " 'Put Down That Paper and Talk to Me!'
> Rapport-Talk and Report-Talk"

> I discovered *that,* in many cases, they didn't think about or even necessarily know communication "rules." (paragraph 3)
> —SUSAN PAGE
> "Essential Traits of Couples Who Thrive"

Studies show *that* if you believe you have calmed down but are still physiologically aroused when you reapproach your spouse, you'll be very susceptible to taking on any emotion he or she expresses. (paragraph 22)

−JOHN GOTTMAN
"The Two Marriages: His and Hers"

Ashley Montagu argued in "The Natural Superiority of Women" *that* females had it all over males [. . .]. (paragraph 1)

−KATHA POLLITT
"Are Women Morally Superior to Men?"

The main thesis of Tannen's book is *that* women's and men's conversation is (not even is *patterned like*) cross-cultural communication (pp. 18, 42, 47). (paragraph 3)

−SENTA TROEMEL-PLOETZ
"Selling the Apolitical"

Gray insists *that* the growth of his empire is merely a response to the outpouring of interest in his work [. . .]. (paragraph 6)

−ELIZABETH GLEICK
"Tower of Psychobabble"

Using Lists

You often can report on information more efficiently if you can group similar examples together in lists. Most of the readings in this chapter contain multiple examples as a way of increasing interest and making advice relevant for different readers. Grouping examples into lists allows writers to include more examples, as you can see in the numbered lists or indented, unnumbered lists in the chapter's readings.

In addition, the readings frequently contain unindented lists within sentences. Sometimes a list needs no introductory colon, usually when it is introduced by *like, such as,* and so forth or when what precedes it is not a complete sentence or clause, as in this example from the readings:

They know who is allowed to use dominant speech acts, *like* commands, orders, explanations, contradiction, doubts, advice, criticism, evaluations, definitions, punishment, attacks, challenges, accusations, reproaches; and who has to apologize, defend, ask for favors, beg, request permission, justify herself, agree, support, adjust, accommodate, and accept someone else's definition of the situation. (paragraph 3)

−SENTA TROEMEL-PLOETZ
"Selling the Apolitical"

More often, lists are introduced by colons, as in the following examples:

But another explanation is that men think women talk a lot because they hear women talking in situations where men would not: on the telephone; or in social situations with friends, when they are not discussing topics that men find inherently interesting; or, like the couple at the women's group, at home alone—in other words, in private speaking. (paragraph 9)

> –DEBORAH TANNEN
> "'Put Down That Paper and Talk to Me!'
> Rapport-Talk and Report-Talk"

For one thing, it seems to explain some important phenomena: that women— and this is a cross-cultural truth—commit very little criminal violence compared with men; that women fill the ranks of the so-called caring professions; that women are much less likely than men to abandon their children. (paragraph 7)

> –KATHA POLLITT
> "Are Women Morally Superior to Men?"

Men are used to dominating women; they do it especially in conversations: they set the tone as soon as they enter a conversation, they declare themselves expert for almost any topic, they expect and get attention and support from their female conversational partners, they expect and get space to present their topics and, above all, themselves [. . .]. (paragraph 5)

> –SENTA TROEMEL-PLOETZ
> "Selling the Apolitical"

Ask about future books, and his answer is, frankly, a little scary: *Men Are from Mars, Women Are from Venus, Kids Are from Heaven,* a parenting book due out in 1998; *Daddy's from Mars, Mommy's from Venus; MAFM, WAFV over 50; MAFM, WAFV over 50 Together Forever; MAFM, WAFV over 50 in the Bedroom; Mars and Venus in the Boardroom; Mars and Venus in the Counseling Room; Mars and Venus Single Again.* (paragraph 3)

> –ELIZABETH GLEICK
> "Tower of Psychobabble"

CITING SOURCES

In reporting on these writers' advice, you will often quote, paraphrase, or summarize what they have said. When you do so, you must cite the authors, identifying them either informally or formally.

Informal Citation

Informal citation allows you to identify all your sources within the text of your essay, mentioning the author, publication, and perhaps the date right in your own sentences. You may also need a phrase or sentence describing the writer in order to establish his or her authority. When using informal citation, you do not identify sources in footnotes or in a works cited list at the end of your essay.

The readings in this chapter rely on informal citation, probably because they are written for the general public. To see how writers use this citation style, look at these examples:

For example, communications researchers Barbara and Gene Eakins tape-recorded and studied seven university faculty meetings. They found that, with one exception, men spoke more often [. . .].

–Deborah Tannen
" 'Put Down That Paper and Talk to Me!'
Rapport-Talk and Report-Talk"

In the 1950s, which we think of as the glory days of traditional sex roles, the anthropologist Ashley Montagu argued in "The Natural Superiority of Women" that females had it all over males [. . .].

–Katha Pollitt
"Are Women Morally Superior to Men?"

Formal Citation

When you use formal citation, you follow a specific style used by a particular academic or professional group. Appendix 2 of this book outlines two of these styles, one from the Modern Language Association (MLA), which is favored by scholars in the humanities, and one from the American Psychological Association (APA), which is favored by scholars in psychology. Ask your instructor which you should follow.

If you are referring to one of the readings in this chapter, cite it as a work in an anthology or edited collection. Depending on your instructor's advice, follow either the recommendations under "A Work in an Anthology" in the "Books" section of the MLA guidelines or those under "A Work in an Edited Collection" in the "Books" section of the APA guidelines. Appendix 2 of this book discusses these options thoroughly and provides examples of each.

Note: Writers usually do not document sources that provide commonly known facts, general background information, or common knowledge, but if you want to make use of some of the background material in this chapter's introductions or reading headnotes—material not written by Tannen, for instance, or the other authors in this chapter—then you have two choices. You can paraphrase the material without giving a citation if it appears to be common knowledge. Or, you can cite Charles R. Cooper and Susan Peck Mac-Donald as authors of *Writing the World,* using the MLA or APA models for an anthology in Appendix 2.

EVALUATING AND REVISING

The following guidelines for revising will help you evaluate your own draft and provide useful advice to other students about theirs. As you read a draft, try to identify what has been done well and to come up with specific ways to make the report clearer or more informative. While revising, focus on the big issues; save spelling and grammar for later.

Since you may need to refer to specific readings, have them handy as you work. If you completed your own information worksheet and writer's notebook tasks on the readings, these will serve you well now as you analyze your own draft or someone else's.

It is a good idea to write out your comments for a classmate's draft on a separate sheet of paper, perhaps following the headings used in this section.

Read to Get a General Impression

Read the draft straight through without marking on it, as if you are one of its intended readers browsing through a magazine in which it appears. Then write three or four sentences summarizing your first impression. What aspect of the essay seems most successful? What do you find most interesting? What one change might make the information clearer or easier to follow?

Read to Analyze the Draft More Closely

Next, number the paragraphs. Then, as you respond to the following questions, refer to specific paragraphs in the draft. Try to analyze the draft with your best understanding of its expected readers' attitudes and knowledge. As you go through the questions below, keep this larger question in mind: What will be engaging, clear, and informative for the readers of this report? Write down what you think is good about the draft as well as specific suggestions for revision.

The Opening.   What strategy is used to open the essay? Are there brief anecdotes, samples of conversation, or other specific observations that will draw a reader in? If not, offer suggestions for making the opening more successful.

The Brief Information about the Context of the Research.   What information about self-help books, problems in communication, or the specific writers being discussed is presented at the beginning? Make suggestions for adding to or clarifying the context of the advice.

The Forecasting Statement and Key Terms.   Put an asterisk in the margin where you find the forecast of what this essay is about and how it will be organized. If you have any uncertainty about the plan being forecast, make suggestions for how to clarify it.

Circle the key terms—both in the forecasting statement and at major transition points throughout the draft. Key terms for this report might include words like *self-help, communication, rapport, hierarchy,* and *defensiveness.* Consider whether the essay's key terms help the reader understand the information presented and set up a clear topical organization. If some of the key terms need to be better defined, make suggestions about what might be added and where to do so.

The Report on the Information.   Find the part of the draft that reports on the advice the four writers in this chapter offer. Within particular topics or subtopics, are the explanations clear and accurate? Note any spots where you find the draft difficult to read or unclear in any way and make suggestions for changes.

Consider, also, the accuracy of the ways the research is presented. If you find that the draft states the writers' advice inaccurately, suggest ways to make the claims more accurate. If there are places where credit needs to be given for particular ideas or examples, suggest where and how to do so. If the essay contains any misstatements, note those also.

Finally, consider whether the information is presented fully enough for the reader. Suggest places where further examples from the readings or personal experience are needed to illustrate the different ways of talking or communicating more effectively. Suggest also places where the reader may need fuller explanations to understand how one type of talk resembles another, what gender differences these researchers found in different types of talk, or how partners can minimize conflict or ill feelings.

The Reception by Critics.   Reactions from critics, if they are included, may be either developed fully in one or two places or woven throughout the report. Identify where these reactions have been introduced. Are they explained fully and placed where they will make most sense to the reader? If not, specify what remedies are needed.

The Cues to Keep Readers on Track.   As you read through the draft, note whether the overall plan stays in the foreground, helping you anticipate where the essay is going and see how different pieces of advice fit into the report. If there are any points where the essay seems to lose its way, note them and look to see whether the key terms have disappeared from the foreground of the essay. Check the beginnings of paragraphs especially, since those are logical spots for the key terms to be useful in carrying out the topical organization.

The Closing.   Look carefully at the closing and consider whether it brings the report to a satisfying close. Tell the writer what you like about the closing and suggest ways it might be made more effective, if necessary.

EDITING AND PROOFREADING

As you revise, you should be concerned primarily with your presentation of the advice about how couples can communicate better or, more specifically, of the role that gender differences play in creating problems in communication. After you have decided on how the larger pieces of the report should fit together, then comes the time to edit, when you begin clarifying your sentences and tightening the connections among them so that each step in the report makes a clear contribution to the overall report.

Examine the connections between all of your sentences. If you sense misdirection or a gap that would break a reader's momentum, try reorganizing one sentence or another or writing new material. Check to see whether you shift terms unnecessarily. Look for sentences that might be combined to better show relationships among ideas. Look also for overly lengthy or garbled sentences that might be broken up into two or three sentences.

As you work on your sentences, look for errors in spelling, capitalization, punctuation, usage, and grammar, consulting a writer's handbook for information about correcting any you find. Ask a friend or classmate to read over your essay to help you recognize and correct errors.

Before you hand in your final revised essay, proofread it with great care and run it through a spellchecker to catch any inadvertent errors.

REFLECTING ON WHAT YOU HAVE LEARNED

After completing this chapter's reading and writing assignments, take time to reflect on what you have learned. Doing so can help you analyze problems you encountered and consolidate your learning. Consider that you have been engaged in two closely related kinds of learning: (1) becoming informed about advice on how couples can communicate more effectively or about the role that self-help writers claim gender differences play in communication problems and (2) reporting that information clearly for others.

Write a page or so reflecting on this accomplishment. The following questions and suggestions may help you begin or extend your reflections.

- What was most challenging for you in understanding the advice on communicating in relationships? What was most surprising? How did you respond to the critics' charges?

- How has your understanding of how people talk been confirmed or changed by both the self-help writers and their critics? What else would you like to know?

- What was most difficult for you in planning your essay? When you began drafting, what was your biggest surprise? Think of the most important revision you made in your draft. How did you come to make this revision?

- What important advice would you give to a writer just starting out on a reporting assignment like this?

- What are you most pleased with in your essay? How would you revise it if you had more time to work on it?

GATHERING ADDITIONAL INFORMATION

To supplement the research in this chapter, you may want to do further reading on men's and women's conversations. Though the readings in this chapter are intended for ordinary readers, most draw on a well-defined body of research by linguists and psychologists. To learn more about the advice in self-help books on relationships or about research on conversations, there are a number of search strategies you can employ.

Self-Help Books

One way to find self-help books is to go to a bookstore large enough to carry a wide selection of self-help books you can browse through. You can also browse through books at an online bookstore and, possibly, online reviews of such books. You might use the readings in this chapter as sample titles to find out what categories your local bookstore or an online bookstore uses for arranging books.

At a public library, you can also find a selection of self-help books, and you can browse magazine indexes meant to be used for nonscholarly research. Ask a librarian for help in deciding which subject headings to use, or try starting with "Marriage, communication and language."

If you are interested in book reviews of particular self-help books, your librarian can show you how to use a *subject search* for the writer's name. You can also look for reviews online by using a subject directory or checking online bookstores at these URLs:

<http://www.amazon.com>

<http://www.barnesandnoble.com> or <www.bn.com>

Scholarly Research

Scholarly research, like the research that Deborah Tannen draws on or that Senta Troemel-Ploetz says would repudiate Tannen, is most likely to be found in books and articles in journals at a college or a university library.

Research in Academic Books. Scholarly research on gender and language is often published as chapters in books whose editors collected a group of journal articles related to one another. To find such collections, you can start with these Library of Congress Subject Headings for finding material in books:

Language and languages — Sex differences

Communication in marriage

Conversation — Sex differences

Women — Language

Sexism — Language

Feminism — Language

Interpersonal communication

Interpersonal relations

Marriage

"Conversation—Sex differences" might be the best subject heading to start finding academic books. Appendix 2 offers further help on subject headings, as will your librarian, who can also show you how to work with the particular search tools in your library.

Research in Academic Journals.   You will find research published in journal articles by using academic indexes. Although general indexes such as *InfoTrac* and the *Readers' Guide to Periodical Literature* may list some references to journal articles on the topic of gender differences in conversation, the best sources of information are the more specialized academic indexes such as *Psychological Abstracts,* the *Social Sciences Index,* and *Sociological Abstracts.* Most community college and some high school and public libraries have the *Social Sciences Index;* you will most likely find *Psychological Abstracts* and *Sociological Abstracts* in college and university libraries. All are published in both print and electronic form; ask the reference librarian which form is available in the library you are using.

Generally you can look for information in these indexes by subject or author. Periodical indexes use subject headings, but they are not always identical to the Library of Congress Subject Headings used for books. One good way to discover which subject headings to use is to try to find an article by an author you already are familiar with from this chapter. Then look to see what subject headings have been used to describe that article.

Sometimes you will have to use more than one subject heading to find exactly the kind of information you need. In *Psychological Abstracts,* for example, you may find research on conversations under the headings "conversation," "social structure," "dominance hierarchy," "human sex differences," and "power." To find articles on the differences in conversation between men and women, you can combine the subject headings on "conversation" and "human sex differences."

If you are interested in reading further research from the 1970s, 1980s, or 1990s, consult the bibliographies in the works listed under "Further Readings" because they will lead you to closely related research.

FURTHER READINGS ON COMMUNICATING IN RELATIONSHIPS

Beck, Aaron T. *Love Is Never Enough: How Couples Can Overcome Misunderstandings, Resolve Conflicts, and Solve Relationship Problems through Cognitive Therapy.* New York: Harper & Row, 1988.

Gottman, John Mordechai. *The Seven Principles for Making Marriage Work.* New York: Crown, 1999.

———. *What Predicts Divorce? The Relationship between Marital Processes and Marital Outcomes.* Hillsdale: Lawrence Erlbaum Associates, 1994.

Gottman, John Mordechai, Lynn Fainsilber Katz, and Carole Hooven. *Meta-emotion: How Families Communicate Emotionally.* Mahwah: Lawrence Erlbaum Associates, 1997.

Hall, Kira, Mary Bucholtz, and Birch Moonwomon, eds. *Locating Power: Proceedings of the Second Berkeley Women and Language Conference, April 4 and 5, 1992, Berkeley, California.* 2 vols. Berkeley: Berkeley Women and Language Group, 1992.

Henley, Nancy M., and Cheris Kramarae. "Gender, Power, and Miscommunication." *"Miscommunication" and Problematic Talk.* Ed. Nikolas Coupland, Howard Giles, and John M. Wiemann. Newbury Park: Sage, 1991. 18–43.

Lakoff, Robin. *Language and Woman's Place.* New York: Harper & Row, 1975.

Maltz, Daniel N., and Ruth A. Borker. "A Cultural Approach to Male-Female Miscommunication." *Language and Social Identity.* Ed. John J. Gumperz. Cambridge: Cambridge UP, 1982. 196–216.

Mills, Sara, ed. *Language and Gender: Interdisciplinary Perspectives.* London: Longman, 1995.

Tannen, Deborah, ed. *Gender and Conversational Interaction.* New York: Oxford UP, 1993.

Thorne, Barrie, Cheris Kramarae, and Nancy Henley, eds. *Language, Gender and Society.* Rowley: Newbury, 1983.

ADDITIONAL WRITING PROJECTS

Here are some additional writing projects that focus on the communication between couples and make use of the readings and ideas in this chapter.

Personal Experience Essay

Tell the story of your own experience with misunderstandings in communicating within a relationship. The incident you choose to relate can come from a personal relationship, from communication in the workplace, or from communication with acquaintances. If parts of this experience are painful or embarrassing, focus only on those you feel comfortable sharing with others.

Purpose and Readers.   Your readers are your classmates who have been reading advice about communicating in relationships. Your purpose is to help them see clearly what happened and understand what the experience was like for you. In addition, try to show them why the experience remains significant for you personally.

Resources to Draw On.   Start by making notes about what you remember. Try to recall as many concrete details as you can about when and where the incident occurred, who was involved, and what specifically was said and done. Also note your feelings — at the time of the experience, soon after it occurred, and now. Some of the examples in this chapter's readings may suggest ways to make your story more concrete and vivid. Check the autobiographical readings in Chapter 4 for further examples of concrete writing.

Tips for Writing a Successful Personal Experience Essay.   You will probably relate your experience in the order in which it happened. Try to make your account memorable and interesting by including many specifics about actions and dialogue. Use vivid verbs, colorful nouns or adjectives, and close imitations of actual conversations whenever possible so that readers have the sense of seeing and hearing real people speak. Finally, reflect on this experience from your present perspective. How does it look to you now? How has it influenced your feelings or beliefs? How has it changed your behavior?

Attach to your essay a page or so of explanations, showing your instructor the connections, as you see them, between the personal experience in your essay and what you have learned from the readings in this chapter.

Report on an Observed Conversation

The writers in this chapter have reported on many conversations they have observed (in the role of participants, friends, counselors, or scientists). Now it is your turn to report on a conversation you observe.

Purpose and Readers.   Your purpose is to offer a detailed report of a sample conversation among men and women to examine whether there are any gender differences in the conversation you observe. Assume that your readers are familiar with the advice in the readings in this chapter, especially with the assumptions in Deborah Tannen, John Gray, and Susan Page that men and women tend to converse differently, and with the kind of criticism Katha Pollitt and Senta Troemel-Ploetz have directed against Tannen and others.

Resources to Draw On.   Find a conversational setting or situation in which you can observe, listen, and possibly take notes on the kinds of conversations occurring there, keeping in mind the sorts of issues discussed in this chapter's readings. You might choose one of the following:

- a cafeteria where you can observe college students in mixed-sex groups talking
- a classroom in which you can observe who talks most and how
- a conversation in an Internet chat group or discussion group
- a party
- a workplace conversation among men and women
- a sporting event where you can observe participants or spectators talking

Begin your observations with a clear sense of what possible gender differences the researchers in this chapter have identified, using what you know from the readings. Then, as you listen to the people you have selected, see what patterns of gender differences you find in their talk. Take as detailed notes as you can about what people say, who talks and how often, who interrupts (or does not interrupt), and so forth. You probably will not find—or be able to discuss—all of the differences these researchers have identified, but try to find one or more patterns that you can connect to the readings in this chapter.

Tips for Writing a Successful Report.   You could begin your report by describing where the participants were, who they were, and what situation led to their conversation (such as mealtime socializing, a meeting to accomplish something specific, and so on). Then report on the nature of the conversation. You may want to summarize the course of the conversation and then organize your observations according to some of the categories in the chapter's readings. You do not *need* to summarize the conversation first; you may decide to just classify what you observe and then report on one category at a time. Use this chapter's sections on classifying, organizing, developing, and revising to help you. Whatever categories you decide on, you can illustrate your findings with concrete examples of talk from the conversation you have observed.

An Interpretation of Humor about Men's and Women's Talk

For this essay, you will use the Web to find samples of humor about men's and women's misunderstandings, and you will then write an interpretation of the humor in light of this chapter's readings.

Purpose and Readers.   In *The 8 Essential Traits of Couples Who Thrive,* Susan Page writes:

> One of the best measures of a society's fundamental beliefs is its sense of humor. [Sarcastic] humor about marriage is rampant in our culture. [Comic strip characters] Blondie Bumstead and Maggie Briggs nagging their husbands and chasing them with rolling pins is supposed to be hilarious. Apparently thousands of people find it funny to see The Lockhorns' utterly miserable relationship portrayed day after day in cartoons that depict their thoughtless, selfish, and mean-spirited behavior toward each other. Endless variations of the classic, "My wife left me ten days ago — but I'm going to wait two weeks before I start to celebrate," are still common fare in comedy clubs.

In other words, humor about relationships shows our discouragement and, possibly, also our desire for something better. You may share this interpretation of Page's and may expand on it or offer a slightly different interpretation.

Your purpose is to interpret a sample of humor about men's and women's communication, studying humor you find on the Web in order to reveal its assumptions about how men and women talk and how they misunderstand each other. Imagine your readers to be men and women who want to understand differing communication styles and get along with each other better. Assume that your readers are aware of the kind of popular humor you find but have not thought much about it. You may want to consider what the humor shows about men's and women's difficulties in understanding each other, their perceptions of the other sex, whether the humor hits its targets fairly, or whether it seems biased or unfair in some way. Your essay will then aim to help your readers understand the humor about communication in ways they might not have thought of before.

Resources to Draw On.   On the Web, you can locate many different forums for discussing gender relations and sites specifically focused on humor about relationships. As of 1999, you could discover a number of samples involving humor about relationships at <http://www.geocities.com/Wellesley/2052/humour.html>. You can begin locating such sites by doing a subject search with the terms *humor* and *relationships*.

Your primary resource for understanding and interpreting the humor you find will be the advice and critiques you have read in this chapter. While you may not need to refer extensively and in detail to this chapter's readings, they should provide the context for your interpreting what you find on the Web.

From the examples of humor that you find, choose one sample that seems particularly relevant to the readings in this chapter. Your sample might consist of a lengthy single piece or a set of related shorter pieces; the sample will be most relevant if it focuses on communication, rather than some other aspect of men's and women's relationships. The sample you choose might humorously illustrate men's and women's difficulties in communicating, or it might contain stereotypical or even offensive views about men's and women's communication — views that you think you can put into perspective using this chapter's readings. Drawing on these readings, you can interpret what experiences, assumptions, fears, misunderstandings, and so on underlie the humorous writing you have found.

Tips for Writing an Interpretation.   You might start by quoting briefly from the sample you have selected or describing where its humor lies. (See paragraphs 18–20 of Tannen's reading in this chapter for an example of concrete description used to launch an interpretation.) From there, you could move into your interpretation, offering a thesis statement about what you think the humor shows about men's and women's communication. Since you will want to divide your subject into parts or subtopics that you can then discuss one by one, you might set up subtopics to correspond to parts of the sample of humor you have selected, or you might use categories from this chapter's readings to set up your subtopics. In either case, be sure to be specific about what you find in the sample you have selected.

Essay Taking a Position

Write an essay that takes a position on whether or not women's conversation shows more concern than men's for intimacy and sharing feelings.

Purpose and Readers.   In the readings, Tannen, Gray, and Page argue that women and men talk differently and that their relationships can be improved if each understands the other better and tries to adjust its conversation in the light of this understanding. Clearly, the sales of self-help books on relationships demonstrate that many people want to improve their relationships and think that self-help advice such as that presented in the chapter readings will help them do so. Pollitt and Troemel-Ploetz, however, argue that such advice is misleading, that men and women who accept this advice do so because it makes them feel good without solving the problem.

Resources to Draw On.   From the readings in this chapter, you are familiar with advice about men's and women's understanding each other better and have a good sense of the critiques of such advice. You also have your own experience of men's and women's conversations to draw on, as well as media images, comic strips, and humor directed at men's and women's misunderstandings. Therefore, you probably already know where you stand on this issue. To support your position, try to recall as many concrete conversations or images of misunderstandings as you can, including where they occurred, who was involved, what was said, and how you felt as a participant or a listener. The readings will suggest ways of categorizing your reasons for agreeing with Tannen, Gray, and Page or for criticizing them in the way that Pollitt and Troemel-Ploetz do.

Tips on Writing a Successful Essay Taking a Position.   You might begin with one or two telling incidents of conversation that illustrate the problem that has given rise to this body of self-help advice. Then you could state your position in a thesis and develop a list of reasons. Taking one reason at a time, you can provide examples of conversation, quotes from experts, and so forth to show how each reason supports your position. You should also be aware of readers' possible questions and objections and build refutations or concessions into your argument. Check the Writer's Guide in Chapter 3 for tips on essays that take a position.

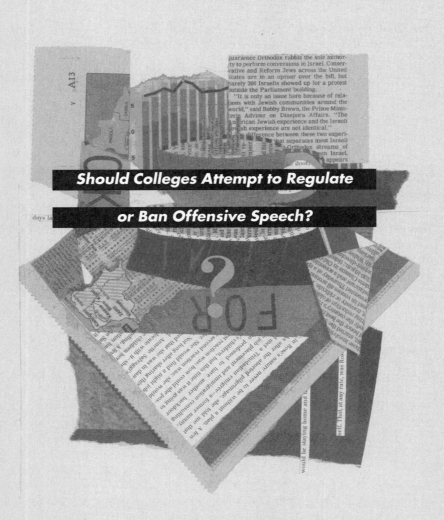

Should Colleges Attempt to Regulate or Ban Offensive Speech?

3

TAKING A POSITION ON A CONSTITUTIONAL ISSUE

Bigotry will not go unchallenged within this community. No one has the right to denigrate another human being on the basis of race, sex, sexual orientation, national origin, etc. We will not tolerate verbal or written abuse, threats, harassment, intimidation or violence against person or property.

> —University of Southern
> California, "Student Life"

When someone calls you a hate name, they are not trying to get into a debate or even a rancorous argument with you. They are telling you that you are less than human, that you have no right to be here, and that your speech is worthless. The typical responses to racist hate speech include fear, flight, or fistfights. People use these words precisely because of the wounding, silencing effect. I suggest that there are some forms of speech we need to limit precisely because we value speech.

> —Mari J. Matsuda, "Assaultive Speech
> and Academic Freedom"

Speech codes have not stopped hate speech. Speech codes are used all too frequently to prosecute and persecute those they would protect. Rather than encourage education, they have enforced a form of ignorance. They have diverted the dialogue from a focus on a fair society to a preoccupation with censorship. They have failed to draw a definitive line between acceptable speech and unacceptable speech. They have trivialized the debate.

> —Paul McMasters, "Free Speech
> versus Civil Discourse"

The following incidents occurred recently on U.S. college campuses. A fraternity held a party that included a "slave auction." Four male students circulated a note on the Internet naming "75 reasons why women (bitches) should not have freedom of speech." Reporting rape and saying "no" to sex were two "freedoms" these students would deny of women. A student sent email to dozens of Asian students saying: "I personally will make it my life's work to find and kill every one of you. OK? That's how determined I am. Do you hear me?" The email was signed "Asian Hater."

In response to such incidents, many colleges and universities have published guidelines in an effort to protect their students from offensive speech directed at them by other students.

Incidents like these—whether spoken, written, or symbolic—are referred to as *speech,* a term from the freedom of speech clause in the First Amendment to the Constitution:

> Congress shall make no law respecting an establishment of religion, or prohibiting the free exercise thereof; or *abridging the freedom of speech,* or of the press; or the right of the people peaceably to assemble, and to petition the government for a redress of grievances.

In developing guidelines or speech codes, however, colleges have found it very difficult to write rules that punish cases of offensive speech without restricting other kinds of speech. Many colleges have found that their attempts at regulating speech have had unexpected effects, as U.S. courts have ruled that college speech regulations are unconstitutional. Thus, colleges may continue to discourage certain kinds of speech, but they may not, as of 1999, punish it. Further complicating the issue is the fact that the Supreme Court had not, through 1999, considered a campus speech case even though it often considers other free speech cases. Consequently, many legal scholars continue to argue that offensive speech on campus can and should be regulated and even punished without violating basic constitutional freedoms.

Like many contemporary issues, the offensive speech debate presents a difficult choice between offering protection to some groups and risking the erosion of speech rights for everyone. In this kind of debate, values and ideals clash. Constitutional issues arise. Is the right of free speech to be protected at all costs? Or might an exception be made to protect college students from speech that insults or demeans them? That is the issue you will read about, discuss, and write about in this chapter. You will also discover that there are informed, responsible arguments on both sides of this issue.

GLOSSARY: WORDS ABOUT WORDS

This chapter concerns words and how they are spoken. It also relies on particular words that identify precisely different types of speakers and their offensive speech. Some of these words will be familiar, but it is important to be aware of their precise meanings as they are used in the chapter—and as you use them yourself in your own discussion and written work.

   This brief glossary provides definitions of some of the words that recur throughout the chapter. You may want to review these words before you begin the readings. This glossary is boxed here for easy reference as you work with this chapter.

animosity: Expressions of resentment and hostility.
badger: To harass or annoy.
bigot, bigotry: Stubborn and intolerant devotion to one's own opinions and prejudices.
defamation, defamatory, defame: The act of speaking or writing in a way that harms someone's reputation.
demean: To lower someone's status or harm someone's reputation.
denigrate: To question the importance of people and undermine their dignity.
deride, derisive: Expressing ridicule or contempt.
epithet: A word or phrase that is abusive or insulting.
harass, harassment: To repeatedly annoy or worry someone.
invective: Insulting or abusive language.
lewd: Vulgar, indecent, immoral, or lustful.
libel, libelous: Speech intended to damage someone's reputation.
obloquy: Abusive language.
political correctness, politically correct: The idea that all speech or writing that might offend the members of any group should be eliminated.
revile, revilings: To verbally abuse someone.
scapegoating: Shifting the blame for one's troubles to other people.
slander: A false and damaging statement about another person.
slur: An insult intended to shame or degrade someone.
stereotype: Oversimplified opinions or prejudiced attitudes held about other people.
stigmatize, stigma: To shame or discredit someone.
vilification, vilify: The act of abusing or defaming someone.
vitriolic: Speech that is harsh or strong.

A LOOK AHEAD: WRITING ABOUT SPEECH REGULATIONS This chapter includes an essay assignment on the issue of whether colleges should attempt to ban offensive speech. Developing such an essay involves asserting your position on the issue, giving reasons why you take that position, and making an argument to support your position. Although most of this support will probably come from the readings, you may want to include personal experiences and anecdotes from other students as well. In addition to arguing in support of your position, you will need to counterargue, that is, to respond to readers' likely questions or objections about your position and to opposing views presented in the readings.

The readings in this chapter are of four kinds. First come articles about specific incidents of offensive speech on college campuses, followed by speech regulations that three colleges have developed in order to discourage or ban offensive speech. Next, excerpts from key Supreme Court cases put the debate within a constitutional context. Finally come nine impassioned arguments about the issue—some in favor of regulating what college students can say to each other, and some opposed. Each set of readings is followed by a writer's notebook, with suggestions for thinking about the readings in terms of your own experience as well as guidance to help you reread the selections critically and prepare to write an essay about this important debate.

CAMPUS SPEECH INCIDENTS

The readings in this section relate specific incidents of offensive speech on three college campuses. Although you personally may never have had anything offensive said to you because of your race, ethnicity, religion, gender, or sexual orientation, many people have had this experience. In fact, almost everyone has experienced hurtful teasing, verbal bullying, or even repeated harassment for one reason or another—for being short or round or tall or skinny, for speaking with an unfamiliar accent, for having unusual interests, for living on the "wrong" side of the tracks.

Verbal harassment, then, is an all-too-familiar American experience and one that raises some fundamental questions about life in a democracy: What rights do individuals and groups have to be protected from hateful speech? How do citizens resolve the conflict between the need for public civility and the free speech protections in the Constitution? Or must we simply endure verbal harassment?

The college you are attending may seem to be a safe place where you do not expect students to be saying offensive things to each other. You may find, however, that other students' experiences are different from yours. As you work through this chapter and interview other students, you may gain a broader perspective and learn specifically what has been said to them.

The three incidents discussed in this section—at the University of California, Riverside; the University of Pennsylvania; and California Institute of Technology—are concrete, typical incidents of offensive speech. Together with your own personal experiences and those of your classmates, these incidents should give you a solid foundation for thinking—and writing—about whether or not offensive speech on campus can or should be regulated.

A CAMPUS CASE:
SPEECH OR HARASSMENT?

Michael deCourcy Hinds

In this 1993 article, Michael deCourcy Hinds, a reporter for the New York Times, *writes about a widely publicized case of verbal harassment. Hinds tells the story of a white University of Pennsylvania student who was charged with racial harassment for words he shouted at a group of African American women students. After this article was published, the university punished the student, Eden Jacobowitz, as outlined in the article. Under pressure from columnists, scholars, and civil rights organizations, however, the university later dropped the charges and punishments. After he graduated from Penn in 1996, Jacobowitz sued the university for "breach of contract and reckless, intentional infliction of emotional distress."*

Even before Jacobowitz was punished, another speech incident occurred at Penn. A group of African American students destroyed nearly all of the copies of the student newspaper because they were angry about a column in the paper attacking "favored treatment of blacks in admissions and disciplinary procedures."

As you read, try to understand not only what happened at Penn but also the public reaction to the university administrators' actions.

Amid preparations for Monday's commencement exercises, University of Pennsylvania officials spent much of today dealing with the racial tension that has plagued the campus over the last semester.

The university's Judicial Inquiry Office held a closed hearing today to determine whether a white student who had called some black students "water buffalo" had violated the university's policy forbidding racial harassment. The policy prohibits racial epithets meant to "inflict direct injury" on people.

The inquiry office will decide within 10 days whether it will dismiss the case or schedule it for a full-blown evidentiary hearing° later this year.

Lawyers at the American Civil Liberties Union° here say the case should have been dismissed, and they vowed to take the case to Federal court if the university penalized the white student.

DIDN'T INTEND RACIAL SLUR

That student, Eden Jacobowitz, said 5 earlier this week that he had intended

---

°**evidentiary hearing:** A carefully planned meeting at which both sides in a dispute present evidence about what happened. °**American Civil Liberties Union:** An organization devoted to protecting individual rights.

no racial slur when he shouted at several black sorority women who were making noise outside his dormitory window. Mr. Jacobowitz, who was born in Israel and speaks Hebrew, said "water buffalo" was a translation of a Hebrew word, *behayma,* which is used as a mild epithet to chide an uncouth individual.

This incident, and a more recent one in which black students threw out nearly the entire press run of the student newspaper because they did not like a columnist's conservative opinions, may not have been as dramatic as the racial unrest on some other college campuses this year.

But the university's handling of the incident has drawn a chorus of criticism and ridicule from civil libertarians° and columnists, who say the university's effort to regulate speech is a prime example of an overzealous attempt to be politically correct.°

The case is drawing special attention because Sheldon Hackney, the president of the university, is President Clinton's nominee to head the National Endowment for the Humanities.

CRITICISM OF UNIVERSITY

University officials said today that Mr. Hackney, who has been an outspoken advocate of free speech when controversial figures like Louis Farrakhan° or Robert Mapplethorpe° appeared on campus or displayed their works, would not discuss the "water buffalo" case while his confirmation hearings are pending.

Criticism of the university revolves 10 around two issues: the university's effort to police free speech and the apparent disparity in the university's response in disciplining black students and white students.

Civil libertarians say that the university should not try to restrict speech, but should try to educate students when they use racial slurs.

The second criticism is that university officials appear to have a double standard in disciplining minority students involved in racial incidents. For at the same time as the university is bringing disciplinary charges against Mr. Jacobowitz, it has taken no action against a group of black students who destroyed 14,000 copies of the student newspaper because they objected to the opinions of a student columnist, Gregory Pavlik, a junior from Delran, N.J., who used his column to attack racial preferences, Martin Luther King Jr., and what he saw as the university's favored treatment of blacks in admissions and disciplinary procedures.

Last month, Mr. Hackney issued a statement about the black students' actions. "Two important university values now stand in conflict," he said. "There can be no compromise

---

°**civil libertarians:** People who strongly support the civil liberties outlined in the Bill of Rights, especially those in the First Amendment. °**politically correct:** Here, not offensive to any group. °**Louis Farrakhan:** Head of the Nation of Islam, a separatist African American group whose leaders have spoken out harshly against whites, especially Jews. °**Robert Mapplethorpe:** An artist (1946–89) whose photographs of nude gay men created controversy.

regarding the First Amendment right of an independent publication to express whatever views it chooses. At the same time, there can be no ignoring the pain that expression may cause."

The university is continuing its investigation of whether the students violated the freedom of expression by trashing the newspapers.

"PATRONIZING PATERNALISM"

Several columnists have criticized 15 Mr. Hackney for what they say is a double standard. George F. Will wrote in an April 29 column, "Hackney's institution has a propensity for behavior both cowardly and bullying, trimming principles to pander° to political fashion." Nat Hentoff, in the May 4 issue of the Village Voice, accused Mr. Hackney of engaging in "patronizing paternalism."° The foreign press has had a heyday, too: A May 7 Toronto Star article, under the headline, "Exactly What Race Is a Water Buffalo?" called the incident "egregiously absurd," noting that water buffalo are not found in Africa, but only in Southeast Asia.

Black leaders of campus groups were reluctant to discuss the Jacobowitz case today. Over the last few months, though, some black students have told reporters that what is important is that the women perceived "water buffalo" as a racial epithet, and that the campus generally is inhospitable to minority students.

University officials would not release the names of the black women involved, or the faculty adviser representing them in the case.

But Mr. Jacobowitz, an 18-year-old freshman from Lawrence, L.I., gave his account of the incident in a telephone interview today. Mr. Jacobowitz, who has a room in the sixth floor of High Rise North residence hall, said that it began around midnight, Jan. 13, when about a dozen black sorority women began "shouting, stomping, singing and screaming things like 'woo, woo.'"

After enduring the noise for about 20 minutes, Mr. Jacobowitz, who said he was trying to write an English paper, said he shouted at the women to "shut up." By that time, he said, lots of other students were shouting, too, but their language was laced with swear words. Mr. Jacobowitz said he did not hear any racial epithets used, but he said the campus police subsequently showed him a list of racial epithets that the women had reported.

TOLD POLICE WHAT HE SAID

The women ignored the white stu- 20 dents' complaints, Mr. Jacobowitz said. "When I got no response, I finally shouted, 'Shut up, you water buffalo,'" he said. "Then I heard one of them say they were looking for a party and I said, "If you're looking for a party, there's a zoo a mile from here.' There was absolutely no racial intention on my part when I said those words, and I

°**pander:** Here, to attempt to please the politically powerful.   °**paternalism:** The belief that others need to be directed for their own good.

did not mean the words to be racist in any way."

The women complained to the campus police, who investigated. All of the white students questioned, except Mr. Jacobowitz, denied shouting. Mr. Jacobowitz said he voluntarily told the police what he had shouted.

In March, the university's Judicial Inquiry Office determined there was a reasonable possibility that [the] university's racial harassment code had been violated, and it tried to reach a settlement with Mr. Jacobowitz.

Mr. Jacobowitz said the inquiry office suggested on March 22 that he settle the case by apologizing for racially harassing the women. In addition, he was asked to agree to being put on dormitory probation, with the understanding that any further violation would cause him to be evicted from university housing.

The settlement would also be noted on his permanent record as well as on his transcript. The transcript notation would be removed in his junior year and would then be expunged, unless he again violated university policies.

DECLINED SETTLEMENT

"I was completely shocked," said Mr. 25 Jacobowitz, who declined the settlement. A hearing was scheduled for April 26, the beginning of final exam week. But on April 15, the campus was jarred by the destruction of 14,000 copies of the student newspaper, which prompted so much publicity about racial tensions on campus that the university postponed the hearing until today.

The black students who removed nearly the entire press run of The Daily Pennsylvanian posted signs taking responsibility for the action, saying that they were not willing to accept "the blatant and voluntary perpetuation of institutional racism against the black community by the D.P. and the university." The signs added, "Sometimes inconvenience is worth the price, think about it."

The black students maintained they had done nothing illegal since the newspapers are free and no limits are set on how many copies a person may take.

SUIT FORCES U.C. RIVERSIDE TO RESCIND FRATERNITY PENALTY

Ralph Frammolino

Ralph Frammolino is a reporter for the Los Angeles Times, *where this article was published in November 1993. Frammolino writes about an attempt at speech regulation at the University of California, Riverside. A fraternity there was disbanded for three years after a Latino student group protested a T-shirt the fraternity produced showing a caricature of two Mexicans on a beach, one holding a beer bottle. The fraternity sued the university for violating its First Amendment rights of free speech, and the court required the university to reinstate the fraternity.*

Frammolino discusses several important aspects of the debate about regulating campus speech: the concept of group libel—insulting speech aimed at a group rather than at an individual; the importance of the First Amendment; the role of off-campus organizations like the American Civil Liberties Union in defending students; the role of the courts in deciding whether punishment for offensive speech violates students' speech rights; and the kinds of punishments colleges have instituted against those accused of offensive speech.

As you read, try to understand why the university acted as it did. Consider, too, the arguments the fraternity used in court against the university's actions. And as you think about the entire incident, keep in mind what punishments were initially attempted but revoked—and what punishments were eventually carried out.

Striking what they called a blow against political correctness,° attorneys for a UC Riverside fraternity have made two top campus administrators promise to undergo 1st Amendment "sensitivity" training and drop their plans to punish group members over T-shirts that depicted stereotypes of Mexicans drinking.

The T-shirts—produced by the Phi Kappa Sigma chapter for its rush week membership drive in late September—caused an uproar on the Riverside campus, prompting school officials to disband the fraternity chapter for three years.

But Phi Kappa Sigma filed suit° in Riverside Superior Court, claiming that the members' right of free speech had been violated. To settle the suit, UC Riverside officials agreed Oct. 28 to rescind° the punishment—and, in a highly unusual step, have the administrators in charge take legal training about the safeguards of the 1st Amendment.

"Basically, we want to let these administrators know that the university is not a place where you can take refuge from the Constitution," said Maura Whalen, spokeswoman for the Individual Rights Foundation, a nonprofit Los Angeles group that represented Phi Kappa Sigma and fraternities that have sued administrators at other campuses over 1st Amendment rights.

The T-shirts in question depicted a 5 beach scene with two Mexican caricatures,° one in sombrero and serape, holding what appear to be beer bottles. The picture is surrounded by the words:

°**political correctness:** The idea that all speech or writing that might offend the members of any group should be eliminated.   °**filed suit:** Phi Kappa Sigma and its lawyers asked the court to overturn all the actions taken against them by U.C. Riverside administrators.   °**rescind:** To cancel or take back.   °**caricatures:** Visual representations of people that exaggerate or distort their features.

"It doesn't matter where you come from as long as you know where you are going."

Whalen said the words are from a song by the late reggae star Bob Marley "that as far as I can tell makes a pretty strong statement against racism." The fraternity gave the T-shirt to members and potential pledges for a "south of the border" party, she said.

The shirts became a controversy on the 8,700-student campus after the Latino student group MEChA — Movimiento Estudiantil Chicano de Aztlan — filed a complaint. UC Riverside spokesman Jack Chappell said the group believed the message, taken with the picture, "was in fact a slur and it was offensive."

The school's inter-fraternity council° recommended that the chapter destroy the T-shirts and banned Phi Kappa Sigma from intramural sports and rush week for a year. Assistant Vice Chancellor Vincent Del Pizzo, however, went further and ordered the chapter dissolved for three years.

Chappell said Del Pizzo considered the T-shirt incident the "last straw" because the fraternity has had 14 violations of campus rules since 1984, including drunken conduct, vandalizing a campus bus stop and wearing T-shirts depicting a skeleton on the back making obscene gestures with both hands.

"The problem was this was the 10 wrong 'last straw' for him to be leveling the suspension that he did," Chappell said. "It happened to be a [constitu-

tionally] protected last straw, and rightfully so."

The fraternity's suit cited the 1st Amendment and a new state law that makes it illegal for high schools and colleges to impose rules contrary to the constitutional provision.

"The irony to all this is the motto of the fraternity is 'Strength Through Diversity,'" said John Howard, the foundation attorney who filed the case. "There's more diversity in this particular fraternity chapter than any other chapter on campus. This is the worst group they could have picked on."

The settlement requires Del Pizzo and Kevin Ferguson, director of campus activities, to take the 1st Amendment training. Del Pizzo declined comment. Ferguson could not be reached.

Howard called the requirement "sensitivity training" that would "make clear to administrators that the 1st Amendment exists for speech you don't like. You don't need the 1st Amendment for speech you do like."

Chappell said the officials have yet 15 to take the training, but there is some thought of inviting former CBS news president and Columbia University professor emeritus Fred W. Friendly to host a "media and society" seminar on campus about how free speech can sometimes collide with civility° and respect for ethnic groups.

Despite the legal settlement, the fraternity chapter still must abide by sanctions imposed by its national office

---

° **inter-fraternity council:** A group of fraternity members representing all fraternities on a campus.
° **civility:** Courtesy, politeness.

requiring a letter of apology to the campus and each chapter member to complete 16 hours of community service in a Latino area.

A member of the fraternity chapter declined comment Wednesday. But an officer at the society's national headquarters in Philadelphia said board members imposed the sanctions because [they] "felt that the chapter was frankly kind of stupid for not realizing that people could be offended."

"Students today believe they live in a bubble," said Alan Preston, Phi Kappa Sigma's executive vice president. "We're trying to send a clear message to other chapters that you have to be aware that you're in the real world. The real world isn't [just] after graduation."

The Riverside incident is not the first time that college administrators have been forced to backpedal from punishing a fraternity for offensive remarks. In March, Cal State Northridge reinstated the Zeta Beta Tau chapter after its members enraged some Latino students with an off-color invitation to a Mexican-theme party.

The fraternity admitted distributing [20] the flyer, which featured song lyrics describing lewd acts with a prostitute named Lupe. Last November, campus administrators suspended the group for 14 months, but the Individual Rights Foundation filed suit, claiming the fraternity's 1st Amendment rights were violated.

CSUN President Blenda J. Wilson agreed to a settlement reinstating the fraternity last April 1 after attorneys advised that the school might lose the potentially costly case. The agreement still required fraternity members to attend cultural diversity workshops and run full-page ads of apology in the campus newspaper.

CALTECH STUDENT'S EXPULSION OVER E-MAIL CONTENTS RAISES CONCERNS

Amy Harmon

Amy Harmon is a reporter for the Los Angeles Times, *where this article on a case of email harassment at the California Institute of Technology (Caltech) appeared in 1995. Harmon reports on a number of issues. As more and more students use the Internet, harassment and "stalking" have come to take place in the form of email. Some states have enacted laws against sending sexually explicit email over the Internet. The most frequent abuse involves romantic relationships, with repeated and sometimes offensive email messages sent by rejected suitors. The problem faced by students, campus administrators, and legislators is how*

*to draw a line between acceptable and unacceptable personal email commun-
ication.*

*As you read, keep in mind that even though the accused Caltech student was
found not guilty in a court trial, Caltech administrators nevertheless dismissed
him from the university for email sexual harassment.*

In a controversial decision that has
polarized the Caltech campus, a
promising doctoral candidate° was
expelled last month for allegedly sexually harassing another student —
largely via electronic mail.

The unusual action has raised new
concerns over the nature of harassment
in a digital age, and the credibility of e-
mail records at a time when the use of
the medium is steeply increasing, both
on and off campus.

Jinsong Hu, 26, who spent six
months in County Jail before being
acquitted° by a Los Angeles Superior
Court jury in June of stalking, insists
that he did not send some of the e-mail
in question and that parts of the mail
he did send were doctored.

Jiajun Wen, Hu's former girlfriend,
also accused him of verbal and written
harassment. But the bulk of the evidence examined in court and in the
university's disciplinary hearings was
electronic mail.

Complaints of e-mail harassment at ₅
many of the nation's universities have
risen sharply over the last 18 months as
students, faculty and staff have gained
increased access to electronic communications.

Given the ease and relative an-
onymity with which e-mail can be sent,
university officials worry that it's
an especially potent tool for harassment. But at the same time, it's often
possible for e-mail to be manipulated
or "spoofed" — made to look as though
it has been sent by someone else —
and thus many schools are treating
e-mail evidence with considerable
caution.

In the Hu case, for example, one of
the apparently harassing e-mail messages that Wen originally told campus
authorities had come from Hu was
later found to have been a joke sent by
a friend of Wen's new boyfriend from
Salt Lake City.

"Forging e-mail is notoriously easy,"
said Gary Jackson, director of academic
computing at Massachusetts Institute
of Technology. "If you get a piece of
ordinary e-mail from me, you have
absolutely no way of establishing that I
sent it."

The Caltech case comes at a time
when policy-makers at the national and
state level are wrestling with myriad
questions about how to govern cyberspace. A congressional committee is
debating several bills that would regulate the distribution of "indecent" material over the Internet — and sexually
oriented or harassing e-mail could fit
that definition. Connecticut recently

°**doctoral candidate:** A graduate student working toward a Ph.D. degree, the most advanced degree
colleges offer.   °**acquitted:** Found to be not guilty.

passed the nation's first anti-computer harassment law.

But important precedents may well be [10] set on university campuses, where most students get a free Internet account and daily tasks are migrating to cyberspace more quickly than anywhere else. Many schools have wired their residence halls to the global computer network, and students are doing homework on-line and attending "virtual office hours."

Caltech may be the first academic institution to expel a student for harassment primarily based on e-mail records. Hu's appeal to Caltech Vice President Gary Lorden was rejected last month.

Students and faculty at Caltech say the case has divided the campus and especially its close-knit Chinese community.

"E-mail is the bread and butter of an institution like this," said Yuk Yung, a geology professor at Caltech. "But it is very hard to prove that the person whose name is on it indeed sent it, and that it has not been tampered with. Especially here, where these kids all have extraordinary computing ability."

Described by his adviser, chemistry and applied physics professor William Goddard, as a brilliant student who scored the highest of nearly 1 million students taking the Chinese equivalent of the GRE exam, Hu was one year away from finishing his degree.

While a university computer expert [15] testified that she traced the offending e-mail back to Hu's account, Hu's defenders argue that Wen had his password, that others had access to his computer—which was often left logged on—and that e-mail is easily edited once it is received.

"Nobody should be convicted or expelled based on unencrypted e-mail," said Hu's attorney, Anita Brenner, who has written several articles on cyberspace and the law. "Particularly in a campus climate of account sharing, sharing of passwords and mail spoofing."

Because of the difficulties involved in authenticating e-mail—and because the social and legal protocols° defining electronic harassment have not yet been fully worked out—many university administrators advise recipients of unwanted e-mail simply to ask the suspected sender to stop. Many schools, including Caltech, also prohibit students from sharing passwords.

Kathleen McMahon, assistant dean of students at UCLA, says e-mail harassment has become prevalent in several forms. Four students were suspended last quarter for planting "e-mail bombs" that disrupted the school's computer system. And there have been several incidents of e-mail threats of violence.

Most common, though, is e-mail harassment, stemming from romantic troubles.

"I'm amazed with the amount of [20] sexual harassment among students and the use of e-mail to express it," McMahon said. "When relationships go bad, instead of stalking the student they

---

° **social and legal protocols:** Here, expectations and rules for using email.

send 10 e-mail messages saying 'I can't believe you won't go out with me.'"

In cyberspace, where facelessness has often led to extreme forms of expression, from angry "flaming" to amorous confessions, some believe such messages may mean less than they do in other forms. Civil libertarians say that moves to restrict or monitor e-mail may violate the 1st Amendment. And, they note, one can simply not read unwanted e-mail.

But anti-harassment advocates say the scope of the Internet and the capability it provides individuals to publish their opinions widely make it particularly dangerous.

Largely in response to the increased usage, the University of California recently drafted a systemwide e-mail policy that critics fear will compromise the privacy of those who use a UC account to log on to the Internet.

Cornell University is grappling with a similar issue this month. University administrators are getting barraged with e-mail from Internet users across the country offended by an e-mail message initially sent among four freshmen titled "Top 75 reasons why women (bitches) should not have freedom of speech."

"I think everybody who got it 25 forwarded it to everybody they knew, and we're receiving a tremendous number of complaints," said Marjorie Hodges, Cornell's legal policy adviser on computer matters. "It's a perfect example of something that might not violate university policies but is indeed offensive and does disrupt university business."

Hodges says individual complaints

regarding e-mail harassment doubled last year and the previous year, and she expects the trend to continue as more members of the campus community go on-line.

MIT's Jackson, whose colleagues started calling him "Dear Abby" after he helped resolve a particularly convoluted e-mail triangle across three campuses, says that most cases can be dealt with simply by getting those involved to ask for it to stop. At MIT, where e-mail has long been the main form of communication, the university has implemented a system called "stop it" to handle harassment complaints.

But the borderline between free speech and harassment can be blurry, especially when electronic harassment takes on particularly ugly forms. Last year, a racist message about Asians was posted to a widely read newsgroup on Chinese literature, under the name of an MIT student.

The student denied having sent the message, but she nonetheless became the recipient of hundreds of angry e-mails. Jackson was unable to identify the actual sender.

Further complicating the unfamiliar 30 territory is the assumed authenticity of electronic records.

"There is a tendency for noncomputer experts to believe anything the computer says because the computer says it," said Steve Worona, a computer expert at Cornell. "But that's just not the case."

There are several tools for encrypting messages and stamping e-mail with an electronic signature to verify the sender, but no good way of telling if an unencrypted message is authentic.

At MIT, Jackson handles about 50 harassment complaints a year. "But if there's been an incident and all the woman has in her hand is a piece of harassing e-mail and that is the sole evidence, there's nothing you can do at that point," he said.

The Caltech case involved four pieces of e-mail. The first one Hu allegedly sent to Wen when they broke up in August, 1994. The other three were apparently sent to Bo Yu, her new boyfriend, in January.

Of those, the first described a sexual 35 experience with Wen. "I would like to talk about our happy life in bed and her body which I know so well," the e-mail printout said, according to court records. The next one continued, "If you are beginning to suffer now, tell Jiajun about it. She knows what it means."

Hu maintains he did not send either of them. He says he first learned of messages allegedly being forged from his account when he tried to sign on one day in early January and found that it had been disabled by a campus computer administrator.

Caltech's dean of graduate students, Arden Albee, says that e-mail is no different than any other form of communication, and therefore falls under the university's harassment policy.

"Just like phone calls, it typically turns out that the system keeps many more records of the e-mail messages than most understand," Albee said.

"These can be traced if the need arises."

Albee was one of three faculty members on the panel that decided to expel Hu. The university said all disciplinary matters are confidential and declined to explain what records the committee relied on to determine who sent the e-mail.

The court case, in which many stu- 40 dents testified on both sides, involved allegations of both verbal and electronic harassment and threats. Hu, who had been held on $150,000 bail, was acquitted after three hours of jury deliberations.

Goddard says the main issue in the university's investigation of Hu was whether he had an alibi for the times when the e-mail message log indicated they were sent. And he did—for two of them. But even then, administration officials noted that he could have written a program to have the computer send the mail while he was no longer at his terminal.

"My own belief is that he didn't send the mail," Goddard said. "And in the worst-case scenario that he did send it, it's not clear to me that it's sexual harassment. It's e-mail."

Goddard has appealed the expulsion to Caltech's provost.

"My personal belief is that the underlying reason they took what I think is a very unreasonable position is that it's the safest thing for Caltech. And that may be true, but on the other hand we're supposed to be here for the students."

A WRITER'S NOTEBOOK
Campus Speech Incidents

The following tasks are designed to help you think about the readings and identify and start to work up material you might use in your own essay.

1. *Consider your own experience.* Write a page or so about the extent to which hateful or offensive speech was a problem at your high school or has been a problem at your college. If it has not been a problem, why do you think that is so? If it has been a problem, who were the perpetrators and who were the victims? What do you think caused and encouraged the offensive speech? Were you involved personally? If possible, tell about two or three specific incidents. The more concrete details you can include, the more useful this material might be in an essay of your own.

2. *Interview other students.* Interview at least three students who are not in your writing class and who come from a different neighborhood or community from your own. Start each interview by telling about two or three typical campus speech incidents. Then ask each student about incidents he or she has witnessed and whether these incidents were directed at individuals or groups. Take detailed notes about who was present, what was said, what happened. You may want to use one or more of these incidents in your own essay.

3. *Reflect on Michael deCourcy Hinds's article.* In paragraph 13, President Hackney is quoted as saying that "there can be no compromise regarding the First Amendment right of an independent publication [the *Daily Pennsylvanian,* the student newspaper] to express whatever views it chooses. At the same time, there can be no ignoring the pain that expression may cause." He might have said the same thing about Eden Jacobowitz's words. Free expression versus possible pain seems to summarize the dilemma here. Write a page or so reflecting on this dilemma in light of the incidents in the Hinds and Frammolino reports and of your own experience as a high school and college student.

4. *Respond to Ralph Frammolino's report.* Write several sentences expressing your own opinion about what happened to the fraternity members. In formulating your opinions, consider some of the following questions: Do you think the fraternity members were treated fairly or unfairly? Should everyone on a college campus be sensitive at all times to the feelings of others? If someone offends other people unintentionally, should he or she be punished? How important is a person's perception that he or she has been offended? How do you explain the contrast between the decision of the court and that of the fraternity's national headquarters? Which quoted statements in the article do you most agree with? disagree with?

5. *Take notes on Amy Harmon's report.* Make brief notes about the email incident at Caltech. Include specific information about what happened and about what was revealed about offensive email at Caltech (paragraphs 1–17, 34–44), UCLA (18–21), Cornell (24–26, 31), and MIT (27–29, 33).

CAMPUS SPEECH GUIDELINES

As a result of incidents like those in the three preceding articles, nearly all American colleges have published guidelines about campus speech. The earliest guidelines, dating from the late 1980s, included specific penalties for offensive speech. Typically referred to as "speech codes," these guidelines were often challenged in court and were consistently declared unconstitutional for violating students' First Amendment speech rights. The courts, however, have never said that colleges could not discourage offensive speech, only that they could not punish students for it. Consequently, recent guidelines have taken a different approach, asserting the importance of civility and community and the dangers of offensive speech directed at either individuals or groups. Some of these guidelines threaten students with unpleasant consequences for offensive speech, but most do not.

Three sets of campus speech guidelines follow. As you read, try to identify the specific kinds of offensive speech the guidelines focus on—and to understand the kinds of communities envisioned at each of the three campuses.

STUDENT LIFE

University of Southern California

The Student Affairs Division has as its fundamental purpose the provision of services and resources to students which will assist them in their total development: physical, social, emotional, cultural, moral and intellectual. As such, the division complements and serves the educational, research and service objectives of faculty and students by designing programs which are an extension of the academic experience. Consistent with this charge, the division has adopted the following statement which informs and guides its policies and actions regarding the USC community.

PRINCIPLES OF COMMUNITY

USC is a multicultural community of people from diverse racial, ethnic, and class backgrounds, national origins, religious and political beliefs, physical abilities and sexual orientations. Our activities, programs, classes, workshops/ lectures and everyday interactions are enriched by our acceptance of one another, and we strive to learn from each other in an atmosphere of positive engagement and mutual respect.

We want to make explicit our expectations regarding the behavior of each member of our community. As adults, we are responsible for our behavior and are fully accountable for our actions. We each must take responsibility for our awareness of racism, sexism, ageism, xenophobia, homophobia and other forms of oppression.

Bigotry will not go unchallenged within this community. No one has the right to denigrate another human being on the basis of race, sex, sexual orientation, nation origin, etc. We will not tolerate verbal or written abuse, threats, harassment, intimidation or violence against person or property. In this context, we do not accept alcohol or substance abuse as an excuse, reason or rationale for such abuse, harassment, intimidation or violence. Ignorance or "it was just a joke" is also not an excuse for such behavior. All who work, live, study and teach in the USC community are here by choice, and as part of that choice should be committed to these principles which are an integral part of USC's focus, goals and mission.

Non-Discrimination Policy

University of Southern California does not discriminate on the basis of color, 5 race, religion, national origin, gender, age, Vietnam veteran status, disability or sexual orientation....

Rights and Prohibited Conduct

Virginia Commonwealth University

Introduction

Virginia Commonwealth University is an academic community given meaning through the mutual respect and trust of the individuals who learn, teach, and work within it. Each member of this community is entitled to certain rights and privileges which must be protected through fair and orderly processes and which are best safeguarded when members act in an orderly and responsible manner. Each member of the University community is equally entitled to the protection of this document....

III. Rights and Prohibited Conduct

Free inquiry and free expression are indispensable to the objectives of an institution of higher education. To this end, peaceful, reasonable, and lawful picketing and other orderly demonstrations in approved areas shall not be subject to interference by the members of the University community. Nor shall any member of the University community be subject to limitation or penalty solely because of the lawful exercise of these freedoms. However, those involved in picketing and demonstrations may not engage in conduct that violates the rights of any member of the University community.

These rules shall not be construed to restrain controversy or dissent, or to prevent, discourage, or limit communication between and among faculty, students, staff, and administrators. The purpose of these rules is to prevent abuse of the rights of others and to maintain public order appropriate to the University.

A. The Right to Academic Freedom and to Equal Educational and Occupational Access

The University is committed to providing an environment conducive to academic freedom, free inquiry, and equal access to educational and occupational opportunities. The principle of academic freedom requires all persons to respect another's dignity, to acknowledge another's right to express differing opinions, to cultivate and to cherish intellectual honesty, and to promote freedom of inquiry and expression. It is therefore the policy of the University that no act of any member of the University community shall serve to restrain or inhibit access to opportunities or the exercise of these freedoms. To that end, no person, either singly or in concert with others, shall willfully:

1. Discriminate against another person on a basis not reasonably related to the educational or job functions involved on the basis of race, ethnicity, sex, religion, color, creed, disability, sexual orientation, marital status, and age.
2. Harass or intimidate any person.
3. Cause physical injury or threaten any person with force or violence.
4. Have in his or her possession any firearm, other weapon, or explosive, regardless of whether a license to possess the same has been issued, without the written authorization of the president of the University. This restriction does not apply to persons whose duties lawfully require the possession of firearms or other weapons.
5. Disrupt or prevent the peaceful or orderly conduct of classes, lectures, meetings, or other University functions, or interfere with the lawful freedom of other persons, including invited speakers, to express their views.
6. Falsify or forge an official University record or document; or file documents with the University with the intent to mislead.
7. Lie, cheat, steal, or plagiarize. Violations of lying, cheating, plagiarism, and stealing will be adjudicated through this or other applicable documents. Student academic violations of lying, cheating, plagiarism, and stealing will be referred to the VCU Honor System for adjudication.

8. Violate any duly authorized University rule or regulation issued pursuant to a specific University function, for example, regulations applicable to social events, the library, or University hospitals.
9. Incite others to commit any act which has been herein prohibited.
10. Bring charges against a member of the University community that are spurious, or that are intended primarily to harass or maliciously defame, or that are designed to intentionally overburden the adjudicatory system.

SEXUAL HARASSMENT OF STUDENTS BY FACULTY AND STAFF

University of Texas at Austin

I. WHAT IS SEXUAL MISCONDUCT OR HARASSMENT?

A. Sexual Misconduct

Sexual misconduct includes implicit or explicit sexual advances, requests for sexual favors or other inappropriate verbal or physical conduct of a sexual nature. Although such behavior may not rise to the level of illegal sexual harassment, it is unprofessional and unacceptable and individuals who engage in it may be subject to disciplinary action.

B. Sexual Harassment

Sexual harassment is a form of illegal gender discrimination. It involves unwelcome advances, requests for sexual favors, or other verbal or physical conduct of a sexual nature when:

1. submission to such conduct is made an explicit or implicit term or condition of employment or one's status as a student in a course, program or activity;
2. submission to or rejection of such conduct is used as a basis for an employment or educational decision affecting an individual; or
3. such conduct has the purpose or effect of unreasonably interfering with an individual's work or educational performance, or creates an intimidating, hostile environment.

C. Examples of Inappropriate Behavior

Examples of conduct that, depending on the circumstances, could be considered to be sexual misconduct or sexual harassment include:

- demanding sexual favors in exchange for a grade, a research assistantship or a letter of recommendation;
- withholding a grade or other benefit in retaliation after a request for sexual favors is rejected; or
- unwelcome and persistent behavior such as:

  requests for dates, sexual propositions, invitations and flirtations made in person or by means of letters, notes, phone calls or e-mail;

  verbal expressions of a sexual nature including comments about a person's body, attire, appearance, or sexual activities;

  sexually suggestive jokes, innuendoes, sounds or gestures including leering;

  anecdotes, questions or comments about sexual activities;

  excessive or inappropriate touching in the form of hugs, pinching, shoulder rubs, pats, brushing up against another's body;

  use of sexually suggestive objects, articles, tapes, pictures or other materials that are unrelated to the subject matter of a course.

In deciding whether conduct involves sexual misconduct or sexual harassment, The University will look at the totality of the circumstances in which it occurred. Those circumstances include the type, frequency and duration of the conduct, the nature of the relationship of the student to the University faculty member, employee or other person who engaged in the conduct, the age of the student, and whether the conduct was welcome or encouraged.

A WRITER'S NOTEBOOK
Campus Speech Guidelines

The following task is designed to help you think about the readings and identify and start to work up material you might use in your own essay.

Analyze the current campus speech guidelines. All of the guidelines seem concerned with developing a certain kind of campus community. Reread each set of guidelines, underlining specific words that describe the sort of community each university is seeking. For example, underline *multicultural, acceptance of one another, positive engagement,* and *mutual respect* in the University of Southern California guidelines. List all the underlined words in your notebook. Then write a few sentences generalizing about the kind of campus community these guidelines hope to foster.

SUPREME COURT CASES AND HISTORICAL BACKGROUND

The debate over regulating speech on college campuses involves not only the abstract principles laid down in the Constitution but also the many cases decided by the U.S. Supreme Court. The brief but important guarantee of freedom of speech in the First Amendment does not offer any specific guidelines—no details about what kinds of speech should be allowed or disallowed. Therefore, people can easily disagree about what freedom of speech means. The actual definition of freedom of speech has evolved through two hundred years of Supreme Court decisions, and the process continues to this day.

When hearing a case, the Supreme Court justices listen to arguments from both sides, usually with attorneys on one side defending a law as constitutional and attorneys on the other side arguing that someone's or some group's constitutional rights have been violated. The justices then debate the case among themselves for many months, both in discussions and in writing, and ultimately vote on it. After the vote, one justice writes a *majority opinion,* and, if the vote was not unanimous, another justice writes a *dissenting opinion.* Other justices may also contribute opinions if they agree or disagree with the decision for different reasons. These written opinions are referred to as Supreme Court cases, or decisions, important documents in American history.

The readings in this section begin with brief excerpts from two Supreme Court cases, *Chaplinsky v. New Hampshire* (1942)* and *Beauharnais v. Illinois* (1952), two typical legal arguments about whether to regulate offensive speech. The language of Supreme Court cases is relatively formal. Sentences tend to be long and may include many legal terms as well as references to previous Supreme Court cases that are the precedents for the current case. A Supreme Court case attempts to justify a decision to readers through step-by-step logical argument.

Following the Supreme Court cases is Samuel Walker's brief history of recent important court decisions on hate speech. Walker focuses on why the federal district courts, guided by Supreme Court decisions like *Chaplinsky* and *Beauharnais,* struck down two universities' attempts to regulate students' speech. He also reviews a more recent Supreme Court case, *R.A.V. v. St. Paul* (1992), which has important implications for the hate speech debate. Finally, Michael W. McConnell describes the Maryland Toleration Act of 1649, the first legal attempt in America to discourage hate speech. Taken together, these readings provide historical context for the debate over whether college campuses should attempt to regulate what students can say to each other.

---

* In a Supreme Court case, the lowercase *v.* stands for "versus," the name of the case is italicized, and the year of the final decision follows in parentheses. In this case, a Mr. Chaplinsky challenged a New Hampshire state law as unconstitutional. Writers often refer to such cases by the first name in the title—for example, *Chaplinsky.*

CHAPLINSKY V. NEW HAMPSHIRE (1942)

U.S. Supreme Court

Walter Chaplinsky, a member of the Jehovah's Witnesses, was handing out religious literature on a Saturday afternoon in 1940 on the streets of Rochester, New Hampshire. When people complained that he was denouncing religion as a racket, the city marshal asked Chaplinsky to stop and later, after Chaplinsky continued his denunciations, warned him again. Chaplinsky responded by saying to the marshal: "You are a God damned racketeer [and] a damned Fascist and the whole government of Rochester are Fascist or agents of Fascists." He was arrested and convicted for violating New Hampshire law 378, which read as follows:

> *No person shall address any offensive, derisive or annoying word to any other person who is lawfully in any street or other public place, nor call him by an offensive or derisive name, nor make any noise or exclamation in his presence and hearing with the intent to deride, offend or annoy him, or to prevent him from pursuing his lawful business or occupation.*

When Chaplinsky and his lawyers appealed his conviction to the Supreme Court, the Court decided that the New Hampshire law was constitutional and that therefore Chaplinsky could be punished for breaking the law. What follows is part of the majority opinion in Chaplinsky, *written by Justice Frank Murphy. This case is important to the campus speech issue because it contains the often-cited "fighting words" rule, which is used to decide whether or not offensive speech is protected by the Constitution. This case is also relevant because of its focus on face-to-face speech intended to insult or demean a person. Although some legal scholars consider* Chaplinsky *to be of little current importance, the Supreme Court has never explicitly rejected the reasoning or conclusions of this case. Consequently, advocates of regulating or banning offensive speech on college campuses continue to rely on this case in their arguments, insisting that the constitutionality of campus speech restrictions is still an open question.*

This case is an important reminder that the First Amendment does not protect every kind of speech. Indeed, the Supreme Court has ruled that some kinds of speech may be forbidden and punished by local, state, or federal authorities. In the first paragraph of this selection from Chaplinsky, *Justice Murphy mentions two kinds of punishable speech: lewd and obscene speech (such as child pornography) and libel (speech intended to damage someone's reputation). Other writers in this chapter, especially Richard Delgado and David H. Yun, extend this list to include the kinds of speech that disrupt learning and a sense of community on college campuses.*

As you read, pay special attention to the reasons Justice Murphy gives for refusing to declare the New Hampshire law unconstitutional.

It is well understood that the right of free speech is not absolute at all times and under all circumstances. There are certain well-defined and narrowly limited classes of speech, the prevention and punishment of which have never been thought to raise any Constitutional problem. These include the lewd and obscene, the profane, the libelous, and the insulting or "fighting" words— those which by their very utterance inflict injury or tend to incite an immediate breach of the peace. It has been well observed that such utterances are no essential part of any exposition of ideas, and are of such slight social value as a step to truth that any benefit that may be derived from them is clearly outweighed by the social interest in order and morality. "Resort to epithets or personal abuse is not in any proper sense communication of information or opinion safeguarded by the Constitution, and its punishment as a criminal act would raise no question under that instrument."° *Cantwell v. Connecticut,* 310 U.S. 296, 309–310.

On the authority of its earlier decisions, the state court° declared that the statute's purpose was to preserve the public peace, no words being "forbidden except such as have a direct tendency to cause acts of violence by the persons to whom, individually, the remark is addressed." It was further said: "The word 'offensive' is not to be defined in terms of what a particular addressee thinks.... The test is what men of common intelligence would understand would be words likely to cause an average addressee to fight.... The English language has a number of words and expressions which by general consent are 'fighting words' when said without a disarming smile.... Such words, as ordinary men know, are likely to cause a fight. So are threatening, profane or obscene revilings. Derisive and annoying words can be taken as coming within the purview of the statute° as heretofore interpreted only when they have this characteristic of plainly tending to excite the addressee to a breach of the peace.... The statute, as construed,° does no more than prohibit the face-to-face words plainly likely to cause a breach of the peace by the addressee, words whose speaking constitutes a breach of the peace by the speaker—including 'classical fighting words,' words in current use less 'classical' but equally likely to cause violence, and other disorderly words, including profanity, obscenity and threats."

We are unable to say that the limited scope of the statute as thus construed contravenes° the Constitutional right of free expression. It is a statute narrowly drawn and limited to define and punish specific conduct lying within the domain of state power, the use in a public place of words likely to cause a breach of the peace....

° **that instrument:** The Constitution.   ° **state court:** The New Hampshire state court that convicted Chaplinsky.   ° **statute:** The New Hampshire law Chaplinsky was convicted of breaking.   ° **as construed:** In this context, as the Supreme Court interprets the New Hampshire law in light of the federal Constitution.   ° **contravenes:** Opposes or is contrary to something.

Nor can we say that the application of the statute to the facts disclosed by the record substantially or unreasonably impinges upon the privilege of free speech. Argument is unnecessary to demonstrate that the appellations "damned racketeer" and "damned Fascist" are epithets likely to provoke the average person to retaliation, and thereby cause a breach of the peace.

BEAUHARNAIS V. ILLINOIS (1952)

U.S. Supreme Court

Beauharnais v. Illinois *(1952) is relevant to the debate over offensive speech on campus because it concerns a group libel law—a law making it illegal to harm the reputation of groups of people. Just as the* Chaplinsky *"fighting words" test may be useful in incidents of individuals insulting other individuals, a prohibition on insulting groups of people might also be a useful precedent when hateful speech is directed toward a student for being in a particular group.*

In this 1952 case, Joseph Beauharnais, president of the White Circle League, an organization that favored racial separateness, was arrested in Chicago and fined $200 for organizing the distribution of pamphlets that portrayed "depravity, criminality, unchastity or lack of virtue of citizens of the Negro race." The pamphlets called on the mayor and the city council of Chicago "to halt the further encroachment, harassment and invasion of white people, their property, neighborhoods and persons, by the Negro." Beauharnais was arrested under an Illinois law that made it unlawful to expose "any class of citizens" to "contempt, derision, or obloquy."

Beauharnais appealed his conviction to the U.S. Supreme Court, claiming that the Illinois law violated his constitutionally protected speech rights. Although the Court upheld Beauharnais's conviction, the vote was 5 to 4, showing how divided it was on whether Beauharnais's speech should be considered unprotected libelous speech or speech protected—legally guaranteed—by the First Amendment.

Following are selections from the majority opinion by Justice Felix Frankfurter and the more famous dissenting opinions by Justices Hugo Black and William O. Douglas. Justice Frankfurter begins by summarizing the history of racial conflict in Illinois.

As you read, notice how strongly divided the Supreme Court members were on this case and consider what the sources of their disagreement were.

Illinois did not have to look beyond her own borders or await the tragic experience of the last three decades to conclude that wilful purveyors of falsehood concerning racial and religious groups promote strife and tend powerfully to obstruct the manifold adjustments required for free, ordered life in a metropolitan, polyglot community. From the murder of the abolitionist Lovejoy° in 1837 to the Cicero riots of 1951, Illinois has been the scene of exacerbated tension between races, often flaring into violence and destruction. In many of these outbreaks, utterances° of the character here in question, so the Illinois legislature could conclude, played a significant part. The law° was passed on June 29, 1917, at a time when the State was struggling to assimilate vast numbers of new inhabitants, as yet concentrated in discrete racial or national or religious groups—foreign-born brought to it by the crest of the great wave of immigration, and Negroes attracted by jobs in war plants and the allurements of northern claims. Nine years earlier, in the very city° where the legislature sat, what is said to be the first northern race riot had cost the lives of six people, left hundreds of Negroes homeless and shocked citizens into action far beyond the borders of the State. Less than a month before the bill° was enacted, East St. Louis had seen a day's rioting, prelude to an outbreak, only four days after the bill became law, so bloody that it led to Congressional investigation. A series of bombings had begun which was to culminate two years later in the awful race riot which held Chicago in its grip for seven days in the summer of 1919. Nor has tension and violence between the groups defined in the statute been limited in Illinois to clashes between whites and Negroes.

In the face of this history and its frequent obligato of extreme racial and religious propaganda, we would deny experience to say that the Illinois legislature was without reason in seeking ways to curb false or malicious defamation of racial and religious groups, made in public places and by means calculated to have a powerful emotional impact on those to whom it was presented. "There are limits to the exercise of these liberties [of speech and of the press]. The danger in these times from the coercive activities of those who in the delusion of racial or religious conceit would incite violence and breaches of the peace in order to deprive others of their equal right to the exercise of their liberties, is emphasized by events familiar to all. These and other transgressions of those limits the States appropriately may punish." This was the conclusion, again of a unanimous Court, in 1940. *Cantwell v. Connecticut, supra,* at 310.

It may be argued, and weightily, that this legislation° will not help matters; that tension and on occasion violence between racial and religious groups must be traced to causes more deeply embedded in our society than the rantings of modern Know-Nothings.° Only those lacking responsible humility will have a

---

°**the abolitionist Lovejoy:** Editor of the *Observer,* an antislavery paper. Lovejoy was murdered by pro-slavery extremists.   °**utterances:** The statements in Beauharnais's pamphlets.   °**The law:** The Illinois law under which Beauharnais was convicted.   °**the very city:** Springfield, the state capital of Illinois.   °**the bill:** The law under which Beauharnais was convicted.   °**this legislation:** The law under which Beauharnais was convicted.   °**Know-Nothings:** Members of the Native American Party of the 1850s, who were strongly opposed to the immigration of Irish Catholics. Justice Frankfurter implies that Beauharnais and his group are like the Know-Nothings.

confident solution for problems as intractable as the frictions attributable to differences of race, color or religion. This being so, it would be out of bounds for the judiciary to deny the legislature a choice of policy, provided it is not unrelated to the problem and not forbidden by some explicit limitation on the State's power. That the legislative remedy might not in practice mitigate the evil, or might itself raise new problems, would only manifest once more the paradox of reform. It is the price to be paid for the trial-and-error inherent in legislative efforts to deal with obstinate social issues.

Mr. Justice Black, with whom Mr. Justice Douglas concurs, dissenting.

This case is here because Illinois inflicted criminal punishment on Beauharnais for causing the distribution of leaflets in the city of Chicago. The conviction rests on the leaflet's contents, not on the time, manner or place of distribution. Beauharnais is head of an organization that opposes amalgamation and favors segregation of white and colored people. After discussion, an assembly of his group decided to petition the mayor and council of Chicago to pass laws for segregation. Volunteer members of the group agreed to stand on street corners, solicit signers to petitions addressed to the city authorities, and distribute leaflets giving information about the group, its beliefs and its plans. In carrying out this program a solicitor handed out a leaflet which was the basis of this prosecution.

I.

That Beauharnais and his group were making a genuine effort to petition their 5 elected representatives is not disputed.... After independence was won, Americans stated as the first unequivocal command of their Bill of Rights: "Congress shall make no law...abridging the freedom of speech, or of the press; or the right of the people peaceably to assemble, and to petition the Government for a redress of grievances." Without distortion, this First Amendment could not possibly be read so as to hold that Congress has power to punish Beauharnais and others for petitioning Congress as they have here sought to petition the Chicago authorities.... And we have held in a number of prior cases that the Fourteenth Amendment° makes the specific prohibitions of the First Amendment equally applicable to the states.

In view of these prior holdings, how does the Court justify its holding today that states can punish people for exercising the vital freedoms intended to be safeguarded from suppression by the First Amendment? The prior holdings°

°**Fourteenth Amendment:** Ensures that the personal rights outlined in the Bill of Rights are available to all Americans, no matter in what states they live.   °**prior holdings:** Earlier decisions of the Supreme Court, which the Court pays close attention to when making a new decision in an area like speech freedoms.

are not referred to; the Court simply acts on the bland assumption that the First Amendment is wholly irrelevant. It is not even accorded the respect of a passing mention. This follows logically, I suppose, from recent constitutional doctrine which appears to measure state laws solely by this Court's notions of civilized "canons of decency," reasonableness, etc.... Under this "reasonableness" test, state laws abridging First Amendment freedoms are sustained if found to have a "rational basis."

The Court's holding here and the constitutional doctrine behind it leave the rights of assembly, petition, speech and press almost completely at the mercy of state legislative, executive, and judicial agencies.... We are cautioned° that state legislatures must be left free to "experiment" and to make "legislative" judgments. We are told that mistakes may be made during the legislative process of curbing public opinion. In such event the Court fortunately does not leave those mistakenly curbed, or any of us for that matter, unadvised. Consolation can be sought and must be found in the philosophical reflection that state legislative error in stifling speech and press "is the price to be paid for the trial-and-error inherent in legislative efforts to deal with obstinate social issues." My own belief is that no legislature is charged with the duty or vested with the power to decide what public issues Americans can discuss. In a free country that is the individual's choice, not the state's. State experimentation in curbing freedom of expression is startling and frightening doctrine in a country dedicated to self-government by its people. I reject the holding that either state or nation can punish people for having their say in matters of public concern.

II.

The Illinois statute upheld by the Court makes it a crime:

1. for "any person, firm or corporation,"
2. to "manufacture, sell, or offer for sale, advertise or publish, present or exhibit in any public place,"
3. any "lithograph [construed to include any printed matter], moving picture, play, drama or sketch,"
4. which portrays "depravity, criminality, unchastity, or lack of virtue,"
5. of "a class of citizens, of any race, color, creed or religion,"
6. and exposes such a class to "contempt, derision, or obloquy,"
7. *or* "is productive of breach of the peace or riots."

This statute imposes state censorship over the theater, moving pictures, radio, television, leaflets, magazines, books and newspapers. No doubt the statute is

---

°**We are cautioned:** In this paragraph and occasionally in subsequent paragraphs, Justice Black takes a sarcastic tone. He is highly critical of the majority opinion written by Justice Frankfurter, and he sometimes becomes bitter and ridiculing.

broad enough to make criminal the "publication, sale, presentation or exhibition" of many of the world's great classics, both secular and religious.

The Court condones this expansive state censorship by painstakingly analogizing it to the law of criminal libel. As a result of this refined analysis, the Illinois statute emerges labeled a "group libel law." This label may make the Court's holding more palatable for those who sustain it, but the sugar-coating does not make the censorship less deadly. However tagged, the Illinois law is not that criminal libel which has been "defined, limited and constitutionally recognized time out of mind." For as "constitutionally recognized" that crime has provided for punishment of false, malicious, scurrilous charges against individuals, not against huge groups. This limited scope of the law of criminal libel is of no small importance. It has confined state punishment of speech and expression to the narrowest of areas involving nothing more than purely private feuds. Every expansion of the law of criminal libel so as to punish discussions of matters of public concern means a corresponding invasion of the area dedicated to free expression by the First Amendment....

The Court's reliance on *Chaplinsky v. New Hampshire,* 315 U.S. 568, is also 10 misplaced. New Hampshire had a state law making it an offense to direct insulting words at an *individual* on a public street. Chaplinsky had violated that law by calling a man vile names "face-to-face." We° pointed out in that context that the use of such "fighting" words was not an essential part of exposition of ideas. Whether the words used in their context here are "fighting" words in the same sense is doubtful, but whether so or not they are not addressed to or about *individuals.* Moreover, the leaflet used here was also the means adopted by an assembled group to enlist interest in their efforts to have legislation enacted. And the fighting words were but a part of arguments on questions of wide public interest and importance. Freedom of petition, assembly, speech and press could be greatly abridged by a practice of meticulously scrutinizing every editorial, speech, sermon or other printed matter to extract two or three naughty words on which to hang charges of "group libel." The *Chaplinsky* case makes no such broad inroads on First Amendment freedoms. Nothing Mr. Justice Murphy wrote for the Court in that case or in any other case justifies any such inference.

Unless I misread history the majority° is giving libel a more expansive scope and more respectable status than it was ever accorded even in the Star Chamber.° For here it is held to be punishable to give publicity to any picture, moving picture, play, drama or sketch, or any printed matter which a judge may find unduly offensive to any race, color, creed or religion. In other words, in

---

°We: The members of the Supreme Court who decided the 1942 *Chaplinsky* case.   °the majority: Supreme Court members who voted with the majority in this case.   °Star Chamber: An informal seventeenth-century English court that sentenced and tortured people without a trial by jury; it was abolished in 1641.

arguing for or against the enactment of laws that may differently affect huge groups, it is now very dangerous indeed to say something critical of one of the groups. And any "person, firm or corporation" can be tried for this crime. "Person, firm or corporation" certainly includes a book publisher, newspaper, radio or television station, candidate or even a preacher.

It is easy enough to say that none of this latter group have been proceeded against under the Illinois Act. And they have not—yet. But emotions bubble and tempers flare in racial and religious controversies, the kind here involved. It would not be easy for any court, in good conscience, to narrow this Act so as to exclude from it any of those I have mentioned. . . .

This Act sets up a system of state censorship which is at war with the kind of free government envisioned by those who forced adoption of our Bill of Rights. The motives behind the state law may have been to do good. But the same can be said about most laws making opinions punishable as crimes. History indicates that urges to do good have led to the burning of books and even to the burning of "witches."

No rationalization on a purely legal level can conceal the fact that state laws like this one present a constant overhanging threat to freedom of speech, press and religion. Today Beauharnais is punished for publicly expressing strong views in favor of segregation. Ironically enough, Beauharnais, convicted of crime in Chicago, would probably be given a hero's reception in many other localities, if not in some parts of Chicago itself. Moreover, the same kind of state law that makes Beauharnais a criminal for advocating segregation in Illinois can be utilized to send people to jail in other states for advocating equality and nonsegregation. What Beauharnais said in his leaflet is mild compared with usual arguments on both sides of racial controversies.

If there be minority groups who hail this holding as their victory, they might 15 consider the possible relevancy of this ancient remark:

"Another such victory and I am undone."

MR. JUSTICE DOUGLAS, dissenting.

Hitler and his Nazis showed how evil a conspiracy could be which was aimed at destroying a race by exposing it to contempt, derision, and obloquy. I would be willing to concede that such conduct directed at a race or group in this country could be made an indictable offense. For such a project would be more than the exercise of free speech. Like picketing, it would be free speech plus.

I would also be willing to concede that even without the element of conspiracy there might be times and occasions when the legislative or executive branch might call a halt to inflammatory talk, such as the shouting of "fire" in a school or a theatre.

My view is that if in any case other public interests are to override the plain command of the First Amendment, the peril of speech must be clear and present, leaving no room for argument, raising no doubts as to the necessity of curbing speech in order to prevent disaster.

The First Amendment is couched in absolute terms—freedom of speech 20 shall not be abridged. Speech has therefore a preferred position as contrasted to some other civil rights. For example, privacy, equally sacred to some, is protected by the Fourth Amendment only against unreasonable searches and seizures. There is room for regulation of the ways and means of invading privacy. No such leeway is granted the invasion of the right of free speech guaranteed by the First Amendment. Until recent years that had been the course and direction of constitutional law. Yet recently the Court in this and in other cases has engrafted the right of regulation onto the First Amendment by placing in the hands of the legislative branch the right to regulate "within reasonable limits" the right of free speech. This to me is an ominous and alarming trend. The free trade in ideas which the Framers of the Constitution visualized disappears. In its place there is substituted a new orthodoxy°—an orthodoxy that changes with the whims of the age or the day, an orthodoxy which the majority by solemn judgment proclaims to be essential to the safety, welfare, security, morality, or health of society. Free speech in the constitutional sense disappears. Limits are drawn—limits dictated by expediency, political opinion, prejudices or some other desideratum of legislative action....

The First Amendment says that freedom of speech, freedom of press, and the free exercise of religion shall not be abridged. That is a negation of power on the part of each and every department of government. Free speech, free press, free exercise of religion are placed separate and apart; they are above and beyond the police power; they are not subject to regulation in the manner of factories, slums, apartment houses, production of oil, and the like.

The Court in this and in other cases places speech under an expanding legislative control. Today a white man stands convicted for protesting in unseemly language against our decisions invalidating restrictive covenants.° Tomorrow a Negro will be haled before a court for denouncing lynch law° in heated terms. Farm laborers in the West who compete with field hands drifting up from Mexico; whites who feel the pressure of orientals; a minority which finds employment going to members of the dominant religious group—all of these are caught in the mesh of today's decision. Debate and argument even in the courtroom are not always calm and dispassionate. Emotions sway speakers and audiences alike. Intemperate speech is a distinctive characteristic of man. Hotheads blow off and release destructive energy in the process. They shout and rave, exaggerating weaknesses, magnifying error, viewing with alarm. So it has

---

°**orthodoxy:** The quality of adhering to an established set of beliefs or practices.   °**restrictive covenants:** Agreements restricting what people can do.   °**lynch law:** Hanging people for possible crimes without due process of law. Named for William Lynch, a nineteenth-century American vigilante.

been from the beginning; and so it will be throughout time. The Framers of the Constitution knew human nature as well as we do. They too had lived in dangerous days; they too knew the suffocating influence of orthodoxy and standardized thought. They weighed the compulsions for restrained speech and thought against the abuses of liberty. They chose liberty. That should be our choice today no matter how distasteful to us the pamphlet of Beauharnais may be.

HATE SPEECH:
THE HISTORY OF AN AMERICAN CONTROVERSY

Samuel Walker

Samuel Walker, a professor of criminal justice at the University of Nebraska law school in Omaha, has written a number of books, including The Color of Justice: Race, Ethnicity, and Crime in America *(1996) and* Hate Speech: History of an American Controversy *(1994), from which this reading comes.*

Walker demonstrates how court interpretations of the First Amendment determine whether speech regulations on college campuses will be allowed and, if so, what kinds. He mentions Chaplinsky *as well as several other Supreme Court cases from the late 1980s and early 1990s —* Doe v. University of Michigan *(1989),* Texas v. Johnson *(1989),* United States v. Eichman *(1990),* UWM Post v. Board of Regents of the University of Wisconsin *(1991),* R.A.V. v. St. Paul *(1992), and* Hustler v. Falwell *(1988) — discussing each case but, with the exception of* R.A.V. v. St. Paul, *not identifying any of them by name.*

Focusing on attempts by the University of Michigan (1988) and the University of Wisconsin (1989) to regulate offensive speech, Walker explains why federal district courts ruled that both universities had violated students' First Amendment rights to free speech. A chief reason was that the justices believed that the regulations were not content neutral. In other words, they thought that the regulations punished speakers for the content *of their speech, something earlier courts had held to be unconstitutional.*

· Unlike Supreme Court cases, which are written for an audience of legal experts, the Walker essay was written for a general readership. It tells three stories, two about an important legal test of university regulations and one about a city law against hateful speech or action. Walker tells about these cases and also comments on what they might mean.

As you read, think about what happens in each case and consider the questions that are raised about regulating or banning offensive speech on college campuses.

THE UNIVERSITY OF MICHIGAN CASE

When the campus speech codes finally reached the federal courts, they met a quick and resounding defeat. The first and only two to be challenged were declared unconstitutional on First Amendment grounds. These decisions reaffirmed the commitment to the protection of provocative and offensive speech. They were soon followed by the Supreme Court's 1992 decision in the St. Paul cross-burning case, which appeared to doom most of the remaining speech codes.

The University of Michigan's policy was the first to reach the courts. It arose out of a series of racist incidents on campus in 1987. On January 27 some unknown people distributed a racist leaflet declaring "open season" on African Americans, referring to them as "saucer lips, porch monkeys, and jigaboos." A week later the campus radio station broadcast some racist jokes. When students demonstrated to protest these events, someone displayed a Ku Klux Klan° costume from a dormitory window. The university president responded with a public statement expressing his outrage at these incidents and reaffirming the university's commitment to a racially and culturally diverse campus. The state legislature entered the picture when the chairman of the House Subcommittee on Higher Education of the Appropriations Committee held public hearings on campus racism. Students, meanwhile, formed a United Coalition against Racism and threatened to file a class-action suit against the university for failing to maintain a nonracist atmosphere on campus.

Responding to this extraordinarily tense situation, the university regents began working on a student code of conduct in early 1988. After much debate they adopted a policy on April 14, to be effective May 31, 1988. The Policy on Discrimination and Discriminatory Harassment of Students in the University Environment prohibited "any behavior, verbal or physical, that stigmatizes or victimizes an individual on the basis of race, ethnicity, religion, sex, sexual orientation, creed, national origin, ancestry, age, marital status, handicap or Vietnam-era veteran status." This included any "express or implied threat to an individual's academic efforts, employment, participation in University sponsored extra-curricular activities or personal safety" or anything that interfered with those activities or "create[d] an intimidating, hostile, or demeaning environment for educational pursuits, employment or participation in University sponsored extra-curricular activities." A second section, with nearly identical wording, prohibited "sexual advances, requests for sexual favors," or other stigmatizing behavior based on gender or sexual orientation. In August the university suddenly withdrew the section relating to a hostile environment but not, for some unexplained reason, the identical section relating to sexual harassment.

°**Ku Klux Klan:** A secret society that advocates white supremacy and limits its membership to American-born white Christians.

There were two aspects of the policy that immediately created alarm among civil libertarians.° First, it did not explicitly require that an offensive expression be directed at an individual. Second, it did not specifically exempt classroom situations. Even worse was the university's attempt to explain how it might be applied. In fall 1989 its Office of Affirmative Action published an interpretive guide, *What Students Should Know about Discrimination and Discriminatory Harassment by Students in the University Environment.* It included some examples of behavior that violated the policy: distributing a [flyer] containing racist threats; a male student's commenting in class that "women students just aren't as good in this field as men"; a dormitory party to which everyone is invited except a student others believe to be a lesbian. Whereas the first example clearly involved a threat, the second represented a statement that could legitimately arise in a discussion of gender differences; the third involved private group behavior rather than speech. A few months later the university withdrew the guide, although without informing anyone on campus, leaving the terms of the policy completely ambiguous. Only later did the university state that the information in the guide was "not accurate."

The policy was challenged by a graduate student in biopsychology who ₅ argued that it infringed on his freedom to teach. Some of the theories in his field relating to biologically based differences between races and genders might prompt in-class discussions that would be perceived as violating the policy. The Michigan ACLU° affiliate agreed to take the case.

On September 22, 1989, the federal district court declared the policy unconstitutional on grounds of vagueness and overbreadth. The first issue confronting the court was whether the policy applied to classroom discussions. It found ample evidence in both the legislative history and its application showing that it did. It cited three instances where students had been disciplined or threatened with discipline under the policy for comments in class. One involved a social work graduate student who said he believed homosexuality was a disease and had counseled clients accordingly. A formal hearing ruled that he did not violate the policy. A second case concerned a business student who read a limerick in a class exercise that ridiculed a famous athlete because of his alleged sexual orientation. This case was settled informally, with the student agreeing to write a letter of apology and attend a gay rap group. The third involved an orientation session in predentistry in which a student commented that he had heard minorities had great difficulty in the course and were not treated fairly. The complaint was filed by a racial minority professor who argued that the comment was unfair and had hurt her chances for tenure. The student was counseled informally and persuaded to write a letter to the professor.

°**civil libertarians:** People who strongly support the civil liberties outlined in the Bill of Rights, particularly the First Amendment.   °**ACLU:** American Civil Liberties Union, a voluntary organization concerned with protecting civil liberties like free speech.

The court accepted the ACLU's argument that the policy was unconstitutionally vague. When asked during the oral argument how he would distinguish between merely offensive speech, which he conceded was protected, and speech that was prohibited by the policy, the university's attorney answered, "very carefully." The court concluded that there was no consistency between the legislative history of the policy, the record of its administration, and the interpretation offered in court. Citing the withdrawal of the explanatory guide and the "eleventh hour" suspension of the section on hostile environment, the court concluded that "the University had no idea what the limits of the Policy were and . . . was essentially making up the rules as it went along."

Several possible remedies for discriminatory and harassing behavior were available to the university. What it could not do—and what this policy did—however, was to prohibit "certain speech because it disagreed with ideas or messages sought to be conveyed." The most recent decision cited in support of this prohibition on content-based restrictions had been delivered by the Supreme Court only three months earlier. In one of the most controversial First Amendment cases in years, the Court upheld the right to burn the American flag. Although burning the American flag was profoundly offensive to millions of Americans, the Court held that to punish that act was to make a distinction based on the content of the message. The flag-burning decision—and the decision the following year overturning the new flag protection act—was extremely relevant to the campus speech code controversy. It is fair to say that many if not most of the students supporting the restriction on hate speech would defend the right of a political radical to burn the flag as a form of protest. The conjunction of the flag-burning and speech-code decisions within a few months of each other in 1989 dramatized once again the earlier lesson of the civil rights movement: that any measure designed to protect powerless groups could easily be used to restrict the political activity of the powerless.

THE UNIVERSITY OF WISCONSIN CASE

Two years later a federal district court in Wisconsin ruled that the University of Wisconsin code violated the First Amendment. The Policy and Guidelines on Racist and Discriminatory Conduct was notable in that it had been drafted with the help of law professor Richard Delgado, whose article on tort remedies° for racist speech and other harmful speech was one of the most influential and widely cited items advocating restrictions. Formally adopted on June 9, 1989, the policy covered "racist or discriminatory comments, epithets or other expressive behavior directed at an individual" where those comments "demean the race, sex, religion, color, creed, disability, sexual orientation, national ori-

---

° **tort remedies:** Legal damages.

gin, ancestry or age of the individual or individuals" or "create an intimidating, hostile or demeaning environment for education" or other university-related activity.

The Wisconsin policy was much clearer and more narrowly drafted than 10 Michigan's in several respects—and thus more likely to survive a First Amendment challenge. First, it explicitly applied only to direct attacks on an individual. Second, the policy itself included illustrative examples: calling someone an offensive name, placing demeaning material in someone's living quarters or workplace, destroying property, and so forth. Most important, it exempted classroom situations: "A student would not be in violation if, during a class discussion, he or she expressed a derogatory opinion concerning a racial or ethnic group." The university also published an explanatory pamphlet with additional examples. This included two classroom situations. In one a male student expresses the view that women are "by nature better equipped to be mothers" and should not be employed in upper-level management positions. The university explained that this was not covered by the policy because it involved "an expression of opinion, contains no epithets, and is not directed to a particular individual." In the second example a faculty member states that certain ethnic groups seem to be genetically predisposed to alcoholism. This was also not covered because the policy did not apply to faculty members. Wisconsin students, in short, had a much clearer picture of what kinds of behavior were forbidden and what ones were not.

Although it was far more carefully drafted than the Michigan policy, the federal district court found the University of Wisconsin policy unconstitutional. The court rejected the university's argument that the policy properly covered only fighting words as defined by *Chaplinsky* and held that the first prong of the *Chaplinsky* definition (words likely to inflict injury) was "defunct"° and that the policy exceeded the scope of the surviving second prong because it was not limited to words that had a tendency to incite an immediate breach of the peace. Moreover, because it singled out racist speech, the policy was an impermissible content-based restriction on speech. The university had argued that it regulated only speech that had harmful effects and minimum social value. The court held that such a balancing test was permissible only in content-neutral regulations.

The court also rejected the university's arguments based on the two most important new rationales for prohibiting hate speech. It rejected the argument that the university had a compelling interest under the Fourteenth Amendment° in increasing the diversity of the student body, noting that the university had offered no evidence that it was not "providing education on equal terms." It also ruled that the concept of a hostile environment did not apply because

---

°"defunct": Here, no longer applicable or to be taken seriously. °Fourteenth Amendment: Ensures that laws apply equally to everyone and that no one be denied equal opportunity.

the *Meritor* decision applied to employment and not to education. Students are not the responsible agents of the university in the same sense that employees are, and consequently the university was not liable for their conduct as was the employer in *Meritor*. The court added that Title VII of the 1964 Civil Rights Act° was a statute° and could not supersede the First Amendment.

Finally, the university's policy was found to be unconstitutionally vague. It was not clear whether it was sufficient for the offending speaker to merely intend to demean the listener (without necessarily accomplishing that end) or whether the words had to actually do so. Along the lines of the decision in the Michigan case, the court cited the inconsistency between the language of the rule and the cases adjudicated to date. The policy stated that words must have the effect of demeaning, whereas the illustrative examples indicated no need to prove that the words in question had any effect on the listener or the educational environment. Nine months later the board of regents formally repealed the policy.

The Michigan and Wisconsin decisions appeared to doom most of the remaining campus speech codes. Two federal district courts had reaffirmed the principle of uninhibited free speech, without content-based restrictions. Moreover, they had rejected the new argument that the prohibition of racist speech was necessary to fulfill the mandate of the Fourteenth Amendment. These were only district court opinions, and it was still possible that higher courts, including the Supreme Court, might reverse one of the two and give new life to the campus speech code movement. It was not to be. Eight months after the decision in the Wisconsin case the Supreme Court gave content-based restrictions on hate speech an even deadlier blow.

CROSS BURNING AS HATE SPEECH

The St. Paul cross-burning case arose in response to the same rise in racist acts 15 that spawned the campus speech codes. In the 1980s there appeared to be a resurgence of violent acts directed at racial minorities (particularly cross burnings), Jews (in the desecration of synagogues and Jewish cemeteries), and homosexuals (in assaults on gay persons, or "gay bashing"). Like campus racist incidents, these acts occurred across the country, even in some unlikely places. Dubuque, Iowa, for example, was the scene of a series of cross burnings in the early 1990s.

In response, virtually every state enacted "hate crimes" legislation or strengthened existing laws. The Anti-Defamation League° was particularly

---

°Title VII of the 1964 Civil Rights Act: Prohibits discrimination in employment based on race, color, religion, sex, and national origin.   °a statute: Here, a law passed by the U.S. Congress. °Anti-Defamation League: Organization founded in 1913 to combat religious and racial discrimination.

active in lobbying for such legislation. Hate crimes laws took several forms. Some created new crimes relating to racial assaults or desecration of religious property. Others enhanced penalties for criminal acts that involved race, religion, or some other protected class. Thus a felonious assault° might incur a harsher penalty if the attack was racially motivated. As with the campus speech codes, there was tremendous variety in these laws: some were narrowly drafted° but others contained very broad language that raised serious First Amendment issues. Such was the case with the St. Paul ordinance.

The St. Paul Bias-Motivated Crime Ordinance made it a misdemeanor to place "on public or private property a symbol, object, appellation, characterization or graffiti" that "arouses anger, alarm or resentment in others on the basis of race, color, creed, religion or gender." The ordinance specifically mentioned "a burning cross or Nazi swastika" as examples of such symbols or objects. The law extended very broadly, covering the mere display of symbols, with no requirement that they be directed toward a specific individual, be intended to harass that person, or be likely to incite a breach of the peace. The prohibition of displays on private property clearly limited what people could do in their own front yards.

A challenge to the law reached the Supreme Court in the context of worsening racial tension, highlighted by the Rodney King incident. Nine months before the oral argument, Los Angeles police officers had savagely beaten King. A videotape of the beating was broadcast innumerable times over the next year, offering unprecedented visual evidence of a seemingly unnecessary act of police brutality. The decision in the cross-burning case came a month after the acquittal of four police officers accused in the beating. The verdict sparked one of the worst riots in American history. For black Americans, the verdict compounded the message of the original King beating: that they could expect no justice in the American legal system. A Supreme Court decision overturning the cross-burning conviction, coming on the heels of the two campus speech code decisions, could reinforce that perception.

There was considerable uncertainty among court watchers about how the justices would rule. This was not the Warren Court,° with its commitment to uninhibited speech. The Burger and Rehnquist Courts° had found sufficient justification to limit First Amendment rights in a number of special contexts: high school newspapers, the military, and prisons. In these situations the Court had been willing to defer to the expressed needs of administrative officials. On

---

°**felonious assault:** An attack on another person that is punishable as a felony, a serious crime. °**narrowly drafted:** Written in very specific language.   °**Warren Court:** The Supreme Court under Earl Warren, chief justice from 1953 to 1969. During this period, the Court was considered politically liberal.   °**Burger and Rehnquist Courts:** Warren Burger was chief justice from 1969 to 1986; William Rehnquist has been chief justice since 1986. Under their leadership, the Court has been considered politically conservative.

the other hand, it had sustained free speech rights in some cases concerning very offensive forms of expression that involved public speech about public figures or issues. Most relevant were the two flag-burning cases of 1990 and 1991. And the crucial factor in those decisions was that Justices Scalia and Kennedy, two of the most conservative members of the Court, had agreed that flag burning was a protected form of expression under the First Amendment. Also relevant was the *Hustler* decision, where the Court had overturned a libel award against *Hustler* magazine for a parody attacking Moral Majority leader Rev. Jerry Falwell. The parody was grossly obscene or hilariously funny, depending on one's political perspective. Offensive or not, the Court had ruled that it was fair comment on a public figure.

The St. Paul case itself involved a relatively low level of violence. A group of 20 teenagers, including Robert Viktora, put together a crudely made cross and burned it on the front lawn of a black family who lived across the street. In some respects the incident was a run-of-the-mill juvenile prank. But there was no mistaking the meaning of the burning cross, the traditional symbol of the Ku Klux Klan. It was a racist incident and, in the context of similar incidents across the country, a matter to be taken seriously. Viktora was charged in juvenile court under the Bias-Motivated Crime Ordinance. Because he was a juvenile at the time of the original action, he was referred to as R.A.V.—hence the name of the ultimate court case.

In what many regarded as a surprising decision, the Supreme Court declared the St. Paul ordinance unconstitutional. The law represented a prohibition on expression based on its content and, Justice Scalia wrote, "that is precisely what the First Amendment forbids." The decision was unanimous, but the justices disagreed sharply over the rationale. The most surprising aspect of the division of opinion was that the more conservative justices were in the majority, striking down the ordinance on broader grounds than the more moderate justices. Scalia, widely regarded as the most conservative of all, wrote the majority opinion.

The St. Paul ordinance was unconstitutional on its face because it prohibited only certain kinds of speech based on their content. It covered fighting words related to race, color, creed, religion, or gender but not similar words related to, for example, "political affiliation, union membership, or homosexuality." Even worse, Scalia argued, the ordinance discriminated among particular viewpoints. The advocate of racial or religious tolerance could use many forms of invective, but that speaker's opponents could not.

Four justices agreed that the ordinance was unconstitutional, but for different reasons. Justices White, O'Connor, Blackmun, and Stevens were generally regarded as the more moderate members of the Rehnquist Court. They argued that the law was unconstitutional because of its breadth. This particular ordinance went too far, they argued, but a prohibition on fighting words that did not involve the exchange of ideas and were used only "to provoke violence or to inflict injury" was compatible with the First Amendment. There was a surprising reversal of roles in this split. The more conservative justices offered the most sweeping, doctrinaire defense of free speech. The moderates, who wanted to preserve some limited basis for restricting hate speech, criticized this approach as "arid, doctrinaire" and "mischievous"—precisely the terms conservatives had used to criticize the activist libertarianism° of the Warren Court.

Coming only weeks after the Los Angeles riots and a heightening of racial polarization, the decision confounded many civil rights activists. Did the First Amendment bar any action against racially motivated cross burning? Some of their complaints resembled the traditional arguments of conservatives angered by constitutional barriers to the social policies they preferred. Scalia anticipated these criticisms and addressed them in the first paragraph of his opinion. The actual cross burning in this case "could have been punished under any of a number of laws," he wrote, citing Minnesota laws on terrorist threats, arson, and criminal damage to property. The decision by no means completely settled the matter: many states had hate crimes laws that were far more narrowly drafted than the St. Paul ordinance. In all likelihood the Court would soon have to consider a case where the distinction between expression and pure conduct was much narrower.

A COMMITMENT STRENGTHENED

From the perspective of the history of the hate speech issue, *R.A.V. v. St. Paul* 25 did not mark the end of an era. Rather, it reaffirmed an American tradition that had developed over the previous half century. On the issue of hate speech, that tradition afforded broad First Amendment protection for offensive and even hateful forms of expression. The depth and strength of that tradition were dramatized in that a unanimous Supreme Court struck down the St. Paul ordinance. The most conservative of the justices affirmed the principle that the First Amendment forbade distinctions based on content—an idea that had been a radical notion only half a century earlier.

AMERICA'S FIRST "HATE SPEECH" REGULATION

Michael W. McConnell

University of Chicago law professor Michael McConnell offers a historical perspective on the debate about banning offensive speech from college campuses. Writing in 1992 in the law journal Constitutional Commentary, *McConnell points*

°**activist libertarianism:** Actively promoting individual rights.

out that Maryland, while still a colony of England in 1649, enacted the first law regulating hateful speech, the Maryland Toleration Act. Designed to protect Maryland's citizens from being called certain religious names that were considered hateful at the time, the law even imposed a fine for using such names. McConnell traces the history of this famous law and argues that it is a "close analogy to the regulation of hate speech on modern American campuses." Colonial Maryland legislators wanted to prevent speech intended to insult people for their religious beliefs. Today's legislators and campus administrators want to prevent speech intended to insult people because they are women, Hispanics, religious fundamentalists, homosexuals, overweight, or members of some other group the speaker does not like.

As you read, you will notice that McConnell is not really advocating campus speech regulations. Instead, he is trying to discover what the Maryland Toleration Act implies for today's attempts to protect college students from offensive speech. McConnell's essay makes clear that hate speech regulation has a rich history, offering lessons of caution as well as hope to those who would regulate or ban offensive speech on college campuses.

Americans have the endearing but frustrating tendency to view every development in public life as if it were happening for the first time. Each issue is a new thing under the sun. Now the issue of "hate speech"—speech that is designed to degrade or injure other people on the basis of their race, ethnic origin, sex, sexual orientation or other sensitive characteristic—is the hot new free speech question. The law reviews are filled with learned analyses. Task forces have been appointed. Colleges and universities are debating the question. Legislation has been introduced in Congress.

Yet to my knowledge, none of the scholarly analyses of the issue has attempted to draw on the American historical experience with this problem. "Hate speech" is one of the oldest public issues in America; the first law was enacted almost 350 years ago. The question traditionally has been framed in these terms: to what extent does a liberal society require social conditions of mutual respect and toleration, and to what extent may the force of law be employed to attain or preserve those conditions? Attention to historical experience may help us to appreciate both the roots of hate speech regulation and some of its pitfalls.

The first hate speech regulation in America was Maryland's Toleration Act of 1649. Maryland had been founded a few years earlier by a Roman Catholic nobleman and friend of Charles I,° Lord Baltimore. Lord Baltimore intended to make Maryland a haven for his fellow Catholics (who at that time were severely persecuted in the mother country) and to extend protection to other dissenters

---

°**Charles I:** King of England from 1625 to 1649.

from the Church of England as well. The Toleration Act, which precedes by forty years the famous act of Parliament° by that name, was enacted by the colonial legislature,° superseding a similar proclamation by Lord Baltimore. As part of legislation establishing the "free exercise" of religion (the first appearance of those words in the laws of this continent), the Act imposed a fine of ten shillings on any person who called another "by such opprobrious terms° as, Heretic, Schismatic, Idolator, Puritan, Independent, Presbyterian, Popish priest, Jesuit, Papist, Lutheran, Calvinist, Anabaptist, Brownist, Antinomian, Barrowist, Roundhead, and Separatist." In the only recorded prosecution under the statute or the predecessor proclamation, a Catholic named William Lewis was fined for "interfering by opprobrious reproaches with two Protestants"—an encouraging sign, since most colonial officials at the time were Catholics.

It may be objected that this statute deals with a subject—religion—far removed from today's concerns of race, sex, sexual orientation, and the like. But we must not commit the anachronism of dismissing religion as a private matter of little weight or consequence. Religion was central to the Maryland colonists' identity, and differences in religion were never far from their minds. Religious discord delivered Lord Baltimore's friend, Charles I, to the scaffold, and England to civil war. Moreover, the immediate problem addressed by the Maryland Toleration Act was not unlike that of today's hate speech regulations on campus. Words were used, then as now, to inflict injury, to humiliate, to ostracize,° and to subordinate. Historian Sanford Cobb said of religious disputants in seventeenth century Massachusetts that they "made of their tongues weapons harder to bear than clubs." The Maryland Toleration Act is thus an exceedingly close analogy to the regulation of hate speech on modern American campuses.

Unfortunately, we do not have much information about the implementation 5 or effects of the Toleration Act. Following the downfall of the King, a Protestant faction seized power in the colony in 1652 and repealed the Toleration Act two years later, replacing it with a law explicitly denying protection to persons who "profess the exercise of the Popish Religion."° Oliver Cromwell° forced the colonists to repeal the 1654 act, thus reinstating the Toleration Act, but in the spirit of the day one would not expect faithful enforcement. Notwithstanding this lack of enforcement, however, three aspects of the Maryland experience seem significant today. . . .

First, the framers of the Maryland statute obviously thought that outlawing hate speech ("opprobrious terms") was consistent with—not in opposition

---

°**Parliament:** The representative governing body of Great Britain, similar to the U.S. Congress. °**colonial legislature:** The Maryland legislature during the time when Maryland was a colony of England. °**opprobrious terms:** Here, disgraceful or hateful expressions. °**ostracize:** To exclude someone from a group. °**Popish Religion:** Roman Catholicism, which is headed by a pope. °**Oliver Cromwell:** Soldier and statesman (1599–1658) who ruled England from 1653 to 1658.

to—a regime of free speech and religion. Restrictions of this sort would advance free discourse and inquiry, because they would enable persons of all groups, including the most socially despised, to participate on equal terms. The Toleration Act did not view religious freedom as meaning only an absence of governmental coercion; it sought to regulate the private sphere to ensure social conditions of toleration.... The hate speech regulators stand in the honorable shoes of Lord Baltimore and the Maryland colonists, who believed that private intolerance, through the use of hurtful epithets, is a significant obstacle to achievement of a society in which persons of all faiths (today we would say all races, sexes, sexual orientations, and the like) can live together peaceably and equally. In a world in which Catholics, for example, are both seriously outnumbered and socially subordinated, a jurisdiction that wants to offer Catholics a hospitable place in which to live must be concerned with the danger that private intolerance will make that objective unattainable. By the same token, if the desired end is a community of inquiry in which all viewpoints and perspectives can be shared, is it unreasonable for university administrators to think that an interventionist policy° is necessary to ensure that some portions of the student body are not silenced and excluded from the discourse?

Second, the framers of the Toleration Act of 1649 had a difficult drafting problem. They were caught between the dangers of vagueness on the one hand and underinclusiveness on the other. How could they define "hate speech" so that they could outlaw it? The problem was particularly difficult because part of the religious exercise they were protecting was the ability to proclaim the faith, which often entails an explanation ("exhortation" might be a better word) of why other religions are false. How could the colonial authorities tell when legitimate discourse ends and "opprobrious terms" begin?

The Maryland drafters did not do a very good job. If their list is taken to be exclusive, there are a number of opprobrious epithets they left out: Socinian, ranter, pagan, Christ-killer, fanatic, hireling, and many more. If the list is taken only to be illustrative, it doesn't solve the vagueness problem. If a Protestant maliciously mocks the Latin of the mass by calling it "hocus-pocus,"° is that covered? If a Unitarian sneers at the credulity of those who believe in a virgin birth, is that covered? Conversely, some of the terms in the Maryland Act seem rather innocent. "Presbyterian," for example, is not an obvious example of an opprobrious epithet. And any of the terms, in a certain context, might be perfectly legitimate. That is the problem with legislation by list. If, however, the Maryland legislators had used another approach instead of listing forbidden epithets, they would have had a different set of problems. They might have

---

°interventionist policy: Taking action to intervene in a problem with the hope of solving it—for example, regulating speech on a college campus in the hope of reducing hate speech.   °hocus-pocus: A corruption of the Latin *hoc est corpus*, "this is my body," a phrase in the Christian communion service.

based the law on the actual intent of the speaker to ostracize or subordinate members of a different faith, which makes it virtually unenforceable. Only the speaker knows his own intent. Or they might have based it on the effect on the hearer, which makes it vaguer than ever and makes speech vulnerable to the reactions of the most sensitive among us.

Modern campus administrators face much the same problem. Like the Maryland legislators, they, too, could publish a list of forbidden epithets, the modern equivalents of "heretic," "schismatic," "papist," or "roundhead." We can all imagine the contents of the list. But no university has opted for that approach, perhaps for reasons of good manners. Instead they opt for vagueness. The University of Michigan interim code—the one instituted *after* the first effort was held unconstitutional by a federal court—forbids "verbal slurs, invectives or epithets referring to an individual's race, ethnicity, religion, sex, sexual orientation," etc., made with the "purpose of injuring the person to whom the words or actions are directed," but excluding statements made as a part of a "discussion or exchange of an idea, ideology, or philosophy." Try to figure out when that will apply.

Given the difficulties of drafting intelligible standards, it should come as no 10 surprise that the enforcement of hate speech codes has been clumsy and unpredictable. Under the original Michigan code, for example, a graduate student was haled before a disciplinary board to account for his statement in a social work class that he believed homosexuality to be a disease and that he intended to develop a counseling program to help patients to overcome it. Another student was "counseled" and required to apologize for commenting in class that "he had heard that minorities had a difficult time in the course and that he had heard that they were not treated fairly." At the same time, some of the more egregious° incidents of racism on campus would apparently fall outside most hate speech codes because they are directed at a general audience rather than at a particular person whom they seek to injure.

Third, the selectivity reflected in the Maryland statute is not random. Several epithets referring to Catholics are listed, because they were precisely the protected class whom the colonial authorities had in mind. There are no epithets pertaining to Jews. There are no epithets pertaining to atheists. There are no epithets pertaining to pagans, Muslims, or other assorted heathen—even though the vast majority of the inhabitants of Maryland in 1649 adhered to religions the legislators would have considered heathen. By interesting contrast, the 1669 Fundamental Constitutions of the Colony of Carolina, drafted in part by John Locke,° which was in other respects less liberal in its protection of religious freedom, explicitly extended its protection to "Jews, heathens, and other dissenters from the purity of Christian religion."

°**egregious:** Here, conspicuously or noticeably bad.   °**John Locke:** English philosopher (1632–1704).

It was no accident that the Maryland legislature outlawed some epithets and not others. Maryland was designed as a haven for religious dissenters, but religious dissenters of a particular kind. Others were not welcome.

We see that same phenomenon in modern hate speech rules, which forbid hate speech directed against certain groups but not against others. You can, for example, call a fellow student a "racist, fascist homophobe," or a "pimply nerd," or a "damn Yankee," with impunity on any campus in America. Epithets like these serve no less to cut off debate, to humiliate, to ostracize, and to exclude; but they are not covered. Modern hate speech rules are intended to protect groups, but only groups of a certain kind. The opinions of significant subgroups of Americans on issues such as race and sexuality are not welcome on most American campuses. And these voices are not often heard. Who wants to be hissed in class? . . .

An examination of the Maryland Toleration Act of 1649 thus suggests that we should not accept too quickly the common position of conservatives and ACLU liberals that hate speech regulation is, in principle, contrary to the requirements of a free society. Our early history shows that lawmakers no less committed to a free society than most of us came to the conclusion that a free, equal, and tolerant society must protect its principles from the forces of intolerance, even when they manifest themselves in speech. But even if we become more sympathetic, in principle, to the concept of hate speech regulation, we should also be aware that there are grave, and perhaps insuperable, difficulties in drafting regulations that are broad enough without being vague. We must be ever conscious of the possibility that, in the guise of regulations for the preservation of toleration, the authorities will use their power over speech to advance their own ideological causes° at the expense of dissenters.

■ ■ ■ ■ ■ **A WRITER'S NOTEBOOK** ■ ■ ■ ■

Supreme Court Cases and Historical Background

The following tasks are designed to help you think about the readings and identify and start to work up material you might use in your own essay. If you need help with tasks that require outlining, summarizing, synthesizing, or evaluating an argument, see Appendix 1.

1. *Summarize part of the Chaplinsky case.* Summarize Justice Murphy's opinion in paragraphs 1–4.

2. *Summarize part of the Beauharnais case.* Justice Frankfurter's argument offers support to someone advocating restrictions on campus speech. Summarize the reasons he gives that the Illinois law was constitutional (paragraphs 1–3).

°**ideological causes:** Causes based on strongly held ideas or beliefs.

3. *Summarize and outline part of the Beauharnais case.* Justice Black's argument should be helpful as you think about some of the difficulties involved in deciding what is hate speech. Write a scratch outline of his argument opposing the majority opinion (paragraphs 4–15). Then, using your outline as a guide, summarize his argument.

4. *Evaluate the Beauharnais case.* Justice Douglas concurs with Justice Black's dissenting opinion but has his own reasons for doing so. Evaluate Douglas's argument (paragraphs 16–21) in the context of the Beauharnais case and the Frankfurter opinion, considering Douglas's purpose, his organization, and the support he gives for his argument. Do you think he presents a successful argument?

5. *Synthesize the Chaplinsky and the Beauharnais cases.* In *Chaplinsky,* Justice Murphy makes an argument favoring a certain kind of speech restriction (paragraphs 1–2). In *Beauharnais,* Justice Frankfurter does the same thing (paragraphs 1–3). Write a synthesis of their arguments, informing readers about their shared points of view on restricting speech.

6. *List reasons from Samuel Walker's essay.* Walker tells why the courts invalidated the Michigan (paragraphs 6–8) and Wisconsin (paragraphs 11–13) attempts to regulate offensive speech. List the main reasons the courts gave for their decisions.

7. *Consider Michael W. McConnell's essay.* In paragraphs 6–13, McConnell discusses the implications of Maryland's colonial experience for modern-day campus speech regulations. He presents three specific implications. In two or three sentences, describe each one.

ARGUMENTS FOR AND AGAINST REGULATING SPEECH ON COLLEGE CAMPUSES

The readings in the preceding sections have provided background for understanding constitutional speech protections in the United States, as well as reports about incidents of offensive speech on various campuses and official speech guidelines from three campuses. In thinking about these readings, you have probably reflected on your own experience with hate speech and perhaps gained additional insight by discussing the issue with other students.

At this point, then, you should be in a good position to compare arguments for and against restrictions on what students can say to each other on college campuses. Although the University of Pennsylvania and some other schools have dropped speech codes that allow for students to be punished or expelled, most schools still publish rules and warnings that seek to regulate or ban certain kinds of speech. In short, the issue is still very much alive.

Some civil rights advocates continue to argue that we must punish offensive speech in order to ensure equal rights for all Americans, even if it means limiting free speech. Recognizing that offensive speech and pornography are currently protected by similar legal arguments, some feminists have added their voices to this argument. Various college groups also argue for more stringent regulations. At the same time, many continue to oppose restrictions on offensive speech.

As you read these arguments, make a list of all of the major reasons given for and against campus speech regulations. You might keep one list of reasons to *support* campus speech regulations (which you will find in the selections by Mari J. Matsuda, Charles R. Lawrence III, Richard Delgado and David H. Yun, and Timothy C. Shiell) and another list of reasons to *oppose* campus speech regulations (which you'll find in the pieces by Paul McMasters, Susan Gellman, and Henry Louis Gates Jr.). Label each reason by author and paragraph number. Compiling such lists will be beneficial to you when you later need to take a position of your own on this issue.

Assaultive Speech and Academic Freedom

Mari J. Matsuda

Mari J. Matsuda, a law professor at Georgetown University, is a frequent contributor to law journals. Her books include Words That Wound: Critical Race Theory, Assaultive Speech, and the First Amendment *(1993, edited with Charles R. Lawrence III and Kimberle Williams Crenshaw) and* Where Is Your Body? and Other Essays on Race, Gender, and the Law *(1996).*

In this reading from Where Is Your Body? *Matsuda strongly advocates regulating speech on college campuses. She uses the term* assaultive speech, *writing from the point of view of those who have felt assaulted or threatened by the speech directed at them. She also uses the term* hate speech, *suggesting that she considers racist and sexist speech to be motivated by hate.*

This reading actually comes from a speech Matsuda delivered at several universities in the late 1980s and early 1990s. As you read, notice how she argues for campus speech regulations on the basis of three related constitutional principles: the equality *of access to and participation in all aspects of college life, the* liberty *from intimidation and oppression on campus, and the* free speech *to debate issues and to dissent from conventional ideas.*

What is a university, what is academic freedom, and how do people with different worldviews come together in the pursuit of knowledge? These are the questions I hope to address today as I consider the problem of campus regulation of racist, sexist, and homophobic speech.

First, I believe we should read the Constitution and the Bill of Rights as a whole. The values of equality and personhood run throughout our founding document. Equality of access and equality of participation are ideals that are central to and definitive of American democracy, particularly in the twentieth century. Hate speech on campus cuts deeply into equality of access for minority group members. To understand this, it is necessary to look at both the quantity and the quality of hate activity on campus. The quantity has increased to the point where few students of color can expect to go through four years of undergraduate education without encountering hate speech. By hate speech I refer to speech the only function of which is to wound and degrade by asserting the inherent inferiority of a group. Similarly, few women will leave our universities without encountering sexual harassment in the form of unwanted advances or a hostile environment created by sexist comments, pornography, or misogynist speech.°

Exposure to these kinds of hate leaves lasting impressions on university students who come to the academy at a formative time in their lives. Students are a population particularly at risk for psychological harm. Younger students are forming their identities, abandoning old peer ties, and seeking out new ones. They are in a transitional stage vis-à-vis families, coming to new understanding about what is good and bad in relationships with parents and siblings; playing out old dramas of interpersonal relationships with new characters; seeking self-knowledge; and considering what they want to do with their adult lives. Older students face the financial uncertainty and self-doubt that comes from returning to school. Many students—younger and older—are economically at risk, holding down part-time jobs, taking out loans, and hoping for financial aid. Some have partners or children or parents whom they are supporting. Some are academically at risk, unsure about how to make it in the maze of large classes, inaccessible professors, fancy-talking classmates, and cultural or class differences that make up the academic world. Even those excelling academically face self-doubt generated by examinations, grades, and job interviewing. Many emotional disorders manifest for the first time in college. Coming to the university is a major life stress event.

This is not the time to subject someone to psychological assault. It is not the time for a student to come back to her dorm room and find an anonymous note calling her ancestors filth, not a time for a student to come to class and find posters advocating the genocide° of everyone of his religion, not a time to walk down the street and face shouts and threats and demeaning and hateful things said about one's body. The administrators and counselors on the front lines of dealing with students, those who know about the students who have changed majors, moved out of the dorm, dropped classes, gone into therapy, and left the university because of harassment know that the problem is a serious one.

A student in Texas told me of studying in her carrel at the library, getting up 5 for a break, and coming back to find someone had drawn swastikas in the margin of her textbook and on her notes.

Another woman, a white woman, told me of walking to school with her moot court partner, an African-American woman, when a passing motorist called out, "Get that n—— bitch off this campus."

A student writer at UCLA spoke of sitting in class listening to a lecture and discovering that someone had written on the wall next to her desk, "Kill all the jews."

°**misogynist speech:** Speech expressing hatred of women.   °**genocide:** The deliberate destruction of a particular political, racial, or cultural group.

On their way to a reception in my honor when I received tenure at UCLA, students who rode the elevator were confronted with graffiti that said, "I want Asian c——nt."

In each of these cases, students were participating in essential activities and daily life at the university—studying, walking to class, listening to the lecture, or attending a social event—when they were attacked out of the blue with a hateful and degrading message. They were ambushed, making the space that once seemed familiar and safe seem threatening and not one's own.

——These students are supposed to keep functioning, and most of them do. 10 Look away from the death threat, refocus on the lecture, and keep on taking notes. Turn the page, keep studying, ignore the swastikas. Continue down the street with your moot court partner, do not be late for class, and forget that someone felt compelled to threaten you and hate you in a public and aggressive way. Feel your knees go weak when the stranger yells from the car and keep walking, head erect, like you have a right to be there.

People manage, but they manage under a burden. Maybe they do not hear all the lecture. Maybe they do not get a full night's sleep, and maybe they do not do as well on the calculus exam. There is a cost, a burden, a price paid for the epidemic of assaultive speech on our campuses, and the cost is paid disproportionately by historically subordinated groups.

The principles of equality and liberty recognize the worth of every human being and the right of each to participate in the institutions of our nation. As Professor Charles Lawrence has pointed out, the case of *Brown v. Board of Education* was, at its core, a case about the way in which racist messages violate the rights of equality and liberty. In *Brown,* the court recognized that no matter how equal the schools, separating children on the basis of race was never constitutionally permissible. Why was this? We separate children all the time, by district, by birth date, and by ability. The reason it was not permissible to separate children by race was that segregation represented a racist ideology.° Jim Crow° embodied white supremacy: white is pure and must remain untainted by the dirt, by the filth, of the Other. The Supreme Court knew this when it decided *Brown,* and it considered substantial testimony about the psychological harm caused by segregation. Separate is never equal, the court found, because of the damage caused by *the message* of racial inferiority. *Brown* thus sets up a set of competing values at odds with the protection of racist speech.

In addition to the liberty and equality interests implicated by hate-speech regulations, there are also First Amendment reasons to ban hate speech. The goal of the First Amendment is to protect dissent, to maximize public discourse, and to achieve the great flowering of debate and of ideas that we need for

---

°**racist ideology:** In this instance, a set of beliefs in which whites are considered superior to blacks and other people of color.   °**Jim Crow:** Jim Crow laws, enacted in the South from 1887 to the 1950s, forced blacks to live segregated from whites. The laws were named after a stereotyped black character in a nineteenth-century song-and-dance act.

democracy to work. Hate speech impedes these goals because hate speech is intended to and has the effect of cutting off debate. When someone calls you a hate name, they are not trying to get into a debate or even a rancorous argument with you. They are telling you that you are less than human, that you have no right to be here, and that your speech is worthless. The typical responses to racist hate speech include fear, flight, or fistfights. People use these words precisely because of the wounding, silencing effect. I suggest that there are some forms of speech we need to limit precisely because we value speech.

Let me give you some examples of hate speech limiting free speech. One of my students was discussing gay-rights issues with friends in a restaurant. A stranger came up to him and said aggressively, "Are you a f——gg——t?" My student said, yes, he is gay and proud of it. Then the assailant escalated his verbal abuse, finally assaulting my student physically. Since the incident, the student tells me, his friends look over their shoulders and size up the room before they discuss gay issues. They speak in hushed tones; sometimes they do not speak. In this case, responding to hate speech with counterspeech resulted in physical assault.

Because physical abuse so often follows verbal abuse in our violent and 15 patriarchal culture,° it does not require actual physical assault for assaultive speech to silence. In San Francisco's Chinatown, community members who testified at a public hearing, many of them participating in the political process for the first time, found that their names and a racist, anti-Asian message were broadcast on the White Aryan Resistance hotline. Many of the speakers feared for their lives. They will think twice before testifying again.

Any university professor who has tried to promote classroom discussion about race, gender, and homosexuality knows how hard it is to get students to express their ideas, feelings, and disagreements about these topics. Our ability to speak across cultural divides is impeded by the feelings of animosity° growing on our campuses. Hate speech shuts down conversations and keeps us from the important work of learning to talk across difference.

Let me emphasize that I believe in the First Amendment. It is absolutely critical, particularly in these days of economic collapse,° that citizens retain the right of dissent, the right to criticize the government. In suggesting that the ugliest forms of hate speech should fall outside First Amendment protection, I make a distinction between dissent, or criticism directed against the powerful institutions° that affect our lives, and hate speech, or speech directed against the least powerful segment of our communities.

It is the lawyer's job to make distinctions in principled ways, and the principle I suggest is that of antisubordination. Our minority students are already at risk for a variety of historical reasons. Many of them come from economically

---

°**patriarchal culture:** A culture in which men have most of the power.   °**animosity:** Feelings of resentment and hostility.   °**these days of economic collapse:** Probably a reference to the economic recession of 1989–92.   °**powerful institutions:** For example, colleges, churches, courts, legislatures, corporations, the Federal Reserve Board, the Internal Revenue Service.

disadvantaged backgrounds. Many are of the first generation in their families to go to college. The antisubordination principle recognizes the historical reality that some members of our community are less powerful and have less access to education. The universities have come a long way in recognizing this, making commitments to affirmative action and to outreach programs to help less advantaged students. Protecting these students from psychological attack is part of that same ethical goal of equal opportunity and inclusion.

Universities bear special obligations for several reasons. First, universities are part of the public trust. They receive government support in the form of subsidies and tax advantages. State universities are supported by taxpayers— by all taxpayers, including the working poor and immigrants who are less often the beneficiaries of a university education. Second, university students are a captive audience. Students cannot choose not to come to class, not to go to their mailboxes, and not to study in the library. When hate speech invades the campus, students have no choice, no place to go to escape the speech. Students are encouraged to think of the university as their home. The university encourages activities in and out of class and promotes a host of extracurricular clubs and events that are critical to the educational experience. The physical confines of the campus are not the anonymous places that city streets are. They are home. And to have ugly messages of hate posted on the walls of a home is much more of an intrusion than, say, a racist march downtown. "Invasion" is a word often used by people who have received hate messages in their dorms, in their churches or synagogues, and in their homes. The right to a sense of personal security in the geographic confines of a home place is something we owe our students.

Finally, universities are not neutral, relativistic, amoral institutions. They [20] stand for something. They stand for the pursuit of knowledge. They stand for ethical striving. They stand for equal opportunity. We wave these values in letterheads, mottos, and catalogs used to recruit students. . . . We are about the pursuit of knowledge and ethics. We do teach values. . . .

A belief in human dignity is at the heart of what we do. Why else try to study and to know all the phenomena of the universe if we do not believe, ultimately, in the glory of life on this planet and the grace of knowing all we can about how to live decent lives while we are here? There is no value-free reason for our existence. We do stand for human dignity, and we must protect the dignity of each of our students. . . .

The unfortunate pattern of response to hate speech has been to do nothing until a serious incident creates a crisis. The crisis is then followed by hastily enacted rules or, worse yet, ex post facto discipline.° These hate incidents are not going to go away. . . . We need to start by gathering information. Every campus should have a system for collecting data about hate incidents. We should

---

° **ex post facto discipline:** Discipline that follows an incidence of campus hate speech.

provide fora° for students to speak out about the discrimination they feel. We need to share this information among campuses, to get a clear picture of the extent of the problem and to develop proactive strategies for dealing with hate. I believe we should draft narrow regulations that will penalize the worst forms of assaultive speech, and I would challenge those who disagree with me to come up with concrete alternative responses to hate speech, including strong nondisciplinary condemnation of bigotry, affirmative action programs, curriculum reform, and other means to improve the campus climate for underrepresented groups. There is a range of alternatives open to us, and I hope we continue to debate and consider them all.

The theme of this lecture is academic freedom.... Academic freedom must include freedom from racist and sexist oppression unless we mean that academic freedom is the sole property of the powerful. I think that the origin of the concept is exactly the opposite. It was the freedom to say that the planets revolve around the sun, even when the church insisted it was the other way around. It was the freedom to expose government corruption, even when the government is paying your salary. This courageous tradition is one we must preserve. It is not the same as the freedom to hurt and degrade the powerless.

Many will disagree with what I have said. I hope we can continue to argue with and learn from one another, letting our speech fill the space made by academic freedom.

IF HE HOLLERS LET HIM GO:
REGULATING RACIST SPEECH ON CAMPUS

Charles R. Lawrence III

Charles R. Lawrence III, professor of law at the Stanford University Law School, has played a major role in the debate about whether to regulate or ban racist speech on college campuses. He favors doing so. In the opening "Newsreel" of this 1990 Duke Law Journal *article, Lawrence presents both perspectives of the debate by contrasting examples of hate speech with typical arguments of civil libertarians who oppose campus speech regulations.*

At Stanford, Lawrence supported the speech regulations drafted by a fellow law professor. Here, he presents those regulations and uses them as the basis for arguing that minority-group students need this sort of protection. Part of his purpose is to show that the "fighting words" concept from Chaplinsky v. New Hampshire *does not adequately explain the situation of face-to-face racial insults.*

° **fora:** Campus meetings for discussing important issues.

Lawrence is convinced that it is unreasonable to expect people who have been subjected to racial insults to fight back on the spot. As you read, try to determine why Lawrence holds this opinion.

NEWSREEL

Racist incidents at the University of Michigan, University of Massachusetts-Amherst, University of Wisconsin, University of New Mexico, Columbia University, Wellesley College, Duke University, and University of California-Los Angeles.

The campus ought to be the last place to legislate tampering with the edges of first amendment protections.

University of Michigan:
  "Greek Rites of Exclusion": Racist leaflets in dorms, white students paint themselves black and place rings in their noses at "jungle parties."

Silencing a few creeps is no victory if the price is an abrogation° of free speech. Remember censorship is an ugly word too.

Northwest Missouri State University:
  White Supremacists distribute flyers stating, "The Knights of the Ku Klux Klan° are Watching You."...

Temple University:
  White Student Union formed....

Memphis State University:
  Bomb Threats at Jewish Student Union.

Arizona State University:
  Shot fired at Hillel Foundation° building.

The harm that censors allege will result unless speech is forbidden rarely occurs.

Dartmouth College:
  Black professor called "a cross between a welfare queen and a bathroom attendant" and the Dartmouth Review purported to quote a black student, "Dese boys be sayin' that we be comin' here to Dartmut an' not takin' the classics...."

Yes, speech is sometimes painful. Sometimes it is abusive. That is one of the prices of a free society.

Purdue University:
  Counselor finds "Death Nigger" scratched on her door.

More speech, not less, is the proper cure for offensive speech.

°**abrogation:** The act of abolishing or putting an end to something.   °**Ku Klux Klan:** A secret society that advocates white supremacy and limits its membership to American-born white Christians. °**Hillel Foundation:** A national Jewish organization of college students.

Smith College:

> African student finds message slipped under her door that reads, "African Nigger do you want some bananas? Go back to the Jungle."

Speech cannot be banned simply because it is offensive.

University of Michigan:

> Campus radio station broadcasts a call from a student who "joked": "Who are the most famous black women in history? Aunt Jemima and Mother Fucker."

Those who don't like what they are hearing or seeing should try to change the atmosphere through education. That is what they will have to do in the real world after they graduate.

University of Michigan:

> A student walks into class and sees this written on the blackboard: "A mind is a terrible thing to waste—especially on a nigger."

People of color, women, and gays and lesbians owe their vibrant political movements in large measure to their freedom to communicate. If speech can be banned because it offends someone, how long will it be before the messages of these groups are themselves found offensive?...

INTRODUCTION

In recent years, American campuses have seen a resurgence of racial violence and a corresponding rise in the incidence of verbal and symbolic assault and harassment to which blacks and other traditionally subjugated groups are subjected. There is a heated debate in the civil liberties community concerning the proper response to incidents of racist speech on campus. Strong disagreements have arisen between those individuals who believe that racist speech, such as that contained in the Newsreel that opens this Article, should be regulated by the university or some public body and those individuals who believe that racist expression should be protected from all public regulation. At the center of the controversy is a tension between the constitutional values of free speech and equality....

I write this Article from within the cauldron of this controversy. I make no pretense of dispassion or objectivity, but I do claim a deep commitment to the values that motivate both sides of the debate. As I struggle with the tension between these constitutional values, I particularly appreciate the experience of both belonging and not belonging that gives to African Americans and other outsider groups a sense of duality....

At Stanford, where I teach, there has been considerable controversy over the questions whether racist and other discriminatory verbal harassment should be regulated and what form that regulation should take. Proponents of regulation have been sensitive to the danger of inhibiting expression, and the current regulation (which was drafted by my colleague Tom Grey) manifests that sensitivity. It is drafted somewhat more narrowly than I would have preferred...but I largely agree with this regulation's substance and approach. I include it here as one example of a regulation of racist speech that I would argue violates neither first amendment precedent nor principle. The regulation reads as follows:

Free Expression and Discriminatory Harassment

1. Stanford is committed to the principles of free inquiry and free expression. Students have the right to hold and vigorously defend and promote their opinions, thus entering them into the life of the University, there to flourish or wither according to their merits. Respect for this right requires that students tolerate even expression of opinions which they find abhorrent.° Intimidation of students by other students in their exercise of this right, by violence or threat of violence, is therefore considered to be a violation of the Fundamental Standard.°

2. Stanford is also committed to principles of equal opportunity and non-discrimination. Each student has the right to equal access to a Stanford education, without discrimination on the basis of sex, race, color, handicap, religion, sexual orientation, or national and ethnic origin. Harassment of students on the basis of any of these characteristics contributes to a hostile environment that makes access to education for those subjected to it less than equal. Such discriminatory harassment is therefore considered to be a violation of the Fundamental Standard.

3. This interpretation of the Fundamental Standard is intended to clarify the point at which protected free expression ends and prohibited discriminatory harassment begins. Prohibited harassment includes discriminatory intimidation by threats of violence, and also includes personal vilification of students on the basis of their sex, race, color, handicap, religion, sexual orientation, or national and ethnic origin.

4. Speech or other expression constitutes harassment by personal vilification if it:
   a) is intended to insult or stigmatize an individual or a small number of individuals on the basis of their sex, race, color, handicap, religion, sexual orientation, or national and ethnic origin; and
   b) is addressed. directly to the individual or individuals whom it insults or stigmatizes; and
   c) makes use of insulting or "fighting" words or non-verbal symbols.°

In the context of discriminatory harassment by personal vilification, insulting or "fighting" words or non-verbal symbols are those "which by their very utterance inflict injury or tend to incite to an immediate breach of the peace," and which are commonly understood to convey direct and visceral° hatred or contempt for human beings on the basis of their sex, race, color, handicap, religion, sexual orientation, or national and ethnic origin.

This regulation and others like it have been characterized in the press as the work of "thought police," but it does nothing more than prohibit intentional

---

°**abhorrent:** Extremely repugnant or disgusting.   °**Fundamental Standard:** The standard or custom at Stanford University of protecting free expression and forbidding discriminatory harassment. °**non-verbal symbols:** Posters, drawings, cartoons.   °**visceral:** Strongly emotional, unreasoning.

face-to-face insults, a form of speech that is unprotected by the first amendment. When racist speech takes the form of face-to-face insults, catcalls, or other assaultive speech aimed at an individual or small group of persons, then it falls within the "fighting words" exception to first amendment protection. The Supreme Court has held that words that "by their very utterance inflict injury or tend to incite an immediate breach of the peace" are not constitutionally protected.

Face-to-face racial insults, like fighting words, are undeserving of first   5 amendment protection for two reasons. The first reason is the immediacy of the injurious impact of racial insults. The experience of being called "nigger," "spic," "Jap," or "kike" is like receiving a slap in the face. The injury is instantaneous. There is neither an opportunity for intermediary reflection on the idea conveyed nor an opportunity for responsive speech. The harm to be avoided is both clear and present. The second reason that racial insults should not fall under protected speech relates to the purpose underlying the first amendment. If the purpose of the first amendment is to foster the greatest amount of speech, then racial insults disserve that purpose. Assaultive racist speech° functions as a preemptive strike.° The racial <u>invective</u> is experienced as a blow, not a proffered idea, and once the blow is struck, it is unlikely that dialogue will follow. Racial insults are undeserving of first amendment protection because the perpetrator's intention is not to discover truth or initiate dialogue but to injure the victim.

The fighting words doctrine anticipates that the verbal "slap in the face" of insulting words will provoke a violent response with a resulting breach of the peace. When racial insults are hurled at minorities, the response may be silence or flight rather than a fight, but the preemptive effect on further speech is just as complete as with fighting words. Women and minorities often report that they find themselves speechless in the face of discriminatory verbal attacks. This inability to respond is not the result of oversensitivity among these groups, as some individuals who oppose protective regulation have argued. Rather, it is the product of several factors, all of which reveal the non-speech character of the initial preemptive verbal assault. The first factor is that the visceral emotional response to personal attack precludes speech. Attack produces an instinctive, defensive psychological reaction. Fear, rage, shock, and flight all interfere with any reasoned response. Words like "nigger," "kike," and "faggot" produce physical symptoms that temporarily disable the victim, and the perpetrators often use these words with the intention of producing this effect. Many victims do not find words of response until well after the assault when the cowardly assaulter has departed.

A second factor that distinguishes racial insults from protected speech is the preemptive nature of such insults—the words by which to respond to such

---

°**Assaultive racist speech:** Racist speech that feels threatening like a physical attack.   °**preemptive strike:** An attack that prevents someone from counterattacking.

verbal attacks may never be forthcoming because speech is usually an inadequate response. When one is personally attacked with words that denote one's subhuman status and untouchability, there is little (if anything) that can be said to redress either the emotional or [the] reputational injury. This is particularly true when the message and meaning of the epithet resonates with beliefs widely held in society. This preservation of widespread beliefs is what makes the face-to-face racial attack more likely to preempt speech than are other fighting words. The racist name-caller is accompanied by a cultural chorus° of equally demeaning speech and symbols.

The subordinated victim of fighting words also is silenced by her relatively powerless position in society. Because of the significance of power and position, the categorization of racial epithets as "fighting words" provides an inadequate paradigm;° instead one must speak of their "functional equivalent." The fighting words doctrine presupposes an encounter between two persons of relatively equal power who have been acculturated to respond to face-to-face insults with violence. The fighting words doctrine is a paradigm based on a white male point of view. In most situations, minorities correctly perceive that a violent response to fighting words will result in a risk to their own life and limb. Since minorities are likely to lose the fight, they are forced to remain silent and submissive. This response is most obvious when women submit to sexually assaultive speech or when the racist name-caller is in a more powerful position—the boss on the job or the mob. Certainly, we do not expect the black women crossing the Wisconsin campus to turn on their tormentors and pummel them. Less obvious, but just as significant, is the effect of pervasive racial and sexual violence and coercion on individual members of subordinated groups who must learn the survival techniques of suppressing and disguising rage and anger at an early age.

One of my students, a white, gay male, related an experience that is quite instructive in understanding the inadequacy and potential of the "fighting words" doctrine. In response to my request that students describe how they experienced the injury of racist speech, Michael told a story of being called "faggot" by a man on a subway. His description included all of the speech inhibiting elements I have noted previously. He found himself in a state of semi-shock, nauseous, dizzy, unable to muster the witty, sarcastic, articulate rejoinder he was accustomed to making. He suddenly was aware of the recent spate of gay-bashing in San Francisco, and how many of these had escalated from verbal encounters. Even hours later when the shock subsided and his facility with words returned, he realized that any response was inadequate to counter the hundreds of years of societal defamation that one word— "faggot"—carried with it. Like the word "nigger" and unlike the word "liar,"

°**cultural chorus:** Here, Lawrence is referring to the many reminders of racist attitudes in our society.   °**paradigm:** Framework.

it is not sufficient to deny the truth of the word's application, to say, "I am not a faggot." One must deny the truth of the word's meaning, a meaning shouted from the rooftops by the rest of the world a million times a day. Although there are many of us who constantly and in myriad ways seek to counter the lie spoken in the meaning of hateful words like "nigger" and "faggot," it is a nearly impossible burden to bear when one encounters hateful speech face-to-face.

But there was another part of my discussion with Michael that is equally 10 instructive. I asked if he could remember a situation when he had been verbally attacked with reference to his membership in a superordinate group. Had he ever been called a "honkie," a "chauvinist pig," or "mick"? (Michael is from a working class Irish family in Boston.) He said that he had been called some version of all three and that although he found the last one more offensive than the first two, he had not experienced — even in that subordinated role — the same disorienting powerlessness he had experienced when attacked for his membership in the gay community. The question of power, of the context of the power relationships within which speech takes place, must be considered as we decide how best to foster the freest and fullest dialogue within our communities. It is apparent that regulation of face-to-face verbal assault in the manner contemplated by the Stanford provision will make room for more speech than it chills. The provision is clearly within the spirit, if not the letter, of existing first amendment doctrine.

The proposed Stanford regulation, and indeed regulations with considerably broader reach, can be justified as necessary to protect a captive audience from offensive or injurious speech. Courts have held that offensive speech may not be regulated in public forums such as streets and parks where a listener may avoid the speech by moving on or averting his eyes, but the regulation of otherwise protected speech has been permitted when the speech invades the privacy of the unwilling listener's home or when the unwilling listener cannot avoid the speech. Racist posters, flyers, and graffiti in dorms, classrooms, bathrooms, and other common living spaces would fall within the reasoning of these cases. Minority students should not be required to remain in their rooms to avoid racial assault. Minimally, they should find a safe haven in their dorms and other common rooms that are a part of their daily routine. I would argue that the university's responsibility for ensuring these students received an equal educational opportunity provides a compelling justification for regulations that ensure them safe passage in all common areas. A black, latino, Asian or Native American student should not have to risk being the target of racially assaulting speech every time she chooses to walk across campus. The regulation of vilifying speech that cannot be anticipated or avoided would not preclude announced speeches and rallies where minorities and their allies would have an opportunity to organize counter-demonstrations or avoid the speech altogether.

PRESSURE VALVES AND BLOODIED CHICKENS: PATERNALISTIC OBJECTIONS TO HATE SPEECH REGULATIONS

Richard Delgado and David H. Yun

Richard Delgado and David H. Yun are law professors, both of whom contribute regularly to law journals. Delgado's most recent books are The Rodrigo Chronicles: Conversations about America and Race *(1995) and* No Mercy: How Conservative Think Tanks and Foundations Changed America's Social Agenda *(1996).*

In this 1994 California Law Review *article, Delgado and Yun challenge four of the most common arguments against any restrictions on speech, including hateful racist speech. Calling these arguments "pressure valve," "reverse-enforcement," "best friend," and "talk back," they dismiss them all as paternalistic, offered in a spirit of "we know what's best for you."*

As you read, try to make connections between this reading and those by Mari J. Matsuda and Charles R. Lawrence III. Like Lawrence's "Newsreel," this reading anticipates some of the chief arguments made by those who oppose speech regulations. Most important, it shows how a careful argument can be constructed against widely held responsible views.

Because of the feasibility of drafting constitutional hate speech regulations, the debate over such rules has shifted to the policy arena.° Four arguments made by opponents of antiracism rules° are central to this debate:

(i)   Permitting racists to utter racist remarks and insults allows them to blow off steam harmlessly. As a result, minorities are safer than they would be under a regime of antiracism rules. We will refer to this as the "pressure valve" argument.

(ii) Antiracism rules will end up hurting minorities, because authorities will invariably apply the rules against them, rather than against members of the majority group. This we will call the "reverse-enforcement" argument.

(iii) Free speech has been minorities' best friend. Because free speech is a principal instrument of social reform, persons interested in achieving reform, such as minorities, would resist placing any fetters° on freedom of expression if they knew their self-interest. This we term the "best friend" objection.

° **policy arena:** That part of public life in which legislators and administrators try to develop public policy about civic problems like hate speech.   ° **antiracism rules:** Rules, like campus speech regulations, that would presumably reduce racism. Delgado and Yun identify the main reasons why people oppose such rules.   ° **fetters:** restraints or limits.

have a First Amendment, anything in the way of legal limitations can be done about such speech.

Prohibitions also turn censored material into "forbidden fruit" and the advocates of racism into martyrs. Whenever any communication—a book, essay, speech, rally, film, play, or work of art—is banned, some persons will suppose it contains a potent and important message that the censors fear, else why would they seek to suppress it? Thus, it arouses more interest than if it had been ignored. Curiosity, if nothing else, will lead some to try to find out for themselves what is being withheld from them.

The would-be communicators whose speech is prohibited also gain more publicity and, quite possibly, more sympathy than they could otherwise hope to achieve. The attempt to prohibit the neo-Nazi march in Skokie brought more attention to Frank Collin, their leader, and to his message, than he could ever have dreamed of achieving on his own. The electoral successes in France of National Front leader Jean-Marie Le Pen may well be due, in part, to the role of martyr he has played to the hilt as a result of the various legal actions brought against him under French law for "inciting racial hatred."

Legal limitations on hate speech are not only likely to be counterproductive, they are simply not the most effective way to deal with the problem. If there is any hope of changing the attitudes of the haters, it can only come, in the short run, from exposing them to more enlightened ways of thinking and, in the long run, through alleviating the causes of their insecurity. Supreme Court Justice Louis Brandeis, in a famous opinion written in 1927, captured the essence of the First Amendment's answer to hate speech when he said: "If there be time to expose through discussion the falsehood and fallacies, to avert the evil by the processes of education, the remedy to be applied is more speech, not enforced silence. Only an emergency can justify repression. Such must be the rule if authority is to be reconciled with freedom. Such, in my opinion, is the command of the Constitution."

■ ■ ■ **A WRITER'S NOTEBOOK** ■ ■ ■

Arguments for and against Regulating Speech on College Campuses

The following tasks are designed to help you think about the readings and identify and start to work up material you might use in your own essay. If you need help with tasks that require summarizing or evaluating an argument, see Appendix 1.

1. *Review your lists of reasons from the readings.* If you prepared lists of reasons as you read the various arguments in this section, compare your lists with those done by one or two classmates. The lists should help you make connections among the arguments in the readings, assess your own position in light of the various arguments, and plan an essay stating your own argument.

2. *Consider Mari J. Matsuda's argument.* Matsuda argues that colleges should ban hate speech in order to ensure that all students have *equal access* to learning and college activities and *equal participation* in college life. To be at all convincing,

she must demonstrate that at least some students lack such access and that they suffer because of it. First, look at the concrete examples she offers in paragraphs 5–8, 14, and 15 and list the kinds of students she has in mind. Then, skimming paragraphs 3, 4, and 9–12, list the main consequences of lack of equal access and equal participation. Finally, write a few sentences expressing your opinion about how successfully Matsuda demonstrates lack of access and participation and the harm it does.

3. *List reasons in Charles R. Lawrence III's argument.* From paragraph 6, list the two reasons Lawrence gives for why he believes that face-to-face insults must be prevented. Then from paragraphs 7, 8, and 11, list the three factors that make it difficult for students to respond to face-to-face insults. These two lists will give you the key parts of Lawrence's argument.

4. *Evaluate Richard Delgado and David H. Yun's argument.* These writers attempt to refute four arguments made by those who oppose any attempt to regulate speech on campus. After reading all four refutations, choose the one you find most convincing, whether you agree with it or not. Evaluate this argument, explaining how it is developed and whether you personally find it convincing.

5. *Summarize part of Timothy C. Shiell's argument.* So what is a university to do? Summarize how Shiell answers this question. Focus your summary on paragraphs 2–6.

6. *Respond to Paul McMasters's argument.* In paragraphs 1–2, look at his list of the problems he sees with college speech codes. Keeping in mind what you have read about in this chapter and your own experience with offensive speech in high school or college, find one problem in the list with which you agree or disagree. Then write several sentences exploring the sources of your agreement or disagreement.

7. *Read Susan Gellman's argument closely.* As an exercise in close reading that will almost certainly give you interesting material to use in an essay, make a list of what Gellman believes are the costs of ethnic intimidation laws to society as a whole. You will find this part of her argument in paragraphs 2–10. Notice the helpful cues Gellman provides to help readers follow her argument. Rely on Gellman's terms, but try to put her argument into your own phrases or sentences. For example, from paragraph 3:

> If legislators and judges restrict what people can say, people will begin to feel that their leaders don't trust them.

> The state puts itself in the position of deciding that only it, not the people, can decide which ideas are important to express.

8. *Evaluate Henry Louis Gates Jr.'s argument.* Since so many writers in this chapter refer uncritically to *Chaplinsky* and *Beauharnais*, it might seem surprising that Gates questions the relevance of these two cases to the hate speech debate. Review his argument in paragraphs 6–14. Then evaluate it, explaining how he develops it and whether you, as a participant in this debate, find it convincing. You may want to review the arguments in each of the two cases.

9. *List reasons in one part of Franklyn S. Haiman's argument.* At the beginning of paragraph 18, Haiman asserts that there are several unfortunate, unintended consequences that follow from banning hate speech. These consequences, he says, are reasons that banning hate speech is not only a bad idea but also a counterproductive one. List the consequences he mentions in paragraphs 18–22.

Now it is your turn. What is *your* position about whether or not speech should be regulated on college campuses? You should find all the material you need to write on this issue in this chapter—reports of speech incidents at various colleges, examples of campus speech regulations, key Supreme Court cases, and arguments for and against regulating campus speech. If you have been doing the work suggested in the writer's notebook sections, you already have completed a lot of writing on this issue. Now is the time to add your own experience, insight, and point of view to the debate.

This Writer's Guide will help you

- plan, draft, revise, edit, and proofread an essay taking a position on whether colleges should attempt to regulate student speech
- work with sources—to gather current information and to cite sources that you draw upon
- consider matters of style, trying out certain sentence patterns that are useful in writing that takes a position
- reflect on what you learned completing this assignment

PLANNING AND DRAFTING YOUR ESSAY

This section provides guidelines and examples to help you plan and draft a convincing essay about campus speech regulations. It will help you

- understand your readers and your writing situation
- select materials
- prepare a prospectus
- organize your essay
- devise a convincing argument
- cite sources

THE WRITING ASSIGNMENT   Write an essay in which you take a position on whether colleges should regulate or ban speech that may be perceived as offensive by individual students or groups of students. In your essay, you will need to help your readers understand the issue, show that you have considered various points of view, provide reasons for your position, and support your reasons by using material from the readings and, perhaps, your own personal experience.

Assume that you are writing your essay for a campus magazine and that it will be read by other college students who favor a position different from yours.

Understanding Your Readers

Assume that your readers know about as much as you knew about the controversial and practical aspects of regulating speech on college campuses before you read this chapter's readings. Your primary purpose is to convince your readers to hear you out and take your argument seriously. Some readers will agree with you; some will not. There will also be readers who will not know what they believe and may remain indifferent or undecided even after reading your argument. You can expect, however, that if you can engage them in thinking about the issue, some of your readers will want to discover what positions are possible. Your goal is to engage all these readers and show them that your argument is reasonable. One key to doing this is to show them that you have considered various positions and anticipated possible questions and objections.

If you yourself have had sexist or racist speech directed at you, you may be more inclined to support speech restrictions on college campuses. Conversely, readers who have never been verbally harassed may oppose speech regulations. To broaden your perspective on how other readers might feel, talk to some of your classmates to find out what they think having read the arguments in this chapter. Talking to classmates who disagree with you may also help you to counter opposing views in your own essay.

If you have never had hateful speech directed at you, it may be difficult to understand the feelings and concerns of those who have. Look carefully at the readings that speak for those who have been subjected to offensive speech. Talk to people who have had this experience.

Assume Authority.   Regardless of the position you take, assume that you are the expert and that you are writing to readers who can benefit from your knowledge. Your job is to tell them what the debate is all about, show them its significance, and invite them to consider your views. You may not be a constitutional scholar, but you have at hand a lot of information on this issue, and it is time for you to put it to use. Accept your authority. Enjoy it.

Selecting Materials

All the readings and writing tasks in this chapter contribute to an understanding of the campus speech issue. Now you can select from those resources materials to support your own position on the issue. The following activities will help you to do so.

List and Review Reasons.   If you prepared a list of reasons when you were reading the arguments, review your list to refresh your memory about the full range of arguments on the issue.

If you have not yet prepared such a list, look at the sections in this chapter containing Supreme Court decisions and arguments for and against regulating speech on campus. Choose several of these readings and list the main reasons the writers give for their positions.

This list will help you see connections among the various arguments. For example, both Matsuda and Lawrence argue that offensive speech must be banned, and they offer the reasons of its physical and psychological effects. You will see that some reasons advanced in one reading may be countered by reasons in another reading. Susan Gellman reasons, for instance, that it is impossible to write hate speech laws that can be easily interpreted and applied, whereas Lawrence insists such laws can be written if narrowed and crafted with care. Looking at a spectrum of reasons will help you decide on those that support your position and will alert you to those that do not—and that must be counterargued.

Commit Yourself to a Position.   What position do you take on banning offensive speech from U.S. college campuses? Choose the position that you find preferable, based on your own experience and on knowledge acquired from the readings. Do not worry if it is difficult for you to choose a position; it may mean that you will find it easier to represent other positions responsibly and to counterargue them effectively.

Identify Key Incidents.   Many campus speech incidents are reported in this chapter. See, for example, the readings by Ralph Frammolino, Michael deCourcy Hinds, Amy Harmon, Matsuda (paragraphs 5–8), Lawrence (paragraph 1), and Samuel Walker (paragraphs 2 and 6). In addition, consider any incidents you yourself have experienced or heard about. Review all of these incidents and decide which ones you find most compelling or illustrative. Which ones might be most useful in presenting the campus speech issue to your readers?

Identify Key Readings.   Which two or three readings may be especially helpful to you for supporting your position? Review these readings and any notebook entries you made on them.

Preparing a Prospectus

At this point, your instructor may want you to prepare a prospectus for your essay, to plot out some of its parts. Engineers, businesspeople, and other professionals write prospectuses for projects in order to win support and funding. In much the same way, a prospectus for an essay enables you to try out your argument for particular readers and to begin thinking seriously about how you will support it.

Here are some guidelines for drafting a two- or three-page prospectus.

1. *List incidents.* List at least three campus speech incidents you would use to present this issue concretely to your readers. Make a note of the source of each incident—your experience, class discussions, readings, whatever.

2. *State your position.* In a sentence or two, state the position you will take on the issue.

3. *List reasons.* List at least three reasons for taking your position seriously. Reasons explain *why* you take a position. You might start quite plainly: "I support/oppose regulating campus speech for the following reasons: _____."

4. *Identify one important reading.* Which single reading do you think will be the most important in providing support for your argument? Explain in two or three sentences why it will be so important.

5. *Anticipate readers' questions or objections.* List at least three questions, objections, or reservations you would expect from readers who oppose your position on this issue.

6. *Identify one reading that challenges your position.* Identify the one reading that poses the greatest challenge to your proposed argument. In two or three sentences, explain why you must argue against it convincingly.

7. *Try to support part of your argument.* Select one reason you listed in item 3 and write at least a page supporting it—arguing for it—with facts, examples, anecdotes, quotations from the readings, and any relevant personal experiences. Do not take time now to consider all the readings. Rely on your memory, notes, and perhaps a quick look at one key reading. Write quickly. Your purpose is simply to try out one part of your argument before you plan your entire essay. You may want to begin directly: "One reason I favor/oppose regulating campus speech is _____."

Organizing Your Essay

Readers generally expect the writer to identify the issue, take a position on it, and provide reasons for that position. They expect writers to support their reasons with quotes from authorities, examples, facts, statistics, analogies, or personal experiences. They also expect writers to consider likely questions and objections and to counterargue published opinions that differ from their own.

Many writers follow a simple two-part plan, first presenting the issue in an engaging, informative way, then arguing and counterarguing convincingly, offering reasons and support for their arguments.

To develop a detailed framework for your essay, you might expand this plan in the following way:

Presentation of the issue
–an engaging opening
–description of the issue
–explanation of the debate and its major positions
–definition of any terms that might be unfamiliar to readers

Argument and counterargument
–position statement (thesis)
–argument for the first reason and counterargument of any questions and objections
–argument for the second reason and counterargument
–argument for the third reason and counterargument
–etc.
–conclusion and reassertion of position

A plan of this sort can serve you well when you draft your essay. It will take some work—some parts may be accomplished in one paragraph, but others may require several paragraphs.

Presenting the Issue.   In addition to describing the issue to readers, you also need to help them see its larger social significance and its importance to them personally. You need to spark their interest and to provide adequate background for your argument.

WRITING AN ENGAGING OPENING.   Try to catch readers' attention and to get them to see the significance of the campus speech issue. You might try one of these approaches:

- Tell the story of one incident of offensive speech from the readings or from your personal experience or interviews.
- List briefly several offensive speech incidents (as Matsuda does in paragraphs 5–8; Lawrence in paragraph 1; Walker in paragraphs 2–6; and Cooper and MacDonald in the introduction to this chapter).
- Relate the incident that led to *Chaplinsky* or *Beauharnais*.
- Declare the issue to be a serious problem (as McMasters does in paragraphs 1–5; as Matsuda does in paragraph 2; as Lawrence does in paragraph 2; as Gates does in paragraphs 1–5; as Shiell does in paragraphs 1 and 9–10; and as Haiman does in paragraph 1).
- Quote someone from each side of the debate and then comment on the quotes so that readers see the important differences between the two.

However you choose to open your essay, keep in mind that you are writing for college students who are not experts on your subject.

DESCRIBING THE ISSUE AND THE DEBATE.   Readers need some information about the issue—its history, its special terms, its constitutional grounding, and an understanding of what people are arguing about and why. Here are several ways to provide this kind of information:

- Describe one of the court cases in this chapter.
- Summarize other recent relevant court cases. (See Walker.)
- Cite a representative reading on each position, summarizing the arguments and quoting memorable passages.
- Tell about one typical offensive speech incident or several different incidents to show the range (as do Frammolino, Harmon, and Lawrence, for example).
- Describe the issue in a general way (as Matsuda and Michael W. McConnell do).
- Contrast the two positions (as Gates does in paragraph 4).

Your own position will, of course, affect how you present the issue and the debate, and you may, in fact, want to use more than one of these options. Whatever approach you take, be careful to present the issue evenhandedly.

DEFINING TERMS. Defining terms is central to this issue. Readers of your essay may need to understand, for example, how *speech* is different from *action*, what *protected* by the First Amendment means, and the differences between *libel, defamation, political speech,* and *offensive speech.*

Take care to define any such terms and to use those terms consistently throughout your essay. *Offensive speech,* for example, may mean many different things. Thus, you would need to define it early in your essay so your readers know precisely what you are talking about.

Plotting Out Your Arguments and Counterarguments. As the heart of your essay, the argument section generally begins with a strong statement of your position, followed by reasons and support and interspersed with counterarguments acknowledging and responding to other positions. (While the next section, "Developing Your Argument and Counterargument," offers help with constructing a thesis, arguing, and counterarguing, the focus in this section is on illustrating options for placing and sequencing the argument and counterargument within the overall essay.)

There are several ways you can arrange an argument section, depending on how you want to sequence your reasons and integrate your counterarguments. Following are examples showing how some writers have done so.

SEQUENCING YOUR REASONS. Some writers begin with the reason readers are least likely to resist. Some open with a reason they can support with personal anecdotes. Others choose to begin with their most controversial reason. There is no set formula to follow, but consider how you can best lead your readers through your argument.

CONSIDERING YOUR COUNTERARGUMENTS. When you counterargue, you acknowledge other positions or questions your readers may have—and you respond to other well-defined positions.

There are basically three ways to integrate counterarguments into your argument. One approach is to counterargue the opposing position as you present each reason for your position. Put your counterarguments first or last, but do so consistently throughout. Examples of this approach can be seen in *Beauharnais,* in the opinions of Justice Frankfurter (paragraphs 2–3) and Justice Black (paragraphs 6–15); Lawrence (paragraphs 7–9); Delgado and Yun; McConnell (paragraph 4); and Gates (paragraphs 6–14 and 15–17).

A second alternative is to consider and fully counterargue the opposing position before you argue for your own position, perhaps even before you state your position. This option has two advantages. It gives you a chance to present the opposing view responsibly—conceding its best points and attempting to refute other points—and shows your readers that you are fair. It also gives readers more background on the issue and prepares them to see your own position as a more attractive or reasonable alternative. McMasters (paragraphs 1–5) and Haiman (paragraphs 8–23) both take this approach.

Or you can counterargue the opposing position toward the end of your essay *after* readers have seen your entire argument. Follow your counterargument by reasserting your position and summarizing your reasoning in your conclusion.

The option you choose depends on your particular understanding of the issue, your plan for supporting your position, and your assessment of your readers.

CLOSING EFFECTIVELY.   Closing may be easier than starting up, but it nevertheless requires imagination. Try to close your essay gracefully and memorably, perhaps even with a flourish. What are some of your options?

- Reassert your position, as Lawrence, McMasters, Gellman, Walker, and Shiell do.
- Summarize your argument, the strategy adopted by Richard Delgado and David H. Yun.
- Quote an authority to support your position, perhaps using a particularly telling quote. See, for example, how Black (in paragraph 15 of *Beauharnais*), McMasters, Gates, and Haiman each use this strategy effectively.
- Frame your argument by referring back to your opening, as Walker does.
- Speculate about what may happen if there is no resolution to the controversy, as McMasters does in paragraph 20 and Gates does in paragraph 20.
- Speculate briefly about actions that could be taken on your campus (or at other schools). Matsuda (paragraph 22) and McMasters (paragraphs 16–19, 21, and 22) take this approach.

You might decide to use one or more of these strategies for your conclusion — or something entirely different. Whatever strategy you adopt, your goal is to convince your readers to take your argument seriously. Since readers tend to remember best what they read last, take advantage of this opportunity to say something memorable.

Developing Your Argument and Counterargument

This section will help you construct a thesis, argue to support your position, and counterargue questions about your argument and well-defined positions that challenge your position.

Constructing a Thesis.   A *thesis* is a clear assertion of your position, in this case on the issue of college speech regulation. A strong thesis establishes some key terms that identify your subject and the reasons for your position. These key terms must be repeated throughout the essay, to help you stay focused on the reasons for your position and to help readers follow your argument. A thesis may also forecast the plan your argument will follow.

You need a tentative thesis in order to start organizing and drafting your essay. Keep in mind, however, that you may revise — or even replace — this thesis several times during the writing process.

Although a thesis and forecast can be delivered in one sentence, they usually require several sentences. Here is Joy Kihara's thesis from a successful essay.

> While very few will argue that it is morally right to
> harass individuals or groups because of their race, gender,
> or beliefs, experience has taught American colleges that it
> is very difficult to formulate speech regulations that are
> both constitutional and effective. I believe it has been a
> wasted effort and counterproductive. The establishment of
> speech regulations may hurt minorities, not protect them.
> Such regulations will never be accepted by the courts and
> will increase and not reduce prejudice.

After carefully presenting the issue and discussing the debate in the first part of her paper, Kihara states her position in this thesis. Notice how direct and assertive the thesis is: there can be no doubt about Kihara's position. After trying out several terms while drafting, she decided on a small set of key thesis terms, ones she repeats throughout the essay: *speech regulations, never be accepted by the courts,* and *increase and not reduce prejudice.* The last two are especially important because they identify the two reasons for her position. Their order here forecasts the order in which she argues for them.

The following thesis by Kathy Quinn appears after she has contrasted the arguments of Mari J. Matsuda and Henry Louis Gates Jr. Notice Quinn's straightforward listing of reasons, which also forecasts the essay's plan.

> Like Henry Louis Gates Jr., I oppose the adoption of rules
> that restrict what students can say to each other on
> college campuses. I believe that speech restrictions would
> hurt minorities and women, would be nearly impossible
> to enforce fairly, and would have several unintended
> effects. I can understand that speech restrictions seem
> irresistibly attractive to students who have been attacked
> verbally on campus, but I believe that even if the
> restrictions were constitutional, they should be opposed
> because they are a dangerous quick fix that those who
> support them most enthusiastically would come to regret.

Here the key terms are *speech restrictions, hurt minorities and women, nearly impossible to enforce fairly,* and *unintended effects.* As Quinn drafted and revised, she found that they held up as terms that identify exactly her reasons and argument and that there was ample evidence in the readings to support these reasons as stated. Notice her use of the word *nearly,* added when she realized that she could not argue that restrictions could never be enforced fairly on any college campus.

This next thesis is from an essay by Edward Hutchinson that supports speech restrictions.

> All colleges need to ban offensive speech. Though the
> arguments against restrictions can seem very convincing, I
> believe the evidence and the need for speech restrictions

```
are even more convincing. Some students come to college
with sexist and racist attitudes, and they need to learn
the harm those attitudes cause and to practice self-
control. Students from groups that have been discriminated
against need an opportunity to gain self-confidence.
Learning requires a willingness, even an eagerness, to
speak. Rules are necessary to ensure fairness in a
voluntary community like a college. Finally, I believe
it is possible to write speech restrictions that are
constitutional.
```

Hutchinson begins by asserting his position and acknowledging that there is a good argument to be made on both sides. He then lists five reasons why he supports speech restrictions, in each case introducing key thesis terms that he repeats throughout the essay.

EXAMPLES FROM THE READINGS. For further examples of thesis statements, examine the following readings: Matsuda (paragraph 2); Lawrence (paragraph 3); Delgado and Yun (paragraph 2); McConnell (paragraph 2); McMasters (paragraphs 6–7); Gellman (paragraph 1; notice her careful forecast of the sequence of her argument); Shiell (paragraph 6); Haiman (paragraph 4; notice also his restatement of his thesis in paragraphs 6 and 23).

Arguing. At the core of any essay that takes a position is an argument. To argue is to give reasons for a position and to support your reasons—to argue for them—with relevant examples, statistics, quotations from authorities, anecdotes, observations, analogies, and so on. This paragraph from Edward Hutchinson's essay illustrates effective support.

```
Self-control and self-confidence create a climate where
learning is possible, but students cannot learn effectively
unless they feel free to speak up. Professor Charles
Lawrence argues in a 1990 Duke Law Journal article: "If the
purpose of the first amendment is to foster the greatest
amount of speech, then racial insults disserve that
purpose." Lawrence believes that hateful speech does not
deserve first amendment protection because its purpose "is
not to discover truth or initiate dialogue but to injure
the victim." Students who are harassed and threatened
because of who they are find that they are not able to
speak up because they are too frightened and angry,
feelings that make thoughtful speech impossible. If
students are worried about offensive speech from other
students or resentful from having experienced it, they are
not likely to be eager speakers in class. They are also
less likely to engage in friendly conversations with
students from groups other than their own. The overall
effect is that students from different groups learn less
about one another.
```

This paragraph supports one of the reasons for Hutchinson's position that campus speech regulations are justified: "students cannot learn effectively unless they feel free to speak up." To support this reason, Hutchinson relies mainly on ideas in the Lawrence reading, quoting Lawrence and paraphrasing information from that reading. In the last three sentences, he offers his own ideas about how fear and anxiety might reduce speech and learning both in and out of the classroom.

In the next example, Heather Flowe argues that speech regulations cannot be justified, giving the reason that such regulations cannot protect students from "codified racist speech," which is subtly indirect.

> Speech regulations would also fail to protect individual students or groups of students from the kind of hateful speech likely to do the most harm: codified racist speech. This type of speech is not blatant name calling--shouted epithets, slurs, or invective. Rather, its hateful message is disguised by sophisticated or even eloquent words and rhetoric. Henry Louis Gates Jr., a specialist in African American studies at Harvard University, points out: "In American society today, the real power commanded by racism is likely to vary inversely with the vulgarity with which it is expressed.[...] The circles of power have long since switched to a vocabulary of indirection" (88-89). Gates gives this example of coded and direct hateful campus speech:
>
>> (A) LeVon, if you find yourself struggling in your classes here, you should realize it isn't your fault. It's simply that you're the beneficiary of a disruptive policy of affirmative action that places underqualified, underprepared and often undertalented black students in demanding educational environments like this one.[...] The truth is, you probably don't belong here, and your college experience will be a long downhill slide.
>>
>> (B) Out of my face, jungle bunny. (188)
>
> Gates asks his readers to consider which of the statements is more likely to be more wounding and alienating to a student who might hear them. Franklyn S. Haiman, a retired professor of communication studies at Northwestern University, reaches the same conclusion as Gates. Haiman writes: "coded messages of group hatred that steer wide of what could be outlawed by any conceivable ban on hate speech are potentially far more harmful to disadvantaged groups than anything a ranting and raving racist might say." Haiman adds: "Yet no one would suggest that, so long as we have a First Amendment, anything in the way of legal limitations can be done about such speech" (194-95). Because the speech most harmful to students cannot ever be captured in a narrowly written set of speech restrictions, we might as well give up on trying to write such restrictions.

Flowe asserts her reason in her first sentence, then relies on well-chosen quotes from two of the readings to support the reason.

EXAMPLES FROM THE READINGS. In the following readings, you can see further examples of the kinds of support Hutchinson and Flowe rely on and other kinds of support as well:

analogy: Gellman (paragraph 17) and Delgado and Yun (paragraph 6)

anecdotes: Lawrence (paragraphs 10–11)

contrast: Haiman (paragraphs 4–6)

effects: Lawrence (paragraphs 6–8) and Shiell (paragraphs 2–3)

examples: Gellman (paragraph 20), Matsuda (paragraphs 5–11), Delgado and Yun (paragraphs 13 and 18), Lawrence (paragraph 12), Shiell (paragraphs 4, 6, and 7), and Haiman (paragraphs 7, 14, 16, and 19–20)

facts: Delgado and Yun (paragraphs 9–10 and 12)

quotations from authorities: McMasters (paragraphs 7, 14, and 20) and Shiell (paragraphs 5 and 8)

Counterarguing. In any argument taking a position on an issue, you need to anticipate readers' objections to and questions about your argument. You also need to acknowledge well-defined opposing views like those in this chapter's readings. Sometimes you may *concede* what you can accept in opposing views, but often you will *refute* what you cannot accept. The following selection from Kathy Quinn's essay opposing speech codes is a good illustration of counterargument. Here Quinn attempts to refute Matsuda's arguments about the psychological harm of hateful speech:

> Matsuda seems to assume that all minority students are
> alike and that they will suffer the same degree of harm if
> they hear racist speech on campus. Without qualification,
> she says they are all "at risk." She also seems to assume
> that all campuses are identical in the harm they inflict
> on minorities. I believe that most minority students would
> reject this way of thinking about the problem and would
> recognize that Matsuda stereotypes minority students when
> she says that they are all helpless and have no resources
> to protect themselves from hate speech. I do believe that
> racist speech can cause pain, but it seems to me that the
> amount of pain depends greatly on the victim's background
> and experience and on the campus situation in which such
> speech occurs. As students experience success at college,
> their self-esteem grows and they become less vulnerable to
> being hurt by racist speech. On most campuses minority
> students are also well organized, which offers some
> protection from hateful speech directed at them as a
> group. The African American and Latino students I know
> personally all belong to student associations. They are

> very supportive of each other and seem very united. I
> think they want an equal chance to do well in college, not
> special protections. I believe that most minority students
> would agree with Susan Gellman's argument in a recent UCLA
> Law Review article that "laws designed to protect people
> from others' hatred are intended benevolently, but carry
> an implicit patronizing and paternalistic message: these
> people are incapable of holding their own without special
> protection."

Although Quinn might have conceded that she finds some value in Matsuda's ideas, she instead attempts to refute her ideas, arguing that her assumptions about minority students are wrong. Notice that she quotes Matsuda directly to show what she finds wrong. When you counterargue opposing views from the readings, it is very important that you represent those views accurately.

You must also present reasons and support for your concessions or refutations in order to convince readers to take your counterargument seriously. Quinn relies on three strategies—asserting her own ideas, reporting personal observations, and quoting an authority (Gellman)—in her refutation of Matsuda.

EXAMPLES FROM THE READINGS. To learn more about how to handle opposing views, look closely at these readings:

Beauharnais, Justice Douglas: paragraphs 17–18 (concession) and 19–22 (refutation)

Gates: paragraphs 14 and 16–17 (refutation), and 25–26 (concession)

Delgado and Yun: refutation throughout

SENTENCES FOR TAKING A POSITION

Certain kinds of sentences are important or even essential in writing that takes a position. Two kinds of sentences are particularly important: (1) sentences that keep readers on track, enabling them to follow the sequence of your argument and to see readily the relationships among its parts; and (2) sentences that mark explicitly their logical relationships to other sentences by using conjunctive adverbs.

You may want to review the material in this section now as a preview of some special kinds of thinking and writing you will be engaged in as you draft and revise your essay. You will find the definitions and examples here most helpful, however, as you revise your essay. At that time, you will want to examine closely the sentence cues you have given readers to keep them on track and the ways you have signaled logical relationships among sentences.

Sentences That Keep Readers on Track

Examples from the readings illustrate sentence cues that keep readers on track within and between paragraphs.

Within Paragraphs.   Within every paragraph, each sentence should be linked logically to the ones before and after it. By using transitional words and phrases, you can make these logical relationships clear, creating what is often called *coherence*. For example, Susan Gellman does this effectively in paragraph 3 of her essay, first promising several reasons and then providing transitional cues (set here in italics) to guide the reader through each one:

> This is troubling for several reasons. *First,* there is the obvious mistrust [. . .]. *Second,* it places the state in the position [. . .]. *Finally,* and perhaps most sobering, it assumes that the government [. . .] .

Paul McMasters uses different kinds of transitional cues in paragraph 4 of his essay:

> the defining process begins to break down *when* the discussion turns [. . .]. *Further* problems develop as the process moves [. . .]. *Finally,* the drafters have to accommodate [. . .] .

Cues are not always as obvious as the ones in these two examples. If you need to impose coherence on a jumbled part of your argument or to signal unmistakably the relations among parts of an argument, however, you may want to use explicit transitional cues.

Between Paragraphs.   A convincing, readable argument follows a logical sequence. To help readers follow the sequence, it is important to use strong transitional cues as you move from one paragraph to another. Such cues nearly always appear at the beginning or end of paragraphs, often as transition sentences. The following examples from the readings illustrate four different kinds of sentence cues.

Susan Gellman's essay, in the section "Costs to Society as a Whole," has a sequence of paragraph-opening cues. Reread this section, beginning with paragraph 2, and notice how the transitions at the outset of these paragraphs mark the stages of the argument:

> "The underlying values of First Amendment jurisprudence [. . .]" (paragraph 2)
>
> "*Beginning with* the most basic of values [. . .]" (paragraph 3)
>
> "*Another* generally applicable [. . .] concern [. . .]". (paragraph 4)
>
> "*Similarly,* there is the 'who decides?' problem [. . .]" (paragraph 5)
>
> "*There is also* a cost to society [. . .]" (paragraph 7)
>
> "*Moreover,* a society's ability to tolerate dissent [. . .]" (paragraph 8)
>
> "*A final set* of costs to society [. . .]" (paragraph 10)

Writers use numerous other words and phrases to cue the stages of an argument. For example, they might begin a new paragraph with *above all, on the other hand, interestingly enough,* or *the major objection.* McMasters takes yet another approach when he poses a rhetorical question (paragraph 6) to mark a turning point in his argument: "So, what have we gained if we succeed in dampening public discourse?"

In addition, you might want to consider using format cues to further emphasize the sections of your argument. Notice how Gellman, for instance, uses subheadings. Consider also your word-processing program's capabilities for bold and various type sizes and styles.

Conjunctive Adverbs for Indicating Logical Relationships

One way to show logical relationships between clauses and sentences is to use coordinating conjunctions like *and, but,* or *so;* subordinating conjunctions like *while, because,* and *although;* and conjunctive adverbs like *however, nevertheless,* and *therefore.*

Conjunctive adverbs are especially important in essays that take positions on issues. The following list includes a number of common conjunctive adverbs and indicates how they might be used. All examples come from readings in this chapter.

> To expand or add: *moreover, further, furthermore, in addition, at the same time, by the same token, that is*
>
> To exemplify: *for example, as an example, thus, for instance*
>
> To qualify: *however*
>
> To show cause or effect: *therefore, consequently, as a result, in effect*
>
> To show concession: *nevertheless*
>
> To show comparison: *similarly*
>
> To show contrast: *instead, on the contrary, rather, by contrast, in opposition, still*
>
> To show emphasis: *indeed, again*

Once you have decided to use a particular conjunctive adverb, how do you decide where to place it? You can usually put conjunctive adverbs at the beginning of a sentence or clause, but sometimes it is better to put them inside. The decision about where to place a conjunctive adverb depends on what you want to emphasize. If you want to emphasize the first part of the sentence, you would probably place the adverb later in the sentence, after the idea you wish to stress, as in these examples from the readings:

> In the case of an ethnically specific intimidation crime, however, the suggestion is that members of the protected group are weaker than everyone else. (paragraph 13)
>
> — SUSAN GELLMAN
> "Sticks and Stones Can Put You in Jail, But Can Words Increase Your Sentence?"

The defamation paradigm, by contrast, compares racist speech to libel [. . .] (paragraph 11)

—HENRY LOUIS GATES JR.
"Let Them Talk"

CITING SOURCES

As you present the issue and develop the argument in your essay, you will frequently quote, paraphrase, or summarize this chapter's readings, and perhaps material from other sources as well. When you use original ideas in this way, you must cite them. In other words, you must identify their sources either informally or formally.

Informal Citation

Informal citation allows you to identify all of your sources within the text of your essay. You mention the author, publication, and perhaps the date right in your own sentences. In some instances, you may also want to include a brief description of the writer to establish his or her authority. When using informal citation, you do not need to identify sources in footnotes or in a works-cited list at the end of your essay.

Many readings, especially those published in newspapers or magazines, rely on informal citation. To see how writers use this citation style in a graceful way, look at these examples from the readings:

Nat Hentoff, in the May 4 issue of the *Village Voice,* accused Mr. Hackney of engaging in "patronizing paternalism."

—MICHAEL DECOURCY HINDS
"A Campus Case: Speech or Harassment?"

"Students today believe they live in a bubble," said Alan Preston, Phi Kappa Sigma's executive vice president. "We're trying to send a clear message to other chapters that you have to be aware that you're in the real world. The real world isn't [just] after graduation."

—RALPH FRAMMOLINO
"Suit Forces U.C. Riverside to Rescind
Fraternity Penalty"

In a speech earlier this year at the Rochester Institute of Technology, John Siegenthaler, chair of the First Amendment Center, put it this way: "For if learning cannot defeat ignorance in the academic community, where debate and Socratic dialogue and love of learning have always been a way of life, there is no hope at all that reason can prevail in the executive suite, on the assembly line, in the church pews, in the military, or in the newsrooms of the nation. If there is no hope for the academy but suppression of thought and speech, there is no hope."

—PAUL MCMASTERS
"Free Speech versus Civil Disobedience"

The doctrine of "fighting words" was promulgated by the Supreme Court in *Chaplinsky* v. *New Hampshire* (1942), in which the Court held that the Constitution did not protect "insulting or 'fighting' words—those that by their very utterance inflict injury or tend to incite an immediate breach of the peace."

—HENRY LOUIS GATES JR.
"Let Them Talk"

Formal Citation

When you use formal citation, you follow a specific style used by a particular academic or professional group. Biologists, for instance, follow a specific style when they write for their scientific journals. Appendix 2 of this book outlines two of these styles: the Modern Language Association (MLA), which is favored by scholars in English and the humanities, and the American Psychological Association (APA) style, which is favored by social scientists. Ask your instructor which you should follow.

If all of your sources are from readings in this book, you should cite the sources as works in an anthology. There are two parts to citing a source: (1) a very brief citation within your essay, called an in-text citation; and (2) a full citation of the source in a list of works cited at the end of your essay. Here is an example of in-text citation done MLA-style in a student essay. The student is quoting from the reading in this chapter by Henry Louis Gates Jr.:

```
Gates asserts that "there are costs also to curtailing
speech, often unpredictable ones" (188).
```

The student writer identifies Gates as the source of the quotation and cites the page number in *Writing the World* from which the quotation is taken.

For every in-text citation, there has to be a corresponding item in the *list of works cited* at the end of the essay. For the in-text citation in the previous paragraph, the student enters this item in the list of works cited:

```
Gates, Henry Louis, Jr. "Let Them Talk." Writing the
    World. Eds. Charles R. Cooper and Susan Peck
    MacDonald. Boston: Bedford/St. Martin's, 2000.
    182-89.
```

You can find additional examples of this type of entry in Appendix 2 under "A Work in an Anthology" in the "Books" section of the MLA guidelines and "A Work in an Edited Collection" in the "Books" section of the APA guidelines. Appendix 2 also offers help with citing other kinds of sources.

Note: You may want to use information in your essay from this chapter's introductions or reading headnotes. If you do so, you need not document facts about authors, titles of readings, or other information likely to be familiar to readers who have been following the debate about college speech regulations. You should, however, document any explanatory or interpretive materials that you paraphrase or quote. To document such material, follow the MLA or APA models given in Appendix 2.

EVALUATING AND REVISING

The following guidelines for revising will help you evaluate your own draft and provide useful advice to other students about theirs. As you read a draft, try to identify what has been done well and to come up with specific ways to improve the presentation of the issue and the argument. As you begin the revision process, focus on the big issues; save spelling and grammar for later.

Whether revising your own draft or helping classmates with theirs, you may need to refer to specific readings, so have them handy as you work. If you prepared a reading-by-reading list of the main reasons for supporting or opposing campus speech regulations, this list should prove helpful now as you analyze a draft about this issue.

If you are reading someone else's draft, it is a good idea to write out your comments on a separate sheet of paper, following the headings used in this section.

Read to Get a General Impression

Even if you are reading your own draft, read it straight through without marking on it, as if you are encountering the essay for the first time in a magazine for college students. Then write three or four sentences summarizing your first impression. What aspect of the essay seems most successful? What is most interesting or surprising? What one major improvement would make the argument more convincing?

Read to Analyze the Draft More Closely

Next, number the paragraphs and mark the point at which the essay divides into two major parts: the presentation of the campus speech issue and the argument for a position on the issue. Reread the draft, keeping in mind that the intended readers may not be very knowledgeable about the campus speech debate. Ask yourself, What do such readers need to know? Write down what is good about the draft as well as specific ideas for revision.

The Opening. What strategy is used to open the essay? How does it draw readers in? Will it engage readers who are not already thinking about this issue? What seems effective about the opening? Does anything need clarifying? Suggest at least one alternative opening.

The Explanation of the Issue. Consider how well the essay explains the campus speech issue. Will readers understand what the debate is about? Have unfamiliar terms been defined? Do you think readers need more — or less — information? If less, what specific material should be cut? If more, what facts, examples, or anecdotes should be added? *What specific readings might serve as possible sources of new material?*

Now look at the opening and the explanation of the issue together. Is the reader likely to continue reading the essay? Has the importance and the significance of the issue been established? How might the essay get off to a stronger start?

The Position.   Does the draft have a clear thesis, stating the writer's position on the issue? Underline the sentences in which the thesis is stated. Circle the thesis key terms. (Key terms could include some of the following: *speech, offensive speech, regulate, restrict, ban, support, oppose, campus, First Amendment, free speech, individual rights, community values, civility, racism, sexism, homophobia, women, ethnic minorities, risk, constitutional, unconstitutional,* or other terms relevant to this issue.) Are all the terms understandable to a reader who is learning about this issue for the first time? If not, are they defined clearly?

Which key terms are carried throughout the essay? Do they provide coherence? Are there any key terms in the thesis that then disappear from the rest of the essay? Might other terms work better for the argument the writer wants to make? What other key terms might be useful?

Does the thesis forecast the steps in the argument, giving the main reasons for the position? If not, or if the forecast seems unclear in any way, what specifically should be done to revise it?

The Reasons and Support.   Find the main reasons that are given to support the position and number them sequentially in the margin. If you cannot do so easily, write down why you think the reasons are unclear.

Identify each reason in a brief phrase. Are there sufficient relevant examples, quotations from experts, facts, anecdotes, and so forth to support each reason? Is more support needed?

What seems especially convincing? Should any reason be dropped from the argument because it is neither relevant nor strongly argued? Can you see other reasons that might strengthen the argument?

The Counterargument.   Reread the draft and note in the margin where each counterargument occurs. Remember that counterarguments may be woven throughout or may be fully developed in one or two places.

Does the draft answer the questions readers may have — and address probable objections? Does it respond to other positions? Sometimes, writers may merely acknowledge objections or other positions, but nearly always they concede or at least attempt to refute them.

How effectively does the draft answer possible questions and objections? If any concessions or refutations are less than convincing, how might they be strengthened? Are there any other questions or objections that need to be considered?

Does the draft fairly and accurately represent the other position(s)? If not, what specifically needs to be added or revised? Does the essay concede or refute such positions? Does it do so gracefully and convincingly? If not, how could the concessions or refutations be made more effective?

The Cues to Keep Readers on Track.   Is it clear where the major parts of the essay—presentation, argument, counterargument—begin and end? Is the argument easy to follow? If not, point out the breaks or gaps. Note any sections that do not clearly fit, which leave you wondering, "Why am I reading this?" Look also for any gaps in the forward movement of the argument.

Are key terms in the thesis used throughout the essay? Identify the key terms of the position statement and then underline each wherever it appears in the essay. Note any paragraphs or pages devoid of key terms.

Look for places where transition sentences may be needed to keep readers on track. Do paragraph-opening sentences lead the reader unmistakably from one section of the essay to the next or from one step in the argument to the next? Is there one thesis key term in each paragraph-opening sentence? If not, the cues may be too weak to carry readers smoothly forward.

The Closing.   Does the essay close in a graceful and memorable way? Are thesis key terms mentioned? What closing strategy is used—summarizing the argument, quoting an authority, framing, or some other? How might the closing be made more effective?

EDITING AND PROOFREADING

As you revise, you should be concerned primarily with your presentation of the issue and your argument. Then comes the time to edit, when you should begin clarifying your sentences and tightening the connections among them. In particular, you will need to check to see that the logical relationships among sentences are clear and that there are adequate cues to keep readers on track through your argument.

Examine the connections between all of your sentences. If you sense misdirection or a gap that would break a reader's momentum, try reorganizing one sentence or writing new material. Check to see whether you shift terms unnecessarily. Look for sentences that might be combined to better show relationships among ideas. Look as well for long or garbled sentences that might be broken up into two or three sentences.

As you work on your sentences, look for errors in spelling, capitalization, punctuation, usage, and grammar, consulting a writer's handbook for information about correcting any you find. Ask a friend or a classmate to read over your draft to help you spot errors.

Before you hand in your final revised essay, proofread it carefully and run it through a spellchecker, trying to make it error free.

REFLECTING ON WHAT YOU HAVE LEARNED

Once you complete this chapter's reading and writing tasks, it is a good idea to take time to think about what you have accomplished and learned. Doing so will help you consolidate your new knowledge and remember it longer.

As you worked your way through the chapter, you were actually engaged in two closely related types of learning: becoming informed about a constitutional issue and taking a position on it yourself. Integrating these two kinds of learning, then, has been your major achievement. Using the following questions as starting points, write a page or so reflecting on this accomplishment.

- What was the most difficult part of understanding the debate over regulating speech on college campuses? What was the most surprising?
- How have your views about regulating offensive speech on college campuses been confirmed or changed? What questions do you still have about this issue?
- What was most difficult for you in planning your essay? When you began drafting, what was your biggest surprise? Think of the most important revision you made in your completed draft. How did you decide to make this change?
- What advice would you give to writers who are just starting an assignment in which they need to take a position on an issue?
- What aspect of your essay seems most effective? How would you revise your essay further if you had more time to work on it?

GATHERING ADDITIONAL INFORMATION

To supplement the readings in this chapter, you may want to do further research about the campus speech issue. For example, you might want to read about other campus speech incidents, review recent arguments for and against speech regulations, read more of the *Chaplinsky* or *Beauharnais* cases, or look up other court decisions on freedom of speech. Following are some suggestions that should help you find other sources on this issue.

Supreme Court Cases

To locate Supreme Court cases about freedom of speech, look at the *Guide to American Law*. In this guide, cases and related materials are arranged by topic in an alphabetical index. In the index, look up "freedom of speech," "hate speech," and "hate crimes." If you find any articles or other resources that look promising to you, your college library will very likely have them or be able to obtain them through interlibrary loan.

Another excellent source is the LEXUS/NEXUS database, which may also be available in your college library. There you can find the full text of Supreme Court cases.

On the Internet, you can gain access to cases and information about the Supreme Court by visiting the Federal Web Locator, a Web page that provides a "quick jump" to the federal judicial branch, which leads you to the Supreme Court's own Web server. The Federal Web Locator is at <http://www.law.vill.edu/

Fed-Agency/fedwebloc.html>. You might also try the Legal Information Institute and Hermes, a Web site that offers Supreme Court opinions issued since May 1990. You can gain access to this site at <http://www.supct.law.cornell.edu/supct>.

Recent Speech Incidents

You will most likely find out about recent speech incidents in newspapers and magazines. Using the Library of Congress Subject Heading (LCSH) "freedom of speech," you might begin by examining any newspaper and magazine indexes your library offers. Check also the *Readers' Guide to Periodical Literature,* which indexes about 200 popular periodicals, and its cousin *Access: The Supplementary Index,* which indexes some magazines not covered by the *Readers' Guide.*

Other indexes may prove more useful, however. *InfoTrac* on CD-ROM covers well over 1,000 magazines and newspapers, offering abstracts of some entries. Look at its Magazine Index and National Newspaper Index. An advantage of *InfoTrac* is that you can narrow your search by using two subject headings. For example, you could combine the subject headings "freedom of speech" and "universities and colleges." Another possibility is the *Alternative Press Index,* which indexes alternative and radical publications.

Finally, you may want to search the CD-ROM *Newsbank,* which provides full-text articles from 500 U.S. newspapers. Ask your librarian about other magazine and newspaper indexes that may be available.

Position Statements on Speech Regulations

In addition to magazine and newspaper indexes, look for position statements in *InfoTrac's Academic Index,* the *Social Sciences Index,* and the *Index to Legal Periodicals.* Ask your librarian to suggest other academic indexes as well. As you begin your search in these indexes, try the heading "freedom of speech." Another index to consider is *Editorials on File,* which reprints editorials arranged by subject from 150 U.S. and Canadian newspapers.

For books, look under "freedom of speech" in your library's card or online catalog. Although very few of the books are concerned solely with speech on college campuses, you may find some with a chapter on campus speech, or you may discover useful references in a book's list of works cited. See also the list of further readings in the section that follows.

The following Web sites offer current news and debates about regulating or banning speech on campus:

The Center for Individual Rights: <http://www.townhall.com/cir>

The Justice on Campus Project: <http://joc.mit.edu/~joc/index>

American Communication Association Academic Freedom Page: <http://www.uark.edu/comminfo/www/campus.speech>

FURTHER READINGS ON REGULATING CAMPUS SPEECH

Abel, Richard L. *Speaking Respect, Respecting Speech.* Chicago: U of Chicago P, 1998.

Delgado, Richard, and Jean Stefancic. *Must We Defend Nazis? Hate Speech, Pornography, and the First Amendment.* New York: New York UP, 1997.

Gates, Henry Louis, Jr., Anthony P. Griffin, Donald E. Lively, Robert C. Post, William B. Rubenstein, and Nadine Strossen. *Speaking of Race, Speaking of Sex: Hate Speech, Civil Rights, and Civil Liberties.* New York: New York UP, 1994.

Greenawalt, Kent. *Fighting Words: Individuals, Communities, and Liberties of Speech.* Princeton: Princeton UP, 1995.

Heumann, Milton, and Thomas W. Church, eds. *Hate Speech on Campus: Cases, Case Studies, and Commentary.* Boston: Northeastern UP, 1997.

Holzer, Henry Mark, ed. *Speaking Freely: The Case against Speech Codes.* Studio City: Second Thoughts, 1994.

Jacobs, James B., and Kimberly Potter. *Hate Crimes: Criminal Law and Identity Politics.* New York: Oxford UP, 1998.

Marcus, Laurence R. *Fighting Words: The Politics of Hateful Speech.* Westport: Praeger, 1996.

Matsuda, Mari J., Charles R. Lawrence III, Richard Delgado, and Kimberle Williams Crenshaw, eds. *Words That Wound: Critical Race Theory, Assaultive Speech, and the First Amendment.* Boulder: Westview, 1993.

Smolla, Rodney A. *Free Speech in an Open Society.* New York: Knopf, 1992. (Chapter 6).

Sunstein, Cass R. *Democracy and the Problem of Free Speech.* New York: Free Press, 1993. (Chapter 6).

Wolfson, Nicholas. *Hate Speech, Sex Speech, Free Speech.* Westport: Praeger, 1997.

ADDITIONAL WRITING PROJECTS

Here are some additional writing projects on the issue of regulating campus speech that make use of the readings and ideas in this chapter.

Personal Experience Essay

Tell the story of your own experience with offensive speech in high school or college. Describe one incident or several related incidents. If parts of this experience are painful or embarrassing, focus only on those you feel comfortable sharing with others.

Purpose and Readers.   Your purpose is to help your classmates see clearly what happened and understand what the experience was like for you. Try to show your readers that you are observant and thoughtful. Help them understand why the experience continues to be significant for you personally.

Resources to Draw On.   Your most important resource will be your memory. A good way to jog your memory is to make notes: List the other people who were present, if any. Jot down details of the setting or scene. Try to recall the exact language or symbols. Outline what happened chronologically—what happened first, next, and so on. Write down what you did after the incident:

whom you talked to, what actions you took, and what other people did. Also note your feelings at the time of the experience, soon after it occurred, and now. Models of this kind of personal experience essay can be found in Chapter 4 in the readings by Luis J. Rodriguez, Nathan McCall, and Rita Williams.

Tips for Writing a Successful Personal Experience Essay. One way to begin is by presenting the context for the incident: what led up to it, whether you were expecting it or were completely surprised, or whether similar incidents had previously occurred on your campus. As you tell your story, try to use vivid descriptions and strong verbs to explain who was there, what was said, what you did, how people were acting, and what you felt at the time. Also try to re-create any conversations that were central to what happened. Unlike other essays, in which a brief anecdote might support a very small part of your argument, this essay consists primarily of personal experience. Consequently, it should be richly detailed and offer readers a memorable example of offensive speech. Finally, reflect on this experience from your present perspective. How does it look to you now? How has it influenced your feelings or beliefs? How has it changed your behavior?

Attach to your essay a page or so of explanation, showing your instructor the connections, as you see them, between the personal experience in your essay and what you have learned from the readings in this chapter.

Policy Proposal

Write a proposal to solve the problem of offensive speech on your campus by instituting regulations and penalties for violating them.

Purpose and Readers. Your purpose is to convince students, faculty, and administrators that speech regulations are necessary and that your proposal will be effective. Another aspect of your purpose is to convince readers that your proposed regulations stand a good chance of winning court approval, should a student who has been punished for violating the regulations decide to challenge them in court.

Resources to Draw On. Your success with this assignment may depend not only on your own understanding of the campus speech issue but also on your willingness to interview people on campus. You might want to talk to several students and perhaps to some teachers, trying out your ideas on them and seeking their help in developing your proposal. Talking to such potential readers should help you strengthen your argument and anticipate opposition to it. This chapter's readings should help you to define the problem and to provide considerable support for your proposed regulations. Note especially the readings by Walker, Matsuda, Lawrence, and Shiell and the sample campus speech regulations.

Tips for Writing a Successful Proposal. You might begin by defining offensive speech and arguing that constitutional regulations can and should be written. Then describe the set of regulations you are proposing for your campus. You need not include every detail, but at least outline the major points of your proposal, the order in which the stages of the proposal might be implemented, and who will be involved in administering the speech regulations. You may want to start with one of the regulations discussed in the readings and then revise or expand it. If possible, contrast your proposed regulations with the ones that now exist on your own campus. Throughout your proposal, try to argue energetically for the timeliness, practicality, and wisdom of your proposal. Be sure, as well, to deal with readers' likely objections and questions.

An alternative to this proposal *for* regulations and penalties would be a proposal to *avoid* regulations and penalties (or to eliminate them if your campus has already instituted them) and instead to devise a campuswide program to reduce offensive speech. The preceding guidelines would apply to this kind of proposal as well.

Report on an Issue

Instead of actually taking a position, write a balanced, comprehensive report about the debate on the issue of regulating campus speech.

Purpose and Readers.   Your purpose is twofold: to convince your readers that the issue is worth learning about and to inform them about the current debate over regulating or banning offensive speech on college campuses. Try to be impartial and to avoid letting readers know your own position on the issue. At first, reporting on an issue might seem easier than taking a position on an issue, but reporting is actually quite challenging because you need to sort through and organize the various arguments so that you can help readers make sense of the debate. Assume that your report will be published in a magazine for college students, and that most readers will not be very knowledgeable about the issue. (See "Understanding Your Readers," page 198.)

Resources to Draw On.   Your main resource is the readings in this chapter, particularly the readings that reveal the various positions in the debate. The articles by Matsuda, Lawrence, Delgado and Yun, and Shiell favor some form of speech regulation, whereas those by McMasters, Gellman, Gates, and Haiman oppose it. If you have time, you could research additional views. (See "Gathering Additional Information," page 216.)

Tips for Writing a Successful Report.   When you report on an issue, you must first understand it very well yourself. You might begin by describing the issue, identifying the main positions, and defining some important terms. Readers also need you to explain the social significance of the issue and to show them how it could be important to them personally. In developing a report of this kind, it is crucial to find a way to categorize the arguments. You might first sort through all the arguments, looking for points of agreement and disagreement. Then you could select the most informative or revealing agreements or disagreements. Organize your report around these categories, perhaps using headings to announce each one. Develop each category by relying on information from the readings. You might want to quote selectively from the readings, letting the best spokespersons state each position. (The Writer's Guide in Chapter 2 may be helpful to you in planning and organizing your essay. Appendix 1 provides guidelines for summarizing information.)

Rhetorical Analysis of a Reading

Select one reading from "Position Statements on Speech Regulation" to analyze. Write an essay in which you describe how this reading works as an argument and evaluate how effective it is for its intended readers.

Purpose and Readers.   Your purpose is twofold: to help readers understand how the argument is organized and to explain what makes the argument convincing or unconvincing. Your readers will be your classmates, who have been discussing the readings and exploring the campus speech debate with you. Because they are familiar with the reading you have chosen to analyze, you need not describe fully what the reading has to say. Instead, as is appropriate in a rhetorical analysis, you can focus on your twofold purpose.

Resources to Draw On.   This chapter provides a number of resources for understanding how an argument that takes a position on an issue is organized and what strategies it relies on to convince its readers. The sections "Organizing Your Essay" and "Developing Your Argument and Counterargument" in the writer's guide should be especially helpful as you describe how your chosen argument works. To evaluate the argument—to decide how convincing or unconvincing it is—consult "Evaluating an Argument" in Appendix 1.

Tips for Writing a Successful Rhetorical Analysis.   For this type of essay, it is usually a good idea to begin by stating your purpose and identifying the author, title, source, and year of the reading. Give your readers a very brief overview of the reading and any information they might need to follow your analysis. Then move to the heart of your analysis, explaining how the argument is put together. For example, how does the reading engage the reader, define key terms, forecast and sequence the argument, support its reasons, and so on? After you have completed this description, change your focus to how *successful* the argument is. For example, does it engage the reader and offer convincing reasons? Does it provide sufficient support for those reasons? Does it consider other positions and successfully respond to those positions? Support your judgments with examples from the reading you are analyzing.

Conservatism? Liberalism? Libertarianism?

4

EVALUATING CIVIC STANCES

■ ■ ■

We hold these truths to be self-evident, that all men are created equal, that they are endowed by their Creator with certain unalienable Rights, that among these are Life, Liberty, and the pursuit of Happiness.

> – The Declaration of Independence, July 4, 1776

We the people of the United States, in order to form a more perfect union, establish justice, insure domestic tranquillity, provide for the common defense, promote the general welfare, and secure the blessings of liberty to ourselves and our posterity, do ordain and establish this Constitution for the United States of America.

> – Preamble to the Constitution of the United States, 1788

The statements on the preceding page are two of the most famous statements in U.S. history. Memorable, moving, and eloquent though they are, these statements are open to multiple interpretations when applied to specific issues. Note, for instance, the various ways the Declaration or the Preamble might be interpreted in the following cases:

- Does the right to liberty include the right to hold large, noisy parties in a quiet neighborhood or the right to smoke cigarettes in restaurants?

- Does the right to pursue happiness include the right to ride a motorcycle without wearing a helmet or the right to use heroin?

- What happens to the idea of "we the people" when citizens cannot agree on how much of the federal budget it takes to "provide for the common defense"?

- Does mandatory sex education in the schools "promote the general welfare" or intrude on the right to liberty?

- Does the government "promote the general welfare" or violate individual liberty if it collects taxes from all Americans to fund public parks or a National Endowment for the Arts?

You have probably heard or argued about some of the issues on this list. Each issue reveals some tension between allowing the individual absolute freedom of choice and allowing government to act on behalf of its members. Whether the government involved is at the town, county, state, or federal level, there will be differences of opinion about the decisions that are made. These differences result in different general beliefs about government—or different civic stances. In this chapter, the term *civic stance* refers to the most frequently adopted beliefs about government size, individual rights or liberties, and economic policies. The term *stances* implies that people's beliefs about government tend to follow particular patterns, and the term *civic* implies the relationship between citizens and their government.

A LOOK AHEAD: EVALUATING A CIVIC STANCE This chapter includes an assignment to write an essay in which you evaluate a civic stance. In this context, *evaluating* means judging one of the three stances to be preferable, on the whole, to the other two and giving reasons why you prefer it. To make such an evaluation, you will need to understand the possible arguments for the stance you prefer and be able to use them to support your own argument. You will also, however, need to understand the other two stances well enough to explain them to a reader and to argue against them.

As you read, concentrate on two things: understanding what a conservative, a liberal, and a libertarian are likely to advocate, and evaluating each of the positions. Ask yourself, What is this writer's argument? What belief is central to this stance? What do I find convincing or unconvincing? Developing your essay will involve constant comparison and contrast as you weigh these competing stances and evaluate their benefits for society.

The readings in this chapter are organized according to three prominent and commonly held civic stances: conservatism, liberalism, and libertarianism. You may at first be tempted to say, "I am an individual, and my civic choices don't follow any pattern at all." Frequently, however, people's underlying beliefs do follow consistent patterns, and the civic choices available to them come in packages anyway, not as separate issues. When you vote for a senator or a mayor, for example, you vote for someone you hope will represent your wishes on a broad array of issues, not just on one issue. The three civic stances you will read about—and choose among—in this chapter are sets of beliefs on a broad array of issues. They are stances you will often encounter in political discussions.

The conservative stance, in general, may be summed up in the words of late Republican U.S. senator Barry Goldwater, an outspoken conservative who ran for president in 1964. In 1960, Goldwater wrote: "The Conservative looks upon politics as the art of achieving the maximum amount of freedom for individuals that is consistent with the maintenance of social order."[1] In other words, the conservative expects government to carry out tasks that individuals cannot do, such as building highways and maintaining police forces and armies. Beyond such tasks, however, the conservative would guarantee a maximum of freedom for individuals.

The liberal, on the other hand, is likely to assign a more active role to government, as revealed in this statement by liberal philosopher Ronald Dworkin:

> Liberals believe, first, that government must be neutral in matters of personal morality, that it must leave people free to live as they think best so long as they do not harm others.[...] The second side of liberalism is economic. Liberals insist that government has a responsibility to reduce economic inequality, both through its management of the economy and through welfare programs that redistribute wealth to soften the impact of poverty.[2]

Both the neutrality toward moral issues, which Dworkin values, and the desire to redistribute wealth would be likely to displease conservatives, who see government as a necessary evil. Liberals, however, generally believe that government regulations are good if they can have good results. Liberals are less likely than conservatives to think that the economy will produce equality all by itself if it is allowed to work freely.

Libertarians are likely to agree with liberals about neutrality toward personal morality but to agree with conservatives—and even more vehemently—that government should not manage the economy. Influential libertarian economist Milton Friedman encapsulates the libertarian argument when he writes:

---

[1]Barry Goldwater, *The Conscience of a Conservative* (Shepherdsville, KY: Victor Publishing, 1960) 13.

[2]Ronald Dworkin, "Neutrality, Equality, and Liberalism," *Liberalism Reconsidered,* ed. Douglas MacLean and Claudia Mills (Totowa: Rowman & Allanheld, 1983) 1. [Reprinted with permission from the *New York Review of Books,* 1983.]

The free man will ask neither what his country can do for him nor what he can do for his country. He will ask rather, "What can I and my compatriots do through government" to help us discharge our individual responsibilities, to achieve our several goals and purposes, and above all, to protect our freedom? And he will accompany this question with another: How can we keep the government we create from becoming a Frankenstein that will destroy the very freedom we establish it to protect?[3]

The libertarian is more likely than the conservative to view government as a necessary evil to be kept under control — or a misshapen Frankenstein monster likely to haunt those who allow it too much power. Some extreme libertarians have even argued that roads could be built and owned privately or that income taxes should be abolished.

You are probably aware that these three civic stances have some strong connections to current political parties. The Democratic Party is frequently associated with liberalism, and the Republican Party with conservatism. Such associations, however, can be misleading. Some Democrats are relatively conservative, and some Republicans are relatively liberal. Some Republicans have been deeply influenced by libertarianism, whereas others have not. Moreover, political candidates often move in more conservative or more liberal directions during elections, depending on how they think they will best gain votes. And there are always periodic redefinitions within parties of what it means to be conservative, liberal, or libertarian in relation to specific current issues. For all of these reasons, then, it is best to focus on the three civic stances without trying to line them up with particular parties or candidates.

It may be clear to you by now that three basic areas of disagreement among conservatives, liberals, and libertarians are about size of government, individual rights or liberties, and government's role in the economy. These topics are discussed within each group of readings. First, writers for each of the stances have an opinion about the appropriate size of government. From the time of the framing of the Constitution, Americans have disagreed about whether government should be larger or smaller and whether the most important governmental bodies should be the local ones (towns, cities, counties, states) or the federal government. This question has generated controversy throughout U.S. history — from the time of the framing of the Constitution, through the time of the Civil War, and continuing to the present day. For example, citizens often question whether national or local educational policies will foster better schools or whether state welfare programs will be superior to those run by the federal government.

Second, conservatives, liberals, and libertarians are likely to disagree about whether the government may regulate individual behavior. One view is that the right to "the pursuit of happiness" can be interpreted to justify government regulation. For instance, some people who assume that heroin addiction causes unhappiness for the individual might also believe that government is justified in preventing heroin use. At the same time, some who champion the individual's

---

[3] Milton Friedman with Rose D. Friedman, *Capitalism and Freedom* (Chicago: U of Chicago P, 1962) 2.

right to *liberty* (or *freedom,* a word used interchangeably with liberty) might deny government the right to regulate heroin use. The Preamble to the Constitution contains similar potential conflicts—the problems of using government regulation to "insure domestic tranquillity" or "promote the general welfare" while also guaranteeing "the blessings of liberty." Many arguments have been waged—and continue to be waged—concerning this tension between individual liberty and the government's right to regulate individual behavior. When can one person's free speech be abridged for the good of another? Is cigarette smoking an individual right or should cigarette smoking be prohibited in public places to safeguard the health of nonsmokers and of smokers themselves? If the government acts to limit access to pornography over the Internet, is it promoting the general welfare or curtailing individual liberty?

A third issue that conservatives, liberals, and libertarians are likely to disagree about is whether the government should intervene in economic affairs. The government already intervenes by taxing Americans to finance Social Security benefits, health care for the poor and the elderly, and public schools and highways. Taxes also support government regulations about workplace safety, environmental protection, fair hiring, and the safety of foods and medicine. Not all of these government interventions are popular, of course, yet many Americans want the benefits they might be entitled to individually, such as unemployment compensation, Social Security, or federal disaster relief.

As you read the various arguments on these issues, you may find it difficult initially to choose one of the three civic stances as preferable to the other two and then to defend your choice. You may even be tempted to choose part of one stance and part of another. This difficult choice is a reflection of the difficult choices individuals are often required to make in their civic lives. When you see the taxes taken out of your paycheck, for instance, you may be tempted to adopt a libertarian stance and say, "No more taxes!" At the same time, you may want the improved roads, college loans, federal disaster relief, or farm subsidies that your taxes support. One thing you will learn in this chapter, then, is that any civic stance involves trade-offs.

You may be aware that conservatism, liberalism, and libertarianism are only a few of the civic stances possible. Anarchism, communism, communitarianism, and democratic socialism are other possible stances that have gained popularity at times in U.S. history. Closely related versions of a civic stance often go under different names. For instance, there are people with roots in liberalism who might nevertheless refer to themselves as "progressives" or "Leftists" or "populists," depending on what kind of policies they prefer and how they see themselves in relation to liberals. There are also conservatives who would disagree with current conservative programs and would distinguish between neoconservatives and paleo-, or traditional, conservatives.

For your essay in this chapter, however, you need not be concerned with any of these other views. Just choose among the three alternatives of conservatism, liberalism, and libertarianism. You should find it challenging and interesting to defend one of these three civic stances.

To aid you in this process, the writer's notebook tasks following each section of readings help you compare what you have read to your own experience and to the views of other students. The notebook tasks also offer guidance as you reread the selections critically and prepare to write your essay about conservatism, liberalism, or libertarianism. You may want to look at the writer's notebook tasks before reading each section.

CONSERVATISM

Conservatism today may be seen as a response to social and economic programs initiated by liberals in the thirty or more years stretching from the New Deal of the 1930s through the 1960s. Contemporary conservatives tend to argue that the liberal social programs instituted in those years to "promote the general welfare" have, instead, discouraged individual responsibility and over-regulated the economy.

When asked to what extent the government can or should intervene in individual behavior, a conservative is likely to promote individual freedom as an ideal but to think that Americans have gone too far in the direction of individual freedom and have abandoned many traditional moral principles. When asked what to do about a rise in teenage pregnancies, for instance, a conservative might answer: "Reemphasize personal morality. Stop teaching birth control in the schools and stop constantly exposing young people to sex in movies and other entertainment." In the realm of individual behavior, then, today's conservatives tend to accept some types of regulation.

When asked about government social programs or economic regulations, however, a modern conservative might say: "Government has grown too large and bureaucratic, too removed from local control; its intrusion into our lives is creating resentment, trampling on our rights, reducing personal responsibility, and stifling the economic growth that will do more for the good of our citizens than any government programs can do." In short, conservatives tend to think that smaller and more local government is preferable to the national government. Conservatives also tend to argue that a free-market economy will do more for the general welfare of society than will government regulation of the economy.

Many conservatives focus on issues of personal morality or behavior, such as family breakdown or crime. As Barbara Dafoe Whitehead writes: "The principal source of family decline over the past three decades has been cultural. It has to do with the ascendancy of a set of values that have been destructive of commitment, obligation, responsibility, and sacrifice — and particularly destructive of the claims of children on adult attention and commitment."[4]

William Bennett, author of the 1993 best-seller *The Book of Virtues,* offers the following ways in which public policies have contributed to what he calls "cultural decline":

---

[4]Barbara Dafoe Whitehead, "The New Family Values," *Utne Reader* May-June 1993: 65. [Excerpted from *Family Affairs* (Summer 1992).]

- We say that we desire from our children more civility and responsibility, but in many of our schools we steadfastly refuse to teach right and wrong.

- We say that we want law and order in the streets, but we allow criminals, including violent criminals, to return to those same streets.

- We say that we want to stop illegitimacy, but we continue to subsidize the kind of behavior that virtually guarantees high rates of illegitimacy.

- We say that we want to discourage teenage sexual activity, but in classrooms all across America educators are more eager to dispense condoms than moral guidance.

- We say that we want more families to stay together, but we liberalize divorce laws and make divorce easier to attain.

- We say that we want to achieve a color blind society and judge people by the content of their character, but we continue to count by race, skin and pigment.

- We say that we want to encourage virtue and honor among the young, but it has become a mark of sophistication to shun the language of morality.[5]

Not all conservatives have the same focus. On the whole, however, when they discuss personal behavior, today's conservatives are likely to emphasize morality and personal responsibility rather than individual liberties; conservatives may even support limits on private behavior. On the other hand, when conservatives discuss the economic realm, they tend to emphasize liberty or freedom—to want smaller government and fewer social programs supported by tax dollars. Although there are some important differences among conservatives, the patterns of concern for personal responsibility and small government nevertheless stand out. The following set of readings provides further insights into the conservative stance.

WHO ARE THE CONSERVATIVES?

Russell Kirk

Russell Kirk, a former history professor, became one of the foremost intellectual influences on modern conservatism after publishing The Conservative Mind *in 1953. A prolific author, he wrote a number of essays and thirty books, including* The Conservative Constitution, The Roots of American Order, *and* The Conservative Reader. *He died in 1994.*

---

[5]William J. Bennett, "Revolt against God: America's Spiritual Despair," *Policy Review* Winter 1994: 24.

This essay is from his 1954 book A Program for Conservatives. *Kirk begins by defining modern liberalism in opposition to conservatism. He then discusses the conservative tradition, beginning with the eighteenth-century British statesman Edmund Burke, who articulated his conservatism in reaction to the French Revolution. Since Kirk was writing in 1954, after the spread of Communism into Eastern Europe, he probably had modern Communism in mind when he criticized abstract government planning. Throughout Kirk's writing, the root of the word* conservative *is apparent: Kirk wants to conserve, rather than to break with, the past. In his view, the past embodies the collective wisdom humans have arrived at through much time and experience. Similarly, Kirk would conserve individual or private ownership of property rather than put property ownership into the hands of government, as modern Communists were doing during much of Kirk's lifetime. Like many conservatives today, Kirk believes that crucial "civil" institutions, such as family, church, and community organizations, are endangered when too much focus is put on either individual rights or government regulation. According to this view, civil institutions need to be strong to provide individuals with the strength and wisdom derived from tradition and experience.*

As you read, note what Kirk says about conserving tradition, "that delicate growth called society." Pay attention as well to his skepticism about the changes that liberal or radical planners might introduce.

The people whom we call "conservative" are not restricted to any social class or any economic occupation or any level of formal education. Some are physicians, and some engine-drivers, and some professors, and some clerks, and some bankers, and some clergymen, and some diemakers, and some soldiers. In a popular magazine, recently, I noticed a passing reference to "the rich conservatives, the well-off liberals, and the poor laboring men." This notion is nonsense. Some millionaires are fanatically radical, and some working men are fiercely conservative, and the well-to-do may be anything under the sun. Conservatism and liberalism and radicalism are states of mind, not of the pocketbook. The United States, throughout most of our history, have been a nation substantially conservative, though rich men have exerted less direct influence upon government here than almost anywhere else in the world. Conservatism is something more than mere solicitude for tidy incomes.

Conservatism, indeed, is a word with an old and honorable meaning—but a meaning almost forgotten by Americans for some years. Even today, although there are many men of conservative prejudices active in national and state politics, few are eager to describe themselves as "conservatives." The people of the United States became the chief conservative nation of the world at the very time when they had ceased to call themselves conservatives at home. For a generation, the word "liberal" had been in fashion, particularly in universities and among journalists. The liberal, in American parlance, has been a man in love with constant change;...commonly the liberal has tended to despise the lessons of the past and to look forward confidently to a vista of endless material progress, in which the state° will play a larger and larger role, and a general equality of condition will be enforced.

This liberal now is a distraught and frightened man, incapable either of serious leadership or serious criticism. It is time for people who know they are *not* liberals or radicals to ask themselves just what they do believe, and what they must call themselves. The traditional system of ideas opposed to liberalism and radicalism is the conservative belief. Already the words "conservative" and "conservatism" are being employed as terms of praise in the popular press and by serious critics of society, and books by conservative writers are receiving an attention that they have been denied most of this century. In politics, as in physics, it is scarcely possible to make progress until you have defined your terms. What is conservatism? Who are the conservatives?

Aristotle was a conservative, and so was Cicero, and there have been intelligent conservatives in every age. John Stuart Mill, a century ago, called conservatives "the stupid party." But the conservatives have outlasted their enemies, or most of their enemies. Modern conservatism, as a regular body of ideas, took form about the beginning of the French Revolution. In England, the founder of true conservatism was Burke, whose *Reflections on the Revolution in France* turned the tide of opinion against the levelling° and destructive impulse of the French revolutionaries. In America, the founders of the Republic had no desire to turn society upside down; and in their writings, particularly in the works of John Adams and in the *Federalist Papers,*° we find a sober conservatism built upon an understanding of history and of human nature....

Edmund Burke, much read in history and much practiced in the conduct of political affairs, knew that men are not naturally good, but are beings of mingled good and evil, kept obedient to a moral law chiefly by the force of habit and custom, which the revolutionaries would discard as so much ancient rubbish. He knew that all the advantages of the civil social existence are the product of intricate human experience over many centuries, not to be amended overnight by some coffeehouse philosopher. He knew religion to be a great benefit to mankind, and established order to be the gift of Providence, and hereditary possessions, and the mass of prescriptive beliefs which we call "prejudices." He set his face, then, against the revolutionaries like a man who of a sudden is attacked by robbers.

° **the state**: A term used to refer to the federal government, state government, or other governmental entities.　° **levelling**: Here, the desire on the part of French revolutionaries to have all people on the same level and to do away with a class system in which some people have more rights, privileges, or wealth than others.　° *Federalist Papers*: Written to defend the proposed U.S. Constitution, the *Federalist Papers* advocated checks and balances that would prevent popular opinion from producing change too rapidly.

Burke had defended the rights of the Americans because they were the traditional and real rights° of actual men, developed through historical processes. He attacked the false concept of the Rights of Man° expounded by the French speculators because he recognized in this abstract notion of rights an insensate desire to be free of all duties toward the past and toward posterity. Burke never favored revolution; he bitterly regretted the American war, and had labored for conciliation, neither repression nor revolution. And the American Revolution, after all, was (as Burke said of the triumph of William and Mary) "a revolution not made, but prevented"; it was an act of separation, but it preserved, rather than destroyed, the traditional framework of life in America. The French Revolution, on the contrary, was intended to uproot that delicate growth called society, and, if not impeded both in the realm of mind and the realm of politics, would end by subjecting all men either to anarchy or to a ruthless master. They would have lost all real rights in the pursuit of pretended abstract rights. . . .

We Americans were from the first a people endowed with strong conservative prejudices, immeasurably influenced by the spirit of religious veneration, firm in a traditional morality, hostile to arbitrary power whether possessed by a monarch or a mob, zealous to guard against centralization,° attached to prescriptive rights,° convinced of the necessity and beneficence of the institution of property. We have reason, I think, to be proud of the healthy and continuous existence of conservative principles here, for three centuries; and it is to be hoped that we will act today in the light of this long conservative development, not lusting after abstract new doctrines, whether those doctrines are called "conservative" or "liberal" or "radical." What we most require is an illumination and renewed recognition of the lofty conservative concepts and institutions which have sustained our nation. . . .

Centralization, extension of the economic functions of government, the increase of taxation and national debts, the decay of family-life and local association, and the employment of state education to enforce uniformity of character and opinion—these influences, and others, are at work among us with dreadful power. We are just beginning to make our way back to the first principles of politics and ethics. The conservative instinct of America, just now reawakening, must draw its vigor from everyone who believes in enduring truth, in liberty under law, and in the political and economic institutions essential to the preservation of a just and free and tranquil society. . . .

°**real rights:** Rights that people already possessed, such as the right to one's property, rather than the sort of abstract rights, such as the right to equality, that French reformers articulated.   °**Rights of Man:** A reference to the *Declaration of the Rights of Man and Citizen,* issued by French reformers in 1789. It stated that "men are born and remain free and equal in rights."   °**centralization:** Here, the concentration of power in a central government rather than in smaller and more local forms of government (such as states, counties, or towns).   °**prescriptive rights:** Rights established by past laws and traditions.

The American conservative, priding himself upon his old antipathy toward abstraction, ought to endeavor to define his own terms. Precisely what is the essence of our American conservatism? I think that the old conservative character of the American nation is marked by these qualities:

(1) A belief in an order that is more than human, which has implanted in 10 man a character of mingled good and evil, susceptible of improvement only by an inner working, not by mundane schemes for perfectability. This conviction lies at the heart of American respect for the past, as the record of Providential purpose. The conservative mind is suffused with veneration. Men and nations, the conservative believes, are governed by moral laws; and political problems, at bottom, are moral and religious problems. An eternal chain of duty links the generations that are dead, and the generation that is living now, and the generations yet to be born. We have no right, in this brief existence of ours, to alter irrevocably the shape of things, in contempt of our ancestors and of the rights of posterity. Politics is the art of apprehending and applying the Justice which stands above statutory law.°

(2) An affection for variety and complexity and individuality, even for singularity, which has exerted a powerful check upon the political tendency toward what Tocqueville calls "democratic despotism." Variety and complexity, in the opinion of conservatives, are the high gifts of truly civilized society. The uniformity and standardization of liberal and radical planners° would be the death of vitality and freedom, a life-in-death, every man precisely like his neighbor—and, like the damned of the *Inferno*, forever deprived of hope.

(3) A conviction that justice, properly defined, means "to each the things that go with his own nature," not a levelling equality; and joined with this is a correspondent respect for private property of every sort. Civilized society requires distinctions of order, wealth, and responsibility; it cannot exist without true leadership. A free society will endeavor, indeed, to afford to men of natural abilities every opportunity to rise by their own efforts; but it will resist strenuously the radical delusion that exact equality of station and wealth can benefit everyone. Society longs for just leadership; and if people destroy natural distinctions among men, presently some Bonaparte will fill the vacuum—or worse than Bonaparte.

(4) A suspicion of concentrated power, and a consequent attachment to our federal principle° and to division and balancing of authority at every level of government.

(5) A reliance upon private endeavor and sagacity in nearly every walk of life, together with a contempt for the abstract designs of the collectivistic reformer.°

°**statutory law:** The laws enacted by legislatures, as opposed to a higher law coming from God or from customs developed over generations.   °**planners:** People who rely on laws and government programs to change people for the better.   °**federal principle:** The principle of power being distributed, in the United States, between the central government and the states.   °**collectivistic reformer:** Someone who believes in reforms that emphasize group (collective) ownership.

But to this self-reliance, in the mind of the American conservative, is joined the conviction that in matters beyond the scope of material endeavor and the present moment, the individual tends to be foolish, but the species is wise; therefore we rely in great matters upon the wisdom of our ancestors. History is an immense storehouse of knowledge. We pay a decent respect to the moral traditions and immemorial customs of mankind; for men who ignore the past are condemned to repeat it. The conservative distrusts the radical visionary and the planner who would chop society into pieces and mould it nearer to his heart's desire. The conservative appeals beyond the fickle opinion of the hour to what Chesterton called "the democracy of the dead"—that is, the considered judgment of the wise men who died before our time. To presume that men can plan rationally the whole of existence is to expose mankind to a terrible danger from the collapse of existing institutions; for conservatives know that most men are governed, on many occasions, more by emotion than by pure reason.

(6) A prejudice against organic change, a feeling that it is unwise to break ₁₅ radically with political prescription, an inclination to tolerate what abuses may exist in present institutions out of a practical acquaintance with the violent and unpredictable nature of doctrinaire reform.

American character being complex, along with these conservative threads are woven certain innovating and even radical threads. It is true, too, that national character is formed, in part, by the circumstances of history and environment, so that such a character may alter, or even grow archaic. Certain powerful influences presently at work among us are affecting this traditional character, for good or ill. It is time, nevertheless, that we acknowledged the predominantly conservative cast of the American mind, since the inception of the Republic, and time that we paid our respects to the strength and honesty of that character. We are not merely the pawns of impersonal historical influences; we have it in our power to preserve the best in our old institutions and in our old opinions, even in this era of vertiginous change; and we will do well, I think, if we endeavor to govern ourselves, in the age that is dawning, by the prescriptive values in American character which have become almost our second nature.

A New Contract with America

Sam Brownback

Sam Brownback was a freshman congressman from Kansas when he published this 1996 article in Policy Review. *Its title refers to the Republican congressional platform for a "Contract with America" in 1994. Brownback grew up on a family farm in Kansas and received degrees in agricultural economics and law; prior to*

1994 he had served as secretary of agriculture for Kansas. When Republican senator Robert Dole retired from the U. S. Senate to run for president in 1996, Brownback was elected to replace him.

This reading reveals Brownback's program for a "new" contract with America. Writing more than forty years after Kirk, Brownback nevertheless shares some of Kirk's basic assumptions: that centralized government and planning are more likely to harm than to promote the general welfare, that solutions lie with individuals, not governments, and that the intermediary institutions of a civil society (families, churches, community organizations, clubs) need to be strengthened.

As you read, note why Brownback would restrict the role of government and who, instead, he would assign the task of promoting the general welfare.

"I love my nation but I fear my government." So read a bumper sticker I saw in Topeka, Kansas, during my first campaign for political office. I was running for Congress and I had to wonder: Was this not the same government that had mobilized the nation to win World War II, that had defeated communism, that had built the interstate highway system? What had gone so desperately wrong? A few months later, I understood perfectly the meaning of that message.

Americans deeply believe in the principles of America, but they don't see them reflected in their government. Americans believe in freedom, democracy, moral values, family, community, and free markets. Yet their government seizes their rights without their consent. Government has become their master, not their servant.

To address these concerns, I ran a campaign in 1994 based on three words: Reduce, Reform, and Return. Reduce the size and scope of the federal government. Reform the Congress. Return to the basic values that had built the country: work and family and the recognition of a higher moral authority.

While many were rightfully skeptical back then that what I said would ever happen, none says so now. We are finally seeing some progress toward reversing a trend thought unstoppable: the growth of government, the irresponsibility of Congress, and the loss of the moral character upon which the nation was founded. The current debate over the budget is about more than simply learning to live within our means. It is a turning point in the history of the federal government. The crucial issue is who should be in charge of major programs like welfare and Medicaid° — the bureaucrats and regulators and members of Congress in Washington, or the American people and their elected state and local representatives.

Our Founding Fathers designed the federal government to be limited. But in the name of compassion, the federal government now tries to do all things for all people. We have discovered, by spending trillions of dollars and taking

5

°**Medicaid:** A federal- or state-sponsored program of medical aid for people who cannot afford regular medical services.

rights and freedoms away from individuals, that government cannot solve all of our problems. Indeed, exceeding the authority for which the system was designed hurts people.

I certainly discovered this in the district I represent.

LeCompton, Kansas, has a population of 750. At the city hall one day, I met Jeff Goodrick, who showed me a ramp that has provided access to the handicapped for 20 years. Under the new Americans with Disabilities Act, the town was told to replace this ramp for an estimated cost of $15,000, even though the design of the old ramp had never denied anyone access to the tiny city hall. The new one was to be slightly longer, with a slightly more gradual slope. The people of LeCompton don't have the money to pay for this new ramp without sacrificing other services essential to their community. Their freedom had been diminished, and for what?

In Erie, Kansas, I walked up and down the main street while I was campaigning. I entered a small repair shop and visited with the owner, Rex Bohrer. He had the thick, callused hands of a man who has not lived a life of leisure. I asked him for his vote. Rex stared up at me from behind an air-conditioner he was repairing and said, "You runnin' for the U.S. Congress?"—to which I answered a timid "yes." He said, "I want to talk to you." He led me to the front of his shop and showed me a government manual containing more than 50 pages of fine print telling him how he must repair refrigerators under new regulations regarding the chemical freon.° He asked, "What the heck am I supposed to do with this? I don't understand this manual, and you tell me that if I violate any provision it could cost me $10,000. What am I supposed to do?"

I didn't know. I certainly do not want to pollute the environment with dangerous chemicals. But here was an honest citizen trying to earn an honest wage who was being directed by an impossibly complex manual and who faces fines of up to $10,000 if he violates any of its provisions. Rex's only recourse is to quit the business that he needs for survival. What is he to do?

In Girard, Kansas, I was speaking to the seniors of Girard High School about **10** the Social Security trust fund. A number of these students had already paid some Social Security taxes. I asked how many of them expected to receive anything from Social Security when they reached the age of 65. Out of nearly 100 students, only four raised their hands. Then I asked how many of them believed in extraterrestrials. About 15 hands went up. This mirrors the responses of young people everywhere. Nationwide, fewer Americans under 25 believe that they will receive anything from Social Security when they retire than believe in UFOs....

In nearly every town hall I visit, I hear complaints about our tax system. The complicated and frequently politically driven statutes° that now make up our tax

---

°**freon:** A chemical often used as a refrigerant; it is believed to deplete the ozone layer.   °**statutes:** Laws.

code compromise our economic growth and provoke class envy. No one can understand the 10,000 pages of tax laws; even the tax lawyers complain about its complexity. When America's taxpayers call the IRS [Internal Revenue Service] for information, they get five different answers from five different agents. Whatever happened to a tax code designed only for raising federal revenue? How did we end up with a system that micromanages our lives and our economy?

Everywhere I go, I hear stories that reveal an overreaching regime distorted by the false notion that centralized authority will lead this nation on the right path. In fact, the American people believe they can handle most of their problems better than the federal government can. They are right.

How has a nation conceived in liberty and opposition to tyranny arrived at a point today where citizens are more fearful of their own government threatening their rights than they are of any other government?

We got off track by forgetting our core principles. But the good news is there is a way out. It's called the Constitution. However much we may have strayed from the precepts of that document, Americans continue to revere it and the principles it enshrines. Ratified by our founding generation and amended by succeeding generations, the Constitution stands equally for self-government and limited government. It is the instrument with which we empowered the federal government in the first place. But it is also the instrument with which we limited that government. If we would only return to those principles of limited government, then our nation, our economy, our liberties, and our social fiber will grow stronger than we have seen for a generation.

The bureaucratic model of growth and prosperity for a nation has been 15 shown wanting all over the world, from communism in the former U.S.S.R., to socialism throughout Europe, to the welfare state in America. Those running for office in 1996 will find that one of the keys to success and leadership will be a vision of hope, of a brighter future with a smaller government—one that is at last turning toward its constitutional principles and away from the idea that a centralized, bureaucratic government will solve all of our problems.

We must create an environment in which Americans look first to themselves and to each other for help, not to their congressmen. We must return to a society where people rely on their communities and do not regard their government as a substitute for civil society.°...

The Constitution gives the federal government a limited number of important enumerated powers—for example, to borrow money, to regulate commerce with foreign nations and among the states, to establish post offices and post roads, to declare war, to coin money, to lay and collect taxes for all these purposes. Powers not granted and enumerated are retained by the states and the people. Much of the federal government literally has no constitutional basis. And that is where we find ourselves today.

° **civil society:** Institutions such as the family, church, community organization, or club in between the individual and government.

The underlying principles limiting the federal government are embodied in our founding documents—the Declaration of Independence, the Constitution, the Bill of Rights, and the Civil War Amendments. These documents paint a picture of government, and the role of government in human affairs, that is subtle and profound....

In the Declaration of Independence, we find the American vision of freedom and responsibility in its purest form. The Declaration's essence is captured in the few short phrases that begin with the most important phrase of all, "We hold these truths to be self-evident." In that simple line, Thomas Jefferson placed us squarely in the natural-law or higher-law tradition, which holds that there are "self-evident truths" of right or wrong. And what is that higher law? It begins with a premise of moral equality—"all men are created equal"—then defines our equality by reference to our "inalienable rights to life, liberty and the pursuit of happiness."

There, in a nutshell, is the moral vision—a world in which moral people are 20 free to pursue their own happiness, constrained only by the equal rights of others to do the same. It is not the responsibility of government to secure our happiness for us. That is our responsibility—and our right. The role of government, rather, is to secure our rights, as the Declaration goes on to say. That is its basic function. But to be just or legitimate, government's powers must be derived "from the consent of the governed."

We have evolved this century from a constitutional government to a government that behaves without regard to constitutional principle. That moral vision in which people have the right and responsibility to pursue their own happiness has been lost. The federal government no longer *derives* its powers from the people—it just takes them. This is why citizens distrust their government so much today. It is time that we re-limit our federal government so it can perform its proper functions well, and leave to the people and the states those functions which the federal government was never intended to perform.

If we can begin to restore a constitutional government, I foresee an America where freedom and responsibility grow for individuals, families, and communities. Freedom and responsibility cannot be separated. Our freedoms never belonged to the federal government, but to the individual. We must make our government return them.

I foresee an America that is the most family-friendly nation on earth. The family, not the government, should be the backbone of society. Government should cease trying to supplant it. When we are careless, legislative initiatives can harm families. By pledging to spare families from additional legislative and regulatory tinkering, we will do more to protect the rights to life, liberty, and the pursuit of happiness than any federal legislative quick-fix.

I also foresee an America where far fewer decisions are made by Washington, and more are made by individuals, markets, or localities. Imagine the federal government, operating within its limited role, serving as a model of efficiency and effectiveness. A federal government focused on its constitutional missions—rather than creating new ones—could become a model for other governments.

So, how do we return to a constitutional government? ... We must develop ²⁵ an agenda to recover the rights of individuals from their government.

A New Contract with America

Call it a new Contract with America—one that passes laws, not merely proposes them.... Our goal should be to implement reforms consistent with those timeless principles embodied in the Constitution.... Here are some broad outlines for such a contract:

I. Reduce Government Spending

We will reduce the size of the federal government by a tangible measurement over a period of four years. My preference would be a reduction of federal spending from 22 percent of our GDP [gross domestic product] to 15 percent or less (which may take longer than four years). Imagine taking these resources from the hands of government and putting them back into the pockets of families and entrepreneurs.

II. Transform the Tax System

We will remove all social engineering° from the U.S. tax code to create a new tax system designed strictly for the purpose of raising revenue efficiently. The power to lay and collect taxes was meant to fund the enumerated powers, not to become a political device in and of itself. Today, we discourage certain behaviors and reward others based purely on the whims of those who control the tax leviathan.°

III. Reorganize the Executive Branch

We will redesign the executive branch to be consistent with its constitutional ³⁰ authority instead of one still operating on 20th-century, centralized government experiments. We will replace the 14 cabinet-level agencies, which impose more than half a trillion dollars worth of regulations upon the U.S. economy each year, with perhaps nine, and restrict their regulatory powers under constitutional principles. The Constitution does not authorize at the federal level, for example, many of the activities within the departments of Housing and Urban Development, Commerce, Education, and Energy.

°**social engineering:** Here, the process of managing human beings through the penalties and rewards of the tax system.   °**tax leviathan:** A large bureaucracy with absolute powers over its citizens. The word *leviathan* is from the title of Thomas Hobbes's treatise (1651) on government.

IV. Create a Constitutional Caucus

We will form a constitutional caucus or commission to evaluate all federal programs for an authorizing principle under the Constitution. A constitutional cleansing of the federal government is long overdue. Furthermore, Congress should require that all legislative proposals cite their precise constitutional authority before they can be enacted. In the case of existing illegitimate programs, Congress should identify and debate which ones should be returned to the states or phased out entirely.

V. Seek Change with Compassion

As we phase out unconstitutional programs, we will implement change with compassion, so that people currently dependent upon federal programs will have time to prepare for the transition and enjoy the empowerment they receive from their new freedoms.

VI. Pay Off the National Debt

We will implement a plan not only to balance the budget, but to run surpluses and pay off our $5-trillion national debt over 30 years, so that our children can decide their own future.

VII. Remove Barriers to Good Citizenship

We will erase from the books all laws, regulations, and other barriers that prevent local voluntary and civic institutions from helping their neighbors. Faith-based and civic institutions that are leading the fight for a civil society should not be stymied and penalized by mountains of federal laws and regulations that merely supplant local acts of kindness with the cold attitude of "government knows best." Why do we have a poverty class at all, when we spend an average of $36,000 in federal, state, and local welfare funds on every family below the poverty level? Because as much as 70 cents of each government anti-poverty dollar doesn't even reach the poor — it is engulfed by administrative overhead and "professional" personnel. We will form a task force to conduct an exhaustive investigation of rules and laws that are interfering with those faith-based and civic institutions that are working to revive their communities and families. Then we will implement its recommendations. Local church and community groups can do far more to bring their people back to self-sufficiency than a central planner could ever hope to achieve.

There are conservatives who believe that, with the proper leadership, the fed- 35 eral government can engineer the comeback of the family and civil society. But we should not yield to such temptations. If we are trying to end social engineering from the left, how can we justify it from the right? Our highest goals should not rely on new legislative initiatives as much as on the proper legislative restraint.

With this platform and this contract with the American people, we will continue to be the party of ideas and of commitment to constitutional principles, to prosperity, to a revived citizenry, and to a government on the side of those who want the culture in America to reflect their basic values. This is more important now than ever before, because government thwarts those values by attempting to replace them. Today, on behalf of the "public good," government crowds out the individual's "pursuit of happiness"—including private investment and private charity—by replacing them with government substitutes.

We face today a set of deep-seated problems—overweening government, massive public debt, and crippling dependence on federal programs. But we face as well a historic opportunity to base our solutions upon our very roots as a nation, and upon our principles as a people—freedom and responsibility.

Let us seize the opportunity before us by recovering those principles. If we restore government to its proper role under our Constitution, we will look back in years to come and say that the moment was right, and we were a match for that moment. And our children and grandchildren will thank us.

CONDOM NATION: GOVERNMENT SEX EDUCATION PROMOTES TEEN PREGNANCY

Jacqueline R. Kasun

Jacqueline Kasun is a professor of economics at Humboldt State University in Arcata, California, and the author of The War against Population *(1988) and other studies of population programs.*

This 1994 article, originally published in the conservative journal Policy Review, *provides a concrete example of how one conservative views a particular public policy issue: sex education. Later in this chapter, you will be able to compare Kasun's views on this issue to those of liberals and libertarians. Writers from all three civic stances agree that teenage pregnancy is not good for teenagers, their babies, or society in general. Beyond that, however, they disagree on some fundamental assumptions. As a conservative, Kasun asks, Who should decide about what promotes the welfare of teenagers—federal or local government? parents? She also asks, in a more general sense, Who should decide on the substance of young people's education?*

As you read, try not to take a stand on sex education itself. Also try not to focus on political party disagreements or on the references to the Clinton administration because political parties often contain ingredients from more than one civic stance. Instead, read Kasun's piece with the goal of seeing what one conservative says about the government's role in sex education.

During the debate over her confirmation last year, Surgeon General Joycelyn Elders° sketched her strategy for combating teen pregnancies and sexually transmitted diseases with her usual sledgehammer bluntness: "I tell every girl that when she goes out on a date—put a condom in her purse." Dr. Elders lamented that schools teach youngsters how to drive but "don't tell them what to do in the back seat."

In fact, they do, and have been doing so for decades in the form of explicit sex-education programs and school-based clinics. And that is the problem. Premarital sexual activity and pregnancy have increased in step with the increase in the programs. One of every 10 teenage girls in the United States now becomes pregnant each year. Studies published by the government family planners indicate that these problems are very likely the result of their programs. For example, one such study found that contraceptive education increased the odds of 14-year-olds starting intercourse by 50 percent.

SEX EDUCATION FOR ALL

None of these facts has ruffled Dr. Elders and her allies in the Clinton administration. Dr. Elders has called for greatly expanding the government commitment to comprehensive sex education from kindergarten through 12th grade, though the surgeon general prefers starting at age three. She wants free contraceptives and abortion referrals through schools and clinics. In his first weeks of office, President Clinton extended the services of federal family-planning clinics and increased their budgets by $100 million. His proposal for health-care reform gives a prominent place to school clinics.

The Clinton administration's expansion of family planning is only the most recent step in a long march° of government-engineered° sex education. In 1964 a private coalition of educators and activists founded the Sex Information and Education Council of the United States (SIECUS) to "expand the scope of sex education to all age levels and groups." Since then, its curriculum has helped form the basis for sex-ed guidelines in most public schools. In 1965 Congress

---

°**Joycelyn Elders:** An African American physician from Arkansas who became President Clinton's controversial surgeon general from 1993 until she was fired in late 1994.   °**long march:** A reference to the Long March (1934–35) made by Chinese Communists under Mao Zedong, which served ultimately to consolidate Communist power.   °**government-engineered:** Refers to government attempts to manage people's behavior.

began to subsidize birth control for the poor. Beginning in 1967, Congress enacted program after program to extend government birth control. This culminated in the Adolescent Pregnancy Act of 1978, which specifically targeted teenagers, even though they were covered in other programs.

Today, sex education is taught from kindergarten through college through- 5 out the nation. In New York, second-graders stand before their classes to name and point to their genital organs. In California, children model genital organs in clay and fit condoms on cucumbers. From such books as *Changing Bodies, Changing Lives,* children are learning alternative forms of sexual expression— including oral sex, anal sex, masturbation, and homosexuality.

At the same time, government-supported "family planning" clinics have blanketed the country, providing young, unmarried men and women with pills, condoms, and abortions—usually without parental notification. School-based clinics, 24 of them in Arkansas alone, often make condoms and other birth-control devices available to children, and even refer teenage girls for abortions without their parents' knowledge. The number of school-based clinics has grown from 12 in 1980 to at least 325 in 1993, according to the Center for Population Options. All told, federal and state expenditures for contraceptive services increased from $350 million in 1980 to $645 million in 1992—not including abortions, sterilizations, and most sex education.

A RECORD OF FAILURE

It is bad enough that public money is being used to advance a sexuality agenda that many families find objectionable. What is inexplicable is that these government efforts continue—trumpeted by our nation's chief medical officer— in the face of mounting and irrefutably negative evidence.

Proponents of sex education argue that government family planning increases the use of contraceptives. It does, but it is most effective at encouraging higher rates of sexual activity, teen pregnancies, and sexually transmitted diseases.

As early as 1980, Melvin Zelnik and John F. Kantner reported in the September/October issue of *Family Planning Perspectives,* a publication of the Alan Guttmacher Institute, that the proportion of metropolitan teenage women who had premarital sex rose from 30 percent in 1971 to 50 percent in 1979. They also reported that the premarital pregnancy rate was increasing even faster than premarital sex activity, despite the increasing availability and use of contraceptives. All of this occurred after more than a decade of increasing sex instruction in public schools.

Studies in the 1980s revealed similar trends. A 1986 Louis Harris poll com- 10 missioned by Planned Parenthood found that 64 percent of 17-year-olds who had contraceptive instruction had engaged in intercourse; the proportion was 57 percent for those who had not had the instruction. Two massive studies of the effects of sex education, published in *Family Planning Perspectives* in 1986, found that young people who had received sex education were more likely to engage in sex at an early age than those who had not received the instruction. These studies were based on two large national probability samples, giving them a high degree of reliability.

SCHOOL-BASED CLINICS

The record has been equally poor for school-based clinics. Douglas Kirby, a supporter of school clinics, published in the January/February 1991 issue of *Family Planning Perspectives* an evaluation of six clinics that tried to reduce pregnancy by providing birth control services to students. The clinics were operating on school grounds in Dallas, Texas; San Francisco, California; Gary, Indiana; Muskegon, Michigan; Jackson, Mississippi; and Quincy, Florida. Mr. Kirby and his comrades reported that the clinics did not reduce pregnancy. Despite this, they suggested ways to improve the effectiveness of the clinics, which included "more outreach."

As an expert witness, I submitted an affidavit to the Supreme Court of the State of New York in 1991; in it I reviewed seven published studies of the outcomes of programs to reduce pregnancy by providing sex education, together with easy access to contraceptives. The programs had been undertaken in Los Angeles, Baltimore, New York, Cleveland, Seattle, Denver, Atlanta, Pittsburgh, St. Paul, and an unnamed "large midwestern city." None of the seven studies presented valid evidence of reductions in pregnancy: Some gave evidence of increases in pregnancy; six of the seven gave evidence of increases in sexual activity.

The Baltimore school clinic program, despite its positive media coverage, needs to be revisited. Laurie Zabin and Janet Hardy, its director, have written several articles and a book about the clinic, claiming it reduced sexual activity and pregnancy among its student clients. However, a careful look at their research methods shows that they manipulated their sample; they omitted the 12th grade from some of their calculations, on the grounds that some of the young women were not sufficiently "motivated" or "advanced"—whatever that means.

Clinic officials have claimed that students "delayed" sexual activity and that teen pregnancies declined. But they based these claims on questionnaires collected from only 96 of the 1,033 girls surveyed at the beginning of the clinic program. They published figures showing that teen sex increased during the operation of the program, but then denied this is what the figures meant.

Last year, Mr. Kirby and others reported on the almost 20 years of experi- 15 ence in the much-publicized St. Paul school clinics, which provide a "full range of reproductive health services," including sex education and prescriptions for birth control. The media have broadcasted claims of significant reductions in student birthrates. Mr. Kirby and his co-authors, however, found "a statistically significant increase in birthrates after the clinics opened." They caution, nevertheless, that the appropriate conclusion is that "the St. Paul clinics had little impact on birthrates." Incredibly, the Center for Population Options concluded that the results prove the need for more "interventions."

SUBSIDIZING ILLEGITIMACY AND ABORTION

Such interventions, however, are simply giving us higher rates of casual sex and illegitimacy. The statistical evidence has been around a long time. Susan Roylance studied 15 states with similar social-demographic characteristics and rates of teenage pregnancy in 1970; in testimony to Congress in 1981 she reported that those with the highest expenditures on family planning showed the largest increases in abortions and illegitimate births among teenagers between 1970 and 1979.

In 1992, I conducted a study of welfare dependency in the 50 states based on data for the mid-1980's (the data for such a study become available only after a lag of three to five years). The results showed that states which spent *more* on birth control per woman ages 15 to 44 had higher proportions of births out of wedlock and higher rates of teenage pregnancy and welfare dependency two years later.

The study also showed that states which provide government-funded abortions do not achieve lower levels of welfare dependency or a lower proportion of births out of wedlock. Instead, those states have significantly higher rates of teenage pregnancy. In *Family Planning Perspectives* of November/December 1990, Shelly Lundberg and Robert D. Plotnick reported similar evidence that easy access to abortion is associated with higher rates of white teenage pregnancy. They also found that easier access to contraceptives and abortions and more generous public assistance are associated with higher rates of premarital births among white teenagers.

The Clinton administration continues to ignore what can no longer be ignored: Government sex-ed programs and school-based clinics either increase teenage sexual activity, pregnancies, and abortion or—at best—have no significant impact. The surgeon general, of all people, ought be aware of the ambiguity. Between 1987 and 1991, during Dr. Elders's vigorous condom and clinic promotion as director of Public Health in Arkansas, the teenage birthrate rose 14 percent.

The Guttmacher Institute, a research affiliate of Planned Parenthood, pub- 20 lished an article concluding that "the existing data do not yet constitute consistent, compelling evidence that sex education programs are effective" in reducing teen pregnancies. Reviewing all the published studies on school clinics, investigators at Northwestern University Medical School and the Department of Health and Human Services concluded: "There is little consistent evidence that school-clinic programs affect pregnancy rates." Even the

National Education Association admits that there is "only meager evidence" that sex-ed programs have any effect on teen sex and illegitimacy.

Why, then, the relentless push for such programs at federal and state levels of government?

The near abandonment of common sense and moral instruction of young people in public education is part of the answer. The simple common sense of an earlier era would have suspected that talking to young people endlessly about sex from kindergarten through college, as is now the pedagogical custom, might encourage experimentation. "The philosophy that directs teens to 'be careful' or 'to play it safe with condoms' has not protected them," says Dr. Joe McIlhaney Jr., president of the Medical Institute for Sexual Health. "It has only enticed them into the quagmire of venereal warts, genital cancer and precancer, herpes for life, infertility, and AIDS." Such views, however, are not in vogue among President Clinton's health and education elites.

Another related reason for the adherence to failed sex-ed programs seems to be a stubborn assumption that sexual information automatically serves as a catalyst for transforming behavior.

As social scientist Charles Murray° has pointedly noted, however, almost 60 percent of the new white teenage mothers in 1991 were unmarried, compared with 18 percent in 1970. In 1991, 92 percent of births to black teenagers occurred out of wedlock, compared with 63 percent in 1970. Hispanics, who account for almost 30 percent of white teenage births, characteristically have higher fertility than other racial groups. The recent increase in teenage fertility, however, is not the result of Hispanic behavior. Fertility among non-Hispanic white teenagers increased by a third between 1986 and 1991, while the rate for Hispanics actually dropped and the rate for blacks increased only 18 percent. Clearly, the big increase occurred among young—and better educated—white women.

Not only were teenagers having rising proportions of births out of wedlock, but as reported by the National Center for Health Statistics, so were women of all ages. In 1960, 5 percent of all new babies were born out of wedlock. In 1991, the number topped 30 percent. This follows nearly three decades of increasingly comprehensive and explicit sex education for our children. Clearly, sexual instruction by itself cannot be expected to promote sexual responsibility. A 1991 *Newsweek* cover story admitted the obvious: "If education alone could affect people's behavior, STDs (sexually transmitted diseases) would be a thing of the past."

BETTER SOLUTIONS

What can be done to reduce risky youthful sexual behavior? There is a role for government, but it is largely negative: Restrictions on access to government-funded birth control and abortion have been followed by significant reductions

---

°**Charles Murray:** Controversial conservative or libertarian writer who argues that government social programs often undermine the family by rewarding irresponsibility.

in pregnancy and childbearing. When Ohio and Georgia stopped paying for Medicaid abortions in 1978, not only did abortion decline but so did pregnancy and births among women eligible for Medicaid.

The number of pregnancies among girls under 18 fell by 15 percent within two years after Massachusetts passed a law requiring parental notification regarding minors' abortions. In 1981, Minnesota passed such a law. The abortion rate among girls 15 to 17 years of age fell by 21 percent between 1980 and 1985, the pregnancy rate fell by 15 percent, and the fertility rate by 9 percent. (Planned Parenthood filed suit to have the law declared unconstitutional.) States that have passed parental consent laws for abortion have seen declines in abortion and teenage pregnancies.

Then what explains the flood of claims, so enthusiastically reported in the media, that government financing of contraceptives, abortion, and sterilizations prevents teenage pregnancy and saves billions in public assistance? The studies, all disseminated by family-planning interests, rely on assumptions rather than evidence. They presume that if women did not have easy access to subsidized government family planning, they would not restrain their sexual activity, nor would they buy their own condoms, but instead would engage in high levels of "unprotected" sex.

This assumption flies in the face of evidence as well as common sense. Considerable research has shown that people do adjust their behavior to the size of the risks they face. People whose houses are insured are more likely to build on flood plains. Economists have an expression—"moral hazard"—for this well-known human tendency to take greater risks, when insurance is more comprehensive and to avoid risk when uninsured. Kristin Luker reported as early as 1977 in *Studies in Family Planning* that women who had ready access to abortion were more likely to risk becoming pregnant.

In addition, the government ought to end or amend its $800,000 ad cam- 30 paign on radio and television to get Americans to use condoms. For one thing, the ads suggest that responsible condom use assures a high level of protection against HIV. But the research findings thus far are simply too controversial to make such claims. A recent study at the University of Texas, for example, found that even with condoms, the risk of HIV transmission can be as high as 31 percent.

Some of the ads even serve as an inducement to teenage sex. In one of them, a popular rock star tells the audience that he is naked and that he uses a latex condom "whenever I have sex." Not exactly a warning of the hazards of uncommitted sexual activity.

The second part of a strategy for curbing teen pregnancies is more affirmative. Leighton C. Ku and others reported in the May/June 1992 issue of *Family Planning Perspectives* that young people who had been taught "resistance skills"— how to say no—engaged in significantly less sexual activity and had fewer sex partners than students given birth-control instruction. In an abstinence-based program in Atlanta public schools, students are 15 times less likely to have sex in the year following the program than teens who took traditional sex education or none at all.

Two popular programs, *Sex Respect* and *Teen-Aid,* have done much to slow down teenage sexual activity, according to studies by the Institute for Research and Education. Both teach that abstinence is the healthiest lifestyle and discuss the emotional risks of premarital sex, as well as the risk of disease. A study of Illinois students enrolled in a *Sex Respect* course found that before the program, 60 percent of the students agreed that abstinence was the best way to avoid pregnancy. After the program, 80 percent of the students favored abstinence.

Despite critics of the program, there is a growing market for abstinence-based curricula. A 1990 study of 1,000 sexually active girls under 16 found that when asked what topic they wanted more information on, 84 percent said, "how to say no without hurting the other person's feelings."

SEX-ED CORRUPTION

After almost three decades of experience and study, the promoters of govern- 35 ment birth control have failed to produce any evidence of its salutary effects. On the contrary, the weight of the evidence, much of it published by its own proponents, shows it to be associated with increases in premarital sex, teenage pregnancy, births out of wedlock, welfare dependency and abortion. Most of the young people who are growing up in this era of government family planning are like my students—unwary, basically decent. But there are others. A *New York Times* story in March 1993 featured an interview with a member of a California gang accused of raping hundreds of girls as young as 10 years old. The boy was candid enough: "They pass out condoms, teach sex education, and pregnancy-this and pregnancy-that. But they don't teach us any rules."

The conclusion must be that government birth control is not merely another useless, wasteful public program. If it were, society could afford to ignore it. The conclusion must be, as the common sense of an earlier generation would have predicted, that government birth control corrupts youth.

■ ■ ■   ■   **A WRITER'S NOTEBOOK**   ■   ■   ■

Conservatism

The following tasks are designed to help you think about the readings and identify and start to work up material you might use in your own essay.

1. *Consider your personal experience with civic life.* Write a page or so telling about your own personal experience with civic life: Have you, for instance, participated in school government? Worked on a political campaign? Helped solve a community problem or helped others in need? Joined a public sports team or recreational group? Participated in a local neighborhood organiza-

tion? Even if you have not had any direct experience in civic life, you may have seen others participating or heard about controversies over local issues. Tell what you have experienced or observed and what you have learned from these situations.

2. *Keep a list.* While reading each argument, keep a list of the key terms or concepts — words like *liberty, rights, equality, individualism, welfare, responsibility, control,* or *regulation* — that the proponents of each stance rely upon. Record the author's name and the paragraph number of each term you select, jotting down perhaps three or four key terms per reading. Keeping this list will help you focus on the differences among conservatism, liberalism, and libertarianism and on the differences of emphases from writer to writer.

3. *Think about your own experience with rights.* The Bill of Rights was added to the Constitution in 1791 to protect the rights to freedom of religion, speech, and the press; the rights to bear arms and to be tried by a jury; and the prohibitions on cruel and unusual punishment and arbitrary government seizure of private property. Despite these protections, however, it is not always clear where one person's rights end and another person's rights begin. Think of an example from your own experience in which tension existed between one person's rights and another's (or one individual's rights versus those of a group). You might pick an incident in which you thought your rights were infringed on. Write a page or so explaining one concrete example. Conclude with a few sentences telling what your experience shows about the concept of rights.

4. *Follow the news.* As you work on this chapter, read a good regional or national newspaper every day and look for columns or interviews that seem written from one of the three civic stances. When you find particularly convincing — or particularly annoying — articles that illustrate conservatism, liberalism, or libertarianism, cut them out and tape them in your notebook. Write brief comments about each one, explaining why you chose it and exactly what it illustrates. You may be able to draw on these articles when writing your essay.

5. *Explain Russell Kirk's statement.* In paragraph 12, Kirk says that "distinctions of order, wealth, and responsibility" are necessary and inevitable, that we should respect private property, and that we should not strive for a "levelling equality." Write a few sentences explaining what you think Kirk means in this paragraph.

6. *Explain one of Sam Brownback's statements.* In paragraph 12, Brownback writes that "the American people believe they can handle most of their problems better than the federal government can." Review some of the examples he gives in paragraphs 7–11, 28, and 34 and then write a half-page or so explaining what you think he means by this statement.

7. *Take a position on Jacqueline R. Kasun's argument.* In paragraph 4, Kasun criticizes "government-engineered sex education," and in paragraphs 6–7 she criticizes the fact that sex education is dictated by government entities rather than by parents or families. Write a page or so agreeing or disagreeing with Kasun's argument that parents are more appropriate than government for making decisions about adolescent sex education and access to birth control. Give reasons for your position and support your reasons with examples from your personal knowledge and experience.

8. *Review key terms and explain conservatism.* If you prepared a list of terms and concepts as you read the arguments in this section, look it over and then try to write a brief explanation of conservatism. Your explanation should be about a page long and include examples from the readings as well as definitions. Use the most important terms or concepts you have identified but put them into your own sentences. Imagine you are writing your explanation for other college students who have not read about conservatism. Working out this brief explanation now will enable you to synthesize what you have learned about conservatism and save you time when you write your essay.

9. *Analyze a cartoon.* The political cartoon below was published in 1996 in *National Review*, a conservative journal. Write a few sentences discussing what you think the cartoon is saying about the IRS (Internal Revenue Service), the federal agency that oversees taxation. (The "public sector" refers to government-run enterprises while the "private sector" refers to private enterprise, businesses attempting to make a profit for their owners or shareholders.) Then explain whether or not you agree with the perspective represented in the cartoon. Does it reflect your own experience? Does it reflect the conservative stance? In what way?

LIBERALISM

Contemporary liberalism is rooted not only in the Declaration of Independence but also in the social and economic programs that began in the 1930s and extended through the 1960s, from President Franklin D. Roosevelt's New Deal to President Lyndon B. Johnson's Great Society. Liberals today continue

"NOW REMEMBER, YOU NO LONGER WORK IN THE PRIVATE SECTOR. IN THE PUBLIC SECTOR, THE CUSTOMER IS NEVER RIGHT."

to believe that the federal government should protect individual liberties and promote the general welfare by providing a safety net for the least fortunate.

Some conservatives argue that solving the problems of today's families requires changes in behavior, such as a renewed commitment to traditional moral standards. To such an argument, a liberal might reply: "The old morality was based partly on the inequality of women, and a return to the family or the moral values of the 1950s would trample on the newly achieved rights of women. Changes in the contemporary American family are the result of women's liberation, economic change, and the need for two-income families." This hypothetical liberal argues, then, that the rights of one group (women, in this example) cannot be subordinated for the sake of a vague general good. Today's liberal tends to value individual rights and to be wary of restrictions on personal behavior.

But this same liberal might answer a conservative very differently when government regulation of the economy is at issue. For example, a liberal might say: "Look at the problems society already has and look at the role of large corporations. Government regulations are there to keep powerful individuals or groups from trampling on the rights of the less powerful but also to help build roads and schools and provide for other benefits that individuals could not achieve on their own." In this liberal argument, government plays a crucial role in promoting the general welfare, refereeing the economy, and reducing inequality.

Barbara Presley Noble, for example, argued in 1994 against critics of big government by citing this list of important safeguards that the federal government has enacted since the 1930s:

- The Fair Labor Standards Act of 1938, which established the minimum wage, the 40-hour work week, and overtime pay and restricted the use of child labor.

- The National Labor Relations Act of 1935, which grants the right of employees to form unions and bargain collectively.

- The Social Security Act of 1935, the employment-based savings program intended to cushion the impact of retirement and old age, unemployment, and the death of the household wage earner.

- The Civil Rights Act of 1964, Title VII of which outlaws discrimination on the basis of gender, race, color, religion or national origin in the workplace.

- The Occupational Safety and Health Act of 1970, governing safety in the workplace.

- The Employment Retirement Security Act of 1974, or Erisa, the devilishly complicated body of law that protects pensions [. . .].[6]

Liberals today are also likely to differ with conservatives about moral values. This difference may occur because liberals distrust what conservatives say about morality or because they think economic policies and conditions—not moral breakdown—are the most important cause of social problems. For instance, Arlene Skolnick makes this liberal contribution to the debate about family values:

---

[6]Barbara Presley Noble, "A Fond Farewell to Big Government," *New York Times* 13 Nov. 1994: F25.

Instead of debating the merits of Murphy Brown or the Waltons vs. the Simpsons, we should be discussing how to help families cope with the real problems of family life [...] the need to have two or more incomes to make ends meet, the unaffordability of housing and health care, the inadequacy of child care, the spread of Depression-era conditions, the disgraceful number of children living in poverty.[7]

Skolnick's point is that family problems derive from economic pressures and that it is somewhat hypocritical to try to solve such problems simply by calling for a return to morality. Ronald Dworkin emphasizes this point as well when he explains the social and economic sides of liberalism:

Liberalism has two aspects, and they are both under powerful attack. Liberals believe, first, that government must be neutral in matters of personal morality, that it must leave people free to live as they think best so long as they do not harm others. But the Reverend Jerry Falwell, and other politicians who claim to speak for some "moral majority," want to enforce their own morality with the steel of the criminal law. They know what kind of sex is bad, which books are fit for public libraries, what place religion should have in education and family life, when human life begins, that contraception is sin, and that abortion is capital sin. They think the rest of us should be forced to practice what they preach. The old issue of political theory—whether the law should enforce a state morality—is once again an important issue of practical politics.

The second side of liberalism is economic. Liberals insist that government has a responsibility to reduce economic inequality, both through its management of the economy and through welfare programs that redistribute wealth to soften the impact of poverty.[8]

As you read the essays by liberals, keep Dworkin's distinctions in mind: that liberals distrust government interference in personal morality but aim to use government to reduce economic inequality.

Today's liberal, then, is more likely than today's conservative to endorse government programs, arguing that the changes in the nature and the size of the economy over the last two centuries require more government intervention and regulation than were required when America was smaller. Liberals sometimes argue that, in the Founders' time, people needed protection *from* tyrannical governments but that now people need government intervention to limit the excesses of modern capitalism and to extend freedom to all citizens.

As you read the following arguments, note particularly what the writers say about freedom, individual rights, and the role of government. Also remember to keep track of key terms and concepts, as you were asked to do for the earlier readings, and to look for newspaper columns and interviews on the three civic stances.

---

[7] Arlene Skolnick, "There's 'Family' at the Microwave," *Los Angeles Times* 9 Aug. 1992.

[8] Ronald Dworkin, "Neutrality, Equality, and Liberalism," *Liberalism Reconsidered,* ed. Douglas MacLean and Claudia Mills (Totowa: Rowman & Allanheld, 1983) 1. [Reprinted with permission from *New York Review of Books,* 1983].

THE TRIUMPH OF LIBERALISM

Roger Rosenblatt

Roger Rosenblatt is an editor and writer whose essays have appeared in the New York Times, Time *magazine, the* New Republic, *and other magazines, as well as on* The Lehrer Report, *a PBS television news show. He has received a number of awards for journalism and is the author of five books.*

In this article, published in the New York Times *in 1996, Rosenblatt defends liberalism against some of its recent critics. Arguing, in part, that liberalism is "robust and established," he first reviews some of the criticisms of liberalism and then defines what he means by the term. He discusses some of the misunderstandings (as he sees it) that have lessened the reputation of liberalism and ends with a review of its accomplishments.*

As you read, note what rights Rosenblatt believes that liberalism has protected and how he thinks liberalism fosters equality.

The America I heard singing° when I was a teen-ager in the late 1950's forced homosexuals into hiding, ignored or derided the disabled, withheld rights from suspects of crimes and kept women in their place, which was usually the kitchen and sometimes an abortionist's back room. It foisted prayers on schoolchildren, paid no attention to the health needs of the impoverished or the elderly, endangered endangered species and threw people out of work because they held an un-American ideology.° In certain places, it denied black Americans the right to sit where they wished to on a public bus, to drink from a public water fountain, to eat in restaurants, to stay in hotels, to go to public schools with whites or to vote.

Every one of these conditions has been corrected or improved by laws and attitudes derived from a philosophy that is held in such low esteem it dare not speak its name. Today, as America enters the 1996 Presidential election year, it is singing two different tunes. One is "Liberalism Is Dead and I'm Feeling So Sad." The other is "Liberalism Is Dead and I'm Feeling So Glad." If this keening and gloating sounds familiar, it is. You last heard it in the election year of 1992. The gloating came most elegantly from Irving and William Kristol, the formidable father-son team of conservative thinkers. In an article in *Commentary,* William, the son, stated that "liberalism is in a deep crisis" and has "a hollowness at the core." Irving wrote in the *Wall Street Journal* that "the beginning of

---

°**I heard singing:** An allusion to "I Hear America Singing," a poem by nineteenth-century American poet Walt Whitman.   °**un-American ideology:** During hearings of the House Un-American Activities Committee in the 1950s, some Americans were accused of being Communists and consequently lost their jobs.

political wisdom in the 1990's is the recognition that liberalism today is at the end of its intellectual tether."

Regrets over liberalism's death arrived in defensive books from equally thoughtful people who celebrated the New Deal and the Great Society as brave last stands against the inevitable, and in statements like that of the former Democratic Presidential candidate Walter Mondale that liberals "kind of used up the old agenda." The final draft of the Democratic Party platform in 1992 openly spurned liberalism by trying to stake out a middle ground between laissez-faire capitalism and the welfare state.° Respected authors sought to redefine the term. Jim Sleeper, Mary D. and Thomas Byrne Edsall and Mickey Kaus, among others, produced books that searched for a liberalism that repudiated liberalism.

What is interesting about these two kinds of attacks, since both are attacks with different motives, is that underneath it all, they take their ardor from the presumption that liberalism is not dead, but robust and established. They are right. "Liberal society is in trouble," says the historian Arthur Schlesinger Jr., "but I would be surprised at a retreat from a basic liberal ethos."...

Liberalism dominates the debate and defines the terms of the debate. The 5 conservative assaults on the L word, which were made most effectively by President Reagan, have been so routine over the past 16 years that there is a whole generation of people under 35 who have never heard "liberal" uttered as anything other than a joke or an insult. Yet they live in a liberal country. Conservatives may have ruined the word but have adopted most of the content of liberalism....

The liberalism I am thinking of is a kind of general cultural-political liberalism, a mixture of the New Deal programs of the 1930's and the individual rights movements of the 1960's, which knocked the wind out of all the callous, restrictive and narrow-minded conditions that I grew up with a few decades ago. It is a malleable philosophy, generous and socially responsible, that governs how people ought to live with one another in a healthy democracy. It is not the specific liberalism of the Franklin Roosevelt era, or the Lyndon Johnson era, or explicitly that of voting rights laws or expanded civil liberties, though it creates and encourages such developments. Rather, it is the sentiment that may be traced back to the Declaration of Independence and the Constitution...and to the moderate Enlightenment° from which those documents sprang, that people are inherently equal, that they have a right to pursue their individuality in an open society and that the state must use its power and authority to secure their rights and to help the needier among them.

°**laissez-faire capitalism and the welfare state:** Laissez-faire is capitalism unrestrained by government regulations or safety nets. *Welfare state* is a general term for a government that takes responsibility for the well-being of its citizens through Social Security, medical insurance, or welfare.
°**Enlightenment:** The eighteenth-century philosophy that emphasized individual rights.

This liberalism is neither dead nor on the run. The country backs away from it in frightened and hardscrabble times. Most observers concede that it needs to make some corrections in its details and attitudes. And from the viewpoint of liberal candidates seeking office, it needs to regain political power to further its aims. But in its competition with conservative thinking for the soul of America, it has won hands down.

"People say that the Great Society failed," says Robert Caro, the historian of the Lyndon Johnson Presidency. "That really is nonsense. Is anyone today suggesting that we resegregate public accommodations, that we have 'colored' and 'white' toilets? It is unthinkable that we would make such retreats. Those aspects of liberalism are now so much a part of America that they are indistinguishable from America. In that sense, America *is* liberalism."....

In a cultural atmosphere in which liberals are assumed to support the purveyors of sacrilege and dirty talk, the purveyors of simpleminded virtue come off as moral leaders, and the public has a choice between the tasteless and the boring. In fact, most liberals who favor the protections of an open society are appalled by its excesses, but they have not made that clear. It has been said that they are in favor of every subculture except that of married, hard-working, home-buying, church-going Americans. The themes raised by conservatives that have been warmly welcomed by the rest of the country are not taxes or a trickle-down economy, but rather an evocation of communal values and morals....

Liberalism is most scorned for its association with big government, even 10 though liberals were against the abuses of Presidential power under President Johnson in Vietnam and President Nixon in Watergate. While originally fearing a too-powerful state, it has been seen as willing and eager to give the state power in order to realize egalitarian° goals. In "Liberal Purposes" (1991), Prof. William A. Galston of the University of Maryland wrote: "A government too weak to threaten our liberties may by that very fact be too weak to secure our rights, let alone advance our shared purposes."

Yet the fact remains that with all of liberalism's missteps and inadequacies, America has signed on to it. There are major areas of activity, like the rights of women and of members of minorities, and the environment, that could not have changed the American landscape without great numbers of people agreeing that they wanted government in their lives. Since the passage of the Civil Rights Act of 1964, the presence of minority-group members in the work force his grown from 11 percent to 23 percent. "Of course we don't have social justice," says Robert Caro, "but we have moved a long way toward it."

Women today make up nearly half the managerial and professional ranks. This is because of big government—Title VII of the 1964 Civil Rights Act, the Equal Pay Act of 1963, the Equal Credit Opportunity Act of 1974. Suzanne

---

°**egalitarian:** Promoting equality.

Braun Levine, editor of the *Columbia Journalism Review*, said, "There has not been a single woman in this country who has not been changed by the last 30 years of activism, and even those who resist what used to be called 'women's lib' are beneficiaries of it."

Even affirmative action, one of the most fragile and hotly contested of liberal programs—debated by both conservatives and liberals—has proved to be wanted, at least in some form, by most Americans....

One of the less noted but highly significant areas in which government has proved indispensable is the environment. According to the Environmental Protection Agency, the effects of the Clean Air Act Amendments of 1990, signed by President Bush, will reduce the country's air pollution by more than 49 billion pounds per year. The number of regions violating the air-quality standards for carbon monoxide has dropped to 9 from more than 40 in the past five years. Sulfur dioxide emissions, which cause acid rain, have been reduced by 2.6 million tons since 1990.

In short, since the 1960's, the public, rather than seeking to reduce a govern- 15 mental presence in the environment, has sought to ratchet it up. Bipartisan support passed the Clean Air Act Amendments in 1990 by 401 to 25 in the House and by 89 to 10 in the Senate. Industry has experienced no serious loss. Du Pont and other chemical companies have been given incentives to develop substitutes for ozone-depleting chemicals. The timber interests in Oregon originally claimed that forest-saving efforts would threaten jobs in the state, but keeping the trees vertical has so increased tourism—while making the state attractive as a corporate location—that now Oregon has the lowest unemployment numbers in a generation.

None of this is to claim that the country is not genuinely concerned with the amount of big government in its life—although there often seems to be as much formulaic reaction against it as there is against "knee-jerk liberalism," or "big business." The reality is that the country very much wants to keep government big.

The triumph of liberalism is not a political victory. Rather it is a triumph of temperament and attitude; it reflects how America wishes to exist. It has been said that liberalism is confounded by an unrealistic optimism about the possibilities of human advancement. But the idea was born in 18th-century rationalism. It picked up 19th-century Romanticism along the way as it moved forward, and the combination of thought may be read in the Constitution—an 18th-century document with 19th-century riders.

The truth of liberalism is that it is both optimistic and pragmatic. It believes in improvement but not in perfectibility. It is often embarrassed by the freedoms it supports and encourages, and by the unwieldiness of the government it promotes. But it believes in the dream of human nobility, which historically has proved equally fanciful and reasonable.

Perhaps, as happens from time to time, America appears to be fed up with liberalism and prepared to shut down its normal impulses for a while. But every such period is followed by a further advance of both freedom and equality, because this is the way the country has wanted to go. Within my lifetime, America has progressed from a nation that quashed human rights and diminished human dignity to one that worries about cultural influences and a budget. Most people would call that a triumph.

They Only *Look* Dead:
Why Progressives Will Dominate the Next Political Era

E. J. Dionne Jr.

E. J. Dionne Jr. is a columnist for the Washington Post. *His first book,* Why Americans Hate Politics *(1991), won several awards and reportedly influenced Bill Clinton in his 1992 presidential campaign. This reading comes from Dionne's 1996 book* They Only *Look* Dead: Why Progressives Will Dominate the Next Political Era. *Using the term* progressive *as a synonym for* liberal, *he predicts that the United States is on the verge of a new era of liberalism, or progressivism.*

Dionne begins by refuting the typical conservative and libertarian argument against government, which he characterizes as a negative argument because it emphasizes freedom from *interference. In contrast, Dionne characterizes liberalism's support of energetic government as positive because it emphasizes* freedom to—*that is, it emphasizes government's role in helping citizens to be free to enjoy good health and not be impoverished in old age; in preserving the environment; and in providing public schools, police protection, parks, and other services.*

As you read, try to understand why Dionne thinks that the marketplace, or free-market capitalism, needs to be regulated. Also keep in mind his distinctions between size *of government and* kind *of government, and* freedom from *and* freedom to.

Those who believe in government's possibilities cannot pretend that they share the new conservatism's view of the state. At the heart of the new conservatism is the belief that government action is not only essentially inefficient but also inherently oppressive. Democratic government, in this telling, has interests all its own that have nothing to do with what the voters want. What's especially important about this idea is that it ultimately sees no *fundamental* distinction between free government and dictatorship. The differences are only a matter of degree, not of kind: The more limited democratic government is, the better; the more active democratic government is, the more it begins to approach the evils of Nazism or communism. "Behind our New Deals and New Frontiers and Great Societies," writes [conservative U.S.] House majority leader Dick Armey,° "you will find, *with a difference only in power and nerve,* the same sort of person who gave the world its Five Year Plans and Great Leaps Forward°—the Soviet and Chinese counterparts." [Emphasis added.]

This an extraordinary and radical claim, effectively equating Roosevelt, Kennedy and Johnson with Stalin and Mao.° If the problem is stated like this, then there is only one choice: Preserving freedom means having government do as little as possible. A government that might levy taxes to provide health care coverage for all or pensions for the old is seen as marching the people down "the road to serfdom," in the evocative phrase of the libertarian economist Friedrich A. Hayek. Better, in this view, to have no health care and no pensions than to have the government embark on this terrible path. Environmental regulations are seen not as preserving streams and forests for future generations; they are viewed as ways of interfering with the free use of private property. Work safety regulations are no longer ways of providing employees with some protections against hazardous machines or conditions; they are seen as "interference in the right of contract."°

This sort of thinking is now so common that it has been forgotten how radically different it is from the tradition on which the United States was founded—a tradition to which contemporary liberals, moderates, conservatives and libertarians all trace their roots. As the political philosopher Stephen Holmes has argued (Holmes, 18, 23), the entire project of freedom going back to America's founders rests not on *weak* government, but rather on an *energetic* government, government strong enough to protect individual rights. Free government° is different in *kind* from despotic regimes because its fundamental purpose—to vindicate the rights of individuals—is different.

Imagine on the one side a dictatorship that has no government-provided social security, health, welfare or pension systems of any type. It levies relatively low taxes which go almost entirely toward supporting large military and secret police forces that regularly jail or kill people because of their political views, religious beliefs—or for any other reason the regime decides. Then imagine a democracy with regular open elections and full freedoms of speech and religion. Imagine further that its government levies higher taxes than the dictatorship to support an extensive welfare state, generous old-age pensions·

°**Dick Armey:** Conservative U.S. House majority leader at the time of Dionne's writing and an unsuccessful candidate in the 1996 Republican presidential primaries.   °**Five Year Plans and Great Leaps Forward:** The economic plans of, respectively, the Soviet and the Chinese Communists.   °**Stalin and Mao:** Joseph Stalin and Mao Zedong, repressive past Communist leaders of, respectively, the Soviet Union and China.   °**right of contract:** The right of individuals to enter freely into contracts, an important element in the political theory of libertarians like Hayek.

and a government health system. The first country might technically have a "smaller government," but there is no doubt that it is *not* a free society. The second country would have a "bigger government," measured as a percentage of gross domestic product,° yet there is no doubt that it *is* a free society. This point might seem obvious, but it is in fact obscured by the presumptions that underlie the conservative anti-government talk now so popular. The size of government is an important issue, but it is not as important as—and should not be confused with—the *kind* of government a society has.

Because the anti-government ideology of the new conservatism views almost 5 all forms of government intervention (beyond basic police protection) with suspicion, it misses entirely the fact that democratic governments can intervene in ways that *expand* individual liberty. At the extreme, it took a very strong national government (and very forceful intervention) to end slavery and literally free four million Americans from bondage. It's worth remembering that supporters of slavery saw abolitionists as "enemies of liberty" interfering with the "property rights" of slaveholders and imposing the federal government's wishes over "the rights of states." Similarly, it took a strong federal government to end segregation in the 1960s and vindicate the right of African-Americans to vote. Such actions were well within the liberal tradition of free government which, notes Stephen Holmes, accepted that there were occasions when "only a powerful centralized state could protect individual rights against local strongmen and religious majorities" (20).

In the current cacophony of anti-government sloganeering, it is forgotten that the ever-popular slogan "equality of opportunity" was made real only by extensive government efforts to offer individuals opportunities to develop their *own* capacities. As Holmes points out, Adam Smith,° the intellectual father of the free market, favored a publicly financed, compulsory system of elementary education. After World War II the government's investment in the college education of millions through the GI Bill simultaneously opened new opportunities for individuals and promoted an explosive period of general economic growth. As Holmes puts it: "Far from being a road to serfdom, government intervention was meant to enhance individual autonomy. Publicly financed schooling, as Mill wrote, is 'help toward doing without help'" (Holmes 23). John Stuart Mill° offers here a powerful counter to those who would insist that government intervention always and everywhere increases "dependency."

Government also fosters liberty by doing something so obvious that it is little noticed: It insists that certain things cannot be bought and sold. We do not, for example, believe that justice in the courts should be bought and sold. We presume that votes and public offices cannot be bought (even if expensive political campaigns raise questions about the depth of our commitment to this

---

°**gross domestic product:** The total value of goods and services produced within a country during a year. °**Adam Smith:** Late-eighteenth-century philosopher and economist. °**John Stuart Mill:** Nineteenth-century British philosopher, author of *On Liberty.*

proposition). We now accept, though we once did not, that it is wrong for a wealthy person to buy his way out of the draft during a time of war. And, of course, we do not believe that human beings can be bought and sold.

But these do not exhaust the instances in which a free people might decide to limit the writ of money and the supremacy of the market.° As the political philosopher Michael Walzer has argued, one of the central issues confronting democratic societies concerns which rights and privileges should not be put up for sale. As an abstract proposition, we reject the notion that a wealthy person should be able to buy extra years of life that a poor person cannot, since life itself ought not be bought and sold. Yet the availability of health care affects longevity, and by making health care a purely market transaction, we come close to selling life and death. This was the primary argument for Medicare° and remains the central moral claim made by advocates of national health insurance. Similarly, we do not believe that children should be deprived of access to food, medicine or education just because their parents are poor. As Holmes puts it, "Why should children be hopelessly snared in a web of under-privilege into which they were born through no fault of their own?"

The current vogue for the superiority of markets over government carries the risk of obscuring the basic issue of what should be for sale in the first place. In a society characterized by growing economic inequality, the dangers of making the marketplace the sole arbiter of the basic elements of a decent life are especially large. Doing so could put many of the basics out of the reach of many people who "work hard and play by the rules." The interrelationship between the moral and economic crises can be seen most powerfully in families where the need to earn enough income forces both parents to spend increasing amounts of time outside the home. One of the great achievements of this century was "the family wage," which allowed the vast majority of workers to provide their families with both a decent living and the parental time to give their children a decent upbringing. The family wage was not simply a product of the marketplace. It was secured through a combination of economic growth, social legislation and unionization. If the marketplace becomes not simply the main arbiter of income, as it will inevitably be, but the *only* judge of living standards, then all social factors, including the need to strengthen families and improve the care given children, become entirely irrelevant in the world of work.

Two questions are frequently confused in the current debate: whether marketplace *mechanisms*° might be usefully invoked to solve certain problems, and whether the solution of the problems themselves should be left *entirely* to the market. This confusion afflicts Progressives and conservatives alike. 10

On the one hand, applying marketplace logic to government programs can be highly useful. One of the most telling criticisms of government is that it does

---

°**the market:** The free, unplanned economy responding to economic supply and demand. °**Medicare:** Government program of medical care for those over sixty-five.   °**marketplace *mechanisms:*** Free-market economic features such as supply and demand or the profit motive.

not live by the disciplines of the market, and can thus—in theory at least—deliver services as shoddily as it chooses, with as large a bureaucracy as it wishes. This argument can become a parody of itself, denying that there are, in fact, good public schools, fine police forces, excellent public parks, great public libraries and the like. But the argument does point fairly to certain limits on the government's capacities. . . . There *are* instances when it is more efficient for government to give each citizen a voucher to purchase services in a competitive marketplace than to provide the services directly. The GI Bill, for example, did not prescribe where veterans would go to college. It let them choose and gave them the means to pay for the education of their choice. Clinton's housing secretary, Henry Cisneros, proposed scrapping federal subsidies for local public housing *agencies* and turning federal aid into housing vouchers that would go directly to poor people. If a given public housing project was so crime-infested and run-down that poor people would choose not to live in it, it could be closed and sold off. An abstract fear of marketplace logic should not impede experiments of this sort.

But supporting market-oriented solutions to problems is *not* the same as suggesting that the market itself, left to its own devices, will solve all problems. If the government had not given the education vouchers to the GIs, many of them would never have gone to college. The market can break down, recessions can throw people out of work, families can lose their health insurance, poor people can lack the money to buy food and shelter for their children. The answer to the most rabid free-market advocates is that the free market is a wonderful instrument that also creates problems and leaves others unsolved. To assert as a flat rule, as Representative Armey does, that "the market is rational and the government is dumb" (Armey 316) is to assume that it is rational to accept problems created by unemployment, low wages, business cycles, pollution and simple human failings; and dumb to use government to try to lessen the human costs associated with them. Mr. Armey might believe that; most Americans do not.

The difference between this era's conservatives and the American Progressive tradition lies in the distinction between two phrases, "freedom from" and "freedom to." Free-market conservatives are very much alive to the importance of what the philosopher Isaiah Berlin called "negative liberty," defined as freedom *from* coercion by the state. American Progressives and liberals share this concern for negative liberty, which is why they accept with the conservatives the need for limited government. Historically, however, Progressives have been more alive to the promise of "positive liberty" and to free government's capacity for promoting it. To be the master of one's own fate—a fair definition of liberty—means not simply being free from overt coercion (though that is a precondition); it also involves being given the means to overcome various external forces that impinge on freedom of choice and self-sufficiency. It means being free *to* set one's course.

From the beginning, therefore, the Progressive project has involved the use of government to give men and women the tools needed for achieving positive liberty, beginning with free elementary and secondary education and moving in the Depression and postwar era to Social Security, unemployment compensation and access to college and to health insurance. (The Progressives, beginning with women's suffrage, were also at the forefront in expanding the realm of freedom for women.) . . .

In our era, conservatives have monopolized the concept of liberty and given it a particular and largely negative definition. Progressives have been cast — and have sometimes foolishly cast themselves — as defenders of coercion and bureaucracy, of government for government's sake. The imperative for Progressives is to rediscover their own tradition as the party of liberty. In a free society *all* parties to the debate should be arguing about the best ways to enhance and advance human freedom. For Progressives, that is and always has been the central purpose of government. . . .

The Progressive's goal is not to strengthen government for government's sake, but to use government where possible to strengthen the institutions of civil society.° Those institutions need protection against the state, but they also need protection from market forces. How, for example, can families be liberated from some of the pressures of the marketplace — through more "family-friendly" tax laws, through better rules on parental leave, through incentives to create more flexible workplaces so parents feel less conflicted between the obligations of work and home? How can government policies strengthen rather than weaken the voluntary sector? Can the poor who live in public housing projects be given more control of their surroundings and a larger stake in their communities? Can rules be written so that employers who feel a sense of loyalty and obligation to their employees will not be punished by the marketplace? Given that the American charitable sector prospered for years on the unpaid labor of women volunteers, how can it be revitalized now that so many women both want and need to work for wages and salaries? . . .

Progressives — liberals — thus need to embrace a politics of liberty and community. They cannot leave the definition of liberty to their conservative adversaries. They need to contest the negative definition of liberty as incomplete. Yes, individuals need to be protected against omnipotent, abusive government. But they also have a right to look to government for help in defending their autonomy and expanding the possibilities of self-reliance. Government should not weaken the bonds of civil society. But government *can* step in to strengthen civil society and protect it against the disruptions created by the normal workings of the economic market. Surely anyone who claims to believe in "family values" should want to relieve families of some of the pressures placed upon them by work and economic distress. As Theodore Roosevelt put it: "No man" — he could have added women — "can be a good citizen unless he has a wage more than sufficient

15

°**institutions of civil society:** Structures like families, neighborhoods, clubs, or volunteer programs that are important in our lives but are not controlled or financed by government.

to cover the bare costs of living, and hours of labor short enough so that after his day's work is done, he will have time and energy to bear his share in the management of the community, to help in carrying the general load" (Roosevelt 146). Long before "civil society" was a fashionable phrase, TR understood its meaning.

A New Progressivism based on these principles would take seriously Bill Kristol's° talk about "the politics of liberty and the sociology of virtue." But it would contest the effectiveness of the new conservative program supported by Kristol and his allies, arguing that liberty and virtue require not only freedom from government coercion, but also the active support of a government that understands not only its limits but also its obligations. It is not enough to preach virtue to a family that finds its living standard falling despite its own best efforts to work, save, invest and care for its children. Such a family surely deserves some support for its own efforts to expand its opportunities—and, at the least, some insurance against the worst economic catastrophes that might befall it.

WORKS CITED

Armey, Dick. *The Freedom Revolution.* Washington, D.C.: Regnery, 1995.

Berlin, Isaiah. *Four Essays on Liberty.* New York: Oxford, 1969.

Holmes, Stephen. *Passions and Constraint: On the Theory of Liberal Democracy.* Chicago: U of Chicago P, 1995.

Roosevelt, Theodore. "The New Nationalism." *Theodore Roosevelt, an American Mind: A Selection from His Writings.* Ed. Mario R. DiNunzio. New York: St. Martin's, 1994.

Waltzer, Michael. *Spheres of Justice: A Defense of Pluralism and Equality.* New York: Basic, 1983.

DUBIOUS CONCEPTIONS

Kristin Luker

Kristin Luker is a professor of sociology and jurisprudence and social policy at the University of California at Berkeley. She is the author of Abortion and the Politics of Motherhood *(1984) and a number of articles on teen pregnancy. This reading comes from her 1996 book* Dubious Conceptions: The Politics of Teenage Pregnancy.

You will see that Luker shares one assumption with Jacqueline R. Kasun: that women who become pregnant as teenagers are less likely to complete their education and take advantage of the opportunities available to those who pursue an

---

°**Bill Kristol:** William Kristol, an influential contemporary American neoconservative.

education first and marry later. Beyond that assumption, however, Luker's views on sex education differ markedly from Kasun's. When Luker writes that "some people think that sex education is part of the problem," you can assume that she has conservative writers like Kasun in mind.

As you read, identify and think about the assumptions that Luker makes about whose responsibility it is to promote the welfare of teenagers. How does Luker's answer to this question differ from Kasun's? Also note that Luker's argument shares some of the same liberal assumptions that are evident in E. J. Dionne Jr.'s reading — the distinction between freedom from *and* freedom to.

In the past twenty years we have acquired a great deal of knowledge about preventing involuntary pregnancy and childbearing among teenagers. But it's the young people who voluntarily get pregnant (although we've seen how passive this "voluntary" choice can be) who elicit the most concern and whom we know the least about helping. And many of the current public-policy proposals seem likely to reverse the gains of the recent past.

This is a dispiriting time to be thinking about teenagers and their pregnancies. We know more than ever about how to help young people avoid getting pregnant and having babies they don't want. We can point with pride to effective public policies that since the 1970s have helped keep early childbearing from reaching truly epidemic proportions, though the numbers of sexually active teens have increased enormously in the United States, as they have in most industrialized countries. Despite their success, these policies have never really addressed the plight of young women who want a baby or of those who don't much care whether they have one or not. Yet here, too, accumulating research has begun to suggest ways of encouraging even these teens to postpone pregnancy, while other research... shows that the reasons for postponement are much less urgent than once thought....

But the dismay and anxiety of the American public in an era of rapid shifts in the economy, in family structures, and in social well-being have led the public discourse about teenagers to become more mean-spirited and irrational than ever. To take one example, government programs have in fact reduced pregnancy rates among teenagers. The political consensus in the 1960s among traditional liberals and traditional conservatives on public funding of contraception has paid off handsomely: today, poor and minority women have the sort of control over their fertility that only middle-class women used to enjoy. And young women have benefited from such programs to a greater extent than most people realize. More and more teenagers have begun using contraception, and using it effectively. Teens can now obtain low-cost or free birth control from a variety of sources (including hospitals, local health departments, and Planned Parenthood clinics), and they make good use of this access: according to one study, about 53 percent of all teenagers—and 72 percent of black teenagers—obtain their first contraceptive from a clinic, whereas about 40 percent of all teens obtain it from a private physician.[1] Between 1969 and 1983 the number of teenagers using family planning clinics increased more than six-fold. By 1988 the figure had doubled again, to approximately 3 million;[2] two-thirds of all teens using contraception identified a family planning clinic as the most recent source of their contraception.[3] During the 1980s, as the economy worsened and medical care became more expensive, clinics became an ever more important source of contraception for teenagers, especially poor ones.[4] In 1983 more than 80 percent of teenage users of clinics came from families living below the poverty level and 13 percent from families on public assistance. Overall, clinic users are likely to be poor and black, and they are younger at first intercourse than people who go to a private physician.

Since the number of sexually active teenagers doubled between 1970 and 1990, it is unlikely that any sort of contraceptive services would have effected a substantial decline in pregnancy rates among teenagers, given that the population at risk doubled. Yet a doubling of the population of sexually active teens did not lead to a doubling of the pregnancy rate, and public funding of contraception is the reason. This enormously successful program—one that has made teens *less* likely to get pregnant than ever before and one whose effects are most visible in poor and minority communities—has been rewarded by having its funding cut almost in half.[5] In part this is due to a resurgence in political opposition to publicly funded contraception, opposition based to some extent on the fact that federal programs have slowed but not reversed the acceleration in the pregnancy rates among teenagers, leading people to see these programs as a failure rather than the considerable success that they are....

[Another] public policy—sex education—seems to be making some progress in preventing teenagers from getting pregnant in the first place. Although sex education has been a feature of American public schools since the Progressive Era, we are just beginning to understand what makes a successful

[1]Melvin Zelnik, M. A. Koenig, and Y. J. Kim, "Source of Prescription Contraceptives and Subsequent Pregnancy among Women," *Family Planning Perspectives* 16 (1984): 6–13.

[2]A. Torres and J. D. Forrest, "Family Planning Clinic Services in the United States, 1983," *Family Planning Perspectives* 17, no. 1 (1985): 30–35; Alan Guttmacher Institute, *Organized Family Planning Services in the United States, 1981–1983* (New York: Alan Guttmacher Institute, 1984); M. Chamie, S. Eisman, J. D. Forrest, M. Orr, and A. Torres, "Factors Affecting Adolescents' Use of Family Planning Clinics," *Family Planning Perspectives* 14 (1982): 126–139; R. Levine and L. Tsolflias, "Publicly Supported Family Planning in the U.S.: Use in the 1980s," Henry J. Kaiser Foundation, 1994.

[3]U.S. Department of Health and Human Services, Public Health Service, Centers for Disease Control, "Use of Family Planning Services in the United States, 1982–1988," *Advance Data from Vital and Health Statistics*, vol. 184 (Hyattsville, Md.: National Center for Health Statistics, 1990).

[4]Levine and Tsolflias, "Publicly Supported Family Planning in the U.S."

[5]Leighton Ku, "Financing of Family Planning Services in Publicly Supported Family Planning Services in the United States" (Washington, D.C.: Urban Institute and Child Trends, Inc., 1993).

program. In 1938 Benjamin Gruenberg, a noted Progressive reformer, found that a majority of the nation's high schools had instituted sex education programs, and most of the rest were considering doing so.[6] In his day "sex education" meant everything from brief lectures about menstrual hygiene to complex discussions of the social, ethical, and moral dimensions of relationships between the sexes—and things are not very different now. At least thirty-one states and the District of Columbia have policies that mandate or encourage sex education, but curricula vary widely in their length and their content, and relatively few have been systematically and rigorously evaluated.[7] We do know from surveys that a great many students receive sex education in school and that the number is increasing over time. One study from the 1970s found that 36 percent of public high schools offered a sex education course; another found that 80 percent of large school districts with junior or senior high schools offered such courses, either separately or as part of another course (say, health or biology).[8] Surveys in the early 1980s found that about 60 percent of young women and 52 percent of young men had taken a course on sex education, and longitudinal surveys suggest that this number is growing—that junior high and high school students today are more likely to have received some sex education than their older brothers and sisters were when they were in school. An analysis of the 1988 National Survey of Family Growth, for example, found that almost 90 percent of teenage girls reported having had sex education by the time they graduated.[9] When asked, even more young people than this report having had sex education, since they include information they have received in nonschool programs such as scout troops, Girls' Clubs and Boys' Clubs, church groups, family planning services, and health clinics, as well as in conversations about sexuality and contraception with their parents.[10]

Some people think that sex education is part of the problem—that by addressing and "normalizing" sexual activity among teenagers, sex education encourages it. This belief has a certain logic, but if sex education does have such an effect at all, it is very weak. One study suggested that taking a sex education

---

[6]Benjamin C. Gruenberg, *High Schools and Sex Education* (Washington, D.C.: Government Printing Office, 1940).

[7]U.S. Senate, Committee on Labor and Human Resources, *Reauthorization of the Adolescent Family Life Demonstration Projects Act of 1981: Hearing before the Subcommittee on Family and Human Services of the Committee on Labor and Human Resources,* 98th Congress, 2nd sess., 1984.

[8]Freya L. Sonenstein and Karen J. Pittman, "The Availability of Sex Education in Large City School Districts," *Family Planning Perspectives* 16 (1984): 19–25.

[9]Calculations by Jane Mauldon and Kristin Luker, based on the 1988 National Survey of Family Growth. See Jane Mauldon and Kristin Luker, "Contraception at First Sex: The Effects of Sex Education," Working paper no. 206, Graduate School of Public Policy, University of California at Berkeley, 1994.

[10]William Marsiglio and F. L. Mott, "The Impact of Sex Education on Sexual Activity, Contraceptive Use and Premarital Pregnancy among American Teenagers," *Family Planning Perspectives* 18, no. 4 (1986): 151–162.

course would increase by 2 percent the odds that a teenager, especially a very young teenager, would be sexually active.[11] Another study found that young men who received some instruction in contraception had their first intercourse slightly earlier than other students, whereas those taking courses that covered AIDS education and "resistance skills" (how to say no) tended to have first intercourse at later ages.[12] Still another study found that students taking sex education courses were less likely to have sex than those who did not take such courses.[13] But careful and rigorous review of all the various studies on the matter suggests that, in general, taking sex education courses has virtually no effect on an individual's propensity to become sexually active.[14]

This is good news, because it is becoming apparent that some sex education programs can reduce pregnancy under certain circumstances. Today, as in Benjamin Gruenberg's time, sex education (or "family life" education, as it is often called) covers a wide range of topics in a variety of formats, and most sex education courses in the United States are less than comprehensive in their approach and substance. Some are extremely short, lasting only five to twenty hours, and they often limit themselves to the safer topics, such as anatomy and physiology; in one family life program offered in New Jersey, students were taught how to fill out the state's income tax form.[15] Teachers may be wary of or feel uncomfortable about discussing contraception, and may do so abstractly and euphemistically rather than directly and concretely. Information about reproductive anatomy is certainly educational, but in the absence of other information it is unlikely to prevent pregnancy.

Another factor limiting the potential effectiveness of sex education courses is the fact that many school districts postpone sex education until the later years of high school, when students are thought to be more developmentally mature. But about one-fourth of Americans do not finish high school, and in some urban areas the figure approaches one-half. This means that a substantial number of young people, and disproportionately high-risk ones at that, may never reach the grade level at which sex education courses are offered. Furthermore, many students become sexually active prior to the grades in which sex education is offered: one study in the 1980s found that about 50 percent of

---

[11]Ibid.

[12]L. C. Ku, F. Sonenstein, and J. Pleck, "Factors Affecting First Intercourse among Young Men," *Public Health Reports* 108 (1993): 680–694.

[13]Frank Furstenberg et al., "Sex Education and Sexual Experience among Adolescents," *American Journal of Public Health* 75, no. 11 (1985): 1331–1332.

[14]Deborah A. Dawson, "The Effects of Sex Education on Adolescent Behavior," *Family Planning Perspectives* 18 (1986): 162–170. Melvin Zelnik and Y. J. Kim, "Sex Education and Its Association with Teenage Sexual Activity, Pregnancy and Contraceptive Use," *Family Planning Perspectives* 14 (1982): 117–126. Kirby et al., "School-Based Programs to Reduce Sexual Risk Behaviors," pp. 339–359.

[15]Lana D. Muraskin with Paul Jargowsky, *Creating and Implementing Family Life Education in New Jersey* (Alexandria, Va.: National Association of State Boards of Education, 1985).

young women and 65 percent of young men received their primary sex education from a partner, not from a course. Among young black men, 81 percent had had intercourse before ever receiving any sex education; among white men the figure was 61 percent; and among Hispanics it was 73 percent.[16] Delaying sex education until the later years of high school, therefore, can seriously compromise whatever effectiveness it may have, because some students never get the information at all and others get it after they have already become sexually active. Not surprisingly, when sex education is given to young people who are already sexually active, it seems to have little effect on their contraceptive and risk-taking behavior.

Increasing worries about early pregnancy and AIDS have led many school districts in recent years to offer sex education courses to younger students and to make such courses mandatory rather than elective. Consequently, many more people are receiving sex education these days, and many more of them are receiving it prior to their first sexual experience. One study found that among women who turned twenty between 1983 and 1985, only 56 percent had had sex education prior to first intercourse; among those who turned twenty between 1991 and 1992, the figure was 81 percent.[17]

After the Adolescent Family Life Act was passed in 1984, the federal govern-   10
ment established about two dozen projects based on a new concept—that of preventing sexual activity rather than providing contraception. One fairly typical example is the Sex Respect curriculum, developed in Illinois and now used in many school districts throughout the country. It is much more prescriptive than other sex education programs, advising that students abstain from sex if they wish to avoid pregnancy. As a group, such "abstinence-based" programs encourage young people to abstain from sex, warn them of the dangers of sexual activity, and, through discussion and role playing, try to give them the communication skills they need in order to implement their decisions. Proponents of this approach believe that providing information about contraception would undermine the goals of these programs.[18] Some of the techniques used, particularly the resistance skills that help teens say no, have been incorporated into other sex education curricula, and some school districts have adopted abstinence-based sex education while also teaching about contraception. The purely abstinence-based curricula (those that give no contraceptive advice or education) are fairly new and have not yet been rigorously evaluated. Like other sex education programs, they can improve students' knowledge and attitudes, but their effects on behavior are less clear.[19] Early research suggests that some parts of

---

[16]Marsiglio and Mott, "The Impact of Sex Education Programs," pp. 151–162.

[17]Mauldon and Luker, "Contraception at First Sex."

[18]Respect, Inc. For an overview, see Colleen Kelly Mast, *Love and Life: A Christian Sexual Morality Guide for Teens* (San Francisco: Ignatius Press, 1986).

[19]S. E. Weed and J. A. Olsen, "Evaluation Report of the Sex Respect Program: Results for the 1988–1989 School Year," Office of Adolescent Pregnancy Programs, Office of Population Affairs, Department of Health and Human Services; S. Christopher and M. Roosa, "An Evaluation of an

the abstinence-based programs can be quite effective. More conventional programs that have incorporated the teaching of resistance skills, for example, do seem to have some success in encouraging young people to postpone their first sexual involvement, but often the postponement is not very great—on the order of six months or so. Other research suggests that conventional programs which are clearly directive in their teaching (as are the abstinence-based programs) rather than neutral in their approach are more likely to change students' behavior. Preliminary data, however, suggest that all of these programs may entail something of a tradeoff: the ones that focus on helping young people say no have little effect on subsequent contraceptive use, and the ones that impart contraceptive skills do not teach young people how to avoid sex.[20] Since American teenagers face one to two decades during which they are sexually mature but not married, programs that urge postponing sex but that have no effect on contraceptive use may worsen the situation.

According to new research, effective sex education programs *can* change adolescents' behavior. Such programs typically begin before students have become sexually active and they are usually strongly prescriptive in nature. Effective programs focus clearly on goals and carefully evaluate what works. Not only do some programs delay the onset of sexual activity, but others lead to greater use of contraception. In comparison to people who have had no sex education, those who have attended a good sex-ed program are more likely to use contraception the first time they have sex, to obtain effective contraception sooner, and to use contraception more reliably in general.[21]

Thus, in view of all the evidence that public policies have done a reasonably good job of containing early pregnancy despite a vast increase in sexual activity among teens, the current conservative initiatives seem paradoxical at best and self-defeating at worst. There are powerful pressures to cut public funding for contraceptive programs, even as these programs are becoming recognized for the success story they are.... Finally, just as we have begun to sort out which sex education techniques work and which ones don't, the very notion of sex education is more contested than it has ever been. In the face of accumulating evidence which suggests that more students than ever are receiving sex education and that well-designed programs can indeed modify adolescents' risk-taking behavior, politically mobilized activists all over the United States are pushing for hasty adoption of abstinence-based programs before rigorous evaluation has been able to show whether they are capable of doing anything other than making adults feel better.

Adolescent Pregnancy Prevention Program: Is 'Just Say No' Enough?" *Family Relations* 39 (1990): 68–72; M. Roosa and S. Christopher, "Evaluation of an Abstinence-Based Adolescent Pregnancy Prevention Program: A Replication," *Family Relations* 39 (1990): 363–367.

[20]Kirby, "School-Based Programs to Reduce Sexual Risk Behaviors," pp. 339–359.

[21]Mauldon and Luker, "Contraception at First Sex."

To put this in the bluntest terms, society seems to have become committed to *increasing* the rates of pregnancy among teens, especially among those who are poor and those who are most at risk. Affluent and successful young women see real costs to early pregnancy and thus have strong incentives to avoid it; but poor young women face greater obstacles, both internal and external. Cutting funding for public contraceptive clinics, imposing parental-consent requirements, and limiting access to abortion all increase the likelihood that a young woman will get pregnant and have a baby. Conversely, providing widespread contraceptive services (perhaps even making the Pill available over the counter), extending clinic hours, and affording greater access to abortion will give at least some poor young women an alternative to early childbearing.

The news is even grimmer when it comes to preventing or postponing childbearing among teenagers who are not highly motivated in the first place. Even as we amass evidence showing that early childbearing is not a root cause of poverty in the United States, we are also realizing more clearly that the high rate of early childbearing is a measure of how bleak life is for young people who are living in poor communities and who have no obvious arenas for success. Here, too, just as we are developing a better sense of what it would take to offer these young women and men more choice in life, the political temper of the times makes even modest investments in young people seem like utopian dreams. Far from making lives easier for actual and potential teenage parents, society seems committed to making things harder.

A quarter-century of research on poverty and early childbearing has yielded 15 some solid leads on ways to reduce early pregnancy and childbearing. But because the young people involved have multiple problems, the solutions aren't cheap. In order to reduce the number of teenagers who want babies, society would have to be restructured so that poor people in the United States would no longer be the poorest poor people in the developed world. Early childbearing would decrease if poor teenagers had better schools and safer neighborhoods, and if their mothers and fathers had decent jobs so that teens could afford the luxury of being children for a while longer. If in 1994 the United States had finally succeeded in creating a national health care system° (becoming the last industrialized country to do so), this change alone would have had a dramatic impact on poor people generally and poor women specifically. Providing wider access to health care, for example, would have eliminated some obstacles to contraception and possibly even to abortion. More fundamentally, it would have meant that young women and men, even if they did have babies and even if they did have them out of wedlock, could have afforded to raise them without going on welfare.

°**national health care system:** In 1994 the Clinton administration's proposed health care system was defeated. Conservatives objected to it as being too large, expensive, and bureaucratic.

A WRITER'S NOTEBOOK

Liberalism

The following tasks are designed to help you think about the readings and identify and start to work up material you might use in your own essay. If you need help with tasks that require summarizing, see Appendix 1.

1. *List liberal accomplishments from Roger Rosenblatt's article.* Toward the end of his article (paragraphs 11–15), Rosenblatt mentions a number of specific accomplishments he attributes to liberalism. Make a list of them.

2. *Summarize part of E. J. Dionne Jr.'s argument.* In paragraphs 8–12, Dionne argues—against both conservatives and libertarians—that the marketplace should not be supreme, that it should not be "the sole arbiter of the basic elements of a decent life." Summarize the argument that Dionne develops in these paragraphs.

3. *Consider Kristin Luker's argument.* If you completed the earlier writer's notebook task asking you to assess Jacqueline R. Kasun's view of government involvement in sex education, look at that now. Then, drawing on your reading of Luker's argument, write a few sentences explaining what Luker approves of in governmental (or public) support of sex education and telling whether you agree more with Luker or with Kasun. Luker's last three paragraphs should help you understand her position.

4. *Review key terms and explain liberalism.* If you prepared a list of key terms and concepts as you read the arguments in this section, look it over and then try to write a brief explanation of liberalism. Your explanation should be about a page long and include examples from the readings as well as definitions. Use the most important terms you have identified but put them into your own sentences. Imagine you are writing your explanation for other college students who have not read about liberalism. Working out this brief explanation now will enable you to synthesize what you have learned about liberalism and save you time when you write your essay.

5. *Analyze a cartoon.* The political cartoon on page 272 appeared in the *Philadelphia Daily News* in December 1996. You can assume it is a liberal cartoon, aimed at either conservatives or libertarians. Write a half-page or so explaining the cartoon and telling whether you think its creator has found an apt target for ridicule or not.

LIBERTARIANISM

Like liberals and conservatives, libertarians can trace their ideas back to the Declaration of Independence, but libertarianism as a modern political movement has gained most of its strength in the last few decades.

The libertarian is likely to side with the liberal on some issues and with the conservative on others, in each case choosing whichever position advocates the greatest liberty. On issues involving individual behavior and civil rights, for instance, the libertarian might side with the liberal, arguing for civil

liberties like freedom of expression. The libertarian, however, is likely to go farther than the liberal, advocating freedom from regulations on illegal drugs, cigarette smoking, youth curfews, pornography, prostitution, gun use, electronic mail, and so on, whereas the liberal would probably accept regulations on some of those behaviors.

On economic issues, the libertarian is likely to side with the conservative or take a more extreme position. When asked about national economic well-being or programs to create jobs, the libertarian might argue: "The government has no role in creating jobs and will only make a mess of things. Cut or abolish income taxes. Reduce government to a minimum. If we can keep the government out of our lives, we'll all be more prosperous."

Though there is an official Libertarian Party, libertarians have probably had more influence on people's ideas than on their votes or their political party affiliations. There is some evidence, for instance, that libertarian views are becoming more popular with some college students, particularly those in the computer sciences, and among employees in computer companies who chafe at government regulations. There is a strong connection between libertarian and conservative ideas for some people, and there are many Republicans who hold both libertarian and conservative sympathies. Many current Republican politicians, for instance, hold some libertarian ideas on issues like free trade, though other conservative Republicans disagree with them. At the same time, however, libertarians are likely to disagree with some conservative beliefs about social behavior. For the essay you will write in this chapter, it will be easier, as suggested before, to avoid equating any one of these civic stances with any particular political party.

The following statement by Harry Browne points up some libertarian beliefs. Browne, who ran for president in 1996 on the Libertarian Party ticket, argues not only that government wastes money but that it encourages behavior most Americans disapprove of:

> By the 1990s the welfare system was a shambles. In 1991 the federal government spent $676 billion on social welfare of one kind or another—20 times the 1962 level—and state and local governments spent $489 billion, largely to qualify for federal welfare programs.
>
> Social welfare spending by all levels of government had increased to $1,165 billion ($1.1 trillion) in 1991, from $63 billion in 1962.
>
> The money spent for public assistance (what we think of as pure welfare) by all levels of government increased to $180 billion in 1991 from $5 billion in 1962—the year President Kennedy promised to reform the system....
>
> Welfare costs us plenty. But it also destroys lives. It perverts the natural incentives of everyone who is touched by it. Here are some examples:
>
> - AFDC (Aid to Families with Dependent Children) pays money to Mom only if there's no Dad at home, so—surprise!—Dad goes away.
>
> - A teenage girl can become independent of her parents by getting pregnant; otherwise, she must live off her parents and obey their rules. Which life is more attractive to most teenagers?
>
> - Federal job-training for welfare recipients circumvents the need for a teenager to stay in school and learn how to make a living.
>
> - The income test for welfare makes a low-paying job seem pointless. This eliminates the incentive for a young person to get the all-important first job, and so he never gains the experience needed to get a job that would pay more than welfare.
>
> - Medicaid reduces the incentive, especially among the young, to avoid injury and disease.
>
> - The availability of welfare reduces the incentive to save for emergencies. And once people don't have savings, what else can they do but go on welfare when trouble strikes?
>
> The people who have been seduced by welfare have become wards of the state, unable to fend for themselves, with no self-respect and no self-confidence.[9]

Browne seems concerned here primarily with the economic aspects of welfare. Some libertarians, though, focus less on economics and more on behavior and the social realm, believing that individuals should be able to engage in any kind of behavior that does not harm others. These libertarians advocate legalizing drugs, for instance, on the grounds that the state has no business

---

[9] Harry Browne, *Why Government Doesn't Work* (New York: St. Martin's Press, 1995) 121.

trying to regulate drug use for the well-being of the individual — that individuals should be free to make decisions about their own lives, even to harm themselves if they so wish.

An example of this social and moral libertarianism can be seen in the remarks of writer and college professor Camille Paglia, who makes the following distinctions in an interview with the editor of *Reason,* a libertarian magazine:

> I feel that government has no right to intrude into the private realm of consensual behavior. Therefore, I say that I'm for the abolition of all sodomy laws. I'm for abortion rights. I'm for the legalization of drugs — consistent with alcohol regulations. I'm for not just the decriminalization but the legalization of prostitution. Again, prostitutes must not intrude into the public realm. I think it's perfectly reasonable to say that civil authorities have the right to say that prostitutes should not be loitering near schools, or on the steps of churches, or blocking entrances to buildings and so on. Prostitution should be perfectly legal, but it cannot interfere with other people's access to the public realm.[10]

This sort of distinction — between private behavior and behavior that harms others — is often important to libertarian arguments. Libertarians may disagree with each other about the *degree* to which there should be liberty from controls and regulations, but they consistently argue for freedom in both the social and the economic realms. Because they advocate liberty so consistently, libertarians may sharply disagree at times with liberals and conservatives.

As you read the following arguments, note what sorts of good libertarians think will come from greater liberty and why. Also remember to keep track of key terms and concepts and to look for newspaper columns and interviews on the three civic stances.

CAPITALISM AND FREEDOM

Milton Friedman

Milton Friedman, an economist and advocate of free enterprise, was awarded the 1976 Nobel Prize in Economics. He has been a professor of economics at the University of Chicago and a fellow at the Hoover Institution, a conservative and libertarian think tank at Stanford University. He is the author of numerous articles and books, including Capitalism and Freedom *(1962), from which this reading comes.*

Friedman did his early economic work during the Cold War period following World War II, when many people thought that the Soviet Union and its Communist allies would do better economically than capitalist countries like the United

---

[10] Camille Paglia, interview with Virginia I. Postrel, *Reason* Aug.-Sept. 1995: 38.

States. Friedman, however, disagreed with this view. When the Communist economies collapsed in the late 1980s and early 1990s, the popularity of libertarianism was renewed because economists like Friedman seemed to have been proved right. Though Friedman is categorized here as a libertarian, his economic ideas are also admired by many conservatives.

As you read, you will see that Friedman shows the typical libertarian preference for minimal government. Try to understand what role Friedman believes government should play in citizens' lives and what benefits—both economic and political—he thinks come from a free economy.

In a much quoted passage in his inaugural address, President Kennedy said, "Ask not what your country can do for you—ask what you can do for your country." It is a striking sign of the temper of our times that the controversy about this passage centered on its origin and not on its content. Neither half of the statement expresses a relation between the citizen and his government that is worthy of the ideals of free men in a free society. The paternalistic "what your country can do for you" implies that government is the patron, the citizen the ward, a view that is at odds with the free man's belief in his own responsibility for his own destiny. The organismic° "what you can do for your country" implies that government is the master or the deity, the citizen, the servant or the votary. To the free man, the country is the collection of individuals who compose it, not something over and above them. He is proud of a common heritage and loyal to common traditions. But he regards government as a means, an instrumentality, neither a grantor of favors and gifts, nor a master or god to be blindly worshipped and served....

The free man will ask neither what his country can do for him nor what he can do for his country. He will ask rather, "What can I and my compatriots do through government" to help us discharge our individual responsibilities, to achieve our several goals and purposes, and above all, to protect our freedom? And he will accompany this question with another: How can we keep the government we create from becoming a Frankenstein that will destroy the very freedom we establish it to protect? Freedom is a rare and delicate plant. Our minds tell us, and history confirms, that the great threat to freedom is the concentration of power. Government is necessary to preserve our freedom, it is an instrument through which we can exercise our freedom; yet by concentrating power in political hands, it is also a threat to freedom. Even though the men who wield this power initially be of goodwill and even though they be not corrupted by the power they exercise, the power will both attract and form men of a different stamp.

How can we benefit from the promise of government while avoiding the threat to freedom? Two broad principles embodied in our Constitution give an

---

°**organismic:** Like a living organism in which individual parts function for the good of the whole.

answer that has preserved our freedom so far, though they have been violated repeatedly in practice while proclaimed as precept.

First, the scope of government must be limited. Its major function must be to protect our freedom both from the enemies outside our gates and from our fellow-citizens: to preserve law and order, to enforce private contracts, to foster competitive markets. Beyond this major function, government may enable us at times to accomplish jointly what we would find it more difficult or expensive to accomplish severally. However, any such use of government is fraught with danger. We should not and cannot avoid using government in this way. But there should be a clear and large balance of advantages before we do. By relying primarily on voluntary cooperation and private enterprise, in both economic and other activities, we can insure that the private sector is a check on the powers of the governmental sector and an effective protection of freedom of speech, of religion, and of thought.

The second broad principle is that government power must be dispersed. If government is to exercise power, better in the county than in the state, better in the state than in Washington. If I do not like what my local community does, be it in sewage disposal, or zoning, or schools, I can move to another local community, and though few may take this step, the mere possibility acts as a check. If I do not like what my state does, I can move to another. If I do not like what Washington imposes, I have few alternatives in this world of jealous nations.

The very difficulty of avoiding the enactments of the federal government is of course the great attraction of centralization° to many of its proponents. It will enable them more effectively, they believe, to legislate programs that—as they see it—are in the interest of the public, whether it be the transfer of income° from the rich to the poor or from private to governmental purposes. They are in a sense right. But this coin has two sides. The power to do good is also the power to do harm; those who control the power today may not tomorrow; and, more important, what one man regards as good, another may regard as harm. The great tragedy of the drive to centralization, as of the drive to extend the scope of government in general, is that it is mostly led by men of goodwill who will be the first to rue its consequences.

The preservation of freedom is the protective reason for limiting and decentralizing governmental power. But there is also a constructive reason. The great advances of civilization, whether in architecture or painting, in science or literature, in industry or agriculture, have never come from centralized government. Columbus did not set out to seek a new route to China in response to a majority directive of a parliament, though he was partly financed by an absolute monarch. Newton and Leibnitz, Einstein and Bohr, Shakespeare, Milton, and

---

°**centralization:** Here, concentrating powers at the national rather than at the state or local levels of government.   °**transfer of income:** Redistributing wealth from rich to poor by means of taxation or other government-sponsored programs.

Pasternak, Whitney, McCormick, Edison, and Ford, Jane Addams, Florence Nightingale, and Albert Schweitzer—no one of these opened new frontiers in human knowledge and understanding, in literature, in technical possibilities, or in the relief of human misery in response to governmental directives. Their achievements were the product of individual genius, of strongly held minority views, of a social climate permitting variety and diversity.

Government can never duplicate the variety and diversity of individual action. At any moment in time, by imposing uniform standards in housing, or nutrition, or clothing, government could undoubtedly improve the level of living of many individuals; by imposing uniform standards in schooling, road construction, or sanitation, central government could undoubtedly improve the level of performance in many local areas and perhaps even on the average of all communities. But in the process, government would replace progress by stagnation, it would substitute uniform mediocrity for the variety essential for that experimentation which can bring tomorrow's laggards above today's mean....

It is widely believed that politics and economics are separate and largely unconnected, that individual freedom is a political problem and material welfare an economic problem, and that any kind of political arrangements can be combined with any kind of economic arrangements.... The thesis [here] is that such a view is a delusion, that there is an intimate connection between economics and politics, that only certain combinations of political and economic arrangements are possible, and that in particular, a society which is socialist° cannot also be democratic, in the sense of guaranteeing individual freedom.

Economic arrangements play a dual role in the promotion of a free society. 10 On the one hand, freedom in economic arrangements is itself a component of freedom broadly understood, so economic freedom is an end in itself. In the second place, economic freedom is also an indispensable means toward the achievement of political freedom.

The first of these roles of economic freedom needs special emphasis because intellectuals in particular have a strong bias against regarding this aspect of freedom as important. They tend to express contempt for what they regard as material aspects of life, and to regard their own pursuit of allegedly higher values as on a different plane of significance and as deserving of special attention. For most citizens of the country, however, if not for the intellectual, the direct importance of economic freedom is at least comparable in significance to the indirect importance of economic freedom as a means to political freedom....

Viewed as a means to the end of political freedom, economic arrangements are important because of their effect on the concentration or dispersion of power. The kind of economic organization that provides economic freedom

---

°**socialist:** A type of society in which the government, rather than individuals, owns property and the means of production.

directly, namely, competitive capitalism, also promotes political freedom because it separates economic power from political power and in this way enables the one to offset the other.

Historical evidence speaks with a single voice on the relation between political freedom and a free market.°.I know of no example in time or place of a society that has been marked by a large measure of political freedom, and that has not also used something comparable to a free market to organize the bulk of economic activity.

Because we live in a largely free society, we tend to forget how limited is the span of time and the part of the globe for which there has ever been anything like political freedom; the typical state of mankind is tyranny, servitude, and misery. The nineteenth century and early twentieth century in the Western world stand out as striking exceptions to the general trend of historical development. Political freedom in this instance clearly came along with the free market and the development of capitalist institutions. . . .

Fundamentally, there are only two ways of coordinating the economic activ- 15
ities of millions. One is central direction involving the use of coercion—the technique of the army and of the modern totalitarian state. The other is voluntary cooperation of individuals—the technique of the marketplace.

The possibility of coordination through voluntary cooperation rests on the elementary—yet frequently denied—proposition that both parties to an economic transaction benefit from it, *provided the transaction is bilaterally voluntary and informed.*

Exchange can therefore bring about coordination without coercion. A working model of a society organized through voluntary exchange is a *free private enterprise exchange economy*—what we have been calling competitive capitalism. . . .

So long as effective freedom of exchange is maintained, the central feature of the market organization of economic activity is that it prevents one person from interfering with another in respect of most of his activities. The consumer is protected from coercion by the seller because of the presence of other sellers with whom he can deal. The seller is protected from coercion by the consumer because of other consumers to whom he can sell. The employee is protected from coercion by the employer because of other employers for whom he can. work, and so on. And the market does this impersonally and without centralized authority.

Indeed, a major source of objection to a free economy is precisely that it does this task so well. It gives people what they want instead of what a particular group thinks they ought to want. Underlying most arguments against the free market is a lack of belief in freedom itself.

°**a free market:** The free, unplanned economy responding to supply and demand—a capitalist, rather than a socialist, economy.

The existence of a free market does not of course eliminate the need for gov- 20
ernment. On the contrary, government is essential both as a forum for determining the "rules of the game" and as an umpire to interpret and enforce the
rules decided on. What the market does is to reduce greatly the range of issues
that must be decided through political means, and thereby to minimize the
extent to which government need participate directly in the game. The characteristic feature of action through political channels is that it tends to require or
enforce substantial conformity. The great advantage of the market, on the other
hand, is that it permits wide diversity. It is, in political terms, a system of pro-
portional representation. Each man can vote, as it were, for the color of tie he
wants and get it; he does not have to see what color the majority wants and
then, if he is in the minority, submit.

It is this feature of the market that we refer to when we say that the market
provides economic freedom. But this characteristic also has implications that go
far beyond the narrowly economic. Political freedom means the absence of coercion of a man by his fellowmen. The fundamental threat to freedom is power to
coerce, be it in the hands of a monarch, a dictator, an oligarchy, or a momentary
majority. The preservation of freedom requires the elimination of such concentration of power to the fullest possible extent and the dispersal and distribution
of whatever power cannot be eliminated—a system of checks and balances. By
removing the organization of economic activity from the control of political
authority, the market eliminates this source of coercive power. It enables economic strength to be a check to political power rather than a reinforcement.

THE COMING LIBERTARIAN AGE

David Boaz

*David Boaz is executive vice president of the Cato Institute, a libertarian think
tank, and the editor of a number of books on libertarian ideas. His articles have
appeared in the* New York Times, *the* Washington Post, *the* Wall Street Journal, *and
the* Chicago Tribune. *This reading is from his 1997 book* Libertarianism: A Primer.

*Boaz begins with assumptions that are based on the political theories of
seventeenth-century philosopher John Locke. Locke believed that natural laws
take precedence over human laws and that people agree to be governed on the
assumption that the government will protect their liberties and not go against natural laws. People's consent to their government was crucial for Locke and became
crucial for the Founders of the United States, who drew from Locke's ideas in*

writing the Declaration of Independence. After developing these ideas in his first few paragraphs, Boaz builds his argument for "a new philosophy of governing."

As you read, note why Boaz asserts that government's legitimate role is a limited one. Try to understand why he thinks our current system is failing because it relies on massive transfer programs. You may want to contrast Boaz's libertarian stance to E. J. Dionne Jr.'s liberal stance, or examine how Boaz's view of individual rights (paragraphs 22–23) compares to the liberal views of both Roger Rosenblatt and Dionne.

Libertarianism is the view that each person has the right to live his life in any way he chooses so long as he respects the equal rights of others. (Throughout this [essay] I use the traditional "he" and "his" to refer to all individuals, male and female; unless the context indicates otherwise, "he" and "his" should be understood to refer to both men and women.) Libertarians defend each person's right to life, liberty, and property—rights that people possess naturally, before governments are created. In the libertarian view, all human relationships should be voluntary; the only actions that should be forbidden by law are those that involve the initiation of force against those who have not themselves used force—actions like murder, rape, robbery, kidnapping, and fraud.

Most people habitually believe in and live by this code of ethics. Libertarians believe this code should be applied consistently—and specifically, that it should be applied to actions by governments as well as by individuals. Governments should exist to protect rights, to protect us from others who might use force against us. When governments use force against people who have not violated the rights of others, then governments themselves become rights violators. Thus libertarians condemn such government actions as censorship, the draft, price controls, confiscation of property, and regulation of our personal and economic lives.

Put so starkly, the libertarian vision may sound otherworldly, like a doctrine for a universe of angels that never was and never will be. Surely, in today's messy and often unpleasant world, government must do a great deal? But here's the surprise: The answer is no. In fact, the more messy and modern the world, the better libertarianism works compared—for instance—with monarchy, dictatorship, and even postwar American-style welfarism. The political awakening in America today is first and foremost the realization that libertarianism is not a relic of the past. It is a philosophy—more, a pragmatic plan—for the future. In American politics it is the leading edge—not a backlash, but a vanguard....

Libertarianism is an old philosophy, but its framework for liberty under law and economic progress makes it especially suited for the dynamic world—call it the Information Age, or the Third Wave, or the Third Industrial Revolution—we are now entering.

THE RESURGENCE OF LIBERTARIANISM

Some readers may well wonder why people in a generally free and prosperous ₅ country like the United States need to adopt a new philosophy of government. Aren't we doing reasonably well with our current system? We do indeed have a society that has brought unprecedented prosperity to a larger number of people than ever before. But we face problems — from high taxes to poor schools to racial tensions to environmental destruction — that our current approach is not handling adequately. Libertarianism has solutions to those problems, as I'll try to demonstrate. For now I'll offer three reasons that libertarianism is the right approach for America on the eve of the new millennium.

First, we are not nearly as prosperous as we could be. If our economy were growing at the rate it grew from 1945 to 1973, our gross domestic product° would be 40 percent larger than it is. But that comparison doesn't give the true picture of the economic harm that excessive government is doing to us. In a world of global markets and accelerating technological change, we shouldn't be growing at the same pace we did forty years ago — we should be growing faster. More reliance on markets and individual enterprise would mean more wealth for all of us, which is especially important for those who have the least today.

Second, our government has become far too powerful, and it increasingly threatens our freedom. . . . Government taxes too much, regulates too much, interferes too much. Politicians from Jesse Helms to Jesse Jackson seek to impose their own moral agenda on 250 million Americans. Events like the assault on the Branch Davidians,° the shootings of Vicki Weaver° and Donald Scott,° the beating of Rodney King,° and the government's increasing attempts to take private property without judicial process make us fear an out-of-control government and remind us of the need to reestablish strict limits on power.

Third, in a fast-changing world where every individual will have unprecedented access to information, centralized bureaucracies° and coercive regulations° just won't be able to keep up with the real economy. The existence of global capital markets means that investors won't be held hostage by national governments and their confiscatory tax systems. New opportunities for

---

°gross domestic product: A measure of the total value of goods and services produced within a country in a year.   °Branch Davidians: Members of a religious group in Waco, Texas, who were killed in 1993 during a seige by the Federal Bureau of Investigation (FBI).   °Vicki Weaver: The wife of white separatist Randy Weaver, she was killed in 1992 by FBI agents who were trying to arrest her husband in Ruby Ridge, Idaho.   °Donald Scott: A rancher in Malibu, California, who was killed by a Los Angeles sheriff's deputy during a hunt for marijuana, which was not found.   °Rodney King: An African American who was severely beaten by Los Angeles police officers after they stopped him for a suspected traffic violation.   °centralized bureaucracies: Federal bureaucracies such as the Internal Revenue Service (IRS) and the U.S. Postal Service.   °coercive regulations: Government regulations such as minimum wage laws that employers must observe.

telecommuting will mean that more and more workers will also have the ability to flee high taxes and other intrusive government policies. Prosperous nations in the twenty-first century will be those that attract productive people. We need a limited government to usher in an unlimited future.

The twentieth century has been the century of state power, from Hitler and Stalin to the totalitarian states behind the Iron Curtain,° from dictatorships across Africa to the bureaucratic welfare states of North America and Western Europe. Many people assume that as time goes on, and the world becomes more complex, governments naturally get bigger and more powerful. In fact, however, the twentieth century was in many ways a detour from the 2,500-year history of the Western world. From the time of the Greeks, the history of the West has largely been a story of increasing freedom, with a progressively limited role for coercive and arbitrary government.

10

Today, at the end of the twentieth century, there are signs that we may be returning to the path of limiting government and increasing liberty. With the collapse of communism, there is hardly any support left for central planning. Third World countries are privatizing state industries° and freeing up markets. Practicing capitalism, the Pacific Rim countries have moved from poverty to world economic leadership in a generation.

In the United States, the bureaucratic leviathan° is threatened by a resurgence of the libertarian ideas upon which the country was founded. We are witnessing a breakdown of all the cherished beliefs of the welfare-warfare state. Americans have seen the failure of big government....

Why is there a libertarian revival now? The main reason is that the alternatives to libertarianism—fascism, communism, socialism, the welfare state—have all been tried in the twentieth century and have all failed to produce peace, prosperity, and freedom.

Fascism, as exemplified in Mussolini's Italy and Hitler's Germany, was the first to go. Its economic centralization and racial collectivism now seem repellent to every civilized person, so we may forget that before World War II many Western intellectuals admired the "new forms of economic organization in Germany and Italy," as the magazine the *Nation* put it in 1934....

The other great totalitarian system of the twentieth century was communism, as outlined by Karl Marx and implemented in the Soviet Union and its satellites. Communism maintained its appeal to idealists far longer than fascism. At least until the revelations of Stalin's purges in the 1950s, many American intellectuals viewed communism as a noble if sometimes excessive attempt

---

° **states behind the Iron Curtain:** The Soviet Union and the Eastern European countries dominated by it after World War II.   ° **privatizing state industries:** The process whereby industries formerly owned by the state are turned over to private ownership and encouraged to make profits. ° **leviathan:** A state with a large bureaucracy and an undemocratic government that is not responsive to the people.

to eliminate the inequalities and "alienation" of capitalism. As late as the 1980s, some American economists continued to praise the Soviet Union for its supposed economic growth and efficiency—right up to the system's collapse, in fact.

When communism suddenly imploded in 1989–91, libertarians were not 15 surprised. Communism, they had argued for years, was not only inimical to human freedom and dignity but devastatingly inefficient, and its inefficiency would only get worse over time, while the capitalist world progressed. The collapse of communism had a profound impact on the ideological landscape of the entire world: It virtually eliminated full-blown socialism as one end point of the ideological debate. It's obvious now that total statism° is a total disaster, leading more and more people to wonder why a society would want to implement *some* socialism if full socialism is so catastrophic.

But what about the welfare states of the West? The remaining ideological battles may be relatively narrow, but they are still important. Shouldn't government temper the market? Aren't the welfare states more humane than libertarian states would be? Although Western Europe and the United States never tried complete socialism, such concerns did cause government control of people's economic lives to increase dramatically during the twentieth century. . . .

Yet today, all over the developed world, welfare states are faltering. The tax rates necessary to sustain the massive transfer programs° are crippling Western economies. Dependence on government has devalued family, work, and thrift. From Germany to Sweden to Australia the promises of the welfare state can no longer be kept.

In the United States, Social Security will start running deficits by 2012— only fifteen years from now—and will be out of money by 2029. Official projections show that Medicare will be out of money as early as 2001 and will be running a deficit of $443 billion by 2006. Economists calculate that an American born in 1975 would have to pay 82 percent of his lifetime income in taxes to keep entitlement programs going, which is why young people are balking at the prospect of working most of their lives to pay for transfer programs that will eventually go bankrupt anyway. A 1994 poll found that 63 percent of Americans between eighteen and thirty-four don't believe Social Security will exist by the time they retire; more of them (46 percent) believe in UFOs than in Social Security (28 percent).

Getting out of the welfare state is going to be a tricky economic and political problem, but more and more people—in the United States and elsewhere— recognize that Western-style big government is going through a slow-motion version of communism's collapse. . . .

° **statism:** A system in which there is centralized government control over economics and planning.
° **transfer programs:** Programs that tax some groups of people in order to help other groups.

KEY CONCEPTS OF LIBERTARIANISM

With that background in mind, I want to spell out some of the key concepts of 20 libertarianism, themes that . . . have developed over many centuries. . . .

Individualism. Libertarian thought emphasizes the dignity of each individual, which entails both rights and responsibility. The progressive extension of dignity to more people — to women, to people of different religions and different races — is one of the great libertarian triumphs of the Western world.

Individual Rights. . . . Individuals . . . have a right to be secure in their life, liberty, and property. These rights are not granted by government or by society; they are inherent in the nature of human beings. It is intuitively right that individuals enjoy the security of such rights; the burden of explanation should lie with those who would take rights away.

Spontaneous Order. A great degree of order in society is necessary for individuals to survive and flourish. It's easy to assume that order must be imposed by a central authority, the way we impose order on a stamp collection or a football team. The great insight of libertarian social analysis is that order in society arises spontaneously, out of the actions of thousands or millions of individuals who coordinate their actions with those of others in order to achieve their purposes. Over human history, we have gradually opted for more freedom and yet managed to develop a complex society with intricate organization. The most important institutions in human society — language, law, money, and markets — all developed spontaneously, without central direction. Civil society — the complex network of associations and connections among people — is another example of spontaneous order; the associations within civil society are formed for a purpose, but civil society itself is not an organization and does not have a purpose of its own.

The Rule of Law. Libertarianism is not libertinism or hedonism. It is not a claim that "people can do anything they want to, and nobody else can say anything." Rather, libertarianism proposes a society of liberty under law, in which individuals are free to pursue their own lives so long as they respect the equal rights of others. The rule of law means that individuals are governed by generally applicable and spontaneously developed legal rules, not by arbitrary commands; and that those rules should protect the freedom of individuals to pursue happiness in their own ways, not aim at any particular result or outcome.

Limited Government. To protect rights, individuals form governments. But gov- 25 ernment is a dangerous institution. Libertarians have a great antipathy to concentrated power, for as Lord Acton said, "Power tends to corrupt and absolute power corrupts absolutely." Thus they want to divide and limit power, and that means especially to limit government, generally through a written constitution enumerating and limiting the powers that the people delegate to government. Limited government is the basic *political* implication of libertarianism, and libertarians point to the historical fact that it was the dispersion of power in Europe—more than other parts of the world—that led to individual liberty and sustained economic growth.

Free Markets.   To survive and to flourish, individuals need to engage in economic activity. The right to property entails the right to exchange property by mutual agreement. Free markets are the economic system of free individuals, and they are necessary to create wealth. Libertarians believe that people will be both freer and more prosperous if government intervention in people's economic choices is minimized.

The Virtue of Production.   Much of the impetus for libertarianism in the seventeenth century was a reaction against monarchs and aristocrats who lived off the productive labor of other people. Libertarians defended the right of people to keep the fruits of their labor. This effort developed into a respect for the dignity of work and production and especially for the growing middle class, who were looked down upon by aristocrats....Modern libertarians defend the right of productive people to keep what they earn, against a new class of politicians and bureaucrats who would seize their earnings to transfer them to nonproducers.

Natural Harmony of Interests.   Libertarians believe that there is a natural harmony of interests among peaceful, productive people in a just society. One person's individual plans—which may involve getting a job, starting a business, buying a house, and so on—may conflict with the plans of others, so the market makes many of us change our plans. But we all prosper from the operation of the free market, and there are no necessary conflicts between farmers and merchants, manufacturers and importers. Only when government begins to hand out rewards on the basis of political pressure do we find ourselves involved in group conflict, pushed to organize and contend with other groups for a piece of political power.

Peace.   Libertarians have always battled the age-old scourge of war. They understood that war brought death and destruction on a grand scale, disrupted family and economic life, and put more power in the hands of the ruling class—which might explain why the rulers did not always share the popular sentiment for peace. Free men and women, of course, have often had to defend their own societies against foreign threats; but throughout history, war has usually been the common enemy of peaceful, productive people on all sides of the conflict....

It may be appropriate to acknowledge at this point the reader's likely suspi- 30 cion that libertarianism seems to be just the standard framework of modern thought—individualism, private property, capitalism, equality under the law. Indeed, after centuries of intellectual, political, and sometimes violent struggle, these core libertarian principles have become the basic structure of modern political thought and of modern government, at least in the West and increasingly in other parts of the world. However, three additional points need to be made: First, libertarianism is not *just* these broad liberal principles. Libertarianism *applies* these principles fully and consistently, far more so than most modern thinkers and certainly more so than any modern government. Second, while our society remains generally based on equal rights and capitalism, every day new exceptions to those principles are carved out in Washington and in Albany, Sacramento, and Austin (not to mention London, Bonn, Tokyo, and elsewhere). Each new government directive takes a little bit of our freedom, and we should think carefully before giving up any liberty. Third, liberal society is resilient; it can withstand many burdens and continue to flourish; but it is not infinitely resilient. Those who claim to believe in liberal principles but advocate more and more confiscation of the wealth created by productive people, more and more restrictions on voluntary interaction, more and more exceptions to property rights and the rule of law, more and more transfer of power from society to state, are unwittingly engaged in the ultimately deadly undermining of civilization.

THE VISION OF THE ANOINTED

Thomas Sowell

Thomas Sowell is a senior fellow at the Hoover Institution, an economist, and the author of a number of articles and books, including The Economics and Politics of Race *(1983),* Preferential Policies: An International Perspective *(1990),* Inside American Education *(1993), and* Race and Culture *(1994).*

This reading is from Sowell's 1995 book The Vision of the Anointed: Self-Congratulation as a Basis for Social Policy. *The "anointed" Sowell refers to in his title are the intellectuals and opinion leaders in politics who, in Sowell's view, are so arrogant about their beliefs that they ignore evidence that does not fit their vision. Sowell's distaste for the arrogance of those who believe that they are the "anointed" comes through in this reading as he criticizes government programs on sex education.*

As you read, notice that Sowell is very critical of the size and the cost of government programs as well as their effectiveness. Note as well that his libertarian position and Jacqueline R. Kasun's conservative stance have many similarities. Sowell, however, puts more emphasis than Kasun on the indoctrination he sees in sex education, the arrogance he finds in its advocates, and the cost of the bureaucracy that oversees such programs. The differences between Sowell's and Kristin Luker's views will be far more obvious.

Among the many crusades which gathered new steam during the 1960s was the crusade to spread sex education into the public schools and through other channels. Among the first acts of the Office of Economic Opportunity in 1964 was making a grant to a Planned Parenthood unit in Texas. From a total expenditure of less than half a million dollars in fiscal year 1965, OEO expanded its financing of sex education more than five-fold by fiscal year 1966. Not only did the federal government begin in the late 1960s to greatly expand its own expenditures on sex education—often known as "family planning" or by other euphemisms—but it also began to mandate that states promote such programs as well. The number of patients served by "family planning" clinics increased approximately five-fold between 1968 and 1978.[1] As early as 1968, the National Education Association in its *NEA Journal* was saying that a federally funded project in a Washington school "demonstrated the need for sex education as an integral part of school curriculum beginning in the early grades." Some of the pregnant girls counseled "reported feeling that if they had studied human sexuality with understanding teachers during elementary school, they would not have become pregnant."[2] Sex education and "family planning" clinics—so called despite their being established to prevent having babies—not only grew rapidly but also changed in the clientele they served. As a study of this era put it:

> Family planning services grew phenomenally from the mid-60s to the mid-70s. In 1964, the federal government made its first family planning grant, which served only married women. By 1970, Congress had passed the first national family planning and population legislation. Federal expenditures grew from $16 million to close to $200 million. In 1969, there were less than a quarter of a million teenagers using family planning clinics; by 1976 this had swollen to 1.2 million.[3]

According to the Alan Guttmacher Institute, a leading research and advocacy organization° promoting sex education, the federal government's support

---

°**advocacy organization:** An organization that exists to promote particular policies.

[1] Aida Tores, Jacqueline Darroch Forrest, and Susan Eisman, "Family Planning Services in the United States, 1978–79," *Family Planning Perspectives,* Vol. 13, No. 3 (May/June 1981), pp. 139, 141.

[2] Patricia Schiller, "Sex Education That Makes Sense," *NEA Journal,* February 1968, p. 19.

[3] Theodore Ooms, *Teenage Pregnancy in a Family Context* (Philadelphia: Temple University Press, 1981), p. 26.

of "family planning services" rose from less than $14 million in 1968 to $279 million a decade later[4]—nearly a twenty-fold increase. By the early 1980s, nearly two-thirds of the money received by "family planning" agencies came from the federal government.[5] What was the purpose of all this activity? "Sex education is considered one of the primary tools to help adolescents avoid unwanted pregnancy," according to a typical comment of the period.[6] Once more, we have the four-stage pattern:°

STAGE 1. THE "CRISIS"

In 1968, it was claimed that "contraception education and counseling is now urgently needed to help prevent pregnancy and illegitimacy in high school girls."[7] The head of Planned Parenthood testified before a congressional sub-committee in 1966 as to the need for sex education "to assist our young people in reducing the incidence of out-of-wedlock births and early marriage necessitated by pregnancy."[8] The incidence of venereal disease among young people was cited by the head of the New York City Board of Education as showing the need for "a crash educational program." An article in the *American School Board Journal* in 1969 depicted sex education as a way of combatting "illegitimacy and venereal disease."[9] *PTA Magazine* likewise urged sex education to combat "the spiraling rate of venereal diseases, the pregnancies before marriage, the emotionally disastrous results of irresponsible sexual behavior."[10]

Similar statements abounded from a variety of sources. But what was in fact the situation when this kind of "crisis" mentality was being used to push for more sex education in the schools? Fertility rates among teenage girls had been *declining* for more than a decade since 1957.[11] Venereal disease was also *declining*. The rate of infection for gonorrhea, for example, declined every year from

---

° **the four-stage pattern:** Earlier in his book, Sowell argues that the "crusades" typically championed by the "anointed" tend to have four stages.

[4] Alan Guttmacher Institute, *Informing Public Change* (New York: Alan Guttmacher Institute, 1980), p. 7.

[5] Cheryl D. Hayes, editor, *Risking the Future: Adolescent Sexuality, Pregnancy, and Childbearing* (Washington, D.C.: National Academy Press, 1987), p. 160.

[6] Ooms, pp. 39–40.

[7] H. S. Hoyman, "Should We Teach About Birth Control in High School Sex Education?" *Education Digest,* February 1969, p. 22.

[8] United States Senate, Eighty-ninth Congress, second session, *Family Planning Program: Hearing Before the Subcommittee on Employment, Manpower and Poverty of the Committee on Labor and Public Welfare* (Washington, D.C.: U.S. Government Printing Office, 1966), p. 84.

[9] Joanne Zazzaro, "Critics or No Critics, Most Americans Still Firmly Support Sex Education in Schools," *American School Board Journal,* September 1969, p. 31.

[10] Robert P. Hildrup, "Why Sex Education Belongs in the Schools," *PTA Magazine,* February 1974, p. 13.

[11] Jacqueline Kasun, *The War Against Population* (San Francisco: Ignatius Press, 1988), p. 144.

1950 through 1959, and the rate of syphilis infection was, by 1960, less than half of what it had been in 1950.[12] This was the "crisis" which federal aid was to solve.

STAGE 2: THE "SOLUTION"

Massive federal aid to sex education programs in the schools, and to "family planning" clinics, was advocated to combat teenage pregnancy and venereal disease. After sex education, according to a "Professor of Family Life," a boy "will find decreased need for casual, irresponsible and self-centered experimentation with sex."[13] Critics opposed such actions on various grounds, including a belief that sex education would lead to more sexual activity, rather than less, and to more teenage pregnancy as well. Such views were dismissed in the media and in politics, as well as by the advocates of sex education. The *New York Times* editorially rejected "emotions and unexamined tradition" in this area[14] and its education editor declared: "To fear that sex education will become synonymous with greater sexual permissiveness is to misunderstand the fundamental purpose of the entire enterprise."[15] As in many other cases, *intentions* were the touchstone° of the vision of the anointed.

STAGE 3: THE RESULTS

As early as 1968, nearly half of all schools in the country—public and private, religious and secular—had sex education, and it was rapidly growing.[16] As sex education programs spread widely through the American educational system during the 1970s, the pregnancy rate among 15- to 19-year-old females rose from approximately 68 per thousand in 1970 to approximately 96 per thousand by 1980.[17] Among unmarried girls in the 15- to 17-year-old bracket, birth rates rose 29 percent between 1970 and 1984,[18] despite a massive increase in abortions, which more than doubled during the same period. Among girls under 15, the number of abortions surpassed the number of live births by 1974.[19] The

---

°**touchstone:** The crucial test of something.

[12] Today's VD Control Problem: Joint Statement by American Public Health Association, American Social Health Association, American Venereal Disease Association, Association of State and Territorial Health Officers in Co-operation with the American Medical Association, February 1966, p. 20.

[13] Lester A. Kirkendall, "Sex Education: A Reappraisal," *The Humanist,* Spring 1965, p. 82.

[14] "Three's a Crowd," *New York Times,* March 17, 1972, p. 40.

[15] Fred M. Hechinger, "Introduction," *Sex Education and the Schools,* edited by Virginia Hilu (New York: Harper & Row, 1967), p. xiv.

[16] John Kobler, "Sex Invades the Schoolhouse," *Saturday Evening Post,* June 29, 1968, p. 26.

[17] Kasun, pp. 142, 144.

[18] Hayes, p. 66.

[19] Ibid., p. 58.

reason was not hard to find: According to the Alan Guttmacher Institute, the percentage of unmarried teenage girls who had engaged in sex was higher at every age from 15 through 19 by 1976 than it was just five years earlier.[20] The rate of teenage gonorrhea tripled between 1956 and 1975.[21] Sargent Shriver, former head of the Office of Economic Opportunity, which led the early charge for more sex education and "family planning" clinics, testified candidly to a congressional committee in 1978: "Just as venereal disease has skyrocketed 350% in the last 15 years when we have had more clinics, more pills, and more sex education than ever in history, teen-age pregnancy has risen."[22] Such candor was, however, the exception rather than the rule among those who had pushed for sex education and birth control ("family planning") clinics.

STAGE 4. THE RESPONSE

Sex education advocates continue to treat as axiomatic° the need for more sex education to combat teenage pregnancy and venereal disease. As late as 1980, and in spite of mounting evidence, the Alan Guttmacher Institute proclaimed: "Teenage pregnancy can, through better education and preventive services, be, if not altogether avoided, at least reduced, and through better maternity, abortion and social services, be reduced in its personal impact on the teenager who does get pregnant." Opposition to sex education continued to be dismissed as a "simplistic view" in the *American Biology Teacher* journal.[23] Congressman James H. Scheuer of New York found that the alarming statistics on rising teenage pregnancy only "highlight the need for strong leadership by the Federal Government in solving this problem."[24] The very possibility that "strong" federal "leadership" might have worsened the situation was not even mentioned. To the Alan Guttmacher Institute as well, an "almost quadrupling" of venereal disease between 1960 and 1972[25] only showed that more "broadly based national programs channeled through the public school system are needed and are long overdue."[26] Opposition to sex education has been depicted as "a threat to a democratic society."[27] When confronted

---

°**axiomatic:** So obvious that evidence is not needed.

[20] Alan Guttmacher Institute, p. 30.

[21] Hearings before the Select Committee on Population, Ninety-fifth Congress, second session, *Fertility and Contraception in America: Adolescent and Pre-Adolescent Pregnancy* (Washington, D.C.: U.S. Government Printing Office, 1978), Vol. II, p. 253.

[22] Ibid., p. 625.

[23] Les Picker, "Human Sexuality Education Implications for Biology Teaching," *American Biology Teacher,* Vol. 46, No. 2 (February 1984), p. 92.

[24] Hearings before the Select Committee on Population, Ninety-fifth Congress, second session.

[25] Paul A. Reichelt and Harriet H. Werley, "Contraception, Abortion and Venereal Disease: Teenagers' Knowledge and the Effect of Education," *Family Planning Perspectives,* March/April 1975, p. 83.

[26] Ibid., p. 88.

[27] Peter Scales, "The New Opposition to Sex Education: A Powerful Threat to a Democratic Society," *Journal of School Health,* April 1981, p. 303.

with the evidence that pregnancy and abortions increased during the 1970s, sex education advocates often deny that sex education was widespread during that decade, by restricting the term "sex education" to *compulsory* sex education, which tended to be mandated later.

Although sex education programs have been sold to the public, to Congress, and to education officials as ways of reducing such tangible social ills as teenage pregnancy and venereal disease, many of the leaders of this movement have long had a more expansive agenda. As a congressional committee report noted gingerly:

> The primary objective of Federal efforts in family life and sex education has been to reduce unwanted pregnancy rates among teenagers, while the primary goal of most sex educators appears to be encouragement of healthy attitudes about sex and sexuality.[28]

In short, however politically useful public concern about teenage pregnancy and venereal disease might be in obtaining government money and access to a captive audience in the public schools, the real goal was to change students' *attitudes*—put bluntly, to brainwash them with the vision of the anointed, in order to supplant the values they had been taught at home. In the words of an article in the *Journal of School Health,* sex education presents "an exciting opportunity to develop new norms."[29] Only in the light of this agenda does it make sense that so-called "sex education" should be advocated to take place throughout the school years—from kindergarten to college—when it could not possibly take that much time to teach basic biological or medical information about sex. What takes that long is a constant indoctrination in new attitudes.[30] An example of such indoctrination may be useful:

> A popular sex instructional program for junior high school students, aged 13 and 14, shows film strips of four naked couples, two homosexual and two heterosexual, performing a variety of sexually explicit acts, and teachers are warned with a cautionary note from the sex educators not to show the material to parents or friends: "Many of the materials of this program shown to people outside the context of the program itself can evoke misunderstanding and difficulties."[31]

Parents who learned of this program and protested were quickly labeled 10 "fundamentalists" and "right-wing extremists," even though they were in fact affluent Episcopalians in Connecticut. Here is an almost textbook example of the vision of the anointed, preempting the decisions of parents as to when and

---

[28] *Fertility and Contraception in the United States: Report Prepared by the Select Committee on Population* (Washington, D.C.: U.S. Government Printing Office, 1978), p. 5.

[29] Sylvia S. Hacker, "It Isn't Sex Education Unless..." *Journal of School Health,* April 1981, p. 208.

[30] See, for example, Thomas Sowell, *Inside American Education* (New York: Free Press, 1992), Chapter 3.

[31] Suzanne Fields, " 'War' Pits Parents vs. Public Policy," *Chicago Sun-Times,* October 17, 1992, p. 19.

how their own children shall be introduced to sex—and dismissing out of hand those with different views. Nor was this episode peculiar to this particular school. Similar things have happened all over the country. Parents are denigrated both in discussions of public policy and in the materials given to students in the schools. A typical comment from "experts" is that "sex and sexuality have become far too complex and technical to leave to the typical parent, who is either uninformed or too bashful to share useful sexual information with his child."[32]

This utter certainty of being right, even to the point of circumventing parents, is completely consistent with the vision, however inconsistent it is with decades of empirical evidence° on the actual consequences of "healthy attitudes toward sex" as promoted by "experts." The key point about the sex education crusade, from the standpoint of understanding the vision of the anointed, is that evidence proved to be as irrelevant here as on other issues.

A WRITER'S NOTEBOOK
Libertarianism

The following tasks are designed to help you think about the readings and identify and start to work up material you might use in your own essay. If you need help with tasks that require summarizing, see Appendix 1.

1. *Summarize part of Milton Friedman's argument and compare it to E. J. Dionne Jr.'s.* Friedman favors economic freedom and makes the sort of argument about marketplace supremacy that Dionne, who espouses liberalism, opposes. If you completed the earlier writer's notebook task asking you to summarize Dionne's objection to marketplace supremacy, review what you wrote now. Then write a page or so summarizing what good Friedman expects to come from economic freedom and telling how his stance differs from Dionne's. You might concentrate on paragraphs 4 and 10–21 in Friedman and paragraphs 8–12 in Dionne.

2. *Consider David Boaz's essay.* In paragraph 16, Boaz addresses a question he expects from his readers: "Aren't the welfare states more humane than libertarian states would be?" Write a few sentences explaining how Boaz answers this question.

3. *Evaluate Thomas Sowell's argument and compare it to Kristin Luker's.* Sowell may be the sort of writer Luker characterizes as wanting to "reverse the gains of the recent past," whereas Luker may be the sort of writer Sowell characterizes as feeling possessed of a morally superior vision. Write a page or so telling which writer you agree with more and why. As you evaluate each argument,

---

°**empirical evidence:** Evidence gained from observation and research.

[32] James Hottois and Neal A. Milner, *The Sex Education Controversy: A Study of Politics, Education, and Morality* (Lexington, Mass.: D. C. Heath and Co., 1975), p. 6.

give examples of your own reactions (or those of your friends) to sex education programs.

4. *Review your key terms and explain libertarianism.* If you prepared a list of key terms and concepts as you read the arguments in this section, look it over and then try to write a brief explanation of libertarianism. Your explanation should be about a page long and include examples as well as definitions. Use the most important terms you have identified but put them into your own sentences. Imagine you are writing your explanation for other college students who have not read about libertarianism. Working out this brief explanation now will enable you to synthesize what you have learned about libertarianism and will save you time when you write your essay.

5. *Analyze a cartoon.* The accompanying political cartoon appeared in the libertarian magazine *Reason* early in 1997, when people first realized that government-mandated air bags in automobiles were dangerous to small children. Write a half-page or so telling what you think its creator is trying to convey and whether you agree or disagree with him.

Now it is your turn. What are your thoughts about which civic stance you prefer? You should find all the material you need to write on this topic in this chapter—a rich debate in the readings, examples, and historical references. If you have been doing the work suggested in the writer's notebook tasks, you already have done a lot of writing yourself on conservatism, liberalism, and libertarianism. Now is the time to add your own experience, insight, and point of view to the conversation.

This Writer's Guide will help you

- plan, draft, revise, edit, and proofread an essay evaluating three civic stances and arguing in favor of one of them
- work with sources—to gather current information and to cite sources that you draw on
- try out certain sentence patterns that are useful in writing that makes an evaluation
- reflect on what you have learned completing this assignment

PLANNING AND DRAFTING YOUR ESSAY

This section provides guidelines and examples to help you plan and draft a convincing essay evaluating civic stances. It will help you

- understand your readers and your writing situation
- select materials
- prepare a prospectus
- organize your essay
- devise a convincing argument
- cite sources

THE WRITING ASSIGNMENT   Write an essay in which you argue for one of three civic stances—conservatism, liberalism, or libertarianism—and defend this stance as preferable to the other two. You need not think the position you prefer is perfect, merely that it is the best of the three. In your essay, you will need to help your readers understand the three stances and why you think the stance you chose is the wisest or most defensible. Provide reasons for your choice and support your reasons with information from the readings and your own personal experience.

Assume that you are writing your essay for a campus magazine that will be read by other college students who may not have encountered formal discussions of these civic stances and may either be uncommitted or inclined to favor one of the stances you reject.

Understanding Your Readers

Although your readers likely have encountered debates—in courses, on radio and TV talk shows, or in newspapers—about issues on which conservatives, liberals, and libertarians differ, they may not have thought about the philosophies that underlie each of these views. Assume that they will probably need help in defining conservatism, liberalism, and libertarianism and in understanding the differences among them. Your readers may already have strong opinions on particular issues—such as whether people should be required to wear motorcycle helmets; whether drugs or cigarettes or pornography should be regulated; or whether the federal tax system is fair. Remember, though, that your argument should not be a one-issue essay about any single law or policy.

As you think about your readers, keep in mind that there is a great deal of ferment concerning these three general civic stances. Some political analysts think that an era of greater conservatism is at hand, others find a rise in libertarianism, and still others predict a resurgence of liberalism. There are conservatives who quarrel with some current definitions of conservatism and liberals who quarrel with some definitions of liberalism. Opinion polls, meanwhile, find that many college students hold a mixture of beliefs—liberal on many issues and conservative or libertarian on others. Imagine, then, that your readers may hold contradictory beliefs in what is a volatile arena of civic stances.

Assume Authority.   Regardless of the stance you take, assume that you are the expert and that you're writing for readers who can benefit from your knowledge. Your job is to help readers who are not so well informed as you to understand these civic stances and consider why you endorse the stance you do. You may not be able to convince anyone to adopt your stance, but you can at least encourage everyone to think more carefully about what stance they themselves might prefer.

Selecting Materials

All the readings and writing tasks in this chapter have contributed to your understanding of these civic stances. Now you can select from those resources the materials you need to support your own stance. The following activities will help you do so.

Select a Stance.   Your first task is to choose the stance that you prefer. You may have a strong conviction about one, or you may feel torn between the merits of one stance and another. Keep in mind that choosing a particular civic stance does not require you to deny all the good points of other stances. In your essay, you can concede that the other stances have some merits.

Identify Key Resources.   Review the readings for the stance you have chosen, this time thinking about why the stance is attractive to you. If you have completed the writer's notebook tasks on this stance, review your work now, along with any relevant entries based on personal experience. Look for entries that might be especially helpful in defending your stance.

List and Review Reasons.   Make a list of five to ten reasons why you prefer this stance, using the readings as well as your personal or family experiences. You will probably find some of the arguments in the readings more relevant and important than others. Make a note of those that seem most compelling.

Review Other Stances.   If you completed the writer's notebook tasks for the readings on the other two stances, review your work and those readings themselves, asking yourself what are the most likely objections or reservations your readers may have about the stance you have chosen. You do not need an exhaustive list, but you should have a clear idea of the two or three objections conservatives are most likely to have about liberals and libertarians, liberals about conservatives and libertarians, and libertarians about conservatives and liberals.

Preparing a Prospectus

At this point, your instructor may want you to prepare a prospectus for your essay, to plot out what it will look like. Engineers, businesspeople, and other professionals write prospectuses for their projects to try out their ideas and win support for them. In much the same way, writing a prospectus for your essay will help you figure out what you might say about the stance you prefer.

Following are some guidelines for drafting a two- or three-page prospectus.

1. *State which stance you prefer.* In a sentence or two, tell which civic stance you prefer—conservatism, liberalism, or libertarianism.

2. *List reasons.* List three to five reasons you will give readers to persuade them that your stance is best. Your reasons may come from the readings, writer's notebook tasks, and personal experience.

3. *Identify one important reading.* Which single reading do you think will be the most important in providing support for your argument? Explain its importance in two or three sentences.

4. *Anticipate readers' objections or reservations.* List at least three questions, objections, or reservations you would expect from readers who prefer the other civic stances.

5. *Identify one reading that challenges your position.* Identify the one reading that poses the greatest challenge to your preferred stance. In two or three sentences, explain why you must argue against it convincingly.

6. *Try to support part of your argument.* Select one of the reasons you listed in item 2 above and write a page or so supporting it with whatever facts, examples, statistics, or anecdotes from the readings—and any relevant personal experi-

ences—come to mind. Do not take time now for a thorough search of the readings; rely on your memory, notes, and perhaps a quick look at one key reading. Write quickly. Announce the reason in the first sentence and then go directly into your support for it. Your purpose is simply to try out one part of your argument before you plan your entire essay.

Organizing Your Essay

Most people are used to hearing debates about civic stances, but their understanding of such stances may be fragmentary. Consequently, your readers will first need to have your clear identification and description of the three stances and then your evaluation, including your reasons for choosing one stance over the other two. So, in your essay you need to present an engaging, informative discussion of the three civic stances, then argue and counterargue convincingly that one stance is preferable to the others, offering reasons and support.

To develop a detailed framework for your essay, you might expand your plan in the following way:

Presentation of the three civic stances
– an engaging opening
– a brief overview of the three stances

Argument for your preferred stance
– statement of your choice (thesis)
– argument to support your choice
– counterarguments to the stances you have rejected
– conclusion and reassertion of the reasons for your choice

While this plan is not the only one you might follow, it can help you draft and revise your essay. Keep in mind, however, that a plan is not a paragraph outline, and as you proceed you may order some parts differently. You may need only one paragraph for some elements but several paragraphs for others. Following are some strategies and resources for accomplishing each part of the plan.

Presenting the Stances.   In addition to informing your readers about the three civic stances, you also need to help them see the social significance and importance to them personally of choosing a civic stance—of discussing these views rationally and openly, listening to others' arguments, weighing and evaluating competing stances, and looking deeper into their own convictions. You want to spark your readers' interest and provide an adequate context for your evaluation of the three stances.

WRITING AN ENGAGING OPENING.   Try to catch your readers' attention and get them to see the importance of learning about the three civic stances. Here are some ways you might begin your essay:

- Relate a personal experience of the benefit or the harm of particular government regulations (as Sam Brownback does).

- Present and comment on a brief quote from an important historical figure that is relevant to the argument you are going to make (as Jacqueline R. Kasun and Milton Friedman do).

- Relate an anecdote you have heard during conversations with classmates or friends that dramatizes an issue involving individual liberties or rights (as Brownback does).

- Briefly quote two or three strikingly opposed differences of opinion that you found in the readings or in newspaper articles and comment on their differences.

Whatever opening you choose, keep in mind that you are writing for students who are not experts on civic stances.

GIVING A BRIEF OVERVIEW.   Your readers need direct information about the three civic stances, basic information they can build on later when they read details of your argument. Here you need to explain the stances clearly and concisely.
    You might try one of these options for presenting your overview:

- Describe each of the three stances in a general way, taking them one at a time.

- Explain each of the three stances by focusing on the one writer who seems to you to present that stance best. You could name the writers and publication sources, quote from each one, and then comment on the quotations.

- Describe each of the three stances very briefly and then compare them to each other, using one or two key issues to make the contrasts among the stances stand out clearly.

Plotting Out Your Argument and Counterargument.   As the heart of your essay, the argument section generally begins with a strong thesis statement of which stance you prefer, followed by reasons and support and interspersed with counterarguments. You have several options for arranging your argument section, depending on how you want to sequence your reasons and integrate your counterarguments. Following are examples showing how various writers have successfully used these strategies.

ASSERTING YOUR PREFERENCE.   As you begin the second part of the essay—justifying your choice of stance—your reader needs a clear statement of which stance you judge to be best. If you hinted at your preference earlier, you still need to reassert your preference and indicate the main reasons for your choice.

SEQUENCING YOUR REASONS.   You need to support the choice you have made and to compare your stance with whatever seems unacceptable and possibly dangerous or offensive about the other stances. In organizing an evaluation, some writers like to begin with what they disapprove of and then move to what they prefer. Others, however, like to begin with what they prefer and then explain what they disapprove of. You need to weigh the possible effects of these alternative arrangements on the reader. Because readers tend to remember best what they have read last, you may want your strongest arguments to appear last. If you make that decision, you will begin with counterargument, explaining what you find faulty about the other two stances, and then give the reasons why your chosen stance is better.

Once you have an overall arrangement in mind, you can decide how to sequence the reasons justifying your preferred stance. There is no set formula for doing this, but one approach is to make a list for yourself of the reasons for the stance you prefer and then take one reason at a time, discussing its importance. Russell Kirk, for instance, lists six beliefs important to conservatism and argues for them one at a time. In similar fashion, Sam Brownback argues for seven proposals in his conservative "Contract with America." Boaz lists nine elements of libertarianism. Though Kirk, Brownback, and Boaz each use slightly different kinds of categories, their tactic of dividing a stance into subparts is a useful one for sequencing the argument part of an evaluation.

INTEGRATING COUNTERARGUMENTS. When you counterargue, you are anticipating and responding to your readers' likely questions and objections and refuting or conceding some of the opposing positions in the readings.

There are basically two ways to integrate counterarguments into an evaluation: you can choose (as Brownback, E. J. Dionne Jr., and Boaz do) to put your counterarguments first, before the reasons for the stance you prefer, or you can begin arguing for the stance you prefer and then criticize the other two stances. If you take this approach, you should reassert your preference at the end of your essay, leaving the reader with a strong sense of the stance you prefer and why.

Here are some of the ways the writers in this chapter have arranged the larger parts of their arguments:

> Brownback moves from anecdotes illustrating the problems of big government (paragraphs 7–12) to his argument describing the conservative position (paragraphs 13–25) and the specific measures conservatism should offer (paragraphs 26–38).

> Rosenblatt begins with the attacks on liberalism and misconceptions about it (paragraphs 2–10) and then defends liberalism for its achievements (paragraphs 11–19).

> Dionne begins by arguing against the conservative (and libertarian) dislike of big government (paragraphs 1–15) and then proceeds to defend the liberal view of government (paragraphs 16–18).

> Boaz begins with a critique of the modern welfare state (paragraphs 5–19) and then moves to what libertarianism can offer (paragraphs 20–30).

CLOSING EFFECTIVELY.   Closing may be easier than starting up, but it nevertheless requires imagination. Try to end your essay gracefully and memorably. You have a number of options:

- Reassert why your chosen stance is preferable.
- Summarize your argument.
- Quote an authority to support your judgment, using a particularly telling quote.
- Frame your argument by referring to the opening of your essay, as Rosenblatt does.
- Speculate briefly about what may happen if Americans adopt what you consider to be a dangerous civic stance.
- Speculate briefly about specific policies implied in the stance you prefer and comment on their potential benefits, as Brownback and Dionne do.

You might decide to use one or more of these approaches for closing—or something entirely different. Whatever approach you use, remember that your goal is to convince your readers to take your evaluation of these stances seriously. Since readers tend to remember best what they read last, take advantage of this opportunity to say something memorable.

Developing Your Argument and Counterargument

This section will help you construct a thesis, argue to support your choice, and counterargue questions about your argument and arguments that challenge your preferred stance.

Constructing a Thesis.   A *thesis* is a clear assertion of your judgment that one civic stance is preferable to the others. Your thesis statement should appear after your overview of the three stances, right at the point at which you begin defending your choice. It should not only name your chosen stance but also identify the reasons you will use. By forecasting your reasons, your thesis statement helps readers follow the development of your argument.

Although thesis and forecast can be delivered in one or two sentences, they usually require several sentences. Here is Laura Lamb's thesis asserting liberalism as her preferred civic stance.

```
Conservatives, libertarians, and liberals all argue
that individuals' independence will benefit both the
community and the individual. However, conservatism
and libertarianism ultimately create dependence because
communities lack support and individuals lack power.
Liberalism, by contrast, truly preserves independence:
it strengthens both communities and individuals because
government protects and promotes equal rights.
```

Lamb begins by asserting the importance of *independence* for each of the three stances. Then she asserts that only liberalism will foster the independence that conservatives, liberals, and libertarians all desire. These three sentences, then, forecast not only what she will say about the three stances but also the sequence of her argument. They tell readers that she will begin with the draw-backs of conservatism, then discuss those of libertarianism, and end with her argument for liberalism.

Here, for contrast, is Konstantine Salmas's thesis statement endorsing the conservative stance:

```
Conservatism is the best civic stance because it puts
trust in the individual: trust that autonomous individuals
are capable of choosing and, with this ability, will
choose the moral life. Choosing the moral life -- a mutual
respect for all those around you, a belief in honesty, a
belief in education and the family -- enables individuals to
feel good about themselves, take responsibility for their
actions, and prepare to deal with the troubles that, at
some point, they will come across.
```

Salmas chooses for his key terms *individual* and *moral* because his preference for conservatism comes from its moral superiority, as he sees it, more than from other considerations (such as rights or economic efficiency). He suggests here that he will not criticize liberalism because it ensures social welfare in the wrong way or tramples on people's rights. Instead, his thesis suggests that what he dislikes about liberalism comes from its *moral* consequences.

As these examples from Lamb and Salmas indicate, an evaluation essay nec-essarily involves some comparisons and contrasts. Your thesis need not focus on every aspect of the stances, but it should identify, by means of a few key terms, the essential reasons you have for preferring one stance over the other two.

EXAMPLES FROM THE READINGS. For further examples of thesis statements, see Kasun (paragraph 2), Friedman (paragraph 2), and Boaz (paragraph 1).

Arguing. Your argument is the central feature of your evaluation—it is where you give reasons for preferring one stance over the others and support those rea-sons with relevant examples, statistics, quotations, anecdotes, observations, analogies, and so on. Since it is also important to give reasons for *not* favoring the other stances, your argument should include comparisons and contrasts.

Here is a paragraph from the argument section of Carolyn Kennedy's essay, which supports conservatism because it favors morality and limited govern-ment intervention:

```
One shocking example of the decay of morality is the decay
of personal responsibility and commitment seen in the
increase of teen pregnancy in this country. Though liberal
critics often argue that economic problems cause teen
pregnancy, Jacqueline Kasun points out in Policy Review
that there are higher rates of teen pregnancy and welfare
```

> dependency in states that spent more, not less, on birth
> control (245). Kasun refers to the National Center for
> Health Statistics, which reports that in 1960 5 percent of
> babies were born out of wedlock whereas in 1991, 30
> percent were, despite increased expenditures on sex
> education (246). The data seem to show that government
> programs will not substitute for moral responsibility. Sam
> Brownback suggests that families will be better off with
> fewer legislative initiatives and more freedom and
> responsibility: "By pledging to spare families from
> additional legislative and regulatory tinkering, we will
> do more to protect the rights to life, liberty, and the
> pursuit of happiness than any federal legislative quick-
> fix" (238). Morality begins on an individual level and is
> taught within a family. Any breakup or breakdown of the
> family is directly related to shattered and collapsed
> concepts of morality.

Kennedy's argument is well focused on her larger thesis about morality, is authoritative, and makes good use of two readings. The information from Kasun provides a statistical foundation for Kennedy to build on, and the quote from Brownback helps her argue that illegitimacy is not a problem to be solved by government. To support your own argument, use information from the readings of the stance you prefer, as Kennedy does here.

Following is another example of argument, from Laura Lamb's defense of liberalism:

> Liberals promote the protection of equal rights through
> governmental regulation, leading to more individuals
> gaining power to control their own lives. Liberal
> journalist Roger Rosenblatt quotes William Galston as
> saying that "a government too weak to threaten our
> liberties may by that very fact be too weak to secure our
> rights, let alone advance our shared purposes." Rosenblatt
> points out that although conservatives and libertarians
> support limits on the power of the government to protect
> the rights of individuals, Americans enthusiastically
> accept the protections liberalism has achieved in
> rights for women and minorities and protection of the
> environment. He lists Title VII of the Civil Rights Act,
> the Equal Pay Act, the Equal Credit Opportunity Act, and
> Clean Air Act amendments as examples of government
> protections that Americans endorse. No institution or
> individual would have the power to protect these rights if
> individuals were left on their own.

Note how Lamb uses one of the readings: first, she quotes Rosenblatt referring to William Galston, then she summarizes some of the examples Rosenblatt uses in his defense of liberalism. When you defend one of these civic stances, you also need to refer specifically to examples from key spokespersons for that stance.

EXAMPLES FROM THE READINGS. In the following readings, you can see further examples of the kinds of support you might use in an evaluation argument:

> personal anecdotes: Brownback (paragraphs 7–11)
>
> brief example: Dionne's example of the "family wage" (paragraph 9)
>
> statistics: Boaz (paragraphs 6 and 18)

Counterarguing.   To argue is also to counterargue—particularly in this essay because your reasons for preferring one civic stance involve your reasons for rejecting the other two. You need to incorporate several strategies of counterargument in your essay. One such strategy is to anticipate readers' possible objections to, and questions about, the stance you prefer so that you can convincingly disarm some of their objections. As part of this process, you need to acknowledge the other two stances, as presented in the readings. You should *concede* whatever you can accept in the other two stances so that your readers do not reject your argument as careless or intolerant, and you should try to *refute* whatever you cannot accept.

In his thesis, Konstantine Salmas stated that conservatism provides the return to morality that America needs. Here, as part of his counterargument to the libertarian stance, he concedes that legalizing drugs might reduce illegal moneymaking:

```
Legalizing marijuana, cocaine, and heroin would be
giving up too much to those individuals who continue to
stretch the limits of right and wrong. The reason
libertarians offer for giving up the war on drugs is that
the program's goal, eliminating the supply of drugs, has
been unsuccessful. But as a conservative I say that by
legalizing drugs of any sort, America is justifying the
use of drugs. Granted, selling marijuana, cocaine, and
heroin on the competitive market would decrease the number
of black-market sellers by undermining prices. Drug
dealing would no longer make millionaires out of dealers,
both in the inner city and urban America. Children who
grow up watching young men dealing and taking the profit
of these deals to purchase Mercedes, gold chains, and
expensive sneakers would be less likely to be attracted to
illegal moneymaking because the market supply would make
these dealers obsolete.
    Regardless of these advantages to making drugs
available on the competitive market, however, as a
country we cannot let the drug use win. How would parents,
communities, even the federal government be able to teach
children that drugs are wrong if we have agreed to
legalize drugs? [...]
```

Note the steps in Salmas's counterargument: In the second sentence of the first paragraph, he uses the word *libertarians* so his readers will be in no doubt about which stance he is counterarguing. With the phrase *But as a conservative,* he states clearly what *he* thinks. In the following sentences, beginning with *Granted,* he makes a concession. Salmas shows himself to be a reasonable person who is willing to think about the libertarian argument and even to concede that it would be good to drive illegal drug dealers out of the market. In the paragraph that follows, however, he returns to his own argument. He clearly signals his readers with the words *Regardless* and *however,* cueing them that although he concedes the value of driving out illegal drug dealers, he does not think legalizing drugs can be morally justified.

EXAMPLES FROM THE READINGS. To learn more about strategies for counterarguing, look closely at these examples from the readings:

> Kasun (paragraphs 16–20) offers evidence to *refute* claims about the value of sex education.

> Dionne (paragraph 1) offers a quote from U.S. House majority leader Dick Armey (a "new conservative" in Dionne's terms or, perhaps, a libertarian), which Dionne then proceeds to *refute.*

> Luker (paragraph 6) *concedes* a concern that people have about sex education but then uses recent research to *refute* the idea that sex education encourages sex.

> Friedman (paragraph 20) *concedes* that there is a role of government as umpire, even though he wants only a minimal role for government.

SENTENCES FOR EVALUATING CIVIC STANCES

Different writing situations often require different kinds of sentences. When you evaluate civic stances, you are sometimes defining or judging and at other times comparing or contrasting. To present each of the stances clearly and relate them to each other, you need to draw distinctions among them. You do not, however, want your readers to feel that they are watching a Ping-Pong match — dizzy from rapidly turning in one direction and then another.

You may want to review the material in this section now as a preview of some of the special kinds of thinking and writing with which you will be engaged as you draft and revise your essay. You will find the definitions and examples here most helpful, however, as you revise your essay, when you will want to examine closely the logical relationships between all of your sentences and the shifts among various verb tenses. (You may also find it helpful to review the section "Sentences That Keep Readers on Track" in Chapter 3.)

Using Repetition Effectively

In your essay, you need to repeat key terms frequently to develop your argument and keep your readers on track. Look, for instance, at how E. J. Dionne Jr. uses the related terms *market* and *marketplace* in paragraphs 8–9 as part of his defense of liberalism and critique of conservatism and libertarianism. To help you see Dionne's use of these terms, the words *market* and *marketplace* are italicized, as are closely related words such as *buying* and *selling:*

> But these do not exhaust the instances in which a free people might decide to limit the writ of *money* and the supremacy of the *market*. As the political philosopher Michael Walzer has argued [...] rights and privileges should not be put *up for sale*. As an abstract proposition, we reject the notion that a *wealthy* person should be able to *buy* extra years of life that a *poor* person cannot, since life itself ought not be *bought* and *sold*. Yet the availability of health care affects longevity, and by making health care a purely *market* transaction, we come close to *selling* life and death. This was the primary argument for Medicare [...].
>
> The current vogue for the superiority of *markets* over government carries the risk of obscuring the basic issue of *what should be for sale* in the first place. In a society characterized by growing *economic* inequality, the dangers of making the *marketplace* the sole arbiter of the basic elements of a decent life are especially large. Doing so could put many of the basics out of [...] reach [...]. The interrelationship between the moral and *economic* crises can be seen most powerfully in families where the need to earn enough income forces both parents to spend increasing amounts of time outside the home. One of the great achievements of this century was "the family wage," which allowed the vast majority of workers to provide their families with both a decent living and the parental time to give their children a decent upbringing. The family wage was not simply a product of the *marketplace*. It was secured through a combination of *economic* growth, social legislation and unionization. If the *marketplace* becomes not simply the main arbiter of income, as it will inevitably be, but the *only* judge of living standards, then all social factors, including the need to strengthen families and improve the care given children, become entirely irrelevant in the world of work.
>
> —E. J. Dionne Jr.
> "They Only *Look* Dead: Why Progressives
> Will Dominate the Next Political Era"

In the first paragraph, Dionne uses a number of closely related terms to raise the question — or sound a warning — about whether everything should be determined by the values of the marketplace. In the second, he introduces a competing value along with a new, repeated term: the *decent* life, which involves a *decent* living and a *decent* upbringing for children. As he builds his argument, he develops another term — *the family wage* — as an alternative to thinking solely in terms of marketplace values. Following these two paragraphs, Dionne continues to use the terms *market* and *marketplace* in nearly every one of his remaining paragraphs.

What you should notice about this example from Dionne is, first, the amount of repetition. Note too, however, that the repetition is not mechanical: as terms are defined, there is a building effect. The argument develops piece by piece, moving from the danger of offering everything *for sale* to suggesting, instead, the importance of a *decent family wage*. Second, the repeated key terms determine what the reader understands to be the issue and help the reader follow the argument. Since the *marketplace* terms are the key terms for the conservative and the libertarian economic views he opposes, Dionne never lets them disappear from the reader's sight while he is arguing against marketplace values.

Giving Readers Clear Signals

Repeating key terms, as Dionne does, helps readers keep track of where the writer is in an argument. It is particularly easy for readers to lose track of a message in this kind of evaluation argument because the writer usually goes back and forth so often between a feature of one stance and a feature of another. In addition to repeating key terms, then, writers in this chapter use a number of strong, clear signals to avoid losing their readers among these back-and-forth comparisons.

Naming the Stances Repeatedly. To evaluate a civic stance — either positively or negatively — you need to refer to it clearly and repeatedly so that your readers can identify at all times exactly which stances you are referring to. This clear identification may sound simple, but it is not always easy to accomplish as you move back and forth from one stance to another.

Here is how Russell Kirk refers repeatedly to conservatism and liberalism in his second paragraph:

> *Conservatism*, indeed, is a word [...]. Even today, although there are many men of *conservative* prejudices [...] , few are eager to describe themselves as "*conservatives.*" The people of the United States became the chief *conservative* nation [...] when they had ceased to call themselves *conservatives* at home. For a generation, the word "*liberal*" had been in fashion [...]. The *liberal* [...] has been [...] commonly the *liberal* has tended to despise the lessons of the past [...].
> — RUSSELL KIRK
> "Who Are the Conservatives?"

Roger Rosenblatt uses the same strategy of repetition in his fifth paragraph:

> *Liberalism* dominates the debate and defines the terms of the debate. The *conservative* assaults on *the L word,* which were made most effectively by President Reagan, have been so routine over the past 16 years that there is a whole generation of people under 35 who have never heard "*liberal*" uttered as anything other than a joke or an insult. Yet they live in a *liberal* country. *Conservatives* may have ruined the word but have adopted most of the content of *liberalism* [...].
> — ROGER ROSENBLATT
> "The Triumph of Liberalism"

Showing the Steps of an Argument.   When you build complex ideas step by step, you need to make sure that your readers can follow the steps. To help her readers focus on her proposed solutions, Jacqueline R. Kasun uses a series of questions at the beginning of paragraphs:

> What can be done to reduce risky youthful sexual behavior? (paragraph 26)
>
> Then what explains the flood of claims, so enthusiastically reported in the media, that government financing of contraceptives, abortions, and steriliza-tions prevents teenage pregnancy and saves billions in public assistance? (para-graph 28)
>
> — JACQUELINE R. KASUN
> "Condom Nation: Government Sex Education
> Promotes Teen Pregnancy"

Each question directs the reader's attention to the argument Kasun will address in that paragraph. Then, in each case, Kasun forcefully states her own point of view and develops her idea further. In effect, the question that opens the paragraph says to the reader: "Pay attention because here is the next step in my argument."

Other writers who use such questions are Dionne (paragraph 16), Boaz (paragraphs 3, 12, and 16), and Sowell (paragraphs 2 and 4).

Using Transitions Effectively.   You also can help your readers by offering clear transitions when you switch your discussion from one stance to another. Here are some examples from this chapter, with the transition words itali-cized.

> Beyond this major function, government may enable us at times to accomplish jointly what we would find it more difficult or expensive to accomplish sever-ally. *However,* any such use of government is fraught with danger. We should not [...]. (paragraph 4)
>
> — MILTON FRIEDMAN
> "Capitalism and Freedom"

> The conservative assaults on the L word, which were made most effectively by President Reagan, have been so routine over the past 16 years that there is a whole generation of people under 35 who have never heard "liberal" uttered as anything other than a joke or an insult. *Yet* they live in a liberal country. Conser-vatives may have ruined the word *but* have adopted most of the content of liber-alism. (paragraph 5)
>
> —ROGER ROSENBLATT
> "The Triumph of Liberalism"

Note that the transitions appear at the point at which the writer turns from a positive to a negative evaluation (or vice versa) and from summarizing what someone has said to criticizing it. Some particularly useful transition words for these purposes are *but, however, nevertheless, yet,* and *although* because they highlight oppositions.

Writers use other signals to continue the thread of an argument. Note how the italicized words in the following passage from Kristin Luker's essay help her readers follow the argument:

> *Some people think* that [...]. *This belief* has a certain logic, *but* if sex education does have such an effect at all, it is very weak. *One study* suggested that [...]. *Another study* found that [...] whereas [...]. *Still another study* found that [...]. *But* careful and rigorous review [...] suggests that, in general, taking sex education courses has virtually no effect on an individual's propensity to become sexually active. (paragraph 6)
>
> —KRISTIN LUKER
> "Dubious Conceptions"

The transitional words and phrases occur early in each sentence and tell the reader immediately where Luker is in her argument: when she is discussing the belief she disagrees with; when she is presenting the evidence that, in her view, is weak *(One study, Another study, Still another study)*; and when she sums up her conclusion *(But* careful and rigorous review [...]). Signals such as these are especially helpful in evaluation arguments because they allow readers to follow the logic of comparisons that move rapidly from one stance to another.

CITING SOURCES

As you develop the arguments and counterarguments in your essay, you will frequently quote, paraphrase, or summarize this chapter's readings, and perhaps material from other sources as well. When you use original ideas in this way, you must cite them. In other words, you must identify their sources either informally or formally.

Informal Citation

Informal citation allows you to identify all of your sources within the text of your essay. You mention the author, publication, and perhaps the date right in your own sentences. In some instances, you may also want to include a brief description of the writer in order to establish his or her authority. When using informal citation, you do not need to identify sources in footnotes or a works-cited list at the end of your essay.

Many readings in this chapter rely on informal citation because they are written for the general public. To see how writers use this citation style, look at these examples:

> "The philosophy that directs teens to 'be careful' or 'to play it safe with condoms' has not protected them," says Dr. Joe McIlhaney Jr., president of the Medical Institute for Sexual Health. "It has only enticed them into the quagmire [...]."
>
> —JACQUELINE R. KASUN
> "Condom Nation: Government Sex
> Education Promotes Teen Pregnancy"

In "Liberal Purposes" (1991), Prof. William A. Galston of the University of Maryland wrote: "A government too weak to threaten our liberties may by that very
fact be too weak to secure our rights, let alone advance our shared purposes."
                                                    —ROGER ROSENBLATT
                                                    "The Triumph of Liberalism"

Formal Citation

When you use formal citation, you follow a specific style used by a particular
academic or professional group. Appendix 2 of this book outlines two of these
styles, one from the Modern Language Association (MLA), which is favored by
scholars in the humanities, and one from the American Psychological Association (APA), which is favored by scholars in psychology. Ask your instructor
which you should follow.

If you are referring to one of the readings in this chapter, cite it as a work in an
anthology or edited collection. Depending on your instructor's advice, follow either
the recommendations under "A Work in an Anthology" in the "Books" section of the
MLA guidelines or those under "A Work in an Edited Collection" in the "Books" section of the APA guidelines. If you cite, for example, material coming from a book,
such as E. J. Dionne Jr.'s *They Only Look Dead: Why Progressives Will Dominate the
Next Political Era,* your in-text reference or "Works Cited" item will list Dionne as the
author of *They Only Look Dead: Why Progressives Will Dominate the Next Political Era*
and *Writing the World* as the anthology in which the Dionne reading appears. Appendix 2 of this book discusses these options thoroughly and provides examples of each.

Note: Writers usually do not document sources that provide commonly
known facts, general background information, or common knowledge, but if
you use some of the background material in this chapter's introductions or
reading headnotes, you have two choices. You can paraphrase the material
without giving a citation if it appears to be common knowledge. Otherwise,
you can cite Charles R. Cooper and Susan Peck MacDonald as authors of *Writing the World,* using the models in Appendix 2.

EVALUATING AND REVISING

The following guidelines for revising will help you evaluate your own draft
and provide useful advice to other students. As you read a draft, try to identify
what has been done well and to come up with specific ways to improve the
presentation and evaluation of the civic stances. As you begin the revision
process, focus on the big issues; save spelling and grammar for later.

Whether revising your own draft or helping your classmates with theirs, you
may need to refer to specific readings, so have them handy as you work. Also
have any writer's notebook entries you wrote close by so you can refer to them by
number.

If you are reading someone else's draft, it is a good idea to write your
comments on a separate sheet of paper, perhaps following the headings in this

section. For your own essay, you can also make comments directly on the draft.

Read to Get a General Impression

Even if you are reading your own draft, read it straight through without marking on it, as if you are encountering the essay for the first time in a magazine for college students. Then write three or four sentences summarizing your first impression. What aspect of the essay seems most successful? What is most interesting or surprising? What one major improvement would make the argument more convincing?

Read to Analyze the Draft More Closely

Next, number the paragraphs and underline the thesis statement. Then mark the point at which the essay divides into two major parts: the presentation of civic stances and the argument for the chosen stance. Reread the draft, keeping in mind that the intended readers may not be very knowledgeable about civic stances. Ask yourself, What do these particular readers need to know? Write down what is good about the draft as well as specific ideas for revision.

The Opening.   What strategy is used to open the essay? How does it draw the readers in if they are not already thinking about this topic? What seems most effective about the opening? What needs clarifying? Suggest at least one alternative opening.

The Overview of the Stances.   Consider how well the essay explains the three civic stances. Do you think readers will need more — or less — information about these stances? If less, what specific material should be cut? If more, what facts, examples, brief quotations, or anecdotes should be added? What specific readings might serve as possible sources of new material?

Now look at the opening and the overview together. Is the opening engaging enough for the reader to want to read further? Have the importance and the significance of the three civic stances been established? How might the essay get off to a stronger start?

The Stance.   Does the draft have a clear thesis, asserting the writer's preferred stance? Underline the sentences in which the thesis is stated. Circle the key terms in the thesis. (Key terms could include some of the following: *conservatism, liberalism, libertarianism, marketplace, welfare, freedom, rights, government,* or other words and phrases relevant to this topic.)

Which key terms are carried throughout the essay to provide coherence? Do any key terms in the thesis then disappear from the rest of the essay? Might different key terms be more appropriate for the argument the writer wants to make?

Does the thesis forecast the steps in the argument, giving the writer's main reasons for the stance chosen? If not, or if the forecast seems unclear in any way, what specifically should be done to revise it?

The Reasons and Support.   Find the main reasons the writer gives for preferring one stance to the other two and number these reasons sequentially in the margin. If you cannot do this easily, write down why you think the reasons are unclear.

Tell whether further examples, quotations, statistics, and so forth are needed, identifying some of the readings that might be used for such examples.

Which reasons seem especially convincing? Should any reason be dropped from the argument because it is neither relevant nor strongly argued? What new reason might strengthen the argument?

The Counterarguments.   Reread the draft and note in the margin where each counterargument occurs. Remember that counterarguments may be woven throughout an argument or fully developed in one or two places. You should be able to find some counterarguments that take readers' specific questions or objections into account and other counterarguments against the other two stances.

How well do they answer such questions and objections? Which concessions or refutations seem particularly effective? If any seem less than convincing, how might they be strengthened? List other questions and objections that should be considered.

How well are the two other stances covered? If a stance is presented unfairly or too sketchily, point out how it might be presented more fully or accurately.

The Cues to Keep Readers on Track.   Note any sections or paragraphs that are confusing, where the direction of the argument seems unclear, or where there are gaps in the reasoning. Is it clear where the major parts of the essay — presentation, argument, counterargument — end and begin? Is the argument easy to follow? Is it logical? If not, point out the breaks or gaps.

Review the key terms in the thesis and note whether there are any paragraphs or pages devoid of key terms.

Look for places where transition sentences may be needed to keep readers on track. Do paragraph-opening sentences lead the reader unmistakably from one section of the essay to the next and from one step in the argument to the next? If not, the cues may be too weak to carry readers smoothly forward.

The Closing.   Does the essay close in a graceful and memorable way? What strategy is used — summarizing the argument, quoting an authority, or some other technique? How might the closing be made more effective?

EDITING AND PROOFREADING

As you revise, you should be concerned primarily with the presentation of the issue and your argument. Then it is time to edit your individual sentences and tighten the connections among them. In particular, you need to check to see that the logical relationships among sentences are clear and that the transitions keep readers on track as they proceed through your argument. Look for sentences that might be combined to clarify relationships among ideas. Look as well for overly long or garbled sentences that might be divided into two or three sentences.

As you work on your sentences, look for errors in spelling, capitalization, punctuation, usage, and grammar, consulting a writer's handbook for information about correcting any you find. Ask a friend or a classmate to read over your draft to help you spot errors.

Before you hand in your final revised essay, proofread it with great care and run it through a spellchecker to try to make it error free.

REFLECTING ON WHAT YOU HAVE LEARNED

Once you have completed this chapter's reading and writing tasks, it is a good idea to take time to think about what you have accomplished and what you have learned. Doing so will help you consolidate your new knowledge and remember it longer.

As you worked through this chapter, you were actually engaged in two closely related kinds of learning: becoming well informed about important civic stances and composing a convincing defense of one stance. Using the following questions as a starting point, write a page or so reflecting on this accomplishment.

- What was the most difficult part of understanding the three civic stances? What was the most surprising thing you learned?

- How has your thinking about conservatism, liberalism, and libertarianism been confirmed or changed?

- What questions do you still have about these stances?

- How have the readings in this chapter affected your viewing of the news, your observations of people around you, and your own thoughts about your identity as an American?

- What was most difficult for you in planning your essay? When you began drafting, what was your biggest surprise? What was the most important revision you made in your draft? How did you decide to make this change?

- What advice would you give to writers who are just starting an assignment in which they need to evaluate civic stances?

- What are you most pleased with in your essay? How would you revise it further if you had more time to work on it?

GATHERING ADDITIONAL INFORMATION

To supplement the readings in this chapter or respond to one of the additional writing projects at the end of the chapter, you may want to find examples of other civic stances or update opinions held by conservatives, liberals, or libertarians.

The *kind* of material you are looking for should guide where you look. In this chapter, you have encountered two kinds of material: (1) opinions on the general philosophical and political benefits of three civic stances; and (2) conservative, liberal, and libertarian opinions on particular current issues, such as sex education. Each kind of material may require a different search strategy.

Opinions on Civic Stances

Opinions on conservatism, liberalism, libertarianism, or other civic stances may be found in both books and articles or short essays.

Books.   Book-length discussions of civic issues may be written by important public officials; nonacademic writers; and academic philosophers, historians, or political scientists who are addressing nonacademic readers. Though you can find books written for other academics, such books may involve detailed discussions about various versions of a particular stance and thus may be less valuable to you than books intended for a less specialized audience. In this chapter, for instance, historian Russell Kirk and journalist E. J. Dionne Jr. both write for a fairly general audience rather than for their peers.

To find books arguing for the three civic stances—or other stances not included in this chapter—consult your library's online catalog using search terms such as *conservatism, liberalism, libertarianism, populism, socialism,* or *progressivism.* You might also want to check the Library of Congress Subject Headings (LCSH) for a book you know. Here, for example, are the subject headings listed in an online catalog's entry for Dionne's *They Only* Look *Dead.*

> United States—Politics and government—1993–
>
> United States—Economic policy—1993
>
> United States—Social policy—1993
>
> Conservatism—United States
>
> Liberalism—United States
>
> Progressivism (US Politics)

You can use these subject headings to find books similar to Dionne's in order to build on what you already know. You could try the same strategy with books by Kirk, Luker, Friedman, Boaz, or Sowell, checking the subject headings assigned to their books and then using them to search in a card or online catalog.

Keep in mind that if you use just one subject heading, such as "United States—Politics and government—1945," you will probably find too much information and will have to sort through many titles to find what you need. If you are using an online catalog, however, you can combine subject headings and narrow your search. For examples, you might want to look for books on "Political participation—United States" and "Conservatism—United States." To combine subject headings, ask a librarian or use the instructions in the online catalog.

Articles or Short Essays.   Articles or short essays may be useful in giving you a more narrowly focused perspective on a particular civic stance. Indexes such as *InfoTrac* will help you find accessible magazine articles, and the *National Newspaper Index* will help you find newspaper articles. The *Social Sciences Index,* which is available in most college libraries, will also contain references to articles on your topic, though some items in this index may be intended for a slightly more academic audience. Since articles often have the same subject headings as books, you might begin your search for articles by using terms like *conservatism, liberalism,* and *libertarianism.*

You can also find short essays on the Internet. There are Web pages for political parties and for foundations, institutes, and publications that consistently take a conservative, libertarian, or liberal stance. Here are some possibilities:

> The Cato Institute — libertarian: <http://www.cato.org>
>
> The Heritage Foundation — conservative: <http://www.heritage.org>
>
> *Reason* magazine — libertarian: <http://www.reasonmag.com>
>
> *Mother Jones* — liberal/left: <http://www.motherjones.com>
>
> *The Nation* — liberal/left: <http://www.TheNation.com>
>
> *National Review* — conservative: <http://www.nationalreview.com>

Many informal opinion groups also have Web pages. Libertarians and conservatives have been particularly active on the Web. You can find such sites by using an index like *Yahoo!,* first choosing a category like "government," and then successive subcategories like "politics," and "political opinion." You should be able to locate at least twenty libertarian sites, eighty conservative sites, and sixty liberal sites, some of which will use the term *progressive.* Remember that some of these sites have been put on the Web by individuals who may not have thought very deeply about competing civic stances, so evaluate carefully what you find.

Opinions on Current Issues

You might want to examine how a conservative, a liberal, or a libertarian reacts to some current issues or events. The ingredients of a particular civic stance tend to shift in relation to current controversies, even though the basics of the stance may remain largely unchanged. For that reason, opinions on current controversies are best found in rapidly published sources like newspapers and magazines. Newspapers, for instance, usually have columnists with known conservative, liberal, or libertarian sympathies who regularly publish opinions on current issues. Indexes like *InfoTrac,* the *Academic Index,* and the *National Newspaper Index* can help you find essays on particular issues. To do so, use search terms that describe the issues themselves, not the terms for the civic stances. Here are some search terms for issues on which conservatives, liberals, and libertarians are likely to disagree:

Civil rights

Gun control

Prayer in the public schools

Birth control — Political aspects

Income tax — Political aspects

Sex education for youth

Assisted suicide

These same subject words can be used to search the Internet, as explained further in Appendix 2.

Another strategy is to identify magazines, journals, and newspapers that tend to reflect conservative, liberal, and libertarian viewpoints, then browse recent issues for editorial opinions on current topics. The magazines with Web pages listed above might be a good place to start.

FURTHER READINGS ON CIVIC STANCES

Conservatism

Buckley, William F., Jr., and Charles R. Kesler, eds. *Keeping the Tablets: Modern American Conservative Thought.* New York: Harper & Row, 1988.

Gottfried, Paul. *The Conservative Movement.* Rev. ed. New York: Twayne, 1993.

Himmelfarb, Gertrude. *The De-Moralization of Society: From Victorian Virtues to Modern Values.* New York: Knopf, 1995.

Kirk, Russell. *The Conservative Mind from Burke to Eliot.* 7th ed. Washington, D.C.: Regnery, 1995.

Nisbet, Robert. *Conservatism.* Minneapolis: U of Minnesota P, 1986.

Liberalism

Bramsted, E. K., and K. J. Melhuish. *Western Liberalism: A History in Documents from Locke to Croce.* London: Longman, 1978.

Damico, Alfonso J., ed. *Liberals on Liberalism.* Totowa: Rowman & Littlefield, 1986.

Gray, John. *Liberalisms: Essays in Political Philosophy.* London: Routledge, 1989.

Yack, Bernard. *Liberalism without Illusions: Essays on Liberal Theory and the Political Vision of Judith N. Shklar.* Chicago: U of Chicago P, 1996.

Young, James P. *Reconsidering American Liberalism: The Troubled Odyssey of the Liberal Idea.* Boulder: Westview, 1996.

Libertarianism

Boaz, David, ed. *The Libertarian Reader: Classic and Contemporary Readings from Lao-tzu to Milton Friedman.* New York: Free Press, 1997.

Crane, Edward H., and David Boaz, eds. *An American Vision: Policies for the '90s.* Washington, D.C.: Cato Institute, 1989.

Hayek, Friedrich A. von. *The Road to Serfdom.* Chicago: U of Chicago P, 1956.

McElroy, Wendy, ed. *Freedom, Feminism, and the State: An Overview of Individualistic Feminism.* 2nd ed. New York: Holmes & Meier, 1991.

Newman, Stephen L. *Liberalism at Wits' End: The Libertarian Revolt against the Modern State.* Ithaca: Cornell UP, 1984.

Nozick, Robert. *Anarchy, State, and Utopia.* New York: Basic Books, 1974.

Poole, Robert W., Jr., and Virginia I. Postrel. *Free Minds & Free Markets: Twenty-five Years of Reason.* San Francisco: Pacific Research Institute for Public Policy, 1993.

Taylor, Joan Kennedy. *Reclaiming the Mainstream: Individualist Feminism Rediscovered.* Buffalo: Prometheus, 1992.

ADDITIONAL WRITING PROJECTS

Here are some additional writing projects on the three civic stances that make use of the readings and ideas in this chapter.

Personal Experience Essay

Tell a story about your own experience with a local, state, or federal government office. Choose a helpful, puzzling, or harmful incident that gave you some insight into government. You might, for example, explain the incident and then tell how you gained some insight into how government can promote or harm the well-being of the individual or how government should intervene or not intervene in regulating individual behavior.

Purpose and Readers.   Assume that your readers are the same as those described earlier for the main assignment in this chapter: people who may have heard terms like *conservative, liberal,* and *libertarian* but have not read or thought much about their own civic stances or about the relation between an individual and government. Your purpose is not only to tell an interesting story about a personal experience but also to help them see its broader implications. They will also want to know your current perspectives and feelings about this incident—how you now explain the experience to yourself.

Resources to Draw On.   Your most important resource will be your memory. Start by making notes about what you remember. Try to recall as many concrete details as you can: when and where the incident occurred, who was involved, and what happened. Also note your feelings—at the time of the experience, soon after it occurred, and now.

Then look at the readings in this chapter, which contain many comments on the relationship between individuals and government (or the state, as it is often referred to). Some writers (like Rosenblatt and Dionne) suggest that the state protects and enhances the individual's well-being, while others (like Kirk and Brownback or Friedman and Boaz) suggest that state bureaucracies or regulations may hamper individual freedoms. You might also examine the essays by Luis J. Rodriguez, Nathan McCall, and Rita Williams in Chapter 5 to see models of stories about a remembered incident. Look as well at the brief stories Brownback uses in this chapter to support his argument for conservatism.

Tips for Writing a Successful Personal Experience Essay.   One way to begin is by first presenting the context for the incident (what led up to it) and then telling what happened. As you tell your story, try to use vivid descriptions and strong verbs to explain who was there, what was said, what you did, how people were acting, and what you felt at the time. Also try to re-create any conversations that were central to what happened. Unlike other essays, in which a brief anecdote might support a very small part of your argument, this essay consists primarily of your personal experience. Consequently, it should be richly detailed and offer a memorable illustration of the experience.

At the end, write a page or so in which you reflect on this experience from your present perspective. What insight has it given you about the relationship between an individual and government? How has it influenced your feelings or beliefs? How has it changed your behavior? This page should show your instructor the connections, as you see them, between the personal experience in your essay and what you have learned from the readings in this chapter.

Essay Taking a Position

Identify one current issue on which conservatives, liberals, and libertarians might disagree and then write an essay in which you take a position on the issue.

Purpose and Readers.   Although this chapter focuses on each civic stance as a package of principles to adopt or not adopt, people often use their civic principles to take a stand on just one issue. In arguments over contemporary issues, and in your essay, the civic stance (conservatism, liberalism, or libertarianism) is not at stake but rather the issue itself. Assume that your readers have encountered some issues such as seatbelt or helmet laws and have opinions about them. Keep in mind, though, that they probably have not thought very deeply about the principles at stake in such issues: whether and when government can or should interfere in personal behavior. Your purpose is to persuade your readers to view a particular issue in the way you do, drawing on your understanding of the kinds of arguments you have read in this chapter.

Resources to Draw On.   Examine the last week or so of your local newspaper, looking for an issue on which conservatives, liberals, and libertarians might be expected to disagree. You might look for local issues (in the city or town where you attend college) or state or national issues. You could also choose an issue referred to in this chapter: environmental regulations, bans on cigarette smoking, sex education, helmet or seatbelt laws, drug legalization, gun controls, or issues involving freedom of expression. Then, drawing on the ideas in this chapter—particularly on the discussions of when or whether the state has the right to interfere in individual behavior—take a position on the issue as a conservative, a liberal, or a libertarian. (You may want to check the Writer's Guide in Chapter 3 for tips on essays that take a position.)

Tips for Writing a Successful Position Essay.   Begin by presenting the issue to your readers, giving them sufficient background information and telling them what the sides of the argument are. Then state your position in a thesis and develop a list of reasons for your position. An effective strategy in this type of essay is to take one reason at a time and provide quotes, statistics, examples, and so forth to show how it supports your position. Also be aware of your readers' possible questions and objections and build refutations or concessions into your argument.

Report on a Civic Stance

The civic stances in this chapter are by no means the only possible stances in modern-day America. A substantial number of Americans hold views such as *populism, progressivism, anarchism, socialism,* or *communitarianism.* Choose one of these other civic stances, find out more about it, and write a report on what the proponents of this stance believe and why.

Purpose and Readers.   Assume that your readers are like you and your classmates: people who have recently gained an understanding of conservatism, liberalism, and libertarianism but know very little, if anything, about other civic stances. Your purpose is to report on one such stance, not to take a position on it or to persuade readers to adopt it. Report on the stance clearly and fairly so that your readers have more information to consider when they choose their own stance.

Resources to Draw On.   You might begin with an encyclopedia of philosophy or the World Wide Web in order to get an overview of another civic stance. Then you can look for more extended discussions in books, magazines, or newspapers. The readings in this chapter on conservatism, liberalism, and libertarianism discuss some of the basic questions involved in thinking about civic stances, and you can draw on that information to look at how proponents of another civic stance might answer the same questions.

Tips for Writing a Successful Report.   When you report on a civic stance, you must first understand it well. You might begin by describing the stance and defining important terms. Even though your purpose is to report on only one stance, you may need to refer to some of the stances discussed in this chapter to distinguish the characteristics of the one you are describing. You need to devise some method of discussing the features of the stance one by one, perhaps drawing on the methods used in this chapter's readings. Like Friedman, for instance, you could divide your discussion into social features and economic features. Like Kirk or Brownback, you could offer a numbered list of the features, or like Boaz, you could discuss key concepts one at a time.

Report on a Controversy

After the spring 1995 bombing of the federal building in Oklahoma City, many Americans were surprised to learn of the existence of militia groups and their estrangement from the federal government. Investigations of government agencies' roles in the Waco, Texas, and Ruby Ridge, Idaho, tragedies stepped up the debate about government's role in both protecting liberties and ensuring public safety. Write a report about militia groups—or some other antigovernment group—and their estrangement from the U.S. government.

Purpose and Readers.   Assume that your readers may not be up to date on current events and may think of Americans' relation to their government as a boring subject. Your purpose is not to persuade your readers to take a position on government or antigovernment groups but rather to report on how such groups view the U.S. government. You may want to convey to your readers that such estrangement from government needs to be considered thoughtfully, either to prevent future tragedies or to understand why such estrangement occurs.

Resources to Draw On.   The World Wide Web has offered a forum for groups that might not have been able to circulate their ideas widely through print media. So use the Web to locate material written by supporters of militia or other antigovernment groups as well as their critics. Identify the arguments that are being made about the government's dual responsibility for protecting individual liberties and ensuring public safety. The Writer's Guide in Chapter 2 may provide you with tips on reporting.

Tips for Writing a Successful Report.   When you report on a controversy, you must first understand what the main positions are and what seem to be the crucial differences of opinion—in this case, between antigovernment groups and their critics. So you need to categorize the issues that lie at the heart of the controversy. The readings in this chapter offer a variety of methods for doing that. You might begin by distinguishing between economic regulations and social regulations, as many of the readings do. Another option might be to begin with the fundamental terms in the Declaration of Independence or the Preamble to the Constitution and then examine how those terms (*liberty, rights, the general welfare*) are interpreted by antigovernment groups and their critics. In addition to your explanation of the controversy, your readers will need an explanation of its social significance. So after examining what antigovernment groups and their critics say about the issues, you might conclude your essay by commenting on whether you think these differences of opinion are likely to become more or less polarized.

What Causes Violence in Young Men?

5

SPECULATING ABOUT
A SOCIAL CRISIS

■ ■ ■

In Littleton, Colorado, high school students Eric Harris and Dylan Klebold, loaded with firearms and homemade pipe bombs, shot and killed twelve classmates and a teacher and wounded twenty-three others.

In Jonesboro, Arkansas, a thirteen-year-old boy and his eleven-year-old cousin opened fire on the children and teachers leaving their middle school. They killed four girls and one teacher and wounded ten others.

In Los Angeles, Ennis Cosby, son of entertainer Bill Cosby, was murdered by an eighteen-year-old male in an apparently random roadside killing.

In rural Franklin, New Jersey, two teenage boys dialed five pizza parlors from a pay phone until they found one that agreed to deliver pizza to a remote, abandoned house. When the deliverymen arrived, they were shot execution style.

In North Carolina, James Jordan—father of basketball star Michael Jordan—was murdered while he slept in his car. Convicted of murdering him were two teenage males who had a record of burglary, forgery, robbery, and assault.

The homicides described on the preceding page occurred recently in the United States.

Highly publicized cases like these have shocked the public and made violent crime by young people a national issue. Insistently, people are asking, "Why is this happening?" Many believe that violence committed by young men is a significant threat not only to the rest of American society but also to the youths themselves. At the same time, some argue that the real crisis lies elsewhere, that adults' neglect of young people and white-collar crime are more important problems. Competing statistics have fueled the debate because crime by young people rose for a number of years and then fell more recently. However, regardless of the arguments about whether such crime is rising or falling, or whether it is more or less dangerous than other kinds of crime, the fact remains that crime by young people is at frightening and unacceptable levels.

Males between the ages of twelve and twenty-four commit more than their share of the violent crimes in the United States, particularly the crimes that are discussed in this chapter: murder, nonnegligent manslaughter, and aggravated assault. These crimes are defined by the Federal Bureau of Investigation (FBI) and the Department of Justice as follows: *Murder* is the intentional killing of another person. *Manslaughter,* a lesser crime than murder, is the killing of another person without the intent involved in murder. There are two kinds of manslaughter. Someone who kills another person without intending to, in an automobile accident for instance, might be accused of *involuntary manslaughter.* More serious is *nonnegligent manslaughter,* which involves some intent but not the level of intent associated with the crime of murder. *Aggravated assault* is an attack on another person that may be intentional or premeditated.

Murder, aggravated assault, and nonnegligent manslaughter are not only at high levels but are also the crimes most associated with young men. By contrast, young women of the same age commit relatively few violent crimes, and even among men in their mid-twenties, the rate of violent crime decreases abruptly. The question, then, is this: What are the likely causes of violence by young men between the ages of ten or twelve and twenty-one?

Many causes have been suggested, including poverty, racism, the breakdown of families, neighborhood segregation, drugs and alcohol, ready access to firearms, and portrayals of violence by the media. These are the causes you will read about, discuss, and write about as you study this chapter.

At the end of each set of readings are some suggestions for keeping a writer's notebook. These are designed to help you understand the descriptions and speculations in the readings and compare what you have read to your own experience and the views of other students. The information you develop in completing these tasks will serve you well when it comes time to plan and write your own essay. So you might want to look ahead to these writer's notebook tasks before you begin reading.

A LOOK AHEAD: WRITING ABOUT VIOLENCE   This chapter includes an assignment to write an essay about what causes young men to commit violent crimes. Writing about causes is a type of argument called *speculating,* in which a writer offers his or her best reasons for thinking something is likely. Although most of your causes and support for them will probably come from the readings, you may want to include your own personal experiences and observations and those of other students as well.

The readings in this chapter are grouped into three sections. Those in the first section offer vivid accounts of recent crimes that have alarmed the public. In the second section, you will find statistical information that helps explain the types and incidence of violent crime. Readings in the final group speculate about the possible causes of violence by young men. Taken as a whole, these readings offer lively debates, some sharp disagreements, and a rich variety of reasons and support for the writers' speculations.

DESCRIPTIONS OF VIOLENT CRIME

The readings in this section include graphic first-person descriptions and newspaper reports of murder, manslaughter, and violent physical assault committed by young men. Although these readings contain some speculation about *why* young men commit crimes, they focus primarily on describing who commits violence, what sort of violence it is, and where it occurs.

When you read writers' speculations later in this chapter about what causes violence and when you write your essay about violence, you can review these cases and consider which ones might be best explained by the speculations you read. You also may be able to use the graphic details in these readings to make your own essay more interesting or persuasive.

As you read the following descriptions of violence, pay attention to how the journalists use vivid descriptions to entice—and even shock—their readers. Note, too, how the writers who reflect on the violence of their own youth provide similarly vivid details to give readers a sense of the circumstances from which the violence arose.

Two Boys, a Debt, a Gun, a Victim: The Face of Violence

Isabel Wilkerson

This account by Isabel Wilkerson is from a series in the New York Times *entitled "When Trouble Starts Young." In this 1994 report, Wilkerson describes a Detroit murder involving ten-year-old Jacob Gonzales and fourteen-year-old Damien Dorris. She weaves together events, statistical data, and comments from experts, yet never loses sight of her subjects, Jacob and Damien, whom she sees as part of "a generation of children born to teen-age mothers" who are "coming of age in neighborhoods already weakened by the addictive power of crack and the destructive force of the drug dealers."*

As you read, pay attention to the details Wilkerson provides about Jacob and Damien as well as the statistics about violence.

DETROIT—It was a wave of the hand from a 10-year-old boy with a Botticelli face° and Dennis the Menace bangs that brought Elizabeth Alvarez to her death on a humid afternoon last August.

The boy, Jacob Gonzales, wheeled around a bank parking lot on the banana seat of a pink bicycle he had stolen and looked for a robbery victim. His accomplice, Damien Dorris, a 14-year-old drug dealer who owed the neighborhood kingpins $430, lay in wait near the automated teller machine.

Mrs. Alvarez, pregnant and the mother of three, was hurrying to get cash for a birthday party. She passed by little Jacob and smiled. "Isn't it a good day?" Jacob said she asked. Jacob nodded in agreement and watched her walk toward the machine. He signaled to Damien when their prey made her withdrawal.

But Mrs. Alvarez refused to hand over her $80, so Damien shot her in the head with a .22-caliber pistol. Jacob looked at the woman, then he backed away. The boys thought the bullet might explode.

They ran off to divide the proceeds. 5 Jacob's take was $20. He bought a chili dog and some Batman toys. Both boys were arrested the next morning.

Damien pleaded guilty to second-degree murder. Jacob, whose detention garb had to be rolled up at the ankles and wrists and secured at the waist to keep from falling off, pleaded guilty to armed robbery. Both boys were sentenced to the maximum term, to remain in state custody until they are 21.

Sitting in an office at a children's home in Flint, Mich., recently, Jacob twirled a pen on a formica-top table, his feet dangling from a chair, not quite touching the floor, and tried to explain that violent day.

"Some stuff bad happened," he said, flipping the pen in the air and catching it before throwing it up again. "It was a game. It wasn't to kill the lady. It wasn't supposed to be like that. It was a game, right?"

The country is facing a crisis of violence among young people unlike any before, criminologists say. Even as overall violent crime has leveled off since 1990 and the number of teenagers has declined, arrests of people under 18 for violent crime rose 47 percent from 1988 to 1992, according to the Federal Bureau of Investigation.

The rise in violence among the 10 young crosses racial, class and geographic boundaries. From 1982 to 1992, F.B.I. statistics show, the rate of arrests for violent crimes rose twice as fast among young whites as among

---

°**Botticelli face:** Alessandro Botticelli (1445–1510) was a Renaissance painter. The faces of the people in his paintings are beautiful and innocent.

young blacks. Still, young blacks were arrested at five times the rate of young whites for violent crimes. Both groups accounted for an equal number of violent crimes. The white rate jumped to 126 arrests per 100,000 whites under the age of 18, from 82. The black rate increased to 677 arrests for every 100,000 blacks under 18, from 533. The high rate of violent crime among blacks is linked to their high rate of poverty, said Dr. Mark Rosenberg, director of the National Center for Injury Prevention and Control at the Centers for Disease Control and Prevention in Atlanta.

"Race is not a cause," Dr. Rosenberg said. "This is an American problem." In studies that take poverty into account, he said, "the differences in the black rate of violent crime and the white rate almost go away."

One in six arrests for murder, rape, robbery or assault is of a suspect under 18, the F.B.I. statistics show, and slayings by these teen-agers have risen 124 percent from 1986 to 1991. In 1992, the F.B.I. said, young people killed 3,400 people nationwide.

The homicide numbers might well have been higher without the medical advances of the past 20 years, particularly improved training and technology that allow doctors and ambulance workers to quickly stop bleeding. "We've been able to salvage people who otherwise would have been killed," said Dr. Robert McAfee, president-elect of the American Medical Association, who plans to focus his tenure on efforts against violence.

A change in weaponry from the knives of the past to the guns of today has been a major factor in the rise in killings by juveniles, criminologists say. But there is also evidence that young people are more violent today than a decade ago, even without weapons. Bureau statistics show that young people committed twice as many assaults without a weapon in 1992 as in 1982, 143,368 to 73,987.

In Indianapolis, for example, two 7- 15 year-old boys pulled a 6-year-old girl into the boys' restroom at school, tore off her clothes and raped her. One pleaded guilty to rape and the other was convicted. Both were put on probation, and their parents were ordered to remove their X-rated videos from the home.

"The Most Dangerous Out There"

Violence among the young is growing at a time when a generation of children born to teen-age mothers is coming of age in neighborhoods already weakened by the addictive power of crack and the destructive force of drug dealers. In many ways, this is the story of Jacob and Damien, each born to a woman on welfare who first gave birth at the age of 14.

Damien was abandoned by his father, and ran away from his mother because, he told court officials, she beat him. Jacob lived in a crack house. His father beat his mother and died violently himself.

Violent Crimes in Suburbs

While violent crime occurs at a disproportionately higher rate in cities than in suburbs and among blacks than among whites, youthful rampages that once seemed confined to inner cities are now striking suburbs and farm towns as well.

Last summer, in the affluent Atlanta suburb of Dunwoody, Ga., three white teen-agers went to the home of a disabled man they knew, tied him in his wheelchair and tortured him for more than 12 hours before stabbing and clubbing him to death. In rural Indiana, three white teen-age girls lured a 12-year-old girl into a car, then beat and stabbed her before burning her alive....

"Unthinkable 20 Years Ago"

In city after city, town after town, there 20 are nightmarish cases that make judges and prosecutors nostalgic for the truants and vandals that once filled their dockets.°

"It is incredible—the ability of the very young to commit the most horrendous crimes imaginable and not have a second thought about it," said Gil Garcetti, the Los Angeles County District Attorney. "This was unthinkable 20 years ago."

THE GROWING YEARS

A Neighborhood of Troubled Heroes

Just about all that Jacob Gonzales has known in his short life is violence. His home on the southwest side of Detroit was a crack house. His father used to beat his mother. Jacob saw his sister shot in the face when he was 4 or 5. His father was shot to death in a bar fight about the

same time. He can rattle off the names and calibers of guns as if they were baseball players and batting averages.

He has seen family friends pull guns on one another and knows the subtleties of detecting a pistol. "You can tell when somebody's carrying a gun," Jacob said. "They hold their side and limp a little."

He was 9 when he took his first drag of marijuana. An older sister gave it to him. His mother, Bonnie, who was raped in the seventh grade, is a welfare recipient with eight children; Jacob is her youngest. Court records show that Mrs. Gonzales drank heavily, used crack and once even sold her children's clothes for drug money.

She failed to show up at Jacob's first 25 court hearings on the armed-robbery charge. She was drunk when she finally came to testify, said Michael Batchelor, the boy's lawyer, who added, "You could smell it." Her testimony was of little help, Mr. Batchelor said. She did not even know her son's birthday.

Drug Dealers as Role Models

"Jake is a product of his environment," Mr. Batchelor said. "He comes from a dysfunctional family. The older neighborhood boys were his heroes. They sold drugs. They had guns. They were his role models. He wanted to be like them."

His heroes were troubled and neglected themselves. Damien Dorris, the 14-year-old who killed Mrs. Alvarez, was abandoned by his father, beaten by his mother and was essentially rearing

---

°**dockets:** Lists of legal cases to be tried in the courts.

himself. He had dropped out of school after the seventh grade and lived with an older teen-age brother. The brother was a drug dealer, the police said, and Damien picked up the trade.

He became a ward of the court° for a time after his mother was accused of beating one of his brothers. His father, Saul Gainey, left the family "in order to deal with personal concerns of his own," according to court records.

Threatening to End His Life

One March day two years ago, Damien reached a breaking point when he was told to leave school after refusing to take off his hat. He climbed atop a railing on a freeway overpass and was threatening to jump when the police pulled him off.

By last summer, he told the police, 30 he had grown bored with drug dealing and was trying to get out. But he had to find a way to pay his $430 debt to his drug suppliers. He told court officials he had been given 24 hours to come up with the money or be killed.

He got his buddy Jacob and two other boys to help him. One left before the shooting, and the police said the other one did not take part. But Jacob carried out his role because, he said, he was hungry, he wanted some money and it was something exciting to do.

Damien told court officials he "didn't plan to shoot the lady," that he "just wanted to rob her." But in case something went wrong, Damien said, he had taken along a gun from his brother's house.

Jacob recalls with childish fascination the preparation for the attack. "He sharpened the bullet so it would go in real good," Jacob said. "It was real pointy."

ALWAYS RUNNING

Luis J. Rodriguez

Luis Rodriguez, a poet and a journalist, is best known for his award-winning autobiography, Always Running: La Vida Loca: Gang Days in L.A. *(1993). He has also published* America Is Her Name *(1998), a bilingual children's book, and, with Joseph Rodriguez and Ruben Martinez,* East Side Stories: Gang Life in East LA *(1998).*

Rodriguez grew up in Los Angeles after his family emigrated there from Mexico. As a young teenager in the late 1960s, he belonged to a gang, but by the time he

---

°**ward of the court**: A young person under the supervision of a court (rather than, in this case, his own parents).

was eighteen he had left the gang and won a prize in an essay contest. He now lives in Chicago and runs Tia Chucha Press.

In this excerpt from Always Running, *Rodriguez writes about his experience as a member of the Animal Tribe gang in Las Lomas, a Chicano neighborhood in East Los Angeles. Unlike the newspaper account by Isabel Wilkerson, this reading offers an anecdote from personal experience.*

As you read, note how the vivid, concrete details paint a picture of a particular kind of violence.

Lomas was reorganizing and recruiting. No longer could one claim Lomas just by being there. Chicharrón invited me to get in.

"They beat on you for about three minutes—that's all," Chicharrón urged. "You get a busted lip. So what? It's worth it."

So later I decided to go to a party in the Hills, fully aware I would join a Lomas set. Like most barrio° parties, it started without any hassle. *Vatos*° and *rucas*° filled every corner in the small house; some ventured outside, smoking or drinking. The house belonged to Nina, this extremely pretty girl whom everyone respected. Nina's mother shuffled in the kitchen, making tacos from large pots of meat and beans simmering on low flames.

The dudes were polite; dignified. *Señora* this and *Señora* that. You couldn't imagine how much danger hung on their every breath.

As the night wore on, the feel of the place transformed. The air was rife with   5 anticipation. Talk became increasingly louder. Faces peeled into hardness. The music played oldies we all knew by heart, and *gritos*° punctuated key verses. Fists smashed against the walls. Just as the food simmered to a boil, the room also bubbled and churned. Weed, pills and hard liquor passed from hand to hand. Outside, behind the house, a row of dudes shot up heroin. In the glow of the back porch light, they whispered a sea of shorn sentences.

A crew of older, mean-eyed *vatos* arrived and the younger guys stacked behind them. Nina's mother showed concern. She pulled Nina into the kitchen; I could see her talking severely to her daughter.

I didn't know these dudes. They were *veteranos*° and looked up to by the homeys.° They had just come out of the joint—mostly Tracy, Chino or Youth Training School, known as YTS, a prison for youth offenders. Chicharrón pressed his face close to my ear and told me their names: Ragman, Peaches, Natividad, Topo...and the small, muscular one with a mustache down the sides of his mouth was called Puppet.

°**barrio:** A neighborhood in which most people speak Spanish.   °*Vatos:* "Dudes," guys.   °*rucas:* Barrio women (literally "old ladies"), used here as slang for "girlfriends."   °*gritos:* Long, deep, soulful, Mexican yells.   °*veteranos:* Veterans of barrio street warfare.   °**homeys:** People from one's own neighborhood.

I then recalled some of their reputations: Natividad, for example, had been shot five times and stabbed 40 times—and still lived! Peaches once used a machine gun against some dudes in a shoot-out. And Puppet had been convicted of murder at the age of 16.

"Who wants in?" Puppet later announced to a row of dark, teenaged male faces in front of him. Chicharrón whispered something in Puppet's ear. Puppet casually looked toward me. They designated me the first to get jumped.°

Topo walked up to me. He was stout, dark and heavily tattooed. He placed **10** his arm around me and then we marched toward the driveway. Chicharrón managed to yell: "Protect your head."

I assumed when I got to the driveway, a handful of dudes would encircle me, provide me a signal of sorts, and begin the initiation. Instead, without warning, Topo swung a callused fist at my face. I went down fast. Then an onslaught of steel-tipped shoes and heels rained on my body. I thought I would be able to swing and at least hit one or two—but no way! Then I remembered Chicharrón's admonition. I pulled my arms over my head, covered it the best I could while the kicks seemed to stuff me beneath a parked car.

Finally the barrage stopped. But I didn't know exactly when. I felt hands pull me up. I looked back at everyone standing around the driveway. My right eye was almost closed. My lip felt like it stuck out a mile. My sides ached. But I had done well.

Hands came at me to congratulate. There were pats on the back. Chicharrón embraced me, causing me to wince. I was a Lomas *loco*° now. Then a homegirl came up and gave me a big kiss on my inflamed lip; I wished I could have tasted it. Then other homegirls did the same. It didn't seem half-bad, this initiation. Later they invited me to pounce on the other dudes who were also jumped in, but I passed.

As the night wore on, Puppet, Ragman, and Nat had the initiates pile into a pickup truck. I was already quite plastered but somehow still standing. Puppet drove the truck toward Sangra.° Elation rasped in our throats.

"Fuck Sangra," one of the new dudes chimed in, and other voices followed **15** the sentiment.

We came across a cherried-out° 1952 DeSoto, with pinstripes and a metal-flake exterior. Puppet pulled the truck up to the side of it. There were four dudes inside drinking and listening to cassette tapes. We didn't know if they were Sangra or what. We followed Ragman as he approached the dudes. One of them emerged from the passenger side. He looked like a nice-enough fellow.

"Hey, we don't want no trouble," he said.

°**jumped** (or **jumped in**): Initiated into a gang.   °*loco*: A "crazy" barrio youth.   °**Sangra**: The barrio surrounding the San Gabriel Mission church.   °**cherried-out**: Shiny and well cared for, better than new.

I knew they weren't Sangra. They looked like hard-working recreational lowriders° out for a spin. But Ragman wouldn't have it. He punched the dude down. A couple of other guys came out of the car, and they too tried to salvage the night, tried to appeal for calm.

"Listen, man, how about a beer," one of them offered.

Nat grabbed his neck from behind and pulled him to the ground, then beat 20 on him. Ragman looked at the other guys who were clearly scared.

"Who don' like it?" he demanded. "Who don' like it . . . you?"

Ragman hit another guy. By then the dudes in the truck had climbed out and bashed in the car, breaking windows and crunching in metal with tire irons and two-by-fours which had been piled in the back of the truck. One dude tried to run off, but somebody chased him down with a wine bottle and struck him on the head. The dude fell down and I saw the wine bottle keep coming down on him, as if it was supposed to break, but it wouldn't.

The driver of the DeSoto tried to pull out, but somebody threw a brick at his head. For a long time, I observed the beatings as if I were outside of everything, as if a moth of tainted wings floating over the steamed sidewalk. Then I felt a hand pull at my arm and I sluggishly turned toward it. Puppet looked squarely into my one opened eye. He had a rusty screwdriver in his other hand.

"Do it, man," he said. Simply that.

I clasped the screwdriver and walked up to the beaten driver in the seat 25 whose head was bleeding. The dude looked at me through glazed eyes, horrified at my presence, at what I held in my hand, at this twisted, swollen face that came at him through the dark. *Do it!* were the last words I recalled before I plunged the screwdriver into flesh and bone, and the sky screamed.

FALLING

Nathan McCall

Nathan McCall, a reporter at the Washington Post, *is the author of* Makes Me Wanna Holler: A Young Black Man in America, *the 1994 autobiography from which this reading comes. McCall recounts his childhood in Portsmouth, Virginia, his three years in prison for armed robbery, his subsequent education, and his career as a journalist. Like Luis J. Rodriguez in the reading that precedes this one, McCall is writing in the 1990s about his youth in the 1960s and 1970s.*

°**lowriders:** Passengers in cars that have been redesigned to hang relatively close to the pavement.

As you read, think about the circumstances involved in this crime—what life was like for the young McCall, who was involved, where and how it happened. As the selection begins, he is writing about his girlfriend, Liz.

In the summer of 1974, Liz came to me and said she'd had a run-in with Plaz. She and a girlfriend were riding bikes past the 7 Eleven when Plaz, hanging around with some other guys, called her a name. "He called me a white girl, so I gave him the middle finger," she said.

That was bad news. Plaz and I had a history that went back several years, when he and those other cats barged in on Denise Wilson and me and raped her. I never got any get-back, but I never forgot it, either. I hated Plaz for that. If I thought I had half a chance of kicking his ass, I probably would have moved on him long before the run-in with Liz.

But I was in no hurry to lock horns with Plaz. . . .

I was nineteen, and he was twenty-two and a much harder cat than me. But he'd cracked hard on my lady. He'd disrespected *me*. Something had to give.

One night, shortly after Liz's run-in with Plaz, she and I took Monroe to a   5 carnival near Cavalier Manor. We were walking along, pushing him in a stroller, when Plaz and three of his boys walked up and confronted us. His eyes blazing, Plaz got within an inch of Liz's face, shook his finger at her, and said, "The next time you flash your middle finger at me, I'm gonna break it off. You hear me?!" Then he scowled at me, looked me up and down as if daring me to say something, and turned and walked away.

I just stood there thinking, *This niggah is gonna make me do something I didn't come here to do.* Not only had he disrespected me again, but he'd done it in *front* of my lady. I *had* to do something. That's when I decided to shoot him.

I told Liz, "Take the baby, put him in the car, and you two go on home."

She got scared. "Where are you going?"

"I'm gonna fuck that niggah up."

She pleaded, "Come on, Nate. We don't have to pay attention to him."   10

I didn't look at her. "Go on home!"

Liz turned and hurriedly pushed the stroller away.

As I walked in the direction Plaz and his boys had headed, I steeled my nerves. Whenever I wanted to do something really crazy like that, something I didn't have the natural heart to do, I had to run a head-game on myself. I had to shut down my mind. I had to block off all thoughts flowing through my brain to prevent me from talking myself out of it. That's the only way I'd be able to go through with it. That's what I did that night. I decided to shoot Plaz and I didn't want to change my mind. I couldn't allow that.

I had a shoulder pouch that I carried with me. In it were some drugs and a .22 pistol. I spotted Plaz and his boys milling around, talking with some other dudes they'd run into. I walked over to the crowd and said to him, "Yo, man. I wanna talk to you."

Flanked by his boys, Plaz really got loud then. He pointed a finger at me and said, "Niggah, you better get outta my face 'fore I stomp your ass! I'm tired a' you and that bitch..." 15

While he talked, I kept my hand inside the pouch, gripping the trigger. Sensing that a rumble was about to jump off, people started crowding around. I saw my buddy Greg in the crowd, looking nervously at Plaz's boys, counting heads. I knew he would go down with me if it came to that.

Moving close enough for me to smell his breath, Plaz poked a finger in my chest and kept on selling wolf tickets. "I'll kick your ass...!"

In one swift motion, I drew the gun, aimed it point-blank at his chest, and fired. *Bam!*

A tiny red speck appeared on the dingy white T-shirt he wore. He fell backward. His arms flew skyward and he dropped to the ground, landing on his back. As soon as they heard the blast, his boys scattered. Everybody around us ran for cover. I walked toward Plaz, looked into his eyes, and saw something I had never seen in him before. Gone was the fierceness that made him so intimidating all those years. In its place was shock. And fear. It was more like terror.

In that moment, I felt like God. I felt so good and powerful that I wanted to 20 do it again. I felt like I could pull that trigger, and keep on pulling it until I emptied the gun. Years later, I read an article in a psychology magazine that likened the feeling of shooting a gun to ejaculation. That's what it was like for me. Shooting off.

I stepped closer and raised the gun to shoot Plaz again, when Greg came up from behind me and called my name. "No, Nate! You don't wanna do that, man!" He carefully pulled the gun from my hand.

The distraction gave Plaz enough time to collect himself. Holding a hand to his bleeding chest, he jumped up from the ground, dashed toward the parking lot, and collapsed between two cars.

The carnival grounds, meanwhile, had turned chaotic. People ran screaming everywhere. It was like one of those movies where a monster is trampling through a city and everybody is running, hollering, fleeing for their lives. It made me feel powerful and light-headed, seeing hundreds of people scattering because of something I'd done....

Only I was confused about what to do next. I didn't know whether to beat my chest and yell at the top of my voice, or shout some pithy, John Wayne-esque remark to be quoted when the shooting was recounted on the streets. I yelled, to no one in particular, "I hope the motherfucka dies!"

A security guard had been standing nearby when I first approached Plaz. I 25 half expected him to walk over and arrest me. I waited for a moment for him to come and slap on the handcuffs. But the guard, apparently rattled by all the commotion, also scrambled for cover.

Greg asked me, "You got a ride?"

I said, "Naw."

He said, "C'mon."

We hopped into his car and drove off. When we got out on the main street, he said, "Where you wanna go?"

I realized that I hadn't thought about that. *Where do you go after you've shot* 30 *somebody?* . . .

There was nowhere else to go but home. I said, "Take me to the crib,° man."

Greg dropped me off and I went into the house. Walking down the hallway to my parents' bedroom, I met my stepfather coming toward me. I said, "I need to talk to you. . . . I just shot somebody."

He was calm. "Is he dead?"

"I don't know."

He thought for a moment, then said, "Let me get dressed. We gotta go to the 35 police station."

During the twenty-minute ride to the station, neither of us spoke a word. The seriousness of what I'd done was dawning on me. Who knows what my stepfather was thinking? After all the run-ins we'd had, he'd known I was headed for something like this. Yet he didn't try to preach to me or say "I told you so." I actually felt glad to have him on my side.

We went downtown, and I turned myself in. It felt strange giving myself up voluntarily to the same people I dodged every day. After interviewing me about the shooting, a detective escorted my stepfather and me into a hallway and told us to wait on a bench. Sitting there in the quiet, I felt so alone. There was no roaring crowd or group of running buddies to pat me on the back and sing my praises. It was just me, sitting there, suddenly powerless again, waiting to face the consequences.

After an hour or so, the detective returned to the hallway, looked at my stepfather, and said, "I'm sorry to keep you waiting out here so long, but Melvin Thompson, the guy your son shot, was rushed to the hospital. They're operating on him. They don't think he's going to make it. If he dies, we're going to have to charge your son with murder."

The word hit me like a sledgehammer. *Murder?!* On TV westerns, when people got shot they just tied a handkerchief around their arm and went on about their business. . . .

Plaz wasn't supposed to die. I thought, *Murder! If he dies, then that will mean* 40 *I have killed someone. Murder?!* I repeated the word silently to myself, over and over, trying to grasp its full meaning.

°the crib: Home.

Then I got a sharp vision of who I really was. I realized I didn't want to be a cold-blooded, baad-assed nigger anymore. I wanted to erase the past few hours, to wipe the slate clean. In desperation, I bowed my head, closed my eyes—tight—and prayed to God to spare Plaz's life. *"Please, God, don't let him die! Please."* I prayed so hard that a listener would have thought Plaz was my dearly beloved brother. My stepfather remained quiet. I don't know if he noticed me praying. At that moment, it didn't matter. I was too busy trying to establish a personal relationship with my Lord and Savior.

After several hours, the detective returned to the hallway. "I've got good news. Thompson pulled through. The doctors said the bullet barely missed his heart. Another fraction of an inch closer and he would've been pushing up daisies." I thanked sweet Jesus.

Oddly, I was released on my own recognizance. I guess it's an indication of how they felt about the value of black life that I wasn't even required to post bond. When I woke up that afternoon, I checked the newspaper and read a brief story about the shooting.

The gravity of what I'd done sank in again, but this time, I looked at it in an entirely different light. Now that I was certain Plaz would live, I felt hard again and I thought about the glory. I had toppled an old-head.°

I got dressed, ate, and went outdoors to catch up with some of the fellas. 45 While walking down Roosevelt Boulevard, I saw a car, filled with a bunch of old hoods, approach slowly. As it cruised closer, heads turned sharply and looked at me. It was some of Plaz's boys. The driver pulled over to the curb, and everybody in the car glared. They started talking to each other—debating, I assumed, whether to jump out and do me in.

Feigning confidence, I reached slowly into my pocket, as though gripping a gun, then stood there and met their gaze. My heart pounded hard. I knew that if they got out of that car, they'd stomp me six feet under. But no one budged. They talked some more, then the driver pulled slowly away from the curb and drove off.

For me, that brief, silent exchange was undeniable proof that I had arrived. I was a bona fide crazy nigger. Everywhere I went after that, guys on the street said, reverently, "Yeah, man, I heard you bust a cap in Plaz's ass." My street rep shot up three full notches. Anybody out there who knew me would think twice about moving against me without a piece. Anybody.

°**old-head:** Older gang member.

FROM ADOLESCENT ANGST TO SHOOTING UP SCHOOLS

Timothy Egan

Timothy Egan, a correspondent for the New York Times, *is the author of several books about the Pacific Northwest:* The Good Rain: Across Time and Terrain in the Pacific Northwest *(1991),* Breaking Blue *(1992), and* Lasso the Wind: Away to the New West *(1998).*

Writing before the Littleton, Colorado, shootings of 1999, in this June 1998 report for the New York Times *Egan describes six earlier school shootings and discusses the patterns he sees in these cases.*

As you read, note particularly what Egan says about the psychological traits of the young men, the kinds of popular culture they most admired, and the shift of adolescent violence from urban to rural locations.

MOSES LAKE, WASH., JUNE 9—Well before the school shootings in Oregon and the South prompted a search to the depths of the national soul, a 14-year-old honors student named Barry Loukaitis walked into his algebra class in this hard little farm town and shot his teacher in the back and two students in the chest.

Guns and violent videos were always around the boy's house. He learned how to fire weapons from his father. And he picked up a pose from the Oliver Stone movie "Natural Born Killers," telling a friend it would be "pretty cool" to go on a killing spree just like the two lead characters in the film.

Dressed in black and armed with three of the family firearms, Barry entered Frontier Middle School in this desert town 180 miles east of Seattle on Feb. 2, 1996, and turned his guns loose on fellow ninth graders.

"This sure beats algebra, doesn't it," Barry said, according to court records, as he stood over a dying boy who was choking on his own blood. He was tackled by a teacher and hauled off to jail, where he promptly took a nap.

A sign soon appeared on a nearby school, bearing a single word: Why? Of late, that question has been asked around the nation, following a spate of multiple-victim school shootings over the last nine months that have left 15 people dead and 42 wounded. People wonder whether something aberrant and terrifying—like a lethal virus, some have called it—is in the bloodstream.

While precise answers may be elusive, the recent killing sprees share a remarkable number of common traits. The first of the rural, multiple-victim student shootings, here in Moses Lake, looks in many respects like a road map of what was to come. From this case and interviews with police officers, prosecutors, psychologists and parents of the attackers—as well as the boys' own words—several patterns emerge:

- Each case involved a child who felt inferior or picked on, with a grudge against some student or teacher. The attackers complained of being fat or nearsighted, short or un-loved—the ordinary problems of adolescence, at first glance. But in fact, most of the assailants were sui-cidal, and of above-average intelli-gence, according to mental health experts who have examined most of the children arrested for the shoot-ings. Their killings are now viewed by some criminologists and other experts as a way to end a tortured life with a blaze of terror.
- The killers were able to easily ac-quire high-powered guns, and in many cases, their parents helped the children get them, either directly or through negligence. Guns with rapid-fire capability, usually semi-automatic rifles that can spray a burst of bullets in a matter of sec-onds, were used in the incidents with the most victims. Single-fire, bolt-action guns or revolvers would not have caused near the damage in human life, the police say.
- To varying degrees, each of the attackers seemed to have been obsessed by violent pop culture. A 14-year-old in West Paducah, Ky., was influenced by a movie in which a character's classmates are shot during a dream sequence, according to detectives. Violent rap lyrics may have influenced one of the boys in the Jonesboro, Ark., case, his mother says. In particular, a song about a stealth killing eerily matches what occurred. The killer who has con-fessed in Pearl, Miss., says he was a fan of violent fantasy video games and the nihilistic rock-and-roll lyrics of Marilyn Manson, as was the boy charged in the Springfield, Ore., shootings last month. The Springfield youth was so enmeshed in violent television and Internet sites that his parents recently unplugged the cable television and took away his computer, a close family friend said.
- The student killers gave ample 10 warning signs, often in detailed writings at school, of dramatic, vio-lent outbursts to come. The boy in Moses Lake wrote a poem about murder, saying, "I'm at my point of no return." Similar jottings were left by the boys in the South and in Springfield. In virtually all of the cases, adults never took the threats and warning signs seriously. Or they simply overlooked them.

"When you look at the overall pat-tern, it's a pretty serious wake-up call," said Dr. Ronald D. Stephens, executive director of the National School Safety Center, which monitors school vio-lence from its headquarters in West-lake Village, Calif. "We are seeing an increasing number of violent, callous, remorseless juveniles.

"What's behind it," Dr. Stephens said, "seems to be a combination of issues that range from the availability of weapons to the culture our kids immerse themselves in to the fact that many youngsters simply have no sense of the finality of death."

People argue, in the age-old debate, that the killers are simply bad human beings or that their actions can be linked to a corrosive family environment—nature versus nurture. Certainly, the recent shootings give plenty of new material for both sides.

Parents of the young killers place blame on the surfeit of guns, the influence of junk culture and children stressed to a snapping point. But they also look at themselves, their broken marriages, their lives of stress and hurry, and wonder how all that affected their children.

"I didn't think about Barry at all," 15 said JoAnn Phillips, the mother of Barry Loukaitis in Moses Lake, in court testimony last year in her son's case.

A few weeks before the shooting, she had told her son that she planned to divorce her husband and that she herself was suicidal, but she was oblivious to how this would affect her son.

"We are responsible for our kids, but you tell me, where did I go wrong?" Gretchen Woodward said in an interview recently in which she discussed her son, Mitchell Johnson, the seventh grader accused, along with Andrew Golden, of killing 5 and wounding 10 in Jonesboro last March.

"I think there's a lot more pressure on our kids today than there was when we were growing up."

THE KILLINGS

Urban Trend Takes Rural Turn

Children have long killed children in the United States. The peak was the 1992–93 school year, when nearly 50 people were killed in school-related violence, according to the School Safety Center.

Most of those killings were in urban 20 schools, and prompted a Federal law banning guns from schools, security measures like metal detectors, and efforts to control the influence of gangs. What is different now is that the shootings are largely rural, have multiple victims and, within the warped logic of homicide, seem to make no sense; many of the victims have been shot at random.

In looking at the 221 deaths at American schoolyards over the last six years, what leaps out is how the shootings changed dramatically in the last two years—not the number, but the type.

Most earlier deaths were gang related, or they were stabbings, or they involved money or a fight over a girlfriend. (Boys are almost always the killers.) Then came the Moses Lake shooting in 1996. Barry Loukaitis, who confessed to the shootings and was found guilty as an adult in trial last fall, did have a target in mind when he walked into the afternoon algebra class—a popular boy who had teased him. He shot the boy dead.

But then he fired away at two other students, people against whom he said he had no grudge. He shot the teacher, Leona Caires, in the back. She died with an eraser still in her hand.

When asked in a tape-recorded session with police why he shot the others, Barry said, "I don't know, I guess reflex took over."

After Moses Lake, shootings of a 25 somewhat similar nature followed. In February 1997 in Bethel, Alaska, a boy armed with a 12-gauge shotgun that had been kept unlocked around the home killed a popular athlete, fired shots at random and then tracked and killed the principal. Like Barry, the 16-year-old Alaskan killer thought it would be "cool," prosecutors said, to shoot up the school.

"He loved what he did," said Renee Erb, who prosecuted the youth, Evan Ramsey. "This was his moment of glory."

By the end of last year, the killings seemed to come with numbing sameness. All but one of the victims apparently were chosen at random in the shootings outside a high school in Pearl, Miss.

"I wasn't aiming at anyone else," said Luke Woodham, convicted this week in the shootings, in a tape-recorded confession played at his trial in Hattiesburg, Miss. "It was like I was there, and I wasn't there."

In West Paducah, Ky., three girls were killed and five other students wounded in a shooting with no apparent motive. "It was kind of like I was in a dream," the accused attacker, 14-year-old Michael Carneal, told his principal.

In March, an 11-year-old steeped in 30 gun culture and a 13-year-old with a troubled past opened fire, in what seemed like a military assault, at students who filed out of Westside Middle School in Jonesboro, Ark.

And finally in Springfield last month—where a boy with a love of guns is accused of mowing down as many students as possible in the crowded school cafeteria, using a semi-automatic rifle taken from his father—the victims were anyone who happened to be in the way, the police said.

People ask why this is now happening in white, rural areas, said Dr. Alan Unis, a University of Washington psychiatrist who did an examination of the Moses Lake assailant for the court. "It's happening everywhere," he said. "One of the things we're seeing in the population at large is that all the mood disorders are happening earlier and earlier. The incidence of depression and suicide has gone way up among young people."

Suicide rates for the young have increased over the last four decades and have leveled off near their all-time highs. More than 1.5 million Americans under age 15 are seriously depressed, the National Institute of Mental Health says. The number may be twice that high, in the view of the American Academy of Child and Adolescent Psychiatry.

Most of the attackers in the recent cases had shown signs of clinical depression or other psychological problems. But schools, strapped for mental health counselors, are less likely to pick up on such behavior or to have the available help, principals at the schools where the shootings happened said.

THE GUNS

Troubled Children and Easy Access

A depressed, insecure child is one 35 thing, and quite common. But that same boy with a gun can be a lethal threat. In all of the recent shootings, acquiring guns was easier than buying beer, or even gas. And these children armed themselves with small arsenals, as if preparing for battle.

The Moses Lake assailant used to play at home with his family guns as if they were toys, friends testified in court. In his confession, Barry Loukaitis said he took two of his father's guns from an unlocked cabinet, and a third one—a .25-caliber semiautomatic pistol—from a family car.

The gun used in the Alaska school shootings was kept unlocked at the foot of the stairs in a foster home where Evan Ramsey was living, according to police.

The shootings in West Paducah, Jonesboro and Springfield were similar in that semiautomatic weapons—capable of firing off dozens of rounds in under a minute—were used to kill children. Weapons of less rapid-fire capability would likely have reduced the death tolls, the police said.

In Jonesboro and Springfield, the parents of the accused assailants followed the general advice of the National Rifle Association and taught their children, at an early age, how to use guns properly. The story of how Andrew Golden, accused in the Jonesboro shooting, was given a gun by Santa Claus at age 6, and was an expert marksman in the Practical Pistol Shooters Club a few years later, has been widely reported.

But less well known is how the other accused Jonesboro killer came by his knowledge of guns. Mitchell Johnson's mother, Mrs. Woodward, said in an interview that she taught her boy how to shoot a shotgun, and then he took a three-week course.

When the boys were arrested after hitting 15 human targets at Westside Middle School, police found nine guns in their possession. Most of them had been taken from the home of Andrew's grandfather, Doug Golden, a conservation officer who says he usually kept his guns unlocked in the house.

The parents of Kipland Kinkel, the boy accused of the Springfield shootings, were not gun enthusiasts, but their son was, according to interviews with family friends. The parents agonized over the boy's gun obsession, finally giving in and buying him a weapon. The father and son took courses in marksmanship and safety, and the guns were kept under lock and key.

But given Kip Kinkel's moods and temper, the parents had debated over whether to get him a single-loading bolt-action weapon or something with more rapid-fire capability. They settled on the more powerful gun, a .22-caliber semiautomatic Ruger rifle. It was a fatal mistake, according to some people who are studying the recent shootings. It was that rifle that Kip used to fire off 50 rounds at Thurston High School.

"The kid had them by the throat," said Dr. Bill Reisman, who does profiling of deviant youth behavior for law-enforcement officials and recently gave a closed-door briefing to community leaders from cities where the school shootings occurred. "They were terrified of his interest in guns, but they went out and bought him guns."

A Kinkel family friend, Tom Jacobson, who played tennis every other week with the boy's father, said the parents were looking for [a] way to control and connect with their voluble child. The parents, Bill and Faith Kinkel, were both killed by their son, prosecutors in Oregon said.

"These were devoted parents in a tight-knit family," Mr. Jacobson said in an interview. "Bill had tried everything with Kip. I think he just ran out of ideas."

THE CULTURE

Too Influenced by Music and Film?

Just as easy to get as guns were videos or cassettes in which murder is a central theme, and often glorified. Jurors in the trial of Barry Loukaitis were shown a Pearl Jam video, "Jeremy," about a youth who fantasizes about using violence against classmates who taunt him. That video, along with "Natural Born Killers," a movie about a pair who kill their parents and then go on [a] nationwide shooting spree, were among Barry's favorites, his friends testified.

"He said it would be fun and a good adventure to go on a killing spree" like the Oliver Stone movie, a neighborhood boy, Zachary Ufkes, said in court.

At least one of the boys accused in the Jonesboro attack, Mitchell Johnson, was a big fan of gangsta rap. Friends and family say a favorite song was one by Bone Thugs-n-Harmony, called, "Crept and We Came," about killings in a massacre-like way.

The boy also played Mortal Kombat, 50 a popular video game that involves graphic killing of opponents, his mother said.

"There are many cultural forces predisposing kids to violent behavior," said the Rev. Chris Perry, a youth minister for Mitchell Johnson at Central Baptist Church, who has talked to the boy three times since the shootings.

"There is a profound cultural influence, like gravity, pulling kids into a world where violence is a perfectly normal way to handle our emotions."

But Mitchell also loved gospel music, the preacher said, and he sang for elderly people at nursing homes. Millions of children listen to violent-themed rap music, play Mortal Kombat and witness killings on television, and do not become murderers.

"Barry Loukaitis was obviously influenced by 'Natural Born Killers,'" said John Knodell, the prosecutor in Moses Lake. "But there are hundreds of thousands of kids who watch these things and don't blow away their schoolmates."

The psychiatrist in the Loukaitis case, Dr. Unis, also is reluctant to blame violent cultural influences.

But he and other experts say there is 55 a syndrome at work, in which a child who sees one shootout on the news may be inspired to try something similar.

"The media or violent videos do not by themselves make the event happen," said Ms. Erb, the prosecutor in Alaska. "But it shows them a way."

THE SIGNS

Cries for Help Often Overlooked

The accused shooters are inevitably portrayed as average children. But a look inside their bedrooms or their journals, or a discussion with their friends shows they left ample clues of trouble to come.

Michael Carneal was known as a slight boy who played baritone sax in the school band in West Paducah, the son of an elder in the local Lutheran

MOSES LAKE, WASH., FEB. 2, 1996

Three killed and one
wounded when Barry
Loukaitis, 14, fired on an
algebra class at Frontier
Middle School. He was
convicted last year of
murder and assault, and
sentenced to two consecu-
tive life terms without
parole, plus 205 years.

BETHEL, ALASKA, FEB. 19, 1997

Two people killed, a stu-
dent and the principal,
when Evan Ramsey, 16,
went on a shooting ram-
page at Bethel High
School. He was convicted
in February of this year of
two counts of first-degree
murder and 15 counts of
assault. He is awaiting
sentencing.

PEARL, MISS., OCT. 1, 1997

Three people killed and
seven wounded when a
boy fired on students at
Pearl High School after
stabbing his mother. Luke
Woodham was found
guilty last week of killing
his mother, and convicted
on Friday of two other
murders.

WEST PADUCAH, KY., DEC. 1, 1997

Three people killed and
five wounded when a stu-
dent opened fire on a
prayer circle outside
Heath High School.
Michael Carneal, 14, has
been charged with the
killings.

JONESBORO, ARK., MARCH 24, 1998

Five people killed and 10
wounded when two stu-
dents who lay in wait in
the grass opened fire on
teachers and students who
had filed out of Westside
Middle School after an
alarm had been pulled.
Andrew Golden (photo-
graph unavailable), 11,
and Mitchell Johnson
(right), 13, have been
charged with the killings,
though they cannot be
tried as adults and could
be released, under
Arkansas law, after they
reach their 18th birthdays.

SPRINGFIELD, ORE., MAY 21, 1998

Four people killed
(including the parents of
the alleged assailant) and
22 injured in a shooting
rampage that started at
home and moved to
Thurston High School.
Kipland Kinkel, 15, has
been formally accused of
the killings, awaits
arraignment next week.

church. After the killings, his principal, Bill Bond, looked at some of his notebook writings and found a child who felt weak and powerless, with an angry desire to lash out at the world.

About a week before the shooting, Michael warned several classmates that "something big was going to happen" and they should get out of the way, detectives said. At least three of the boys accused in other cases did the same thing.

The Alaskan assailant warned spe- 60 cific students the night before the killings to go up on a second-floor balcony. "These kids didn't tell anyone," said the prosecutor, Ms. Erb. "Instead, they got right up there the next day to get their view of the killings."

In his ninth-grade English class, Barry Loukaitis wrote a poem about murder that ended this way:

I look at his body on the floor,
Killing a bastard that deserves to die,
Ain't nothing like it in the world,
But he sure did bleed a lot

Kip Kinkel read a journal entry aloud in his English class about killing fellow students. Most of the attackers were also suicidal, writing notes before the killings that assumed they would die.

Luke Woodham's journal writings from Mississippi were particularly graphic. He left a last will and testament, leaving music cassettes to the older boy who is said by police to have influenced him. "I do this to show society, 'Push us and we will push back,'" he wrote. "I suffered all my life. No one ever truly loved me. No one ever truly cared about me."

Dr. Reisman said parents and teachers should be alarmed by such writings. Animal abuse, arson and a sudden interest in death and darkness are red flags, he said.

Often the assailants live in the 65 shadow of successful older siblings, Dr. Reisman added. But the most common element is deep depression, which is near epidemic among American youth, he said.

"They'll all have depression, in the state in which they do these things," Dr. Reisman said. "When they're cornered, the first thing they say is, 'Kill me.' It's suicide by cop."

THE STREETS OF LOS ANGELES

Rita Williams

Rita Williams writes fiction as well as reviews and articles for the LA Weekly, *in which this 1991 essay originally appeared. Here she recounts her experience of driving at night in Los Angeles and being stopped by black teens who held a gun to her head in an attempted carjacking. Writing as an African American who has known what it is to feel black rage and who has fought "for the civil rights of kids such as these," Williams describes her own reactions to the incident as she reflects on what motivated these young men.*

As you read, note how Williams is surprised by her own expectations of the young men who stop her.

It's 10:30 on a Saturday night in Los Angeles, and I am trying to drive up La Cienega Boulevard, but even at this hour, the turgid flow of traffic is maddening. I decide to cut over to Crescent Heights, which should move faster. As I swing right onto Airdrome, a pedestrian steps in front of my car. This strikes me as very wrong, but I stop.

When the guy moves around toward my side, I see why it feels odd. He is a young black kid, braced in a combat stance, and he is pointing a gun at me. Before the fear slams my sense shut, I register a baby face with dimples, a sensuous pink mouth, and a Batman cap with the bill sideways on his head. His eyes are what makes me lose hope. He looks bored.

Panic wrestles with paralysis as I contemplate flooring it and running him down. But he would definitely shoot me, and I can tell from the size of the barrel that if he gets off even one round, it will be lethal.

He walks toward my door, and the closer he gets, the more I feel my system become drowsy with fear. But my thoughts surge through a list of protests so naive that it surprises me. Having worked for years to transform my own black rage into something constructive, I had not realized I felt entitled to some kind of immunity. Instead, I am now staring down the cannon of this kid who is acting out *his* black rage.

Then two more guys appear, quiet   5
as eels, a foot from my car door. I sense rather than see them, because I can't tear my eyes away from the escape route ahead. I struggle not to slide completely into shock. My unlocked car door swings open.

"Get out," the kid demands. His voice is close behind me to the left. The muscles at the base of my head twitch as he gently rests the gun barrel at the base of my brain stem. I fantasize about the trajectory of the bullet passing through the left rear of my skull and exploding out my right temple. I know I should do exactly as he says, but I'm too scared to move.

Then I remember something familiar about this kid's stance. His teachers were probably cops. He has that same paramilitary detachment. Long ago, I was taught that when a jacked-up cop shakes you down, you keep your hands in plain sight and don't make any fast moves. That lesson was learned fighting for the civil rights of kids such as these. I hope now it will work to protect me from them.

"I *said* get out of the car, bitch," the kid snaps.

The layers of contempt in the word *bitch* make me wonder whether the plan is rape. I decide that exposing my entire body to his rage would be suicidal, so I don't move at all. But I have another problem. I'm angry. And that has to be contained.

This is not the first group of bullies I [10] have faced. At the WASPy prep school° I attended in rural Colorado, "nigger" was the nicest name they called me. It got so virulent I used to eat my meals on a tray in the lavatory. One day I saw myself in the mirror, cowering on the can, scarfing down my lunch, and I realized this was the bottom. Nothing they could say to me could be worse than this, so I took my tray into the lunchroom.

From then on, it was open season. They went at me with a renewed vengeance. Then one evening before study hall, I once more lost my nerve. I just couldn't stand it, so I walked away from school—which could have gotten me expelled. They loved it. And that was it. I picked up a rock and decided to fight. And to my surprise, the chase ended, the name-calling stopped. Now, even though these kids are black, it feels just like my old school. The first kid drags a jagged fingernail across my throat as he tries to yank me out of the car. But even though I haven't moved, I am no longer immobile. My grip on the steering wheel tightens, even as his pulling me slams my head against the roof of the car. After a halfhearted go at it, he stops and moves away from the car. There is whispering among the boys, and I pick up the phrase "bitch must be crazy."

Then I hear the guy who has been standing the farthest away approach the car. He croons, "Ah, man. Man, this is a sister. We can't be ripping off no sister."

I don't get it. Then I realize that, in the dark, they could not tell that I was black. But in this epidemic of black-on-black violence, I would never expect my race to protect me. If anything, it should make them rip me off with impunity.

But the compassion flowing toward me from this young man is unmistakable. He has interceded for me. And I'm sure that he is taking a tremendous risk by doing so. I also know that this delicate dynamic could shift back in a breath. But I have to look at him anyway. "Thank you," I say, then floor it.

It's a good thing the car finds the way [15] back home, because I can't remember how to get there. When I am finally safe, I only want to immerse myself in the mundane. I definitely do not want to call the police. But somebody else might be in danger. So I have to do something. I call the police.

After speaking with several impatient and indifferent male officers, I'm transferred to the dispatch commander. Now the voice is that of a woman, a black woman. Hope for understanding, maybe even some empathy, comes back.

"You wish to make a report?" she asks.

"Please," I say.

"What was the location of the incident?"

I give her the information. Then I [20] notice her tone shift when I tell her

---

°**WASPy prep school:** The acronym WASP stands for white Anglo-Saxon Protestant.

that the one kid let me go because I was a "sister."

"These kids were black?"

"Yes," I reply, and before I can say anything else, she interrupts me. "Will that be all?"

I can't quite let it go. So I ask her, "What do you think of how I handled this situation?"

"Listen, lady, anybody who'd drive around in L.A. at night without their door locked is crazy and, second, you ought to have run those fools down. Then we could have sent a cruiser to take them to the morgue. You can believe they would have done the same to you. I don't understand you stopping in the first place."

I feel dumb. She does have a point. 25 My door should have been locked, but... I prepare to launch into a self-defensive diatribe, when it hits me that this black woman, and the cops I spoke to before, and the kids who tried to hold me up would all concur that I have been the fool this evening.

She tells me that she will send a cruiser out, but since I can't identify any suspects, I shouldn't expect much.

A WRITER'S NOTEBOOK
Descriptions of Violent Crime

The following tasks are designed to help you think about the readings and identify and start to work up material you might use in an essay.

1. *List causes.* For each reading you study in this chapter, list the causes its writer offers to explain violent crime. Record which reading suggests or states which cause and jot down the number of the paragraph in which each is stated. Although these first readings are primarily descriptive, most of the writers indicate in some way what might be causing the violence among young men (see, for example, paragraphs 10, 14, and 17 in the reading by Isabel Wilkerson), so you can begin your list now. It is also a good idea to include causes the writers say are *not* influential (see, for example, paragraph 11 in Wilkerson). Later, when you plan your essay about violence, this list can help you choose causes you believe to be most likely.

2. *Interview students.* Interview at least three students, both men and women, who are not in your writing course, allowing at least ten minutes for each interview. Begin by briefly explaining the basic facts about violent crime among young men: that they are far more likely than young women or older men to commit violent crimes, that such crimes often occur in suburbs and small towns as well as in inner-city neighborhoods, and so on. Ask the students what factors they think account for this violence by young men and which factors do *not*, in their view, contribute to the problem. Take notes about the causes they mention. Later, you may want to do brief follow-up interviews to get their reactions to specific arguments proposed in the readings. When you plan and draft an essay on violence, the information you gain from these interviews will help you assess what your readers — other college students — know and believe about violent crime.

3. *Discover incidents of violence.* Try to find two or three other people who have observed violence by a young man. Few individuals may have observed a murder, but some may have seen a violent attack, perhaps a fight that resulted in a severe beating. Ask each person to describe in detail what happened and what might have caused the incident. Take notes. Then write a page or so about one of the incidents, describing it for someone who has never observed violence by a young man.

4. *Consider your own experience.* Write a page or so about your own fears of violent crime. Be specific about where you live, places or situations you think should be avoided, and the basis for your fears. Or write about your *lack* of fear of violent crime, including a discussion of places and situations and an explanation of why you are not fearful of such crime.

5. *Find current examples of violence in the media.* For a week or so, check your local newspaper and a national newspaper every day and collect published accounts of violence by young men. As you find articles, jot down source and publication information (date, page numbers). In addition, watch local and national television news for reports of violence and take notes on any relevant incidents, including the date and source of the report. Insert all of the accounts into your notebook, along with any notes you have taken. When you write your essay, this information may help you present your argument.

6. *Review Isabel Wilkerson's report.* From interviews, observations, and reading, Wilkerson has selected events and facts that inform and alarm readers about violence by young men. Review her report and choose the fact in it that alarms you the most. Write a few sentences identifying the fact and explaining why you find it troubling.

7. *Reflect on your experience and the Luis J. Rodriguez and Nathan McCall essays.* Recall your own experience with violence — as a victim, a witness or onlooker, or a participant. Before writing about the experience, skim the Rodriguez and McCall readings, noticing how they rely on concrete details: people's names, descriptions of physical appearance, remembered dialogue, and the sights and sounds of the scene or action. Write a page or so describing your experience of violence, using specific, vivid details to show what happened.

8. *Analyze McCall's essay.* Reread paragraphs 13, 19, 37, and 44 of McCall's account to see what he was thinking and feeling at different points during the period he describes. Write a page or so in which you try to explain McCall's feelings and speculate about why he acted as he did.

9. *Consider Timothy Egan's report.* Egan's report on the recent school shootings suggests different patterns from those in the situation Wilkerson describes. Pick out one or two parts of the patterns Egan describes and write a half-page or so telling what you find most interesting and convincing in his account of patterns in these school shootings.

10. *React to Rita Williams's account.* Just as many people are shocked by the violence in schools, Williams is shocked by violent young black men who should, she believes, have seen her as a "sister." Explain, in a few sentences, what it is that so shocks Williams. Then write a half-page or so about your own reactions to her account.

STATISTICS: PATTERNS OF VIOLENCE

While the readings in the previous section offer descriptions of specific violent acts, this section presents *statistics,* or numerical data, about violent crime in general. It is important to study statistics, particularly those collected by the FBI, to get a sense of overall criminal patterns, which may not be clear from individual cases.

In developing an essay about violent crime, you may want to use statistics in several ways: (1) to help you decide which causes of violence seem most likely; (2) to support the causes you choose; or (3) to introduce or close your essay in a compelling way. Keep in mind, however, that statistics have limitations. Because they focus only on averages within large populations, statistics do not predict what will happen in a particular instance or with a particular individual. Following are some basic FBI statistics about the violent crimes that are the focus of this chapter: murder, nonnegligent manslaughter, and aggravated assault.

Who Commits Violence

Among males and females under eighteen years of age, males are far more likely than females to be arrested for violent crimes. Table 5.1 shows at a glance the significant differences in the numbers of murders and aggravated assaults committed nationwide by the two sexes in 1996.

Statistics also reveal that *young* men commit more than their share of violent crimes. Table 5.2 shows that murder arrests are at their highest rates among young men in their late teens and early twenties.

When crime statistics are analyzed to see which age group is committing which types of crime, different patterns emerge between young men's crimes and crimes committed by older people. In 1990, for instance, 37.7 percent of the murders recorded by the FBI were by people between eighteen and twenty-four, whereas only 16.8 percent of the gambling crimes were committed by people in that age group.[1] Crimes like gambling and arson are more

Table 5.1
Arrests, by Offense Charged and Sex, 1996

	Males under 18	Females under 18
Murder and Nonnegligent Manslaughter	1,907	132
Aggravated Assault	40,320	10,240

Source: U.S. Department of Justice, Federal Bureau of Investigation, *Crime in the United States, 1996* (Washington, D.C.: GPO, 1997) 219.

---

[1]U.S. Federal Bureau of Investigation, *Crime in the United States, 1990.* U.S. Department of Commerce, Bureau of the Census, *Current Population Reports,* Series P-25, no. 1057.

Table 5.2
Male Murder Offenders, by Age, 1996

Age (in years)	No. of Male Offenders
5–8	3
9–12	13
13–16	934
17–19	2,522
20–24	3,042
25–29	1,688
30–34	1,291
35–39	1,008
40–44	685
45–49	452

Source: U.S. Department of Justice, Federal Bureau of Investigation, *Crime in the United States, 1996* (Washington, D.C.: GPO, 1997) 16.

prevalent among older people. Statistical analyses show other differences as well. Longtime sexual offenders, for instance, seem to remain sexual offenders well into middle age, but murder and aggravated assault tend to be committed less frequently by males as they reach their late twenties.

Where Violence is Committed

Statistics about *where* crimes are likely to be committed can sometimes help pinpoint social conditions that may contribute to crime. Place is important in several of the accounts in the preceding section: Isabel Wilkerson, Luis J. Rodriguez, and Rita Williams all suggest a connection between violence and big cities, and Timothy Egan notes that violence may be increasing in smaller cities, rural areas, and suburbs. Table 5.3 provides the FBI statistics on the rates for some crimes in three types of places.

Table 5.3
Crime Rates per 100,000 Inhabitants, by Place, 1996

Place	Murder and Nonnegligent Manslaughter (rate per 100,000)	Aggravated Assault (rate per 100,000)
Metropolitan Areas	8.1	424.2
Cities outside Metropolitan Areas	4.5	349.7
Rural Counties	4.7	177

Source: U.S. Department of Justice, Federal Bureau of Investigation, *Crime in the United States, 1996* (Washington, D.C.: GPO, 1997) 63.

As Table 5.3 shows, crimes of violence occur more often in metropolitan areas than in suburbs or rural locations. Despite some dips and rises from one year to another, the number of crimes in the suburbs and rural areas has consistently remained lower than the number of crimes in cities.

The preceding statistics are just some of the data that are available about violent crime. Like the earlier article by Isabel Wilkerson, the readings in the next section contain further statistics. You may also want to consult yearly government publications, using the advice in "Gathering Additional Information" (later in this chapter) or in Appendix 2.

A WRITER'S NOTEBOOK

Statistics: Patterns of Violence

The following tasks are designed to help you think about the readings and identify and start to work up material you might use in your own essay.

1. *Present the problem.* Writers sometimes use statistics to impress on readers the seriousness of a problem. With this purpose in mind, look again at the statistics in the preceding tables. Then choose the data that you think best convey the alarming nature of the problem of violence by young men. Write a few sentences explaining those statistics, presenting information to readers to convince them that the issue is serious.

2. *Find statistical facts.* Ask a reference librarian to show you the most recent copy of *Statistical Abstracts of the United States.* From the statistics on murder, manslaughter, or aggravated assault, select one piece of data that you find particularly important in relation to young men. Photocopy the page, include it in your writer's notebook, and write a half-page or so telling why you consider this information so interesting or significant. Or, if you have access to the World Wide Web, go to the National Criminal Justice Reference Service (NCJRS) Web site at <http://www.ncjrs.org> or the Bureau of Justice home page at <http://www.ojp.usdoj.gov> and then follow a link that interests you until you find some statistics about violence among young men. Select one piece of data and write a half-page or so explaining why you think the information is important. (See Appendix 2 if you need help with library or Internet research.)

POSSIBLE CAUSES OF VIOLENCE BY YOUNG MEN

In the preceding sections, the readings have offered some descriptions of violent incidents and some statistics. If you have read these, you have probably also considered your own reactions to, or experiences with, violent crime and those of people you know. At this point, then, you should be ready to consider possible causes—*why* some young men may commit violent crimes. Since some of the earlier descriptive accounts mention possible causes, you may have already begun to form your own ideas about the likely causes of this social crisis.

Here is a way to begin sorting kinds of causal arguments about violence: Assume that the relatively greater tendency of young males to engage in violence has been true of other times and other places, not only contemporary America. Whatever makes young men in different societies and different times prone to violence may be called *background* causes. Some might argue that male hormones lead young males to commit more violence; if so, hormones are a *background* cause because they are always there. A second kind of cause might be called *triggering,* or *precipitating,* causes; these are the most temporary and accidental causes (e.g., easy access to a gun, a sudden fit of anger, the absence of a police officer), but in most cases there are some underlying circumstances that make the triggering or precipitating cause possible.

The readings in this section are about this third kind of cause: the *circumstances* affecting which young men are most likely to commit violence and when and where they do so. *Circumstances* are the various influences in a person's life — poverty, inequality, family, neighborhoods, codes of conduct, and the like — that might incline someone toward violence. Note that guns might be said to be either a *triggering* cause — if they are simply the method a violent person uses to express his anger — or a *circumstance* related to cultural images and values if a young man sees guns as a sign of masculinity or has a fascination with guns themselves. The writers in this section differ with one another not about background causes but about which circumstances are most likely to cause violence.

When crime statistics show that some kinds of violence in the United States are much more prevalent than they were several decades ago, it is logical to assume not that the background causes have changed but that circumstances have changed. Because of such changes, a particular young man might now be more likely to commit a violent act.

The following readings are arranged roughly according to the circumstances they focus on: neighborhoods, families, ideas and other cultural influences. These groupings are not the only way to organize the possible causes of violence, but they should help you as you begin to compare writers' arguments and think about your own. The first three readings — by Susan Straight, William Julius Wilson, and Elijah Anderson — focus on neighborhoods and how poverty, joblessness, or inequality within city neighborhoods may promote violence. Next, David Popenoe argues that some family circumstances may put young men at greater risk for violence, and, to offer an alternative to Popenoe's argument, Mike A. Males argues instead that adults' violence in the home lies behind youths' violence in the streets. The third group of readings — by Carl M. Cannon, Todd Gitlin, Andrew Lam, Gary Ross, and Myron Magnet — cover a wide variety of influences, including media images, attitudes, and cultural ideals.

The readings in this section are important in a number of ways. By informing you about some of the causal speculations others have made, they will help you enter the debate confidently and write an authoritative essay. The readings will immerse you in the kinds of reasons and support central to a causal argument, including personal experience, interviews, cases, and statistics. They also demonstrate a variety of argumentative stances, from calmly professorial to urgently personal. Finally, the readings illustrate how writers lead their readers step by step through a causal argument, combining diverse kinds of support, quoting various sources, and weaving all this material together into a persuasive piece of writing.

As you read, keep a list of all the causes these writers give for the violence committed by young men. To keep track of this material, list the paragraph number(s) in which you find each cause.

THE GUN IN THE CLOSET

Susan Straight

Susan Straight, a novelist and short story writer, is the author of Aquaboogie *(1990),* I Been in Sorrow's Kitchen and Licked Out All the Pots *(1992),* Blacker Than a Thousand Midnights *(1994), and* The Gettin Place *(1996). During her lifetime she has seen Riverside, California, change from a rural town of orange groves and wild oat fields to a "sprawling part-urban, part-rural city of 250,000 people." In this reading, first published in* Harper's *magazine in 1994, Straight recounts how she, a white woman, and her African American husband, Dwayne, have seen the city where they grew up become more dangerous.*

Straight is the first of several authors in this section to focus on neighborhoods. As the statistics in the preceding section indicated, crime occurs more often in large cities than in suburban and rural areas.

As you read, notice what Straight says about her neighborhood and how circumstances there have changed since her childhood.

Our house is on a street that was once an orange grove, too. During the Twenties and Thirties the land was sold off and new wood-frame houses were built on long narrow lots (we still have irrigation-ditch rights through several backyards). As teenagers, we used to cruise through this neighborhood at night wishing we could live here, even admiring the wisteria on what is now our home.

Back then we knew a few people who "packed."° But they owned guns for specific reasons. Dwayne's older brother had close friends and roommates who had guns because they were dealing drugs. Other men we knew kept guns

---

°**packed:** Carried a gun.

around the house for hunting. Dwayne's father and uncles, who'd grown up in Oklahoma, surviving in part on game they shot, lived in rural Riverside and had old rifles; his cousins shot and roasted pigeons and rabbits in the fields.

Now those fields and groves bristle with ten new homes per acre, each house and tract walled off for safety and privacy. During the late 1980s, pushed by high real estate prices in Los Angeles, record numbers of home buyers poured into Riverside, giving this county one of the fastest growth rates in the nation. But the good jobs that drew people here in the Forties—those at Kaiser Steel and in the defense industry, where our relatives and neighbors worked—are disappearing. So the new homeowners must drive hours to work elsewhere, often leaving their kids unattended after school. Many of these recent residents fled gang violence in Los Angeles only to find their kids starting new gangs in rural Riverside inside the walls. These kids cruise like we did, but there's a difference now: they're likely to be "strapped." They don't have hunting guns, they have handguns. And the boys and men who live around here do, too: I've found spent shells from .357- and .22-caliber guns on the sidewalk by our fence.

• • •

Dwayne spends his days working with young criminals at a juvenile detention center in Riverside. When he first started there ten years ago, he would come home each evening and rail against loose gun-control laws that allowed so many firearms on the streets. But I haven't heard Dwayne mention gun control for a while now. Every day he watches and feeds and supervises his fifty juvenile charges, who are awaiting trial for their violent crimes. He listens to the grisly details of these incidents and hears no remorse in their voices. He has made up his mind. "Nothing but young fools out there. They don't even *see* me—they just see that I'm an obstacle blockin' them from something they want. I'm not gonna get killed by a fool. I'll be prepared," he says.

When I hear Dwayne talk like this I wonder what has happened to him. But I 5 know that he's not alone in his thoughts. One of Dwayne's colleagues, T, a Chicano supervisor at the facility who lives in a historic Mexican-American neighborhood in Riverside, told us, "See, in the old barrios,° you couldn't get away with robbing and shooting people because everyone knew everyone. But not with these new kids. They're not scared of anything. Now it's up to the people to take back the neighborhoods, man. Hey, when these kids know we're all ready and armed, and they know they might get killed, they're gonna have to stop."

The night we talked in the garage Dwayne told me that he had bought his .380 handgun two years before, after a woman was murdered during a botched carjacking while she was shopping during her lunch hour. He had purchased the Ruger 9-millimeter more recently, after he met the "Pimp-Style Hustlers" at

---

°**barrios:** Neighborhoods in which most people speak Spanish.

his detention center. This group of teenagers was brought to Dwayne's facility after an eight-day spree of robbery, attempted kidnapping, and carjacking. They were white, black, Filipino, and Latino boys from one of the new, "master-planned" communities near here, one of those housing tracts where the parents often get off the freeway after dark and get back on before the morning light. The boys were earning "stripes"—robbing or shooting people for the right to gain entry into the group. The rampage ended when several tried to steal a car from a mother of two outside her gym; they killed her instantly with a bullet to the neck.

Dwayne's co-workers can recite a list of people who were murdered over older-model, essentially worthless cars. "Come on, man," one of Dwayne's colleagues says with disgust. "These three white kids jacked that teacher for his old Toyota pickup? And they gotta kill him?"

I can hear it in the tone of their voices—there's something especially appalling to them about feeling unsafe in their own steel shells. This is southern California, after all. You are nothing without a car, and now you are nothing over a car.

"It's not even enough for these guys to get the money and the car. They *want* to shoot you. I know," Dwayne says one night, sitting wearily at the kitchen table after work. "They're bold now. They don't care. They don't think."

When Dwayne mouths these words I know what he is thinking: nothing can 10 guarantee his or my safety, not his six-four, 240-pound frame, not the fact that he is a father of two and stays clear of trouble. But what he is saying is that he will not feel helpless. He will buy guns. He will learn to shoot. Dwayne, his co-workers, his brothers, our neighbors—all of them will do anything to ward off vulnerability. They are men, all races, mostly old-fashioned and living in often dangerous circumstances, with people and property to protect.

• • •

For me guns have always been alarming, blind threats to *him*, a tall black man. When he told me that five of his co-workers were now carrying 9-millimeter handguns in their cars, and that he had considered it, I was angry and frightened. How could he even *think* about doing something that might increase his chances of a tragic confrontation with the police? Dwayne has always been careful about this. I've seen him dangle his hands limply from the driver's window, waiting patiently for the police to approach after his car had been pulled over. "And if you have a gun in the glove compartment or under the seat, and you get stopped by the cops?" I ask him, my voice shaking with frustration.

We sit in the kitchen, silent for a long time, listening to voices passing outside.

I suppose it was inevitable, but I was surprised nonetheless the day I got caught in the sound of popping caps and flying bullets. The day was completely ordinary. I was picking up my baby girl from my mother-in-law's after work and had paused on the sidewalk to read my mail, which is why I was so slow and oblivious when the sounds began to crackle from the corner. Suddenly I heard my sister-in-law in the yard next door shouting at me.

All I could see was the doorknob of the heavy-meshed security screen, so far away. I heard more pops, heard running, and I bent my head awkwardly, trying to be smaller as I scrambled for the knob, my neck moving like a turtle's.

Once inside, I slammed the door and ran to the back room, where my 15 mother-in-law held the sleeping baby and sighed with resignation. "Who's shooting now?" she asked.

It turned out that W, a young man who lives a few doors down, had been making the wrong hand gestures on that corner, and when a carload of rival young men shot at him with a .25 rifle, he had run behind me toward safety. The bullets flew past us both while I lingered in the driveway.

Now in the afternoons I find myself wondering about the group of boys who crowd around the mailbox by our fence, the shiny black curls, the straight curves of red hair, the slicked-back brown ponytails, the plaid shirts and huge, cavernous pants—camouflage, I think. They can't appear afraid; they have to look tough, dress to blend in, carry the right piece, because otherwise all they are is scared.

These are the boys my daughters watch from the windows and the lawn. My older girl likes our redheaded neighbor, whom Dwayne had in detention twice last year. I like him, too—the way he laughs with smaller kids, the ancient bike he rides. His parents are alcoholics, I know, and he is rarely supervised. I wave at him, my daughters smile flirtatiously, and I wonder if he has a gun. Another neighborhood boy, one of four sons, is in detention now for robbing a pizza delivery man. He used a BB gun, for which he was derided by staff and detainees at Dwayne's job. And his younger brother, four years old, is my four-year-old's "boyfriend," according to his mother. He's brown-skinned and shy, and I can't help but wonder whether he, too, will end up incarcerated under Dwayne's watchful eye.

Who will our daughters go out with? Dwayne and I ask each other. Will there be any teenage boys left by then? Or are they all going to kill one another?

• • •

Even our porch frightens me. It's bare and open and faces the avenue. I used to 20 sit here for hours when the girls were babies, rocking them and watching the endless streams of pedestrians and traffic. My daughters learned some of their first words here: Volkswagen, do-do-si-cu (motorcycle), heli-coppa, and boom-truck, the ones with huge, pounding speakers.

These nights when I sit on this old porch after the girls are asleep, rocking in the ancient plastic glider my parents gave us, I stare at the cars and imagine that someone might not like my face bobbing here. Or maybe the police will chase another carjacker from Thrifty.° Or someone else's target might walk past on the sidewalk and hover near me. I have no camouflage.

I go inside. In the small room where I work, the radio plays rap. "I'm cruisin' with my Glock cocked," the rapper Ice Cube sings. "You coulda had a V-8

°**Thrifty:** A drugstore.

instead of a 3-8 slug to your cranium, I got six and I'm aimin' 'em." I think of W, the shadow that flew behind me that day in front of my mother-in-law's house. Recently, he was involved in a fight at a funeral reception for a slain friend, and he ran shooting after the man into the parking lot of my niece's elementary school, Dwayne's old school. It was afternoon, and the stream of departing children cowered as W fired several shots and then fled. He was out on bail shortly after, and I see him on the street almost every day. Dwayne can't talk about it without beginning to shout.

WHEN WORK DISAPPEARS

William Julius Wilson

William Julius Wilson, a prominent Harvard University sociologist, is the author of a number of articles and books, including The Truly Disadvantaged: The Inner City, the Underclass, and Public Policy *(1987), an influential book about the relation between urban poverty and violence. This reading comes from Wilson's 1996 book* When Work Disappears: The World of the New Urban Poor. *Like Susan Straight, Wilson looks at how particular kinds of neighborhoods are associated with increased violence.*

Wilson did much of his research in Chicago in the 1970s and 1980s, when there was an ongoing debate over poverty's role in causing violence. At the time, some researchers had speculated that poverty creates an underclass whose habits of behavior, rather than poverty itself, cause their problems. Wilson, however, looked to the economic changes that have transformed cities over the last few decades. In his view, the "truly disadvantaged" live in neighborhoods that middle-class jobholders have fled, where concentrated poverty is accompanied by "social disorganization."

At the beginning of this reading, Wilson compares the current situation in Chicago to an earlier situation described by Chicago researchers St. Clair Drake and Horace Cayton. In their 1945 book Black Metropolis: A Study of Negro Life in a Northern City, *these researchers found a "color line" in several areas of the city, blocking blacks from making progress. Evaluating the same neighborhoods in 1962, Drake and Cayton expressed hope for new prosperity and integration in what they called "Bronzeville" (three sections of Chicago's black community: Washington Park, Grand Boulevard, and Douglas).*

As you read, note the differences between the current jobless ghetto and the earlier facts about Bronzeville. Note, too, the connections Wilson makes between joblessness and weak social organization in poor city neighborhoods.

The most fundamental difference between today's inner-city neighborhoods and those studied by Drake and Cayton is the much higher levels of joblessness. Indeed, there is a new poverty in our nation's metropolises that has consequences for a range of issues relating to the quality of life in urban areas, including race relations.

By "the new urban poverty," I mean poor, segregated neighborhoods in which a substantial majority of individual adults are either unemployed or have dropped out of the labor force altogether.[1] For example, in 1990 only one in three adults ages 16 and over in the twelve Chicago community areas with ghetto poverty rates held a job in a typical week of the year. Each of these community areas, located on the South and West Sides of the city, is overwhelmingly black. We can add to these twelve high-jobless areas three additional predominantly black community areas, with rates approaching ghetto poverty, in which only 42 percent of the adult population were working in a typical week in 1990. Thus, in these fifteen black community areas—comprising a total population of 425,125—only 37 percent of all the adults were gainfully employed in a typical week in 1990. By contrast, 54 percent of the adults in the seventeen other predominantly black community areas in Chicago—a total population of 545,408—worked in a typical week in 1990. This was close to the citywide employment figure of 57 percent for all adults. Finally, except for one Asian community area with an employment rate of 46 percent, and one Latino community area with an employment rate of 49 percent, a majority of the adults held a job in a typical week in each of the remaining forty-five community areas of Chicago.

But Chicago is by no means the only city that features new poverty neighborhoods. In the ghetto census tracts of the nation's one hundred largest central cities, there were only 65.5 employed persons for every hundred adults who did not hold a job in a typical week in 1990.[2] In contrast, the nonpoverty areas contained 182.3 employed persons for every hundred of those not working. In other words, the ratio of employed to jobless persons was three times greater in census tracts not marked by poverty.

Looking at Drake and Cayton's Bronzeville,° I can illustrate the magnitude of the changes that have occurred in many inner-city ghetto neighborhoods in recent years. A majority of adults held jobs in the three Bronzeville areas in 1950, but by 1990 only four in ten in Douglas worked in a typical week, one in three in Washington Park, and one in four in Grand Boulevard. In 1950, 69 percent of all males 14 and over who lived in the Bronzeville neighborhoods

---

° **Bronzeville**: Drake and Cayton's term for the African American communities in Chicago comprising Douglas, Washington Park, and Grand Boulevard.

[1] The figures on adult neighborhood employment presented in this section are based on calculations from data provided by the 1990 U.S. Bureau of the Census and the *Local Community Fact Book for Chicago—1950* and the *Local Community Fact Book—Chicago Area, 1960.*

[2] Kasarda (1993).

worked in a typical week, and in 1960, 64 percent of this group were so employed. However, by 1990 only 37 percent of all males 16 and over held jobs in a typical week in these three neighborhoods.

Upon the publication of the first edition of *Black Metropolis* in 1945, there was much greater class integration within the black community. As Drake and Cayton pointed out, Bronzeville residents had limited success in "sorting themselves out into broad community areas designated as 'lower class' and 'middle class.'... Instead of middle-class *areas,* Bronzeville tends to have middle-class *buildings* in all areas, or a few middle-class blocks here and there."[3] Though they may have lived on different streets, blacks of all classes in inner-city areas such as Bronzeville lived in the same community and shopped at the same stores. Their children went to the same schools and played in the same parks. Although there was some class antagonism, their neighborhoods were more stable than the inner-city neighborhoods of today; in short, they featured higher levels of what social scientists call "social organization."

When I speak of social organization I am referring to the extent to which the residents of a neighborhood are able to maintain effective social control and realize their common goals. There are three major dimensions of neighborhood social organization: (1) the prevalence, strength, and interdependence of social networks; (2) the extent of collective supervision that the residents exercise and the degree of personal responsibility they assume in addressing neighborhood problems; and (3) the rate of resident participation in voluntary and formal organizations.[4] Formal institutions (e.g., churches and political party organizations), voluntary associations (e.g., block clubs and parent-teacher organizations), and informal networks (e.g., neighborhood friends and acquaintances, coworkers, marital and parental ties) all reflect social organization.

Neighborhood social organization depends on the extent of local friendship ties, the degree of social cohesion, the level of resident participation in formal and informal voluntary associations, the density and stability of formal organizations, and the nature of informal social controls. Neighborhoods in which adults are able to interact in terms of obligations, expectations, and relationships are in a better position to supervise and control the activities and behavior of children. In neighborhoods with high levels of social organization, adults are empowered to act to improve the quality of neighborhood life—for example, by breaking up congregations of youths on street corners and by supervising the leisure activities of youngsters.

Neighborhoods plagued by high levels of joblessness are more likely to experience low levels of social organization: the two go hand in hand. High rates of joblessness trigger other neighborhood problems that undermine social

---

[3]Drake and Cayton (1962), pp. 658–60.
[4]Sampson and Groves (1989), Sampson (1992b), and Sampson and Wilson (1995).

organization, ranging from crime, gang violence, and drug trafficking to family breakups and problems in the organization of family life.

Consider, for example, the problems of drug trafficking and violent crime. As many studies have revealed, the decline in legitimate employment opportunities among inner-city residents has increased incentives to sell drugs.[5] The distribution of crack in a neighborhood attracts individuals involved in violence and lawlessness. Between 1985 and 1992, there was a sharp increase in the murder rate among men under the age of 24; for men 18 years old and younger, murder rates doubled. Black males in particular have been involved in this upsurge in violence. For example, whereas the homicide rate for white males between 14 and 17 increased from 8 per 100,000 in 1984 to 14 in 1991, the rate for black males tripled during that time (from 32 per 100,000 to 112).[6] This sharp rise in violent crime among younger males has accompanied the widespread outbreak of addiction to crack-cocaine. The association is especially strong in inner-city ghetto neighborhoods plagued by joblessness and weak social organization.

Violent persons in the crack-cocaine marketplace have a powerful impact on the social organization of a neighborhood. Neighborhoods plagued by high levels of joblessness, insufficient economic opportunities, and high residential mobility are unable to control the volatile drug market and the violent crimes related to it. As informal controls° weaken, the social processes that regulate behavior change.

As a result, the behavior and norms in the drug market are more likely to influence the action of others in the neighborhood, even those who are not involved in drug activity. Drug dealers cause the use and spread of guns in the neighborhood to escalate, which in turn raises the likelihood that others, particularly the youngsters, will come to view the possession of weapons as necessary or desirable for self-protection, settling disputes, and gaining respect from peers and other individuals.

Moreover, as Alfred Blumstein pointed out, the drug industry actively recruits teenagers in the neighborhood "partly because they will work more cheaply than adults, partly because they may be less vulnerable to the punishments imposed by the adult criminal justice system, partly because they tend to be daring and willing to take risks that more mature adults would eschew."[7] Inner-city black youths with limited prospects for stable or attractive employment are easily lured into drug trafficking and therefore increasingly find themselves involved in the violent behavior that accompanies it.

°**informal controls:** Controls that are not formal laws but may nevertheless be effective. When an adult in a neighborhood tells a young person to behave and he or she obeys, that is a type of informal control.

[5]Fagan (1993).

[6]Blumstein (1994).

[7]Blumstein (1994), p. 18.

A more direct relationship between joblessness and violent crime is revealed in recent research by Delbert Elliott of the University of Colorado, a study based on National Longitudinal Youth Survey data collected from 1976 to 1989, covering ages 11 to 30. As Elliott points out, the transition from adolescence to adulthood usually results in a sharp drop in most crimes as individuals take on new adult roles and responsibilities. "Participation in serious violent offending behavior (aggravated assault, forcible rape, and robbery) increases [for all males] from ages 11 and 12 to ages 15 and 16, then declines dramatically with advancing age."[8] Although black and white males reveal similar age curves,° "the negative slope of the age curve for blacks after age 20 is substantially less than that of whites."

The black-white differential in the proportion of males involved in serious violent crime, although almost even at age 11, increases to 3:2 over the remaining years of adolescence, and reaches a differential of nearly 4:1 during the late twenties. However, when Elliott compared only *employed* black and white males, he found no significant differences in violent behavior patterns among the two groups by age 21. Employed black males, like white males, experienced a precipitous decline in serious violent behavior following their adolescent period. Accordingly, a major reason for the racial gap in violent behavior after adolescence is joblessness; a large proportion of jobless black males do not assume adult roles and responsibilities, and their serious violent behavior is therefore more likely to extend into adulthood. The new poverty neighborhoods feature a high concentration of jobless males and, as a result, suffer rates of violent criminal behavior that exceed those in other urban neighborhoods.

The problems of joblessness and neighborhood social organization, including crime and drug trafficking, are...reflected in the responses to a 1993 survey...conducted on a random sample of adult residents in Woodlawn and Oakland, two of the new poverty neighborhoods on the South Side of Chicago. In 1990, 37 percent of Woodlawn's 27,473 adults were employed and only 23 percent of Oakland's 4,935 adults were working. When asked how much of a problem unemployment was in their neighborhood, 73 percent of the residents in Woodlawn and 76 percent in Oakland identified it as a *major* problem. The responses to the survey also revealed the residents' concerns about a series of related problems, such as crime and drug abuse, that are symptomatic of severe problems of social organization. Indeed, crime was identified as a major problem by 66 percent of the residents in each neighborhood. Drug abuse was cited as a major problem by as many as 86 percent of the adult residents in Oakland and 79 percent of those in Woodlawn. 15

°**age curves:** Here, the rise of crime in adolescence and its fall with age, which resembles a bell-shaped curve on a graph.

[8]Elliott (1992), pp. 14–15.

Although high-jobless neighborhoods also feature concentrated poverty, high rates of neighborhood poverty are less likely to trigger problems of social organization if the residents are working. This was the case in previous years when the working poor stood out in areas like Bronzeville. Today, the nonworking poor predominate in the highly segregated and impoverished neighborhoods.

The rise of new poverty neighborhoods represents a movement away from what the historian Allan Spear has called an institutional ghetto—whose structure and activities parallel those of the larger society, as portrayed in Drake and Cayton's description of Bronzeville—toward a jobless ghetto, which features a severe lack of basic opportunities and resources, and inadequate social controls.

What can account for the growing proportion of jobless adults and the corresponding increase in problems of social organization in inner-city communities such as Bronzeville? An easy answer is racial segregation. However, a race-specific argument is not sufficient to explain recent changes in neighborhoods like Bronzeville. After all, Bronzeville was *just as segregated by skin color in 1950* as it is today, yet the level of employment was much higher then.

Nonetheless, racial segregation does matter. If large segments of the African-American population had not been historically segregated in inner-city ghettos, we would not be talking about the new urban poverty. The segregated ghetto is not the result of voluntary or positive decisions on the part of the residents who live there. As Massey and Denton have carefully documented, the segregated ghetto is the product of systematic racial practices such as restrictive covenants,° redlining° by banks and insurance companies, zoning,° panic peddling° by real estate agents, and the creation of massive public housing projects in low-income areas.

Segregated ghettos are less conducive to employment and employment preparation than are other areas of the city. Segregation in ghettos exacerbates employment problems because it leads to weak informal employment networks and contributes to the social isolation of individuals and families, thereby reducing their chances of acquiring the human capital skills, including adequate educational training, that facilitate mobility in a society. Since no other group in society experiences the degree of segregation, isolation, and poverty concentration as do African-Americans, they are far more likely to be disadvantaged when they have to compete with other groups in society, including other despised groups, for resources and privileges.

To understand the new urban poverty, one has to account for the ways in which segregation interacts with other changes in society to produce the recent escalating rates of joblessness and problems of social organization in inner-city ghetto neighborhoods.

°**restrictive covenants,** °**redlining,** °**zoning,** °**panic peddling:** Forms of economic discrimination that have kept African Americans from moving out of the ghetto.

WORKS CITED

Blumstein, Alfred. 1994. "Youth Violence, Guns, and the Illicit-Drug Industry." Working paper, H. John Keinz III School of Public Policy and Management.

Drake, St. Clair, and Horace Cayton. 1945; rev. ed. 1962. *Black Metropolis: A Study of Negro Life in a Northern City*. New York: Harcourt Brace Jovanovich.

Elliott, Delbert S. 1992. "Longitudinal Research in Criminology: Promise and Practice." Paper presented at the NATO Conference on Cross-National Longitudinal Research on Criminal Behavior, July 19–25, Frankfurt, Germany.

Fagan, Jeffrey. 1993. "Drug Selling and Licit Income in Distressed Neighborhoods: The Economic Lives of Street-Level Drug Users and Dealers." In *Drugs, Crime, and Social Isolation*, edited by G. Peterson and Adele V. Harrell, pp. 519–35. Washington, D.C.: Urban Institute Press.

Kasarda, John D. 1993. "Inner-City Concentrated Poverty and Neighborhood Distress: 1970–1990." *Housing Policy Debate* 4 (3): 253–302.

Local Community Fact Book — Chicago, 1950. 1953. Chicago Community Inventory, University of Chicago.

Local Community Fact Book — Chicago Area, 1960. 1963. Chicago Community Inventory, University of Chicago.

Massey, Douglas S., and Nancy A. Denton. 1993. *American Apartheid: Segregation and the Making of the Underclass*. Cambridge: Harvard University Press.

Sampson, Robert J. 1986. "Crime in Cities: The Effects of Formal and Informal Social Control." In *Communities and Crime*, edited by Albert J. Reiss Jr. and Michael Tonry, pp. 271–310. Chicago: University of Chicago Press.

———. 1988. "Urban Black Violence: The Effect of Male Joblessness and Family Disruption." *American Journal of Sociology* 93: 349–82.

———. 1992. "Integrating Family and Community-Level Dimensions of Social Organization: Delinquency and Crime in the Inner City of Chicago." Paper presented at the International Workshop on Integrating Individual and Ecological Aspects of Crime, August 31–September 5, Stockholm, Sweden.

Sampson, Robert J., and Walter Groves. 1989. "Community Structure and Crime: Testing Social Disorganization Theory." *American Journal of Sociology* 94: 774–802.

Sampson, Robert J., and William Julius Wilson. 1995. "Toward a Theory of Race, Crime, and Urban Inequality." In *Crime and Inequality,* edited by John Hagan and Ruth Peterson, pp. 37–54. Stanford: Stanford University Press.

Spear, Allan. 1967. *Black Chicago: The Making of a Negro Ghetto*. Chicago: University of Chicago Press.

THE CODE OF THE STREETS

Elijah Anderson

Elijah Anderson, professor of social sciences at the University of Pennsylvania, is the author of A Place on the Corner *(1978); the award-winning book* Streetwise: Race, Class, and Change in an Urban Community *(1990), a study of how people get along in a poor urban neighborhood in Philadelphia; and* Code of the Street: Decency, Violence, and the Moral Life of the Inner City *(1999).*

This 1994 article from the Atlantic Monthly *complements the essay by William Julius Wilson. Both writers look at the circumstances of the inner-city poor, and both think the causes of violence are to be found in the connections among poverty, racial discrimination, and city neighborhoods. Wilson and Anderson differ, however, as to exactly* how *these circumstances may contribute to violence. Wilson focuses on large-scale economic changes, whereas Anderson focuses on behavior within a neighborhood, behavior that comes from the desire for respect and the competition between decent values and street values. Although Anderson and Wilson would not necessarily disagree, their different accounts show that there are many ways in which poverty in inner-city neighborhoods might lead to violence.*

As you read, think about the two competing sets of values Anderson describes. What is the code of the streets and how does it lead to violence?

Of all the problems besetting the poor inner-city black community, none is more pressing than that of interpersonal violence and aggression. It wreaks havoc daily with the lives of community residents and increasingly spills over into downtown and residential middle-class areas. Muggings, burglaries, car-jackings, and drug-related shootings, all of which may leave their victims or innocent bystanders dead, are now common enough to concern all urban and many suburban residents. The inclination to violence springs from the circumstances of life among the ghetto poor—the lack of jobs that pay a living wage, the stigma of race, the fallout from rampant drug use and drug trafficking, and the resulting alienation and lack of hope for the future.

Simply living in such an environment places young people at special risk° of falling victim to aggressive behavior. Although there are often forces in the community which can counteract the negative influences, by far the most powerful being a strong, loving, "decent" (as inner-city residents put it) family committed to middle-class values, the despair is pervasive enough to have

---

°**at special risk:** Anderson is careful not to suggest that ghetto poverty always causes violence. He uses the expression "at special risk" to indicate that ghetto poverty increases the likelihood of violence.

spawned an oppositional culture, that of "the streets," whose norms are often consciously opposed to those of mainstream society. These two orientations—decent and street—socially organize the community, and their coexistence has important consequences for residents, particularly children growing up in the inner city. Above all, this environment means that even youngsters whose home lives reflect mainstream values—and the majority of homes in the community do—must be able to handle themselves in a street-oriented environment.

This is because the street culture has evolved what may be called a code of the streets, which amounts to a set of informal rules governing interpersonal public behavior, including violence. The rules prescribe both a proper comportment and a proper way to respond if challenged. They regulate the use of violence and so allow those who are inclined to aggression to precipitate violent encounters in an approved way. The rules have been established and are enforced mainly by the street-oriented, but on the streets the distinction between street and decent is often irrelevant; everybody knows that if the rules are violated, there are penalties. . . .

At the heart of the code is the issue of respect—loosely defined as being treated "right," or granted the deference one deserves. However, in the troublesome public environment of the inner city, as people increasingly feel buffeted by forces beyond their control, what one deserves in the way of respect becomes more and more problematic and uncertain. This in turn further opens the issue of respect to sometimes intense interpersonal negotiation. In the street culture, especially among young people, respect is viewed as almost an external entity that is hard-won but easily lost, and so must constantly be guarded. The rules of the code in fact provide a framework for negotiating respect. The person whose very appearance—including his clothing, demeanor, and way of moving—deters transgressions feels that he possesses, and may be considered by others to possess, a measure of respect. With the right amount of respect, for instance, he can avoid "being bothered" in public. If he is bothered, not only may he be in physical danger but he has been disgraced or "dissed" (disrespected). . . .

This hard reality can be traced to the profound sense of alienation from 5 mainstream society and its institutions felt by many poor inner-city black people, particularly the young. The code of the streets is actually a cultural adaptation to a profound lack of faith in the police and the judicial system. The police are most often seen as representing the dominant white society and not caring to protect inner-city residents. When called, they may not respond, which is one reason many residents feel they must be prepared to take extraordinary measures to defend themselves and their loved ones against those who are inclined to aggression. Lack of police accountability has in fact been incorporated into the status system: the person who is believed capable of "taking care of himself" is accorded a certain deference, which translates into a sense of physical and psychological control. Thus the street code emerges where the influence of the police ends and personal responsibility for one's safety is felt to begin. Exacerbated by the proliferation of drugs and easy access to guns, this volatile situation results in the ability of the street-oriented minority (or those who effectively "go for bad") to dominate the public spaces....

CAMPAIGNING FOR RESPECT

...At an early age, often even before they start school, children from street-oriented homes gravitate to the streets, where they "hang"—socialize with their peers. Children from these generally permissive homes have a great deal of latitude and are allowed to "rip and run" up and down the street. They often come home from school, put their books down, and go right back out the door. On school nights eight- and nine-year-olds remain out until nine or ten o'clock (and teenagers typically come in whenever they want to). On the streets they play in groups that often become the source of their primary social bonds. Children from decent homes tend to be more carefully supervised and are thus likely to have curfews and to be taught how to stay out of trouble.

When decent and street kids come together, a kind of social shuffle occurs in which children have a chance to go either way. Tension builds as a child comes to realize that he must choose an orientation. The kind of home he comes from influences but does not determine the way he will ultimately turn out—although it is unlikely that a child from a thoroughly street-oriented family will easily absorb decent values on the streets....

In the street, through their play, children pour their individual life experiences into a common knowledge pool, affirming, confirming, and elaborating on what they have observed in the home and matching their skills against those of others. And they learn to fight. Even small children test one another, pushing and shoving, and are ready to hit other children over circumstances not to their liking....

In addition, younger children witness the disputes of older children, which are often resolved through cursing and abusive talk, if not aggression or outright violence. They see that one child succumbs to the greater physical and mental abilities of the other. They are also alert and attentive witnesses to the verbal and physical fights of adults, after which they compare notes and share their interpretations of the event. In almost every case the victor is the person who physically won the altercation, and this person often enjoys the esteem and respect of onlookers....

Those street-oriented adults with whom children come in contact—including mothers, fathers, brothers, sisters, boyfriends, cousins, neighbors, and friends—help them along in forming this understanding by verbalizing the messages they are getting through experience: "Watch your back." "Protect yourself." "Don't punk out." "If somebody messes with you, you got to pay them back." "If someone disses you, you got to straighten them out." Many 10 parents actually impose sanctions if a child is not sufficiently aggressive. For example, if a child loses a fight and comes home upset, the parent might respond, "Don't you come in here crying that somebody beat you up; you better get back out there and whup his ass. I didn't raise no punks! Get back out there and whup his ass. If you don't whup his ass, I'll whup your ass when you come home." Thus the child obtains reinforcement for being tough and showing nerve....

Self-Image Based on "Juice"

By the time they are teenagers, most youths have either internalized the code of the streets or at least learned the need to comport themselves in accordance with its rules, which chiefly have to do with interpersonal communication. The code revolves around the presentation of self. Its basic requirement is the display of a certain predisposition to violence. Accordingly, one's bearing must send the unmistakable if sometimes subtle message to "the next person" in public that one is capable of violence and mayhem when the situation requires it, that one can take care of oneself....

Even so, there are no guarantees against challenges, because there are always people around looking for a fight to increase their share of respect—or "juice," as it is sometimes called on the street. Moreover, if a person is assaulted, it is important, not only in the eyes of his opponent but also in the eyes of his "running buddies," for him to avenge himself. Otherwise he risks being "tried" (challenged) or "moved on" by any number of others. To maintain his honor he must show he is not someone to be "messed with" or "dissed."...

An important aspect of this often violent give-and-take is its zero-sum quality. That is, the extent to which one person can raise himself up depends on his ability to put another person down. This underscores the alienation that permeates the inner-city ghetto community. There is a generalized sense that very little respect is to be had, and therefore everyone competes to get what affirmation he can of the little that is available. The craving for respect that results gives people thin skins. Shows of deference by others can be highly soothing, contributing to a sense of security, comfort, self-confidence, and self-respect. Transgressions by others which go unanswered diminish these feelings and are believed to encourage further transgressions. Hence one must be ever vigilant against the transgressions of others or even *appearing* as if transgressions will be tolerated. Among young people, whose sense of self-esteem is particularly vulnerable, there is an especially heightened concern with being disrespected. Many inner-city young men in particular crave respect to such a degree that they will risk their lives to attain and maintain it.

The issue of respect is thus closely tied to whether a person has an inclination to be violent, even as a victim. In the wider society people may not feel required to retaliate physically after an attack, even though they are aware that they have been degraded or taken advantage of. They may feel a great need to defend themselves *during* an attack, or to behave in such a way as to deter aggression (middle-class people certainly can and do become victims of street-oriented youths), but they are much more likely than street-oriented people to feel that they can walk away from a possible altercation with their self-esteem intact....

In impoverished inner-city black communities, however, particularly among 15 young males and perhaps increasingly among females, such flight would be extremely difficult. To run away would likely leave one's self-esteem in tatters. Hence people often feel constrained not only to stand up and at least attempt to resist during an assault but also to "pay back" — to seek revenge — after a successful assault on their person. This may include going to get a weapon or even getting relatives involved....

By Trial of Manhood

On the street, among males these concerns about things and identity have come to be expressed in the concept of "manhood." Manhood in the inner city means taking the prerogatives of men with respect to strangers, other men, and women — being distinguished as a man. It implies physicality and a certain ruthlessness....

Central to the issue of manhood is the widespread belief that one of the most effective ways of gaining respect is to manifest "nerve." Nerve is shown when one takes another person's possessions (the more valuable the better), "messes with" someone's woman, throws the first punch, "gets in someone's face," or pulls a trigger. Its proper display helps on the spot to check others who would violate one's person and also helps to build a reputation that works to prevent future challenges. But since such a show of nerve is a forceful expression of disrespect toward the person on the receiving end, the victim may be greatly offended and seek to retaliate with equal or greater force. A display of nerve, therefore, can easily provoke a life-threatening response, and the background knowledge of that possibility has often been incorporated into the concept of nerve.

True nerve exposes a lack of fear of dying. Many feel that it is acceptable to risk dying over the principle of respect. In fact, among the hard-core street-oriented, the clear risk of violent death may be preferable to being "dissed" by another. The youths who have internalized this attitude and convincingly display it in their public bearing are among the most threatening people of all, for it is commonly assumed that they fear no man.... When others believe this is one's position, it gives one a real sense of power on the streets. Such credibility is what many inner-city youths strive to achieve, whether they are decent or street-oriented, both because of its practical defensive value and because of the positive way it makes them feel about themselves. The difference between the decent and the street-oriented youth is often that the decent youth makes a conscious decision to appear tough and manly; in another setting—with teachers, say, or at his part-time job—he can be polite and deferential. The street-oriented youth, on the other hand, has made the concept of manhood a part of his very identity; he has difficulty manipulating it—it often controls him....

AN OPPOSITIONAL CULTURE

The attitudes of the wider society are deeply implicated in the code of the streets. Most people in inner-city communities are not totally invested in the code, but the significant minority of hard-core street youths who are have to maintain the code in order to establish reputations, because they have—or feel they have—few other ways to assert themselves. For these young people the standards of the street code are the only game in town. The extent to which some children—particularly those who through upbringing have become most alienated and those lacking in strong and conventional social support—experience, feel, and internalize racist rejection and contempt from mainstream society may strongly encourage them to express contempt for the more conventional society in turn. In dealing with this contempt and rejection, some youngsters will consciously invest themselves and their considerable mental resources in what amounts to an oppositional culture to preserve themselves and their self-respect. Once they do, any respect they might be able to garner in the wider system pales in comparison with the respect available in the local system; thus they often lose interest in even attempting to negotiate the mainstream system.

At the same time, many less alienated young blacks have assumed a street-oriented demeanor as a way of expressing their blackness while really embracing a much more moderate way of life; they, too, want a nonviolent setting in which to live and raise a family. These decent people are trying hard to be part of the mainstream culture, but the racism, real and perceived, that they encounter helps to legitimate the oppositional culture. And so on occasion they adopt street behavior. In fact, depending on the demands of the situation, many people in the community slip back and forth between decent and street behavior. [20]

A vicious cycle has thus been formed. The hopelessness and alienation many young inner-city black men and women feel, largely as a result of endemic joblessness° and persistent racism, fuels the violence they engage in. This violence serves to confirm the negative feelings many whites and some middle-class blacks harbor toward the ghetto poor, further legitimating the oppositional culture and the code of the streets in the eyes of many poor young blacks. Unless this cycle is broken, attitudes on both sides will become increasingly entrenched, and the violence, which claims victims black and white, poor and affluent, will only escalate.

°endemic joblessness: Joblessness that is permanent rather than just occasional or temporary.

LIFE WITHOUT FATHER

David Popenoe

David Popenoe, professor of sociology at Rutgers University, is a well-known researcher and writer on the family and former cochair of the Council on Families in America. His 1988 book Disturbing the Nest: Family Change and Decline in Modern Societies *examines the ways in which the family has become less important in modernized societies. This reading comes from his 1996 book* Life without Father: Compelling New Evidence That Fatherhood and Marriage Are Indispensable for the Good of Children and Society.

During the last two or three decades, there has been a lively debate about whether fathers and marriage are necessary for the well-being of children. In the early 1990s, the sides were sharply divided, with some lamenting the decline of the nuclear family and others defending single mothers. Since then, however, the lines in the debate have blurred. Some point out that the importance of two parents can be stressed without blaming single mothers. Others argue that new research shows greater than expected negative effects of divorce on children. Not everyone agrees. Popenoe has been criticized for his views and has entered vigorously into the debate.

As you read, pay attention to why Popenoe thinks children need fathers and why he believes a father's influence in the home can help prevent violence. Keep in mind that Popenoe is engaging in a lively debate and is marshaling all the supporting data he can to make his case. Note, too, that he deals with differing views within his own argument. For example, he asks questions (as in paragraph 13) and then spells out his opponents' reasons before countering with reasons of his own.

THE DECLINE OF FATHERHOOD

The decline of fatherhood is one of the most basic, unexpected, and extraordinary social trends of our time. The trend can be captured in a single telling statistic: in just three decades, from 1960 to 1990, the percentage of children living apart from their biological fathers more than doubled, from 17 percent to 36 percent. If this rate continues, by the turn of the century nearly 50 percent of American children will be going to sleep each night without being able to say good night to their dads.

No one predicted this trend, few researchers or government agencies have monitored it, and it is not widely discussed, even today. But its importance to society is second to none. Father absence is a major force lying behind many of the attention-grabbing issues that dominate the news: crime and delinquency; premature sexuality and out-of-wedlock teen births; deteriorating educational achievement; depression, substance abuse, and alienation among teenagers; and the growing number of women and children in poverty. These issues all point to a profound deterioration in the well-being of children....

FATHERS: ESSENTIAL BUT PROBLEMATIC

Across time and cultures, fathers have always been considered by societies to be essential—and not just for their sperm. Indeed, until today, no known society ever thought of fathers as potentially unnecessary. Biological fathers are everywhere identified, if possible, and play some role in their children's upbringing. Marriage and the nuclear family—mother, father, and children—are the most universal social institutions in existence. In no society has non-marital childbirth been the cultural norm. To the contrary, a concern for the "legitimacy" of children is another cultural near universal: The mother of an illegitimate child virtually everywhere has been regarded as a social deviant, if not a social outcast, and her child has been stigmatized.

At the same time, being a father is universally problematic for men and for their societies in a way that being a mother is not. While mothers the world over bear and nurture their young with an intrinsic acknowledgment and, most commonly, acceptance of their role, taking on the role of father is often filled with conflict, tension, distance, and doubt. Across societies, fathers may or may not be closely engaged with their children, reside with the mother, or see their father role as highly important.

The source of this sex-role difference can be plainly stated. Men are not bio-   5
logically as attuned to being committed fathers as women are to being committed mothers. Left culturally unregulated, men's sexual behavior can be promiscuous, their paternity casual, their commitment to families weak. Yet in virtually all societies, especially modern societies, both child and social well-being depend on high levels of paternal investment: the time, energy, and resources that fathers are willing to impart to their children.

That men are not perfectly attuned to fatherhood in biological terms is not to say that fathering behavior is foreign to the nature of men. Far from it. Evolutionary scientists tell us that the development of the fathering capacity and high paternal investments in offspring—features not common among our primate relatives—have been a source of enormous evolutionary advantage for human beings. Because human young are more dependent on adults for a longer period of their lives than any other species and human mothers require a great deal of help if their children are to survive, a key to human evolution was the capturing of male effort to the goal of childrearing. It is almost certainly the case that the human family is the oldest social institution, at heart a biological arrangement for raising children that has always involved fathers as well as mothers.

In recognition of the fatherhood problem—that fatherhood is essential but also somewhat problematic—human cultures have realized that sanctions° are necessary if paternal investments are to be maximized. The main cultural carrier of sanctions is the institution of marriage, a major purpose of which is to hold men to the reproductive pair bond. Simply defined, marriage is a relationship within which a community socially approves and encourages sexual intercourse and the birth of children. It is society's way of signaling to would-be parents of children that their long-term relationship together is socially important. As evidenced by the vows of fidelity and permanence that almost universally are part of the wedding ceremony, an important purpose of marriage is to hold the man to the union. Margaret Mead once said, with the fatherhood problem strongly in mind, that there is no society in the world where men will stay married for very long unless culturally required to do so.

FATHERHOOD AND MARRIAGE

Today, because the great social complexity of modern societies requires longer periods of socialization and dependency for children than ever before, the need for adult investments in children has reached new heights. In order to succeed economically in an increasingly technological society, children must be highly educated. In order to succeed socially and psychologically in an increasingly complex and heterogeneous culture, children must have strong and stable attachments to adults. Nonfamily institutions can help with education, but family and close-kin groups are essential for socioemotional success. Parents and other close relatives are still the persons most likely to have the motivational levels necessary to provide the time and attention that children need to feel loved and special.

Yet at the time when the childrearing task is ever more demanding and male assistance with the task is ever more important, cultural sanctions holding men to marriage and children have dramatically weakened. Marriage, once both sacred and economically essential for survival, is today based solely on the fragile tie of affection for one's mate. And whereas the institution of marriage once legally bound a couple with a high degree of permanence, marriages can now be broken unilaterally on a whim.

The United States has by far the highest divorce rate in the industrialized 10 world. The chance that a first marriage occurring today will end in divorce stands at around 50 percent—by some estimates as high as 60 percent. The chance in the middle of the last century was around 5 percent. In the past three

---

° **sanctions:** Rules or other mechanisms (such as social disapproval) that a society uses to encourage members to behave in ways that the society values.

decades alone, the divorce rate has doubled or tripled, depending upon how one calculates it. . . .

There has emerged in the last decade or two a tendency for women to go it alone. It would be nice, many of these women report, if the perfect man came into the picture. But he is not around, so I am going to have a child anyway. . . .

With this kind of cultural acceptance, it is little wonder that the percentage of out-of-wedlock births in America has increased 600 percent in just three decades, from 5 percent of all births in 1960 to 30 percent in 1991.[1] If the percentage keeps climbing at its current rate, 40 percent of all births (and 80 percent of minority births) will take place out of wedlock by the turn of the century.[2] . . .

THE FATHERHOOD DEBATE

Could it be that the era of fatherhood is at an end, that the fatherhood problem can be resolved by simply getting rid of fathers and perhaps substituting someone or something else in their stead? Is there something new and different about modern societies that makes single parenthood a reasonable option and makes these societies increasingly immune from the age-old proscription against illegitimacy? Have we become so free and individualized and prosperous that the traditional social structures surrounding family life no longer have the importance that they have had in all of human history to date?

Positive answers to these questions have been forcefully argued. The argument contains these key elements:

- Women no longer need men for provision or protection, the traditional male family roles. For provision, most women now have independent access to the labor market; and if they don't, they have access to government-supported welfare programs. For protection, women have the police, and in any event it is usually their male partner from whom they must be protected.
- Both single mothers and their children have been unfairly stigmatized over the generations. This has been grossly unfair to mothers as well as to the children who did absolutely nothing to bring about their plight. Societies today are able, thankfully, to correct this age-old injustice.
- Male-female family life is inherently inequitable, a patriarchal institution wherein men have always dominated women. Men are selfish, irresponsible, psychologically untrustworthy, even intractable. If women are to achieve true equality, therefore, we must find some alternative to the nuclear family.

---

[1]U.S. Department of Health and Human Services. *Vital Statistics of the United States, 1991*. Vol. 1, *Natality*. Washington, DC: GPO, 1993. Among blacks, the increase has been from 23% to 68%.

[2]Congressional testimony of Lee Rainwater, Harvard University. Cited in William J. Bennett. 1994. *The Index of Leading Cultural Indicators*. New York: Simon and Schuster, p. 47.

- Men frequently leave their wives and children in the lurch, especially in times of crisis, either through psychological withdrawal or outright desertion. It is safer for a woman never to begin counting on a man.
- It is not clear that fathers any longer provide something unique to their children. There is not much they do that mothers do not, or cannot, do just as well.

There is some truth, of course, to each of these points. Many women to- 15 day are perfectly capable, in economic and other terms, of raising children by themselves. The traditional stigma against illegitimacy is something that few people want to bring back. There does seem to be some kind of inherent inequality between men and women, if nothing more than that men are bigger and stronger and more aggressive. The selfish, irresponsible male is not uncommon. And since some fathers and mothers do carry out the same childrearing activities, the question of why we need both is a reasonable one to ask.

But the aim . . . is to try to convince you that this no-father argument is fundamentally wrong. If we continue down the path of fatherlessness, we are headed for social disaster.

FATHERS AND MOTHERS

. . . In my many years as a functioning social scientist, I know of few other bodies of evidence whose weight leans so much in one direction as does the evidence about family structure: On the whole, two parents — a father and a mother — are better for the child than one parent.[3]

There are, to be sure, many complicating factors to the simple proposition that two parents are best. Family structure is only a gross approximation of what actually goes on within a family. We all know of a two-parent family that is the family from hell. A child can certainly be well-raised to adulthood by one loving parent who is wholly devoted to that child's well-being. But such problems and exceptions in no way deny the aggregate finding or generalization. . . .

What does the social science evidence about family structure and child well-being actually show? Researchers Sara McLanahan and Gary Sandefur recently examined six nationally representative data sets containing over twenty-five

---

[3]It should be noted that social science evidence is never conclusive, on this or any other matter we will be taking up in this book. The world is too complex; the scientific method can only imperfectly be applied to the study of human beings; researchers have biases; and people may not always be telling investigators the truth. These are but a few of the many problems endemic to the social sciences. The best use of the social science evidence is to help confirm or disconfirm. Does the evidence generally support a proposition or not? If it does, fine; if it does not, one had better have a good explanation as to why that proposition may still be true.

thousand children from a variety of racial and social-class backgrounds. Their conclusion:

> Children who grow up with only one of their biological parents (nearly always the mother) are disadvantaged across a broad array of outcomes... they are twice as likely to drop out of high school, 2.5 times as likely to become teen mothers, and 1.4 times as likely to be idle—out of school and out of work—as children who grow up with both parents.[4]

Sure, you may say, that is because one-parent families are poorer. But here is 20 the researchers' conclusion about the economic factor:

> Loss of economic resources accounts for about 50 percent of the disadvantages associated with single parenthood. Too little parental supervision and involvement and greater residential mobility account for most of the rest.[5]

Many other researchers... have come up with similar conclusions. The evidence covers the full range of possible effects, from crime to school achievement. Social analysts William A. Galston and Elaine Ciulla Kamark report, for example, that

> The relationship [between family structure and crime] is so strong that controlling for family configuration erases the relationship between race and crime and between low income and crime. This conclusion shows up again and again in the literature.[6]

Based on such evidence, a strong case can be made that paternal deprivation, in the form of the physical, economic, and emotional unavailability of fathers to their children, has become the most prevalent form of child maltreatment in America today.

THE UNIQUENESS OF FATHERS

What is unique about fathers when compared to mothers? Studies show that virtually all children clearly distinguish a mother role from a father role, even if some contemporary adults do not seem to be able to.[7] Fathers and mothers differ, just as males and females differ. Part of the reason is cultural, to be sure, but only part. Inborn biology is also a major contributor....

---

[4]Sara S. McLanahan. 1994. "The Consequences of Single Motherhood." *The American Prospect,* 18:48–58, esp. 49.

[5]McLanahan. *Consequences,* p. 52.

[6]Elaine Ciulla Kamark and William A. Galston. 1990. *Putting Children First: A Progressive Family Policy for the 1990s.* Washington, DC: Progressive Policy Institute, pp. 14–15.

[7]Henry B. Biller. 1993. *Fathers and Families: Paternal Factors in Child Development.* Westport, CT: Auburn House.

Across all cultures, the "natural and comfortable" way most males think, feel, and act is fundamentally different from the way most females think, feel, and act. Differences between men and women have been found universally with respect to four behavioral/psychological traits: aggression and general activity level; cognitive skills; sensory sensitivity; and sexual and reproductive behavior.[8] Perhaps the greatest difference is in aggression and activity level. Almost from the moment of birth, boys tend to be more aggressive and in general to have a somewhat higher activity level than girls....

How do the inherent male-female differences express themselves in dissimilar fathering and mothering behaviors? In dealing with infants, there is an enormous and obvious difference that stems from the woman's having carried the child in utero and from her ability to breast-feed. But beyond that, as Alice Rossi has noted based on an accumulating body of evidence, "In caring for a nonverbal, fragile infant, women have a head start." They are more able to read an infant's facial expressions, handle with tactile gentleness, and soothe with the use of voice.[9] With toddlers, while women provide comfort and emotional acceptance, men typically are more active and arousing in their nurturing activities, fostering certain physical skills and emphasizing autonomy and independence.

Even with older children the father's mode of parenting is not interchange- 25 able with the mother's. Men typically emphasize play more than caretaking, and their play is more likely to involve a rough-and-tumble approach.[10] In attitude and behavior, mothers tend to be responsive and fathers firm; mothers stress emotional security and relationships, and fathers stress competition and risk taking; mothers typically express more concern for the child's immediate well-being, while fathers express more concern for the child's long-run autonomy and independence.

The importance of these different approaches for the growing child should not be underestimated. All children have the need for affiliation with others but also the drive to go off on their own, to be independent. They need both the personal security brought by strong social ties ("roots") and the push away from the group toward eventual autonomy ("wings"). They need a parent who

[8]Eleanor E. Maccoby and Carol N. Jacklin. 1974. *The Psychology of Sex Differences.* Palo Alto, CA: Stanford University Press. J. Archer and B. Lloyd. 1985. *Sex and Gender.* New York: Cambridge University Press. Robert Pool. 1994. *Eve's Rib: Searching for the Biological Roots of Sex Differences.* New York: Crown.

[9]Alice Rossi. 1987. "Parenthood in Transition: From Lineage to Child to Self-Orientation." Pp. 31–81 in Jane B. Lancaster, Jeanne Altmann, Alice Rossi, and Lonnie R. Sherrod, eds., *Parenting Across the Life Span: Biosocial Dimensions.* New York, NY: Aldine de Gruyter, p. 69.

[10]M. W. Yogman. 1982. "Development of the Father-Infant Relationship." Pp. 221–280 in H. E. Fitzgerald, B. M. Lester, and M. W. Yogman, eds., *Theory and Research in Behavioral Pediatrics 1.* New York: Plenum Press; J. L. Roopnarine and N. S. Mounts. 1985. "Mother-Child and Father-Child Play." *Early Child Development Care* 20:157–169.

says "strive, do better, challenge yourself," along with one who comforts them when they fall short.

For boys in modern societies, in order to counterbalance a common behavioral tendency, it is important, if they are to excel in life, to stress affiliation with family and community. For girls, for the same reason, it is important to stress independence. But for both sexes the resolution and balancing of these forces is one of the key components of maturation and personal achievement.

Certainly in a pinch, men and women, fathers and mothers, can play each other's parts in the script of life. Indeed, people can be taught to do almost anything. But most men and women are not predisposed or well-motivated to take on even temporarily the behavior and attitudes of the other sex. And most children want and need and can easily detect the real thing. Fatherless children are therefore at a distinct psychological disadvantage, as a growing body of evidence attests.

THE UNATTACHED MALE

Apart from enhancing children's lives, there are other good reasons why it is important for men to be engaged in parenting. One socially crucial reason is contained in this caveat: Every society must be wary of the unattached male, for he is universally the cause of numerous social ills. The good society is heavily dependent on men being attached to a strong moral order centered on families, not only to help raise children but to discipline their own sexual behavior and to reduce their competitive aggression.

Family life is a considerable civilizing force for men. It is not uncommon to 30 hear men say, for example, that they will give up certain deviant or socially irresponsible behavior only when they have children, for then they feel the need to set a good example. Long ago the great sociologist Emile Durkheim noted that married men experience a "salutary discipline"; marriage forces men to master their passions, but it also encourages the regular work habits and self-sacrifice required to meet the family's material needs.[11]

A high proportion of male criminals are unattached. Unattached men are more likely to behave criminally and violently than attached men; they are also more likely to die prematurely through disease, accidents, or self-neglect....

So even those who disagree that fathers are essential to sound childrearing and feel sanguine about unmarried women taking on the task by themselves still should worry about how the men left out will be spending their time. Do we really want a society filled with single men, unattached to children, leading self-aggrandizing and often predatory lives?

---

[11] Emile Durkheim. 1951. *Suicide: A Study in Sociology.* New York: Free Press.

JUVENILE DELINQUENCY AND VIOLENCE

Of all the negative consequences of fatherlessness, juvenile delinquency and violence probably loom largest in the public mind: There are too many little boys with guns. A 550 percent increase in reported violent crime has occurred since 1960, while the population has gone up by only 41 percent. The segment of the population with the fastest-growing crime rate is juveniles. Serious violent crime used to be an adult phenomenon, but arrests of juveniles for murder went up by 128 percent between 1983 and 1992. A study of the officially recorded criminality of two groups of Philadelphia boys, those born in 1945 and those born in 1958, found that the later group was three times more likely to commit violent crimes and five times more likely to commit robberies.[12] Killers and killed alike are younger than ever.

One can point to many recent changes in our society that have fed this outburst of violence among juveniles, including the lethal combination of guns and drugs in our inner cities, the decline of low-skilled jobs, and the violent themes of popular culture. But behind it all there lurks the strong probability that a key underlying cause is the rapid growth of fatherlessness. Many people have an intuitive presumption that fatherlessness must be related to delinquency and violence, and based on the research that has been conducted, the weight of evidence strongly buttresses that presumption. Juvenile delinquency and violence are clearly generated disproportionately° by youths in mother-only households and in other households where the biological father is not present.[13]

What is the evidence? First, there are large-scale studies of statistical associ- 35
ation. A statistical review of fifty major studies on the effects of family structure on delinquency concluded that "the effect of intact versus 'broken' families is a consistent and real pattern of association°...the prevalence of delinquency in broken homes is 10–15 percent higher than in intact homes."[14] Similarly, a review of all significant studies of the impact of divorce on children conducted

---

°**disproportionately:** Popenoe makes another statistical point here: that the percentage of juvenile delinquents coming from mother-only households represents a higher (and therefore "disproportionate") percentage of the total number of juvenile delinquents than might be expected, given the percentage of mother-only households in the population.   °**pattern of association:** Though delinquency and broken families seem to be associated, it is not clear that one causes the other.

[12]Paul E. Tracy, Marvin E. Wolfgang, and Robert M. Figlio. 1990. *Delinquency Careers in Two Birth Cohorts.* New York: Plenum Press.

[13]We do not have the evidence to demonstrate *conclusively* that fatherlessness is a major cause of increased delinquency and violent behavior among adolescents and young adults. Given the complexities of the issue, fully conclusive evidence will probably never exist. Nevertheless, the present evidence is substantial and convincing.

[14]L. Edward Wells and Joseph H. Rankin. 1991. "Families and Delinquency: A Meta-Analysis of the Impact of Broken Homes." *Social Problems* 38(1):71–93 (p. 87).

in the past few decades found that "research on antisocial behavior consistently illustrates that adolescents in mother-only households and in conflict-ridden families are more prone to commit delinquent acts."[15]

Comparable findings come from the National Surveys of Children, a major longitudinal study done in two waves. The study found that family disruption "was associated with a higher incidence of several behavior problems, negative effects being greatest with multiple marital transitions."[16] The behavior problems included depression/withdrawal, antisocial behavior, impulsive/hyperactive behavior, and school behavior problems. One important finding was that a child living with a custodial parent of the opposite sex is especially prone to problem behavior. Given the makeup of most single-parent families, this applies mainly to boys living with their mothers.

Reviewing all such studies, criminologists Michael R. Gottfredson and Travis Hirschi concluded in their influential work *A General Theory of Crime* that "in most (but not all) studies that directly compare children living with both biological parents with children living in 'broken' or reconstituted homes, the children from intact homes have lower rates of crime."[17] The findings of the large-scale social surveys are corroborated by° those of so-called ecological studies that examine the association of factors in particular areas of cities or geographic regions. From such studies, Gottfredson and Hirschi concluded that "such family measures as the percentage of the population divorced, the percentage of households headed by women, and the percentage of unattached individuals in the community are among the most powerful predictors of crime rates."[18]

Sixty percent of America's rapists, 72 percent of adolescent murderers, and 70 percent of long-term prison inmates come from fatherless homes.[19] . . . This is no statistical artifact. Fathers are important to their sons as role models. They are important for maintaining authority and discipline. And they are important in helping their sons to develop both self-control and feelings of empathy toward others, character traits that are found to be lacking in violent youth.

Unfortunately, the die for the near future has already been cast. The teenage population is expected to rise in the next decade by as much as 20 percent,

---

° **corroborated by:** Reinforced by.

[15] David H. Demo and Alan C. Acock. 1988. "The Impact of Divorce on Children." *Journal of Marriage and the Family* 50(3):619–648 (p. 639).

[16] James L. Peterson and Nicholas Zill. 1986. "Marital Disruption, Parent-Child Relationships, and Behavior Problems in Children." *Journal of Marriage and the Family* 48(2):295–307 (p. 295).

[17] Michael R. Gottfredson and Travis Hirschi. 1990. *A General Theory of Crime.* Stanford, CA: Stanford University Press, p. 103.

[18] Ibid., p. 103. See also Robert J. Sampson. "Urban Black Violence: The Effect of Male Joblessness and Family Disruption." *American Journal of Sociology* (1987) 93:348–382.

[19] Data provided by the National Fatherhood Initiative.

even more for minority teenagers, as the children of the baby boomers grow up. This has prompted criminologist James Fox to assert: "There is a tremendous crime wave coming in the next 10 years." It will be fueled not by old, hardened criminals but by what Fox calls "the young and the ruthless"—children in their early and mid-teens who are turning murderous. In 1993 there were 3,647 teenage killers; by 2005 he expects there will be 6,000 of them.[20] If fatherlessness continues to increase, we face even more dangerous times ahead. . . .

There is strong evidence that tendencies toward antisocial behavior first 40 emerge in childhood and are relatively stable across the stages of life into adulthood.[21] This is especially true of male aggressiveness. Most adult criminals, in other words, manifested antisocial tendencies already in childhood (that is not to say that all antisocial children become adult criminals). . . .

Which childhood experiences are most important? Family, neighborhood, peer group, and popular culture all play some role. General agreement exists within the social science community, however, that antisocial behavior in children is heavily a product of the socialization and social control processes employed by parents. James Q. Wilson, one of America's leading criminological experts, attests: "A large body of data has demonstrated beyond much doubt the powerful effect on aggressiveness and delinquency of being raised in a family that is discordant, lacking in affection, or given to inappropriate disciplinary practices."[22]

In their recent reanalysis of the pioneering data set first collected in the late 1930s and early 1940s by Sheldon and Eleanor Glueck of the Harvard Law School, researchers Robert J. Sampson and John H. Laub found strong corroborating evidence for the importance of early childhood experiences. The Gluecks' data set, designed to uncover the causes of delinquency and adult crime, compared the life course from childhood to adulthood of five hundred delinquents with five hundred nondelinquents, all of whom were white males who grew up in the Boston slums. The Gluecks collected data from a wide variety of sources, including teacher reports, psychiatric interviews, health and welfare records, employer assessments, and extensive interviews with the subjects and their families. Sampson and Laub reached this conclusion: "Low levels of parental supervision, erratic, threatening, and harsh discipline, and weak parental attachment were strongly and directly related to delinquency."[23]

A recent authoritative report entitled *Violence,* prepared by the Panel on the Understanding and Control of Violent Behavior of the National Research

---

[20] Quoted in Joe Urschel. "Expert Seeks Classroom of Millions." *USA Today,* April 11, 1995, p. 1.

[21] Robert J. Sampson and John H. Laub. 1992. "Crime and Deviance in the Life Course." *Annual Review of Sociology* 18:63–84.

[22] James Q. Wilson. 1991. *On Character.* Washington, DC: AEI Press, p. 59.

[23] Robert J. Sampson and John H. Laub. 1993. *Crime in the Making.* Cambridge, MA: Harvard University Press, p. 247.

Council, summarizes what we now know: "Researchers have identified many correlates and antecedents of aggressive childhood behavior that are presumed to reflect psychosocial influences [including] early family experiences: harsh and erratic discipline, lack of parental nurturance, physical abuse and neglect, poor supervision, and early separation of children from parents."[24] The report continues: "Numerous studies show that violent offenders tend to come from certain types of family backgrounds. In particular, they tend to have been subjected to physical punishment, they tend to have alcoholic or criminal parents, and they tend to have disharmonious parents who are likely to separate or divorce."[25]

Where do fathers fit into this picture? A major contribution of involved fathers, according to researchers, is to teach their children two key character traits: self-control and empathy. People with antisocial and criminal tendencies lack both of these traits; that is, they "tend to be impulsive, insensitive, physical (as opposed to mental), risk-taking, short-sighted, and nonverbal, and they will tend therefore to engage in criminal and analogous acts."[26]

The lack of self-control in adulthood is closely associated with the absence of powerful and necessary "inhibiting forces" in early childhood, forces which can now be identified with some clarity following several decades of intense study by social scientists.[27] These inhibiting forces consist of parental child-rearing practices which are able "to set clear rules, to monitor behavior, and to make rewards contingent on good behavior and punishment contingent on bad behavior."[28] The development of empathy in children, in turn, is strongly associated with childrearing approaches that involve reasoning with children (rather than disciplining without reasoning), teaching about the consequences of their actions on others, and eschewing authoritarian and/or harsh disciplinary methods.[29]

It is entirely possible, of course, for a single mother to follow these childrearing practices and bring up children who possess a high degree of social control and empathy, but it is certainly more difficult for one parent than for two.

---

[24] Albert J. Reis, Jr., and Jeffrey A. Roth, eds. 1993. *Understanding and Preventing Violence.* Washington, DC: National Academy Press, p. 105.

[25] Ibid., p. 368.

[26] Gottfredson and Hirschi. 1990, p. 90.

[27] Ibid., p. 255.

[28] Ibid., p. 68.

[29] Nancy Eisenberg and Paul H. Mussen. 1989. *The Roots of Prosocial Behavior in Children.* Cambridge: Cambridge University Press. For the development of both self-control and empathy, in addition, it is important for children to be strongly "attached" to their parents, to regard their parents with love and respect, and for the children's parents to be good role models (and especially not be criminals themselves!).

THE SCAPEGOAT GENERATION

Mike A. Males

Mike A. Males, a journalist and social ecologist, is the author of a number of articles on youth and social issues. He is a former youth program worker who has published in the Lancet, *the* New York Times, *the* Progressive, Adolescence, *and elsewhere. He wrote the entry on children's violence in the* Encyclopedia of Violence in America *as well as the 1996 book* The Scapegoat Generation: America's War on Adolescents, *from which this reading comes.*

Males argues that statistics about violence by young men have been greatly exaggerated and misused by the media and politicians and that the underlying cause of violence by young men lies in their having been treated violently by their parents. Males's argument could be placed alongside the earlier readings arguing that poverty causes violence, because he thinks it is poverty that causes abuse within the family as well as violence outside the family. Males also offers an alternative perspective on David Popenoe's argument about the family.

As you read, note Males's distinction between violence in the home and violence in the streets and try to understand the role he thinks poverty plays in creating the conditions for violence and how adults' violence is related to youths' violence.

When a 3-year-old Los Angeles girl was murdered in an apparent gang killing in September 1995, the press headlined the story and President Clinton rightly called a "day of mourning" for child victims of street violence. When a 3-year-old Beverly Hills boy was murdered by his 37-year-old father three weeks later, the story drew little attention or politician outrage. When a national child abuse commission reported in April 1995 that 2,000 American children per year are murdered by their parents and caretakers, Clinton and other leaders didn't bother to comment.[1] But the September 1995 decision by Time-Warner Records to cut loose its rap music label was widely hailed by politicians as a victory over youth mayhem. The official view must be that the words of rap songs are a bigger incitement to teen violence than the fists, sticks, sexual assaults, and other substantiated physical brutalities inflicted on 350,000 children and adolescents every year by the adults they should be able to trust the most.[2] . . .

[1]U.S. Advisory Board on Child Abuse and Neglect (1995, April), *A nation's shame: Fatal child abuse and neglect in the United States.* Washington, DC: U.S. Congress. See also Rivera C (1995, 26 April). Child abuse in U.S. at crisis level, panel says. *Los Angeles Times,* pp. A1, A23.

[2]National Center on Child Abuse and Neglect (1995, April). National child abuse and neglect data system. *Child maltreatment, 1993.* In U.S. Bureau of the Census (1993). *Statistical abstract of the United States, 1995.* Washington, DC: U.S. Department of Commerce, Table 346.

From the Washington and media depiction, no one would guess another fact shown in FBI figures[3] year after year: Two-thirds of all murdered youths are slain by adults, not by other youths. In a 1993 tabulation of 11,000 murders by age of victim and killer, the FBI reported that 70 percent of the murderers of children/youths and 92 percent of the slayers of adults were adults. But grownup voters and media patrons don't want to hear about that, so it is not officially talked about....

I recently asked a guard at Chino, a prison 40 miles east of Los Angeles stuffed with 2,500 of California's most dangerous 16–24-year-old rapists, murderers, and batterers, how many had been violently abused at home. "One thousand percent," he said. I asked the same question 1,200 miles away and a few years earlier of the superintendent of Montana's Pine Hills youth detention center, Al Davis:

> "All of our kids at Pine Hills have been neglected or abused in one way or another," Davis said. "...In most cases, we should leave the kid home and send the parents to Pine Hills."

A remarkable study in Sacramento, California, found that while only 1.4 percent of the county's children ages nine to twelve had come to the attention of child protective authorities due to victimization by abuse or neglect, the same 1,000 children accounted for half of the city's arrests for crimes committed by youths in that age group.[4]

Bureau of Justice Statistics reports show that while youths predominate in street violence, adults are the aggressors in home violence. Parents are six times more likely to murder their teenage children than the other way around.[5] And like nearly all youth and adult behaviors, the two are linked. A 1992 National Institute of Justice study found that child abuse is a factor in at least 40 percent of the nation's violent crime.[6]

President Clinton vows to punish his stock villain, "13-year-olds...with automatic weapons,"[7] but neglects to discuss the fact that 49-year-olds (Clinton's age) murder twice as many people.[8] In the equation of rising American brutality, young age is the most politically expedient characteristic to blame—

[3]FBI (1994). *Uniform crime reports for the United States 1993*. Washington, DC: U.S. Department of Justice, Table 2.7.

[4]Liederman D (1995, 17 November). Does America really care about its teen parents? Phoenix, AZ: Address to the annual conference of the National Organization on Adolescent Pregnancy, Parenting, and Prevention. Washington, DC: Child Welfare League.

[5]Bureau of Justice Statistics (1994, July). *Murder in families*. Special Report, NCJ-143498. Washington, DC: U.S. Department of Justice, Tables 1, 2, 8.

[6]Widom CS (1992, October). *The cycle of violence*. Washington, DC: U.S. Department of Justice, p. 1.

[7]Associated Press (1994, 14 November), Washington, DC.

[8]FBI (1994), *op cit*, Table 38.

and among the least-important real-world characteristics. There is no such thing as "youth violence," except in the same sense that there is "Sagittarian violence" (One in 12 killers! Tripled since 1960!) or "Smith violence" (The leading name of U.S. murderers!) or "Brown-eyed violence" (don't even calculate).

Most people, especially experts, would find such a statement—"there is no such thing as youth violence"—incredible. They would point to the doubling in homicide and 70 percent rise in violent crime arrests among 13–19-year-olds in the last decade, the gangland drive-bys, the 135,000 school gun toters, the pipe-stabbings and wildings and cold-eyed sixth grade shootists. Yet all of these are predictable results of the doubling in youth poverty over the past 20 years. A nation that adds 6 million young to its poverty rolls—especially under circumstances in which older age groups are becoming richer—can expect an increase in street violence among youths compared to adults. It is a tragic and unnecessary development. But it is not one that should be generating the pious shock and bewilderment among those familiar with the causes of violence.

Youth violence is primarily a sociological issue, flowing from the larger conditions in which minority youths are raised. The stresses and violence of growing up impoverished push marginal youth toward violence, as the 16-fold higher murder arrest rate for black Los Angeles teenagers compared to white L.A. teens...demonstrates. Adults subjected to similar levels of poverty are similarly violent. Yet national and state youth violence policies continue to mistreat it as a "psychological" problem located within the heads of adolescents, a strategy that guarantees no option other than to lock up ever-growing numbers of nonwhite youths under conditions in which most can never be released to society. *The most effective anti-violence policy that can be adopted is to raise fewer children in poverty....*

GENDER AND VIOLENCE

Violent crime, both in its high incidence and rising trend, is a male issue. In 1993, FBI *Uniform Crime Reports*[9] showed that males under the age of 20 were involved in 7,180 homicide arrests, compared to 430 for teenage females. Teenage males accounted for 94 percent of the homicide and 88 percent of the violent crime arrests involving teenagers.

Females age 15–19, in contrast, had lower murder arrest rates than men in 10 their 50s. Further, while murder arrests among teenage males have skyrocketed since the mid-1980s, those among females have been stable. In 1993, females age 10–19 accounted for 8 percent of the nation's over-10 population, but less than 2 percent of its murder arrests and just 3 percent of its violent crime

---

[9]U.S. Federal Bureau of Investigation (1994), *op cit,* Table 39 and previous annual, table of arrests by offense, age, gender.

arrests. Teenage female violence, while occasionally media sensationalized, is not a threat to public safety.

Violence is not simply a male, but an adult male issue. Like teenage males, adult males accounted for nine in ten violent crime arrests involving adults in 1993. Adult men over age 20 accounted for two-thirds of all violent crime arrests in 1993. Of particular concern, men ages 20–44 — the age most likely to be parents — accounted for just 24 percent of the over-10 population, but comprised 55 percent of the nation's homicide and 57 percent of its violent crime arrestees. No presidential commissions, Congressional hearings, or *Newsweek* cover stories on middle-aged male slaughter.

Predictably, officials have sought to blame the least culpable group — teenage females — for male violence. In 1994, Surgeon General Joycelyn Elders claimed that children of unwed teenage mothers account for nearly all crime. This claim was based on the "evidence" of a few hours' of uncontrolled surveys in a New York central-city ward where virtually all parents are severely impoverished blacks or Hispanics. And as usual, the media tagged along. *Time* magazine, citing no reason and zero documentation, blamed "14-year-old mothers" for "all these 16-year-old predators."[10] Perfect: The whole violence enchilada, from alpha to omega, birth to murder, is the fault of teenagers.

Except that the statement is factually ridiculous. The proportion of young men arrested (a staggering 25 percent per year for 18–24-year-olds)[11] far exceeds the proportion ever born to unwed teenage mothers (8 percent per year).[12] Even if every unwed teen mom's son grew up to be a thug and was arrested every year, only one-third of violent crime could be explained thereby. Teenage mothers are no more likely to raise poorly developed children than adult mothers from similar backgrounds.[13] Yet it is likely that offspring of teenage mothers are disproportionately likely to be arrested, just as it is known that children of poorer, nonwhite mothers comprise a large majority of violent crime arrests....

POVERTY AND VIOLENCE

The official/media-generated crisis of "children killing children" (and innocent adults) collapses in one simple calculation: Divide the arrest rate for murder or violent crime (which includes murder, rape, robbery, and aggravated assault)

[10] Gibbs N (1994, 20 June). The vicious cycle. *Time*, pp. 27–28.

[11] Law Enforcement Information Center (1995). *Crime and delinquency in California, 1993*. Sacramento, CA: California Department of Justice, Tables 33, 35.

[12] Center for Health Statistics (1994). California resident live births, 1993, by age of father and mother, race (printout). Sacramento, CA: Department of Health Services.

[13] Geronimus AT, Korenman S, Hillemeier MM (1994, September). Does young maternal age adversely affect child development? *Population and Development Review* 20, 585–609.

for each age group by the number of persons in that age group living in poverty. The result: The fact that teenagers are more likely to live in poverty than adults in their 20s and 30s fully explains the higher rates of murder and violent crime among teenagers. Let us take 1992 as the most recent year for which both crime and poverty figures are available (Table 5.4).

For every 1,000 persons living in poverty, 1.2 murder and 35 violent crime 15 arrests can be expected for teens, a rate lower than that of persons age 20–24 and similar to that of persons age 25–34. In older age groups, violent crime declines geometrically, as do poverty rates. Poverty does not seem to provoke the same kind of public violence (the kind usually resulting in arrest) among persons over age 40 as among persons in their teens, 20s, and 30s, perhaps because most habitually violent people have been killed or incarcerated by that age. Or it may be that poverty is not a straight-line predictor of violence. Above a certain threshold—with respect to blacks and Latinos ages 15–34 in particular—widespread poverty appears to foster a "critical mass" of groups who operate outside the law (i.e., gangs) and who therefore enforce their interests by means of violence,[14] increasing the violent crime rate more than poverty alone would predict.

There is no discernible difference in violence between adolescents and the adults of the age groups who are raising them. Teenagers do not respond to poverty more or less violently than do grownups; teenagers just experience

Table 5.4
Poverty Has Similar Effects on Teenage and Adult Violence

	Arrests for:			Arrests per 1,000 Persons Living in Poverty	
Age	Homicides	Violent Crimes	Population below Poverty Level	Homicides	Violence
9–12	40	11,011	3,440,000	0.1	3.2
13–19	6,693	196,135	5,550,000	1.2	35.3
20–24	6,109	157,179	3,120,000	2.0	50.4
25–34	5,920	240,335	5,540,000	1.1	43.4
35–44	2,766	113,930	3,940,000	0.7	28.9
45–59	1,393	40,091	3,320,000	0.4	12.1
60–older	408	8,895	5,100,000	0.1	1.7

Sources: U.S. Federal Bureau of Investigation (1994). *Uniform Crime Reports for the United States, 1992.* Washington, DC: U.S. Department of Justice, Table 38; U.S. Bureau of the Census (1994). *Poverty in the United States, 1992.* Current Population Series P60-185. Washington, DC: U.S. Department of Commerce, Table 5.

[14]See Blumstein (1995, August), *op cit,* pp. 5–6.

more poverty. Once the poverty factor is removed, "teen violence" disappears, and with it all the agonized why-why-why saturating the media and political landscape (usually fanned by experts who should know better) whenever the cameras roll to another teen murder scene.

The uniquely rising rate of poverty among youths parallels the unique rise in violent crime among youths. This trend shows up most clearly in the disparity in poverty between young and old. In 1959, children were 1.4 times more likely than adults to live in poverty. By 1969, after the successes of the war on poverty, the child/adult poverty ratio bottomed out at 1.2. For a brief five years or so, the U.S. flirted with the standard of other industrial societies in having only a slightly higher child than adult poverty level. It was a standard the rising self-centeredness of post-1970 grownups could not sustain. As young-family poverty programs were selectively dismantled in the 1970s and '80s while adult anti-poverty measures retained generous funding, the number of children living in poverty rose by 6 million.

In 1992, children were 2.1 times more likely [than] adults to live in poverty, a gap wider than any in the decades in which statistics have been kept. By the late 1980s, these rising numbers of tots born into poverty from the mid-1970s on were maturing into teenhood. Predicting a rise in youth violence beginning in the late 1980s from that pattern is not exactly sociological rocket science.

In California of 1993, one in four black, and one in five Hispanic, males ages 18–24 is arrested for a felony every year. This is many times the white and Asian arrest rate.[15] The large disparity in poverty among racial/ethnic groups is the single most consistent social factor explaining the large difference in violence among these groups. Poverty should not be misunderstood as some kind of imperative, however. Most poor people are not violent. As Table 5.4 indicates, 96 percent of all poor people will not be arrested for a violent offense and 99.9 percent will not commit murder in a given year. But the ongoing criminological debate over whether poverty *causes* an *individual* to be violent is not as important to the study of youth violence as is its effect on entire populations. No serious observer disputes the larger fact that if 6 million poor are added to any population (as we have done for youth since 1970), that population will display more violence.

This is not a concept we have trouble grasping when adults are impover- 20 ished. What Los Angeles County Children's Services director Peter Digre reports from practical experience is what research has amply showed: "We've learned from past experience that whatever undermines the economic well-being of families immediately translates into increased child abuse."[16]

. . . If the U.S. wants less juvenile violence, serious consideration needs to be

---

[15]Law Enforcement Information Center (1995), *op cit.*

[16]Terry GP (1995, 22 October). Peter Digre: Trying to protect children enmeshed in the welfare-reform plans. *Los Angeles Times*, p. M3.

given to the societally inflicted violence of raising three to 10 times more youth in poverty than other Western nations.[17]...

Adult Violence against Youth

The only political candidate I have encountered who made adult violence against children a major campaign theme was Mike McGrath, the Lewis and Clark county attorney who ran for the office of Montana attorney general in 1988. "In my years in law enforcement, I have never seen a serious criminal who wasn't abused as a child," McGrath told me. "Most were physically abused, some were sexually abused, and all of them were emotionally abused. People are raised to be criminals."...

McGrath lost, though not by a wide margin. Analysts agreed with McGrath that the child abuse theme was not a vote-enhancer. Not like, say, blaming Beavis and Butt-head.

However uncomfortable it makes adults to hear about it, along with poverty, household violence against children and teens is the foundation of youth crime. Yet officials seem unable to comprehend that violence, like cigarette smoking and other behaviors, does not *begin* with adolescents. It is the manifestation of years of negative childhood experiences and conditions. Within the official and media preoccupation with youth crime as the major category of violence, adult violence against children and teenagers is distinctly downplayed, except when celebrities or spectacle are involved. It is under-investigated, under-reported, and under-prosecuted.

The U.S. Advisory Board on Child Abuse and Neglect reported in April 1995 25 that violence, mostly by adult parents and caretakers, kills 2,000 children and seriously injures 140,000 more per year. Worse still, the Board found, was the indifference:

> When it comes to deaths of infants and children...at the hands of parents or care-takers, society has responded in a strangely muffled, seemingly disinterested way.... Little money has been spent to understand this tragic phenomenon. The true numbers and exact nature of the problem remain unknown, and the troubling fact of abuse or neglect often remains a terrible secret that is buried with the child.[18]

No presidential addresses or multi-cabinet press conferences ensued. Shalala° and the Centers for Disease Control continued their tradition of silence on

---

°**Shalala:** Donna Shalala, head of the Department of Health and Human Services in the Clinton administration.

[17]For information on age, income, and generation issues, see U.S. Bureau of the Census (1994). *Money income of households, families, and persons in the United States: 1992.* Current Population Series, P60-184. Washington, DC: U.S. Department of Commerce.

[18]U.S. Advisory Board on Child Abuse and Neglect (1995, April). In Rivera C (1995, 26 April), *op cit,* p. 1.

the issue of child abuse, symptomatic of an official dereliction that did not go unremarked in the Board's "scathing assessment" of child protective services and federal responses.

"You can call the Centers for Disease Control and Prevention and find the number of children who had a brown recluse spider bite last year, but you certainly can't get correct information on child abuse and neglect," University of Oklahoma child abuse expert Barbara Bonner testified.[19] The board found that professionals—doctors, teachers, social workers—failed to report seven in 10 cases of suspected child abuse to authorities. Those that were reported, even homicides, were "routinely" reduced to lesser charges or not prosecuted at all.

Of the 1 million cases of physical or sexual abuses of children and youths reported to overworked child protection authorities in the most recent available year (1993), 232,061 cases of physical abuse and 139,326 cases of sexual abuse of children were substantiated.[20] False reports are believed to be very few; lack of investigative resources accounted for most of the reports not substantiated. Underreporting is much more likely. A 1985 survey of 2,600 adults nationwide found 22 percent had been sexually abused as children at an average age of 10 by abusers who averaged around 30 years old.[21] A dozen years of tabulations of child abuse and neglect cases by the American Humane Association likewise consistently found offenders averaged over 30 years old. Substantiated cases of violent abuse and sexual offense against children by their parents and caretakers quadrupled from 1976 through 1993.[22]

The 370,000 confirmed cases of violent and sexual offenses in 1993 against children and youths, overwhelmingly by adult offenders, can be compared to the 350,000 arrests of children and youth for violent and sexual offenses (including all violent crimes plus misdemeanor assaults and sex offenses) reported by the FBI for 1993.[23] Although adult violence against children/youth and crimes of violence by children/youth are both distinctly under-reported, crimes against juveniles are more often unreported than crimes against adults.[24] The enormous hype surrounding "youth violence" (primarily in public locations) can be contrasted with the muted official and media concern

[19] Rivera C (1995, 26 April), *op cit*, p. A23.

[20] National Center on Child Abuse and Neglect (1995, April), *op cit*.

[21] Timnick L (1985, 25 August). The Times Poll: 22 percent in survey were child abuse victims. *Los Angeles Times*, pp. A1, A34.

[22] American Humane Association (1989). In U.S. Bureau of the Census (1993). *Statistical abstract of the United States, 1992*. Washington, DC: U.S. Department of Commerce, Table 301.

[23] FBI (1993), *op cit*, Table 38. Estimates involving crime reports prorate tabulated arrests upward in ratio to population of U.S. versus population of crime reporting area.

[24] Children often overlooked in crime reports (1994, November/December). *American Nurse*, 20. See also, National Victim Center (1992). *Rape in America*. Washington, DC, p. 6.

regarding what appears to be an equivalent or greater volume of adult violence against juveniles (primarily in homes).

The cliché that the American home is a violent place for children is sug- 30 gested from a number of sources:

> Interviews with national probability family samples reveal that a full 18 percent of children have been the object of a "severe violent act" (more serious than spanking or slapping... [including being] kicked, bit, punched, beat up, burned or scalded, and threatened with or used a gun or knife) by their parents at some time in their lives, with 11 percent experiencing an event in the past year.[25]

This works out to 7 million children subjected to at least one "severe violent act" by their parents every year, not including spanking and whipping (which the U.S. Supreme Court has ruled would constitute "cruel and unusual" punishment if inflicted on adults). Assuming (absurdly conservatively) that none of these 7 million parentally assaulted children suffered more than one violent assault per year, that would be approximately 19,000 kickings, beatings, bitings, burnings, punchings, and threats or attacks with weapons aimed *against* American children by their parents *every day*.

A 1985 study of 1,000 families by family violence researcher Murray Straus found that parents inflicted nearly twice as many severe, and nearly four times as many total, violent acts on their teenage children [as] the other way around.[26] Other studies indicate Straus's findings may be conservative. A 1988 survey of 1,146 parents found that 80 percent of the children under age 10, two-thirds of the 10–14-year-olds, and one-third of the 15–17-year-olds were hit or struck by their parents within the previous year. Parents are nearly four times more likely to commit simple assault, and twice as likely to commit severe or aggravated assault, against their teenage children [as] the other way around. Two thousand to 5,000 children are killed by their parents every year, with most called "accidents."[27] ...

"Violence Begets Violence"

"Teenage" violence is so interrelated with adult violence that analyzing it separately obscures more than it illuminates. As Straus notes, "family training" is the genesis of violence.[28] Children who are violently and sexually abused are three times more likely than non-abused youths to behave violently them-

---

[25] Dodge KA, Bates JE, Pettit GS (1990, 20 December). Mechanisms in the cycle of violence. *Science* 250, 1678, 1683.

[26] Straus MA (1985). Family training in crime and violence. In Straus MA, Lincoln AJ (1985). *Crime and the family.* Springfield, IL: Charles C Thomas, p. 168.

[27] Hutchings N (1988). *The violent family.* New York: Human Sciences Press, p. 93.

[28] Straus MA (1985), *op cit,* p. 168.

selves, even when such variables as parental income and marital status are held constant. Teenage mothers, incarcerated youths, and other youth populations at risk were victimized by severe violence and sexual abuse while growing up at much higher levels, typically 60 percent to over 90 percent.[29]

Pre-teen years appear to be the time in which a storehouse of rage builds up in abused children.[30] From age 10–12 to age 13–14, the rate of homicide arrests multiplies nine-fold. It jumps another five-fold by age 16, and redoubles yet again by age 18. Thus an 18-year-old is 100 times more homicidal than an 11-year-old. Even so, 1,999 out of every 2,000 18-year-olds will not kill anyone.

Violence rises in late teenage years as youths acquire the strength, skills, and independence to retaliate against previous victimizations. This latter potential illustrates the tragedy of misdirected reprisal. The hostility of abused children is not usually brought to the door of the abuser.

The link between adult and youth violence has been well established. A 1992 National Institute of Justice [NIJ] comparison of the criminal records of 908 abused/neglected youths with 667 non-abused youths found that "violence begets violence . . . being abused or neglected as a child increased the likelihood of arrest as a juvenile by 53 percent, as an adult by 38 percent, and for a violent crime by 38 percent." The study reported that in addition to being more crime prone:

> The abused and neglected cases were also more likely to average nearly 1 year younger at first arrest (16.5 years versus 17.3 years), to commit nearly twice as many offenses (2.4 percent versus 1.4 percent), and to be arrested more frequently (17 percent of abused and neglected cases versus 9 percent of comparison cases had more than five arrests).[31]

Thus teens and adults who were abused or neglected as children not only commit 40 percent more crimes than non-abused persons, they commit twice as many crimes per criminal than their non-abused counterparts. This indicates that the overall crime volume among individuals abused or neglected as children is approximately 2.4 times higher than those whose childhoods were free of violence and neglect. The NIJ findings should be considered conservative, since the absence of "official records" of abuse or neglect in the non-abused sample does not guarantee at least some of the control group had been abused as well. Child abuse and neglect, as noted, are notoriously under-reported.

A 1990 study of 300 students reported in *Science* magazine likewise found that abused children were nearly three times more aggressive than non-abused

---

[29] Boyer D, Fine D (1992), *op cit*, and Braun E, Lustgarten K (1994), *op cit*.

[30] See Miller A (1983). *For your own good: Hidden cruelty in child-rearing and the roots of violence.* New York: Farrar Straus & Giroux; Miller A (1990). *Banished knowledge: Facing childhood injuries.* New York: Doubleday.

[31] Widom CS (1992, October), *op cit*, pp. 1, 2.

children even when other factors such as family income, divorced and single parenting, and family discord were taken into account. Abused children committed 30 percent more aggressive acts in real life and were rated as consistently more violent both by their teachers and peers. Due to probable "under-reporting of abuse" in the so-called non-abused sample, "our estimates of the magnitude of the effects of abuse may actually be underestimates," the authors said.[32]

Repeated studies in Philadelphia, Los Angeles, and other cities found that while most youth and young-adult gangs are not violent, so-labeled "scavenger" or "territorial" gangs are. Of those that perpetrate most gang violence:

> The research indicates without question that most gang members are impoverished school drop-outs with a history of violent victimization at home and in their communities, who commit crimes to get by, and whose affiliation with their gang may be the only reason they have for liking themselves and feeling proud.[33]

Instead of focusing on the adult violence that precedes youth violence, the [40] official response has been to "suppress gangs"—with concomitant growth in their size and violence....

Adult violence against youth often remains a hidden, family crime; violence by youth is both public and subject to emotional anecdote. For example, while the media and officials claim school violence has risen drastically and that "135,000 kids bring guns to school every day,"[34] the annual *Monitoring the Future* report of over 2,000 public high school seniors finds no rising trend. In 1976, 5.0 percent of the white seniors and 6.7 percent of the black seniors reported being injured by someone with a weapon at school. In 1993, these figures were 4.3 percent and 6.4 percent, respectively.[35] "Victimization rates of high school seniors changed little between 1976 and 1993," the National Center for Education Statistics reported.[36] Reports of other types of school violence and crime were similarly stable.

The "adult factor" explains why theories that blame violence on youth proclivities, while popular, inevitably fail fundamental real-world tests of validity. While all adolescents are exposed to equivalent levels of youth-based influences, such as media violence or "peer pressure," real-world violence is highly concentrated in certain demographic groups. Why, in fact, do boys commit nine times more violent crimes than girls? Why are murder rates among black male youths ten times higher (and rising several times faster) than murder

---

[32] Dodge KA, Bates JE, Pettit GS (1990, 20 December), *op cit*, pp. 1681–1682.

[33] Prothrow-Stith D, Weissman M (1991), *op cit*, p. 104.

[34] National Commission on the Role of the School and Community in Improving Adolescent Health (1990), *op cit*, p. 4.

[35] Maguire K, Pastore AL, Flanagan TJ (1994). *Sourcebook of criminal justice statistics—1993.* Washington, DC: U.S. Department of Justice, Table 3.69.

[36] National Center for Education Statistics (1995). *The condition of education, 1995.* NCES 95-273. Washington, DC: U.S. Department of Education, p. 134.

among white, non-Hispanic male youths? Why are California teenagers a dozen times more likely to commit murder than Montana teenagers? It is here that efforts to explain "youth violence" as a phenomenon separate from "adult violence" fail most profoundly across a wide variety of pragmatic tests.

The difference is that black, male, urban, California youth are exposed to far different kinds of adult influence and conditions than are rural, white, Montana teens. Correlations of youth violence rates with corresponding violence rates of adults of their gender, race, era, and region reveal powerful associations.° Both over time, for the last four decades, and by geographic region of the U.S., youth violent crime arrests and adult violent crime arrests are almost perfectly correlated: Where one is high, the other is high also. These near one-to-one correlations indicate that 90 percent of the youth violence rate over time and by geographic location is explained by the same factors that cause adult violence. In short: *Youth violence and adult violence are not separate behaviors; they are one and the same phenomenon.*

But the parallel nature of youth and adult behavior described [here] is not automatic. If conditions between the young and old become sufficiently divergent, separate youth trends may emerge. Beginning in the mid-1980s, during a period of intensive legal and programmatic efforts to combat "teen violence," youth violent crime arrests began to climb rapidly. Crime among California teenagers rose earlier, and more rapidly, than among youths nationwide, even though (perhaps partly because) the state pioneered "get tough" policies in the 1970s. The poverty rate among California youth also rose at a record pace during this period, from 15 percent in 1980 to 29 percent by 1995. The demographic variables underlying both youth and adult violence rates are so decisive—and converge around the variable of "poverty"—that they dwarf the "age" factor unfortunately chosen to name the issue.

Honey, I Warped the Kids: The Argument for Eliminating Movie and TV Violence

Carl M. Cannon

Carl Cannon wrote this 1993 article for Mother Jones, *a magazine that takes its name from union organizer Mary Harris "Mother" Jones (1830–1930) and is dedicated to exposés and politics. Cannon's is the first of several readings that*

° Correlations . . . powerful associations: Statistical tests indicating what events typically occur together.

*focus on how ideas in American culture help foster violence. Cannon concentrates
on ideas that come from television and, in his opinion, help encourage actual violence. To develop his argument, he summarizes a number of studies on TV violence.*

*As you read, pay attention to how Cannon uses the research studies and other
kinds of support to bolster his view.*

Tim Robbins and Susan Sarandon implore the nation to treat Haitians with
AIDS more humanely. Robert Redford works for the environment. Harry Bela-
fonte marches against the death penalty. Actors and producers seem to be constantly speaking out for noble causes far removed from their lives. But in the
one area over which they have control — the excessive violence in the entertainment industry — Hollywood activists remain silent.

The first congressional hearings on the effects of TV violence took place in
1954. Although television was still relatively new, its extraordinary marketing
power was already evident. The tube was teaching Americans what to buy and
how to act, not only in advertisements, but in dramatic shows, too.

Everybody from Hollywood producers to Madison Avenue ad men would
boast about this power — and seek to use it on dual tracks: to make money and
to remake society along better lines.

Because it seemed ludicrous to assert that there was only one area — the
depiction of violence — where television did not influence behavior, the TV
industry came up with this theory: Watching violence is cathartic.° A violent
person might be sated by watching a murder.

The notion intrigued social scientists, and by 1956 they were studying it in 5
earnest. Unfortunately, watching violence turned out to be anything but cathartic.

In the 1956 study, one dozen 4-year-olds watched a "Woody Woodpecker"
cartoon that was full of violent images. Twelve other preschoolers watched
"Little Red Hen," a peaceful cartoon. Afterward, the children who watched
"Woody Woodpecker" were more likely to hit other children, verbally accost
their classmates, break toys, be disruptive, and engage in destructive behavior
during free play.

For the next 30 years, researchers in all walks of the social sciences studied
the question of whether television causes violence. The results have been stun-
ningly conclusive.

"There is more published research on this topic than on almost any other
social issue of our time," University of Kansas Professor Aletha C. Huston,
chair of the American Psychological Association's Task Force on Television and
Society, told Congress in 1988. "Virtually all independent scholars agree that
there is evidence that television can cause aggressive behavior."

There have been some 3,000 studies of this issue — 85 of them major
research efforts — and they all say the same thing. Of the 85 major studies, the

---

°**cathartic:** Having the effect of releasing emotions or tensions.

only one that failed to find a causal relationship between TV violence and actual violence was paid for by NBC. When the study was subsequently reviewed by three independent social scientists, all three concluded that it actually did demonstrate a causal relationship.

Some highlights from the history of TV violence research: 10

• In 1973, when a town in mountainous western Canada was wired for TV signals, University of British Columbia researchers observed first- and second-graders. Within two years, the incidence of hitting, biting, and shoving increased 160 percent.

• Two Chicago doctors, Leonard Eron and Rowell Heusmann, followed the viewing habits of a group of children for 22 years. They found that watching violence on television is the single best predictor of violent or aggressive behavior later in life, ahead of such commonly accepted factors as parents' behavior, poverty, and race.

"Television violence affects youngsters of all ages, of both genders, at all socioeconomic levels and all levels of intelligence," they told Congress in 1992. "The effect is not limited to children who are already disposed to being aggressive and is not restricted to this country."

• In 1988, researchers Daniel G. Linz and Edward Donnerstein of the University of California, Santa Barbara, and Steven Penrod of the University of Wisconsin studied the effects on young men of horror movies and "slasher" films.

They found that depictions of violence, not sex, are what desensitizes 15 people. They divided male students into four groups. One group watched no movies, a second watched nonviolent X-rated movies, a third watched teenage sexual-innuendo movies, and a fourth watched the slasher films *Texas Chainsaw Massacre, Friday the 13th, Part 2, Maniac,* and *Toolbox Murders.*
`All the young men were placed on a mock jury panel and asked a series of questions designed to measure their empathy for an alleged female rape victim. Those in the fourth group measured lowest in empathy for the specific victim in the experiment—and for rape victims in general.

The anecdotal evidence is often more compelling than the scientific studies. Ask any homicide cop from London to Los Angeles to Bangkok if TV violence induces real-life violence and listen carefully to the cynical, knowing laugh.

Ask David McCarthy, police chief in Greenfield, Massachusetts, why 19-year-old Mark Branch killed himself after stabbing an 18-year-old female-college student to death. When cops searched his room they found 90 horror movies, as well as a machete and a goalie mask like those used by Jason, the grisly star of *Friday the 13th.*

Or ask Sergeant John O'Malley of the New York Police Department about a 9-year-old boy who sprayed a Bronx office building with gunfire. The boy explained to the astonished sergeant how he learned to load his Uzi-like firearm: "I watch a lot of TV."

Numerous groups have called, over the years, for curbing TV violence: the 20 National Commission on the Causes and Prevention of Violence (1969), the U.S. Surgeon General (1972), the National Institute of Mental Health (1982), and the American Psychological Association (1992) among them.

During that time, cable television and movie rentals have made violence more readily available while at the same time pushing the envelope° for network television. But even leaving aside cable and movie rentals, a study of TV programming from 1967 to 1989 showed only small ups and downs in violence, with the violent acts moving from one time slot to another but the overall violence rate remaining pretty steady—and pretty similar from network to network.

"The percent of prime-time programs using violence remains more than seven out of ten, as it has been for the entire 22-year period," researchers George Gerbner of the University of Pennsylvania Annenberg School of Communication and Nancy Signorielli of the University of Delaware wrote in 1990. For the past 22 years, they found, adults and children have been entertained by about 16 violent acts, including two murders, in each evening's prime-time programming.

They also discovered that the rate of violence in children's programs is three times the rate in prime-time shows. By the age of 18, the average American child has witnessed at least 18,000 simulated murders on television.

But all of the scientific studies and reports, all of the wisdom of cops and grief of parents have run up against Congress' quite proper fear of censorship. For years, Democratic Congressman Peter Rodino of New Jersey chaired the House Judiciary Committee and looked at calls for some form of censorship with a jaundiced eye. At a hearing five years ago, Rodino told witnesses that Congress must be a "protector of commerce."

"Well, we have children that we need to protect," replied Frank M. 25 Palumbo, a pediatrician at Georgetown University Hospital and a consultant to the American Academy of Pediatrics. "What we have here is a toxic substance in the environment that is harmful to children."

Arnold Fege of the national PTA added, "Clearly, this committee would not protect teachers who taught violence to children. Yet why would we condone children being exposed to a steady diet of TV violence year after year?"

°**pushing the envelope:** Extending limits or reducing constraints.

THE SYMBOLIC CRUSADE AGAINST MEDIA VIOLENCE IS A CONFESSION OF DESPAIR

Todd Gitlin

Todd Gitlin has been director of the mass communications program at the University of California, Berkeley, and teaches at New York University. The author of a number of studies of television and mass media, he has written Inside Prime Time *(1983) and* The Twilight of Common Dreams: Why America Is Wracked by Culture Wars *(1995). This 1994 article, originally published in* The American Prospect, *challenges the arguments presented by Carl M. Cannon.*

As you read, note the distinctions Gitlin makes. In paragraph 1, for instance, he says that he is not defending TV violence, and in paragraph 4, he concedes that TV violence is unpleasant. He argues, however, that it is not the cause *of killing. Note the reasons Gitlin gives to support his belief.*

Guns don't kill people, picture tubes do. Or at least that seems to be the message behind the clangor of current alarms about television violence. Don't misunderstand: I have denounced movie violence for more than two decades, all the way back to *The Wild Bunch* and *The Godfather.* I consider Hollywood's slashes, splatters, chainsaws, and car crashes a disgrace, a degradation of culture, and a wound to the souls of producers and consumers alike.

But I also think liberals are making a serious mistake by pursuing their vigorous campaign against violence in the media. However morally and aesthetically reprehensible today's screen violence, the crusades of Senator Paul Simon and Attorney General Janet Reno against television violence, as well as Catharine MacKinnon's° war against pornography, are cheap shots. There are indeed reasons to attribute violence to the media, but the links are weaker than recent headlines would have one believe. The attempt to demonize the media distracts attention from the real causes of—and the serious remedies for—the epidemic of violence. . . .

That media violence contributes to a climate in which violence is legitimate—and there can be no doubt of this—does not make it an urgent social problem. Violence on the screens, however loathsome, does not make a significant contribution to violence on the streets. Images don't spill blood. Rage, equipped with guns, does. Desperation does. Revenge does. As liberals say, the drug trade does; poverty does; unemployment does. It seems likely that

---

°Catharine MacKinnon: A feminist and law professor who argues against pornography not because of its explicit sexual content but because she sees it as causing violence against women.

a given percent increase in decently paying jobs will save thousands of times more lives than the same percent decrease in media bang-bang.

Now I also give conservative arguments about the sources of violence their due. A culture that despises and disrespects authority is disposed to aggression, so people look to violence to resolve conflict. The absence of legitimate parental authority also feeds a culture of aggression. But aggression per se, however unpleasant, is not the decisive murderous element. A child who shoves another child after watching a fist fight on TV is not committing a drive-by shooting. Violence plays on big screens around the world without generating epidemics of carnage. The necessary condition permitting a culture of aggression to flare into a culture of violence is access to lethal weapons....

The symbolic crusade against media violence is a confession of despair. 5
Those who embrace it are saying, in effect, that they either do not know how to, or do not dare, do anything serious about American violence. They are tilting at images. If Janet Reno cites the American Psychological Association report *Violence and Youth,* she also should take note of the following statements within it: "Many social science disciplines, in addition to psychology, have firmly established that poverty and its contextual life circumstances are major determinants of violence.... It is very likely that socio-economic inequality—not race—facilitates higher rates of violence among ethnic minority groups.... There is considerable evidence that the alarming rise in youth homicides is related to the availability of firearms." The phrase "major determinant" does not appear whenever the report turns to the subject of media violence.

The question for reformers, then, is one of proportion and focus. If there were nothing else to do about deadly violence in America, then the passionate crusade against TV violence might be more justifiable, even though First Amendment absolutists° would still have strong counter-arguments. But the imagebusting campaign permits politicians to fulminate photogenically without having to take on the National Rifle Association, or for that matter, the drug epidemic, the crisis of the family, or the shortage of serious jobs. To the astonishment of the rest of the known world, we inhabit a political culture in which advocates of gun control must congratulate themselves for imposing restrictions on the purchase of certain semi-automatic weapons, or a five-day waiting period before the purchase of a handgun....

There is no space here to address properly the plague of real-world violence. But let that discussion proceed with proper respect for the gravity of the situation. As for *media* violence, let it be criticized for the right reasons and in the right spirit. To be loathsome, popular culture doesn't have to be murderous. To disapprove of media violence, we don't need a threat of government action to

---

°**First Amendment absolutists:** Those who give the highest priority to the U.S. Constitution's First Amendment protection of speech rights and freedoms.

rectify morals by fiat. The proper disapproval would have recourse to categories of judgment that make Americans nervous: aesthetic and moral standards and the intersection of the two. The democracy of taste has not been hospitable to judgments of this order. We aren't content to condemn trash on the grounds that it is stupid, wasteful, morally bankrupt; that it coarsens taste; that it shrivels the capacity to feel and know the whole of human experience.

Let a thousand criticisms bloom. Let reformers flood the networks and cable companies and, yes, advertisers, with protests against the gross overabundance of the stupid, the tawdry, and the ugly. Let them demand of local TV stations that the news cameras find something else to photograph besides corpses....

Not least, let the reformers not only turn off the set, but criticize the form of life that has led so many to turn, and keep, it on.

LOVE, MONEY, PRISON, SIN, REVENGE

Andrew Lam

Andrew Lam, an associate editor at Pacific News Service, came to the United States with his family at the time of the fall of Saigon, when the Vietnam War ended in 1975. He has been a Rockefeller Fellow at UCLA, and his work has appeared in the New York Times *and the* Nation. *In this reading, published in the* Los Angeles Times Magazine *in March 1994, Lam explores a 1991 shooting incident in Sacramento, California, during which three of four young Vietnamese gunmen (two of them brothers) were killed. He presents the story, in part, to discover what caused the violence. Implicitly, he asks, Why did the journey of these boys end so differently from my own?*

As you read, note the differences Lam mentions between the wave of Vietnamese immigrants who arrived in 1975 and those who arrived later, referred to as boat people, who underwent terrible hardship to leave Vietnam in small handcrafted boats. Note, too, the ideas named in his title — love, money, prison, sin, revenge. According to Lam, how did the Vietnamese and American cultures, high-tech consumerism, Hong Kong videos, and the legacy of the Vietnam War contribute to the Sacramento shooting?

On the afternoon of April 4, 1991, 15 years, 11 months and 27 days after the end of the Vietnam War, four Vietnamese youths armed with semiautomatic pistols stormed into a Good Guys electronic store on Stockton Boulevard in

Sacramento and held 41 people hostage. Speaking heavily accented and broken English, they issued what the *Sacramento Bee* described as "a series of bizarre demands." They wanted a helicopter to fly to Thailand so they could fight the Viet Cong,° $4 million, four bulletproof vests and 40 pieces of 1,000-year-old ginseng roots.

While a crowd, some enthusiasts equipped with their own camcorders, gathered across the street, TV reporters informed viewers that three of the gunmen were brothers—Loi Khac Nguyen, 21; Pham Khac Nguyen, 19, and Long Khac Nguyen, 17—and that the last, Cuong Tran, 16, was Long Nguyen's best friend. The Nguyen brothers had come from a poor Vietnamese Catholic family headed by an ex-sergeant of the South Vietnamese army.° All four were altar boys. Three of the youths had dropped out of school or had been expelled. None had been able to find a steady job.

The gunmen could be seen on live television behind the store's glass doors, strolling back and forth with their firearms, bound hostages at their feet. Sacramento County Sheriff Glen Craig, who had implanted listening devices in the store, reported that the gunmen were jubilant at seeing themselves and hearing their names on TV—"Oh, ah, we're going to be movie stars!" The sheriff had also told reporters that the gunmen belonged to a loosely knit gang called Oriental Boys—an error, as it turned out, since police couldn't prove membership in any gang.

As the siege wore on, negotiations between the gunmen and the taut-faced, gray-haired sheriff reached a stalemate. The gunmen, for their part, had grown increasingly edgy and refused to negotiate after authorities met only part of one demand—providing them with a single bulletproof jacket. Sheriff Craig, on the other hand, later told reporters that the four would not "focus on any single demand. They were attempting to gain notoriety, attention and, perhaps, some transportation out of the country."

Eight-and-a-half hours later, after the gunmen wounded two of the [5] hostages, a SWAT team raided the store on live television. Three of the young men were killed immediately, but not before one of them sprayed the hostages with bullets, killing two employees—John Lee Fritz and Kris Sohne—and a customer—Fernando Gutierrez—and wounding eight more. Loi Nguyen, the oldest, and the one who wore the bulletproof jacket, was seriously wounded. His trial on 49 felony counts and three counts of murder is set for July 11. He is pleading not guilty.

As I watched this tragedy unfold on my TV set that night, I remember being overwhelmed by an irrational fear. It was the fear that the Vietnam War had

---

°**Viet Cong:** A guerrilla member of the North Vietnamese Communist forces who fought against the South Vietnamese and their U.S. allies.   °**South Vietnamese army:** The side allied with the United States during the Vietnam War.

somehow been renewed by those gunmen and by those helicopters hovering over the store. And though I was on the safe side of the TV screen now and judging their barbaric acts, I was not without this singular sense of foreboding: Six years ago I could have been one of them.

If the story of the Good Guys ended in carnage on the linoleum floor of an electronics store, it began an ocean and an epic journey away, nourished by numerous subterranean streams. It is those streams I am foundering in. I am at once too close and too far from their story. Though an American journalist now, I came to this country as a Vietnamese refugee, the son of a South Vietnamese army officer. The young men and I, through our fathers, are veterans of a civil war we never actually fought. In their demands, I hear the thematic echo of vengeance, which forms and shapes all Vietnamese youths who grow up in America. Perhaps all this binds me to the Good Guys hostage-takers nearly two decades after the last U.S. helicopter hovered over a burning Saigon° before heading toward the South China Sea.

When I asked for directions, the blond kid on Stockton Boulevard rattled off names of generic American landmarks in an amiable tone: Midas...Shakey's pizza...Carl's Jr....man, you can't miss it.... Turn left at the House of Fabrics. Next to it, you'll see the Good Guys.

Inside, the first thing you noticed was yourself. Walk through the glass door and a dozen camcorders gave you back your reflections on the various TV sets. For as little as $549, you could be (oh, ah) your own movie star.

I saw but tried not to look at my own faces on those TV screens. The faces, 10 my faces, appeared expressionless, the thick brows slightly raised, touched perhaps by a tinge of skepticism. I do not believe in instant fame, had always thought Andy Warhol's prediction° an odd American curse.

But teen-agers are daily worshipers in this secular temple of high-tech consumerism, their eyes mesmerized by the *son et lumière*. At the Nintendo counter, five Asian teens vied to compete for world championship of Street Fighter II. At the cellular phone display, two Latino girls pretended to gossip, using those palm-sized communicators. And at the store's far end, a hundred or so TV sets formed a kind of electronic wall that talked and sang and showed the shopper the panorama of America — talk shows, soap operas, commercials. A fat housewife described her sex life on a dozen or so screens. In a hushed tone, she related intimate details of her marital betrayal to Oprah and 14 million other people — "I never told anybody this but..." — and managed to blush.

°**Saigon:** The capital of South Vietnam, and the center of U.S. efforts on behalf of the South Vietnamese. When Saigon fell to the North Vietnamese Communists in 1975, U.S. troops and officials evacuated, taking with them top South Vietnamese military advisers.   °**Andy Warhol's prediction:** Andy Warhol, a twentieth-century artist, predicted that everyone would have fifteen minutes of fame.

It is here, in this American postmodern public square,° that the ethnic private meets the mainstream public. At dinnertime on the night of the Good Guys siege, Papa and Mama Nguyen suddenly saw their three eldest boys holding American hostages at the neighborhood electronics store. One can assume that their sons were simultaneously watching their own drama on dozens of TV sets. It is a kind of instantaneous real-life opera made popular by television these days, the blood opera with all nuances flattened so that viewers get only a reporter's sound bites and vivid endings. Narrative is shaved to the bone, history and background ignored.

That sort of ignorance is peculiarly American, or so it seems to many of the 12,000 Vietnamese in the Sacramento area. A few who watched the siege recall a dangerous combination of arrogance and confusion among the TV reporters and especially the authorities. "They ran around like chickens without heads," said one Vietnamese man who volunteered to help the police but was turned away. "The boys were Vietnamese Catholics and the sheriff initially had a Laotian [Buddhist] monk° at the scene," he said.

Yet clues that would have helped the sheriff and the journalists unlock the gunmen's psyches were just minutes from the Good Guys, in Little Saigon. In a mini-mall a mile or so away, a video store called Ngoc Thao (Precious Herb) catered to a Vietnamese clientele. Colorful posters of gangsters and cops holding Uzis and of ancient swordsmen in silk brocades flying above temple rooftops covered the walls and glass windows. Here, as in many other video stores frequented by local Vietnamese in Sacramento, one can find 1,000-year-old ginseng roots—the precious cure-all usually discovered by the lucky hero in kung fu° epics—or other magical panaceas and cursed swords. They're in hundreds of Hong Kong videos, dubbed in Vietnamese, that line the shelves.

The cashier, a heavily made-up woman, was having a busy day. Like a high 15 priestess with holy water, she dispensed pieces of Asia's fabled past to hordes of homesick Vietnamese.

"Sister, when is the Royal Tramp video coming out? I've been waiting for months."

"Sister, we want 'Dragon Palms' and 'The Revenge of Black Orchid.' I hear the woman in 'Orchid' is the best fighter and, like a man, kills everyone who assassinated her parents."

"Aunty, how much does a karaoke machine cost? Everybody in my family is dying to be a rock 'n' roll star."

°**postmodern public square:** Unlike the town square of a largely homogeneous village in early America where people met face to face, today's "postmodern" world brings together a variety of cultures through the instant communication the media make possible. °**Vietnamese Catholics...Laotian monk:** Since the boys were Catholic, a Buddhist monk was not appropriate. °**kung fu:** Various Chinese arts of self-defense, including karate.

At the entrance, an 8-year-old holding a plastic bag filled with kung fu videos was his old man's pride and joy. Papa urged youngest son to say something to a friend, an army buddy wearing a fatigue jacket. Youngest son shrugged, then, without enthusiasm, recited a quote from a movie:

"Honorable father, I must leave you now and find a mentor to learn the martial art way. I will avenge our family honor after I have mastered the Iron Palms of Death." 20

The two men laughed and applauded the mythological voice of China, a voice that provides a kind of parochial snare in the Americanization process.° Thanks to CNN, satellite dishes, cable TVs, VCRs, jumbo jets, camcorders and fax machines, integration turns retro-future-active. Technology renews old myths, shrinks oceans, packages memories, melts borders, rejuvenates old passions, redefines the assimilation process. For Asian children immigrating to America today, their parents' homelands are no longer as far away as they were for children in earlier times. The American-born Vietnamese boy who mouths ancient wisdoms may not know their meaning, may never, for that matter, master the Iron Palms of Death, but somehow Asia has already exuded mysticism into his soul. Indeed, the alluring incense, the singsong languages, the communal and familial Confucian values° of loyalty and obligation, the old-world gestures of self-sacrifice and revenge—all that earlier generations of American-born Asians tried so hard to exorcise—is now in style, evidenced in the Little Saigons and Little Seouls° that dot so many California urban landscapes.

Two days after the Good Guys siege, a *Sacramento Bee* photo that ran the length of the page showed the Nguyen brothers' parents standing in their living room as if facing a firing squad. Though stricken with grief, Bim Khac and Sao Thi Nguyen admitted journalists into their tiny two-bedroom unit in the Laura Dawn Manor Apartments, a two-story structure rented out mostly to Southeast Asian families.

The photo shows a sagging sofa, a VCR and, of course, a large TV set. On top of the TV stands a South Vietnamese flag—three red horizontal stripes against a gold background—representing a country that no longer exists. On the opposite wall, a three-tier shrine displays crucifixes, statues of Mary, Joseph and Jesus and various martyred saints, all with mournful faces.

The Nguyens and their six children spent four months in a refugee camp in Indonesia before coming to the United States in the early 1980s. In Sacramento,

---

°**parochial snare in the Americanization process:** Lam suggests that because news from home (in this case, China) can be transmitted instantaneously, today's immigrants are able to hold on to their parochial (or home) values and therefore resist Americanization.   °**Confucian values:** Confucius, a Chinese philosopher (551–479 B.C.), emphasized devotion to parents and ancestors.   °**Little Saigons and Little Seouls:** Neighborhoods in which Vietnamese or Koreans in the United States partly re-create their home cities.

they were receiving Aid to Families with Dependent Children.° The ex-sergeant from the South Vietnamese army, who is active in church, said through an interpreter that he was no help to his children when it came to explaining American things such as homework or news on TV. Still, wasn't what he wanted for his children the same as what any Vietnamese parent wants—that they do well in school but keep "Vietnamese traditions"?

"Please tell the people of Sacramento I am very sorry for what my sons have 25 done," the patriarch offered. Asked how his quiet, obedient boys wound up becoming hostage-takers, Nguyen and his wife provided only a miserable silence.

This is the silence of an older generation of Vietnamese refugees who no longer feel anchored anywhere but in their impoverished homes. The exterior landscape belongs to America, strange and nonsensical, not their true home. Inside, many Vietnamese refugees tend to raise their children with stern rules—the way they themselves were raised back home. Vietnamese is spoken, with familial personal pronouns—youngest son, older sister, aunt, father, great uncle, and so on—lacing every sentence to remind the speakers and the listeners of their status in the Confucian hierarchical scheme of things.° These parents are unprepared for children who lead dual lives, who may in fact commit rash and incomprehensibly violent acts—not at all the docile and obedient Vietnamese children they had hoped to raise.

"They are no longer really Vietnamese, nor are they really Americans," said a former teacher, who recently came from Vietnam and now lives on welfare in Sacramento, of his own children. He called their tangled assimilation "crippled Americanization."

For Loi, Pham and Long Nguyen and Cuong Tran, who failed school and grew up between the Good Guys electronics store and the Ngoc Thao, there existed two separate notions—notoriety and revenge, revenge being the stronger impulse. One encourages public displays (i.e., confessing on "Oprah," or holding shoppers hostage and giving incoherent speeches) that may lead mainstream America to acknowledge that they exist. The other fulfills the old man's extraterritorial passion—"helicopters to Thailand to kill Viet Cong"—and rejects America as the wasteland.

To grow up Vietnamese in America, after all, is to grow up with the legacy of belonging to the loser's side and to endure all that entails. To grow up in America is to desire individual fame and glory, a larger sense of the self. Driving on Stockton Boulevard, it suddenly occurs to me that, while I myself might have learned to walk that strange Vietnamese American hyphen, it continues to hurl young and hapless Vietnamese down into a dark and bottomless pit.

° **Aid to Families with Dependent Children:** A federal program available to poor families with children.   ° **Confucian hierarchical scheme of things:** In the Confucian way of ordering human relations, people of different ages and classes are not all seen as equals; older people, for instance, are accorded more importance and respect than younger people.

After Good Guys, the media offered a variety of explanations. One had to do 30 with the chronology of waves, as in waves of Vietnamese immigrants. The first wave of refugees who came to America in 1975, my wave, comprised intellectuals, educators, army officers, skilled civil servants, professionals—Vietnam's best and brightest—those who had not experienced Vietnam under communist rule. This wave adjusted readily to American life, to an America of the 1970s that was economically stable and motivated, in part by guilt, to be generous to the newly arrived: There were English as a Second Language teachers, low-interest loans, job-training programs.

The later wave, the boat people who came in the '80s, were a different group—people who had been traumatized by re-education camps, cannibalism, rape, robbery, drowning at the hands of sea pirates, people who had suffered a chaotic and broken society back home under communist hands. These less-skilled, less-educated refugees were ill equipped to adjust to a less generous America.

But there were deeper currents that fed this second-wave refugee family that the media failed to detect. According to one Vietnamese who has been a social worker and knows the family well, the Nguyen parents had been burned not once but twice by communism. They fled to the South in 1954 when Catholics were persecuted by Ho Chi Minh° and his army, and they fled Saigon as boat people a few years after the communists ransacked the South in 1975. Communist crimes, Viet Cong crimes, human-rights abuses by the Hanoi° regime—all are meticulously documented by Vietnamese Catholic newspapers and magazines in the United States. The Viet Cong, whom the eldest Nguyen boy barely remembered, nevertheless figured as the prime villains in the household cosmology—the chief cause of their family's suffering in America, the robbers of their father's dignity, the blasphemers of the crucifix in their church, called the Vietnamese Catholic Martyrs.

The Nguyen brothers and Cuong Tran (whose more-affluent Chinese Vietnamese parents, unlike the Nguyens, refused to open their doors to journalists) were reportedly Hong Kong movie fanatics. All four youths watched the highly stylized films whose sword-crossing heroes and gun-toting detectives and gangsters duked it out amid Hong Kong high-rises, filling their waking dreams with homilies to honor, fraternal loyalty, betrayal and, of course, revenge.

To many Vietnamese living in Sacramento, these Hong Kong videos are the real culprit in the Good Guys shootout. Gangster films like John Woo's "A Better Tomorrow" and "Bullet in the Head" were the rage among Vietnamese youth in the late 1980s. It was in re-enacting these gang-shooting scenes, some

---

°**Ho Chi Minh:** Communist president of North Vietnam from 1945 to 1969.   °**Hanoi:** The capital of North Vietnam.

speculate, that the gunmen coolly flipped coins to decide which of the hostages would take the first bullet.

In "Bullet in the Head," three best friends—blood brothers from Hong 35 Kong looking to make a name for themselves (they have been losers up to this point)—travel to Vietnam during the war to smuggle illegal ampicillin. With the help of an assassin, they end up fighting everyone, including the Viet Cong. Though profit was their original quest, they are searching for their lost souls— they cannot decide whether they are good guys or bad guys. Along the way, the brothers are captured by the Viet Cong and tortured. They escape when Army of Republic of Vietnam helicopters arrive and attack the Viet Cong stronghold.

What moves the plot along and prompts young Vietnamese viewers to whooping-oohing cheers, is the escalating interplay of terror and death from one scene to the next, culminating in a betrayal of camaraderie and leading to vengeance. A few weeks after Good Guys, Sacramento police received a mysterious letter signed by the Brothers of the Dragon.

"On 4-4-91 you have killed our brothers in Sacramento for no reason," it announced. "For this reason there must be revenge. The Brothers of the Dragon have decided in a meeting a lesson will be made." On the margins of the letter were the Vietnamese words that embody the Hong Kong video gangster mythos, words that many Vietnamese gang members have tattooed on their own skin: *Tinh, Tien, Tu, Toi, Thu*—Love, Money, Prison, Sin, Revenge.

WHY?

Michael Ramirez

Michael Ramirez, a Pulitzer Prize–winning political cartoonist, is president of the Association of American Editorial Cartoonists and an editorial cartoonist for the Los Angeles Times. *The son of a Japanese mother and a Mexican American father, Ramirez describes himself as a political conservative and an "equal opportunity offender" in the political subjects he chooses to comment on.*

This cartoon appeared in the Los Angeles Times, *following the 1998 Jonesboro, Arkansas, school shootings. It features the question "Why?" which is central to this chapter.*

As you look at the cartoon, note all the small details to see what Ramirez considers the possible causes of the Jonesboro tragedy and, possibly, other school shootings or other violence by young men.

MOVING BEYOND BLAME

Gary Ross

Gary Ross is a writer and director of films such as Big *and* Dave, *for which he wrote the screenplays, and* Pleasantville, *which he wrote and directed.*

In April 1999, eighteen-year-old Eric Harris and seventeen-year-old Dylan Klebold entered their high school in Littleton, Colorado, with firearms and home-made bombs hidden under their trench coats and killed thirteen people, wounding another twenty-three. Since the high school was in an affluent suburb and the killers were middle-class video game players; since so many people were killed; and since the event had been preceded by a series of other school shootings (see the Egan reading in this chapter), the event triggered a flood of commentary from media figures, politicians, psychologists, video game opponents, gun control advocates, and others. Here Ross enters into the discussion because of growing charges that the entertainment industry (video games, the

Internet, Hollywood films, rap music, and so on) should bear part of the blame for violence.

As you read, note how Ross defends the movie business and yet still points to cultural causes of violence.

LOS ANGELES – Ever since the tragedy in Littleton, Colo., the American preoccupation with finding a simple answer has been churning nonstop. In a nation that reduces everything to box scores ("Conventional Wisdom" in *Newsweek,* etc.), the media and its pundit class° have been obsessed with finding the *immediate* cause, like a zealous cop hellbent on making an early collar.

My industry (the movie business), in a pre-emptive first strike, said the cause was guns. Gun lovers of course said the cause was movies. Politicians, depending on their place in the political spectrum, said the cause was one, the other, or both.

And no sooner were these first accusations traded than the natural defenses began. "Guns don't kill people, people kill people." "Movies don't kill people, people kill people." "Video games don't kill people, people kill people." (This N.R.A.° construct is almost as specious as "guns don't kill people, bullets kill people," but even the N.R.A. wouldn't go that far.)

Let's just assume for a minute that all these things *are* involved. In other words, instead of shifting blame, what if we search our souls for culpability?

Guns kill people and movies kill people and video games kill people and it soon becomes obvious that the list doesn't stop there.

It may not reduce to a tidy sound 5 bite or a convenient political enemy, but the simple truth is that whatever debases the culture (Springer),° degrades the value of human life (Doom),° panders to violent impulses (local news), trivializes human relationships (Springer again) or isolates us from one another (paradoxically, the Internet) can contribute to a situation like Littleton. It is absurd to say that this problem occurred in the absence of social forces, but it is equally absurd to blame a single one.

In the book "Finding the Heart of the Child," the psychiatrist Edward Hallowell cogently lists many of the factors that contribute to the kind of alienation that allows something like Littleton to occur. These include changing family structure (single-parent homes, two-career homes); the breakdown of communities, villages and neighborhoods; cynicism about government and social institutions; the decrease in a sense of security, job permanence or close personal relationships; the decline of

---

°**pundit class:** Writers, critics, TV personalities, and others whose views are often sought and publicized when major events occur.   °**N.R.A.:** National Rifle Association, a group that frequently lobbies against gun control laws.   °**Springer:** Talk-show host Jerry Springer.   °**Doom:** Video game in which users practice shooting animated characters.

genuine spirituality as an ethical force in the culture; an explosion of information that creates anxiety over one's worth or abilities; a lack of respect for older people and an overreliance on "self" to find the meaning of life.

In comparison to that list, the movies/guns paradigm withers. How many of us who have an impact on the culture have contributed (however unwittingly) to the social forces that Dr. Hallowell identifies?

When conservative Republicans fought to have night basketball removed from the crime bill of several years ago, they were eroding a sense of community that can prevent this kind of isolation. When prime-time magazine shows peddle yet another "hard hitting" investigation of yet another corrupt local official, they are feeding our cynicism about social institutions by elevating the exception to the rule. When advertisers exploit perfect bodies on perfect men and women to sell their less-than-perfect products, they are exacerbating the anxiety that adolescents feel in regard to their self-worth. (Littleton has shown us this is no benign thing.) When the local news leads its broadcast with a homicide three nights a week, it is committing the very desensitization that it decries when it covers a story like Littleton.

So how do you program a V-chip° for all of that?

It seems to be a vicious circle. When 10 problems seem overwhelming, we grasp for sound-bite solutions as a way of convincing ourselves that the problems are not insoluble and the alienation is not that deep. Of course, the hollowness of this just increases the feelings of futility and alienation, but for a moment we feel better. For a moment we feel assuaged by the passion play that modern news has become: a hero gets elevated, a villain gets vanquished, a sinner gets stoned, a victim is avenged.

Since only an acceptance of personal responsibility can possibly break this deadlock, let me start now. I will not defend the role of movies in the culture. Despite my deep and abiding passion for the First Amendment,° I will not even defend our right to make them. Let me say that movies *can* contribute to this desensitization. And let me promise that, on each screenplay, I will ask myself what the ramifications are to the culture in which I live and the children who may see these films.

But what should we ask after that?

°**V-chip:** Proposed device to allow parents to block undesirable TV programs for their children.
°**First Amendment:** The right to free speech.

THE DREAM AND THE NIGHTMARE: THE SIXTIES' LEGACY TO THE UNDERCLASS

Myron Magnet

Myron Magnet, an editor at Fortune *magazine, is the author of* The Dream and the Nightmare: The Sixties' Legacy to the Underclass *(1993), from which this reading comes. The book's subtitle provides a clue to understanding Magnet's argument. He believes that the "Haves"—people in positions of power and authority— shape the ideas other people adopt. According to Magnet, the plight of the "Have-Nots" comes not so much from economic circumstances as from the cultural beliefs and attitudes that influence behavior, and he sees the values of the Have-Nots as coming from the ideas of the cultural elite of the 1960s—the Haves. As Magnet puts it, this elite "radically remade American culture, turning it inside out and upside down to accomplish a cultural revolution whose most mangled victims turned out to be the Have-Nots."*

In the reading that follows, Magnet applies his views to the problem of violent crime. He begins by tracing two competing traditions in the history of ideas: the relatively modern idea that people are naturally good and that violence and aggression are the fault of society, and the older idea that people are not naturally good and that societies therefore create laws to control the selfish tendencies of individuals. Magnet believes the latter and thus disagrees with William Julius Wilson's argument that economic changes are at the root of changes in behavior. In fact, Magnet argues against Wilson in paragraph 24.

As you read, follow Magnet's argument that "man's instinctual aggressiveness" (paragraph 5) necessitates social control and that ideas from the 1960s have increased violence.

Theories of crime have to make an assumption about whether men are predisposed by nature to force and violence or whether violence gets into their hearts from some outside source.... [A] key assumption of the new culture of the Haves...is that men are intrinsically peaceful creatures, inclined not to disturb their fellows and, when necessary, to cooperate harmoniously with them. As nature formed them, they don't attack and invade each other. Crime is an artificial growth, grafted onto human life by the development of societies and governments....

These ideas were always alive in American culture, but they became dominant only at the start of the sixties. Michael Harrington gave voice to this interpretation of crime just as it was becoming widespread. Speaking of black delinquents and then of all delinquents, he concluded in *The Other America*: "[T]heir sickness is often a means of relating to a diseased environment."[1] Ramsey Clark, Lyndon Johnson's attorney general and assistant attorney general in the Kennedy administration, is a luminous example of how quick were the Haves at their most established to embrace such an understanding of crime as part of the new era's revolutionized worldview. Clark takes an utterly uncompromising tack. "[C]rime among poor blacks...flows clearly and directly from the brutalization and dehumanization of racism, poverty, and injustice," he wrote in 1970, summing up his experience as the nation's top law enforcement officer. "[T]he slow destruction of human dignity caused by white racism is responsible."[2]...

[T]he other great tradition of political philosophy spring[s] from Plato and [is] strengthened by such architects of the Western imagination as St. Augustine, Hobbes, Burke, even Freud.

This other tradition, for most of history the dominant stream in Western political philosophy, best explains the origin of crime. This tradition takes as its starting point the irreducible reality of human aggression. It holds that as men come from the hand of nature—or as they have been transformed by original sin, according to the Church Fathers'° version of the theory—they are instinctively aggressive, with an inbuilt inclination to violence....

The fundamental purpose of the social order, of the civilized condition itself, is to restrain man's instinctual aggressiveness, so that human life can be something higher than a war of all against all. The great seventeenth- and eighteenth-century political theorists, most notably Thomas Hobbes, imagined that that restraint was accomplished by a social contract: driven to desperation by the universal warfare that made their lives "solitary, poore, nasty, brutish, and short," in Hobbes's famous phrase, men in the early ages of the world entered into an agreement, by which each man renounced his unlimited freedom of aggression in order to promote the security of all. And because it could only be effective if some authority existed to enforce it, the contract also established a governmental apparatus armed with the power to punish infractions, further prompting everyone to keep his word. As James Madison expressed his thought in Number 10 of *The Federalist:* "[W]hat is government itself but the greatest of all reflections on human nature?"...

Looked at through assumptions like these, crime takes on an entirely different appearance from the one it has in Ramsey Clark's eyes and in the culture of the Haves today. Not only does the social order not *cause* crime, it is the very thing

5

°**Church Fathers:** Early Christian writers who described the teachings and practices of the Roman Catholic Church.

[1] Michael Harrington, *The Other America: Poverty in the United States,* rev. ed. (New York: Penguin, 1971), p. 136.

[2] Ramsey Clark, *Crime in America: Observations on Its Nature, Causes, Prevention and Control* (New York: Simon & Schuster, 1970), p. 51.

that *restrains* crime to the remarkable extent that it is restrained. The social order is precisely what makes man's life something other than a scene of constant mutual invasion, in which all live in continual fear and danger of violence....

[T]hough the whole governmental structure of force and threat—police, judges, and prisons—is a key means by which society restrains aggression and crime, it isn't the principal means, according to this tradition. The most powerful curb isn't force at all: it is the *internal* inhibition that society builds into each person's character, the inner voice (call it reason, conscience, superego, what you will) that makes the social contract an integral part of our deepest selves.

So while to prevent crime we should worry about whether judges are too lenient or legal procedures too cumbersome, it is still more crucial to ensure that the inner barriers to violence and aggression are strongly in place. This is a cultural matter, a matter of how people bring up their children, a matter of the messages that get passed from the community to the parents and thence to the children. The object is both to transmit the necessary prohibitions against aggression to each individual and to win each individual's inner, positive assent to the social endeavor.

Paradoxically, the hardest of hard realities—whether people commit crimes or not—comes down to a very large extent to nothing more than values and beliefs in the world within the individual. Do we deeply believe thou shalt not kill, thou shalt not steal—so deeply that these injunctions are a constituent part of our deepest selves? Do we believe in an idea of justice that embraces us and our community? Do we value such qualities as honor, duty, mercy, honesty, kindness? Do we subscribe enough to the values of our community that we would feel guilt or shame to have transgressed against them, dismay or outrage that others should have flouted them? ...

When crime flourishes as it now does in our cities, especially crime of mind- 10 less malice, it isn't because society has so oppressed people as to bend them out of their true nature and twist them into moral deformity. It is because the criminals haven't been adequately socialized. Examine the contents of their minds and hearts and too much of what you find bears out this hypothesis: free-floating aggression, weak consciences, anarchic beliefs, detachment from the community and its highest values. They haven't attained the self-respect or the coherent sense of self that underlie one's ability to respect others.

This is a predictable result of unimaginably weak families, headed by immature, irresponsible girls who are at the margin of the community, pathological° in their own behavior, and too often lacking the knowledge, interest, and inner resources to be successful molders of strong characters in children. Too many underclass mothers can't enforce the necessary prohibitions for children—or for themselves. And most underclass families lack a father, the parent that

---

°**pathological**: Abnormal, sick.

Freud, wearing his psychoanalyst's hat rather than his political philosopher's, sees as the absolutely vital agent in the socialization of little boys and in the formation of their superegos.

When the community tells people from such families that they are victims of social injustice, that they perhaps are not personally to blame if they commit crimes, and that it is entirely appropriate for them to nurse feelings of rage and resentment, it is asking for trouble. Worse, the new culture holds that, in a sense, such crime isn't pathological; it is something higher and healthier. It is rebellion—the manly response that Americans have shown to oppression since the Boston Tea Party, the response that Robin Hood and his outlaw band gave to injustice before America was even thought of....

Such a view of the admirably defiant criminal still holds the underclass in thrall.° "They want us to settle for a little piece of nothing, like the Indians on the reservation," as one inner-city resident who grew up in a Harlem housing project said recently, summing up his vision of the larger society. "They got us fighting and killing each other for crumbs. In a way, the ones in jail are like political prisoners, because they refused to settle for less."[3]

How deep the glorification of the criminal runs today can be seen in the "near folk-hero status," as the *New York Times* calls it, that murderer Larry Davis won in Harlem and the Bronx in 1986. Charged with killing and robbing six drug dealers in cold blood, Davis dodged from hideout to hideout as police closed in on him during a seventeen-day manhunt, which ended in a pyrotechnic, TV-style shootout at a Bronx housing project. Davis wounded six policemen before being captured and led out in handcuffs, cool and uninjured, to the acclaim of a cheering crowd of project residents. All through the manhunt, and after its bloody end, ghetto residents told tales of his larger-than-life outwitting and resisting the police, speaking of him with thrilled, emphatic admiration as "the dude who elude." This Scarlet Pimpernel° of the projects later was acquitted of five of the murders, convicted of one, and also jailed in connection with the shootout.[4]

The cultural revolution left none of the barriers to crime undisturbed. Not 15 only did it undermine the inner inhibitions, but it also weakened the external deterrent, the threat of official punishment. Guided by the idea that society systematically oppresses the poor and the black, the Haves increasingly hampered the governmental apparatus that upholds the law by force.

Government, according to this view [that society oppresses the poor and the black], tends almost reflexively to be an instrument of injustice against the

---

°**in thrall:** Bound by a particular way of thinking.   °**Scarlet Pimpernel:** A daring, heroic figure who outwitted his enemies in a historical novel set during the French Revolution.

[3] "As Many Fall, Project's Survivors Struggle On," *The New York Times* (February 6, 1991).

[4] "Larry Davis Convicted in Killing of a Drug Dealer," *The New York Times* (March 15, 1991).

Have-Nots, above all in its law enforcement capacity. As William Ryan put it in *Blaming the Victim,* all experts know that "the administration of justice is grossly biased against the Negro and the lower class defendant; that arrest and imprisonment is a process reserved almost exclusively for the black and the poor; and that the major function of the police is the preservation not only of the public order, but of the social order—that is, of inequality between man and man."[5] However overwrought, Ryan's statement contains this element of somber truth: racial discrimination did taint police treatment of blacks when Ryan was writing, and in the South police did act as oppressors of blacks, as the nation learned indelibly when Freedom Riders were arrested in Jackson and elsewhere in Mississippi in 1961 or when Chief Bull Connor viciously attacked civil rights demonstrators with police dogs, clubs, cattle prods, and fire hoses in Birmingham, Alabama, in 1963.

Properly indignant at such viciousness, the majority culture responded by throwing a cordon around the government's police functions, aiming to confine the police within the narrowest channel so they couldn't surge out of control. In this effort, federal judges took the lead. With their ideas continually renewed by a flow of talented clerks newly minted from the nation's top law schools, the judges were part of the advance guard of the resulting cultural changes. They had the moral authority and political power to take new ideas and transform them into the concrete reality of law almost overnight, anointing them in the process as normal and right. Accordingly, out of the impulse to curb the police functions of the state came the well-known string of 1960s court decisions that succeeded in tying down criminal law enforcement with as many strands as Gulliver in Lilliput.°

Still, it was a big step from the shameful doings of Bull Connor to the conclusion that the entire governmental apparatus for controlling crime across the nation was an engine of injustice. And it was an even bigger step to the conclusion that the proper remedy for such instances of police lawlessness as did occur was to free proven criminals—as distinct from Freedom Riders or civil rights demonstrators—rather than to dismiss and punish the responsible officials.

As with so many elements of the cultural revolution, these key court decisions of the sixties produced long-term unintended consequences. Anxious to protect citizens from a tyrannical abuse of police power, the judges erected safeguards that turned out to hinder ordinary, untyrannical policemen from bringing common criminals to justice. From *Mapp* v. *Ohio* in 1961 through *Miranda* v. *Arizona* in 1966, the Supreme Court decisions that proceeded from fears of police tyranny aimed to prevent juries from hearing evidence

---

° **Gulliver in Lilliput:** In Jonathan Swift's *Gulliver's Travels* (1726), the giant Gulliver was tied down by the six-inch people of the imaginary island Lilliput.

[5] William Ryan, *Blaming the Victim,* rev. ed. (New York: Vintage, 1976), p. 217.

obtained in ways that the Court, ever more punctiliously, deemed unconstitutional....

The inevitable result was that criminals became harder to convict, and 20 punishment for crime became rarer. As the judges issued their rulings on suppressing evidence in the sixties, the prison population declined. By the mid-seventies, the average Chicago youthful offender got arrested over thirteen times before being sent to reform school. In big cities, more than nine felony convictions in ten result not from trials but from plea bargains, in which penalties are lighter and criminals are left with at least some sense of having beaten the system. Today, thanks partly to plea bargaining, your chance of *not* going to jail if you're *convicted* of a serious crime is two to one.[6]

As it became possible to suppress key evidence and literally to get away with murder, crime took off. In the sixties, the overall crime rate doubled. And between 1961 and now, while the murder rate "only" doubled, the rape rate quadrupled, and both the robbery and assault rates quintupled.[7]...

For all Americans, the wholesale overturning of the bars to crime and disorder has scrambled the moral order. What becomes of the sense of justice when, almost daily, people violate the fundamental principle of the social contract? What becomes of the sense of personal responsibility for actions when people are not held accountable even for the most evil deeds? With the ground on which the sense of values rests giving way beneath their feet, no wonder many reel with moral vertigo.

For all Americans, Haves and Have-Nots alike, the weakening of the protections against crime and disorder has debased urban life, overlaying it with fear and suspicion as well as real injury. The disproportionate number of crimes committed by underclass lawbreakers has heightened racial hostility, straining the social fabric. Straining it too are the menacing rowdiness and graffiti, the dope selling, and the occupation by the homeless of public spaces everywhere....

However much the erosion of the barriers to crime and disorder disrupted the lives of the Haves, that disruption pales compared to the disruption it inflicted on the lives of the Have-Nots. More than any economic change of the William Julius Wilson variety, it is the explosion of violent crime that has turned inner cities into blighted wastelands, virtual free-fire zones. Repeated holdups and street robberies of employees drove out small tradesmen and larger businesses alike. Crime made fear ever-present for hardworking, law-abiding ghetto citizens—who, though you might not think so from reading William Julius Wilson on the flight of upwardly mobile blacks from the ghetto, certainly do exist.

---

[6] Richard E. Morgan, *Disabling America: The "Rights Industry" in Our Time* (New York: Basic Books, 1984), p. 76.

[7] FBI Uniform Crime Reports.

The almost daily reports of gunfire crackling outside the projects, of people 25 cowering on the floor of their apartments, of innocent passersby getting caught in the crossfire, become numbing by their very familiarity. But it is true that a young black man has a greater chance of being murdered in the inner city than a soldier had of being killed in the jungles of Vietnam. It is true that you can send your kid to the grocery store and never see him again alive. It is true that an East New York high school, in a painfully ghoulish accommodation to anarchy, has recently established a "Grieving Room," where students gather to mourn slain classmates. In the last four years, seventy have been shot or stabbed, half of them fatally. . . .

The achievements of civilization rest upon the social order, which rests in turn upon a mutual agreement to forswear aggression. In the ghetto, the agreement is in tatters, the police are hamstrung, and the life of the civilized community is being stomped out by force and violence. In cities in which civilization should have reached its apogee, gang-ridden ghetto areas have regressed to some dark age when human life was organized around predatory, roving bands with continually shifting memberships. It is as if the peaceful citizens of those neighborhoods really were under the cruel yoke of the banditti of ruffians that Thomas Paine° imagined as introducing violence and crime into the early ages of the world.

After a nine-year-old girl in a crime-ravaged Brooklyn ghetto had just been shot in the head by a thug's stray bullet, a neighbor—a law-abiding family man living across the street from a crack house—lamented: "Our lives have been reduced to the lowest levels of human existence." In such an anarchy, it's a wonder not when people fail to achieve the civilized excellences but when, like the family man quoted above, they succeed.

The primary function of any society is to guarantee the social contract. What but anarchy can you expect if the legitimate force of society has eroded?

A WRITER'S NOTEBOOK

Possible Causes of Violence by Young Men

The following tasks are designed to help you think about the readings and identify and start to work up material you might use in your own essay. If you need help with tasks that require summarizing or evaluating an argument, see Appendix 1.

1. *Review list of causes.* If you compiled a list of causes of violence by young men as you read the arguments in this section, discuss your list with one or two of your classmates and compare it to theirs. With the help of your classmates and instructor, you may be able to add some causes of violence to your list and better understand some of the more difficult selections.

°**Thomas Paine:** American political philosopher (1737–1809) of the revolutionary era.

2. *React to Susan Straight's argument.* Write a page or so explaining what causes seem most important in contributing to violence in Riverside. You might focus on paragraphs 1–6, 17–19, and 22 in Straight.

3. *Summarize William Julius Wilson's argument.* Although many people believe that poverty or unemployment may cause high crime rates in cities, exactly *how* they do so is not altogether obvious. Focusing on paragraphs 8–15, summarize how Wilson thinks that the jobless ghetto fosters violence among young men.

4. *Connect your experience to Elijah Anderson's ideas.* Write a page or so of personal observations about when and how young men are pressured to act out a particular type of manhood. Drawing on your experiences at home, in the workplace, or at school, focus on one or two specific examples. As you comment on these personal examples, connect your comments to some of Anderson's ideas.

5. *Consider Anderson's argument.* Write a half-page or so explaining how the desire for respect in the code of the streets may cause violence.

6. *Explain David Popenoe's view.* Although many writers have offered statistical evidence that violence comes disproportionately from fatherless young men, such evidence may not be convincing without further explanation of *how* fatherlessness can cause violence. Reread Popenoe's essay, especially paragraphs 22–28 and 40–46, then write a page or so explaining how, in Popenoe's view, growing up without a father can increase the likelihood that young males may commit violence.

7. *Summarize Mike A. Males's argument.* Summarize Males's argument in paragraphs 21–38 that "household violence against children and teens is the foundation of youth crime" (paragraph 24).

8. *React to Males, Timothy Egan, and Popenoe.* Males criticizes policies about youth violence for "mistreat[ing] it as a 'psychological' problem located within the heads of adolescents" (paragraph 8). Both Egan and Popenoe might disagree. Egan quotes several authorities who attribute youth violence to "mood disorders" and depression (paragraphs 32–34 and 65–66), and Popenoe connects youth violence to the absence of fathers (paragraphs 33–39). Write a page or so reacting to any two of these three authors' arguments, telling which of the two you are more inclined to agree with and why.

9. *Explain Carl M. Cannon's and Todd Gitlin's main points.* Write a page or so first explaining each writer's main point and then explaining which view you find more persuasive and why.

10. *Link Cannon's and Gitlin's arguments to your own reactions.* Write a few sentences reflecting on your personal reactions to media violence and its influence on you. Then watch one TV drama or movie and write a page or so describing any violence you see and reflecting on it in light of the ideas in Cannon's or Gitlin's article.

11. *Think about Andrew Lam's essay.* Lam describes a number of concrete images and cultural beliefs that may contribute to young men's willingness to engage in violence. Choose one such image or belief that you think Lam might be right about and explain why Lam thinks it encourages violence.

12. *Analyze Michael Ramirez's cartoon.* After examining all the small details of the Ramirez cartoon, write a half-page or so on the possible answers to the "Why?"

the mother asks. Conclude with a few sentences about which of the readings in this chapter Ramirez seems most in agreement with.

13. *Reflect on Gary Ross's essay.* In paragraph 5, Ross names a number of "social [or cultural] forces" that "can contribute to a situation like Littleton." Write a page or so reflecting on what you personally have seen of social forces that debase the culture, degrade the value of human life, pander to violent impulses, trivialize human relationships, or isolate us from one another.

14. *Evaluate Myron Magnet's view.* Review paragraphs 15–21 and then write a page or so evaluating Magnet's view that ideas from the 1960s have contributed to an increase in violence.

Now it is your turn. What do you think are the causes of violence by young men? The readings in this chapter provide a rich supply of material to draw upon to write an essay on this issue: arguments and counterarguments about possible causes, vivid descriptions of violence, and statistical information. As you develop your essay, you can also draw on any writer's notebook entries you have made, on your own personal experience, and on current news items about violence you may have collected.

This guide will help you turn your materials into a convincing causal argument. More specifically, it will help you

- plan, draft, revise, edit, and proofread an essay that speculates about the causes of violence among young men
- work with sources—to gather additional information and to cite sources that you use
- construct certain kinds of sentences required in speculating about an issue
- reflect on what you have learned completing this assignment

PLANNING AND DRAFTING YOUR ESSAY

This section provides guidelines and examples to help you plan and draft a convincing essay about violence by young men. It will help you

- understand your readers and your writing situation
- select materials
- prepare a prospectus
- organize your essay
- devise a convincing argument
- cite sources

THE WRITING ASSIGNMENT   Write an essay in which you speculate about why young men commit violent crime. Begin by deciding whether you think violence is most likely to be caused by circumstances in neighborhoods, families, or ideas.

You may want to develop an argument about how one cause leads to another or about how several causes combine to foster violence. Whatever approach you take, plan on considering and counterarguing causal speculations that challenge your own. Assume you are writing your essay for a magazine that informs general readers about social, political, and economic issues affecting all Americans. Your goal is to persuade readers of the reasonableness of your speculations.

Understanding Your Readers

Your readers—college students and other adults who are generally well informed about social and political news and issues—may at first seem to be a difficult audience to write for. Keep in mind, however, that few adults are better informed than you are right now about violence among young men and its possible causes. Your information comes from diverse, current sources, and, if you interviewed other students about their thoughts on this issue, you have already gained insights into the knowledge and attitudes of people who are not immersed in the study of violence.

Your readers may or may not have experienced violent crime, and they may or may not hold views like those of the people you may have interviewed. You may need to help them focus on nondomestic murder, nonnegligent manslaughter, and assault, rather than on other types of crime. And you will certainly need to maintain a consistent purpose for your readers, making it clear that you are speculating about causes of violent crime rather than, for instance, offering solutions. Many of your readers will not need to be convinced that violent crime among young people is a social crisis, but they may not have thought or read much about its possible causes. Other readers may believe that such crime has always existed or that it doesn't really affect them. For those readers, try to offer enough vivid details or telling statistics to get their attention and make them concerned about the problem.

Assume authority. Regardless of the causes you write about, assume that you are the expert and that you are writing for readers who can benefit from your knowledge. Your job is to tell them what the social crisis is all about, establish the seriousness of the problem, and invite them to consider your views. Accept your authority. Enjoy it.

Selecting Materials

The readings and writing tasks in this chapter have made a wealth of materials and resources available to you—more information and ideas, in fact, than you can possibly use in one essay. Your next step is to choose from all this material the facts, experiences, and speculations that will enable you to construct an effective argument. The following activities will help you to do so.

Choose a Category of Circumstance. When experienced writers research a complex issue, they look for ways to organize large amounts of information and to focus on a particular aspect of the issue. In this chapter, the speculations about violence are grouped into three categories of circumstances. What kinds of circumstances will you focus on in your essay?

- *Neighborhoods*—This category allows you to speculate about how poverty, joblessness, lack of opportunity, discrimination, or bad neighborhoods may promote violence. The readings related to neighborhoods are those by Susan Straight, William Julius Wilson, Elijah Anderson, and, to a lesser degree, Andrew Lam.

- *Families* — This category allows you to speculate about how and whether circumstances within the family may promote violence. The relevant readings are those by David Popenoe and Mike A. Males and, to a lesser degree, Timothy Egan, Anderson, and Myron Magnet.

- *Ideas* — This category allows you to speculate about how some of the following ideas may promote violence: cultural beliefs; attitudes; and images and values stemming from the media, including television (drama, docudrama, news, advertising), movies, and pornography. The readings that view ideas as a cause of violence are written by Carl M. Cannon, Todd Gitlin, Gary Ross, Lam, and Magnet.

Choosing one of these three categories of circumstances will help you get started. If you commit yourself tentatively to one of these three, you may feel less tempted to try to cover every possibility and can therefore concentrate on rereading the arguments most relevant to you. Such a tentative choice will allow you to begin developing your causal argument.

List and Choose Causes.   After you have chosen one of the three categories, select three to five related causes within that category. To help you make your selection, review any writer's notebook entries you made and any relevant readings. If you prepared a list of causes when you were reading the selections, review your list to refresh your memory and highlight the causes you might want to speculate about. If you did not prepare a list of causes as you were reading the essays, make a limited list of whatever causes you think you will use in your essay.

As you look again at the readings in a particular category, keep in mind that authors writing about one kind of circumstance may nevertheless offer different, or even contradictory, views. For example, William Julius Wilson and Elijah Anderson both present arguments about neighborhoods. Wilson, however, discusses a sequence of historical and economic changes in the ghetto whereas Anderson stresses codes of behavior that work in combination with poverty and inequality. Wilson and Anderson might each agree that the other's argument is important and valid, but they each restrict themselves to a particular set of causes. Similarly, Lam and Magnet both point to ideas and cultural beliefs as sowing the seeds of violence, but Lam's focus is on images of warriors and Magnet's on beliefs from the 1960s.

Identify Key Readings.   Identify one reading that you think will be especially useful in supporting your argument and the one that poses the biggest challenge to your argument — one you may need to counterargue most imaginatively. Also, identify any related writer's notebook entries that may be especially helpful. Reread those you select purposefully, looking for facts, anecdotes, expert opinions, and other information that will help you speculate convincingly.

Preparing a Prospectus

At this point, your instructor may want you to prepare a prospectus for your essay, to plot out some of its parts. Businesspeople, scientists, and other professionals often write prospectuses for projects to win support and funding for them. In much the same way, preparing a prospectus for your essay helps you determine whether you have enough resources to develop your argument and whether your causes may seem convincing. Most important, you can show your prospectus to others, who can ask you questions and give advice.

Here are some guidelines for drafting a two- or three-page prospectus.

1. *Identify the category of circumstance.* Identify the category of circumstance you will focus on—neighborhoods, families, or ideas—and write a few sentences explaining your choice. You can be tentative for now.

2. *List causes.* From the category you have chosen, list the particular causes you want to discuss, such as lack of social services, pressure to gain respect, or lack of discipline from a father figure. Try to sequence the causes logically so that one leads to the next or is a precondition for the next until violence results.

3. *Identify one important reading and relevant personal experience.* Identify the one reading that will be most important in providing support for your speculation and explain in two or three sentences why it can help you develop your argument. If you plan to rely on personal experience for support as well, briefly identify the experience(s).

4. *List other readings.* List any other readings you may draw on for support.

5. *Anticipate readers' objections or reservations.* List two or three major objections or questions you would expect from someone who does not agree with you. Choose one of these objections and write a few sentences explaining why it poses a challenge to your argument.

6. *Identify one reading that challenges your position.* Identify the one reading that poses the biggest challenge to your argument. In a sentence or two, explain how you can counter that challenge most convincingly.

7. *Try to support part of your argument.* Select one cause you listed in item 2 and write a page or so supporting it with facts, examples, and quotations from the readings, and also with any relevant personal experiences, observations, or interviews. Do not take time now to consider all of the readings. Rely on your memory, notes, and perhaps a quick look at a key reading. Write quickly. Your purpose is to try out one small part of your argument before you plan your entire essay.

Organizing Your Essay

Readers familiar with essays that speculate about the causes of a social problem or crisis have certain expectations about how the argument will unfold. When these expectations are fulfilled by the plan of the argument, readers are able to move ahead confidently and better understand the material. For example, readers of an essay about why young men commit violence might expect to find the crisis described at the beginning, followed by an overview of current speculations about violence. They would then expect the writer's own argument, backed up by statistics, quotes from authorities, anecdotes, examples, and any relevant personal experiences. In addition, readers would probably be disappointed if the writer ignored their own questions about the argument or overlooked causes they had previously considered important.

To fulfill readers' expectations, many writers follow a simple two-part plan, first presenting the crisis in an informative and engaging way, drawing readers into the essay, then arguing and counterarguing imaginatively and convincingly about possible causes, providing support for their views. In some essays, the presentation may be as long as the argument, but whatever the balance between these two basic parts, both should be developed with care.

To develop a more detailed framework for your essay, you might expand this plan in the following way:

Presentation of the crisis

– an engaging opening
– information about the crisis
– overview of frequently offered speculations

Arguments and counterarguments

– thesis and forecast
– argument for the first cause
– argument for the second cause
– argument for the third cause
– counterarguments to readers' objections and questions
– an effective closing

A plan of this sort will serve you well as you draft and revise your essay. Keep in mind, however, that a plan is not a paragraph outline. You may need only one paragraph for some elements but several paragraphs for others. The next sections provide some strategies and resources to help you accomplish each aspect of the plan.

Presenting the Crisis.   In addition to describing the crisis to readers, you also need to help them see its larger social significance and its importance to them personally. You want to spark their interest and to provide adequate background for your argument.

WRITING AN ENGAGING OPENING.   Your opening must be compelling enough to make your readers want to read further and must also anticipate the argument you are going to make. You might, for example, try one of these strategies:

- Relate your own experience with violence (as Straight does in paragraphs 1–3) or an experience of someone you interviewed, as in the articles by Wilkerson (paragraphs 1–8) and Lam (paragraphs 1–5).

- Summarize several brief incidents of violence from the readings or newspaper clippings you may have collected.

- Retell in some detail one violent incident from a reading, such as the incidents in the selections by McCall, Rodriguez, Straight (paragraphs 13–16), Williams, or Lam.

- Present a few of the most surprising or troubling statistics about the crisis, as Popenoe does at the outset of his article or Males does throughout.

- Highlight the significance of the crisis, as Anderson does in his first paragraph.

Whatever strategy you choose, be sure your opening leads naturally to your argument. For instance, if your focus is on media images of violence, you may want to summarize incidents in which teenagers seem obsessed with particular kinds of music or fictional warriors. If your focus is on families, you may want to use incidents or statistics that point up changes in family life.

PROVIDING INFORMATION ABOUT THE CRISIS. Your readers need some general information about the crisis—statistics on the prevalence of the problem, examples of violent incidents, definitions of essential terms, and so forth. Here are some ways you might provide this kind of information:

- Define what kind of violence you will be concerned with and identify the 12-to-24-year-old age group you are focusing on.

- Contrast the incidence of violence by young men with the incidence by women or older men (see Males and Table 5.1 in "Statistics").

- Give examples of violent incidents from the readings or your interviews, if you did not already do so in your opening.

- Present statistics on the crisis, as Wilkerson does in paragraphs 9–15.

A comprehensive introduction might include all of these kinds of information.

GIVING AN OVERVIEW. To orient your readers to the argument you are going to make, provide an overview of the differing speculations about the causes of violence in this chapter's readings, such as joblessness, inequality, disintegrating neighborhoods, lack of fathers, cultural glorification of warriors, and so on. Describe some of the most prominent causes briefly so that readers get an idea of the arguments that respected writers have made. At this point, it may be best not to reveal the causes *you* consider most likely; save that for the argument section of your essay.

Presenting a balanced overview shows that you have a good understanding of the crisis and can help readers put together scattered information and arguments they may already be familiar with. A thoughtful overview also provides a context for your own argument.

Plotting Out Your Argument and Counterargument. As the heart of your essay, the argument section usually begins with a statement of your thesis, followed by the causes you prefer and support for them, along with counterarguments acknowledging and responding to other views. Before you begin writing, however, you need to decide how to organize your argument. Following are some suggestions.

SEQUENCING YOUR CAUSES. Putting the causes of violence you have chosen to discuss in logical order is a particularly challenging part of planning, requiring your most original, creative reasoning. Look, for instance, at the readings by Susan Straight, William Julius Wilson, and Elijah Anderson. All are about neighborhoods, yet these three writers develop their arguments in strikingly different ways, supported by different kinds of facts, observations, and anecdotes. What these essays have in common—most noticeably those by Wilson and Anderson—is a logical, step-by-step sequence, an organization that shows how one cause can readily lead to another, which, in turn, can lead to violence. Try to arrange your own causes in a logical sequence, perhaps in some order like this: when X exists, Y is more likely to happen, and as a result Z may then occur. (The list you made for step 2 of your prospectus should be helpful here.) As you develop your essay, then, you can take each step or element in order and fully support it before you go to the next step.

INTEGRATING COUNTERARGUMENTS. When you counterargue, you acknowledge questions your readers might have and concede or refute other frequently argued causes. There are several ways to do this.

One option is to integrate your counterarguments into each step of your own argument, which you might arrange like this:

Give the first step in your argument

–back it up with statistics, examples, anecdotes, and other kinds of support
–concede or refute readers' likely objections to this particular speculation about the cause of violence by young men
–concede or refute causes in the readings that would challenge the cause you are speculating about

Give a second step, and so on.

Another option is to separate counterarguments from your argument by putting them in a different part of your essay, either before or after you begin your own argument. Examples of this approach can be seen in paragraphs 1–4 of Gitlin's essay, in which his counterarguments precede his argument, and in the readings by Popenoe (paragraphs 13–15) and Magnet (paragraphs 16–21), in which the counterarguments are concentrated in one place.

CLOSING EFFECTIVELY. An effective closing will add weight to your argument. This is your last chance to have an impact on your readers, so try to close your essay memorably. Following are some options:

- Summarize your argument.
- Speculate briefly about what may happen if the high rate of violence by young men is not reduced soon, as Anderson does in paragraph 21.
- Refer to an anecdote you began with, as Wilkerson does in paragraph 33.
- Quote an authority's statement about the seriousness of the crisis, as Cannon does in paragraph 26.
- Explain the obstacles to resolving the crisis.

You may decide to use one or more of these strategies—or something entirely different. Whatever strategy you follow, take advantage of this opportunity to say something memorable.

Developing Your Argument and Counterargument

This section offers strategies for writing the central part of your essay, in which you offer your own speculations and counterargue the challenges to them.

Constructing a Thesis. At the point at which you turn from presenting the crisis to making your causal argument, a strong, clear thesis statement will help readers understand and appreciate your argument. A thesis statement should do three things: (1) signal that this is the point at which your essay shifts from presenting to arguing; (2) state your causal argument in a specific and interesting way; and (3) forecast the path your argument will take. Your thesis statement thus serves as a sort of road map for your readers. It tells them that your argument starts here, alerts them to pay attention to your plan, and helps them follow it.

The following example is from an essay by student Susan Durik. Note her thesis statement, which has been underlined.:

```
Politicians, police, parents, and teenagers are asking
themselves, "Why this increase in violence?" While many
point to the increase in drug use, the economy, and lack
of opportunity, these are only symptoms of the real root
causes. The root cause is the breakdown of the family and
religious values that since the beginning of time have
kept society from disintegrating into violence. A variety
of circumstances are responsible for this disintegration
of family and religious values, but while the picture is
complex, the main culprits are the media, the influence of
ideas from the 1960s, and feminism.
```

In her thesis statement, Durik asserts her causal argument strongly: violence by young men is caused by the breakdown of values, to which three "culprits" contribute. Note that in Durik's mind family values and religion are connected in such a way that she is not arguing for two unrelated kinds of causes: she has chosen the category of *ideas* to focus on.

Durik's thesis also forecasts the path her argument will take: it will follow the influences of the 1960s, the media; and feminism. By listing these three causes, she not only promises readers an interesting and specific causal argument but also offers them a road map to follow. The thesis statement—and the argument itself—would be less effective if Durik had stopped at claiming that the breakdown of values was the cause of violence. By specifying *which* values have broken down, she tells readers that her argument will offer more than generalities.

One way of stating a thesis is to state it directly, as Durik does. Note the strong, confident tone of Durik's statements: "The root cause is," "circumstances are responsible," "the main culprits are." Another way is to signal how your own view differs from the prevailing view by writing a sentence that uses a phrase like "I believe" or "I think."

Here are two other examples of students' thesis statements. The first is by Jacqueline Kushner:

> One cause of children's tendencies toward violence is violence in the media.

The second is by Eric Dallaire:

> Economic problems often drive desperate people to commit acts of violence. Los Angeles, the site of the destructive riots over the Rodney King verdict, serves as a model for urban violence. Severely economically depressed, South Central Los Angeles had been teeming with anger for years before the verdict. High unemployment, low economic prospects, little opportunity for job mobility, and deteriorating race relations fueled the fires that scorched Los Angeles. Poverty is linked to violence because impoverished citizens feel betrayed in that they lack the opportunities and the material wealth others have, so they do not feel bound by laws.

EXAMPLES FROM THE READINGS. For further examples of thesis statements, examine the readings by Wilson (paragraphs 7–8), Anderson (paragraph 2), Popenoe (paragraph 2), Males (paragraph 8), Gitlin (paragraph 2), and Magnet (paragraph 4).

Arguing.   Your argument is the most important part of your essay. The key to a successful argument is to set out carefully and convincingly a specific line of reasoning. Keep in mind that *speculating* means arguing about likelihoods, possibilities, and probabilities—not about certainties. Human beings behave in complex ways that are not always predictable. In speculating about the causes of violence, then, you enter the realm of likelihood, not certainty.

In the arguments in the readings in this chapter, each author has arranged his or her causes of violence in some sort of probable sequence. Anderson, for instance, argues that in circumstances of poverty and inequality, neighborhoods can develop a code of behavior. Then, once a young man is challenged, it is likely that he will act in a particular way; and when he acts in that way, it is likely that violence will occur. Anderson does not argue that all young men will react this way, but that the combined causes of poverty, inequality, and a particular code of behavior increase the likelihood of some young men resorting to violence. Your essay should also point to some probable sequence. Though you and another writer may both begin with the same circumstance, such as families, the specific causes you focus on and the ways you relate them logically to one another will be unique to your essay.

In the following example, student Keller Hackbusch discusses one of the specific ways that family breakdown may cause violence: the absence of fathers.

> It is my belief that what contributes most to violence is family breakdown caused by the absence of a father figure. David Popenoe states in his 1996 book Life without Father that 36 percent of American children were living without their fathers in 1990, compared to only 17 percent in 1960 (369). Popenoe cites research suggesting that fathers help their children learn self-control; since people with criminal tendencies tend to lack self-control and to be impulsive and short sighted, some children growing up without fathers are more likely to lack the self-control they might otherwise have learned. Timothy Egan's account of school shootings shows that several of the boys involved were impulsive and short sighted. Barry Loukaitis, for instance, after shooting a boy he had a grudge against, said that he shot several others because "reflex took over," and Luke Woodham said: "It was like I was there, and I wasn't there" (339). These are not the statements of young men who act patiently with a rational view of the future.

Several things work well in this paragraph. First, the choice of a particular cause — absence of a father — narrows the argument and allows Hackbusch to use two examples from Timothy Egan's account. To further support his argument, Hackbusch could have said more about the family backgrounds of the boys involved in the murders. He might also have looked at Isabel Wilkerson's account for more instances of absent fathers.

Second, Hackbusch effectively uses information from Popenoe's essay to support his own point. He does not just summarize Popenoe's material but makes the connection between Popenoe and Egan. It may be tempting, at times, to organize an essay around the readings, explaining the views of one source and then the views of another. It is far better, however, to organize your essay by topic. For instance, if each source contributes to the same idea—in this case, that fathers are important—then an essay that moves from source to source will seem sprawling and weak. Hackbusch wisely avoids this problem by focusing on a topic—one specific way in which a father's presence may prevent violence—and then offering support from several readings.

Later in his essay, Hackbusch uses the same strategy when he discusses how teen motherhood contributes to violence:

> Another way that family breakdown can increase the chance of violence is that often a single and very young mother is trying to take care of problem kids. The mother may be not only young but also immature. How can someone who is a kid herself take care of another child? (It isn't always just one kid, either.) Popenoe writes that out-of-wedlock births increased 600 percent between 1960 and 1990 and may soon account for 40 percent of all births and possibly 80 percent of minority births (372). Many of these out-of-wedlock births occur to teenage girls who then bring up babies alone.
>
> The problems associated with teenagers becoming parents are obvious from a 1994 <u>New York Times</u> article by Isabel Wilkerson. Damien Dorris, the 14-year-old drug dealer who shot Elizabeth Alvarez, and his 10-year-old accomplice, Jacob Gonzalez, both had mothers who first gave birth at the age of 14. Damien's mother was abandoned by his father, and Damien was beaten by his mother. Jacob was the eighth child in his family; his father was shot in a bar fight, and his mother drank heavily and used crack. The odds are stacked against the mothers of these two boys; they were not even in high school when they gave birth. Magnet states that violence is an unquestionable result of "unimaginably weak families, headed by immature, irresponsible girls who are at the margin of the community, pathological in their own behavior, and too often lacking the knowledge, interest, and inner resources to be successful molders of strong characters in children" (411). Magnet's statement may sound harsh, but I believe that he is right.

By combining concrete details from the case Wilkerson describes and references to the readings by Popenoe and Magnet, Hackbusch brings authority to these paragraphs.

Another way to support an argument is to draw on your own knowledge or experience—as student Jacqueline Kushner does here, arguing that ideas coming from the media are an important cause of violence:

> I hold that the media, not just the news media but the advertising media, are strong influences on how young people act and behave. I am arguing not that advertisers

encourage young people to act aggressively or commit
violent crimes but that advertisers set a standard for
behavior. They set the norms for what is "cool," what is
"in," what is acceptable and what is not. They tell us
that women are sexy when they are submissive and that men
are irresistible as predators. They tell us that a real
man will go out and take what he wants, that a real man is
a hunter in today's urban world, that a real man is free,
wild, and independent. They tell us to be assertive, to be
go-getters, to "just do it." They tell us that we need an
attitude to survive on the streets, a "new attitude," and
they show a six-foot-five man stalking the streets of New
York in his Air Jordans. They show us the "good life,"
lounging poolside in California with palm trees lining the
streets and a bunch of kids cruising around in a $50,000
convertible. The message that the urban poor are getting
from this is mixed: they are told to go out and take what
they want, be unstoppable, and at the same time they are
shown things that are impossibly out of reach. As a
result, we get Larry Demery and Daniel Green killing James
Jordan for his car. Why not? Their futures may appear
bleak to them, and they may feel they have nothing to
lose. But they have probably been given the message
somewhere along the line that the car is more important
than a human life, and that driving the car is the most
important thing. They have been instructed to live for the
day, to take what they want. So they did. They weren't
thinking long-term. Why should they?

Kushner uses concrete details to make this paragraph persuasive. If the entire
paragraph consisted of general statements like "advertisers set a standard for
behavior" or "They tell us that women are sexy," the passage would not be effective. But references to actual ads—the "Just do it" of the Nike ad and the stalking man with his Air Jordans—grab our attention and convey authority.

As you construct your argument, imagine that an open-minded reader is
peering over your shoulder, urging you to take your argument one step further by saying, "Exactly *how* does *that* cause violence?" Keeping this hypothetical questioner in mind will help you remember to develop your argument
with specific causal reasoning, supported by concrete particulars, instead of
relying on generalizations.

EXAMPLES FROM THE READINGS. In the following readings, you can see further
examples of the kinds of support Hackbusch and Kushner rely on and other
kinds of support as well:

  statistics: Wilson (paragraphs 2–3 and 9), Popenoe (paragraphs 10, 12, and
  33), and Males

  personal anecdotes: Williams and Straight (paragraphs 13–17) evidence from research studies: Wilson (paragraph 13), Cannon (paragraphs 6, 9, and 11–15), Popenoe (paragraphs 36–40), and Males

extended single example: Lam and Magnet (paragraph 14)

historical comparisons: Wilson (paragraphs 4–5), Popenoe (paragraphs 3–7), and Males

definition: Wilson (paragraph 6)

quotations from researchers: Wilson (paragraph 12), Popenoe (paragraphs 19–21 and 42–43), Males (paragraphs 26, 36, and 39), and Cannon (paragraph 22)

quotations from police officers or public figures: Males (paragraphs 3, 20, and 28), Cannon (paragraphs 18–19), and Lam (paragraph 4)

examples of specific media images, movie heroes, song lyrics: Straight (paragraph 22) and Lam (throughout)

Counterarguing.   While writing your essay, assume that your readers may believe that some other cause of violence by young men is more likely than the ones you focus on; assume, too, that your readers are open-minded enough to consider your argument seriously. In other words, as you address your readers' possible objections, proceed as though you have a chance to change their minds.

Take a look at how Susan Durik counterargues as she continues her argument that a breakdown in values causes violence.

> The foremost culprits are the media, because of their power to shape our thinking. Many individuals have criticized the media for their portrayal of violence, which leaves watchers desensitized to incidents of violence. Since 1956, there have been hundreds of studies on whether or not watching TV causes violence. Carl Cannon, in his argument for ending TV violence, cites University of Kansas professor Aletha C. Huston, chair of the American Psychological Association Task Force on Television and Society. Huston told Congress in 1988: "Virtually all independent scholars agree that there is evidence that television can cause aggressive behavior."
>
> I think Huston and others, however, have missed the point. While the "selling" of violence contributes to aggressive behavior, the problem lies in the "selling" of excitement and in attacks on the family and religion in a secular culture that is spiritually and emotionally bankrupt. Alexander Cockburn, in a March 1994 Los Angeles Times article, compares our society to Japan's. Japan has long had a tradition of respect for authority and of proving one's manhood through accomplishment. The Japanese are renowned in this country for being good students. Although their country is flooded with violent media,

```
including pornography and depictions of rape, they have
nowhere near the incidence of gang-related violence that
we do. The case of Japan shows that strong families have
more influence on children than what they watch on TV.
However, in the United States, feminism, economic forces,
and the media have greatly weakened the family.
```

Durik does several things well here. In her first paragraph, she presents the media-creates-violence argument, giving it enough space and weight to represent it fairly. Only then does she counterargue strongly in the second paragraph, saying, "I think [they] have missed the point." By first giving an impartial representation of the argument she is going to counterargue, she establishes her credibility as a fair-minded writer. In the second paragraph, she takes issue not so much with Cannon's argument that images and ideas can cause violence but with his specific assumptions about how they do so. To counterargue Cannon's assumption that the selling of violence is what is harmful about television, Durik presents her belief that the selling of excitement is most important because it helps undermine traditional values. To develop this argument, she compares Japanese society to that of the United States. Her detailed comparison illustrates that counterargument involves more than merely disagreeing with another argument: Durik takes pains to support one of the reasons behind her disagreement.

In counterarguing, you may *refute* an opposing view, as Durik does; you may also *concede* that it has some merit before you proceed to find fault with it. Another student, Helane Adams, takes the latter approach in the following paragraph. While arguing that media violence is an important cause of violence by young men, she nevertheless concedes that media violence is not the sole cause of violence:

```
The media cannot, of course, take full responsibility for
the outbreak of violence in our men. Media figures are in
part just giving people what they want. Many even argue
that the connection between crime and the media has not
been proven and that to have the media modify their
programming to account for child viewers would ruin their
business. We should ask, however, which is the greater
evil: loss of business or the destruction of American
children? Combined with the rage many young people already
experience because of social or economic conditions, media
sources are a lethal weapon in the hands of movie and
television producers. The media may merely reflect many
aspects of our society's reality, but these reflections
can, in turn, cause violence by young men looking for a
way out of a desperate situation.
```

By conceding that media violence is not the only cause of real-world violence — that to some degree it merely reflects violence that is already present in society — Adams increases her own credibility. She shows herself to be a reasonable writer who is willing to consider and accommodate differing points of view, rather than simply dig in her heels with her own argument.

EXAMPLES FROM THE READINGS. To learn more about how to handle opposing views, look closely at these examples from the readings: Popenoe (paragraphs 14–16 and 19), Males (paragraphs 6–8 and 12–13), Gitlin (paragraphs 1–4), and Magnet (paragraphs 15–21 and 24).

SENTENCES FOR SPECULATING

Different writing situations often require different kinds of sentences, even within the same essay. For example, when you speculate about causes, you may sometimes need to use straightforward, neutral sentences to present an issue. At other times, however, you may need to write sentences that draw attention to an argument. Note also the three kinds of signals that are most useful in a causal argument.

You may want to review the material in this section now as a preview of some of the special kinds of thinking and writing with which you will be engaged as you draft and revise your essay. You will find the definitions and examples here most helpful, however, as you revise your essay, when you will want to examine closely the logical relationships between all of your sentences and the shifts among various verb tenses. (You may also find it helpful to review the section "Sentences That Keep Readers on Track" in Chapter 3.)

Using Verbs Effectively

Whether you are presenting a neutral overview, making your own argument, or counterarguing, the verbs you use can help you fulfill your purpose.

Reporting Neutrally.   To report what someone has said without passing judgment on the accuracy of the statement, use neutral verbs like *says, states, concludes,* and *writes:*

> "Race is not a cause," Dr. Rosenberg *said.* (Isabel Wilkerson, paragraph 11)

> From such studies, Gottfredson and Hirschi *concluded* that [...]. (David Popenoe, paragraph 37)

Drawing Attention to an Argument.   At times you may want to report what someone has said and also draw attention to its being an *argument,* not necessarily a fact or a certainty. You might report in this way because you want to be scrupulously careful not to claim more than is justified or because you want to distance yourself from the statement, as in this example:

This has prompted criminologist James Fox to *assert:* "There is a tremendous crime wave coming in the next 10 years." It will be fueled not by old, hardened criminals but by what Fox *calls* "the young and the ruthless"—children in their early and mid-teens who are turning murderous. (paragraph 39)

> —DAVID POPENOE
> "Life without Father"

By using the verb *assert,* Popenoe signals to readers that Fox is making an argument or assertion, not simply reporting a fact, and that Popenoe cannot by himself substantiate Fox's claim. The verb *calls* has the same purpose: together, *assert* and *calls* suggest that Popenoe is carefully noting the element of tentativeness in Fox's argument. In effect, Popenoe is saying that not everyone would agree with Fox and that the coming "crime wave" is not a proven fact.

You might also want to draw attention to an arguable statement in order to counterargue it, as in the following example:

Government, *according to this view,* tends almost reflexively to be an instrument of injustice against the Have-Nots, above all in its law enforcement capacity. As William Ryan put it in *Blaming the Victim* [. . .]. (paragraph 16)

> —MYRON MAGNET
> "The Dream and the Nightmare:
> The Sixties' Legacy to the Underclass"

By mentioning Ryan as the owner of this view, Magnet is able to make clear his disagreement with him. Magnet first quotes Ryan, then concedes that there is an element of truth in what Ryan says, and finally attacks Ryan's view.

One way to keep the source of an argument in plain sight is to use statements like "As William Ryan put it," as Magnet has done. Another important way is to use a special set of verbs followed by a *that* clause, such as *claims that, argues that, contends that, asserts that, theorizes that,* or *speculates that.*

Signaling Steps in a Causal Argument

Clearly signaling where you are in your argument helps your readers follow the argument and understand the distinctions you are drawing. Signals are especially important when an argument shifts gears—from presenting to arguing, from arguing to counterarguing, or from one part of an argument to another. Following are three kinds of signals that are used in this chapter's readings.

Question and Answer. One way of calling attention to an important point in an argument is by posing a question—which you then answer. Both William Julius Wilson and David Popenoe occasionally use a question and answer to draw attention to moves in their arguments:

What can account for the growing proportion of jobless adults? [...] An easy answer is racial segregation. (paragraph 18)

—WILLIAM JULIUS WILSON
"When Work Disappears"

What is the evidence? First, there are large-scale studies of statistical association [...]. Which childhood experiences are most important? Family, neighborhood, peer group, and popular culture all play some role [...] (paragraphs 35, 41)

—DAVID POPENOE
"Life without Father"

Transitions. Common transition words can signal how one idea adds force to the preceding idea or changes direction from it. Here are some of the ways Wilson and Popenoe use them.

But Chicago is by no means the only [...]. (Wilson, paragraph 3)

In contrast, the nonpoverty areas [...]. (Wilson, paragraph 3)

As a result, [...]. (Wilson, paragraph 11)

Moreover, as Alfred Blumstein pointed out, [...]. (Wilson, paragraph 12)

Yet at the time [...]. (Popenoe, paragraph 9)

But behind it all [...]. (Popenoe, paragraph 34)

Unfortunately, the die for the near future [...]. (Popenoe, paragraph 39)

Some of the transitions you use will draw attention to the causal relationships that you are arguing for. Here are examples from the readings:

As a result, the behavior and norms in the drug market are likely to influence the action of others. [...] Drug dealers cause the use and spread of guns in the neighborhood to escalate, which *in turn* raises the likelihood [...] (Wilson, paragraph 11)

However, in the troublesome public environment of the inner city, as people increasingly feel buffeted by forces beyond their control, what one deserves in the way of respect becomes more and more problematic and uncertain. This *in turn* further opens the issue of respect to sometimes intense interpersonal negotiation. (Anderson, paragraph 4)

You do not want to overdo—or automatically insert—any one of these signals, an *I believe,* a question and answer, or an adverb of transition. Used with care, however, they can help writers ensure that their readers follow the shifts in their arguments.

CITING SOURCES

As you speculate about causes in your essay, you will frequently quote, paraphrase, or summarize this chapter's readings and perhaps material from other sources as well. When you use original ideas in this way, you must cite them. In other words, you must identify their sources either informally or formally.

Informal Citation

Informal citation allows you to identify all of your sources within the text of your essay. You mention the author, the publication, and perhaps the date of publication right in your own sentences. In some instances, you may also want to include a brief description of the writer to establish his or her authority. When using informal citation, you do not need to identify sources in footnotes or in a works-cited list at the end of your essay.

Many of the readings, especially those published in newspapers or magazines, rely on informal citation. To see how writers use this citation style in a graceful way, look at these examples from the readings:

> "We've been able to salvage people who otherwise would have been killed," said Dr. Robert McAfee, president-elect of the American Medical Association, who plans to focus his tenure on efforts against violence. (paragraph 13)
>
> —Isabel Wilkerson
> "Two Boys, a Debt, a Gun, a Victim:
> The Face of Violence"

> "There is more published research on this topic than on almost any other social issue of our time," University of Kansas Professor Aletha C. Huston, chair of the American Psychological Association's Task Force on Television and Society, told Congress in 1988. (paragraph 8)
>
> —Carl M. Cannon
> "Honey, I Warped the Kids:
> The Argument for Eliminating
> Movie and TV Violence"

Formal Citation

When you use *formal citation,* you follow a specific style used by a particular academic or professional group. Biologists, for instance, follow a specific style when they write for their scientific journals. Appendix 2 outlines two of these styles: the Modern Language Association (MLA) style, which is favored by those in English and the humanities, and the American Psychological Association (APA) style, which is favored by social scientists. Ask your instructor which of these styles you should follow.

If you are referring to one of the readings in this chapter, cite it as a work in an anthology or edited collection. Depending on your instructor's advice, follow either the recommendations under "A Work in an Anthology" in the "Books" section of the MLA guidelines or those under "A Work in an Edited Collection" in the "Books" section of the APA guidelines. If you cite, for example, material coming from an article such as Isabel Wilkerson's, you will list Wilkerson as the author of the article, "Two Boys, a Debt, A Gun, a Victim:

The Face of Violence" as the title of the article, and *Writing the World* as the anthology in which the article appears. Appendix 2 of this book discusses these options thoroughly and provides examples of each.

Note: Writers usually do not document sources that provide commonly known facts, general background information, or common knowledge, but if you want to make use of some of the background material in this chapter's introductions or reading headnotes—material not written by Nathan McCall, for instance, or the other authors in this chapter—then you have two choices. You can paraphrase the material without giving a citation if it appears to be common knowledge. Otherwise, you can cite Charles R. Cooper and Susan Peck MacDonald as authors of *Writing the World,* using the models in Appendix 2.

EVALUATING AND REVISING YOUR ESSAY

The following guidelines for revising will help you evaluate your own draft and provide useful advice to other students about theirs. As you read a draft, try to identify what has been done well and to come up with specific ways to improve the presentation of the crisis and the argument. As you begin the revision process, focus on the big issues; save spelling and grammar for later.

Whether revising your own draft or helping your classmates with theirs, you may need to refer to specific readings, so have them handy as you work. If you prepared a reading-by-reading list of the causes of violence by young men, this list should prove helpful now as you analyze a draft about this issue.

If you are reading someone else's draft, it is a good idea to write out your comments on a separate sheet of paper, perhaps following the headings used in this section.

Read to Get a General Impression

Even if you are reading your own draft, read it straight through without marking on it, as if you were encountering the essay for the first time in a magazine about social and political issues. Then write three or four sentences summarizing your first impression. Does this essay offer a fresh, persuasive, and complex understanding of what causes violent crimes by young men? What aspect of the draft do you find most successful or interesting? What one major improvement would make the argument more convincing?

Read to Analyze the Draft More Closely

Next, number the paragraphs and underline the thesis statement. Then mark the point at which the essay divides into two major parts: the presentation of the crisis and the argument. Reread the draft, keeping in mind that the intended readers may not be very knowledgeable about the causes of violence by young men. Ask yourself, What do these particular readers need to know? Write down what is good about the draft as well as specific ideas for revision.

The Opening.   How does the opening engage the reader's interest? Are there vivid anecdotes or shocking statistics to draw the reader in? If not, suggest at least one alternative opening.

The Information about the Crisis.   First, consider whether the essay offers enough general information about the crisis. The focus of the essay should be clear to readers — it will discuss what *causes* violence and what crimes of violence are most often committed by young men. Are essential terms defined? Note any ways in which the initial information may need to be presented more clearly. Then consider whether the essay establishes the seriousness of these crimes of violence. What statistics or anecdotes in the readings might help establish this?

Now look at the opening and the information about the crisis together. Is the reader likely to continue reading the essay? Has the significance of the problem been established? If the essay incorporates statistics, are they relevant and clearly explained? How might the essay get off to a stronger start?

The Overview of Frequently Offered Speculations.   Does the essay present an impartial overview of the differing speculations about the causes of violence by young men? Are there descriptions of some specific causes, such as joblessness, poverty, or media violence? Does the overview provide a good context for the argument that follows? If not, suggest ways that it might be improved to better prepare readers for the balance of the essay.

The Thesis.   Put an asterisk in the margin where you find the thesis statement. Is the thesis stated clearly and forcefully? Or does it seem too general or uninteresting? If the latter, suggest ways to strengthen it.

Circle the key terms in the thesis. (Key terms might include *poverty, jobs, code of the streets, family breakdown,* or *violent images* — important words and phrases that are used throughout the essay and that identify which category and, more specifically, which causes the writer will focus on.)

Does the thesis also offer readers a road map for the essay? What might be done to make the forecast more complete or helpful?

The Argument.   Find the part of the essay that directly presents the causal argument. Are the causes presented in a logical sequence? If they don't seem to follow naturally from one to the other, suggest a more probable sequence.

Taking each step of the argument in turn, list ways it might be strengthened. Ask yourself, What more might be done to provide convincing causes of violent crime by young men? Suggest specific kinds of support, especially examples, statistics, anecdotes, and quotations from the relevant readings. Also suggest ways personal experiences and observations might be presented in a more compelling way.

The Counterargument.   At each step in the argument, consider questions and objections readers are likely to have. Note any other objections or questions that need to be considered. Where, if at all, do the writer's counterarguments need to be strengthened? Identify competing causal arguments that should be refuted or parts of competing arguments that might be conceded. What specific readings should be counterargued?

Should the counterarguments be rearranged in any way? Should they come earlier or later in the essay? Remember that counterarguments may be woven throughout an argument or fully developed in one or two places.

The Cues to Keep Readers on Track.   Think about how effectively the essay is organized. It should move along clearly without causing readers to lose track of the argument or lose interest. What parts of the essay are confusing? Where does the direction of the argument seem unclear? Are there gaps in reasoning? Point out any instances you find and suggest possible remedies.

Look to see whether the key terms in the thesis are referred to consistently throughout the essay. Note any places where terms shift in meaning or where causes disappear from mention for any significant portion of the essay.

What specific changes would make the essay easier to follow? For example, should different terms be used? Should paragraphs be combined or separated? Are more or clearer transitions needed? Also consider whether any parts of the essay should be moved to another place.

The Closing.   Does the essay close in a graceful and memorable way? Does it reassert the importance of the causes argued for throughout the essay? Is key language used? How might the closing be strengthened?

EDITING AND PROOFREADING

As you revise, you should be concerned primarily with your presentation of the issue and your argument. Then comes the time to edit, to begin clarifying your sentences and tightening the connections among them so that each step in your reasoning makes a clear contribution to the overall argument.

Examine the connections between all of your sentences. If you sense misdirection or a gap that would break a reader's momentum, try reorganizing one sentence or the other or writing new material. Check to see whether you shift terms unnecessarily. Look for sentences that might be combined to better show relationships among ideas. Look as well for overly long or garbled sentences that might be broken up into two or three sentences.

As you work on your sentences, look for errors in spelling, capitalization, punctuation, usage, and grammar, consulting a writer's handbook for information about correcting any you find. Ask a friend or a classmate to read over your essay to help you spot errors.

Before you hand in your final revised essay, proofread it carefully and run it through a spellchecker to try to make it error free.

REFLECTING ON WHAT YOU HAVE LEARNED

Once you complete this chapter's reading and writing assignments, you may want to reflect on what you have learned. Doing so will help you consolidate your new knowledge and remember it longer.

As you worked your way through this chapter, you were actually engaged in two closely related kinds of learning: becoming informed about a social crisis and its causes and composing a convincing causal argument of your own. Integrating these two kinds of learning, then, has been your major achievement. Using the following questions as starting points, write a page or so reflecting about this accomplishment.

- What was the most difficult part of understanding the causes of the high rate of violence by young men in the United States today? What was the most surprising?

- How have your attitudes about the causes of violence been confirmed or changed? What questions do you still have about this social problem?

- What was most difficult for you in planning your essay? When you began drafting, what was your biggest surprise? Think of the most important revision you made in your draft. How did you decide to make this change?

- What advice would you give to writers who are just starting an assignment in which they need to speculate about a cause?

- What aspect of your essay seems most effective? How would you revise your essay if you had more time to work on it?

GATHERING ADDITIONAL INFORMATION

To supplement the readings in this chapter, you may want to do further research into the causes of violence by young men. The *kind* of material you are looking for should guide where you look. In this chapter, you have encountered three kinds of material: personal accounts and reports of violence, statistics, and causal arguments. Since each kind requires a different search strategy, the following tips should prove helpful in finding other sources on this issue.

Personal Accounts and Reports of Violence

Personal accounts may come from autobiographies written by people who have experienced violence or from magazine articles written by victims or observers of violence. Since personal accounts tend to be of interest to a general readership, they often can be found not only in college libraries but also on newsstands and magazine racks and in public libraries.

For help in finding book-length autobiographies containing descriptions of violence, ask a librarian for assistance. He or she may be able to suggest some relevant book reviews. Personal accounts of violence are also frequently found in magazines written for general readers. You can look in *InfoTrac* or other indexes like the *Readers' Guide to Periodical Literature,* the *Expanded Academic Index,* or *Periodicals Abstracts,* which cover general-interest magazines and journals. Begin your search using search terms such as *juvenile offenders, school violence, violence in children, youth and violence.*

Newspaper reports, such as those in this chapter by Isabel Wilkerson, Timothy Egan, and Rita Williams, also offer descriptive details and facts that may be useful to you. To find such reports, look in *Newsbank,* the *National Newspaper Index,* or other newspaper indexes. You might start your search by using terms such as *juvenile delinquency, juvenile homicide,* or *school violence.* Many national newspapers are also available on the Web. Use a search directory to find their Web pages. The *New York Times,* for instance, may be found at <http://www.nytimes.com/>.

Statistics

Locating statistics requires a different search strategy. The U.S. government is the best source of statistics on violence because they are gathered by the Bureau of the Census, the FBI, and its parent agency, the Department of Justice. Key government statistics on violence are available in the reference section of most libraries as well as on the Internet. Look for the following compilations:

- *Uniform Crime Reports for the United States,* published annually by the FBI
- *Sourcebook of Criminal Justice Statistics,* published annually by the Department of Justice
- *Youth Indicators: Trends in the Well-Being of American Youth,* published annually by the Department of Education
- *Statistical Abstract of the United States,* published annually by the Bureau of the Census

If you have access to a large research library with a government documents collection, you will be able to find more detailed and more technical government reports. Ask a librarian for help since government documents are organized somewhat differently than materials in the rest of the library.

If you are using the Internet, you can locate many of the same government statistics that are available in print sources. You may also be able to find crime statistics for local areas if their police departments have home pages with reports on crime. Here are some good places to begin a Web search:

National Criminal Justice Reference Service — The NCJRS home page provides links to many other useful sources because it is a collection of clearinghouses supporting many government bureaus. It is located at <http://www.ncjrs.org>.

U.S. Department of Justice, Bureau of Justice Statistics — This home page is located at <http://www.ojp.usdoj.gov/bjs/>.

U.S. Department of Justice, Federal Bureau of Information (FBI) — The FBI publishes its yearly *Uniform Crime Reports* both in print form and online. These statistics are likely to be available online up to a full year before the print form reaches libraries. The FBI home page is located at <http://www.fbi.gov>.

Other Web sites containing facts on violence may be found by using a search tool such as Yahoo! and following the links from search categories like "government" or "law." (See Appendix 2 for additional information on Internet search tools.)

Causal Arguments

In addition to personal accounts, newspaper reports, and statistics, you may want to find causal arguments, such as those in the last set of readings in this chapter. Causal arguments are often written by professional researchers, many of whom hold positions in universities, and are generally published in scholarly books or journals. These are most likely to be found in college or university libraries rather than in public libraries.

Books. Books about violence will not be absolutely up to date in their information; they are useful not for discovering current facts but for reading extended, well-developed arguments. To locate books in your library's card or online catalog, try the following search terms: *violence in television, violence in children, violent crimes, juvenile delinquency.*

In addition, you may want to use some search terms about families or ideas — particularly if you are highlighting one of these circumstances as the most important cause of violence. If, for instance, you want to examine arguments about the family, you could look at these Library of Congress Subject Headings (LCSH):

Fatherless family—United States

Fatherhood—United States

Fathers—United States

Paternal deprivation—United States

Children of single parents—United States

The preceding headings are those designated for David Popenoe's book *Life without Father.* By using the Library of Congress Subject Headings for a book you know, you may be able to locate similar or related studies. See Appendix 2 for more information about using the LCSH.

Articles.   You can also look for causal arguments in magazines or research-oriented journals. The essay by Elijah Anderson, for example, originally appeared in *Atlantic Monthly,* a journal whose articles may be found in many of the same general indexes, mentioned above, in which you would find personal or newspaper accounts: *InfoTrac,* the *Expanded Academic Index,* the *Readers' Guide,* and the *National Newspaper Index.* You might, therefore, have located Anderson's article by using a general database in either a public or a university library. Since different libraries use different indexes or different names for their indexes, check with your reference librarian for the name of the indexes available in whatever library you are using.

Some articles appear in journals that are read almost exclusively by college professors, students, and professional researchers. These articles are more difficult to read because they usually assume a certain level of expertise. They may, however, provide you with considerable detail about research on a particular subject. To find scholarly articles, look in specialized indexes in a college or university library, such as *Sociofile,* the *Expanded Academic Index,* and *Criminology Abstracts.*

FURTHER READINGS ON CAUSES OF VIOLENCE

Anderson, Elijah. *Code of the Street: Decency, Violence, and the Moral Life of the Inner City.* New York: Norton, 1999.

Gabarino, James. *Lost Boys: Why Our Sons Turn Violent and How We Can Save Them.* New York: Free, 1999.

Gibson, James William. *Warrior Dreams: Paramilitary Culture in Post-Vietnam America.* New York: Hill & Wang, 1994.

Gottfredson, Michael R., and Travis Hirschi. *A General Theory of Crime.* Stanford: Stanford UP, 1990.

Jankowski, Martin Sanchez. *Islands in the Street: Gangs and American Urban Society.* Berkeley: U of California P, 1991.

Males, Mike A. *The Scapegoat Generation: America's War on Adolescents.* Monroe: Common Courage, 1996.

Prothrow-Stith, Deborah, with Michaele Weissman. *Deadly Consequences: How Violence Is Destroying Our Teenage Population and a Plan to Begin Solving the Problem.* New York: HarperCollins, 1991.

Snyder, Howard N., and Melissa Sickmund. *Juvenile Offenders and Victims: A Focus on Violence.* Pittsburgh: National Center for Juvenile Justice, 1995.

Tonry, Michael. *Malign Neglect: Race, Crime, and Punishment in America.* Oxford: Oxford UP, 1996.

Wilson, James Q., and Richard J. Herrnstein. *Crime and Human Nature.* New York: Simon & Schuster, 1985.

Wilson, William Julius. *The Truly Disadvantaged: The Inner City, the Underclass, and Public Policy.* Chicago: U of Chicago P, 1987.

ADDITIONAL WRITING PROJECTS

Here are some additional writing projects on the causes of violence by young men that make use of the readings and ideas in this chapter.

Personal Experience Essay

Tell the story of your own experience with violence by young men, as a participant or as an observer. If parts of this experience are painful or embarrassing for you, focus only on those you feel comfortable sharing with others.

Purpose and Readers.   Your readers are your classmates who have been reading about violence by young men. Your purpose is to help them see clearly what happened and to understand what the experience was like for you. In addition, try to show them why the experience remains significant for you personally.

Resources to Draw On.   Your most important resource will be your memory. Start by making notes about what you remember. Try to recall as many concrete details as you can: when the incident occurred (year, season, time of day), where it occurred (city or area, specific location, key objects, vehicles, roads, and the like that were relevant to what happened), who was involved (as doer, as victim), and what happened (what specifically was said and done). Also note your feelings at the time of the experience, soon after it occurred, and now. Some of the readings in this chapter may suggest ways to make your story more concrete and vivid. Look, for example, at the writers' descriptions of sights (Isabel Wilkerson), sounds (Luis J. Rodriguez and Susan Straight), smells and bits of dialogue (Nathan McCall), physical objects (Timothy Egan and Andrew Lam), and young men's body language (Rita Williams).

Tips for Writing a Successful Personal Experience Essay.   You will probably relate your experience in the order in which it happened. Try to make your
account memorable and interesting by building some suspense as you move
from beginning to end. Also try to include many specifics about actions and
dialogue. Use vivid verbs, colorful nouns and adjectives, and close imitations
of actual conversations whenever possible so readers have the sense of seeing
and hearing real people speak. Finally, reflect on this experience from your
present perspective. How does it look to you now? How has it influenced your
feelings or beliefs? How has it changed your behavior?

Attach to your essay a page or so of explanations, showing your instructor
the connections, as you see them, between the personal experience in your
essay and what you have learned from the readings in this chapter.

Report on Statistical Information

Every year, law officers, government officials, and the public question whether
the United States is becoming a more or less violent country. Newspapers
often report on whether the problem of violence is increasing or diminishing.
You, too, can write a balanced report on the current level of violence by young
men. You may want to focus on the incidence of one crime — murder, nonnegligent manslaughter, or aggravated assault — or report on all three crimes.
Whatever you decide, be sure to base your report on the most reputable
recent statistics, such as those gathered by the FBI.

Purpose and Readers.   Your purpose is to present facts clearly and to report
fairly about *what* is happening, not to argue about *why.* In many ways, your
purpose resembles that of government sources and newspapers that track
yearly rises or declines in crime: They do so because people want to know
whether the problem is growing or diminishing. Assume that your readers are
educated adults who like to keep up with current news. Some of them may be
parents or others who have been alarmed by recent reports of violent crime
among the young.

Resources to Draw On.   You might begin by consulting the section on statistics in this chapter and the readings that contain relevant statistics, such as
the essay by Males. You could then look for other statistics, either more recent
data or statistics that allow you to compare data from different years. All of
this information will help you expand your understanding of the facts themselves. In addition, you can examine the readings to see the various ways that
statistics can be presented — separately from the text (in tables, for instance),
within quotations, or in your own words. Two resources that are likely to be
helpful are the most recent editions of the *Statistical Abstract of the United
States* and the FBI's *Uniform Crime Reports,* both of which are discussed in "Statistics" on page 440–41.

Tips for Writing a Successful Report. Write a report on the statistics that interest you most and seem to provide a clear picture of some aspect of violence by young men. You may want to devise your own tables or figures or include parts of published tables or figures in your report. As you develop your essay, be careful not to argue but instead to report objectively on the information you find. One possible approach would be to compare the incidence of murder, nonnegligent manslaughter, and aggravated assault in two time periods or two years. Then you could look at the crimes one by one, reporting on the differences between the earlier and later periods. Another approach would be to look at only one crime, such as murder, and to report on its incidence in cities, rural areas, or different parts of the United States, perhaps comparing one decade to another. Whatever statistics you decide to write about, try to present your facts in an orderly fashion so that readers can grasp them easily. It is also a good idea to photocopy the statistics you use and include the photocopies with your essay so that your instructor can see where your data came from.

Essay Speculating about Effects

Write an essay speculating about one or more of the long-term effects of violence by young men. You might, for example, consider the psychological effects on the victims and on the larger community, the monetary costs to society in the form of prisons or other costs, or the effects on schools and learning, on racial and ethnic relations, or on the communities and neighborhoods in which violence occurs.

Purpose and Readers. Speculating about effects is the flip side of arguing about causes, and much of the worry about causes of crime comes from the worry about its effects. Assume that your readers are adults who are interested in current events and have read about shocking incidents of violence such as the cluster of schoolyard shootings in 1998 and 1999. They are asking, Could this happen to us or our community? What is happening to us as a society? The purpose of your essay is to provide some answers to these questions.

Resources to Draw On. In speculating about the long-term effects of violence by young men, you could start with the statistics and accounts of violence in this chapter and then speculate about what may result later. Consider the three categories of circumstances presented in the readings: neighborhoods, families, and ideas and cultural influences. Perhaps you think neighborhoods will become more — or less — violent, or that there will be further breakdowns in the family, or that the family of the future will take different directions. Maybe you foresee a change in the media or other cultural influences due to the concern about violence. Whatever your inclinations, use this chapter's readings to think about the future, not merely the past.

Tips for Writing a Successful Speculative Essay.   Choose one effect or a related series of effects and write an essay speculating about it. First present the crisis and explain to your readers those effects that are already widely agreed on. Then speculate about what seem to you to be the most likely long-term effects. If you have chosen to focus on effects on neighborhoods, for instance, you can sequence the effects you think will occur, discuss them one by one, and explain why each is likely. The same kind of approach should work if you focus on other types of effects, such as economic or psychological ones. Review the writer's guide in this chapter for more information on speculating.

Essay Taking a Position

Write an essay that takes a position on whether or not stricter gun control laws will help prevent violence by young men.

Purpose and Readers.   Controversy surrounds the issues of gun possession and gun control. Some argue that guns do not cause violence but are merely the tools of people who engage in violence. Others, however, argue that guns are a direct cause of violence, that without the easy availability of guns, young men would be far less likely to engage in violence and the violence they do engage in would be less destructive. Your purpose in this essay is to take a position within this debate and to convince your readers of your point of view. Assume that your readers know there is such a debate but have not made up their minds where they stand on the issue.

Resources to Draw On.   The readings in this chapter provide accounts of school violence (Egan and Ross), the growth of guns in Riverside, California (Straight), and young men's fascination with guns (Lam). In addition, you can use the World Wide Web to explore this debate. Locate some of the arguments from both sides by searching for the terms *gun control* and *gun rights* and following interesting links they suggest. If you want to examine some of the current laws, you can check the U.S. Bureau of Alcohol, Tobacco and Firearms site at <http://www.atf.treas.gov/core/firearms/firearms.htm>. When you have a good sense of the arguments on either side of the debate, decide what your own position is. You might want to limit your discussion to gun control laws in your state or city, if you can readily find such information (there are some Web sites about gun control laws in particular states).

The Successful Essay.   You might begin with one or two telling incidents of violence that illustrate the possible benefits or problems with gun controls.

Then you could state your position in a thesis and develop a list of reasons. Taking one reason at a time, you can provide statistics, quotes from experts, examples, and so forth to show why each reason supports your position. You should also be aware of readers' possible questions and objections and build refutations or concessions into your argument. You may want to check the Writer's Guide in Chapter 3 for tips on essays that take a position.

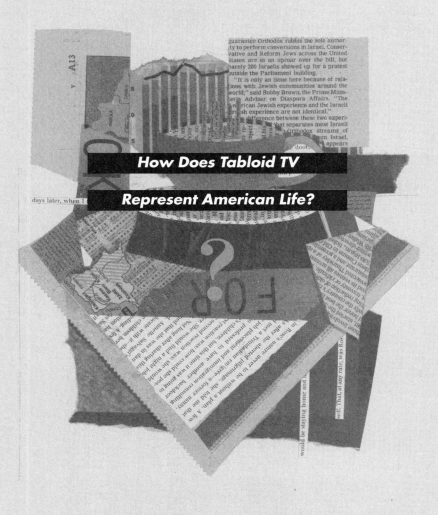

How Does Tabloid TV Represent American Life?

INTERPRETING POPULAR CULTURE

■ ■ ■

After a wing collapses on a twisting stunt plane during an air show, the plane dives into a lake and disappears beneath the water. Weeks later, her first time at the lake since the accident, the wife of the pilot talks tearfully to a television reporter. She always traveled with her husband, she says, and announced his stunt routines; they were childhood sweethearts; and the three children miss their father, who had no life insurance. Somber music opens and closes the show, and the crash is replayed numerous times.

Sharry (no last name given), a former *Playboy* model, sits in a wheelchair in her living room. A married woman with two young children, she has had a serious automobile accident, which has left her a paraplegic. She denies that she was drunk at the time of the accident, though the police report says she was. She refuses to accept that she will never walk. She says she misses "power shopping and walking" but hopes one day to have a career in "fraud investigation."

At a distance, two men are stripping parts off a parked car, and a reporter informs viewers that one out of every forty-two cars is stripped, one every twenty seconds. A man in the neighborhood says, "The police pass by and don't even bother." The television crew has planted a 1987 Mercury on a street leading to a freeway on-ramp. The camera crew watches from a distance. Within two hours the hubcaps have been stolen. After dark, two men break in and steal the radio and battery. The reporter neither explains how this particular case is resolved nor interviews someone who might propose a solution to the problem.

If you recognize the television stories described on the preceding page, you have probably been watching tabloid TV or reading the *National Enquirer*—or perhaps watching the late-evening news, which has adopted many tabloid features. The half-hour programs of tabloid TV present stories within a magazine-like format and offer a sensationalistic version of the news. The best-known tabloids have been *Hard Copy, Inside Edition, American Journal,* and *Extra.* In the nineteenth century, the term *tabloid* was used to identify short summaries of important news events, but by the 1920s the term became associated with newspapers that focus on crime and violence and that feature very large headlines and many photographs. The *New York Post* is an example of a contemporary tabloid newspaper. The *National Enquirer* and the *Star,* often referred to as supermarket tabloids, are other examples of the genre.

Tabloid TV has been very popular in America in recent years. In their heyday, the major tabloids aired five times a week in pre-prime time (6:30 to 8:00 P.M.). The two most popular tabloids, *Inside Edition* and *Hard Copy,* were available on almost every local television station in the country. In a 1995 Gallup Poll, 24 percent of respondents said they regularly watched tabloid TV, and 40 percent said they sometimes watched it. By comparison, 43 percent said they regularly watched such newsmagazines as *60 Minutes* or *20/20,* and 43 percent said they sometimes watched them. All of the tabloids are syndicated, produced by specialized companies that then sell them to the networks (CNN, ABC, CBS, Fox, etc.). Some of these production companies are associated with the movie industry.

This chapter looks at tabloid TV as a television genre and invites you to explore some of the possible influences of tabloid TV on viewers. During your study of tabloid TV, you will be asked to view several programs in one series and guided to take careful notes about them. Doing so will enable you to participate in basic research on popular culture.

Given the dazzling variety of popular-culture forms and even the large number of TV genres—talk shows, soap operas, cop shows, situation comedies, local news, and more—why analyze tabloid TV? Popular culture, especially television, is being studied seriously in several academic disciplines, especially in the social sciences. Since television viewing is the single most common cultural experience of all Americans, many researchers consider it worthy of serious study. They believe that scholarly studies of television can tell us something about how television viewing influences young people, how it affects people's choices of leisure activities, how it shapes viewers' attitudes toward politics and responsible citizenship, and how it affects or reflects numerous other aspects of American life.

Studying tabloid TV, then, will introduce you to the study of popular culture and prepare you for other courses involving the study of popular culture. It will also give you an opportunity to learn how to interpret critically a form of popular culture that you have previously watched for entertainment.

The first section of this chapter shows you how to view tabloid TV critically and to gather data on the shows you watch. The next section, a set of readings, introduces the history, development, and style of tabloid TV and some of the issues surrounding the genre. A subsequent set of readings deals with the critical perspective from which you will be interpreting tabloid programs.

At the end of each section are some suggestions for keeping a writer's notebook. The tasks are designed to help you to compare what you have viewed or read to your own experience and that of other students; they also offer guidance as you reread the selections critically and prepare to write a research report about tabloid TV. You might want to look ahead at these tasks before you begin your viewing and reading.

A LOOK AHEAD: WRITING ABOUT TABLOID TV   This chapter includes an assignment to write a research report that interprets tabloid TV from a social perspective. Developing such a report involves demonstrating how, in your view, a particular tabloid series represents social life. As in making any argument, you will need to state your position concisely in a thesis and support your thesis with detailed examples — in this case, from tabloid TV programs you have been watching. In addition to presenting your own interpretation of tabloid TV, you will need to take other interpretations into account and counterargue — that is, respond to — them if necessary.

VIEWING TABLOID TV CRITICALLY

To learn how to critically view tabloid TV, read this section all the way through, including the writer's notebook tasks at the end. The guidelines that follow will help you

- orient yourself to the viewing task
- watch closely and gather data
- interpret what you have seen

BECOMING ORIENTED

If you are not already among the 20 million Americans who watch a tabloid TV series each week, start watching one or two different series to become familiar with the tabloids. If possible, watch two different series on the same night. The shows that are available may change, but look for such titles as *Inside Edition, Hard Copy, American Journal,* or *Extra.*

You can watch them Monday through Friday and sometimes Saturday, usually between 6:30 and 8:00 P.M. Check a local newspaper for times and channels.

As you watch, notice that each half-hour program is usually divided into three to five major segments and sometimes one collection of very brief segments. Consider, too, the kinds of subjects in each segment and their range or diversity. Pay attention to the graphics and the sound effects as well as the anchors and reporters, especially their appearance and manner. Think about how the two tabloid series are alike and different. Remember that you are watching not only to orient yourself to this television genre but also to choose a series to interpret.

WATCHING CLOSELY AND GATHERING DATA

After class discussion and reflection, choose one series to interpret. You may want to choose the series that best fits your schedule, or your instructor may encourage you and your classmates to watch the same series. All series feature the same kinds of subjects, but different series may give more or less attention to celebrities, personal calamities, or investigative reports.

For the duration of this assignment, plan to watch at least five or six programs in the series you have chosen, gathering data on fifteen or more program segments. Later, as you begin drafting and revising your research report, you may find that you need to watch even more programs to gather sufficient support for your interpretation.

Critical Viewing

The key to successful *critical* viewing of television is to find a new way to be in the same room with a television set. In other words, you need to transform a familiar situation of passive leisure into an unfamiliar situation of *active, purposeful* attention. People who interpret and write about popular culture have proposed that active attention requires defamiliarization—being able to see something familiar as strange or even foreign, as though you have never seen it before. How do you defamiliarize television so that you can learn more about it? The following tips may help:

- Take notes as you watch.
- Gain knowledge of tabloid TV from the readings.
- Videotape a program and watch it a second time.
- Watch a tape with other students in class and stop it after each segment for discussion and further note-taking.

At first you may find it difficult to sustain active attention when you watch a program, but it should gradually get easier with practice.

Gathering Data about a Series

To gain information to be able to describe a series in your report, you will need to take careful notes about its characteristics. Use the following list as a guideline for the features to focus on, including the specific details you might otherwise overlook.

1. Time, channel, network, producer
2. Anchor(s): name, age, dress, hairstyle, manner (posture, body language, ways of relating to anchor and reporters), language (reserved, friendly, chatty, formal), way of previewing upcoming segments or future programs
3. Setting for anchor(s): type of space, furnishings, background (objects, colors, other details)
4. Interviewers and reporters: names, personal styles, attitudes toward persons interviewed
5. Graphics: series logo, titles of segments, words on the screen
6. Sound: music, sound effects
7. Typical advertisements: several examples, perhaps all the ads before, during, and after one segment

Here is an example of notes taken about one feature of a series:

Setting for anchors:
Tony Cox substituting for main anchor, blonde Deborah Norville. Not in studio but at the location of one of the segments—O.J. Simpson civil trial in Los

Angeles. Cox an African American. Norville is also frequently on location rather than in the studio. Cox is sitting in a director's chair somewhere I can't identify. Maybe balcony of a hotel room—a lower floor because behind him is an L.A. scene. Sunshine. Slight smog haze. Palm trees. Looks like the edge of a park more than downtown. Parked cars on a street, cars moving on the street. No sound from the traffic. No people on the sidewalks. Actually a very peaceful scene. Cox does not move around or gesture. Just sits and talks at the camera. See only his upper body with the scene behind until he is joined late in the segment by a reporter who has been at the trial. Setting doesn't seem to go with the downtown courthouse Simpson trial.

The preceding notes take the form of words, phrases, and full sentences. They are neither polished nor revised, and their organization reflects the order in which the writer noticed certain details. The concrete details may or may not find their way into the writer's final report, but they are important because they help the writer remember this particular setting. Continuing to watch other programs, the writer will gradually add notes about other settings for anchors—and, of course, about other characteristics of the series.

Gathering Data about Program Segments

In the series you have chosen, the segments in each program will provide most of the data for your interpretation and most of the support for your findings. Since not all segments of a program will be relevant to your report, your interpretation probably will be based on a small group of segments from several different programs. As you work and watch, be sure to name and identify each separate segment and to take detailed notes about it.

The guidelines below are designed to help you collect all the information you need to write a successful report. At first, it may be difficult to do so much note-taking. Keep in mind, however, that the more details you record about each segment, the easier it will be to recall the segment when you are planning and drafting your report. Jot down specific details about each of these items.

1. Day and date of the program
2. Title of segment (if the segment is not titled, make up a title of your own)
3. Subject or topic of the segment
4. Setting: name(s) and description(s) of the location(s)
5. Characters: names and descriptions of the people in the segment, their appearance, way of talking, whether they speak at all
6. Summary: the basic parts of the story, what happens to those involved
7. Main point: the major idea a viewer is supposed to grasp, the primary reaction that is intended

Here is an example of notes taken while watching a program segment about baby-sitting:

Title: Can You Trust Your Baby-Sitter?
Florida couple, both work full time—hired a baby-sitter for 1 year old son. Interviewed the sitter, liked her. She had references. Then tape shows sitter hitting child on couch and in crib with a hair brush. Sound of child crying. Sitter doesn't say anything—just hits child. Woman in her thirties maybe, a little overweight, dark hair. Parents noticed big change in child's behavior—didn't want to get off the couch. Hired Baby Watch Franchise to secretly videotape sitter in living room and bedroom. Brief interview with franchise owner— explains the service they offer. Parents fired the sitter and called the police, accusing her of child abuse, with the video as evidence.

Sitter named Sara Conception Azevedo. Handcuffed, walking with a police officer—at jail or courthouse. Reporter goes to her house and knocks on door— knocking sound probably faked—but no one comes to the door. Azevedo never talks. Narrator's voice and music are the prominent sounds in the segment. Mother says two or three sentences about how sad she is, but she does not appear. Segment ends with a closeup of an empty crib with baby music playing.

People who are on camera during the segment: anchor, reporter, Azevedo, child, franchise owner, policeman. Parents are not on camera. Only voices are those of anchor, narrator, child, franchise owner, mother. Taped segments in home are replayed. Azevedo moves slowly, deliberately, like someone who is in control. Point seems to be you can't trust anybody.

To record these notes, the writer wrote almost continuously while watching the segment. The notes follow the story from beginning to end, describing the setting and the people, detailing their actions and interactions, their appearance, and what they say. Sounds are noted, and specific names are included. Instead of making many comments, the writer focuses on the action and the people. The writer added the last paragraph during the commercial break following the end of the segment. It makes general comments about how the segment was presented and states a possible point of the segment, a point about social relations.

INTERPRETING TELEVISION FROM A SOCIAL PERSPECTIVE

Interpretation often begins with a question or an insight. It involves making connections and testing out ideas. You probably have experienced moments of active, critical TV viewing, times when you have had ideas of your own about the impact of television on your life and on the lives of others. You may have read about research that links violence to television viewing, or you may have heard political leaders criticize television for undermining viewers' morals. When you react to such ideas, you become a more active, critical television viewer. You begin to interpret what you watch.

This chapter invites you to interpret television in a systematic way and to adopt a social perspective. To take such a perspective means to look closely at *the way social relations are represented* in television programs. Think of *social* as including all possible temporary or long-term relationships among people— couples, families, friends, classmates, neighbors, coworkers, shoppers, citizens, and so forth. Think of *represent* as meaning "translate"—turning events from the real world into some version of reality. Keep in mind that TV representations always have a point of view, always are selective, and thus always change or distort reality. Nevertheless, these representations exert a powerful influence on how viewers see reality.

To take a social perspective on tabloid TV means to look closely at how it represents people and social life in America. It means to look attentively at what kinds of people appear on the programs and how they interact with each other.

After you have taken careful series and program-segment notes, it is time to consider questions of interpretation. Think about these questions as you reflect on your notes for a program segment:

1. *What kinds of people appear and how are they represented?* Are they young or old, men or women, attractive or unattractive, poor, middle class, or wealthy, educated or uneducated? What ethnic groups are represented? Are people straight or gay, married or unmarried, rural, suburban, or urban? Are they celebrities or ordinary people? Are they people with exceptional skills and training or average people? What kinds of people are slighted or ignored?

2. *How do people relate to each other?* Are the relationships portrayed based on trust or distrust? What is the predominant way men and women or children and parents relate to each other? Do Americans from different ethnic, religious, class, or income groups seem to get along or to be in conflict? Does the cooperation, aggressiveness, violence, or manipulation shown seem more or less common than your personal experience would lead you to expect?

3. *How do program staff relate to people in the stories?* Do anchors and reporters evaluate relationships or simply present them? If they evaluate, what kinds of judgments do they make?

The following example is a social interpretation of the earlier program-segment notes on "Can You Trust Your Baby-Sitter?"

> White couple with baby are betrayed by a poor Hispanic woman—she lies to them and abuses their child. The franchise owner is a white male—he's the hero of the story, I suppose. The policeman is a white male too. All seem to be in their thirties. Only the whites speak—the wife, franchise owner. We never see the family's house or neighborhood, but from the room sizes and furnishings on the secret video I think the neighborhood must be middle class. So we get a crime inflicted on the white middle class by an inner-city person of color.
>
> The relationship here is basically one of betrayal. Lack of trust is the problem—you really can't trust anyone, no matter how trustworthy they may seem. Fear of violence is also involved. This segment must increase the fear and maybe even guilt of parents who both must work and hire others to care for children. Everybody must be checked out by experts before you let them into your home. *Inside Edition* would probably say they are providing a public service by warning parents of certain dangers.

Focusing on notes and recollections from one segment, this writer tries out a social interpretation. The interpretation is exploratory and tentative. The writer does not try to be right or even wise but rather to discover some plausible meanings in the segment. Before reaching any conclusions about how the tabloids represent social life in America, the writer would need to interpret several other segments. This will be your task as well as you proceed through the chapter.

A WRITER'S NOTEBOOK
Viewing Tabloid TV Critically

The following tasks are designed to help you think about tabloid TV and identify and start to work up material you might use in your own essay.

1. *Become oriented to tabloid TV.* Watch one or two programs—from different tabloid TV series if possible—and take notes about each program segment so that you can tell your classmates about the series and program segments you watched. What seems special or unusual about these tabloids? What makes them different from other television programs you watch?

2. *Gather data about a series.* Choose one tabloid TV series to watch several times over the next two or three weeks. In your notebook, enter the categories of series characteristics listed in the "Gathering Data about a Series" section in this chapter above and allow enough space for notes. As you watch the series over the next few weeks, jot down notes in each category until you have enough data to describe the series in detail to someone who has never seen it.

3. *Gather data about program segments.* Start a new section in your notebook and call it "Program-Segment Data and Analysis." As you watch each program in the series you have chosen, note as many details as possible about each program segment. The guidelines in the "Gathering Data about Program Segments" section in this chapter should help you.

4. *Interpreting television from a social perspective.* After watching each program, select one segment to interpret. Question what you have seen in order to reflect on what the segment means. Write phrases and sentences to capture your insights. Later you may think of other insights to add to your notes. You may want to use the questions in the "Interpreting Television from a Social Perspective" section in this chapter to guide your interpretation.

GLOSSARY: WORDS ABOUT WORDS

In this chapter's readings, you will encounter several terms having to do with economics, production, and marketing of tabloid TV. This glossary introduces these special terms. You may want to review the glossary before you begin the readings and then later refer to it as needed.

cable channels: Television channels brought into a home by cable for which a monthly fee is paid. Noncable channels are broadcast directly to television

(continues on next page)

(continued from previous page)

receivers, and no fee is paid for this broadcast. Most viewers pay for cable service to receive a larger number of channels and programs.

demographics: In the case of television, the characteristics of age, gender, race, income, and so forth of viewers of a program, which is key information for advertisers.

FCC: Federal Communication Commission, an agency of the U.S. government, which sets nationwide rules governing the television industry.

market size: The number of viewers of a television program relative to the number of viewers watching similar, competing programs.

network affiliation: Most local television stations have a network affiliation — that is, they offer exclusively or primarily the programs provided by a national network like ABC or Fox. Some local stations are owned by a national network.

prime time: 7:30 or 8:00 to 10:00 P.M., Monday through Friday.

producers: Television companies that produce programs and sell them to television networks. Producers include King World, Westinghouse Group W, and Viacom. Tabloid TV programs are made and distributed by such producers.

ratings: A system of ranking television programs by the number and type of viewers they attract. The higher the ratings, the more advertising revenues a program brings in.

syndication: The production of television programs for sale to national networks and local stations. Tabloid TV programs are syndicated, rather than produced by networks like ABC or CNN.

TABLOID TV AS A TELEVISION GENRE:
ITS HISTORY AND FEATURES

The readings in this section provide background information that will help you interpret tabloid TV. They introduce you to the history of tabloid TV, differentiate it from other kinds of TV news and entertainment, and describe some of its special strategies and effects. Ever since tabloid TV became an easily recognizable genre of American television in the late 1980s, it has attracted the attention of media reviewers, cultural critics, and scholars. All are represented in this section.

HERE COME THE NEWS PUNKS

Max Robins

Max Robins is senior editor at TV Guide *and writes frequently about media issues. Writing for the media magazine* Channels *in 1988, Robins offered one of the first reports on early tabloid television.* Channels *is read by a wide variety of people working in television—reporters, producers, executives, and advertisers.*

After describing America's Most Wanted, *a crime show that invites viewers to call in tips about perpetrators of unsolved crimes, Robins focuses on* A Current Affair, *an early tabloid show that began in 1986 and continued until 1998. It may seem at first that Robins dislikes tabloid TV, but if you read closely, you will see that he presents a balanced view. Notice, for example, that he and others criticize conventional 1988 TV news as bland and gray.*

As you read, pay attention to what Robins says about the distinctive style and content of the early television tabloid shows, the kinds of shows they displaced, and the kind of audience they attracted.

The ascension of the news punks rankles the journalism establishment: How dare they soil the fourth estate?° "The old rules of journalism are pretty much out the window. The ethic is to grab an audience and get it to watch," opined Pulitzer Prize-winning critic Ron Powers on a recent *Nightline.* "What we're

---

°**fourth estate:** The public media—newspapers, magazines, and television, particularly in their role as government watchdogs and interpreters of the culture.

seeing now is the blueprint for a new kind of value-free, content-free, high-impact programming that calls itself news but is really something else."

Powers' analysis is too facile, too black and white. Certainly, the news punks' hell-bent approach can lead to abuse — when Geraldo crashes through a door in a televised live drug bust there's always the possibility that innocent parties will have their faces splashed nationwide. Still, the news punks' aggressive stance can break news and inform, heightening awareness of important topics. [Talk-show host Morton] Downey, for all his fractiousness, at least has people talking about social and political issues. Their willingness to exploit the visual properties of the medium, to stir things up, cannot be dismissed.

"Even in the worst of these shows, the audience comes away with something they didn't know before," says Rivera. "You can't say that about the game shows they replace. Rather than go 'tut tut tut' about the decline of quality TV, look at what's being offered."

Each of these programs has a distinct personality, but they all share an interactive quality. The best of them deliver a visceral hit — they create an emotional link between TV and viewer. Like it or not, the news punks are 1990s TV. They are heating up the cool medium, changing the programming equation and showing how news and information can make money.

"The problem with TV is not that there's too much controversy," says Phil 5
Donahue. This despite the fact that grandpa-news-punk Phil admits he has to work a lot harder with Geraldo and company encroaching on his turf. "It's that [TV programming] is too bland."

A lot of the people who will decide if these programs fly agree. "I hate how sanitized the medium has become," says Post/Newsweek Stations Inc. chairman Joel Chaseman. The genre, he explains, offers an alternative to game shows and sitcom reruns. "At least the producers of these shows are trying to escape the grayness that's out there."

The best examples of tabloid content with visuals and audio to match are *A Current Affair* and *America's Most Wanted*. Both programs, from the belly of Murdoch's Fox beast,° rely on dramatizations of crimes and were initially produced on minuscule budgets. Both have been surprise successes for Fox. *A Current Affair*, produced at Fox's WNYW in New York, went into national syndication last October and now clears more than 75 percent of the country. *America's Most Wanted*, produced at WTTQ in Washington, has been the Fox network's most-watched program, occasionally doing better than Big Three° fare.

°**Murdoch's Fox beast:** Rupert Murdoch, an Australian citizen, owns Twentieth Century Fox Television, an American company. Some critics have blamed Murdoch for the sudden appearance of American tabloid television.   °**Big Three:** ABC, CBS, and NBC, the three major American non-cable radio and television networks.

• • •

America's Most Wanted's searing buzz-saw guitar theme leads back in from a commercial. It's time to pay attention. Host John Walsh rests against the desk on the studiously disheveled police-office set. Save for the giant *America's Most Wanted* logo on the wall and a TV monitor, it looks like the set of *Barney Miller.*

"You can make a difference," says Walsh, after presenting a piece about a man accused of firing two bullets into the head of his neighbor, who survived to play himself in the reenactment. "If you know the whereabouts of this fugitive, let us know what you know."

Two more segments of violent mayhem, including one where a couple is suspected of beating their young daughter to death, play out. Walsh again urges viewers with information to call in, and the credits roll. The bank of operators off to the left of the set are fielding calls at a rate that would give a home-shopping network pause. Various law-enforcement types related to the different cases linger nearby to field any promising tips.

There's no doubt that the interactive component of *America's Most Wanted* 10 has propelled it to success. The program got the kind of publicity boost that is a producer's dream when a criminal profiled on the first episode was apprehended via a tip called in to the program's 800-CRIME 88 hot-line. After seven months on the air, 17 bad guys had been apprehended through viewer tips.

Fox has heavily promoted the crime-stopper component of the program. It makes good business sense to do so, despite such critics as the *Los Angeles Herald Examiner's* David Gritten, who calls the show "video vigilantism." This is not such a bad thing in the view of Fox vice president Thomas Herwitz, who would have us believe that Fox's prime motivation in airing the show is public service and that the money coming into the network is secondary. "We've always viewed [*America's Most Wanted*] as a special project aimed at serving the needs of our viewers, who are more concerned than ever about crime," says Herwitz. "Advertisers are saying that to be a part of it is to be in an environment perceived as doing something for the public good."

No such illusions exist about *America's Most Wanted's* alter ego, *A Current Affair.* Advertisers such as Honda, Mitsubishi and Manufacturers Hanover are presumably buying time on *A Current Affair* because of the show's appeal to a relatively upscale audience. And when Canada Dry runs a spot showing a young, affluent couple sipping ginger ale, talking about restaurants where they serve sun-dried tomatoes, somebody clearly believes yuppies are tuning in. In eight of the 14 markets where *A Current Affair* goes head to head with *Wheel of Fortune,* it beats the game show in the all-important 18-to-49 group.

There is a perception that tabloid TV's rise is in part a result of "two-tiered TV," where what's left of the broadcast audience after VCRs and cable have taken their bites are lumpen proles:° blood, guts and sex fans. But *A Current Affair's* audience

---

°**lumpen proles:** The lumpen proletariat, the least educated or lowest class in a society.

proves a taste for the sensational transcends class. "In New York we're doing better numbers than two of the network affiliate newscasts in $40,000-plus households," boasts Twentieth Century Fox Television v.p. of research Steve Leblang.

"Most people like to see other people's dirty laundry," says Katz Television v.p. and director of programming John von Soosten, attempting to dissect *A Current Affair*'s appeal. "They love to peer into people's houses, see their tragedies and feel glad it's not them. Most people are voyeuristic."

The arch trio that created *A Current Affair*—two Australians, executive pro- 15 ducer Ian Rae and senior producer Peter Brennan, along with producer Joachim Blunck—thrive on feeding the peeping masses. Veterans of Murdoch's News America organization, they are expert at tapping sensationalism's mother lode and giving it their own particular spin. Having veteran newscaster Maury Povich, with his comfortable "can you believe this?" demeanor, as their anchor cum foil, lets them zip from tawdry star profile to gruesome small-town murder in a slick half hour.

Fox's power news-punk trio revel in the controversy they create. They are building a raucous video beachhead for Murdoch's global media machine. When *Los Angeles Times* critic Howard Rosenberg wrote that *A Current Affair* was so foul it had to be watched with a gas mask, they laughed about sending him one. When a new field producer, a man with blond hair several inches past his shoulders, was hired, Brennan told him, "When you come to work for us, mate, whatever you do, don't cut your hair." Fox news punks love to contrast their freewheeling style with the button-down culture of network news.

"TV has developed a habit of going and doing issues—Oprah does wife beating or sexual whatever," says Brennan. "We single out the individual's story and let him be the symbol of what the issue is. It's nothing new, *60 Minutes* has been doing it for years. You're dealing with a direct one-on-one relationship with the subject of the story and the audience. *A Current Affair* is about extraordinary things happening to ordinary people."

"You walk a very fine line with [*A Current Affair*]. We don't do hookers, lesbianism or incest," adds Ian Rae. The executive producer wants everyone to know his program has standards. It's not simply a grab bag of the sensational.

"We might tell a hell of a story, like the one we did the other night," Rae explains, relishing the memory of a favorite segment. "It was about a couple in love, and we told the whole love story right down to the moment they wanted to get married and made that horrific discovery—they were brother and sister. It wasn't a story about incest. The word was never uttered and never would be. It was a real human story—a tragic love story. We were very careful about that."

From *A Current Affair*'s early days two years ago as a New York-based nightly 20 show operating on a meager $35,000 a week, it has managed to break the kind of stories that make headlines and ratings, such as the first TV interview with Baby M's mom, Mary Beth Whitehead. The streak continued as the program went national and the budget increased to roughly $150,000 to $200,000 a week. When *A Current Affair* had an exclusive of a home videotape showing preppy murderer Robert Chambers, out on bail, frolicking with a bevy of nubile girlfriends, the program made national news and in some markets scored the kind of ratings associated with a network hit. In New York, *A Current Affair* scored a 20.9 rating and a 34 share, wiping out *Wheel of Fortune*. Granted, that was in the city where Chambers' sensational crime occurred, but as far away as San Francisco it scored a 20 share, beating out *Evening Magazine* and *Entertainment Tonight*.

"*A Current Affair* begins where *20/20* left off," observes a veteran network news executive. "Watch. Someone will take it the next step and on a network level do a national tabloid newscast. Maybe it will be Murdoch. If there's a summit in the Soviet Union, it will do a piece on Russian sex."

News Caliente:
Tabloid TV with a Latin Accent

Silvana Paternostro

Silvana Paternostro is a freelance writer born in Colombia but living in the United States. She writes about women's issues in Latin America today, as in her book In the Land of God and Man: Confronting Our Sexual Culture *(1998). Writing in the 1993* Columbia Journalism Review, *Paternostro introduces her readers to Spanish-language versions of tabloid TV. The* Review *is read by a wide range of people working in print, radio, and television news journalism.*

Paternostro discusses two Spanish-language programs, Noticias y Más *and* Ocurrió Así, *which are popular with Hispanics in the United States and with viewers in Latin America as well. Appearing five years after* A Current Affair *was launched in 1986, these Spanish-language programs were clearly influenced by* A Current Affair *and other U.S. tabloids.*

As you read, consider the extent of the U.S. influence and why Paternostro thinks Hispanics were especially receptive to tabloid television.

Tune in to your local Spanish-language television station and see a woman who cries tears of glass to demonstrate God's glory, or a mother who, to earn money to feed her family, dances with a boa constrictor. Flick to the competing Spanish channel and observe voluptuous women in string bikinis on Rio de Janeiro's beaches, or hear the story of the boy who castrated a pig with his teeth. Stick around: the following segment could be an update of the U.S. mission to Somalia,° or Bill Clinton's next political Gordian knot.°

Univisión and Telemundo, which together reach about 90 percent of the Spanish-speaking households in the U.S. through more than 800 stations, have concocted a new version of tabloid journalism: *Hard Copy* meets CNN's *Headline News,* plus salsa—Latin America's magic realism° meets the news camera. The shows, which started a little more than two years ago, mix news, consumer information, virgin apparitions,° and teenage suicide pacts. Univisión's *Noticias y Más* (News and More) and Telemundo's *Ocurrió Así* (It Happened This Way) are among the most popular programs on Spanish-language television—so popular among the 24 million U.S. Hispanics that they recently expanded from thirty minutes to a full hour. In Latin America, they are aired in nearly every country.

As news shows, they are earning recognition. At the regional Emmy ceremony in Miami last year, *Ocurrió Así* walked off with four awards. *Noticias y Más* won three, including one for outstanding investigative reporting, for a story about an ultraconservative branch of the Catholic church accused of "brainwashing" Spanish girls into becoming nuns.

But the programs also face sharp criticism. It was during a filming of a story for *Ocurrió Así* last January that a man shot and killed his ex-wife before a running Telemundo camera. Producers had planned a story about a man in mourning after his teenage daughter's suicide. As a crew filmed him placing flowers on the daughter's grave, his former wife, whom he blamed for the suicide, arrived unexpectedly. While Telemundo's reporter was pressing the nervous woman to talk about the daughter's suicide, the father shoved the reporter aside and began shooting. Some viewers were shocked that the network chose to show the entire episode.

That same week, Univisión's *Noticias y Más* aired a slapdash story about a   5 visit by the president of Guatemala to a topless nightclub in New York City. After the story provoked headlines all over Guatemala, it became clear that president Jorge Serrano Elías had been in the restaurant part of the establishment, not the go-go section, with his two sons, his defense minister, and various U.N. delegates. The network apologized for the segment's "tone."

Univisión's *Noticias y Más* was conceived by Guillermo Martínez, who heads the network's news department, to look much like a local news show, complete with sports and weather reports. Advertising for the show, however, puts the emphasis in *Noticias y Más* on the *Más,* or more. In a popular Spanish-language

---

°**U.S. mission to Somalia:** In 1992, 30,000 American soldiers were sent to Somalia in an effort to prevent massive deaths from starvation and to attempt to bring peace among warring political leaders.   °**Gordian knot:** A difficult or insoluble problem, from a knot tied by King Gordius of Phrygia and cut by Alexander the Great (356–323 B.C.) with his sword. Gordius asserted that the knot could be untied only by the first ruler of all of Asia. Alexander was that person.   °**magic realism:** Many Latin American writers use this technique, in which the fantastic is portrayed with realistic detail. °**virgin apparitions:** A reference to the claimed sightings of the Virgin Mary, the mother of Jesus.

magazine, a glossy ad for the newscast shows a smug-looking journalist sitting in a steaming cauldron, videocamera in hand, while in the background a skull hangs from a branch. The copy reads: "Everything is possible on *Noticias y Más.*"

Telemundo, for its part, hired Fran Mires, a former producer of a now-defunct U.S. tabloid show, *Inside Report.* "I didn't speak Spanish, but I had the perfect training for these sensational news magazines," she says. Mires started *Ocurrió Así* in October 1990 with a segment about a girl who was kidnapped, raped, and mutilated in Texas. She won a regional Emmy for it.

Mixing news and horror is not new in Latin America, where many leading dailies dedicate extensive space to the coverage of violent crimes and accidents, usually accompanied by a bloody photograph. Martínez freely admits that *Noticias y Más* includes gore. "But," he adds, "there are a lot of soft touches." A recent segment of his show profiled a blind professor who built a school in a hamlet in the Colombian desert.

Mires does such stories on *Ocurrió Así,* too. She recently did a piece about a blind child, also in Colombia, who bicycles around telling neighbors they have calls at the public telephone booth. "If I took this story to American producers," says Mires, "they'd say, 'Get out of here. It's too nice, not sexy. There is no shock value.'"

To add sex appeal to its own mix, Mires hired a Chilean former Miss Universe to present the entertainment news. She recently interviewed Geraldo Rivera, in Spanish. 10

THE BIG SLEAZE

Krista Bradford

Now a reporter for WNBC-TV in New York City, Krista Bradford has also been a television reporter and anchor in St. Louis, Los Angeles, Denver, and Boston. From 1987 to 1992, she worked for several tabloid TV series.

In this personal and highly critical 1993 essay, which appeared in Rolling Stone *magazine, Bradford introduces readers to the life of a reporter on a tabloid TV show. In the style of many other* Rolling Stone *articles, Bradford's language is informal and even occasionally profane, perhaps reflecting the trashiness she sees in the tabloids.*

As you read, pay particular attention to Bradford's social concerns: How do the tabloids view ordinary Americans? What groups of people are regularly excluded from the tabloids? What kinds of relationships are featured?

Beginning in 1987, I worked in the subterranean world of tabloid television, a world where the truth is far less important than the sexy story. I learned that interviews are regularly purchased and that tabloid TV cuts deals, agreeing to cover notorious characters favorably—Manuel Noriega,° for instance—and lobbing only softball questions. I've overheard conversations in which field producers have threatened celebrities with damaging information if they didn't cooperate. I have watched reality become fiction in the edit bays as news footage was intercut with movie scenes and music videos and tarted up with sound effects and music.

The world of trash TV is awash in Australian journalists whose perspective on American life is so distorted it's as if they were standing on their heads. I started first as a reporter and substitute host for *A Current Affair,* then later became one of five correspondents for the weekly Fox newsmagazine show *The Reporters.* Following its demise and about nine months of unemployment, I accepted a job as senior correspondent for *Now It Can Be Told,* a nationally syndicated show hosted by Geraldo Rivera, which aired for about a year until August 1992. It was my latest tabloid experience. Now I've decided it will be my last.

Now, I know what you're thinking: "Hey, lighten up. These shows are meant to entertain, to have a little fun with the news. This kind of TV is all a harmless romp." But is it? Behind its campy humor, its tits-and-ass raunchiness, its rubbernecking at the oddities of American life, there is something decidedly *mean* about tabloid television. Because sometimes *people* get in the way of a good story. And the bigwigs of trash TV don't really give a damn.

As someone who has worked in TV news since the age of eighteen, I fit in the world of tabloid because I was a misfit. At seventeen, I interned for Joan Lunden at KCRA-TV, in Sacramento, California. I cut an audition tape and hit the road, landing at a Monterey station that had just lost its female anchor. I got the job. I later reported for local news operations in St. Louis, Los Angeles, Denver and Boston. Growing up in television news is akin to prolonged high-level exposure to cultural radiation—you don't mature, you mutate. There is something decidedly *warped* about being celebrated for your ability to read aloud or for the way you look on TV. It does something to a person. It made me cranky not being taken seriously as a journalist.

In 1986, some ten years after I started my career, I lost my job as weekend ⁵ anchor and weekday reporter at the ABC affiliate in Boston, WCVB-TV. My contract wasn't renewed. Looking back, I don't really blame them, and I don't really blame myself for what I did next.

I flew to Manhattan to consider taking a job as a reporter for *A Current Affair.* Back then, even the *New York Times* praised the show, which had not yet gone national: "Forget now the pejorative notions that cling to the phrase," said the

---

°**Manuel Noriega:** Leader of Panama prior to 1989, he was arrested by the U.S. military and convicted in Florida on charges of drug smuggling and money laundering.

Times. "*A Current Affair* is tabloid journalism at its best. It is zippy and knowledgeable, and when it falls on its face, at least it's in there trying." But instead of
spending the afternoon in the show's Upper East Side offices at Fox TV station
WNYW, I was directed to the Racing Club, a dark, smoky bar across the street,
where I watched some of my prospective colleagues get pissed—as in drunk,
not angry. That's what these journos called it.

It was in this bar that I met producer Peter Brennan, the mastermind who
molded *A Current Affair* before moving on to produce Paramount's sleazier son of
Affair, Hard Copy. There was something lovable about Brennan—the way
he affectionately called everyone Bubba, his pink cheeks and graying hair
reminiscent of a fellow who preferred chimneys and soot to elevators. He winked
knowingly and nodded warmly his approval of me while he nursed a single drink
that day. There was something about my WASPy° manner that he liked. Later he
told me what it was: that I could make the unseemly appear somehow seemly,
that I could wade waist deep through the muck of tabloid and emerge unsoiled.
Eventually, ABC's *PrimeTime Live* correspondent Judd Rose would give me some
more-accurate career advice: "There's only so long you can be a diamond swimming in a sea of shit before you end up a shit-covered diamond."

On my first day at *A Current Affair,* some six months after its debut, I was
asked to portray Jessica Hahn in a reenactment of her alleged rape by the televangelist Jim Bakker.° I was horrified. I wasn't an actress, I was a journalist, for
God's sake. I was supposed to pretend I was the now infamous "bimbo"
Jessica—to "act" like I was being sexually assaulted? I refused.

But aside from that hitch in the beginning, I grew to like the wacky stories,
the travel and the adventure offered by *A Current Affair.* The show had a deli-
cious sense of humor. The stories often featured a Joe Six-Pack° who had gotten
his life turned so inside out that it was as if he were wearing underwear for a
hat—it was nearly impossible not to laugh at the village idiot. There was the
guy who faked his own plunge to his death over Niagara Falls. And the forest
ranger who was damn sure he saw Bigfoot. And there was Sheriff Corkey, who
had rented a video camera to make X-rated movies with his wife. Naturally,
they returned the camera with the racy video still inside. Naturally, duplicates
were made, providing endless entertainment to law-enforcement officers across
the country and grist for *A Current Affair.*

Even the grisly murder stories were fascinating at first. I felt like Truman 10
Capote° as he was reporting *In Cold Blood.* I spent weeks psychoanalyzing
a murderer and sex offender who was trying to con his way out of prison. I

°**WASPy:** Having the characteristics of a typical white Anglo-Saxon Protestant. °**Jim Bakker:** A
1980s American televangelist, Bakker served a jail term for misusing donors' money. His assistant,
Jessica Hahn, accused him of raping her, but he has written that their one-time sexual encounter
was consensual. °**Joe Six-Pack:** A derogatory term for an average working-class man. °**Truman
Capote:** American author (1924–84) whose famous nonfiction book *In Cold Blood* reported on the
murder of five members of a small-town Kansas family and the fate of their killers.

pushed one convict's buttons enough that he broke down and cried (known as "passing the onion" in the trade). I thought that I just might find the key to what caused these people to kill. But after doing enough of these stories, I eventually came to the conclusion that they killed because they were crazy.

I soon started noticing things I wished would go away—only they didn't. *A Current Affair* didn't like doing stories about gays, people of color or unattractive women. I drew this conclusion, as did many of my colleagues, based on the standard questions we were asked when we would propose a story: "What color is he/she, mate?"—followed by "Are there pictures?" to confirm the physical description. Stories that were about these unwanted people generally were not pursued. Former *Hard Copy* reporter Alexander Johnson, who became a correspondent for *Now It Can Be Told* and now reports for *A Current Affair,* is one of the few blacks in the genre. He does not deny that the racism exists. "That's an area I would not want to comment on," Johnson told me. "It's very sensitive."

At *The Reporters,* I worked on a story about violence at the United States–Mexico border. I later discovered that the field producer had negotiated with two brawny young men to videotape American vigilantes beating up illegal immigrants. I didn't know whether this assignment would incite these strapping gents to rustle up some frightened Mexicans for the money. Hell, I didn't know if these men would fake an attack. I urged my superiors to reconsider the story. Instead, they gave it to another correspondent.

Spend any time with the Australians or British Fleet Streeters,° and their attitude about race makes itself apparent—for their distinctive vocabulary is rife with racial slurs.° And it was my impression that they never felt that there was anything offensive about this. Once, on a flight to Los Angeles, I asked fellow correspondent Steve Dunleavy (known as the Dog) to help me with the *New York Times* crossword puzzle. With all seriousness, he took the paper and puzzled over the clue: a five-letter word for a person of Asian descent. He returned my newspaper with the answer proudly penciled in: *slope.* (For the record, Dunleavy said the slur is "out of character" for himself and that his recollection of the incident "is diametrically different.")

Geraldo Rivera may be tabloid's exception to the racist rule. His staff is the most integrated shop I've seen. And *A Current Affair* may be cleaning up its discriminatory act. A November 23rd, 1992, report in *Variety* said, "Gone, according to a veteran staffer, is the old unwritten rule of what the show wouldn't cover—gays, urban (read black and Hispanic) America." Right. Gone are most of the managers primarily responsible for *A Current Affair's* questionable editorial decisions. They have moved on to the other tabloid shows.

°**British Fleet Streeters:** Reporters who were trained on Fleet Street, the center of the London newspaper district.   °**racial slurs:** Insults intended to shame or degrade someone of a different race from the speaker.

While I was preparing this story, *Hard Copy*'s public-relations person, Linda 15 Lipman, sent me a compilation videotape, which struck me as strange, since I had not yet formally contacted the show. Later, Lipman refused me interviews because, she said, the show had heard I was investigating racism in tabloid. With that, I decided to take a look at this mystery tape, and sure enough, *Hard Copy* had sent me a collection of its stories that featured blacks, as if that were proof it did not practice prejudice. (I contacted all the shows requesting interviews; I was turned down by *Hard Copy* and *Inside Edition*. *A Current Affair*'s publicist limited my request for interviews, none of which ever materialized.)

At first, I felt liberated by the creative freedom tabloid offered to experiment with longer stories—up to twenty minutes instead of the average minute-and-a-half package you see on your local news. We could use music, sound effects and reenactments, and the possibilities seemed inspiring. But now you can consider me a purist. My trouble with sound effects came after *Now It Can Be Told* producers had edited in the sound of an explosion to accompany pictures of the space shuttle *Challenger* breaking up in the sky for promotional teasers coming in and out of every commercial break.

The story was about NASA's withholding information from family members and investigators about the fate of the astronauts. The producers insensitively played the tape over and over again, never stopping to consider the feelings of family members and friends. And the *Challenger* didn't explode; rather, it was torn apart by aerodynamic forces, as I explained in my report—but now after having heard the blast, I'm sure most of the people who saw it are certain the *Challenger* blew up.

While I was a correspondent with *The Reporters*, the show reenacted the Tampa, Florida, murder of Karen Gregory, showing a photograph of her dead body in the promotional teasers. Her family and friends claimed that the reporter, in order to gain their cooperation, promised them there would be no such sensational scenes. "They told us this was going to be good, respectable journalism; we all fell for it," said David Mackey, a Tampa therapist and a friend of the victim's. Back then, correspondent Steve Dunlop told me he did make that promise, only to be overruled. At the time, Bob Young, executive producer of *The Reporters*, explained Dunlop's promise was out of order. "That reporter misspoke," said Young. "He didn't have the authority to say that. It never should have been said." Young went on to say that the objectionable material was dropped from the story and that he had "no moral problems" with the final version.

And that is my main complaint about tabloid television. Rarely do its producers have trouble sleeping. I never heard discussions of ethical dilemmas. They do not pause to consider the consequences—for the ratings° justify the means....

°ratings: A system of ranking television programs by the number of viewers they attract; the higher the ratings, the more advertising money a program brings in.

So why, you might wonder, did I stay in a profession so low, so lacking in 20 dignity? Well, I'll tell you. The pay and the perks were generous. I went to Vietnam, El Salvador, Brazil, Thailand, Cuba and other places. I was asked to do a lot of things, and I did some of them, like trying to buy Ben Johnson's° story. I was upbraided by TV critics for hugging a subject on camera. I did a story on strippers. But gradually I learned how to define and enforce my own boundaries. By the time I reached *Now It Can Be Told,* I routinely refused what I believed to be unethical or distasteful assignments. But by then, it was too late. I'd been slimed. I was caught in the tabloid trap. Network executives advised me to go back to local news. And I did.

So maybe my five years in the big sleaze has made me a bit oversensitive. All around me I see tabloid's corrupting influence—in local news, in political campaigns, in movies of the week, even creeping into the staid network newsmagazine shows, which are resorting more frequently to hidden cameras and other tabloid techniques. Not that hidden cameras are necessarily always bad; at least these shows have been known to weigh the consequences of invading people's privacy.

TV Tabs' New Tone

Frank Houston

Frank Houston is a former editor at Columbia Journalism Review *and a freelance writer. In this 1996 essay for that journal, he insists that some of the tabloids have improved by "opting for more sober, in-depth reporting."*

Houston argues that Inside Edition *and* A Current Affair *have assumed a "new tone" in order to appeal to higher-income viewers, who enable tabloids to charge more for advertisements and thereby make higher profits. He singles out increased budgets and staffs and attention to investigative reporting as evidence of the new approach.*

As you read, notice what Houston says has changed and what seems to have remained the same about these tabloids.

Once the province of royal scandal and Elvis sightings, television's syndicated tabloid news shows are sporting a new look. The gossip quotient is down at

---

°Ben Johnson: Canadian runner disqualified from participating in the 1992 Olympics after failing a drug test.

shows like *Inside Edition, American Journal,* and *A Current Affair,* and investigative journalism is up. While the tactics of tabloid television—parking-lot ambushes and hidden cameras—haven't changed, the targets have. The shows are digging up consumer fraud and rooting out political misdeeds with the same zeal they once applied to stories about topless donut shops and Joey Buttafuoco.°

The shows, scattered across TV's syndicated landscape five evenings a week, playing to an estimated audience of more than twenty million in the early hours leading up to and including prime time, still include the Hollywood prattle proffered by *Extra* and *Entertainment Tonight* and the entertainment-and-sensation recipe of Viacom's *Hard Copy. Hard Copy,* in fact, with a heavy investment in the O.J. story, won the tabloid ratings race last year.

But the other tabloid news shows have begun opting for more sober, in-depth reporting. King World's *Inside Edition* has always had investigative pieces, but in recent years it has had more of them, and the pieces have had more impact. Meanwhile, Twentieth Television, owned by Rupert Murdoch's News Corporation, has taken its *Current Affair* in a similar direction with a complete overhaul this year.

One reason for this is that advertisers are increasingly looking beyond pure ratings numbers to just who is watching. A mix of higher-quality stories tends to mean better demographics.° Instead of asking who has the most viewers, "The question now is, can this particular show deliver women aged eighteen to thirty-four, or will another show give us men twenty-five to fifty-four who make more than $75,000 a year," says David Bartlett, president of the Radio and Television News Directors Association. "What we're seeing here is a shake-out period for a lot of these programs. They've got to improve the program in the eyes of the target audience."

Behind the scenes in this effort are two tabloid veterans, producers Bob 5 Young and John Tomlin, who worked on *A Current Affair* when it began life in 1986 as the original TV tab. In 1988 Young and Tomlin jumped ship to launch the rival *Inside Edition,* envisioning an "upmarket" tab° (the original anchor was David Frost). The show has steadily beefed up its investigative presence, especially in consumer reporting, looking, for example, into safety problems at U-Haul, food inspection, and insurance fraud. King World's other tab, *American Journal,* has reported on fast-food health violations and adulterated beef in the nation's supermarkets, among other stories.

One of the biggest victims of this investigative streak has been Chrysler Corp. A series of *Inside Edition* stories illustrated why the National Highway Traffic

---

°Joey Buttafuoco: A tabloid sensation after his young girlfriend, Amy Fisher, shot his wife.
°demographics: The categories (age, gender, race, income, etc.) of viewers of a television program.
°"upmarket" tab: A tabloid that appeals to wealthier viewers.

Safety Administration (NHTSA) had been investigating a flaw in the rear-door latch that caused the liftgates of Town and Country, Dodge Caravan, and Plymouth Voyager minivans to open in collisions in which thirty-seven people have died in the last decade. *Inside Edition*'s Steve Wilson first reported the story in January 1995. When Chrysler preempted a Safety Administration finding (and a possible recall) in March by instigating a replacement program, Wilson showed the new latch to be inadequate, too. The federal agency continued its investigation and has since raised its standards for minivan rear-door latches.

But the story didn't end there. Last summer, producers Young and Tomlin moved back to *A Current Affair,* and they brought the Chrysler story with them. This time, they focused on the public relations firm, Maritz, that was answering questions from concerned minivan owners. An undercover camera revealed operators telling hotline callers that there were no safety problems with the minivan's latch, contrary to established facts. When officials of the government agency learned of the segment, they issued a strong rebuke to Chrysler, saying "NHTSA at no time found the latches to be safe."

A Current Affair began remaking its image after finishing a distant third in the ratings race last year. The revamping started with a new anchor, Jon Scott (who was lured away from *Dateline NBC*), twenty new investigative staff members, a new Washington bureau, and a $4 million marketing campaign. A commercial, in which a dump truck rumbles through a suburban neighborhood and then winds up plunging off a cliff, explained the approach: "We took out the trash." *A Current Affair* even changed its "bug," or logo, in the corner of the screen, to prevent viewers from mistaking the new show for the old. "If the old *Current Affair* was synonymous with sleaze," says Young, "we'd rather they just saw the content." The show's first segment of the new season was about an all-expenses-paid charity golf vacation for members of Congress in Sun Valley, Idaho, where corporations paid thousands of dollars for the right to bend a legislator's ear on the links. In *Inside Edition*'s "Senators' Ski Cup," reporter Wilson is called a "horse's ass" by a discomfited Missouri Senator Christopher "Kit" Bond, who is seen skiing the slopes of Park City, Utah, free of charge alongside corporate sponsors from American Express, USWest, and Delta. The style of the piece—which opens to the strains of "Chariots of Fire"—is an odd intersection of Michael Moore's "Roger and Me"° and *ABC World News Tonight*'s "Your Money" segments.

In fact, that intersection is emblematic of the middle ground emerging between the tabs and the network news magazines. Rosemary Armao, executive director of Investigative Reporters and Editors, is one who doesn't see "a

---

°"Roger and Me": A documentary film attacking the competence of former president of General Motors Roger Smith.

great dividing wall" between the tabloids and the "so-called 'legitimate' journalism" of the networks. "If you cut out the alien landings and the checkbook journalism, is it so different?" Actually, *Inside Edition*'s investigative unit doesn't pay for interviews; the new *Current Affair* will shy away from the practice and will say so when it does pay.

Jacquee Petchel, a senior producer for investigations at WCCO-TV, a CBS- 10 owned and operated station in Minneapolis, says the distinction in the eyes of the viewer between tabloid and mainstream is largely illusory, anyway. "Viewers remember what they saw, not where they saw it," she says. "When people criticize a story that's shoddily done, it reflects on all of us. Whenever somebody attempts to do a better job, it's good for all of us."

GLUED TO THE SET

Steven D. Stark

Steven Stark is a political commentator on popular culture for NPR and CNN, a writing instructor at the Harvard Law School, and a journalist. This reading comes from Stark's 1997 book Glued to the Set: The 60 Television Shows and Events That Made Us Who We Are Today.

Stark argues that tabloid TV in the United States was inspired by Entertainment Tonight, *a celebrity-interview show that began in 1981. He attempts to demonstrate that* Entertainment Tonight *and the tabloid TV shows complement each other perfectly in the way they represent social life, the first taking a relentlessly upbeat view, the latter a cynical view. Stark also discusses other influences on the emergence of tabloid TV, including 1960s values and the feminist movement. He also notes that some American habits are apt to make many people in the United States favor the tabloids.*

As you read, try to understand Stark's speculations about what so attracts the American television audience to tabloid TV.

Over the years, *Entertainment Tonight,* or *ET* as it's affectionately called, has nightly plumbed the heights of celebrity and show-business gossip, covering an average of 12 Hollywood Walk of Fame ceremonies, 17 awards ceremonies, and 27 celebrity obituaries a year. At last count, Arnold Schwarzenegger had been interviewed over 200 times, and Shirley MacLaine more than 150.

This is the show that made the world safe for anchors Mary Hart and John Tesh—who left in 1996 to pursue his New Age music career. Never have so many (a staff of almost 200) talked so much (at last count to 179 stations covering 95 percent of this nation, and 17 foreign countries) about so little. *ET,* wrote the *Los Angeles Times'* Howard Rosenberg, "excels at the say-nothing interview," and "seems never to have met a film it didn't like or a story it couldn't transform into a flesh market." This was a "news" show on Prozac: Everything was repackaged as something relentlessly upbeat.

ET didn't create the culture that blurred the distinctions between politics and show business, or gossip and news, as anyone who ever listened to Walter Winchell more than 50 years ago knows. As early as 1952, *Today* was pioneering television's attempts to merge the worlds of news and entertainment, and *People* magazine did the same on the print side later. *ET* helped accelerate these changes, however, and, if nothing else, made the world safe for celebrity birthdays. (The show has almost 4,000 on file!) Indeed the practice of reporting box-office gross and ratings winners—now done even by the *New York Times*—was popularized by this show.

ET was the ultimate in the triumph of TV style over substance: The show did all this while presenting itself as if it were the *CBS Evening News,* complete with anchors and reports from the field which sounded and looked like news. Yet it wasn't—at least until the *CBS Evening News* began to imitate *ET* and the other tabloid shows that were this show's mirror image, with its own reports about celebrity scandals and the like. *ET* also helped change the look of news on the networks with its high-tech graphics of split screens, spin frames, animation, charts, and inserts. Bill Moyers once complained of his stint with CBS: "In meeting after meeting, *Entertainment Tonight* was touted as the model—breezy, entertaining, undemanding.... Instead of... gathering, weighing, sorting and explaining the flux of events and issues, we began to be influenced by the desire first to please the audience." The theorist Neil Postman once wrote:

> Whereas television taught the magazines that news is nothing but entertainment, the magazines have taught television that nothing but entertainment is news. Television programs, such as "Entertainment Tonight," turn information about entertainers and celebrities into "serious" cultural content, so that the circle begins to close: Both the form and content of news becomes entertainment.

The relentlessly upbeat style of *Entertainment Tonight* also became the model   5 for much of television news, especially on local stations. "I'm not saying that *Entertainment Tonight* is directly responsible for this," cultural analyst Mark Crispin Miller once told a reporter. "But I will say that people are so habituated to a certain level of hysterical cheer, so habituated to a constant stream of happy endings, that it has become harder and harder than ever for them to tolerate any downbeat or discouraging reports or images." After *ET* became popular, with nightly ratings that virtually equaled any of the network newscasts, it became *de rigueur* for local news stations to hire their own entertainment "reporters," whose job was to deliver similar flattering celebrity profiles and puffball reviews.

The inevitable string of clones followed: Fox's *Entertainment Daily Journal*, eventually an entire network, E!, devoted just to entertainment hype. (E!, a writer once said, is like "a science-fiction movie in which a Hollywood publicist takes over your brain.") Once *ET* showed how "news" could be repackaged as a salable syndicatable commodity, more tabloid shows, such as *A Current Affair* and *Inside Edition*, rushed in to help broaden (and often pollute) the definition of news throughout the medium.

An *ET* reporter was once quoted as saying that, in the beginning, *Entertainment Tonight* was supposed to be more like a traditional news broadcast. "But then," the source said, "the research showed that if you want more people to watch, you've got to program what they want, and research revealed that viewers were more interested in celebrity coverage than in hard news." Over the years, that puffy celebrity coverage has been the *ET* claim to fame—or black mark, given your opinion of a program which has been defined as a press agent's dream. "[T]he show has dropped almost all pretense of being anything but an arm of the Hollywood publicity machine," Richard Zoglin wrote in *Time* in 1994. The show seems to feature an odd emphasis on health matters—perhaps because, in the kingdom of Hollywood, no one is supposed to grow old. The *Entertainment Tonight* segments that are said to have attracted the most mail are Elizabeth Taylor's hip surgery, Michael Landon's announcement that he had pancreatic cancer, Jim Nabors' need for a liver donor, and the word that Bill Bixby had prostate cancer.

The line between celebrity-reporter and celebrity-subject on this show is so exceedingly gray that *ET* once did a piece on coanchor Mary Hart's new album of lullabies. (Hart's other claim to fame is that the *New England Journal of Medicine* once reported that the sound of her voice was triggering epileptic seizures in a viewer.) Of course, there is more to such an obsequious attitude toward celebrity than just pleasing the audience, as the research demands: *Entertainment Tonight* is owned by Paramount, which is in the entertainment business that this show endlessly promotes.

ET wouldn't have been possible until the 1980s, when satellite technology made it possible for local stations easily to receive quick feeds of syndicated shows sold to stations independently by huge production companies. Like *Wheel of Fortune* and *Jeopardy!* (two other eighties success stories), the show was also aided by FCC rules which effectively prevented the networks from beginning their prime-time broadcasts until 8:00 P.M. The thought was that this would eventually encourage local stations to produce their own shows.

Instead, beginning in the eighties, many local stations turned to this show, 10 as well as to tabloid news shows earlier in the afternoon, like *A Current Affair* (premiering in 1987), *Inside Edition* (premiering in 1988), and *Hard Copy* (premiering in 1989). All three of these other "news" shows offered a smattering of the same celebrity gossip as *Entertainment Tonight*, but focused instead on the seamier side of fame—particularly if it involved sex—and sensational crime stories reminiscent of the New York tabloids and the *National Enquirer.* "It's the evening news without all those boring stories from foreign countries," wrote *Entertainment Weekly*'s Bruce Fretts about *Hard Copy,* which assigned 30 staffers to cover the O. J. Simpson murder case.

The ratings of these syndicated "Tabloid Three" would soon rival the traditional newscasts for the three networks, which then took the predictable step of beginning to ape the tabloids to win over their audience. *Inside Edition* did a special interview with Tonya Harding, and CBS's Connie Chung followed just days later. *Hard Copy* got a scoop on alleged molestation charges against Michael Jackson, and the reporter then appeared on the *CBS Morning News.* In 1993, for the first time, news about the entertainment industry and its stars became among the Top Ten most heavily reported subjects on the evening newscasts of all of the three major networks.

If *ET* was overly saccharine, then *A Current Affair, Hard Copy,* and *Inside Edition* frequently offered up a nightly dose of acid—which is why TV analyst Ron Powers once called these shows and *ET* "two halves of the same whole." "We are a fearful, angry nation," he once said. "So [on tabloid shows] we demonize a culture we have allowed to spring up, while at the same time, I think the country takes refuge in celebrity worship. It's withdrawal into two complementary, mutually reinforcing forms of fantasy." These scrappy news shows, which wore their tabloid populism on their sleeves and appealed to a working-class audience, came to do so well in the ratings that *Entertainment Tonight* eventually hired away Linda Bell Blue of *Hard Copy* to produce its show—a move soon reflected in innovations like the upbeat *ET* viewer poll on whether South Carolina child-murderer Susan Smith should be executed. The characterization of news on *Entertainment Tonight* was merging with the downbeat ethos of the tabloids to offer a truly alternative vision of national "journalism"—a sharp, raffish contrast to the way in which Walter Cronkite° and his cohorts had once defined it.

All of these syndicated "news" shows were the outgrowth of a renewed emphasis on gossip and scandal throughout the news which began to flourish in the 1980s when a former Hollywood actor became president. After a while, it became hard to tell where the entertainment news about Hugh Grant stopped and the political news about Bill Clinton and Paula Jones or Gennifer Flowers began. Part of the reason for the focus on sexual scandal was—for lack of a better term—the pornographication of American culture. Frankness is one thing, but beginning in the eighties, Americans could now routinely find in their VCR stores the kind of sexual exhibitionism they had to travel to Times Square to view in earlier decades. Throughout the culture, standards for public discourse—and news—thus widened considerably.

°**Walter Cronkite:** Highly respected CBS news anchor (1962–81).

Part of the increased exposure to gossip was also due, oddly, to the transformation of a slogan from the sixties: "The personal is political." In the 1960s, that credo was intended to mean, broadly, that how people choose to live and work is a political statement. In the years following, however, the motto came to stand for the privacy-eroding proposition that the public had a right to know even the most private details of both a politician's and an entertainer's life.

The feminization of American culture—through the women's movement— 15 also had the unintended effect of broadening the acceptability of gossip news. In her bestselling *You Just Don't Understand,* linguist Deborah Tannen wrote that what has traditionally been labeled as gossip by men is often a positive way in which women discuss the world in order to understand and build relationships. As women have gained power, this private phenomenon has become a more accepted public form, though it is far more destructive in the hands of journalists (caustic cynics by professional nature) than in those of two people talking over coffee.

Before he died, Republican strategist Lee Atwater also offered another theory as to why crime and scandal news could now infatuate the public more than ever. "Bull permeates everything," he said. "In other words, my theory is that the American people think politics and politicians are full of baloney. They think the media and journalists are full of baloney. They think big business is full of baloney." In this atmosphere, crime and gossip news are appealing because they purport to show viewers something authentic and spontaneous. If voters think that all candidates are packaged by consultants, and stars by publicists, stories about drug use or sexual liaisons reveal those shielded celebrities in unrehearsed moments. In an age of hype and fabrication, the tabloid shows purported to offer reality.

As Alexis de Tocqueville° noted long ago, Americans have always been drawn to gossip—the better to demonstrate why the famous are no better than anyone else. If "No man is a hero to his valet," it is not surprising that, in an egalitarian country which glorifies the common man and woman, everyone becomes a kind of valet. The flip side of that sentiment, however, is that a culture needs leaders to set standards and build aspirations. Gossip—even the positive kind about Hollywood celebrities—ultimately erodes trust in figures we once admired. "The celebrity media cater to a double impulse—to admire and to envy the famous," USC professor Leo Braudy once said. Thus what these shows built up, they soon destroyed, as *Entertainment Tonight* produced the admiration, and the *Hard Copy* types supplied the envy. And, in each case, they obscured the definition of real achievement. Daniel Boorstin° got it right: Once upon a time, American society had heroes. Now, it just has celebrities.

°**Alexis de Tocqueville:** French traveler in America who wrote *Democracy in America* (1834).
°**Daniel Boorstin:** U.S. historian.

THE REALITY EFFECTS
OF TABLOID TELEVISION NEWS

Graham Knight

Graham Knight, a Canadian scholar who teaches at McMaster University, is the author of "The Reality Effects of Tabloid Television News," which appeared in 1989 in Communication: For and Against Democracy *(edited by Marc Raboy and Peter A. Bruck). Knight presents a brief history of tabloid journalism and television. As an academic, he writes in a style different from that of the journalists who authored the earlier readings in this section. His sentences and paragraphs are longer. He assumes more knowledge on the part of his readers, and he is concerned less with particular tabloid series and personalities than with the general characteristics of tabloid TV.*

Considering local television news and national tabloids together, and seeing little difference between them, Knight believes that sensationalized local news may have been the precursor of tabloid TV. After establishing this historical context, he focuses on the unique technical characteristics of tabloid TV, particularly its "reality effects." These techniques, which are achieved primarily through sound and dramatization, are intended to make the tabloids seem real to viewers and therefore engage them more easily.

As you read, try to gain a solid grounding in the history of print and television tabloids. Try as well to understand the reality effects that define tabloid TV as a television genre.

The association of the word "tabloid" with journalism and the news media is a fairly recent one. It dates from the turn of the [twentieth] century when "tabloid" was applied metaphorically from its initial chemical-medicinal context where it referred to anything given or taken in a compressed or condensed form—a meaning much like that of the similar term "tablet." Tabloid news referred initially to the bulletin-like presentation of short, condensed summaries of the most newsworthy aspects of events and issues. Later, after World War I, this meaning was generalized to denote the smaller, more compact physical size of the tabloid newspaper as a whole, in contrast to the still more conventional broadsheet.°

This literal definition, however, does not capture the rich web of associations and connotations that has developed around tabloid journalism. Substantively and formally, tabloid journalism means much more than just the size of

---

°**broadsheet:** A newspaper with full-size pages.

the newspaper or the stories inside. It is a distinct news idiom° which has developed historically from roots in the earlier scandal and gossip sheets, the human interest magazine, the sports press, the "yellow" journalism° of the late nineteenth century, and the "muckraking" journalism° of the earlier twentieth century. This genealogy has set tabloid journalism apart as a difference of *degree* rather than *kind* from other forms of news. Tabloid still operates within the broad organizational and representational parameters° of news production; its distinctiveness is one of topic, accent, emphasis, and style.

In these respects, two characteristics have stood out in the evolution of the tabloid press. The first is a substantive emphasis on coverage of events and issues concerning *moral disorder* and its effects. Unlike the more highbrow news media, tabloid journalism has generally eschewed coverage of weighty political and economic issues in favour of an emphasis on the more immediate instances of deviance, conflict, and the threat to or disruption of everyday life. Crime, corruption, scandal, human tragedy, and suffering—particularly associated with sex, violence and (illicit) money—continue to form the staple ingredient for tabloid news. And it is this focus on the immoral and the illegal that has earned tabloid a reputation for exaggeration, over-dramatization, appealing to the prurient, and what W.T. Stead of the *Pall Mall Gazette* referred to as "the demon of sensationalism."

The second, and related, characteristic is a stylistic emphasis on the *subjective* in news coverage. Events and issues are personalized to an extent that makes nearly every tabloid news story a "human interest" story: the accent is on the individual and the emotional, on "people"—what they "feel" and how they react. This personalization now extends beyond the participants to the news personnel themselves. The conventional guarantee of journalistic objectivity—rendering the author/narrator anonymous in order to represent a particular point of view as the general, common point of view—has been increasingly set aside, particularly in tabloid news where the presence and personality of the reporter or columnist are often played up to enhance "credibility" and identification. Tabloid journalism promotes itself on the claim that its reporters and writers are "involved," that they "care," and this focus on the subjective and the personal has earned tabloid a reputation for bias and trivialization.

Both of these features of the tabloid press were carried over intact into television. Tabloid television news began effectively in the early 1970s with the "happy talk" format of "Eyewitness" and "Action News" shows in major U.S. metropolitan areas like New York, Los Angeles, and Chicago. Aspects of the genre spread to Canada in the mid to late 1970s, primarily, again, in the larger, 5

°**"yellow" journalism:** Sensationalized reporting.   °**"muckraking" journalism:** A type of exposé journalism that attempts to correct social problems.   °**representational parameters:** Guidelines for how news should be presented.

more competitive urban markets. In one sense at least, the recency of tabloid television news is puzzling inasmuch as television has developed in many ways in North America as a generally tabloid medium. Certainly, tabloid's affinity for the subjective, the close, the local, is something that is shared by television to a great extent, as is the preoccupation with moral disorder and deviance. For this reason, it is perhaps more difficult to specify a distinctively tabloid television format; it is a question not so much of major differences in style and content as of differences in detail and the ways these are combined. Indeed, many of these details have now become institutionalized as standard practices in television news production, particularly at the local level, and to that extent tabloid's success may well eventually threaten its idiomatic distinctiveness.

The historical context within which tabloid television news arose and grew represents the confluence of several developments. The first is simply the growing popularity of television news in the late 1960s and early 1970s. Until then, news had generally been seen as an audience and revenue loser. Costly to produce, especially at the local level where audience size was more restricted, and not especially popular with viewers, news had been produced primarily to fulfill government requirements for public service, informational broadcasting, and secondarily as a way to build up something of a local station "image." But television coverage of the conflicts of the late 1960s, the Vietnam war in particular, together with the changing representation of the war from an "objectified," top-down perspective to a closer, more subjective look at those actually conducting the fighting (on the U.S. side at least), seems to have been the catalyst for a change in news viewing habits.

The second development that contributed to the emergence of tabloid television news was the growing competitiveness for viewers and advertising revenues that occurred with the intensification of the economic crisis in the early 1970s. Particularly in larger markets, television stations began to market and advertise themselves in terms of their local image. News provided an important ingredient in this construct, given that it was, and is, usually the main form of in-house production in which local stations engage, the bulk of their programming coming from independent producers via network affiliation and/or syndication. What is important about this, as any other form of competition, is that stations competed by avoiding direct competition, by striving to provide essentially the same service, but with a difference. . . .

Third, technology figures in this context in at least two ways. Growing competition for audiences and revenue was intensified by the expansion of cable services. Cable reception has had the effect of breaking down the older forms of local markets—defined by the restricted reception capacity of individual television sets—and reconstituting them on a larger, more regional scale. The newscast, as the mainstay of the station's local image, therefore became more important in attracting and maintaining local audiences in the face of competition from neighbouring stations available on cable. The audience carryover effect—from the early evening news into "prime time"—became more crucial because of cable's effect on market size.

At the same time, technology was also having an effect on news at the point of production through the replacement of film with videotape as the standard medium for visual and audio recording. Video had a number of immediate organizational effects: tape is reusable and therefore cheaper, the equipment is lighter, more compact, and portable, and the editing time is shorter, allowing more time each day for news-gathering out in the field. But from the point of view of representational form, the importance of tape is its perceptual and semiotic effects.° The visual effect of tape is that it heightens the sense of rawness and immediacy, and reinforces television's conventional ideological claim to "liveness." The unmediated visual quality of tape, particularly when used in close-up, adds to tabloid's accentuation of the subjective, its "feeling" for reality, by helping to construct more forceful lines of identification and (self-) recognition for the viewer. . . .

. . . The claim that television can better record "the action" is often contra- 10 dicted by its strategic inability to be at the scene as the action is actually taking place. To repair this loss, and gloss over the contradiction between claim and capacity, television attempts to provide a substitute form of action, a simulated action, a series of "action effects" that form part of television's broader repertoire of "reality effects" and give tabloid television its hyperactive effect.°

Action effects are constructed chiefly through the control of pace and movement, narratively and discursively.° The most obvious way this is achieved is through editing: visual images tend to be cut fairly rapidly, at five to six second intervals, on average, for local news, with tabloid newscasts at the faster end of the scale. In voice-over° sections, which, despite the emphasis on "actuality" images, still comprise the single largest narrational element in most news reports, the visual editing is usually more rapid still, at three to four seconds. For voice-overs, this editing pace has been common for some time, and this is largely dictated by the need to correspond the visual images with the single-sentence, segmental format of news script delivery. But for other narrational elements like sound bites,° interview clips, and stand-ups,° the speed of the visual editing has probably increased in recent years, particularly with tabloid style news. It is, for example, very common for tabloid editing to break up longer (more than ten seconds) interview clips with the regular use of cutaways° such as reporter listening shots.

°**semiotic effects:** Here, meanings in the use of tape itself.   °**hyperactive effect:** Appearance of frantic activity.   °**narratively and discursively:** The visual elements of a television story or segment (the narrative part) and the verbal interaction (the discursive part).   °**voice-over:** A reporter's voice being heard over sounds or images of the event being reported.   °**sound bites:** Brief statements.   °**stand-ups:** Scenes in which a reporter stands and speaks directly at the camera.   °**cutaways:** Movements of the camera away from the scene or from the person being interviewed.

Even within the fixed visual frame, the tabloid camera continues to simulate action effects through movement of various kinds—panning, zooming, and tracking. Panning is used mainly to add movement to otherwise static longer shots of inanimate objects—buildings, streets, landscapes—used as visual signifiers in voice-over narration. Panning serves to extend the spatial frame of the story in a fluid way, without the abruptness of the visual cut. "Tracking" shots, where the camera follows after movement of some kind, are commonly used to create the impression of active pursuit, for example, of news subjects who are reluctant to be interviewed and are attempting to walk away from the camera. The "action/reality effect" is enhanced by the jerkiness of the visual frame as the camera moves after its subject. Zooming is used to generate an effect of visual intensification, usually to complement or contrast with some point of emphasis in the audio. It is used most commonly in interview shots, where the focal length is shortened to achieve a tighter facial close-up, particularly in an attempt to capture visual evidence of emotion or stress of some kind on the part of the subject.

Complementing the action effects of visual movement and editing is the way in which the audio is used to produce an impression of continuity and "seamless" narration. Sound is crucial to television flow, especially in tabloid news where the rapid editing generates a highly segmented visual structure. Continuous audio serves to offset the potentially disruptive effect of visual cutting by sewing disparate images together, by means, primarily, of the narrational and discursive voices of the reporter and newsroom anchor, and secondarily by that of interview subjects.

Like the use of music as a continuity device (mainly in fictional representations), the voice can be used to vary and control the pace and tone of signification. Tabloid makes greater use of this variability of the voice, coupled with more extensive use of facial and bodily gesturing, to generate lines of identification with and for the audience. The pace of delivery (by studio anchors and by reporters in voice-overs and stand-ups) is slightly quicker, the tone more modulated, the flow more continuous, the look less often diverted from direct address to the camera-viewer. Breaks between "tell" stories are now signified less by audible pauses and the visible shuffling of paper, than by changes in camera angle and/or focal length.

The way in which sound produces action effects has to do not only with 15 pace and flow, but also with its fullness. One of the audio techniques that tabloid television exploits is to overlap different audio sources at the same time, creating a fuller sense of sound by drawing on its ambient, unfocused quality. This is most evident in voice-over segments where "actuality" sound is preserved as background to the reporter's narration. It used to be the practice, until the 1960s at least, to erase the actuality sound from voice-over visuals, so that the only sound present was that of the reporter's or anchor's voice. Today it is standard practice in television news to keep actuality sound in, but usually in a muted, and at times barely discernible form. With tabloid news, however, the level of actuality sound is maximized, to a point where, if increased further, it would interfere with the audibility of the voice-over. This not only creates a fuller sense of sound, but also contributes to the "action/reality effect" of the image by presenting evidence of the real. Very often, the content of this sound is quite irrelevant to the content of the news story; its presence is to authenticate the scene of representation as real.

Television is a medium that mixes fiction and nonfiction, yet it takes their distinction very seriously, and goes to great pains to ensure that the boundaries are clearly marked. At the same time, conventions associated primarily with one spill over into the other. Up to the mid-1960s, for example, music, which is a normal feature of drama and other forms of television entertainment, was often added to lengthy voice-over stories, particularly in "softer," more feature-like news coverage. Today, music is confined to the opening segment of the newscast, where it normally conveys a sense of immediacy and action, and is rarely, if ever, added to news reports where it would contradict the logic of reality effects.

A fictional technique that is used, especially by tabloid, is that of the "dramatization" or re-enactment of a (type of) news event. This is done mostly in the case of "news-they-can-use" coverage — "they" being usually the police, or possibly some other governmental agency — where the event entails the kind of (presumed) drama and conflict that television can rarely capture in process. Violent street crimes, like purse-snatchings, muggings, and sexual assaults, are the most likely candidates for dramatization, particularly when a series of similar incidents has given rise to a news-mediated "crime wave" and concomitant moral panic about public safety. Dramatizations not only provide a substitute representation of action, but also, as part of their justification, appeal to viewer identification. For this reason, they are only effective when that line of appeal is based on solidly consensual ground, socially and morally.

A WRITER'S NOTEBOOK

Tabloid TV as a Television Genre

The following tasks are designed to help you think about the readings and identify and start to work up material you might use in your own essay. If you need help with tasks that require annotating, outlining, or summarizing, see Appendix 1.

1. *List the characteristics of tabloid TV from Max Robins and Silvana Paternostro.* Both Robins and Paternostro discuss a number of special characteristics — concerning style, features, and content — of tabloid TV. Make a list of the specific characteristics each mentions. Robins, for example, introduces several characteristics of the tabloids in his first two paragraphs, including "grab an audience," "value-free, content-free, high-impact programming," and "aggressive stance," and more features in paragraphs 3–7 and paragraph 12. Making these lists should help you find characteristic patterns more easily.

2. *Explain Krista Bradford's views.* Write a few sentences explaining Bradford's views about the tabloids' attitudes toward ordinary people (paragraphs 9, 21) and toward gays, people of color, and women (paragraphs 11–15).

3. *Consider the appeal Frank Houston discusses.* List the specific investigative reports Houston mentions or describes in paragraphs 5–8. Write a few sentences speculating about the appeal of these investigations to upmarket viewers.

4. *Summarize part of Steven D. Stark's article.* Underline the words and phrases Stark uses in paragraphs 10–12 to characterize tabloid TV. Then summarize his discussion in paragraphs 13–17 about the major cultural changes that he believes created a climate for the gossip and scandal offered by the tabloids.

5. *Test Graham Knight's ideas about moral disorder and subjective style.* Knight says that tabloid TV can be characterized by its emphasis on *moral disorder* and its *subjective style* of news coverage (paragraphs 3–4). Test out this characterization by applying it to all of the segments in one half-hour program. Take detailed notes as you watch, and then write a page or so reporting what you learn, giving specific examples from the program.

6. *Apply Knight's action effects.* List the *action effects* Knight discusses in paragraphs 11–15 and then look for them in one tabloid TV program. Take careful notes as you watch each segment and then write a page or so reporting what you learn, giving specific examples from the program.

7. *Test Knight's ideas about the influence of tabloid TV on local news shows.* Knight argues that local TV news has had a tabloid style for a long time. Watch one local news program, possibly a late-night program, to discover whether it resembles tabloid TV as Knight describes it in paragraphs 3–4 and 11–15. Write a page or so about what you learn, incorporating specific examples from the program.

SOCIAL PERSPECTIVES ON TABLOID TV

The four readings in this section take a social perspective on tabloid TV. In other words, they are concerned with basic questions about how the tabloids represent social life: What kinds of people appear? How are they represented? How do they relate to each other? Considering such questions will influence what you notice in the tabloid segments you view and how you interpret those segments.

Although they all focus on how the tabloids represent people and social relations, the readings offer quite different views. Philip Weiss believes that tabloid TV offers a nonelitist and realistic view of ordinary people and families who are usually an invisible segment of American life. Jib Fowles argues that television unifies Americans socially by creating a common national culture, whereas Robert Lichter and his coauthors hold that television's representation of social life can sometimes be at odds with reality. Finally S. Elizabeth Bird asserts that the tabloids divert poor women from questioning the status quo.

As you read and discuss these readings, and as you continue to view and interpret a tabloid series, you will decide which of these authors' views you find most convincing. Whatever your decision, it will be grounded in your own research—in your viewing of tabloid program segments, in your notes about them, and in your interpretations of certain segments in writer's notebook tasks.

BAD RAP FOR TV TABS

Philip Weiss

Philip Weiss is a contributing editor for the Columbia Journalism Review, *which published this article in 1989. Like Krista Bradford, Weiss is concerned about the social representations on tabloid TV. Unlike her, however, he sees positive social values in the tabloids. For example, what Bradford views as contempt for ordinary Americans and families, Weiss sees as genuine interest in those lives. He believes that television without the tabloid programs would provide a limited view of social life.*

As you read, notice how Weiss supports his view that there is social value in the tabloids.

I watched trash TV for several weeks early this year. I avoided the talk shows that were so busy trying to outdo one another with outrage…and focused on magazine shows that are more traditionally journalistic because, unlike the talk shows, they contain real reporting. These magazine shows are geared for "the prime-access hour" right before prime time.° As I began watching, two programs—*Inside Edition,* a King World production that seems to specialize in exclusive interviews with killers, and *This Evening,* a Westinghouse Group W venture that calls itself "The Heart Behind the Headlines"—were being launched to take on Fox's *A Current Affair,* which pioneered tabloid television, becoming nationally syndicated in September 1988. Fox, which is controlled by Rupert Murdoch,° also produces *The Reporters,* which has no anchor but has several self-dramatizing reporters and whose Saturday night audience is smaller than that of *West 57th,* the CBS magazine show that airs two hours later. *West 57th* is not tabloid TV—its point of view is too thoughtful, its technique too subtle—but it's worth recalling that a couple of years back, before the dawn of trash TV, *West 57th* was reviled by *60 Minutes* staff and other traditionalists for its

---

°**prime time:** The television viewing period from 8:00 to 10:00 P.M., Monday through Friday.
°**Rupert Murdoch:** Australian owner of Twentieth Century Fox Television, a U.S. television network.

disregard of verbal narration in favor of visual information and for its borrow-ings from music videos. Today, trash TV is even more indiscriminate in its pick-ings, scavenging the magnetic-tape universe for inspiration—home video, handheld cameras, police video, answering-machine tapes, even pornographic video. The journalism on these shows is often harrowing, but the form can be daring, and the tabs' assault on sobriety and self-seriousness is welcome.

The lack of seriousness is the first thing you notice about tabloid TV. Halfway through February, *Current Affair* anchor Maury Povich, a protean talent who looks by turns horny, sentimental, cool, and distraught, became pious during a piece about the NBC entertainment series *Nightingales*. *Nightingales* features nurses who change costumes a lot on camera, and Povich said it hurt the profes-sion; he sympathetically interviewed a nursing official about misrepresentation. But even as she complained, the screen was filled with *Nightingales* nurses hop-ping onto desks and hiking their whites, nurses in lingerie, libidinous nurses. Bill O'Reilly, *Inside Edition*'s pleasant counterman, can be just as offhand. Kissing off a never-ending series of jiggle stories° pinned to the publication of *Sports Illustrated*'s annual bathing-suit issue, O'Reilly said that because February was the ratings-sweeps month° there was going to be a lot of steamy material on the air and said so with such teflon irresponsibility you half-admired him for it. Both these guys have a video cool a la David Letterman, dissociating themselves from certain gestures even as they perform them: the banality and immediacy of the medium are more powerful than any effort to hold out. Nancy Glass, the anchor of *This Evening*, isn't quite so airy; she actually seems sincere.

The *Nightingales* piece was part of an insistent theme on these shows: if you think we're bad, you're not watching other stuff. O'Reilly often reads tabloid newspaper headlines to mock the real tabs' standards, and one night Povich went into a campy lather about New York's porn cable station. "Prime time becomes slime time," he said, though as he railed we got lewd glimpses (the previously uncharted terrain these shows explore is largely the bottom, which at times is dis-played virtually unclothed) of, for instance, bikini-clad mudwrestlers.

The daily TV tabs generally air three segments a night and, apart from TV and celebrity stories, the typology is stories of smalltown ignorance, stories that reveal authority (often in the form of a pastor or plastic surgeon) as wickedly hypocritical, and stories of family violence.

The untrustworthy family is the central narrative of much of this journal-   5 ism. Whenever a piece begins with the image of a happy couple you can be sure someone is about to be betrayed, flayed, made a fool of, sprayed with gunshot, burned to a still-living crisp after a visit to Disneyland, or shot outside the hot

---

°**jiggle stories:** Stories that show women's breasts or bottoms jiggling.   °**ratings-sweeps month:** During the month of February, the number of people watching a television program counts the most toward what its network can charge for advertisements.

tub while balancing several women. The family's an unstable unit, it's full of lies. "In two years I had ten lovers . . . that's not very many," says a jailed *Inside Edition* interviewee who turns out to have shot her children. "I thought she was having a weight problem," a mother says on *A Current Affair* of the pregnancy her daughter concealed from her for nine months, but typically the reporter doesn't believe it and undercuts her with doubting lines. When a Texas girl was accused of scheming to rub out her parents, once allegedly rat-poisoning their food, she made both *A Current Affair* and *Inside Edition* the same night. "She didn't allow us to drink the coffee that she had put it in," the mom told *A Current Affair,* clinging to the innocence of the demon seed, who the reporter says is "every bit as unfeeling as" Charles Manson.°

Sociopolitical angles in these pieces are suppressed. *A Current Affair's* exclusive on jazz pianist Billy Tipton, who on his death was revealed to be a woman, might have had political impact—the music world didn't welcome women, so she became a man. Instead, it was reduced to a where's-the-salami saga in which the focus was his former wife's dubious anatomical ignorance ("Yet she too claims she found out the truth only after Bill's death").

Just the same, many of the family-deceit stories confirm a Dostoyevskian° view of existence with an actuality few nonfiction media° approach. Some undermine the very idea of family. When a woman living with the boyfriend who shot her, crippling her from the waist down, says matter of factly, "We've had our ups and downs, like everybody has—we've fought," we're to understand that the two are like us. And when a deeply alienated man charged with trying to kill the wife who's just said she still loves him says for his part, "I'm inclined to believe that I'm thinking about a person and continuing to love a person who no longer exists," we're pressed to identify with his dissociated cast of mind.

These reports are no more dishonest journalistically than sensationalist tales from tabloid papers, and to say that they're unworthy of airtime is priggishly elitist, especially when you consider that the American appetite for news and information on TV seems to be growing. Some of the criticism reflects a class bias. The subjects of these stories are usually middle or lower-middle class (far below network journalists). And while these shows occasionally fulfill the classic journalistic duty of keeping authority honest, the ripoffs and frauds they chronicle tend to be small change compared to the higher stakes of *60 Minutes.* The best piece of journalism I saw in five weeks was an inspired investigation on *Inside Edition* of traffic deaths and injuries related to Domino's Pizza's policy of guaranteeing delivery within thirty minutes. It's hard to imagine that sort of exposé being aired on a

---

° **Charles Manson:** Criminal mastermind behind infamous 1969 murders.   ° **Dostoyevskian:** Having the perspective of Fyodor Dostoyevski (1821–81), a Russian writer who expressed a bleak view of human existence.   ° **nonfiction media:** Books or documentary films that deal with actual people or events.

quiche-targeted° vehicle. (The next night Domino's advertised on *Inside Edition,* thus displaying a shrewd understanding of video's leveling quality; as it spurts off into the air, all information is rendered equally trivial.)

To gain some sense of the relative class stance of the tabloids and an established magazine show, compare two social pieces with twist endings from *60 Minutes* and *The Reporters.* On February 19, a bubbly, empathetic Diane Sawyer took up the story of a man running a boys orphanage in Guatemala. After an upbeat beginning the mood changes abruptly: *60 Minutes* learned after it had prepared the segment that the man faced accusations as a child molester. Sawyer seems genuinely saddened. She struggles on camera to overcome her disbelief, and this struggle becomes the emotional focus of the piece.

As for the *Reporters* piece, it was, of course, much farther out on the cultural 10 tundra, reporter Rafael Abramovitz peering in on a husband and wife who plan to continue living together with their children in England after poppa has surgery to make him a woman. Abramovitz is hairy and macho and speaks in an I've-seen-it-all slur that mocks all pieties, but the story line of every episode calls for him to lose the weariness and get wound up about some new evil—like a transsexual daddy. Still, with everyone in the family being so accepting about the operation, he hasn't gotten outraged until the trick ending, when he discovers—"a couple of hours" before going on the air, he claims—that the couple is wanted in California for solar-energy investment scams.

So Abramovitz is confirmed once more as a tough guy, while Sawyer exits with pale hand pressed against her lovely brow, trying not to acknowledge what she sees. As a piece of journalism, the Sawyer story was more nuanced and less manipulative, but who's to say that its attitude about life is more realistic? Compare the generally satisfied view of New York life that pervades the *New York Times* with the hard-boiled view of the *New York Post.* Is the *Post* wrong? Of course not. Nor is tabloid television. . . .

This isn't to say that the shared values of the tabs aren't often offensive. Old-fashioned men abound in these formats, notably the dandy Australian (jile for jail, plie-ons for plans) Steve Dunleavy of *The Reporters,* who always manages to include a scene of his own jousting (twice shadowboxing with his subject, once holding a gun). He wears a cowboy hat and jeans and, in an ambush interview of a doctor who has been altering women's genitals by performing what he calls "love surgery," he carries some kind of shiv—maybe a letter opener. Abramovitz gets thrown out of the doctor's office, missing the climactic encounter that usually caps his act. "I really wish there was someone to confront about it all but the sad thing is that everyone points to someone else, and in the end no one is willing to be held accountable," he apologizes to us.

This Evening represents a refreshing departure from those values. Anchor Nancy Glass, sunny and professional, seems to have been put behind the desk

---

°**quiche-targeted:** Here, television program aimed at the upper-middle class.

to capture a women's audience, and the show tilts to women's-magazine-like stories: the memories of a Vietnam nurse, the scourge of the "obsessive-compulsive disorder" in the daily lives of an alleged five million Americans.

As bad as is the male-restorationism° on most shows are the shows' cheap frauds. Stories are continually sold as the "inside look," "behind closed doors," the "naked truth," when more often than not the program has nothing to deliver but gossip and speculation. In its exposés of what really happened between Madonna and Sean Penn, then Tom Hayden and Jane Fonda, *A Current Affair* offered mainly interviews with celebrity reporters. (Free-lancers and authors take note: all the shows exalt as experts anyone who commits words to print, *This Evening* once quoting three print people on a Madonna story.) The show simply lied to its viewers. At other times the manipulations are annoying. Through video sleights, the programs frequently fade from one face to another, often from a victim to an innocent person—as if to suggest that the former's fate could just as easily befall the latter. These gestures are of a piece with the dramatizations these shows employ so ruthlessly: shadows on the wall of a woman taking a hammer to her husband, a faceless actor grabbing a tin of kerosene to blow up his son, a corpse in a wheelbarrow with hand dangling from blanket, a detective opening the trunk and reeling away from the smell of the decomposing body. Unhappily, these dramatizations° are not always labeled as such.

But complaints that dramatization blurs the line between entertainment and 15 news or that the use of music to torque the emotions violates sacred norms of nonfiction TV are tiring. The upholders of network tradition have been moaning about the breach of the wall between entertainment and news so many times—between Fred Friendly locating it in 1966 when CBS ran *I Love Lucy* instead of congressional hearings on Vietnam, to author Peter J. Boyer expressing horror last year over CBS's exploitation of emotional "moments" in stories—that it's about time we get out of the prison of that conservative model. Filmmaker Errol Morris, after all, won the critics' praise for *The Thin Blue Line,* his documentary about an unjust conviction in a capital case in Texas, though he used a lot of dramatization and even B-movie° effects.

The thing to bear in mind is that the trash shows are add-ons; they're not shoving out more highbrow stuff, not directly anyway. In most cases the time slots they occupy used to feature entertainments. Meanwhile, for all their fulminating against the tabloids, mainstream newscasters haven't set a noble standard—just remember what a superficial presidential campaign they gave us last year.° In fact, the tabloids may have a beneficial effect in fragmenting network

---

°**male-restorationism:** The process of trying to restore men's traditional roles.   °**dramatizations:** Reenactments of actual events.   °**B-movie:** A cheaply produced movie.   °**last year:** 1988, the year Republican George Bush and Democrat Michael Dukakis were candidates for president.

audiences further, in making the television landscape more varied, even in reducing the self-importance of so many television newspeople.

And there are things to learn from these shows. Because they are battling it out with people who are devoted to VCRs, they're open to the democracy of video in a way that few other commercial programmers are. Many stories seem to run just because the home-video footage the producers could get was good—like a brawl at a bridal shower in California that a neighbor taped one night, right down to police manhandling the celebrants. Another *Current Affair* piece, this one on a woman who went to a hot tub party to blow her fickle man away, was a wired wacky salad of taped immediacies. There was her testimony at her trial, videotaped, her taped threat on another woman's answering machine months earlier, police video of the hot tub, and the police tape of the first report on the shooting, in which a witness, struggling to explain what had happened just seconds ago, cried, "It's like the *Fatal Attraction* movie." In a gripping story about a Detroit crack ring on *This Evening,* the most startling footage was made up of home movies the dealers had taken of themselves ("Can we throw these [singles] away, because we got $500,000?" a half-naked man says with odd charm, standing at a table full of money, and the cameraman says, "I'll tell you what we can do, we can give it to the poor"), and the producers of the piece were forced to compete with this gritty style in their own shots from the streets. Then there was the creepiest story I saw all month, a *Current Affair* piece about a man (a Detroiter again) who surreptitiously made videotapes of a lover and then humiliated her by leaving them on her neighbors' porches and windshields....

The tabs surely owe something to porn videos if only in their occasional employment of a mindless soundtrack to cover salacious visual material. Povich ends each show with a leer and the line, "Until next time, America," as though the show had been a dinner-time quickie with the viewer, and the rubber-faced lewdness his role calls for, the alacrity with which he moves through a half dozen expressions and voices (from furry soft to wired and mean) is a motility reminiscent of the veteran porn star. But that's who Povich is up against. In a hyped and bogus-sounding sex survey, *A Current Affair* once noted that 19 percent of its respondents watch X-rated video at home and that 20 percent made their own X-rated videos. These figures are surely swollen, but they speak to the central challenge of the tabs, to intrigue households with something approaching the intimacy of the spontaneous, shaky, but indisputably authentic work of millions of amateur camera people.

The moment I'll remember longer than any other of my weeks of watching had just that feel. Video made *Inside Edition*'s report on the pizza scandal possible— nighttime shots from a tail car of drivers breaking the law—and when Matt Meagher confronted a driver in a Domino's lot, the frankness of the driver's response was a video artifact. This man was not threatened by the camera, which is no longer Fred Friendly's mythic one-ton pencil° confronting the subject but a familiar, approachable household gadget. So the driver said, Yes, he sped, he sped because he needed the money for his family, his wife, the kid. His explanation was so fresh and sincere it tended to crowd out Meagher's outrage, and when Meagher asked the man his name he didn't blink but leaned past the reporter to look half-amused at the camera and call it out unashamed — Roger Something! — like an intimacy to a friend, us, viewers of the world. He'd commandeered the videotape to pull us to his side, a scene that was raw, direct, and unsettling in a way journalism too rarely is.

WHY VIEWERS WATCH

Jib Fowles

Jib Fowles is a professor of media studies at the University of Houston, Clear Lake. He is author of Advertising and Popular Culture *(1966) and* The Case for Television Violence *(1999). This reading comes from his book* Why Viewers Watch: A Reappraisal of Television's Effects *(1991).*

   Fowles argues that television unifies Americans socially by creating a common national culture. Though he acknowledges that television can create "harrowing social change" by removing partitions between people (for example, between men and women or between adults and children), he believes that television offers positive social values. He focuses on prime-time television, but his arguments apply to tabloid TV as well, in its pre-prime-time slot.

   As you read, try to discover the social values Fowles finds in TV.

Television's fictions serve to bind up Americans.... As a consequence of the great popularity of the medium with individuals, television has become a universal force, and the creator of a national culture. In contrast to all other national cultures in history, which were shared in unevenly by the citizenry because of geographical or social displacement, what is remarkable about the televised culture of the United States is the pervasiveness of it. All Americans are aware of the same mediated figures,° the same national issues, the same products, the same lessons in behavior and values, the same language usage, the same dress styles, the same sense of tempo, and on and on, endlessly, through all the myriad aspects of what

---

°**Fred Friendly's mythic one-ton pencil:** Friendly, a television pioneer, believed that many people who were comfortable being interviewed by newspaper reporters with their notepads and pencils were initially frightened by the television camera, which he referred to as a "one-ton pencil."
°**mediated figures:** People presented by the media.

constitutes a culture. As individuals they may not embrace all or any of these features; familiarity—having seen it on television—is sufficient for social cohesion.°

This cultural commonality has been decades in arriving. At the beginning of the television era, the wide variance in viewing times and preferred content reflected the social divisions of the time. Initially the highly educated watched less, and only highly selectively, while the less well educated were more indiscriminate viewers. But as the years went by, viewing habits of various demographic groups° became more alike than different. Steiner (1963) and then Bower (1973, 1985) demonstrated the convergence in types of selections and amount of viewing. Making allowance for the opportunity to view, the viewing behaviors of blacks and whites, educated and less well educated, rich and poor, rural and urban, male and female, were coming to resemble each other more and more. George Comstock noted that "what people choose to view is much more alike than one would guess from differences in their backgrounds and in what they think and say about television" (1989, p. 46). Americans are watching the same sorts of programs, and thereby are being oriented to a mainstream culture.

For example, viewers of prime time shows, no matter what demographic group they may belong to, now exhibit similar habits. "If one classifies programs into about seven major categories," write Patrick Barwise and Andrew Ehrenberg, "the way in which people allocate their time across categories varies surprisingly little between subgroups of the population" (1988, p. 26). Daytime viewing audiences used to be skewed toward rural, poorer females; the viewership now draws more equally from men and women, rural and urban, rich and poor (Cassata & Skill, 1983, p. 163). Because viewers of television news come proportionally from all groups, news programming has served as a knowledge leveler, reducing the information gap between the better educated and the less educated (Neuman, 1976; Robinson & Levy, 1986, p. 84). If the programs, whether entertainment or information, are lost to a household, as when a set is broken or stolen, no class of Americans feels the deprivation any more or less than any other class; nowadays all grieve equally (Winick, 1988, p. 233).

At the beginning of the 1980s it was thought that the commonality which television was imparting to the nation would prove to be short-lived. The growing number of cable channels,° which were going to be "narrowcasting" to specific audiences, were sure to segment the population once again. While cable channels did proliferate, the splintering of the audience did not result, however. The content carried on the extra stations differed little qualitatively from the network programming, and so did little to attract a particular following. Despairing, W. Russell Neuman proposed a new law of mass communication: The more video programming that is available, the less diverse the viewing menu of the average audience member (1988, p. 346).

°**social cohesion:** The unification of people into one social or cultural group.   °**demographic groups:** People grouped according to income, gender, age, religion, and so forth.°   **cable channels:** Television channels brought into viewers' homes by cable, for which the viewers pay a monthly fee.

The chief reason that the amplitude of channels has not re-divided the audi- 5
ence has to do with the manner in which Americans have come to watch television. Detailed analyses of viewing data by Goodhardt et al. (1987) and Barwise
and Ehrenberg (1988) have produced revelations about viewing behavior.
Viewers are not loyal to the particular programs they state they like, nor even to
the types of programming (sports, for example) they say they prefer. Rather,
they scan a great number of programs, watching some of this and some of that.
Viewers choose variety above commitment or routine. Because viewers are frequently shifting through the channels, the audience for any one show does not
consist of either partisans of that show or a specific demographic group, but
instead will be a cross-section of the viewership available at the time of broadcast. When more cable offerings came along, spectators simply incorporated
them into their cycle of channels. In Heeter and Greenberg's study of cable television viewing, they found that, for sets monitored every minute, there [were]
an average of 34 channel changes per household per day; the number would
have been much higher with continuous monitoring (1988, p. 294). The audience with cable service is getting exposed to the same common culture as the
audience without; it just comes in more, if smaller, portions. Barwise and
Ehrenberg predict that "narrowcasting," featuring specialized programs for targeted audiences, will not be substantial in the future (1988, p. 154).

The result of increased similarity of viewing practices among Americans is
likely to be an increased similarity of thoughts and outlooks. Comstock
observes, "There is substantial evidence in behalf of the view that television
contributes to the way people perceive the world and that the result is a somewhat more commonly held way of thinking and believing" (1989, p. 277). One
piece of evidence comes in the form of a 1982 study by W. Russell Neuman. He
was probing the extent of cultural homogenization° in America by seeing if
thoughtfulness regarding programs varied according to educational levels.
Were the more educated the more reflective, as one might guess? A sample of
viewers were interviewed by telephone immediately after watching certain programs and asked if they had had any thoughts about the make-up of the program or how the program pertained to wider concerns. There was very little
difference in the number of reflections according to educational level. Since
earlier studies had indicated a positive relationship between education and
reflection, Neuman took "the lack of differentiated response in this case as possible evidence of a cultural leveling phenomenon"° (p. 486).

Whether this "cultural leveling," or the removal of past distinctions, is good
or bad must be the subject of interpretation. TV prigs are made resentful
when gradients° are removed and a mass culture arises; their vilification can be

---

°**cultural homogenization:** A process whereby people become increasingly alike in their
knowledge, interests, ideals, and values.   °**cultural leveling phenomenon:** The possibility that
people in different social groups are becoming much more alike.   °**gradients:** Different levels or
distinctions.

boundless. At another level of sophistication, Joshua Meyrowitz has looked with uneasiness at some aspects of the convergence of exposure levels (1985). Since, thanks to television, everyone is privy to the same things, there can no longer be the private communication domains that once lent structure to society. In the video age, the world of children and the world of adults are no longer demarcated; the led know as much as the leaders do; males and females no longer have their separate realms. The removal of these partitions—between child and adult, president and populace, men and women—can create harrowing social change.

But by the same token, television's dissemination of a common culture brings with it many benefits. It radically changes the nature of social life by abandoning old patterns of exclusion and installing new ones of inclusion. Now everyone can belong—if only in their minds; no one needs to feel unknowledgeable about the majority culture. This is certainly consonant with democratic ideals. The sphere of televised culture encompasses all Americans, and links all of society as does no other force. The speed and complexity of modern life might cause things to fly apart were it not for the omnipresent nightly dose of simple fantasies from the nation's storyteller.

WORKS CITED

Barwise, Patrick, & Ehrenberg, Andrew. (1988). *Television and its audience.* Newbury Park, CA: Sage.

Bower, Robert T. (1973). *Television and the public.* New York: Holt, Rinehart & Winston.

Bower, Robert T. (1985). *The changing television audience in America.* New York: Columbia University Press.

Cassata, Mary, & Skill, Thomas. (1983). *Life on daytime television: Tuning-in American serial drama.* Norwood, NJ: Ablex.

Comstock, George. (1989). *The evolution of American television.* Newbury Park, CA: Sage.

Goodhardt, G.J., Ehrenberg, A.S.C., & Collins, M.A. (1987). *The television audience: Patterns of viewing.* Brookfield, VT: Gower.

Heeter, Carrie, & Greenberg, Bradley S. (1988). *Cableviewing.* Norwood, NJ: Ablex.

Meyrowitz, Joshua. (1985). *No sense of place: The impact of electronic media on social behavior.* New York: Oxford.

Neuman, W. Russell. (1976). Patterns of recall among television news viewers. *Public Opinion Quarterly, 40,* 115–123.

Neuman, W. Russell. (1982). Television and American culture: The mass medium and the pluralist audience. *Public Opinion Quarterly, 46,* 471–487.

Neuman, W. Russell. (1988). Programming diversity and the future of television: An empty cornucopia? In Stuart Oskamp (Ed.), *Television as a social issue* (pp. 346–349). Newbury Park, CA: Sage.

Robinson, John P., & Levy, Mark R. (1986). *The main source.* Newbury Park, CA: Sage.

Steiner, Gary A. (1963). *The people look at television.* New York: Knopf.

Winick, Charles. (1988). The functions of television: Life without the big box. In Stuart Oskamp (Ed.), *Television as a social issue* (pp. 217–237). Newbury Park, CA: Sage.

PRIME TIME:
HOW TV PORTRAYS AMERICAN CULTURE

S. Robert Lichter, Linda S. Lichter, and Stanley Rothman

In 1994, S. Robert Lichter, Linda S. Richter, and Stanley Rothman, academics who have long studied the influence of TV on American viewers, published Prime Time: How TV Portrays American Culture. *This selection is from a chapter in that book. Like other writers in this section, these authors have clear ideas about how TV influences Americans' views of social life. Moreover, their argument reflects recent academic research on the effects or influences of TV. They ask, Whose agenda determines the kind of TV we watch and the social relations we see there—the establishment, the New Left, or the New Right?*

As you read, pay attention to how they answer this question and what else they have to say about the representation of social life on TV.

The world of prime time is preeminently a social world rooted in the interactions and institutions of American society. Even shows set in the Old West or outer space bear the marks of contemporary America in their plots, characters, and dialogues. And the changing schedules and program genres, from the squeaky clean suburban sitcoms of the 1950s to the steamy miniseries of the 1990s, have carried changing messages about personal relations, occupational roles, moral values, and social structures. To some degree these changes reflect parallel developments in American society. But they also show an internal consistency that can be at odds with external reality....

Thirty years ago television's content reflected a more traditional social order, more conservative assumptions about how society works, and more restrictive standards about the propriety of program material. This distant world was dominated by the private lives of traditional families and the protection of society by high-minded law enforcers. It was a world in which social institutions worked, and political concerns rarely intruded into the private lives of the populace. The military assured our national security, and the churches looked after our spiritual values. Moral codes were clear cut and transgressors were punished. Business executives were good guys, and even when bumbling bosses offered amusement, backtalk from workers was a rarity. In general, life's problems were manageable, and the people in charge could usually be trusted to manage them pretty well.

This world began to disappear in the middle 1960s, as television discovered political issues, social conflict, and populist appeals.° By decade's end some characters were calling for social change, others were confronting newly hostile authority, and still others were posing moral dilemmas in the sphere of

---

° **populist appeals:** Appeals to the interests and values of ordinary people.

sexual behavior, race relations, and professional conduct. Within a few years, pointed social and political commentary had become as integral a feature of successful sitcoms as wacky redheads and slightly precocious kids once were. The gangsters and low-lifes who were once the main threat to law and order were joined by a phalanx of evil executives and crooked cops. The establishment became a villain, and the good guys had to fight the system in order to make it work. Private life was laden with conflict, as families had to face a new range of social problems and workers and bosses exchanged sarcastic barbs. As surcease from this increasingly conflicted world, television offered its characters new opportunities for sexual gratification. But even the current epidemic of heavy breathing is punctuated by debates over the boundaries of normal behavior and the appropriateness of moral standards.

This, then, is the world that survives in the current prime-time schedule — sarcastic, sometimes cynical, and apt to cast a jaundiced eye on the very standards and sensibilities the medium embraced so enthusiastically a mere generation ago. To call this a less conservative or more liberal version of reality contains some truth but probably carries more weight than these unwieldy labels can safely bear. Some of the change is best characterized as populist — an anti-establishment upsurge of resentment against the rich and powerful. But populism itself has partisan variants, which were expressed in the rise of both a "New Left" and a "New Right" on the recent political landscape.

The New Left's anti-establishment flavor was directed against institutions 5 like business, the military, and religion. Government, in the guise of "old politics," was depicted as a tool of the military-industrial complex and derided for its failure to control economic powers or to protect civil liberties.° New Left populism scorned traditional moral restrictions and endorsed "alternative lifestyles," including sexual experimentation, feminism, and more egalitarian° family groupings. It castigated the "system" as an instrument of upper-status white males that oppressed blacks, women, homosexuals, and other minorities outside the charmed circle of wealth and power. It embraced the banner of society's victims and endorsed strong government action to make politics more open (the "New Politics") and society more egalitarian and pluralistic.°

The New Right was equally anti-establishment, but its goals and villains were quite different. Its target was the liberal Eastern establishment, comprised of government do-gooders, activist judges, woolly-headed intellectuals, and an adversary media. This populism mistrusted government not as the handmaiden of repressive capitalism but as an intrusive tax collector on a quixotic mission of economic redistribution and social leveling.° It embraced "tradi-

---

°**civil liberties:** Examples are freedom of speech, the right to live anywhere, the right to vote, the right to meet with other people for any purpose.   °**egalitarian:** Promoting equality.   °**pluralistic:** Having different ethnic, social, or religious groups pursuing their own interests within one common culture.   °**social leveling:** The phenomenon of people in different social groups becoming more alike.

tional values," including a patriarchal family° and more restrictive standards of sexual morality. It condemned the coddling of criminals and catering to minority "special interests" at the expense of hard-working, God-fearing middle Americans. It called for a return to old-fashioned virtues like free enterprise,° personal responsibility, patriotism, and religious faith.

These competing strands of populism diverge sharply in the values they uphold and the "establishments" they oppose. Both arose as self-conscious movements in the 1960s, although the populist Right attracted little media attention except in its incarnation as a "silent majority" until the Reagan years, when it became very vocal indeed. Meanwhile, the contemporaneous rise of populistic material in television entertainment clearly drew upon the left-wing variant far more than the right-wing. The changes in television's social agenda—increasing criticism of business, the police, and the military; endorsement of sexual diversity and experimentation; women's rights, racial and cultural pluralism—have paralleled the development of Left populism.

This is not to say that TV entertainment has followed this agenda unreservedly or has engaged in anything like a radical critique of American society. As we have seen, the "politics" of TV entertainment are mainly a matter of either legitimizing or criticizing social norms and modes of conduct. But beginning from a relatively apolitical and traditional perspective on the social order, TV has meandered and lurched uncertainly along paths forged by the politics of the populist Left.

We can demonstrate this point more systematically with regard to social institutions. To illustrate TV's changing view of the establishment, we combined . . . 139 shows that addressed the theme of honesty vs. corruption in business, politics, and the justice system. Before 1975, 47 percent of these shows indicted the system and 53 percent exonerated it. After 1975, 70 percent condemned the institution as corrupt, and only 30 percent upheld its honor. Moreover, nearly as many shows (sixty-nine) raised this issue in the study's last decade as in the first two decades combined (seventy). So establishment corruption has become a much more common theme of TV entertainment in both relative and absolute terms since 1975.

Although the direction of change is evident, the extent of change varies from 10 one topic to another. For example, television is still relatively traditional in the roles it assigns to female characters but aggressively feminist in the plots that directly address the status of women. Similarly, shows rarely cast such traditional authority figures as clergy or policemen as bad guys, but scripts are increasingly likely to attack religious intolerance or corruption in the criminal justice system.

°**patriarchal family:** A family in which the father has authority over other family members.   °**free enterprise:** An economic environment in which private businesses operate for profit with minimal government controls.

These examples illustrate more than that the politics of TV entertainment is a mixed bag. They also reveal something about the nature of the mix. The conservative side of television appears mainly in the aspects of life it takes for granted. Few would argue that writers and producers are consciously trying to keep women in their "place" by casting decisions that place them in traditional roles. They are simply populating the screen in terms of social arrangements and interactions that they take for granted, at least until activist groups protest.

This is one complaint of critics on the Left, who argue that television reinforces the status quo° by portraying it without criticism. As Donald Lazere puts it, the messages of TV entertainment (and other mass media) "assure us that there are no irreconcilable conflicts within the present social order and that those presently in power are capable of resolving every social problem if we just trust them." Similarly, Larry Gross of the Annenberg School of Communications argues that "the basic reality of the television world is the reality of the American middle-class establishment; its morality is the conventional and rigid Sunday-school morality of the middle class; its heroes and villains are those of the great silent majority." Just by presenting the world as it is without criticizing it, the argument goes, mass entertainment legitimizes its imperfections and thereby helps to perpetuate them.

There is still some truth in this criticism, but it applies far more to the program schedule of a generation ago than to today's prime-time world. Some series, especially traditional family comedies like "Full House," represent holdovers from the early years. But they are not pervasive enough to reverse the trends that began in the late 1960s and have continued unabated since then, as our statistical analysis shows. In fact, the absence of any measurable "Reagan reaction" during the 1980s belies the assertion that television follows the election returns. The internal dynamic of social trends on prime time remained impervious to conservative trends in public discourse on the other coast. If anything, the ascendance of conservative politics in Washington may have accelerated television's leftward tendencies by alarming and mobilizing the predominantly liberal Hollywood community. . . .

Similarly, the networks' much-ballyhooed sensitivity to outside pressure has undoubtedly acted as a brake on the engines of change, but it cannot shift them into reverse. For some pressure groups have been more successful than others. It is difficult to imagine producers submitting their scripts to the fundamentalist Coalition for Better Television for prior review, as they have done for the Gay Media Task Force. Hollywood's response to special interest complaints is dictated not only by the amount of pressure these pressure groups generate, but also by the perceived righteousness of their cause.

Television's America may once have looked like Los Angeles' Orange County 15 writ large—WASPish,° businesslike, religious, patriotic, and middle American.

°**reinforces the status quo:** Maintains social and economic arrangements just as they are.   °**WASPish:** Like white Anglo-Saxon Protestants, presumably the most favored group in American society.

Today it better resembles San Francisco's Marin County—trendy, self-expressive, culturally diverse, and cosmopolitan. Some aspects of this world, like the casual acceptance of recreational sex, turn the Left's argument on its head. One could just as easily argue that television is reflecting controversial social changes and, by presenting them as legitimate, accelerating their acceptance across the country.

In many other areas of life, moreover, television offers a picture of life that clearly does not reflect the status quo. One example is the workplace, where workers tell off bosses and warm personal relationships are infinitely more important than economic productivity. Another is ethnic relations. In prime time's pluralistic paradise all racial and ethnic groups live and work together harmoniously, threatened only by the occasional bigot, who is either defeated or sees the error of his ways. Perhaps the clearest divergence from reality is in television's portrayal of criminals, which inverts the real-world portrait of FBI crime statistics. In real life violent crimes are committed disproportionately by blacks, youths, and low-income groups. In prime time violent criminals are mainly wealthy white, mature adults, especially businessmen.

FOR ENQUIRING MINDS

S. Elizabeth Bird

This reading comes from S. Elizabeth Bird's 1992 book-length study of contemporary American tabloid newspapers and magazines, For Enquiring Minds: A Cultural Study of Supermarket Tabloids. *Her research, which focuses on women who regularly read the* National Enquirer, *is a good example of an academic study of popular culture.*

Though Bird studied readers of print tabloids, her findings and speculations apply equally well to viewers of television tabloid shows. Bird acknowledges the diversion and pleasure that poor, working-class women derive from reading the Enquirer. *She questions, however, whether the tabloids offer anything that would give these women the "power to change their lives." She concludes that the tabloids encourage poor women to accept their subordinate social position rather than help them secure a better future for themselves and their families.*

As you read, notice Bird's concern with the problem of romanticizing tabloid readers and viewers. Consider, too, whether you find her overall argument convincing. Keep in mind that some of the television tabloids appeal to the middle class, a different audience from the one Bird studied.

...My research on tabloid readers suggests that an important element in their readings is indeed a form of resistance to dominant values—an awareness, for example, that they "should" be reading about news and current affairs but find these boring and irrelevant. The perception that tabloids offer "untold stories" about anything from government waste to a movie star's romance is important to them because it suggests some sense of knowing and control over things that are really out of control.

But a sense of pleasure in a feeling of control is not the same as actually having control. And resistance is not subversion. Readers may feel empowered, but that does not change their subordinate position in the class structure. There may be a range of possible readings of tabloids, but a radical reading° is not one of them....It is highly improbable that the most creative reader could, for instance, construct a feminist, secular, or liberal reading of tabloids. In effect, what tabloids seem to do very effectively is show that being subordinate really is not so bad....

In fact, tabloid readers are, for the most part, people with little real power who would dearly love to have more. But they are not radicals; they are not out to change the system. Willis discusses aspects of working-class experience: "A quite marked degree of disenchantment with the prevailing system and a degree of knowledge of exploitation...can coexist with a calm acceptance of the system and belief that there is no systematic suppression of personal chances in life. Suppression is recognized, but as no more than a random part of the human condition" (1977, 165). And if suppression is random, change may also be random, and subject to the many faces of fate that are presented in tabloids. While Willis was writing about Britain, his point is easily transferable to the United States. In fact, it may be even more relevant here, where a sense of "working-class" consciousness is less developed. Ideals of individualism—the dream that any ordinary person might become a star or a president—tend to ensure even less of a sense of "systematic suppression" in this country.

As Gitlin points out, the optimistic interpretations of cultural studies appear to claim resistance to dominant ideology° as a political act, when it clearly is not: "it is pure sloppiness to conclude that culture or pleasure is politics" (1990, 192). In fact, the pleasure that tabloid readers derive from the political message of tabloids may actually replace real political action, giving as it does an illusion of "insider knowledge." The feeling of getting closer to the power center, based on the erection of widespread conspiracy theories, may seem empowering; actually it just confirms that, in reality, they are infinitely far from the center. The tabloids offer fables and moral tales that help readers cope with

---

°**radical reading:** Here, a reading that would recommend major political reform or attack the tabloids for failing to do so. In the next sentence, Bird identifies three types of radical readings: feminist, secular, and liberal.   °**dominant ideology:** The dominant view in a society about human life and culture.

their disenchantment, giving them undeniable pleasure. But because there is pleasure in learning to live with and enjoy aspects of subordination, including the possibility that fate may intervene, does not mean that there is no pain, no frustration, no anger that the Wheel of Fortune has passed by yet again.

Another troubling point that emerges from a consideration of the "banality 5 of cultural studies" (Morris 1988) is the question of relativism. The optimistic voice of cultural studies suggests that there are innumerable readings of a text and that readers will choose the one that works best for them.... [S]ome people may read tabloids as scientific, and that may indeed be a strategy of resistance against what is seen as a dominant scientific establishment. From an optimistic, relativistic standpoint, there is no problem with this; if it gives a reader pleasure, it is positive....

But there is a problem. Schudson applauds the more recent view of consumers of mass culture as active and creative. "But this is not or should not be to admit all cultural forms equal, all interpretations valid, all interpretive communities self-contained and beyond criticism" (1987, 66). Tabloids themselves are supremely relativistic. Tabloid writers repeatedly absolve themselves from responsibility with their assertions of objectivity; they do not have to believe anything, merely to find someone authoritative who does. We have seen that few if any readers believe everything in the tabloids. But the message of tabloids is that anything is potentially believable, and all things are possible. Do we accept and even celebrate the "divergent rationality"° of readers who think fossilized dinosaur eggs can hatch or that the earth is regularly visited by aliens? Is it such a wonderful, constructive thing that some tabloid readers firmly believe they will win the lottery, or that celebrities' lives are really much worse than their own? Petrified eggs do not hatch, and anyone who believes they do is likely to be dismissed by the educated as stupid, uneducated, or both. Espousing many aspects of the "divergent rationality" of the tabloids simply ensures that proponents advertise their subordinate class to the world. As Willis writes, resistance against dominant ideology, although pleasurable, may actually block people from upward mobility. "Resistance is thus an intimate part of the process of reproducing capitalist-class relations"° (1977, 82).

In an enthusiasm for the power of the audience, it is easy to invest too much in an empowerment that may be illusory. There is not one, single "reading" of tabloids; there are not even only two or three. But there are not infinite numbers of readings, either; tabloids cannot be anything to anybody. Like much popular culture, tabloids consistently preach the lesson that there is little anyone can do to change the world except hope for a miracle. In that respect, they

---

° "**divergent rationality**": A kind of thinking that is different from mainstream thinking. ° "**reproducing capitalist-class relations**": Maintaining wealth and income disparity among classes (lower, middle, upper) in countries with capitalist economies, like the United States, England, or Brazil.

are...much like a great deal of folklore. While in certain situations folklore can be genuinely subversive in a way tabloids are not, most folk narratives help people cope with daily existence and their position in the pecking order by telling tales that dramatize values that are essentially conservative. They provide rich material for fantasy and hold out hope of sudden, magical change, but people who are overly ambitious or greedy meet bad ends. For while it has rarely been analyzed as such (Green, 1983), folklore too is ideological in that it reinforces and repairs hegemony,° "defining a reality that citizens freely accept, a reality whereby the natural or inevitable right of the ruling class is popularly taken for granted" (Schudson 1987, 53).

Schudson writes of his discomfort with much recent research that has offered "a salutary new valuation of popular culture combined with an undiscriminately sentimental view of it" (1987, 51). Like Morris, he points out the other side of the optimistic view of cultural studies: "with the recognition of the active role of audiences in constructing the works they engage, there is a danger of romanticizing and sentimentalizing audiences as they exist in certain inhumane social conditions" (p. 64).

For example, my interpretation of female readings of tabloids suggests that women read actively and creatively, inserting tabloid narratives into their oral culture and their lives. They value tabloids highly because the papers validate their concerns for family and interpersonal relations. Yet many had lived or were living very difficult lives, victims of spouse abuse, lack of money, and the generalized oppression of being an "old-fashioned housewife." Tabloids, like romances, help them cope with their lives and feel good about themselves, but they do not give them power to change their lives....

In this study, I have tried to narrate a previously "untold story" of the super- 10 market tabloids. Working within the theoretical tradition of cultural studies, my aim has been to understand the relationship between tabloid writer, text, and audience, an interplay that succeeds in producing a supremely popular cultural commodity. The tabloid charms its readers and beckons them into a world where life is dangerous and exciting. But when the journey is done, it soothes them with assurances that, be it ever so humble, there really is no place like home.

Works Cited

Gitlin, Todd. 1990. "Who Communicates What to Whom, in What Voice and Why, about the Study of Mass Communication?" *Critical Studies in Mass Communication* 7(2): 185–96.

Green, Archie. 1983. "Interpreting Folklore Ideologically." In Richard M. Dorson, ed., *Handbook of American Folklore*. Bloomington: Indiana Univ. Press, 351–58.

°**hegemony:** Domination over others.

Morris, Meaghan. 1988. "Banality in Cultural Studies." *Discourse* 10(2): 3–29.

Schudson, Michael. 1978. *Discovering the News: A Social History of American Newspapers*. New York: Basic Books.

Schudson, Michael. 1987. "The New Validation of Popular Culture: Sense and Sentimentality in Academia." *Critical Studies in Mass Communication* 4: 51–68.

Willis, Paul. 1977. *Learning to Labour: How Working Class Kids Get Working Class Jobs*. London: Saxon House.

A WRITER'S NOTEBOOK

Social Perspectives on Tabloid TV

The following tasks are designed to help you think about the readings and identify and start to work up material you might use in your own essay.

1. *Consider your own experience.* Describe your current TV-viewing habits by writing down what you watch in a typical week. List specific programs and times. Do you think you watch a lot of television or not very much? What do you consider significant or unusual about your TV viewing?

2. *List important information from Philip Weiss's essay.* In paragraphs 7, 10, and 15–18, Weiss discusses the positive social values of tabloid TV. List each specific tabloid example he mentions, identifying each in a brief phrase and noting the positive social value he sees in it. Include the paragraph number of each item in your list. To get you started: In paragraph 7, Weiss mentions a segment reporting on a woman who was paralyzed when her boyfriend shot her. He comments that viewers would feel identification and sympathy for the woman. In the next paragraph, he asserts that this segment is worthy of airtime.

3. *List important information from Jib Fowles's argument.* List the phrases Fowles uses to identify the social benefits he attributes to TV, noting the paragraph number for each phrase. To get you started: Fowles begins by noting that television functions to "bind up Americans" and that it is the "creator of a national culture."

4. *Evaluate Fowles's argument.* To learn more about the credibility, emotional appeal, and logic of Fowles's argument, evaluate it.

5. *List television representations of social life from the reading by S. Robert Lichter et al.* In paragraphs 9–10 and 15–16, the authors discuss the way TV influences viewers' perceptions of social life in America. Reread these paragraphs and list the influences, noting the paragraph number of each influence. As you compile your list, keep in mind that the authors' views are sometimes implied in their criticisms of other social theorists rather than stated directly. To get you started: In paragraph 3, the authors say that television shows us evil executives and crooked cops.

6. *Capture the main points in S. Elizabeth Bird's essay.* Bird asserts that her research has led her to a pessimistic view of the influences of print tabloids on their readers. List the reasons why she holds this view, noting the paragraph number of each reason. Keep in mind that Bird sometimes states her reasons

directly and sometimes conveys them by quoting other researchers. To get you started: In paragraph 2, Bird says that the tabloids influence readers to accept their subordinate positions.

7. *React to one of the arguments in this section.* Choose one reading in this section that you tend to agree with or one you tend to disagree with. Write a page or so explaining your agreement or disagreement in light of the tabloid TV programs you have been watching.

Now you are ready to bring together all you have learned about tabloid TV. Your goal is to write a research report that interprets tabloid TV from a social perspective, using the series you have been watching as the special example. You are in an enviable position as a writer: You know a great deal about the history and characteristics of tabloid TV, and you have also sampled a wide range of opinions on the tabloids. Most important, you have taken pages of notes while viewing a tabloid series and have started to interpret those notes from a social perspective. Now is the time for you to decide how the series you have been watching represents social life in America.

This Writer's Guide will help you

- plan, draft, revise, edit, and proofread a research report that interprets tabloid TV from a social perspective
- work with sources — to gather current information and to cite sources that you draw upon
- construct certain kinds of sentence patterns that are useful in writing that interprets popular culture
- reflect on what you learned completing this assignment

THE WRITING ASSIGNMENT   Write a research report that interprets tabloid TV from a social perspective. Your essay should answer the following question: How, in your view, does tabloid TV represent people and social life in America? You will need to devise a thesis that asserts your interpretation of tabloid TV and support your thesis with detailed examples from the series you have been watching. Your purpose is to convince your readers that your interpretation of tabloid TV should be taken seriously.

Many colleges have research forums for undergraduates. These forums invite students to submit carefully researched reports, and a committee of faculty and students chooses the best reports for publication or presentation. Write your report as though you are submitting it to such a forum. Assume that it will be evaluated by a committee that has experience in interpreting the influence of television on American culture.

PLANNING AND DRAFTING YOUR REPORT

This section provides guidelines and student examples to help you plan and draft an effective report about tabloid TV. It will help you

- understand your readers and your writing situation
- select materials
- prepare a prospectus
- organize your essay

- devise a convincing argument
- cite sources

Understanding Your Readers

Assume that your readers have watched a lot of television and are familiar with cultural studies. In fact, as you develop your report, you may assume that your readers—whether students or instructors—have probably completed a cultural studies research project. Thus, they will understand your method of interpretation—looking critically at one aspect of popular culture. They will also recognize that cultural studies research is worthwhile for what it reveals about us as a country—about our values, concerns, and priorities; you will not need to convince them that this is so.

You will need to demonstrate to them, though, that you are a serious student of the tabloids. You are in a good position to do so. Your authority comes from the reading you have done, from the social perspective you have adopted, and from the evidence you have collected while critically viewing a tabloid TV series. Although you may not be an expert on the subject, you are still very knowledgeable.

Interpreting popular culture and supporting your interpretation in a carefully argued report, you will be engaged in a special kind of research and writing that is widely practiced in college and university humanities and social science departments and by social analysts and critics at large. Because these researchers refer to their research publications as "research reports," we follow that convention in calling your essay for this chapter a "report." Recognize, however, that you will be writing what we call "argument" elsewhere in this book. It is thesis centered and developed by reasoned, supported argument and counterargument.

Selecting Materials

All of the TV viewing, note-taking, reading, and other writing tasks in this chapter have contributed to your understanding of tabloid TV. Now you can select from these resources the materials that will best support your interpretation of tabloid TV from a social perspective. The following activities will help you to do so.

Make a Judgment.   If you have not already done so, decide whether you believe that the representations of people and their relationships by tabloid TV weaken or strengthen social life in America. Your decision may reflect your own long-standing attitudes toward television in general or toward tabloid TV, or perhaps you will be influenced by one or more of the readings. Whatever the source of your decision, it will determine the thesis and the argument of your essay and will guide you in choosing examples from tabloid TV programs to support your argument.

Search the Readings for Thesis Ideas.   Reexamine the social-perspective readings, this time looking for key ideas or claims the authors make about how people and social relationships are represented on tabloid TV. From one of these can come a tentative thesis statement that will bring your essay into focus and guide the remainder of your work on this assignment. Philip Weiss in "Bad Raps for TV Tabs," for example, makes several claims about the tabloids:

> the typology is stories of smalltown ignorance (paragraph 4)
>
> stories that reveal authority (often in the form of a pastor or plastic surgeon) as wickedly hypocritical (paragraph 4)
>
> stories of family violence (paragraph 4)
>
> The untrustworthy family is the central narrative (paragraph 5)
>
> Many of the family-deceit stories confirm a Dostoyevskian view of existence. [...] Some undermine the very idea of family. (paragraph 7)

Weiss makes other claims in these paragraphs, but those listed above are concerned directly with how tabloid TV represents people and social life. The point is to be selective, looking for claims that reflect a perspective on people, relationships, and social life. The claims singled out above might lead to the following thesis statements for a research report interpreting tabloid TV from a social perspective:

- Tabloid TV weakens viewers' confidence in marriage and the family by frequently representing families as unstable and untrustworthy. Typical family relationships are deceitful and violent.

- Tabloid TV makes viewers unnecessarily suspicious of authority figures by representing them as hypocrites. With only two exceptions in the eight segments I viewed in which authorities appeared, they were represented as something less than or different from what they appeared to be.

You might want to borrow one of the above thesis statements—or one of the others listed below—or use them as models for your own thesis. Your goal is to construct a thesis that reflects what has caught your attention in the representations in the tabloid series you have been viewing. Then you must support this thesis through numerous examples from that series. The examples should be directly relevant to the thesis and presented in some detail, telling what happened, who was there, what was said, where it happened, what attitude was conveyed by the reporter, and so on. Such details are crucial, especially for readers who may be resistant to your thesis. Strong, vivid details may serve to convince them to take your thesis seriously.

Following are examples of other possible theses based on claims in the readings:

> Like all of television, tabloid TV brings Americans together into one inclusive social and cultural group, thereby strengthening democracy.
>
> — JIB FOWLES
> "Why Viewers Watch"

Criticisms of tabloid TV reflect a bias against the lifestyles and values of the lower middle class, the working class. Such criticisms are elitist. By paying attention to the working class, even though not always showing working-class members in a flattering light, tabloid TV does its part to keep them in view as a valued part of American society.

> — PHILIP WEISS
> "Bad Rap for TV Tabs"

Tabloid TV celebrates cultural diversity but only superficially, ignoring deep-rooted ethnic and cultural differences.

> — S. ROBERT LICHTER, LINDA S. LICHTER,
> and STANLEY ROTHMAN
> "Prime Time: How TV Portrays
> American Culture"

Except for celebrities, people represented on tabloid TV have relatively low social status and income, little opportunity to better their lives, and no apparent political awareness. They are subordinate and do not seem to be concerned about it. They make no effort to change the status quo.

> —S. ELIZABETH BIRD
> "For Enquiring Minds"

Notice that while these thesis statements necessarily rely on terms from the readings, the sentences are the writer's own. While theses may either stay close to a reading's claims or spin off from them, the language of each thesis centers it unmistakably in a social perspective on popular culture and makes clear the writer's judgment that tabloid TV either weakens or strengthens social life.

Many other theses can be derived from the social-perspective readings in this chapter. Staying close to the readings when you attempt to construct your thesis will help ensure that your eventual thesis reflects a social perspective — how people and their relationships are represented. It will not be enough for your thesis merely to assert your like or dislike of tabloid TV. For example, this would not be an appropriate thesis because it expresses only a personal judgment or preference: It is an understatement to call tabloid TV trash TV. I personally find it trivial and uninformative.

Review Your Viewing Notes.   With a tentative thesis in mind, review the notes you took while viewing a tabloid series to see whether you have enough information on specific programs and segments to support your thesis. It is especially important that you use details from a number of segments for this report since you want to generalize about the cultural impact of the entire genre based on your interpretation of one typical series. After looking over your notes, you may discover that you need to view or interpret more programs, reinterpret segments you have already viewed, or take notes on entirely new segments.

Preparing a Prospectus

At this point, your instructor may want you to prepare a prospectus for your report, to plot out some of its parts. Engineers, businesspeople, and other professionals regularly write prospectuses for projects to test their ideas and win support for them. In much the same way, a prospectus for a research report enables you to try out your argument for particular readers and to begin to think seriously about how you will support it.

Here are some guidelines for drafting a two- or three-page prospectus.

1. *Identify the tabloid series.* Name the tabloid TV series you have viewed and interpreted.

2. *Identify the most important reading.* Identify the one reading that contributed most to your thinking about tabloid TV and to your judgment about whether the tabloids weaken or strengthen social relationships and social life in America. Write a few sentences explaining the importance of this reading.

3. *State your thesis.* Construct a clear thesis statement based on your most important reading. Reread the essay unhurriedly, underlining the main ideas the writer offers about tabloid TV. Reflect on these ideas and try to come up with a thesis that reflects the social perspective of the reading and at the same time expresses your personal views about the influence of tabloid TV. You may discover that you need to reword the thesis two or three times to get it approximately right, or you may want to try a different thesis by focusing on other ideas in the reading.

4. *List the steps in a possible argument.* After going over your viewing notes, jot down a few steps to show how you might present your findings to your readers. What will you do first, next, and so on to support your thesis? It may help to think of these steps as reasons why, after viewing several tabloid TV programs in one series, you arrived at your thesis. For example, if your thesis concerns women's limited roles on tabloid TV, your support might demonstrate that women are typically represented as idle, indulgent celebrities; dangerous to their families; obsessed with their bodies; or passive and dependent on men. These four reasons, along with appropriate examples, might be the four steps in your argument.

5. *Find support for your thesis.* Once you have a tentative idea about how your argument might unfold, identify in a phrase or two each program segment you plan to rely on for support. Remember that each segment must contribute specific details and examples to support your argument. For a focus on women's limited roles, a writer might use program segments like these: a Korean bride of an American soldier kills their child and tries to kill herself; a beauty queen tries to kill her romantic rival; a paraplegic former *Playboy* model denies that her drunkenness caused her accident and has unrealistic plans to become a fraud investigator; a female photographer talks about the celebrities she photographs, not her work and career.

6. *Try to support one part of your argument.* Select one step or reason in item 4 above and write at least a page supporting it—arguing for it—with one or more examples from the notes on the program segments you watched. Do not, for now, attempt a thorough search of your material. Rely on your memory and

notes. Write quickly. Your purpose is simply to try out one part of your argument before you plan your entire report. You may want to begin with a sentence like the following: "Tabloid TV often portrays women as dangerous to their families, backing up my contention that women's roles in tabloids are very limited."

Organizing Your Report

Although a research report is essentially an argument, a genre familiar to most readers, it has a few special features. Research reports are usually written for readers who know something about the subject under study and about the methodology of the research. They generally follow a conventional format, beginning with a statement of purpose, a description of the subject, and a description of the research method. Since your report will be read and evaluated in an academic setting, the first part of it should incorporate these features. The next part of your report, which presents your thesis and findings, will look like any argument essay that supports a position: a step-by-step argument that incorporates details from the tabloid programs you watched and counterargues readers' possible reservations about your findings.

A successful research report, then, must accomplish two things: it must present the subject studied and the method of interpretation, and it must provide extensive support for the thesis. To provide a detailed framework for your report, you might expand this two-part plan in the following way:

Presentation of the subject (tabloid TV) and your social perspective for interpretation
 – statement of the purpose of the study, along with a brief definition of tabloid TV
 – description of tabloid TV as a television genre
 – description of your tabloid TV series and your method for viewing and analysis

Argument and counterargument
 – thesis statement
 – argument to support your thesis
 – counterargument of your readers' possible reservations about your thesis or argument
 – counterargument of possible alternative interpretations of your program-segment notes
 – conclusion and reassertion of your thesis

A plan of this sort will serve you well when you draft your report. It will take some work—some sections may be accomplished in one paragraph, but others may require several paragraphs.

Presenting the Subject and Perspective.   The information that you need to cover in this part may take up as much as a third of your report. Unlike other essays, a research report does not include a typical introduction. Instead, you should begin immediately with your statement of purpose.

PURPOSE OF THE STUDY.   In a few sentences, state the purpose of your study and define tabloid TV briefly (you will define it more fully later on). Explain what you have studied and why, mentioning the social perspective that has guided your interpretation. From your statement of purpose, you should be able to develop a title for your report. It should be as brief as possible but should indicate the subject and research perspective of your report.

DESCRIBING TABLOID TV AS A TELEVISION GENRE.   Briefly describe tabloid TV as a television genre, a type of television program with unique characteristics. You need not evaluate the genre here; just describe it objectively. Some of the readings contrast tabloid TV with conventional television news and cop shows, and you may want to do so as well. Also identify the most popular tabloids.

To recall how other writers describe tabloid TV, check the following paragraphs in these readings. These readings also contain much of the information you will need for this section of your report.

Max Robins (paragraphs 4, 12, 13, 15, 16, 20)

Frank Houston (paragraphs 1–5)

Graham Knight (paragraphs 1–9)

Krista Bradford (paragraphs 6–9)

Steven D. Stark (paragraphs 12–17)

Philip Weiss (paragraph 4)

DESCRIBING YOUR TABLOID TV SERIES.   Describe the tabloid TV series you have interpreted. Identify the network, time, anchors, setting for the anchors, reporters or interviewers, graphics, sound, typical number of program segments, and typical advertisements.

PRESENTING YOUR METHOD FOR VIEWING AND ANALYSIS.   Readers will want to evaluate the soundness of your method for viewing the tabloid series. You need to reassure them that you have followed a systematic plan of viewing, note-taking, and interpreting. Identify the number of programs and segments you viewed. Then present the key questions you relied on to guide your interpretation and describe your strategy of note-taking. Describe briefly how you evaluated your viewing notes in order to select examples to support your thesis.

In this first part of your report, you might consider using headings to indicate to readers exactly how you have organized the material. The following are effective, but you may want to come up with other ones. Since the statement of purpose serves as the introduction to your report, it does not need a heading.

Tabloid TV as a Television Genre

Inside Edition (name of the series you analyze)

Method for Viewing and Analysis

Plotting Out Your Arguments and Counterarguments.   As the heart of your report, the argument section begins with a concise thesis statement, followed by reasons to support your thesis, which is based on your research findings. Following are some ideas about how to organize this part of your report. (Ultimately, you will probably need only two headings: Findings and Conclusion.)

STATING YOUR THESIS.   Observing the standard conventions of a research report, you would nearly always assert your thesis after introducing your study and before arguing to support your findings. These readings present a thesis statement early: Robins (paragraph 4), Weiss (paragraph 4), Fowles (paragraph 1), and Bird (paragraphs 1 and 2).

SEQUENCING YOUR REASONS.   Allow considerable space to provide the reasons for your thesis and several detailed examples from relevant tabloid segments. These provide the primary, if not exclusive, support for your thesis. Think carefully about how to sequence reasons. You may want to begin with the least convincing reason and end with the most convincing, or you may want to begin with the reason most likely to be accepted and conclude with the most controversial reason. Fowles, for example, begins by arguing that all Americans watch television in much the same way (paragraphs 3–5) and then argues that this similarity of viewing practices leads to similar thoughts and outlooks (paragraphs 6–8).

INTEGRATING YOUR COUNTERARGUMENTS.   Your readers will probably have at least a few questions or objections about the way you argue to support your thesis. In addition, some readers may think your supporting evidence from the tabloid segments suggests other conclusions than the ones you have asserted in your thesis. If you can anticipate any of these objections or alternative interpretations, you may concede or refute them at appropriate points in your argument. One option is to integrate counterarguments as you go along, mentioning them as readers follow your own argument. Another approach is to deal with all counterarguments together, either at the conclusion or at the beginning of your argument.

Several writers integrate counterarguments as they develop their own arguments: Bradford (paragraphs 3 and 20), Weiss (paragraphs 7 and 8), Fowles (paragraph 7), and Lichter et al. (paragraph 12).

CLOSING EFFECTIVELY.   To close a research report, it is often a good idea to reassert your thesis and the main points of your argument. Framing an argument in this way makes it more memorable for readers. You might also quote an author who agrees with you or save a particularly convincing part of your support for the conclusion.

Various strategies of concluding an argument are illustrated by readings in this chapter:

- Reassert a thesis, as Houston (paragraph 9), Fowles (8), and Bird (10) do.
- Speculate about implications of an argument, as Bradford does (paragraphs 19–20).

- Quote an authority to support a position, as Houston (paragraphs 9 and 10) and Stark (17) do.
- Use a particularly telling example, as Weiss does (paragraph 19).

Whatever strategies you choose, your goal is to convince your readers to take your argument seriously. Since readers tend to remember best what they read last, take advantage of this opportunity to make an important final statement.

Developing Your Argument and Counterargument

This section will help you construct a thesis, argue to support your thesis, and counterargue readers' objections and different interpretations from your own.

Constructing a Thesis. This section offers further examples of theses and discusses some of the issues involved in formulating a workable thesis.

While writing research reports on tabloid TV, some students devised the following thesis statements:

```
• Even though many women today hold powerful, important
  jobs, tabloid TV represents women as either frivolous,
  self-indulgent celebrities or people too stupid to avoid
  dangerous situations.              -Jennifer Driggers
• Tabloid TV loves celebrities, especially women. When it
  represents celebrity women, it focuses on their bodies,
  clothes, men, or troubles, not on their talents or
  achievements.                         -Tamara Richards
• Tabloid TV, like all television, contributes to social
  change by removing partitions between groups of people
  who used to be mysterious to each other--adults and
  children, men and women, ordinary people and glamorous
  celebrities.                              -Frank Chin
• Tabloid TV contributes to greater social sympathy and
  cohesion by telling stories that reveal the tragedies,
  frustrations, and triumphs of ordinary people.
                                           -Alberto Salas
```

Notice, first, that each thesis asserts the writer's judgment about whether tabloid TV weakens or strengthens social life. Driggers and Richards believe that tabloid TV weakens social life by focusing on the least accomplished women, whereas Chin and Salas believe that tabloid TV strengthens social life by contributing positively to social change and cohesion. Notice, too, that each thesis mentions specific aspects of the tabloids, forecasting what is to be discussed in the rest of the report. Driggers singles out "frivolous, self-indulgent celebrities" and women "too stupid to avoid dangerous situations." Richards offers a contrast between "talents or achievements" and "bodies, clothes, men, or troubles." Chin and Salas also single out specific aspects of the tabloids' influences on social life.

These specifics signal readers that these writers have been viewing a tabloid series carefully and critically. Instead of general impressions, these theses offer thoughtful insights and precisely chosen words and phrases—the essential key terms in a successful thesis. Key thesis terms are hardly ever discovered immediately and are sometimes discovered only after a draft of a research report is well under way. Consider, for example, Salas's thesis. His key terms are *social sympathy, cohesion, tragedies, frustrations,* and *triumphs. Cohesion* came from the Fowles reading. *Sympathy* arrived after Salas tried out *understanding* but rejected it as lacking any suggestion of shared feelings that might contribute powerfully to social cohesion by keeping people's relationships close. The other three terms joined the list only after Salas had tried repeatedly, while reviewing his viewing notes and interpretations, to name the range of situations in which he observed ordinary people represented in tabloid segments—situations of tragedy, frustration, and triumph. Key terms like these, which should reappear frequently, help keep readers on track, particularly at points where they look for direction, like first sentences of paragraphs.

A workable thesis aids readers by forecasting the argument, providing an overview, and predicting the steps of the argument. For example, as soon as they see her thesis, experienced readers know that Driggers will begin by demonstrating that, in all the tabloid segments she viewed, a low percentage represented women holding "powerful, important jobs." She will then demonstrate by describing several segments in detail that women are frequently represented as "frivolous, self-indulgent celebrities." Finally, she will demonstrate that women are also frequently represented as "too stupid to avoid dangerous situations."

An argument cannot succeed without a workable thesis. Notice, as an experienced viewer and interpreter of tabloid TV, your high level of confidence that these students' theses can actually be supported by examples from typical tabloid programs. You can no doubt remember segments in which ordinary people experienced tragedies, frustrations, or triumphs or celebrity women were represented solely for their bodies, clothes, men, or troubles.

EXAMPLES FROM THE READINGS. For further examples of successful thesis statements, examine the following readings: Bradford (paragraphs 3 and 16–19); Weiss, Fowles, and Lichter et al. (paragraph 1 in each); and Bird (paragraph 2).

Supporting Your Interpretation. The heart of your report is your argument, in which you support—argue for—your thesis with examples from the tabloid series you have been watching. The following selections from student essays illustrate some basic strategies for providing such support.

The first student example is from a report by Donald Ferris. It focuses on tabloid TV's representation of childhood as a time of loss and danger. Ferris first argues that a surprising number of *Inside Edition* segments show children being killed or injured in their homes by their parents or other adults. He then argues that children are shown to be in just as much danger *outside* their homes:

```
Children are also frequently shown being killed or injured
outside their homes. For example, one Inside Edition
segment tells the story of a Knoxville, Tennessee, child
```

who died after an emergency-room doctor refused to accept
her. The ambulance driver was forced to take her to
another hospital, and she died on the way there. This
tragedy was investigated, and the hospital authorities
backed the doctor. The ambulance driver said that he had
taken children to this hospital before and they had been
admitted and treated. The reporter interviews the girl's
parents, who appear to be young and poor. They sit on a
couch, holding hands. The father quietly answers the
reporter's questions about the investigation while the
mother looks down at a photo of the child she holds in her
lap. They seem bewildered and resigned. Then we see the
front of the hospital and the emergency room entrance. No
one at the hospital would talk to the tabloid reporter.
In another segment, viewers learn that 150 juveniles
(children under age 18) have been executed for crimes in
the United States since 1975. The United States is one of
only eight countries, including Iran and Iraq, that
execute 16- and 17-year-olds. Twenty-one states allow the
execution of 16-year-olds. In a Texas prison, the tabloid
reporter interviews two 17-year-olds awaiting execution by
lethal injection. Both seem confused and depressed and do
not think they should be executed. The reporter also
interviews the parents of the people they killed. The
parents predictably show little sympathy for the killers.
In a third segment, children are revealed to be in danger
from a shampoo for lice called Lindane. Many parents have
called the National Reticulosis Association complaining
about the shampoo. Eighteen countries have banned it, but
our Environmental Protection Agency defends it. Drug
companies have said it is safe if used as directed. The
reporter interviews a doctor, who says you can absorb it
through your skin. Viewers are given a phone number to
call for information about the dangers of Lindane. These
three segments give viewers the impression that the world
outside the home is truly a dangerous place for children
and that danger is everywhere--in products bought off the
shelf in drug stores, in a legal system that treats
children like adults, and even in hospitals. Not one
segment in the programs I viewed showed children enjoying
positive, supportive experiences.

Almost all of the sentences in this paragraph are devoted to specific supporting examples. In addition, each of the three examples is presented in
enough detail so that readers can imagine it and therefore judge for themselves whether it offers convincing support for Ferris's interpretation. To back
up his view that tabloid TV represents children as endangered from forces outside their homes, he includes only the relevant details from each segment he
viewed. Notice as well how Ferris's opening sentence signals to readers that he

is introducing a new reason for his interpretation. His use of the word *also* connects the first part of his argument to this part, and the word *outside* announces the contrast with the first part.

As he presents his material, he uses three phrases—"for example, one segment," "in another segment," and "in a third segment"—to mark clearly the beginning of each separate example. Then, after his third example, he declares explicitly the significance of the examples both to his thesis and to this "outside" step in the argument. The three examples could be presented in three separate paragraphs. In relatively formal research reports, however, as in much academic writing, paragraphs may be lengthy, bringing together much more related material than you will find in informal writing and in typical magazines and newspapers.

The second student example comes from a report by Elizabeth O'Connor, who argues that tabloid TV represents families in the 1990s as highly unstable and likely to experience threat, crisis, or disintegration. The following paragraph comes early in the essay, where O'Connor argues that tabloid TV represents men as the major cause of family instability.

> When mothers destroy a family on tabloid TV, they usually do so by killing a husband in order to protect a child from the father or by killing themselves out of desperation over personal abuse or child abuse. In one segment I viewed, an abused mother killed her child and tried to kill herself. In another, the mother killed her husband, who she said had been sexually abusing their daughter. In contrast, men threaten or destroy their families by having affairs, as I observed in four of six segments in which men created family crises. For example, one segment reminded viewers of President Kennedy's many affairs, and another segment revealed the laughable affair of Reverend Jim Bakker and his secretary Jessica Hahn. In both of these cases, the family held together. Just as often on the tabloids, however, affairs lead to the destruction of the family.
>
> In the first of two examples I observed, Dennis Rodman, the basketball star, is reported to have felt abandoned when his father left the family. His father, Philander Rodman, now lives in the Philippines with two wives. He has twenty-seven children from all of his marriages. We see photographs of him with one of his wives and several children. The reporter says that Philander wants Dennis to bring him to the United States so that they can have a "man to man talk," but Dennis is not interested. The reporter says that Dennis feels close only to his mother and sisters from his father's first marriage. In the second example, the reporter tells viewers that a married high school coach, Harvey Kochel, went to jail for a year for writing love letters to a fifteen-year-old girl student at his school. Over the years several girls and their parents had

```
complained to the school principal about Kochel's sexual
advances, but according to the reporter, the principal had
ignored the complaints. When the reporter interviewed
Kochel after his release from prison, Kochel claimed
that he was now a Christian and that God had forgiven
him. He was met at the prison by a former student, and
they announced plans to marry. We do not learn anything
about his former family. In these two segments, Kochel
and Rodman express no regret or guilt over destroying
their first families. They show no awareness of the
harm that was likely done to their wives and children.
They assume they have been forgiven or deserve to be.
Although viewers may be aware that half of all marriages
in the United States end in divorce, they might get the
impression from watching Inside Edition that the other
half are likely to end that way soon. I believe that
the tabloids should reflect the realities of our times,
but I question why stable families are so rarely seen.
```

This selection demonstrates that not all examples must be detailed. O'Connor mentions several relevant segments but elaborates only the ones involving Philander Rodman and Harvey Kochel. She very carefully prepares us for her argument that men are represented as destroyers of families; then, after she details the two examples, she makes their relevance explicit and reminds us of her position. As Ferris did in his paragraph, O'Connor clearly introduces the two examples, using the following phrases: "in the first of two examples I observed" and "in the second example."

EXAMPLE FROM THE READINGS. Because their purposes differ from yours, few of the readings mention specific tabloid TV segments. Only one reading develops segments into examples of the kind you will be developing to support your interpretation. You may want to turn to the Weiss reading to see how he goes about presenting segments as examples in paragraphs 5, 7, 9, 10, 17, and 19.

Counterarguing. Counterargument—anticipating readers' questions or objections and alternative views—is integral to all argument. In arguing to support interpretations of research data, however, counterargument may not be featured in the way it almost always is when you speculate about causes or consequences or take a position on issues. The difference is that in reading an argument supporting an interpretation, your readers rarely have immediate access to the data you are using. For example, unless your readers have been watching the same tabloid series you are writing about, they have no way of knowing whether you are using examples responsibly or might be ignoring program segments that fail to support your interpretation. Consequently, readers must assume that you have been ethical in the way you have used the examples available to you. They can, nevertheless, question the relevance of the examples to your thesis and whether your argument is logically organized and internally consistent.

In the previous student example, Elizabeth O'Connor anticipates readers' likely questions and reservations toward the end of the last paragraph. When she writes that "viewers may be aware that half of all marriages in the United States end in divorce," she shows that she is anticipating what her readers may be thinking: What is so unusual about these examples? It is hardly news that men leave their wives and that many of them then neglect their children. By assuring readers that she is aware of divorce statistics, she gains authority to suggest that the tabloids represent family life too grimly and negatively.

In the full report of her research, O'Connor does not counterargue alternative interpretations, but she might have. Some readers, for example, might view her examples as relevant support for the thesis that women and children are nearly always well rid of a man who is unfaithful and self-indulgent. These readers might also notice that neither segment reports on what happened to the divorced wives and children. They might conclude, therefore, that O'Connor has no sound basis for her argument. Instead, they could argue that the examples represent only the too-frequent necessity of dissolving a bad marriage. To avoid losing these readers, O'Connor would need to concede or refute this alternative interpretation. Acknowledging such an interpretation does not mean that you must jettison your own. You need, however, to come up with a strategy for conceding or refuting the alternative interpretation.

EXAMPLES FROM THE READINGS. To learn more about counterarguing readers' likely questions or objections to the writer's argument, see Robins (paragraph 2), Weiss (paragraphs 11–15), Fowles (paragraph 7), and Lichter et al. (paragraphs 11, 15–16). Fowles (paragraphs 4–5) illustrates counterargument of possible alternative interpretations.

SENTENCES FOR INTERPRETING POPULAR CULTURE

Different writing situations often require different kinds of sentences, even within the same essay or report. When you interpret a tabloid series, you write many sentences that introduce examples from program segments. You may also write sentences in which you distinguish carefully between current and past actions in a particular segment. Study the following sentence strategies and tips for matching verb tenses within examples and refer to them as you revise.

Introducing Examples That Support Your Argument

As you develop your argument, you need to integrate supporting examples smoothly into your report. You will usually use two or more examples together, so you need to mark their sequence clearly for your readers. Examples from the readings illustrate how you might do so.

DATES WHEN SEGMENTS ARE TELEVISED.   Silvana Paternostro uses the dates of two segments to introduce them into her argument in paragraphs 4 and 5 of her essay:

It was during a filming of a story for *Ocurrió Así last January* that a man shot and killed his ex-wife [. . .].

That same week, Univison's *Noticias y Más* aired a slapdash story about a visit [. . .].

By mentioning when the segments aired, she not only introduces them but also marks them as separate from each other.

QUOTATIONS FROM SEGMENTS.   Philip Weiss introduces two examples in one paragraph by quoting especially revealing remarks. He does this in paragraph 5 of his essay, in which he argues that the tabloids represent the family as unstable and untrustworthy:

"In two years I had ten lovers. [. . .] That's not very many," says a jailed *Inside Edition* interviewee [. . .].

"I thought she was having a weight problem," a mother says on *A Current Affair* of the pregnancy of her daughter [. . .].

WHEN CLAUSES.   Weiss introduces a third example in paragraph 5 with a *when* clause:

When a Texas girl was accused of scheming to rub out her parents, once allegedly rat-poisoning their food, she made both *A Current Affair* and *Inside Edition* the same night.

In paragraph 7, he continues this pattern, using a *when* clause followed by a quotation:

When a woman living with the boyfriend who shot her, crippling her from the waist down, says matter of factly, "We've had our ups and downs, like everybody has—we've fought," we're to understand that the two are like us.

And *when* a deeply alienated man charged with trying to kill the wife who's just said she still loves him says for his part, "I'm inclined to believe that I'm thinking about a person and continuing to love a person who no longer exists," we're pressed to identify with his dissociated cast of mind.

REFERENCES TO "STORY."   A tabloid TV program segment generally takes a narrative form: most segments tell a story that has a beginning and an ending, characters who interact with each other, and a point. A good way to introduce examples is to refer to them as stories. Reread Weiss's paragraph 17 and notice how he relies on the word *story* to introduce four examples:

Many *stories* seem to run

Another *Current Affair piece* [with *piece* used as a synonym for *story*]

In a gripping *story* about a Detroit crack ring

Then there was the creepiest *story* I saw all month

FOR EXAMPLE.   You may introduce examples by referring to them as *examples,* as in the two student paragraphs in the section "Supporting Your Findings." Elizabeth O'Connor adopts this sensible strategy:

In the first of two *examples,* I observed

In the second *example*

Donald Ferris also adopts this strategy and combines it with the term *segment:*

For *example,* one *segment* tells the story

In another *segment,* viewers learn

In still another *segment*

Whatever strategy you choose to introduce examples, it is best to stay with that pattern for the entire set of examples in that part of your argument. By predictably marking the beginning of each example in a particular section, you help create coherence in your argument.

Matching Verb Tenses When Presenting Examples

When you present examples to support your argument, you need to use present-tense verbs for actions occurring during the TV tabloid segment and past-tense verbs for actions or events completed prior to the filming of the segment. Depending on the topics and the way the segment is put together, you may have to shift tenses or maintain the same tense throughout the example.

SHIFTING TENSES.   Since the principles of tense selection and shifting are so abstract, a concrete illustration should prove helpful. Consider student Donald Ferris's paragraph in the section "Supporting Your Interpretation," in which he relates details of a segment about a young girl who apparently died because the doctor on duty at an emergency room would not accept her. The following list paraphrases some of the clauses Ferris uses in his example, which begins in the past tense, shifts to the present tense, and returns to the past tense.

Past tense

driver *was forced* to take her to another hospital

she *died*

authorities *backed* the doctor

driver *said*

he *had taken* children there before

they *had been admitted* and treated

Present tense

reporter *interviews* parents

who *appear* to be young and poor

they *sit* on a couch

the father *answers* questions

the mother *looks* down

she *holds* a photo in her lap

they *seem* bewildered

then we *see* the front of the hospital

Past tense

no one at the hospital *would talk* to the reporter

Ferris uses these present- and past-tense clauses to reconstruct the reporter's story. What he learns during the reporter's interview of the couple is in the present tense, and what he learns from the reporter about what happened previously is in the past tense. In other words, the interview is the current dramatic center of the story; what happened earlier is background.

MAINTAINING THE SAME TENSE. Not all examples require tense shifts. In Ferris's paragraph, a second example — based on a segment about capital punishment for 16 and 17 year olds — is presented all in present tense:

The United States *is* one of only eight countries [. . .] that *execute* 16- and 17-year-olds.

Twenty-one states *allow* the execution of 16-year-olds.

the tabloid reporter *interviews* two 17- year-olds

Both *seem* confused [. . .].

The reporter also *interviews* the parents [. . .].

The parents *show* little sympathy [. . .].

As in the preceding example, what Ferris learns from the interview is in present tense. He also puts the statistical information in present tense because the statistics inform viewers about the *present* status of the law on capital punishment, not about *past* events in the story. The present tense may be appropriate for presenting other kinds of information as well. Ask your instructor if you are not sure whether to use present or past tense.

CITING SOURCES

As you present the subject of tabloid TV and develop the argument supporting your interpretation, you will frequently quote, paraphrase, or summarize material from your tabloid series, as well as information from this chapter's readings. When you use original ideas in this way, you must cite them. In other words, you must identify their sources either informally or formally.

Informal Citation

Informal citation allows you to identify all of your sources within the text of your essay. You mention the author, publication, and perhaps the date right in your own sentences. When using informal citation, you do not need to identify sources in footnotes or in a works-cited list at the end of your essay.

Some of the readings in this chapter rely on informal citation because they are written for the general public. To see how writers use this citation style, look at these examples from Steven D. Stark:

> Over the years, that puffy celebrity coverage has been the *ET* claim to fame — or black mark, given your opinion of a program which has been defined as a press agent's dream. "[T]he show has dropped almost all pretense of being anything but an arm of the Hollywood publicity machine," Richard Zoglin wrote in *Time* in 1994.
>
> — STEVEN D. STARK
> "Glued to the Set"

> In her best selling *You Just Don't Understand,* linguist Deborah Tannen wrote that what has traditionally been labeled as gossip by men is often a positive way in which women discuss the world in order to understand and build relationships.
>
> — STEVEN D. STARK
> "Glued to the Set"

Formal Citation

When you use formal citation, you follow a specific style used by a particular academic or professional group. Appendix 2 of this book outlines two of these styles, one from the Modern Language Association (MLA), which is favored by scholars in the humanities, and one from the American Psychological Association (APA), which is favored by scholars in psychology. Ask your instructor which you should follow.

If you are referring to one of the readings in this chapter, cite it as a work in an anthology or edited collection. Depending on your instructor's advice, follow the recommendations under "A Work in an Anthology" in the "Books" section of the MLA guidelines or those under "A Work in an Edited Collection" in the "Books" section of the APA guidelines. If you use an example from a book such as Jib Fowles's, for instance, you would cite Fowles as the author of *Why Viewers Watch* and *Writing the World* as the anthology in which the Fowles reading appears. If you cite an example from an essay, such as Krista Bradford's "The Big Sleaze," you would list Bradford as the essay's author, "The Big Sleaze" as the essay's title, and *Writing the World* as the anthology in which it appears. Appendix 2 of this book discusses these options thoroughly and provides examples of each.

Note: Writers usually do not document sources that provide commonly known facts, general background information, or common knowledge, but if you want to make use of some of the background material in this chapter's introductions or reading headnotes, then you have two choices. You can paraphrase the material without giving a citation if it appears to be common knowledge. Otherwise, you can cite Charles R. Cooper and Susan Peck MacDonald as authors of *Writing the World,* using the models provided in Appendix 2.

EVALUATING AND REVISING

The following guidelines for revising will help you evaluate your own draft and provide useful advice to other students about theirs. As you read a draft, try to identify what has been done well and to come up with specific ways to improve the presentation of the research method and of tabloid TV as a television genre and the argument to support the interpretation. As you begin the revision process, focus on the big issues; save spelling and grammar for later.

Whether revising your own draft or helping classmates with theirs, you may need to refer to specific readings, so have them handy as you work, as well as material you have entered in your writer's notebook.

If you are reading someone else's work, it is a good idea to write out your comments on a separate sheet of paper, perhaps following the headings used in this section.

Read to Get a General Impression

Even if you are reading your own draft, read it straight through without marking on it, as if you are encountering the research report for the first time. Then write three or four sentences summarizing your first impression. What aspect of the report seems most successful? What is most interesting or surprising in the support for the interpretation? What one major improvement would make the argument more convincing?

Read to Analyze the Draft More Closely

Next, number the paragraphs and also mark the point at which the report divides into two major parts: the presentation of tabloid TV and of the writer's purpose and method of study, and the argument for a social interpretation of a tabloid series. Reread the draft, keeping in mind that the interested readers are familiar with studies of popular culture. Ask yourself, What do these particular readers need to know? Write down what is good about the draft as well as specific suggestions for revision.

The Statement of Purpose. Examine the statement of purpose closely because it plays a crucial role in opening the report and gaining readers' interest. Describe what seems to be working well. Advise the writer on ways to strengthen the statement.

The Description of Tabloid TV as a Television Genre. Consider whether the writer adequately informs readers about tabloids in general. Are the tabloids defined and distinguished clearly from related kinds of TV or print genres? Do you think readers need more—or less—information? If less, what specific material should be cut? If more, what specific information from the readings might be added?

The Description of the Series.   Consider whether the report adequately describes the series under study. Does it provide a clear picture of what the series is like—anchors, reporters, typical subjects, sounds and graphics, attitude toward people and viewers, and so on? What further information about the series do readers need?

The Method for Viewing and Analysis.   Like the opening statement of purpose, this section should make it clear to readers that the writer is a careful, systematic researcher. Tell the writer how the research plan might be described more clearly and completely. Evaluate whether readers might be confused by any aspects of the method as presented.

The Thesis.   Underline the sentences in which the thesis is stated. Does the thesis statement make a clear judgment about the social representations in the tabloids? Does it clearly reflect a social perspective on the tabloids? Has the writer used key words and phrases? Do the key terms seem to be accurate and workable? Might other words be better for the argument the writer wants to make? If so, suggest them. Does the thesis forecast the argument to come? If not, how might the thesis be improved?

The Support for the Argument and Counterargument.   Readers will not accept the thesis of the report unless the examples are interesting, detailed, and relevant. How many examples from the tabloid TV programs are included? Are they sufficiently detailed? Where are more or fewer examples needed? Explain any places where general references to programs should be replaced by specific examples.

Notice also whether the support is organized into a logical, step-by-step argument. Are reasons given for including each example? Point out any gaps or inconsistencies and suggest better ways to sequence the material if necessary.

How well does the report address readers' possible reservations about the argument and support? Does it mention possible alternative interpretations of the findings? If not, suggest possible reservations and alternative interpretations. If these are mentioned, what aspects of the counterargument seem especially insightful and convincing? Suggest ways to make it more convincing.

The Cues to Keep Readers on Track.   Note any sections or paragraphs that do not clearly fit, which leave you wondering, "Why am I reading this?" Look also for any gaps in the forward movement of the argument. Is it clear where the major sections of the report—statement of purpose, description of the tabloid genre, presentation of the series viewed, findings, argument—end and begin?

Are the key terms in the thesis used throughout the report? Identify the key terms in the thesis and underline each one wherever it appears. Note any paragraphs or pages devoid of key terms.

Look for places where transition sentences may be needed to keep readers on track. Does each paragraph-opening sentence lead the reader unmistakably from one section of the report to the next or from one step in the argument to the next?

The Closing. Does the essay close in a memorable way? What strategy is used? Does it reassert the thesis and repeat key terms? Does it bring the report to a satisfying close? How might the closing be made more effective? Is there anything in the readings that might be used to make it stronger?

EDITING AND PROOFREADING

As you revise, you will be concerned primarily with your presentation of the research study and your argument. Then comes the time to edit, when you begin clarifying your sentences and tightening the connections among them. In particular, you need to check to see that your sentences proceed logically and keep readers on track.

Examine the connections between all of your sentences. If you sense misdirection or a gap that would break a reader's momentum, try reorganizing one sentence or writing new material. Check to see whether you shift terms unnecessarily. Look for sentences that might be combined to better show relationships among ideas. Look as well for long or garbled sentences that might be broken up into two or three sentences.

As you work on your sentences, look for errors in spelling, capitalization, punctuation, usage, and grammar, consulting a writer's handbook for information about correcting any you find. Ask a friend or a classmate to read over your draft to help you spot errors.

Before you hand in your final revised report, proofread it carefully and run it through a spellchecker, trying to make it error free.

REFLECTING ON WHAT YOU HAVE LEARNED

Once you complete this chapter's reading and writing tasks, it is a good idea to take time to think about what you have accomplished and learned. Doing so will help you consolidate your new knowledge and remember it longer.

As you worked through this chapter, you were actually engaged in two closely related types of learning: becoming informed about a form of popular culture and learning how to interpret and report on it. Integrating these two kinds of learning, then, has been your major achievement. Using the following questions as a starting point, write a page or so reflecting on this accomplishment.

- You viewed several tabloid programs and took notes about many program segments. Then you practiced interpreting certain segments from a social perspective. What was the most difficult part of this basic research process? What was the most surprising?

- How have your views about tabloid TV been confirmed or changed? What questions do you still have about this television genre?

- What was most difficult for you in planning your research report? When you began drafting, what was your biggest surprise? Think of the most important revision you made in your draft. How did you decide to make this change?

- What advice would you give to writers who are starting to work on a research report about popular culture?

- What aspect of your report seems most effective? How would you revise your report further if you had more time to work on it?

GATHERING ADDITIONAL INFORMATION

To supplement the readings in this chapter, you may want to do further research. For example, you might want to know more about the history or economics of the tabloid TV genre or more about the debate over the social consequences of television in general. Following are some suggestions to make your research efficient and productive.

Reports on Tabloid TV

To find reports about the tabloids as a television genre, first check your library's indexes to magazine and newspaper articles. You may already be familiar with the *Reader's Guide to Periodical Literature,* which indexes about 200 popular periodicals, and its cousin *Access: The Supplementary Index,* which indexes some magazines not covered by the *Reader's Guide.*

Other indexes may prove more useful, however. Your library may have an index called *InfoTrac* (in some libraries the name may differ). *InfoTrac* covers well over 1,000 magazines and newspapers, offering abstracts of some entries. Look at its *Magazine Index* and *National Newspaper Index.* It may appear in different forms, such as online or on CD-ROM. Another possibility is the *Alternative Press Index,* which indexes alternative and radical publications. Ask your librarian about other magazine and newspaper indexes that may be available.

As you begin your search, you might try these subject headings:

Television broadcasting — Social aspects

Television — Social aspects

Television and politics

Television and women

You might also look up the authors of this chapter's readings. Since an author may have written other articles about tabloid TV, the subject headings displayed by the article entry may provide leads for additional searches. For example, the *InfoTrac* subject headings for Frank Houston's article "TV Tabs' New Tone" include "sensationalism in television" and "investigative reporting."

At this writing, information about tabloid TV on the Internet seems limited, but you should find some sources by using the subject heading "tabloid television." In addition, two tabloid TV series have their own Web sites:

Extra   http://www.extratv.com

Inside Edition   http://www.insideedition.com

Neither of these sites offers research reports by cultural studies specialists. Instead, they provide scheduling information, news about the series, profiles of anchors and reporters, summaries of current program segments, and previews of upcoming programs.

Arguments about How Television Represents Social Life

Arguments about the social representations on tabloid TV can be found in both magazines and books. So you can use the magazine indexes mentioned previously, as well as your library's card or online catalog to locate books under the same Library of Congress Headings listed earlier. You may also want to look at arguments about television in general. A great deal of material exists on this broader topic, and you may be able to apply some arguments about television to your arguments about tabloid TV.

Arguments about the social representations on tabloid TV may also appear in academic journals. Try *InfoTrac's Academic Index* or other specialized indexes. *Communication Abstracts*, for example, covers television. Ask a reference librarian about your library's specialized indexes.

You may find useful readings and subject headings through online or *InfoTrac* searches for the four authors in the section "Social Perspectives": Philip Weiss, Jib Fowles, S. Robert Lichter et al., and S. Elizabeth Bird. An author search on S. Robert Lichter, for example, reveals that he has written other books about television in addition to *Prime Time: How TV Portrays American Culture.* Furthermore, the subject headings used to describe *Prime Time,* "Television broadcasting—Social aspects—United States" and "Television programs—United States—History and criticism," may lead you to promising additional current material.

FURTHER READINGS
ON TELEVISION AND POPULAR CULTURE

Fowles, Jib. *Why Viewers Watch: A Reappraisal of Television's Effects.* Rev. ed. Newbury Park: Sage, 1992.

Hallin, Daniel. *We Keep America on Top of the World: Television Journalism and the Public Sphere.* New York: Routledge, 1993.

Langer, John. *Tabloid Television: Popular Journalism and the "Other News."* New York: Routledge, 1998.

Mayer, Martin. *Making News.* Boston: Harvard Business School, 1993.

Monaco, Paul. *Understanding Society, Culture, and Television.* Westport: Praeger, 1998.

Stark, Steven D. *Glued to the Set: The 60 Television Shows and Events That Made Us Who We Are Today.* New York: Free Press, 1997.

Winch, Samuel P., and David Boeyink. *Mapping the Cultural Space of Journalism.* Westport: Praeger, 1997.

ADDITIONAL WRITING PROJECTS

Personal Experience Essay

Tabloid TV often features the extraordinary experiences of ordinary people. Think of some of your own personal experiences that might have promise as tabloid TV segments. The experiences could be humorous, sad, or tragic. Maybe your car rolled over three times but you were uninjured. Or you were burning leaves or trash in the backyard, and the flames raced across dry grass and burned down your neighbor's garage. Or one of your pets was killed in a freak accident. Maybe something unexpected or frightening occurred at school or at work. Identify two or three experiences to write about.

Purpose and Readers.   Your readers are your classmates, who have been watching tabloid television programs. Your purpose is to demonstrate to them that you understand the kind of human-interest story the tabloids feature and to entertain them with your remembered stories. You also want to offer some insights into the social significance of the tabloid-like personal experiences you have chosen.

Resources to Draw On.   Your main resource is your own memory. You also could talk to other people involved in the experiences in order to recall more specific details. Make notes about what happened, listing the other people who were present, details about the setting or scene, and conversations that occurred. Outline—chronologically—what happened first, next, and so on. Also note your feelings—during the experience, soon afterward, and now. Models of this kind of personal experience essay can be found in the selections by Luis J. Rodriguez, Nathan McCall, and Rita Williams in Chapter 5.

Tips for Writing a Successful Personal Experience Essay.   Simply narrate your experiences as though you were writing autobiography or prose fiction. Assume that if one of your experiences were produced, someone else would turn your written narrative into a visual tabloid segment. Tell the stories concretely and dramatically, using vivid description and strong verbs. Give details of the setting or scene and the people involved. Reveal their size, shape, and dress and show them moving, gesturing, and talking. Try to reconstruct any conversations that were central to what happened. Arrange your narrative so that readers can easily follow the series of events and personal interactions that occurred. Try to create suspense as the story moves along and to reveal your own emotions and those of the other participants.

After you have told your potential tabloid TV stories, write another page or so explaining to your instructor the connections, as you see them, between the personal experiences in your essay and what you have learned from the readings in this chapter.

Rhetorical Analysis of a Reading

Select one reading from "Social Perspectives on Tabloid TV" to analyze. Write an essay in which you describe how this reading works as an argument and evaluate how effective it is for its intended readers.

Purpose and Readers. Your purpose is twofold: to help readers understand how the argument is organized, and to show what makes the argument convincing or unconvincing. Because your readers will be your classmates, who will be familiar with the argument you are analyzing, you need not describe fully the content of the reading. Instead, you can focus on its argumentative strategies and your evaluation of its effectiveness.

Resources to Draw On. Chapter 3 provides a number of resources for understanding how an argument is organized and what strategies it relies on to convince its readers. The sections "Organizing Your Essay" and "Developing Your Argument and Counterargument" should be especially helpful as you describe how your chosen argument works. To evaluate the argument—to decide how convincing or unconvincing it is—consult "Evaluating an Argument" in Appendix 1.

Tips for Writing a Successful Rhetorical Analysis. For this type of essay, it is usually a good idea to begin by stating your purpose and identifying the author, title, source, and year of publication of the reading. Give your readers a very brief overview of the reading and any information they might need to follow your analysis. Then move to the heart of your analysis, explaining how the argument is put together. For example, how does the argument engage the reader and sequence the argument? Concentrate not on content but on the argument's organization and strategies. After you have completed this explanation, shift your focus to how *successful* the argument is. For example, does it offer convincing reasons? Does it provide sufficient support for those reasons? Does it anticipate readers' likely questions or objections and successfully respond to them? Support your judgments with examples from the reading.

Report on an Issue

Write an essay in which you write a balanced, comprehensive report about the debate on the social influences of tabloid television. As you know from the readings in this chapter, some writers argue that tabloid television is an asset, strengthening social relations and democracy in a number of ways. Others argue that tabloid TV fragments social relations and weakens democracy. Without taking sides yourself, help readers understand what each side is saying.

Purpose and Readers.   Your purpose is to inform readers about the arguments over the social influences of tabloid TV. Your readers are other college students who occasionally watch television news but rarely, if ever, watch one of the popular tabloid television series. Assume that they watch television for information, diversion, and entertainment—not from a critical perspective. As you develop your report, try to be objective and yet to generate interest in the ideas on both sides of the debate.

Resources to Draw On.   Your chief resource is the readings in "Social Perspectives on Tabloid TV," which adequately define the debate, though you might want to research additional views. (See "Gathering Additional Information" and "Further Readings on Television and Popular Culture.") The introduction of this chapter will help you establish a context for the debate, and the Writer's Guide in Chapter 2 provides help with planning and drafting an essay that aims to explain unfamiliar material to readers.

Tips for Writing a Successful Report.   Begin by describing the issue to your readers in a way that will help them see its significance. You may want to use a quotation or an example—something to spark their interest. Give them enough background information so that they can follow your presentation, then discuss the major points at the heart of the debate and support these points with relevant information from the readings. By paraphrasing, summarizing, and quoting, you can incorporate materials from the readings into your report. (See Appendix 1 for guidelines on these strategies.) Strive to offer a balanced presentation that gives equal attention to all positions. Even if you favor one view over another, do not let your readers know your preference. The authority of your report comes from your impartiality and your command of the information in the readings.

Research Report

Using the guidelines in this chapter, write a research report about representations of social life in some television genre other than tabloid TV. There are many possibilities: situation comedies, cop shows, hospital dramas, talk shows, cartoons, and so forth. Analyze the genre from a social perspective.

Purpose and Readers.   Your purpose is to convince readers that they should take seriously your interpretation of a television genre. Your readers are other students who have also completed research on the social influences of various forms of popular culture, including television. Assume that they will neither question your topic nor challenge your research methods. Try to establish your authority with your readers by carrying out a careful research study and reporting it convincingly. (For more information about the purpose and readers for this kind of report, see "Understanding Your Readers" in this chapter.)

Resources to Draw On.   Because this assignment is based directly on the main assignment in this chapter, you can take advantage of many of the resources and strategies you used while studying tabloid TV. Whatever television genre you analyze, the readings in "Social Perspectives on Tabloid TV" will help you think critically about the way social life is represented on television. The section "Viewing Tabloid TV Critically" outlines a systematic method that can be used to analyze social representations in any television genre. The writer's notebook tasks at the end of that section should help you organize, record, and interpret your findings. If you want to learn more about the genre you choose to analyze, look for it by name in your library catalog and other indexes. Or go online and use various tools to search for the genre or for prominent current programs in that genre. Of course, your most important resource will be the programs that you watch while you are working on this assignment.

Tips for Writing a Successful Research Report.   Begin by stating the purpose of your research study and identifying the television genre you are analyzing. Name and briefly describe several programs in the genre and try to describe its general characteristics. Then explain how you went about doing your analysis. For example, readers will want to know how many different series and programs you watched. Move on to a concise thesis statement about how social life was represented by the genre you studied. Then present an argument supporting your thesis. This argument, the heart of your essay, has to be convincing if your essay is to succeed with your readers. Give reasons to support your thesis and back up your reasons with plentiful examples from the programs you watched. If you anticipate questions or objections from your readers, you might want to address those directly in your argument.

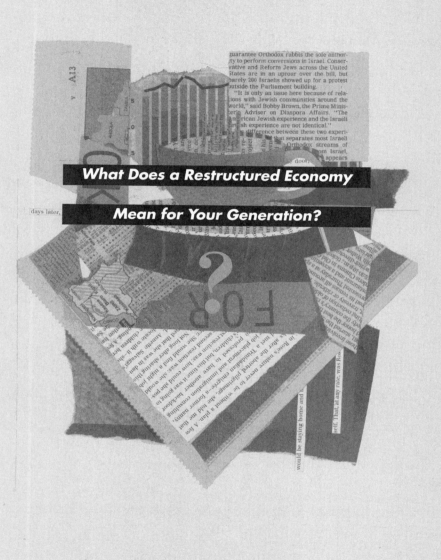

What Does a Restructured Economy

Mean for Your Generation?

7

SPECULATING
ABOUT THE FUTURE

■ ■ ■

The average income of individuals and families has declined.

The gap in income between the richest and the poorest has widened, and poverty has increased.

Many traditional industries have disappeared or declined, and new technologies have emerged.

Large federal debt and large trade imbalances have become the norm.

Corporate mergers and downsizing have led to lower pay and reduced benefits.

There has been a huge increase in two-earner families, with women—especially young mothers—flooding into the workplace.

$\mathbf{T}$he changes listed on the previous page illustrate the fundamental restructuring the American economy has undergone since the early 1970s. Because of these changes, and many others, your economic opportunities may be quite different from those of your parents and grandparents. This chapter discusses America's recent economic changes and what they may mean for you and your generation. Think of your generation as including all of those born approximately fifteen years before and after you were born. The size and the needs of the generations just ahead of yours will greatly influence your opportunities, as you will learn.

For many middle- and late-middle-age Americans, the restructured economy has resulted in a lower standard of living compared to the standard enjoyed by individuals and families in the 1950s and 1960s. Families with a relatively high standard of living own a home; drive a late-model car or two; contribute to children's college expenses; take vacations; have job security, a retirement plan, and adequate health coverage; and may, in addition, have some savings. Many families today, however, do not enjoy such benefits. Census data show that in terms of current dollars, the average individual and family today have less money than the average individual and family had from the late 1940s to the mid-1970s. For some Americans, then, there has been an unexpected downward social movement—a slide from the upper-middle class into the lower-middle class or from the middle class into poverty.

Not every individual or family, of course, has experienced a declining living standard or suffered downward mobility. Many professionals, business owners, and corporate executives and managers are doing very well. People with college degrees and advanced graduate training in fields like computer science, medical research, and engineering have achieved a high standard of living. Those who have moved up through the ranks in state and federal bureaucracies have also prospered. Two-income families in occupations with relatively low top earnings, such as physical therapy, nursing, teaching, and law enforcement, have been able to make a comfortable living. And the phenomenal growth of the stock market over the course of the 1990s generated considerable wealth for smart investors.

As you will learn from the readings, however, some individuals and families in all of these categories have suffered serious economic setbacks during the 1980s and 1990s. Many economists attribute such setbacks primarily to a restructuring of the economy rather than the usual ups and downs of a capitalist economy.

Economists debate the details and the magnitude of the decline in the standard of living, but they agree that the economy has been fundamentally restructured. Liberal economists, for instance, may decry some aspects of the restructuring and call for legislation to correct what has occurred. Conservative economists, on the other hand, may applaud the restructuring and argue that once the federal budget deficit is reduced, everyone's standard of living will rise.

As you learn about the restructured economy, you will be able to think seriously about the opportunities that may be available during your lifetime. Will you have extended periods of job security and a chance for advancement based on achievement and merit? Will you have freedom from discrimination and harassment on the job and safe and healthful working conditions? Will you have continuing access to further education and training, both on and off the job? What about affordable health care, a retirement plan, accumulation of modest wealth (savings, home ownership, investments), and money for leisure activities? Will you have the opportunity to put down roots and contribute to a community, to raise and educate children?

GLOSSARY: WORDS ABOUT WORDS

In this chapter's readings, you will encounter several terms having to do with the restructured economy and with ways economists talk about the economy. This glossary introduces these special terms. You may want to review the glossary before you begin the readings and then later refer to it as needed.

assets: Property of different kinds that one may own — such as money, material goods, real estate, and stocks and bonds.

birth cohort: A group of people born in the same time period and therefore subject to the same demographic, economic, and historical forces.

business cycle: A period of years when economic activity goes from low to high and then cycles back again to low.

capital gains: Money earned from an asset (such as stocks, bonds, or real estate) between the time it is bought and the time it is sold.

Consumer Price Index (CPI): A measure of the cost of living, derived from the actual cost of a list of typical consumer purchases such as food, clothing, entertainment, and transportation.

demography/demographics: The study of populations.

Fortune 500: *Fortune* magazine's yearly list of the 500 most prosperous American corporations.

Great Depression: From 1929 to 1939, a time of weak economic activity, high unemployment, and great personal hardship for many Americans.

inflation: A general increase in prices; inflation was 2 to 3 percent in the mid-1990s as measured by the Consumer Price Index.

median: The midpoint in a distribution of numbers; *median income* is the midpoint in income in a highest-to-lowest list of incomes of all families in the United States.

monetary: Of or relating to money.

postwar: Usually refers to the period after World War II, which ended in 1945.

recession: A period when unemployment is high, demand for goods and services slows, and factory output declines. The average price of publicly traded stocks may decline.

(continues on next page)

(continued from previous page)

stock market: Stocks are shares of the value of a business. Stocks are bought and sold for individuals and groups of investors by members of stock exchanges like the New York Stock Exchange or the NASDAQ National Market. In 1997, 43 percent of Americans owned stocks, either as individual investors or as purchasers of stock mutual funds, in part through company pension plans or retirement accounts.

A LOOK AHEAD: WRITING ABOUT THE ECONOMY   This chapter includes an assignment to write an essay in which you speculate about the consequences of the new economy for your generation. Developing such an essay involves describing the main features of the economy, deciding on some likely short- and long-term consequences, and arguing to support the consequences you consider most likely to occur. Although most of this support will probably come from the readings, you may also want to include your own personal experiences in the workplace as well as information from interviews with people in your parents' and grandparents' generations who have been in the workplace before and during the momentous developments that have led to the current U.S. economy. In addition to arguing in support of the consequences you choose, you will need to counterargue — that is, respond to — questions or objections concerning your position, as well as consequences in the readings that challenge your own.

The first readings in this chapter cover several features of the restructured economy, including falling wages, the wealth gap, job insecurity, contingent or temporary work, and the shift of manufacturing from the United States to low-wage countries. Next, two readings about generation size and conflict establish the economic demands to be made on your generation by the baby boomers. The final readings speculate about the short- and long-term consequences of the new economy for your generation. The writer's notebook tasks following each set of readings help you to compare what you have read to your own experience in the workplace and to that of family members and friends. The notebook tasks also help you to read critically and prepare to write an essay about this important development.

UNDERSTANDING THE RESTRUCTURED ECONOMY

The readings in this section provide detailed information about these features of the restructured economy: falling wages, the growing wealth gap between the rich and the rest of society, the increase in contingent work, job insecurity, and the loss of American jobs to overseas workers. What you read may surprise you, and it may worry you. Though some of these trends could moderate or even reverse during the next decades, projections suggest that most of them will continue.

The information in these readings is important in two ways: it will give you a basis for evaluating the subsequent section of readings that speculate about the consequences of this restructured economy, and it will allow you to present some of the main facts about the restructured economy in your essay.

MEET THE MEDIAN FAMILY

Andrew Hacker

Andrew Hacker teaches political science at Queens College in New York City and has written Money: Who Has How Much and Why *(1997). His other books include* U/S: A Statistical Portrait of the American People *(1983) and* Two Nations: Black and White, Separate, Hostile, Unequal *(1992). This article first appeared in 1996 in* Time, *a popular weekly newsmagazine sold nationwide.*

Hacker offers a fictional account of Carol and Paul Median, a recently married couple in their early thirties (the median *is the midpoint in a distribution of numbers, in this case the distribution of yearly incomes earned by Americans in 1995.) The Medians live "just south of Bloomington, Indiana," the population midpoint of the country. To help readers follow and absorb the economic information he offers about marriage and career, Hacker creates this typical middle-class couple and compares their lifestyle, careers, and future prospects to that of their fictional parents.*

This reading establishes the importance of statistics and generational comparisons in understanding the new economy. It also addresses specific features of the economy, including two-income families, the shrinking middle class, the challenge posed by new technologies, corporate mergers and downsizing, job insecurity, declining incomes, and increasing income and wealth inequality. By noting the phenomena of delayed marriage and uncertainty about having children, Hacker also speculates about some consequences of the new economy—the central task in this chapter's essay assignment.

As you read, think about the lifestyle and the careers of this typical middle-class couple and how different their lives are from those of their parents.

This is a story about Carol and Paul Median, she 32 and he 34, married for one year and living just south of Bloomington, Indiana. They are as average as can be. Last year Paul earned $28,449, and Carol made $23,479, precisely the midpoint paychecks for men and women their age. It also happens that their part of Indiana is the population center of the U.S. Since no real-life couple is truly typical, however, I have created the fictional Medians, going by Census figures,° to give a sense of the exact middle of American life. In ways good and bad, the Medians' life is far different from the previous generation's. To gain some perspective, one must look back to 1970 to see how their parents lived when they were about the same age.

Both Paul and Carol have full-time jobs. She works for a large book manufacturer, supervising a team of compositors, who tap copy into computers. As it happens, her dad once did that job, which then required casting hot lead. It was considered "men's work." As was common at that time, it paid a high union wage, and Carol's mother never worked. Today there are mainly women at the consoles, and they aren't unionized. (In fact, only 11% of private workers are, down from 28% in 1970.) Carol loves what she does, and her boss just told her she will soon be promoted.

Paul's situation is dicier. He's a loan officer at a local bank. On paper, he is listed as management. But there may be some title inflation here: a recent Department of Labor report found some 16 million people listed as managers, executives or administrators, which means most of them must be fairly far

---

°**Census figures:** Statistics about life in America published by the U.S. Bureau of the Census.

down the ladder. And that really describes Paul. His problem is that in the last year, half the people in his department have been let go.

It's not that business is bad. In fact, the bank is prospering. For efficiency's sake, it has installed LOANEX, a software system that supplants much of Paul's judgment. It is an "experience-based" program containing far more data than any loan officer could have in his head. Would-be borrowers type in answers to questions that appear on the screen. Credit reports are then factored in, after which the software says yes or no. Only if it prints out MAYBE is Paul's input needed, and this seems to be happening less and less. Nor do things look better higher up the ladder: his bank is in the midst of being absorbed by an out-of-state firm with a reputation for thinning executive ranks. Paul, a college graduate, never thought he might one day be applying for jobless benefits. His father spent his entire career in the same company, where his security was never in doubt. The firm always found a niche for him. No one talks or acts that way in the milieu Paul knows.

By many measures, it looks as if Paul's and Carol's parents had things a lot ⁵ better. Their counterpart year, 1970, was at the height of the postwar era. During the prior quarter-century, real income almost doubled, raising American living standards to an all-time high. Countries on every continent sought to emulate the American way. However, it soon emerged that economies elsewhere—first in Europe, then in Asia—could match products once made only in the U.S. America's per capita output° has now° been passed in Finland, Norway, Switzerland and Sweden. Since 1970, most Americans have been working longer and harder to stay in place. Paul's paycheck buys less than a median salary did a generation ago. Moreover, his and Carol's parents managed well with only their fathers' earnings. Today two-thirds of all households depend on two or more incomes, yet find themselves barely ahead.

But interyear comparisons can be deceptive. How much a dollar buys is measured by the Consumer Price Index [CPI], which is based on a typical mix of purchases. If salaries seemed to go further in 1970, one reason is that shopping lists were simpler. Paul and Carol recall the days of Keds and typewriters and turntables. Today the CPI includes Nikes, laser printers and multiple-CD changers, which cost more because they do more. Even bread has been upgraded: croissants and exotic grains have replaced blander white loaves. Paul and Carol have two cars; in 1970 only 28% of families did. Moreover, Paul and Carol's high-tech vehicles have higher price tags relative to their family budget. Like a growing number of Americans, they want to think they are middle class, but the symbols of that status are growing more complicated and costly. Paul and Carol dine out a lot or take home prepared meals. And when they find such pleasures straining their budget, they feel their living standard is dropping.

°**per capita output:** The average amount of goods and services produced by each person in the United States.   °**now:** 1996.

While the Medians occupy the middle, they have less company there than their parents did. The income pyramid° is changing. More households are now in the under-$20,000 tier, when measured in inflation-adjusted dollars, because of declining wages and a rise in single-parent families. But there has also been a burgeoning at the top. The number of families with $60,000 or more has grown, while those at over $100,000 have actually tripled. The result: a shrinking and insecure stratum in the middle. Let's see how Paul and Carol are responding to these new configurations.

Paul worries about being fired, while Carol has been told she can anticipate an ascending career. Part of the difference is luck: Paul's bank was acquired by a firm bent on downsizing. But that's not the full story. Recall how Paul seemed resigned to being replaced by LOANEX, as if it were impossible to mount a response. Yet something similar has been happening at Carol's company. It has started asking authors to submit their manuscripts on computer disks so their work can go directly into the typesetting system. Might that mean axing Carol's job? She didn't wait to find out: "I showed my boss that we would need to devise bridge programs so the author's stuff will jibe with the book's format." He gave her the go-ahead, and that will be her new job. She didn't need Bill Gates° to tell her that new technologies generate new opportunities.

Carol may be fictional, but is she exceptional? Less than one might think. There is increasing evidence that women are doing better at adapting to new challenges in the world of work. If more are being hired and promoted, it is not just to meet affirmative-action goals or avoid discrimination suits. In increasing instances, they surpass men in the attitudes and abilities employers are looking for. This can be seen early in high school, where girls get better grades. "We listened more carefully to the teachers' assignments," Carol recalls, "while the guys thought they knew it all." The upshot is that more women are accepted by colleges and now outnumber men on campuses. They account for almost 55% of bachelor's degrees, and more than half the enrollments at leading law and medical schools. Many professors note that women are better at organizing their work and write with greater clarity. Of course, parity is still a long way off. Says Carol: "Too few of us raise our hand or advance ideas unless we are called on." She must also overcome perceptions that a woman's voice carries less authority. Yet women have been winning elections up through the state level, and to do so they must win over men. The next step should be executive suites.

The Medians' home life is as fraught with uncertainty as their jobs. Paul and 10 Carol were not so unusual in delaying marriage: today 30% of men and 20% of

---

°**income pyramid:** Until recently the American income pyramid was shaped like a true pyramid, wide at the bottom, broad in the middle, very narrow at the top, representing a huge poor and working class, a large middle class, and a very small upper class. Now it seems that the bottom level is even larger, the middle level smaller, and the upper level larger.   °**Bill Gates:** Founder and head of Microsoft Corporation and the richest person in America.

women are single as they enter their 30s. In 1970 most men were married by 23, most women by 21. Like many members of their generation, Paul and Carol had lived with other people, but those relationships didn't work out. This time they hope to make it last, even while knowing that more than half of all marriages now end in divorce. It is not that people their age are especially selfish or difficult as companions; but they do have a strong sense of self and wish to delineate their own lives. Some of Carol's girlfriends tried to talk her out of taking Paul's name. Marriage, yes; but not too early or all-embracing. . . .

The Medians have no children yet. This would have stood out in 1970, when 92% of women Carol's age had already given birth. "My mom had her third by the time she was 32," she notes. "I want a child, but the time has to be right." Here too the statistics put Carol right in the middle. The current projection is that a typical 1,000 American women will end up having 2,046 children, which is below replacement level. Immigration is the chief reason our population keeps growing.

Some of Carol's diffidence stems from her impending promotion, which will require extended hours and travel. Yet even short of that, the years once reserved for parenthood are seen today as a time for fun. She and Paul are avid skiers, a budget item that can come close to the cost of an additional family member. More than six times as many Americans take vacations abroad now as in 1970; such jaunts are not easily enjoyed with children in tow.

Above all, having children bespeaks a confidence in the years ahead. Such a vision generated the baby boom, the peak years of the postwar period. In those years, citizens willingly invested in education, from kindergarten through graduate school, because they wanted the forthcoming generation to be the best in the world. Today that spirit is strangely lacking. It does not bode well for the next generation of Medians, who may have trouble keeping up with their predecessors, just as Paul and Carol have.

THE STATE OF WORKING AMERICA 1998–99

Lawrence R. Mishel, Jared Bernstein, and John Schmitt

Lawrence R. Mishel is research director of the Economic Policy Institute, a private foundation interested in widening the debate about economic growth, prosperity, and opportunity. He has coauthored The Myth of the Coming Labor Shortage *(1991) and* The Prosperity Gap: A Chartbook of American Living Standards *(1997). Jared Bernstein and John Schmitt are both labor economists at the Economic Policy Institute. Between 1995 and 1996, Bernstein was deputy chief economist at the U.S. Department of Labor. Schmitt has conducted economic research in El Salvador and also worked there for the United Nations peacekeeping mission. Together, the three have coauthored several editions of* The State of Working America. *This reading comes from the 1999 edition.*

The authors here report on a prominent feature of the restructured economy: falling wages for most families and individuals from the early 1970s through the 1990s. They consider falling wages and widening wage disparities to be the "most important problem" facing the United States, and they judge the continued drop in wages after the economic recovery from the recession of the early 1990s to be "historically unique." First they focus on trends in the median yearly incomes of all families and of dual-earner families. Next they illustrate the growing disparity in median yearly family incomes at five income levels, from lowest to highest. Finally, they demonstrate that recent generations (or birth cohorts, as they call them) are having less success than earlier generations at increasing their incomes during a career.

This reading includes a number of tables and figures. To interpret each, start by looking at the title and the headings of the columns (across the top) and the rows (down the side). Once you have oriented yourself in this way, the function of each number and the relationships among numbers in the same and different rows and columns will become clear. In their discussion, the authors also take readers through key parts of each table. As you read such passages, take the time to find each number in the table, perhaps even underlining or circling it and then drawing lines to other numbers in order to make important numerical relationships clear.

Focus on what the authors say about changes in family incomes from 1947 to 1997 and women's contributions to family income since the early 1970s. Note also the differences in family incomes during all time periods and the widening of those differences in the 1980s and 1990s.

The slow and uneven growth of family income since the early 1970s is the most important economic problem confronting American families.... The 1990s recovery, despite racking up some impressive numbers on aggregate economic indicators such as unemployment and recent productivity growth,° provides an excellent example of the income problem. For the first time in the postwar period, family income fell four years in a row, declining each year from 1989 to 1993. The initial decline was attributable to the recession that began in 1990, but the median continued to fall as the recovery got under way in 1991 and

---

°**productivity growth:** Economic productivity is measured by the average hourly output, or production, of all workers. Productivity increases as workers' hourly output increases. Historically, wages have increased as productivity has increased.

1992. In 1994, median family income finally responded to overall growth, and it has increased each year since (the most recent available data on family income are from 1997). Nevertheless, the median family—the family in the middle of the income scale—was only slightly better off (by $285 in 1997 dollars) in 1997 than it was at the peak of the last business cycle, in 1989. This is also historically unprecedented: in every prior recovery, the income of the typical family had, by this point, far surpassed its level of the prior peak. But in the 1990s, thanks to the continued surge of income inequality, the relationship between the growing economy and improving living standards has eluded all but the wealthiest families.

Even with the growth that has occurred since 1994, by 1997 the income of the median family was essentially back where it started in 1989, despite a 9% increase in productivity over the period. . . .

Why have income trends continued to be so negative in the 1990s? Along with overall slow growth, the primary reason, at least through 1996, is the continuing wage deterioration among middle- and low-wage earners, now joined by white-collar and even some groups of college-educated workers. Another key factor in understanding recent income trends is the contribution of working wives.

In the 1980s, many families compensated for the fall in hourly compensation, which was particularly steep for male workers, by working more hours (either through more family members working or through longer hours by those employed). This strategy—working longer for less—is most notable among married-couple families, in part because these families tend to have more potential workers than do families headed by one person. In fact, in the absence of increased hours and earnings by working wives in married-couple families in the 1980s, the incomes of the bottom 60% of families would have fallen.

In the 1990s, however, there was a slowdown in the growth (for some, even 5 a decline) of hours and earnings among working wives in married-couple families, particularly among low- and middle-income women. Unlike the prior decade, wives' contributions were no longer sufficient to offset the lower earnings of husbands, whose wages continued to fall (only husbands in the top fifth experienced wage increases). By 1996, the bottom 80% of married-couple families would have experienced flat or declining incomes in the absence of wives' work; even with wives' contributions, families in the bottom 40% lost economic ground in the 1990s. . . .

MEDIAN INCOME GROWS SLOWLY IN 1980S, DECLINES IN 1990S

Income growth over the last two business cycles—1979–89 and 1989–97—was slow and the gains were unequally distributed. Tables 7.1 and 7.2 show changes in family income, adjusted for changes in consumer prices, in various cyclical peak (or low-unemployment) years since World War II. . . .

Table 7.1
Median Family Income,* 1947–97 (1997 dollars)

Year	Median family income*
1947	$20,102
1967	35,076
1973	40,978
1979	42,483
1989	44,283
1997	44,568

Total increases

1947–67	$14,974
1967–73	5,902
1973–79	1,505
1979–89	1,800
1989–97	285

* Income includes all wage and salary, self-employment, pension, interest, rent, government cash assistance, and other money income.

Source: Authors' analysis of U.S. Bureau of the Census data.

Table 7.2
Annual Growth of Median Family Income, 1947–97 (1997 dollars)

Period	Median family income growth		Adjusted for family size*
	Percent	Dollars	Percent
1947–67	2.8	$749	n.a.
1967–73	2.6	984	2.8
1973–79	0.6	251	0.5
1979–89	0.4	180	0.5
1989–97	0.1	36	0.1

* Annualized growth rate of family income of the middle fifth, divided by the poverty line for each family size.

Source: Authors' analysis of U.S. Bureau of the Census data.

Family income increased substantially in the two decades immediately following World War II (1947–67). During that time, median family income increased by $14,974, for an annual rate of growth of 2.8% (Table 7.2). Family incomes continued to grow into the early 1970s, but since 1973 they have risen slowly. In 1989, the median family's income was $1,800 greater than it was in 1979, translating into growth of just 0.4% per year from 1979 to 1989, or only two-thirds of the sluggish 0.6% annual growth of the 1973–79 period and only one-seventh the rate of the postwar years prior to 1973 (Figure 7.1). In fact, the $1,800 income growth over the 10 years after 1979 equals the amount that incomes rose every 22 months in the 1967–73 period.

The recession that began in 1990 and ended in 1991 (or in 1992 in terms of unemployment) significantly reduced incomes through 1993. Despite income growth from 1993 to 1997, the median family income in 1997 was only 0.6%, or $285, above its 1989 level. This small 1989–97 income growth appears to reflect more than the unemployment accompanying a normal business cycle downturn. First, considering the mildness of the 1991 recession (unemployment rose by 2.1 percentage points, which is less than in the usual downturn), we would have expected median family income to recover much sooner, as it did following much deeper recessions. Second, the income decline reflects several ongoing and new structural shifts in income growth, such as the falloff in wages among white-collar and college-educated workers that preceded the recession.

The fact that the median income took eight years to return to its pre-recessionary peak is historically unique. Typically, job growth, falling unemployment, and increasing productivity—all of which occurred in the recovery

Figure 7.1
Annual Growth of Median Family Income, 1947–97

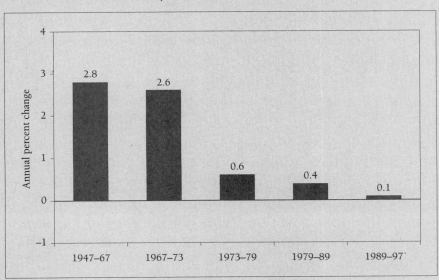

Source: U.S. Bureau of the Census.

that began in 1991—would have helped return median family income to its previous level. But as we show below, increasing income inequality and continued earnings declines through 1996 have eroded the incomes of all but the top 5% of families....

ONLY DUAL-INCOME, MARRIED COUPLES GAIN

The only type of family that experienced income growth over the 1980s and the 1990s was married couples with a wife in the paid labor force (Table 7.3). 10

Table 7.3
Median Family Income by Family Type, 1947–97 (1997 dollars)

| Year | Married couples | | | Single | | |
	Total	Wife in paid labor force	Wife not in paid labor force	Male-headed	Female-headed	All families
1947	$20,619	n.a.	n.a.	$19,472	$14,405	$20,102
1967	37,322	$44,020	$33,652	30,128	18,986	35,076
1973	44,301	51,812	38,826	36,527	19,712	40,978
1979	46,477	53,921	38,403	36,455	21,429	42,483
1989	49,893	58,590	37,209	36,043	21,281	44,283
1997	51,591	60,669	36,027	32,960	21,023	44,568
Annual growth rate						
1947–61	3.0%	n.a.	n.a.	2.2%	1.4%	2.8%
1967–73	2.9	2.8%	2.4%	3.3	0.6	2.6
1973–79	0.8	0.7	−0.2	0.0	1.4	0.6
1979–89	0.7	0.8	−0.3	−0.1	−0.1	0.4
1989–97	0.4	0.4	−0.4	−1.1	−0.2	0.1
Share of families						
1951*	86.7%	19.8%	66.9%	3.0%	9.9%	100.0%
1967	86.4	31.6	54.8	2.4	10.6	100.0
1973	85.0	35.4	49.7	2.6	12.4	100.0
1979	82.5	40.6	41.9	2.9	14.6	100.0
1989	79.2	45.7	33.5	4.4	16.5	100.0
1997	76.6	47.3	29.3	5.5	17.8	100.0

*Earliest year available.

Source: Authors' analysis of U.S. Bureau of the Census (1996) and unpublished Census data.

Incomes among married couples where the wife was not employed declined 0.3% over the 1980s and 0.4% in the 1990s (1989–97). Similarly, the slight fall in income experienced by single-parent families in the 1980s accelerated somewhat in the 1990s. This was a dramatic turnaround for female-headed families, since their incomes grew 1.4% per year in the 1973–79 period. . . .

This pattern of income growth suggests that it was only among families with two adult earners that incomes grew in the post-1979 period. The data in Table 7.3 also show sizable growth in the importance of working wives. In 1979, the share of married couples without a wife in the labor force was about equal to that of those with a wife in the labor force (41.9% versus 40.6% of all families). By 1997, married couples with two earners (assuming the husband worked) made up 47.3% of all families, while one-earner married couples were proportionately fewer in number, 29.3% of the total.

While this shift toward two-earner families has been a major factor in recent income growth, this shift appears to be attenuating, since the rate at which wives (and women in general) have been joining the labor force has slowed in recent years. . . . For example, among married-couple families, wives joined the paid labor force at an annual rate of 1.3% in the 1970s, 0.8% in the 1980s, and 0.5% in the 1989–97 period (not shown in table). Furthermore, . . . the hours of working wives grew more slowly in the 1990s relative to the 1980s.

Married-couple families, although still predominant—they represented 76.6% of all families in 1997—make up a smaller share of families than they did in the 1950s and 1960s. There has been a continuing rise in the importance of female-headed families; in 1997 they represented 17.8% of the total. Although this phenomenon has been the focus of increased attention in recent years, the share of female-headed families grew more quickly in the 1967–79 period than in the period since 1979. Note also that the median incomes of these female-headed families actually grew over the 1967–79 period, when their share of the population of families was increasing. . . .

Examined as a whole, family income growth was stagnant over the 1989–97 period (Table 7.3, last column), with losses experienced by single-headed families and families with wives not in the paid labor force. Families with working wives were the only family type to achieve income growth over this period; their incomes rose a modest 0.4% per year. As we show below, this growth was driven primarily by the increase in annual hours of work by wives.

GROWING INEQUALITY OF FAMILY INCOME

The vast majority of American families have experienced either modest income 15 growth or an actual erosion in their living standards in recent years, while the small minority of upper-income families have experienced substantial income growth. The result has been an increase in inequality such that the gap between the incomes of the well-off and those of everyone else is larger now than at any point in the postwar period. The rich have gotten richer, low-income and even poor families are more numerous and are poorer than they have been in decades, and the middle has been "squeezed." This section examines the income trends of families at different income levels and the dramatic growth of income inequality in the 1980s and 1990s.

Table 7.4 shows the share of all family income received by families in different segments of the income distribution. Families have been divided into fifths, or "quintiles," of the population, and the highest income group has been further divided into the top 5% and the next 15%. The 20% of families with the lowest incomes are considered the "lowest fifth," the next best-off 20% of families are the "second fifth," and so forth....

The upper 20% of families received 47.2% of all income in 1997. The top 5% received more of total income, 20.7%, than the families in the bottom 40%, who received just 14.1%. In fact, the 1997 share of total income in each of the three lowest-income fifths—the 29.8% of total income going to the bottom 60% of families—was smaller than the 34.5% share this group received in 1979....

Table 7.4
Shares of Family Income by Income Fifth and Top 5%, 1947–97

Year	Lowest fifth	Second fifth	Middle fifth	Fourth fifth	Top fifth	Breakdown of top fifth	
						Bottom 15%	Top 5%
1947	5.0%	11.9%	17.0%	23.1%	43.0%	25.5%	17.5%
1967	5.4	12.2	17.5	23.5	41.4	25.0	16.4
1973	5.5	11.9	17.5	24.0	41.1	25.6	15.5
1979	5.4	11.6	17.5	24.1	41.4	26.1	15.3
1989	4.6	10.6	16.5	23.7	44.6	26.7	17.9
1997*	4.2	9.9	15.7	23.0	47.2	26.5	20.7
Percentage-point change							
1947–67	0.4	0.3	0.5	0.4	−1.6	−0.5	−1.1
1967–73	0.1	−0.3	0.0	0.5	−0.3	0.6	−0.9
1973–79	−0.1	−0.3	0.0	0.1	0.3	0.5	−0.2
1979–89	−0.8	−1.0	−1.0	−0.4	3.2	0.6	2.6
1989–97	−0.4	−0.7	−0.8	−0.7	2.6	−0.2	2.8

* These shares reflect a change in survey methodology leading to greater inequality.

Source: Authors' analysis of unpublished Census data.

The 1980s was a period of sharply increasing income inequality, reversing the trend toward less inequality over the postwar period into the 1970s. Between 1979 and 1989, the bottom 80% lost income share and only the top 20% gained. Moreover, the 1989 income share of the upper fifth, 44.6%, was far greater than the share it received during the entire postwar period and even higher than the 43% received in 1947. Even among the rich, the growth in income was skewed to the top: between 1979 and 1989, the highest 5% saw their income share rise 2.6 percentage points (from 15.3% to 17.9%), accounting for the bulk of the 3.2 percentage-point total rise in the income share of the upper fifth....

The increase in inequality continued unabated over the 1989–97 period. For example, the share received by the top 5% grew from 17.9% in 1989 to 20.7% in 1997.... Comparing the bottom two rows of the table reveals that the rate of share loss among the bottom 80% was slower than that of the 1980s. However, note that these two rows compare a 10-year to a seven-year period; correcting for this difference reveals that inequality grew at a similar annualized rate in both periods....

Figure 7.2 presents a revealing picture of incomes growing together in the 20 first 30 years of the postwar period and growing apart thereafter. The bars in each panel represent the annual growth rate of average income by income fifth over the periods 1947–79 and 1979–96. The top panel, covering the years 1947–79, shows strong and even growth. In fact, over this period, growth was slightly faster at the bottom of the income scale relative to the top, i.e., growth was equalizing. The bottom panel shows a very different pattern. Since 1979, the annual growth of family income has been negative for the bottom fifth, falling 6.4% per year. Income growth has been flat for the next fifth and positive for the top three fifths. Note that between 1947 and 1979 income grew 0.4% per year more slowly in the top relative to the bottom fifth (found by subtracting one rate of growth from the other); since 1979, income has grown 2.0% more *quickly* in the top relative to the bottom fifth. Thus, the 1947–79 equalizing pattern of growth has sharply reversed in the post-1979 period....

FALLING BEHIND THE EARLIER GENERATIONS

It is especially important to note that the incomes of individuals and families generally follow a life-cycle pattern. Typically, a person, after completing schooling, starts earning income in a relatively low-paying entry-level job, sees fast income growth as job changes, accumulated experience, and seniority occur over the next two decades, and obtains slower income growth in his or her later working years. As Figure 7.3 shows, young families (headed by a person in his or her twenties) in 1996 had much lower incomes than families headed by a middle-aged person (in his or her forties or fifties). It also shows that incomes grow relatively rapidly as the household head proceeds through

Figure 7.2
Family Income, Average Annual Change

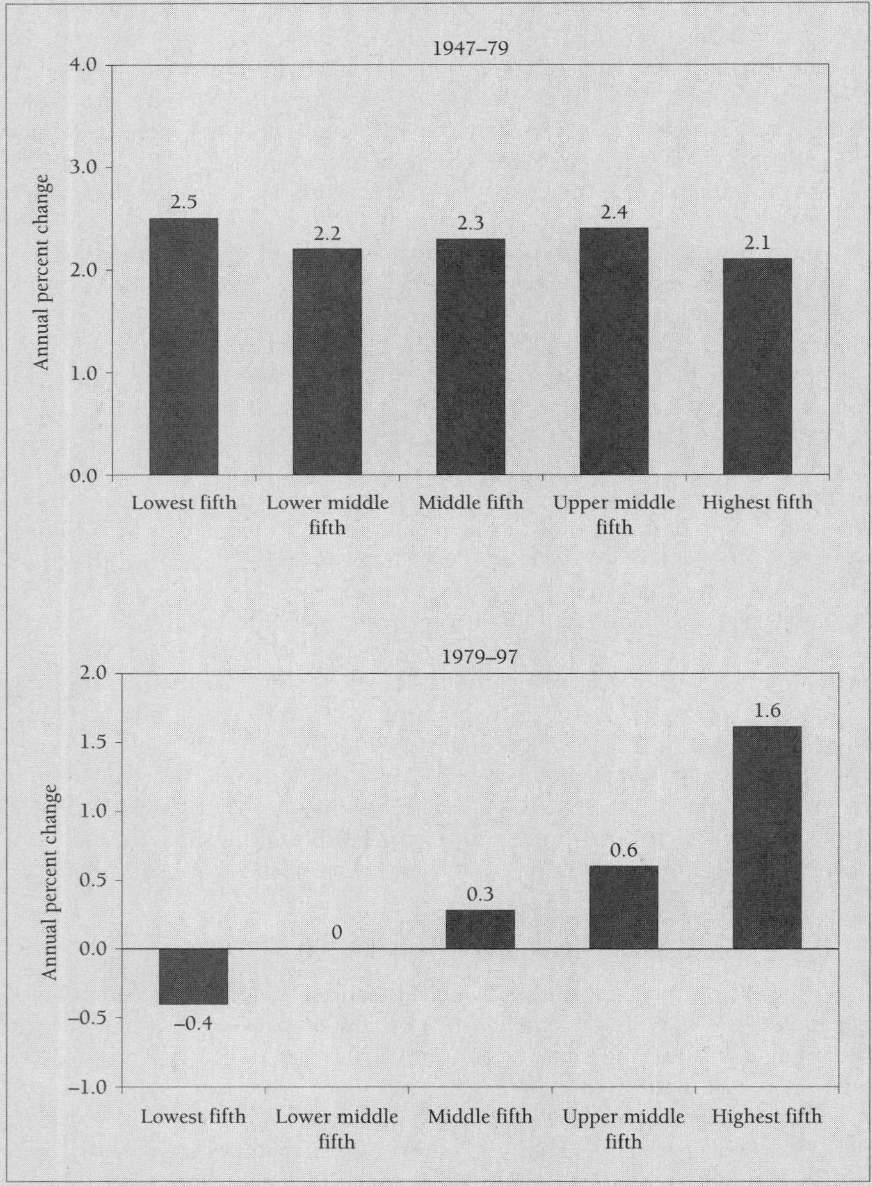

Source: Authors' analysis of U.S. Bureau of the Census (various years).

Figure 7.3
Median Family Income by Age of Householder, 1997

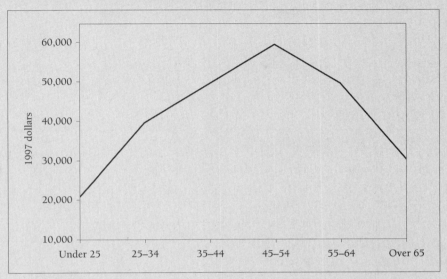

Source: U.S. Bureau of the Census.

his or her thirties and forties, and that income growth slackens and then declines as the household head approaches retirement years.

Viewed this way, the income growth of families as a whole over a 10-year period depends both on how high incomes are for young families when they start out and on how fast incomes grow as families progress through their life-cycle pattern. In fact, the slow growth of median family incomes in recent years is most accurately portrayed as young families starting off with lower incomes than their predecessors while older families proceed to higher incomes at a historically slow pace.

One way to examine income growth over the life cycle is to examine the income trajectories of "birth cohorts" (a group of people born in the same years) over time, as in Table 7.5. The first column shows the median income, in 1996 dollars, of males age 25–34 in the years 1956 through 1996. The second column tracks the median income of 35- to 44-year-olds over these periods. We focus exclusively on males' median incomes, since trends in female income are confounded by large changes in labor supply over this period.

This type of table allows two related types of analyses. By comparing the income levels down each column, we can compare levels across cohorts, such as the different income levels experienced by 25- to 34-year-olds, at different

Table 7.5
Median Income by Male 10-Year Birth Cohorts, 1956–96

Year	Ages 25–34	Ages 35–44	Ages 45–54
1956	$22,321	$24,251	$22,851
1966	29,004	32,561	30,836
1976	30,949	37,841	37,228
1986	27,432	37,467	39,735
1996	25,179	32,167	36,232
Percent change			
1956–66	29.9%	34.3%	34.9%
1966–76	6.7	16.2	20.7
1976–86	−11.4	−1.0	6.7
1986–96	−8.2	−14.1	−8.8

Source: U.S. Bureau of the Census, Income Website.

points in time. Thus, reading down column 1 shows that the median income of young males age 25–34 was about 19% lower in 1996 than in 1976. We can also track a particular cohort's progress through time by reading along the diagonal (more on this approach below)....

...This table tracks three cohorts over 20 years: the first cohort moves from 25 1956, when its members were 25–34, with median income of $22,321 (1996 dollars), to 1976, when they were 45–54, with median income of $37,228. Similarly, the second cohort can be tracked from 1966 (median income $29,004) to 1986 (median income $39,735). While each of these cohorts started out higher than the previous one, their incomes grew successively more slowly. For example, the median income of the first cohort grew 67%, that of the second cohort grew 37%, and that of the third cohort grew 17% (from $30,949 to $36,232). In fact, for this third cohort, as it moved from ages 35–44 in 1986 to 45–54 in 1996, its median actually fell, from $37,467 to $36,232, a 3% decline.

In sum, we find that, while each cohort continues to experience some measure of the expected age-income profile revealed in Figure 7.3, over the last 20 years each successive cohort has been worse off than the preceding cohort at the same age. This break in upward income mobility across cohorts raises the issue of whether the most recent cohorts (those age 25–34 in 1986 and 1996) will ever achieve incomes in their "prime age" equal to those of the earlier postwar cohorts. Given continued slow income growth and falling real wages, it is possible that the recent (and some future) cohorts will have lifetime incomes inferior to those of their parents' generations.

CONCLUSION

The most important development regarding contemporary income trends is the slow and unequal growth that continues unabated. Over the 1979–89 period, rapid income growth among upper-income families and stagnant or falling incomes for the bottom 60% of families led to sharp increases in inequality. At the same time, the income of the median family grew more slowly (0.4% per year) than over any other postwar business cycle.

Since 1989, median family income growth has been stagnant for most family types, and the 1997 median is just $285 (in 1997 dollars) above its 1989 level. In prior recoveries, the income of the median family had far surpassed its pre-recession level by this point in the business cycle. In fact, our analysis of an important source of family income growth in the 1980s — the contributions of working wives — shows that this source was insufficient to counteract the negative hours and earnings trends in the 1990s that beset the bottom 40% of prime-age, married-couple families. Finally, younger families starting out in the 1980s or 1990s have done so from lower income levels than earlier generations, and their likelihood of pulling ahead in later years has fallen.

HOW THE PIE IS SLICED

Edward N. Wolff

Edward Wolff, professor of economics at New York University, studies productivity growth and income and wealth distribution. A managing editor or associate editor of three economics journals, Wolff has authored, coauthored, and edited several books, among them Productivity and American Leadership *(1989),* International Comparisons of the Distribution of Household Wealth *(1987),* Research in Economic Inequality *(1993), and* Top Heavy: A Study of Increasing Inequality of Wealth in America *(1995). In 1995 Wolff published a concise version of* Top Heavy *in the liberal magazine* American Prospect, *from which this reading is taken.*

This reading introduces still another feature of the current economy: wealth inequality, or, as it is sometimes referred to, the wealth gap. Income inequality is also a feature of the economy, but income and wealth inequality, though related, are significantly different, as Wolff demonstrates. Income inequality refers to the low yearly income of full-time workers in relation to the high yearly income of their managers and the chief executive officers and board chairs of corporations. This is the income gap, which presently is wide and growing, as the previous reading by Lawrence R. Mishel, Jared Bernstein, and John Schmitt shows. Wolff addresses the wealth gap—the difference between the accumulated wealth of the middle class and the rich in the form of property, investments, and savings. This gap, too, has been growing for the last twenty years.

As you read, keep in mind the difference between current income and accumulated wealth. You might want to start with paragraph 10, in which Wolff describes what he means by wealth. Then read to discover how wealth is accumulated and kept and whether those in the middle class without wealth have a chance to accumulate any in the new economy.

...As many people have noted, median family income has failed to grow. The picture is even more stark for gains in wealth than for gains in income. New research, based on data from federal surveys, shows that between 1983 and 1989 the top 20 percent of wealth holders received 99 percent of the total gain in marketable wealth, while the bottom 80 percent of the population got only 1 percent. America produced a lot of new wealth in the '80s—indeed, the stock market boomed—but almost none of it filtered down....

The most recent data suggest that these trends have continued. My preliminary estimates indicate that between 1989 and 1992, 68 percent of the increase in total household wealth went to the richest 1 percent—an even larger share of wealth gain than between 1983 and 1989. As a result, the concentration of wealth reached a postwar high in 1992, the latest year for which data are available. If these trends continue, the super rich will pull ahead of other Americans at an even faster pace in the 1990s than they did in the '80s.

Figure 7.4
Winners and Losers in the 1980s

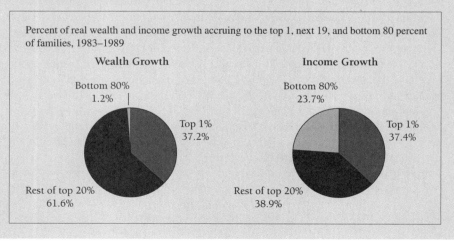

Percent of real wealth and income growth accruing to the top 1, next 19, and bottom 80 percent of families, 1983–1989

Wealth Growth

Bottom 80%
1.2%

Top 1%
37.2%

Rest of top 20%
61.6%

Income Growth

Bottom 80%
23.7%

Top 1%
37.4%

Rest of top 20%
38.9%

Figure 7.5
Concentration of Wealth

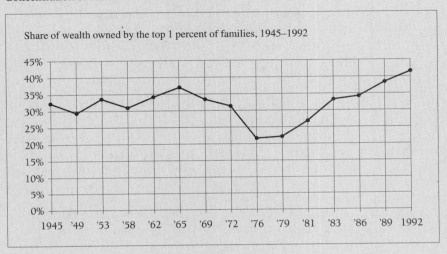

Share of wealth owned by the top 1 percent of families, 1945–1992

Growing inequality in the distribution of wealth has serious implications for the kind of society we live in. Today [1995], the average American family's wealth adds up to a comparatively meager $52,200, typically tied up in a home and some small investments. While *Forbes* magazine each year keeps listing record numbers of billionaires—in 1994 *Forbes* counted 65 of them in the U.S.—homeownership has been slipping since the mid-1970s. The percentage of Americans with private pensions has also been dropping. And, with their real incomes squeezed, middle-income families have not been putting savings aside for retirement. The number of young Americans going to college has also begun to decline, another indirect sign of the same underlying phenomenon. In fact, international data now indicate that wealth is more unequally distributed in the U.S. than in other developed countries, including that old symbol of class privilege, Great Britain.

Economic worries may be at the root of much of the political anger in America today, but there is almost no public debate about the growth in wealth inequality, much less the steps needed to reverse current trends. The debate needs to start with an understanding of how and why America's pie is getting sliced so unequally.

REVERSAL OF FORTUNES

The increasing concentration of wealth in the past 15 years represents a reversal of the trend that had prevailed from the mid-1960s through the late 1970s. The share of total wealth owned by the rich depends, to a large extent, on asset   5 values° and therefore swings sharply with the stock market, but some trends stand out (see Figure 7.5). During the twenty years after World War II, the richest 1 percent of Americans (the "super rich") generally held about a third of the nation's wealth. After hitting a postwar high of 37 percent in 1965, their share dropped to 22 percent as late as 1979. Since then, the share owned by the super rich has surged—almost doubling to 42 percent of the nation's wealth in 1992, according to my estimates.* ...

By the 1980s the U.S. had become the most unequal industrialized country in terms of wealth. The top 1 percent of wealth holders controlled 39 percent of total household wealth in the United States in 1989, compared to 26 percent in France in 1986, about 25 percent in Canada in 1984, 18 percent in Great Britain, and 16 percent in Sweden in 1986. This is a marked turnaround from the early part of [the twentieth] century when the distribution of wealth was considerably more unequal in Europe (a 59 percent share of the top 1 percent in Britain in 1923 versus a 37 percent share in the U.S. in 1922).

The concept of wealth used here is marketable wealth—assets that can be sold on the market. It does not include consumer durables such as automobiles, televisions, furniture, and household appliances; these items are not easily resold, or their resale value typically does not reflect the value of their consumption to the household. Also excluded are pensions and the value of future Social Security benefits a family may receive.

Some critics of my work, such as the columnist Robert Samuelson of the *Washington Post,* argue that a broader definition of wealth shows less concentration. To be sure, including consumer durables, pensions, and entitlements to Social Security reduces the level of measured inequality. The value of consumer durables amounted to about 10 percent of marketable wealth in 1989; including them in the total reduces the share of the top 1 percent of wealth holders from 39 percent to 36 percent. Adding pensions and Social Security "wealth," which together totaled about two-thirds of marketable wealth, has a more pronounced effect, reducing the share of the top 1 percent from 36 percent to 22 percent. However, even though pensions and Social Security are a source of future income to families, they are not in their direct control and cannot be marketed. Social Security "wealth" depends on the commitment of future generations and Congresses to maintain benefit levels; it is not wealth in the ordinary meaning of the term.

Moreover, the inclusion of consumer durables, pensions, and Social Security does not affect trends in inequality. With these assets included, the share of the richest 1 percent reached its lowest level in 1976, at 13 percent, and nearly doubled by 1989 to 22 percent. Nor does it affect international comparisons. For example, using this broader concept of wealth, we still find that the share

---

°asset values: See paragraph 10 for a list of asset values, or marketable assets.

* See my monograph *Top Heavy: A Study of Increasing Inequality of Wealth in America* (New York: Twentieth Century Fund, 1995) for technical details on the construction of this series.

Figure 7.6
...And the Rich Get Richer

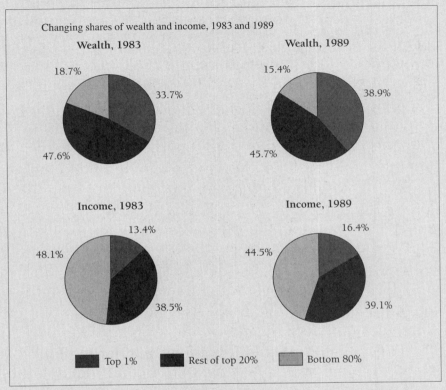

Changing shares of wealth and income, 1983 and 1989

Wealth, 1983

18.7%
33.7%
47.6%

Wealth, 1989

15.4%
38.9%
45.7%

Income, 1983

13.4%
48.1%
38.5%

Income, 1989

16.4%
44.5%
39.1%

■ Top 1%   ■ Rest of top 20%   ■ Bottom 80%

Sources: Author's computations from the 1983 and 1989 Survey of Consumer Finances; Kennickell and Starr-McCluer, 1994.

of the top 1 percent in the U.S. is almost double that of Britain in 1989 — 22 percent versus 12 percent.

WHY THE RICH GOT RICHER

Part of the explanation for growing wealth concentration lies in what has hap- 10 pened to the different kinds of assets that the rich and the middle class hold. Broadly speaking, wealth comes in four forms:

- homes;
- liquid assets,° including cash, bank deposits, money market funds, and savings in insurance and pension plans;

° **liquid assets:** Assets that can be readily sold.

- investment real estate° and unincorporated businesses;° and
- corporate stock,° financial securities,° and personal trusts.°

Middle-class families have more than two-thirds of their wealth invested in their own home, which is probably responsible for the common misperception that housing is the major form of family wealth in America. Those families have another 17 percent in monetary savings of one form or another, with only a small amount in businesses, investment real estate, and stocks. The ratio of debt to assets is very high, at 59 percent.

In contrast, the super rich invest over 80 percent of their savings in investment real estate, unincorporated businesses, corporate stock, and financial

Figure 7.7
The Composition of Household Wealth, 1989

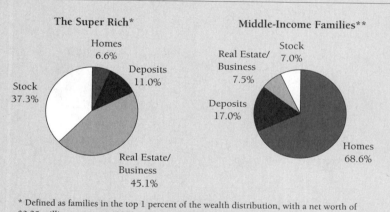

* Defined as families in the top 1 percent of the wealth distribution, with a net worth of $2.35 million or more in 1989.
**Defined as families in the middle quintile, with incomes between $21,200 and $34,300 in 1989.

Homes refers to owner-occupied housing; *Deposits* to liquid assets (cash, bank deposits, money market funds, cash surrender value of insurance, and pension plans); *Real Estate/Business* to investment real estate and unincorporated businesses; *Stock* to corporate stock, financial securities, personal trusts, and other assets.

Source: Author's computations from the 1989 Survey of Consumer Finances.

°**investment real estate:** Houses, land, buildings, and businesses that are bought for the purpose of selling them later for a profit.   °**unincorporated businesses:** A privately owned business that can be sold by the owner.   °**corporate stock:** Shares of a corporation purchased through a stock exchange.   °**financial securities:** Usually, bonds that are bought from corporations or government agencies. Like stocks, bonds are a type of investment for savings and eventual profit.   °**personal trusts:** Family members may make investments for other family members that are held "in trust" by a trustee for payment at a later time.

securities. Housing accounts for only 7 percent of their wealth, and monetary savings another 11 percent. Their ratio of debt to assets is under 5 percent.

Viewed differently, more than 46 percent of all outstanding stock, over half of financial securities, trusts, and unincorporated businesses, and 40 percent of investment real estate belong to the super rich. The top 10 percent of families

Figure 7.8
Assets Held Primarily by the Wealthy

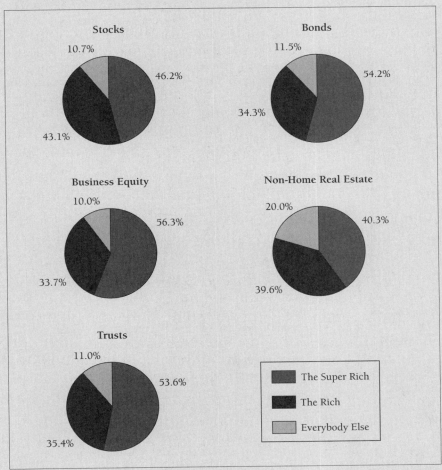

Families are classified into wealth class on the basis of their net worth. In the top 1 percent of the wealth distribution (the Super Rich) are families with a net worth of $2,350,000 or more in 1989; in the next 9 percent (the Rich) are families with a net worth greater than or equal to $346,400 but less than $2,350,000; in the bottom 90 percent (Everybody Else) are families with a net worth less than $346,400.
Source: Author's computations from the 1989 Survey of Consumer Finances.

as a group account for about 90 percent of stock shares, bonds, trusts, and business equity, and 80 percent of non-home real estate. The bottom 90 percent are responsible for 70 percent of the indebtedness of American households.

Thus, for most middle-class families, wealth is closely tied to the value of their homes, their ability to save money in monetary accounts, and the debt burden they face. But the wealth of the super rich has a lot more to do with their ability to convert existing wealth—in the form of stocks, investment real estate, or securities—into even more wealth, that is, to produce "capital gains." . . .

According to my estimates, the chief source of growing wealth concentra- 15 tion during the 1980s was capital gains. The rapid increase in stock prices relative to house prices accounted for about 50 percent of the increased wealth concentration; the growing importance of capital gains relative to savings explained another 10 percent. Increased income inequality during the decade added another 18 percent, as did the increased savings propensity of the rich relative to the middle class. The declining homeownership rate accounted for the remaining 5 percent or so.

In short, wealth went to those who held wealth to begin with. For those who didn't have it, savings alone were not sufficient to amass wealth of great significance.

DISPOSABLE WORKERS

Janice Castro

Janice Castro, an associate editor at Time *magazine, writes about politics, business, and health care policies. Some of her major reports have been on the high cost of medical care, quality in American manufacturing, the state of the U.S. workforce, and Japanese investment in the United States. She was a principal writer for* Time*'s 1992 special issue on women. This reading appeared in a March 1993 issue of* Time.

Castro reports on the increasing reliance of American business on "disposable," or "contingent," workers—workers who, whether they work part-time or full-time, have no job security and usually have no benefits like health care. Young people in high school and college and others who want time to pursue other interests have long held part-time or temporary full-time jobs. Now, however, more and more adults are being forced to work this way, "fundamentally changing the relationship between Americans and their jobs," Castro says. (To update Castro's still timely and comprehensive 1993 report, by the end of 1996, 24 percent of the work-

force was employed contingently and 70 percent of corporations made at least
some use of contingent staffing, according to a report by the National Association
of Part-Time and Temporary Employees; and in 1999 Manpower Inc. was still the
largest employer of any kind in the United States.)

As you read, think about what contingent work might mean for your generation.

The corporation that is now the largest private employer in America does not
have any smokestacks or conveyor belts or trucks. There is no clanging of
metal on metal, no rivets or plastic or steel. In one sense, it does not make anything. But then again, it is in the business of making almost everything.

Manpower Inc., with 560,000 workers, is the world's largest temporary
employment agency. Every morning, its people scatter into the offices and factories of America, seeking a day's work for a day's pay. As General Motors
(367,000 workers), IBM (330,500) and other industrial giants struggle to survive by shrinking their payrolls, Manpower, based in Milwaukee, Wisconsin, is
booming along with other purveyors of temporary workers, providing the
hands and the brainpower that other companies are no longer willing to call
their own.

Even as its economy continues to recover, the U.S. is increasingly becoming
a nation of part-timers and free-lancers, of temps and independent contractors.
This "disposable" work force is the most important trend in business today, and
it is fundamentally changing the relationship between Americans and their
jobs. For companies large and small, the phenomenon provides a way to
remain globally competitive while avoiding the vagaries of market cycles° and
the growing burdens imposed by employment rules, antidiscrimination laws,
health-care costs and pension plans. But for workers, it can mean an end to the
security and sense of significance that came from being a loyal employee. One
by one, the tangible and intangible bonds that once defined work in America
are giving way.

Every day, 1.5 million temps are dispatched from agencies like Kelly Services
and Manpower—nearly three times as many as 10 years ago. But they are only
the most visible part of America's enormous new temporary work force. An additional 34 million people start their day as other types of "contingent" workers.
Some are part-timers with some benefits. Others work by the hour, the day or the
duration of a project, receiving only a paycheck without benefits of any kind.
The rules of their employment vary widely and so do the attempts to label them.
They are called short-timers, per-diem workers, leased employees, extra workers, supplementals, contractors—or in IBM's ironic computer-generated parlance, "the peripherals." They are what you might expect: secretaries, security

---

°**market cycles:** In free market economies, there are cycles of growth and recession, times when
jobs are plentiful and profits are high and times when jobs are scarce and profits are low.

guards, salesclerks, assembly-line workers, analysts and CAD/CAM° designers. But these days they are also what you'd never expect: doctors, high school principals, lawyers, bank officers, X-ray technicians, biochemists, engineers, managers—even chief executives.

Already, one in every three U.S. workers has joined these shadow brigades 5 carrying out America's business. Their ranks are growing so quickly that they are expected to outnumber permanent full-time workers by the end of [the 1990s]. Companies keep chipping away at costs, stripping away benefits or substituting contingent employees for full-time workers. This year° alone, U.S. employers are expected to use such tactics to cut the nation's $2.6 billion payroll costs as much as $800 million. And there is no evidence to suggest that such corporate behavior will change with improvement in the economy.

Once contingent workers appear in a company, they multiply rapidly, taking the places of permanent staff. Says Manpower chairman Mitchell Fromstein: "The U.S. is going from just-in-time manufacturing° to just-in-time employment. The employer tells us, 'I want them delivered exactly when I want them, as many as I need, and when I don't need them, I don't want them here.'" Fromstein has built his business by meeting these demands. "Can I get people to work under these circumstances? Yeah. We're the ATMs of the job market."

In order to succeed in this new type of work, says Carvel Taylor, a Chicago industrial consultant, "you need to have an entrepreneurial° spirit, definable skills and an ability to articulate and market them, but that is exactly what the bulk of the population holed up inside bureaucratic organizations doesn't have, and why they are scared to death." Already the temping phenomenon is producing two vastly different classes of untethered workers: the mercenary work force° at the top of the skills ladder, who thrive; and the rest, many of whom, unable to attract fat contract fees, must struggle to survive.

The flexible life of a consultant or contract worker does indeed work well for a relatively small class of people like doctors, engineers, accountants and financial planners, who can expect to do well by providing highly compensated services to a variety of employers. David Hill, 65, a former chief information systems officer for General Motors, has joined with 17 other onetime auto-industry executives (median salary before leaving their jobs: $300,000) to form a top-of-the-line international consulting group. "In the future," says Hill, "loyalty and devotion are going to be not to a Hughes or Boeing or even an industry, but to a particular profession or skill. It takes a high level of education to suc-

---

°**CAD/CAM:** Computer-aided design/computer-aided manufacturing. °**This year:** 1993. °**just-in-time manufacturing:** Manufacturing products when there is a demand for them rather than stockpiling in anticipation of a demand. °**entrepreneurial:** Interested in organizing and managing a business. °**mercenary work force:** Workers who are more concerned about the money they will make than about establishing a long-term relationship with an employer.

ceed in such a free-flowing environment. We are going to be moving from job to job in the same way that migrant workers used to move from crop to crop."

The number of people employed full time by Fortune 500 companies has shrunk from 19% of the work force two decades ago to less than 10% today. Almost overnight, companies are shedding a system of mutual obligations and expectations built up since the Great Depression, a tradition of labor that said performance was rewarded, loyalty was valued and workers were a vital part of the enterprises they served. In this chilly new world of global competition, they are often viewed merely as expenses. Long-term commitments of all kinds are anathema to the modern corporation. For the growing ranks of contingent workers, that means no more pensions, health insurance or paid vacations. No more promises or promotions or costly training programs. No more lawsuits for wrongful termination or other such hassles for the boss. Says Secretary of Labor Robert Reich:° "These workers are outside the traditional system of worker-management relationships. As the contingent work force grows—as many people find themselves working part time for many different employers— the social contract is beginning to fray."

As the underpinnings of mutual commitment crumble, time-honored 10 notions of fairness are cast aside for millions of workers. Working temp or part time often means being treated as a second-class citizen by both employers and permanent staff. Says Michelle Lane, a former temp in Los Angeles: "You're just a fixture, a borrowed thing that doesn't belong there." Being a short-timer also can mean doing hazardous work without essential training, or putting up with sexual and racial harassment. Placement officers report client requests for "blond bombshells" or people without accents. Says an agency counselor: "One client called and asked us not to send any black people, and we didn't. We do whatever the clients want, whether it's right or not."

Workers have little choice but to cope with such treatment since most new job openings are the labor equivalent of uncommitted relationships. More than 90% of the 365,000 jobs created by U.S. companies last month [February 1993] were part-time positions taken by people who want to work full time. "The fill-ins are always desperate for full-time jobs," says one corporate personnel officer. "They always ask." Richard Belous, chief economist for the National Planning Association in Washington, has studied the proliferation of tenuous jobs. "If there was a national fear index," he says, "it would be directly related to the growth of contingent work."

Many professionals like the freedom of such a life. John Andrews, 42, a Los Angeles antitrust attorney, remembers working seven weeks without a day off as a young lawyer. He prefers temping at law firms. Says he: "There's no security anymore. Partnerships fold up overnight. Besides, I never had a rat-race

---

° **Robert Reich:** Secretary of labor (1993–96) during President Clinton's first term.

mentality, and being a lawyer is the ultimate rat-race job. I like to travel. My car is paid for. I don't own a house. I'm not into mowing grass."

But most American workers do better with the comfort and security of a stable job. Sheldon Joseph was a Chicago advertising executive until he was laid off in 1989. Now he temps for $10 an hour in a community job-training program. Says the 56-year-old Joseph: "I was used to working in the corporate environment and giving my total loyalty to the company. I feel like Rip van Winkle.° You wake up and the world is all changed. The message from industry is, 'We don't want your loyalty. We want your work.' What happened to the dream?"

Employers defend their new labor practices as plain and simple survival tactics. American companies are evolving from huge, mass-production manufacturers that once dominated markets to a new species of hub-and-network enterprises° built for flexibility in a brutally competitive world. The buzz phrase at many companies is "accordion management"—the ability to expand or contract one's work force virtually at will to suit business conditions.

Boardroom discussions now focus on what are called "core competencies"— 15 those operations at the heart of a business—and on how to shed the rest of the functions to subcontractors or nonstaff workers. Managers divide their employees into a permanent cadre of "core workers," which keeps on shrinking, and the contingent workers, who can be brought in at a moment's notice. Most large employers are not even certain at any given time how many of these helpers are working for them—nor do they usually care. Says a manager: "We don't count them. They're not here long enough to matter." Some analysts wonder whether America's celebrated rise in productivity per worker (2.8% last year) [1992] is all it seems to be, since so many of those invisible hands are not being counted. So profound is the change that the word core has evolved a new meaning, as in "she's core," meaning that she is important and distinctive because she is not part of the contingent work force.

No institution is immune to the contingent solution. Imagine the surprise of a Los Angeles woman, seriously injured in an auto accident, when she recently asked a radiology technician at the hospital about a procedure. "Don't ask me," he snapped. "I'm just a temp." In Appleton, Wisconsin, the Aid Association for Lutherans is using temps to keep track of $3.6 million in relief funds for victims of Hurricane Andrew. The State of Maine uses temps as bailiffs and financial investigators. IBM, once the citadel of American job security, has traded 10% of its staff for "peripherals" so far. Says IBM administrative manager Lillian

---

° **Rip van Winkle:** A fictional character who woke after a twenty-year sleep to find the world had changed. ° **hub-and-network enterprises:** Companies in which managers and production may be widely separated geographically, such as a shoe company with headquarters in Los Angeles and factories in South Carolina, Mexico, and China.

Davis, in words that would have been unimaginable from a Fortune 500 executive 20 years ago: "Now that we have stepped over that line, we have decided to use these people wherever we can."

Indeed, managers these days can hire virtually any kind of temp they want. Need an extra lawyer or paralegal for a week or so? Try Lawsmiths in San Francisco or Project Professionals in Santa Monica, California. Need a loan officer? Bank Temps in Denver can help. Engineers? Sysdyne outside Minneapolis, Minnesota. CAD/CAM operators? You don't even need to buy the equipment: in Oakland, California, Western Temporary Services has its own CAD/CAM business, serving such clients as the U.S. Navy, the Air Force, Chevron, Exxon and United Technologies. Doctors and nurses? A firm called Interim in Fort Lauderdale, Florida, can provide them anywhere in the country. Need to rent a tough boss to clean up a bad situation? Call IMCOR, a Connecticut-based firm that boasts a roster of senior executives expert at turnarounds. Says IMCOR chairman John Thompson: "Services like ours are going to continue to flourish when businesses change so rapidly that it's in no one's interest to make commitments. Moving on to the next place where you're needed is going to be the way it is. We will all be free-lancers."

Behind this profound change in the workplace are the impersonal market forces of the new global economy. Americans must now compete for jobs with the growing legions of skilled workers in developing economies from Asia to Eastern Europe. U.S. executives have taken to talking of global "market prices" for employees, as if they were investing in cattle futures. "We understand it's just business, but it's still awfully demeaning," says Deb Donaldson, a part-time retail sales clerk in Moline, Illinois. Manpower's Fromstein dismisses such complaints of exploitation, pointing out that his own profit margins are razor thin (1.3%). Says he: "We are not exploiting people. We are not setting the fees. The market is. We are matching people with demands. What would our workers be doing without us? Unemployment lines? Welfare? Suicide?"

Employers are also responding to factors closer to home. They are embracing such cutbacks not simply to slash up to 40% of payroll costs, though that might be inspiration enough. They are also freeing themselves from inconvenient labor and equal-employment requirements. Says Ronald Cohen, a senior partner of Cohen & Co., a regional accounting firm based in Cleveland, Ohio: "You don't need to worry about the incredible compliance problems° and potential litigation if you fire someone." Using disposable workers also means that companies rarely have to train them. Moreover, getting rid of such workers

---

°**compliance problems:** Employers must observe various federal and state regulations protecting full-time employees from discrimination and harassment, unfair and arbitrary policies, and unsafe working conditions.

is easy when they don't measure up. Says Robert Uhlaner, senior vice president of Quantum Consulting in Berkeley, California: "You can try them out. The best thing about it is that you never have to face firing people—because you never really hire them in the first place."

In the long run, however, this scramble to shed full-time staff may be as 20 harmful to American industry as it is to the American work force—since a well-trained work force is the greatest asset of a nation's industries. Analysts, including Labor Secretary Reich, have pointed out that in a borderless world, capital and production are portable; thus, the key resources of companies as well as nations are the skills and ideas of its people. The reduction in corporate programs for training and developing employees—one of the long-term effects of the temping of America—leads to a disinvestment in the nation's human capital. By discouraging commitment and initiative, managers risk poisoning the well of their most important asset.

President Clinton has called for more "good jobs at good pay" for workers. But even as he gears up his plan to retrain American workers, companies are abandoning their traditional role of nurturing new talent. Richard Belous argues that government training programs may have to help repair the damage. Schools must also do a better job.

The best solution, however, may be to find ways to reduce some of the forces that are pushing companies to rely more heavily on disposable workers. Creating a system of universal health insurance might be a start: properly designed, it could reduce one of the costs of taking on full-time employees as well as make life easier for contingency workers. If employers are required to provide extensive benefits to workers, though, such a plan may backfire, triggering new job eliminations.

There is no going back to old-fashioned lifetime employment. Companies need flexibility. Thus the long-term social costs of all the well-intentioned work-force rules that have accrued over the past few decades may have to be reconsidered.

For now, most citizens will have to scramble to adapt to the new age of the disposable worker. Says Robert Schaen, a former comptroller of Chicago-based Ameritech who now runs his own children's publishing business: "The days of the mammoth corporations are coming to an end. People are going to have to create their own lives, their own careers and their own successes. Some people may go kicking and screaming into the new world, but there is only one message there: You're now in business for yourself." —*With reporting by John F. Dickerson, Jane Van Tassel/New York and William McWhirter/Chicago*

DISCONNECTED

Barbara Rudolph

Journalist Barbara Rudolph has written for Forbes *and* Time *and has recently published* Disconnected: How Six People from AT&T Discovered the New Meaning of Work in a Downsized Corporate America *(1998), a study of six people who lost their jobs at a major U.S. corporation in the mid-1990s.*

This reading, taken from the opening of Disconnected, *introduces another feature of the restructured U.S. economy: job insecurity. In today's workplace, employees understand that they cannot expect a lifelong career with one employer. By tracing the history of job security in the twentieth century, Rudolph makes clear that there has been only a brief period of relative security, from the 1940s to the 1970s. Through the 1930s, jobs were less secure than they are today. Nevertheless, as she argues, since the late 1970s there has developed a changed relationship between employers and employees, a new social contract, that has led to job insecurity.*

As you read, try to understand why there was a period of relatively secure employment from the 1940s to the 1970s and why there has been a period of relatively insecure employment since then.

Middle-class job security began to erode in the late 1980s, when a wave of white-collar layoffs began. The prototypical victim was the fifty-year-old neighbor down the street who, to everyone's surprise, lost his job after fifteen years with the company. He wasn't fired, exactly; his position was eliminated in a reorganization. College-educated white-collar workers, most of them men, were especially stung by the force of these layoffs. Still, it was not until the presidential campaign in the winter of 1996 that the dimensions of this change were fully appreciated by middle-class Americans, resulting in a national debate about downsizing and job insecurity.

THE HISTORY OF JOB SECURITY

We start you in a Chevrolet, and we bury you in a Cadillac.
—GENERAL MOTORS EXECUTIVE, circa 1960

What we think of as "job security" had a relatively brief tenure in American history. It was one component of a uniquely halcyon° chapter in U.S. economic development that began at the end of World War II and ended around the time of

---

°halcyon: Peaceful and prosperous.

the first OPEC oil shock° in 1973. During this postwar boom, the gross national product (GNP), productivity, and median family income were all on the rise.

For the first three decades of the century, as historian Sanford Jacoby recounts in *Employing Bureaucracy,* the average U.S. worker knew that he would be laid off at least once during the year. But by the late 1930s, the newfound strength of labor unions (by 1940, one in three manufacturing workers belonged to a union) and government pressure in the midst of the Great Depression gave birth to corporate paternalism. One result was that between 1935 and 1940, the number of workers covered by pension and health insurance plans soared.

At the core of the emerging new workplace was a social contract between employer and employee—in its purest form, an exchange of loyalty for security. This unwritten pact assumed a long-term attachment between worker and employer. It also had the critical effect of insulating workers from fluctuations in the economy that affected the value of their labor in the outside market.

The organization, meanwhile, acquired a stable and experienced pool of labor. Companies could exploit their employees' firm-specific knowledge—the awareness of a particular organization's strengths, quirks, and culture that only comes with time. Moreover, by this exchange of loyalty for security, the corporation was able to harness the very spirit of its workers, that special commitment which can be given freely but never bought.

As the postwar workplace evolved, the largest U.S. companies offered the most stable jobs. Even in the 1950s and 1960s, though, when the names of mighty American corporations like General Motors, Sears, Roebuck, and United States Steel had such resonance, they employed only a small fraction of the workforce. In 1965, for example, only 16 percent of all workers (11.3 million people) were employed by Fortune 500 firms. (The ratio of 16 percent still held in 1979, when the Fortune 500 payrolls reached 16.2 million, as it did in 1996, when 20.4 million of 134 million Americans worked for Fortune 500 companies.) Yet these corporations had a presence in the workplace that transcended their number of employees. They were the public face of American business, symbols of postwar prosperity; to many smaller firms (and their workers), they represented the ideal employer.

Their stature reflected the fact that the U.S. economy of the 1950s and 1960s was far more cohesive than it is today. A handful of brand-name firms within a few key sectors—most notably manufacturing and transportation—struck the dominant chords. It was a world of three television networks and one phone company, a single computer giant, and a small clique of regulated airlines.

By 1980, however, the postwar American economy had been transformed. A relatively simple structure had become complicated and diffuse. The service

°OPEC oil shock: In 1973 the Organization of Petroleum Exporting Countries (OPEC) raised oil prices, producing a sharp rise in gasoline prices that led to difficult economic times in the United States.

sector was exploding, technology was flourishing, and manufacturing had receded into the shadows. The U.S. economy inevitably became more differentiated—and more closely linked to a global market.

Shared Sensibility

The postwar workplace inspired and sustained a particular sensibility in the men and women who filled its cubicles and corner offices. It was shaped by the experience of a class and a generation: the college-educated, white-collar, middle-class baby boomers.

This sensibility was defined by a shared expectation of *what work means*— 10 shared notions of the connection between work and personal identity. In describing this sensibility one uses words, like *dignity* and *fraternity,* that are now almost unthinkable in a corporate context. Job security made these feelings possible, because it gave people a sense of control over their working lives. Safety allowed them to aspire to loftier ideals, to some larger meaning and purpose in their jobs.

The workplace itself seemed predictable and manageable. Employees knew that if they respected the conventions of the corporate organization, they could master its hierarchy through talent and sheer perseverance. Was this world governed by fair play and selflessness? Of course not; the free market has always obeyed a rough sort of justice. But this environment encouraged a fundamental faith that one could shape and control the course of one's working life.

People approached their careers as a ladder to be climbed. Jobs were clearly defined, and paths of advancement plainly marked. Work histories followed a linear narrative line. Company men of the baby-boom generation did not need to spend thirty years at one firm, like their fathers. For William Whyte's organization men, who came of age in the Great Depression and valued security above all else, the totems of corporate distinction—the country club memberships, the plaques of appreciation (more ornate with each passing decade), the heavy gold watches of retirement—were respected as legitimate status symbols, and with a pristine faith that their children could never share. Yet these sons and daughters joined their own corporate organizations with a similar basic expectation: if they wanted to burrow into the bureaucracy, and stay for decades, they believed that they could. They could choose to follow their fathers' course even if they ultimately decided to reject it. This choice was a powerful freedom.

• • •

The baby boomers went to work in good faith. But while their fathers had happily submerged themselves in the organization as "team players," the baby boomers thought of themselves as individualists. Whereas their fathers had idealized the corporation, their perspective was more skeptical. This was in keeping with the tenor of the 1960s, of course, when "big business" was a popular target. In 1967, *The Graduate*'s famous line, "I just want to say one word to you, just one word... plastics," became part of the national dialogue; that same year, thousands of demonstrators assailed Dow Chemical's management as hateful "baby killers." Still, among the men and (occasionally) women who made their living within the corporate structure, the firm was generally seen as a benign force.

For the growing ranks of the professional middle class—lawyers, engineers, and doctors, as well as company men (a group defined less by its financial status than by its college education)—the old workplace offered the possibility of real autonomy. These men and women could aspire to not merely jobs but careers, even if they did not always find them. They could invest themselves in their work and hope to find some meaning in their labor.

Company men and women were loyal. The emotion was born of a sense of 15 belonging to a larger community. Employees felt a personal identification with the organization; they believed that they shared the same fate. This sense of citizenship encouraged them to serve the long-term interest of the organization. Without it, the company man, in whatever incarnation, would not exist.

Where did this visceral faith come from? For many it was a family heritage. It is easy now to forget how commonplace it was to meet second- and third-generation employees at companies such as Eastman Kodak, IBM, and especially AT&T (where many can still be found). The family legacy took root, reinforced by decades of easy prosperity, as the memory of the Depression faded.

The company was personified. A prevailing metaphor became a cliché, but it was grounded in a perceived truth: the company was a family. People trusted the organization, which is why so many could ultimately feel betrayed. Old-fashioned, unreconstructed employee loyalty was essentially a kind of love....

...People unconsciously repeat their own family dynamics, assume old roles, and act out old patterns of conflict in any organization. This behavior is inevitable in the workplace, the most important social environment outside the home. During the heyday of the "good" corporation, the identification was particularly intense. The company *was* family for many of its employees.

Loyalty could often take the form of unquestioned obedience to an impersonal, omnipotent bureaucracy. Managers could not refuse a transfer. Even the most absurd, unreasonable privileges of rank were respected. Freethinkers and whistle-blowers met with deep suspicion. The essential goodness of the corporation was never called into question.

Creative Destruction

Capitalism is by nature a form of change and never is, never can be, stationary.
—JOSEPH SCHUMPETER

A confluence of changes, both inside and outside the firm, caused the old cor- 20 porate structure and sensibility to come undone. Global competition and the rise of new technologies in the 1970s and early 1980s forced companies to reconceive their operations. To bolster profits, they needed to cut costs, and reducing payroll expenses—in other words, firing people—was an obvious place to start. As U.S. manufacturing came under global siege, the recession of the early 1980s sparked widespread layoffs of factory workers. Eventually, though, American industry became much more productive and competitive — producing more with fewer hands.

Layoffs of white-collar workers followed about a decade later, in the late 1980s. The rise of the service economy meant that many more Americans worked in white-collar jobs, so by definition that group was more vulnerable to downsizing. It had become clear, too, that as the ranks of middle managers had swelled in the 1970s and 1980s, many companies had become overstaffed.

Another factor was the rise of "investor capitalism," as Michael Useem has described the far-reaching influence of institutional shareholders,° including mutual funds and retirement plans held by millions of American households. These stockholders cajoled and compelled companies to restructure, to down-size — to do anything to drive the stock price up. As executive compensation was increasingly tied to a company's stock performance (with CEO paychecks reaching historic and often outrageous levels during the 1990s bull market°), investor capitalism became increasingly entrenched. Still more white-collar downsizing was often a crude form of mob psychology, as CEOs made the fashion of "re-engineering" synonymous with systemic layoffs.

All this downsizing was part of a deep transformation of the workplace. Rapid changes in technologies, shorter product cycles,° and relentless competitive pressures meant that companies had to reinvent themselves continually. This almost perpetual state of flux necessarily diminished the storehouse of firm-specific knowledge that long job tenure had provided.

Most importantly, these changes intensified the demand for flexibility (a word that has become a staple of management guides) from both employers and workers. This flexibility appears most vividly in so-called contingent or alternate work relationships, in which an employee works for a company as an independent contractor, a part-timer, or through a temporary agency. Though there is a debate about how best to define this sector of the labor pool, there is no doubt that the category is rapidly expanding. The prevalence of outsourcing is another illustration, as more and more companies limit their ranks of permanent workers, by hiring outside firms to take over not only clerical work but financial, information technology, and human resources functions as well.

For many men and women trying to make their way in an organization, the 25 word *flexibility* masks a corrosive uncertainty. In a world of constant flux, one never quite stands on solid ground.

°**institutional shareholders:** Large groups such as retirement associations that hold huge amounts of stock.   °**bull market:** A period of time when the average value of stocks rises. (During a bear market, the average value of stocks falls.)   °**product cycles:** The time between the introduction of a new product (for example, a personal computer, sport utility vehicle model, shade of lipstick, managed-care contract, or walking-shoe design) and its replacement by a newer product.

Detachment and Disjunctions

Today, as they confront these changes, people are reassessing their notions of what work means. Yet old hopes still linger. In the voices of today's company men and women one hears a wistfulness, a tension between fading expectations and sharpening reality.

Compared with their baby-boom predecessors, Americans presently in their twenties and early thirties, members of Generations X and Y, have come of age with toughened expectations of what any corporate organization can provide. They generally expect to change jobs—and careers—more frequently than their older siblings and parents.

From both older and younger workers, then, there echoes the hopeful refrain of the flexible worker: "I must manage my own career." But what does this really mean, and who is most likely to achieve it? Fraternity is fleeting. For many, the sense of a collective purpose has been overtaken by individualism, and any surviving loyalty must be qualified. The emotional bond between a worker and an employer in this new environment becomes entirely conditional, and to speak of loyalty or trust in this context now becomes absurd.

Who will flourish in this new environment? People who can be not only flexible but also emotionally detached. They neither want nor expect the organization to act as their family manqué.° As the organization lurches about, they will instinctively find their equilibrium: They won't take corporate changes and disruptions personally. And they certainly won't take them to heart.

In this context, restlessness will prove to be an asset. This is an environment 30 in which people constantly look over their shoulders, ready to jump at a moment's notice to another department, another project, or another company.

Some workers will find freedom in this motion, enjoying the challenge of the chase. In *White Collar Blues,* Charles Heckscher describes the emergence of a new professional loyalty, in which people make a "commitment to a mission or task rather than to a company." They engage in an enterprise for a prescribed period of time, then move on.

The trick in all this is timing. Finding the next mission or project as soon as the present one ends is no simple task. Here the laws of the market will prevail, and those employees whose skills and talents are in demand will have the edge. Now employers have little incentive to teach their workers the skills they will need in the open market. How can a company justify such an investment when both the worker and the employer feel only a contingent connection to each other?

In the wake of dislocation and shared uncertainty, class boundaries blur. If middle-class workers have lost so much of their job security and feel such an attenuated sense of purpose in their work, how can they distinguish themselves from the working class? They can no longer assume, as they once did,

---

°family manqué: A substitute family.

that they work for something more than a wage. It was this expectation, more than the obvious gulf between physical and mental labor, that once set them apart from the working class.

Even so, there can be no question that class issues are very much with us. In fact, they form an interesting subtext to the economic debate about downsizing.

SOME WHO LOST JOBS IN EARLY '90S RECESSION FIND A HARD ROAD BACK

Tony Horwitz

As a reporter for the Wall Street Journal, *Tony Horwitz won the Pulitzer Prize in 1995 for national reporting. Now a writer for the* New Yorker *magazine, he has authored three books:* One for the Road *(1999),* Baghdad without a Map *(1992), and* Confederates in the Attic *(1998), a national best-seller and* New York Times Notable Book of the Year.

In this 1998 Wall Street Journal *report, Horwitz explores job insecurity from the perspective of ten "middle managers in major firms," ages thirty-nine to sixty-one, who lost their jobs in the early 1990s. He met with this group for roundtable discussions in 1993 and 1998. His report blends comments from economists with details about what happened to the men after they lost their jobs. Each of the ten men has a different story to tell, but their experiences as a group reveal interesting patterns or themes. For example, the younger men—those between ages thirty-nine and forty-four—were more likely to find new jobs as good as the ones they lost.*

As you read, try to understand why these men lost their jobs at the peaks of their careers and why most of them are having such difficulty finding new jobs that make full use of their skills and experience. Also notice the ways in which their views of themselves and their opportunities changed after they lost their jobs.

WAYNE, PA.—At most reunions, friends swap tales of the good old days. But when former members of a support group called Executives in Transition gather at a restaurant on Philadelphia's Main Line, the talk is of pay cuts, job-interview woes, and painful readjustments to the 1990s economy.

"I answered one ad for a managerial position and it turned out to be a firm that retails soft-core porn," recalls one of the men, a former corporate-telecommunications manager. "I did a phone interview with them, I was that desperate. Never heard back."

Another man phoned a prospective

employer to ask why he didn't land a job interview, only to learn that his resume had been prescanned electronically for "action verbs" that failed to turn up. "I've had the privilege of being rejected by a computer," he says.

Ben Linfoot, at least, has found steady work as a field sales representative for a computer firm. But he's earning far less than he did a decade ago as a marketing executive, and feels he's using "only 20%" of his skills. "Everybody knows what the rules of corporate life are now," he says, ticking off several to loud "amens": Forget job security, forget upward mobility, and most of all, forget the past. "The tough part," he concludes, "is realigning yourself to what is, not what used to be."

HISTORY OF WOE

What used to be, for these men and 5 thousands like them, was well-paid and seemingly secure employment as middle managers in major firms. But downsizing and white-collar layoffs in the early 1990s put much of that world in jeopardy. The men at the Wayne restaurant were among 10 displaced managers who met with this reporter in the summer of 1993.

Now, exactly five years later, the economy keeps booming and unemployment remains at historic lows. Yet, to a surprising degree, these men have not fully shared in the recovery. Even those who have returned to full-time jobs, or found lucrative self-employment, feel scarred by their experience and apprehensive about the future.

"It's like living in California on an earthquake fault," says Bill Kane, a for-

mer bank vice president who now is self-employed as a telecommunications consultant. "It looks calm out there, but underneath, you have this feeling that it could all get shaky again and leave you falling through the cracks."

Economists are still trying to make sense of what happened to the job market during the early 1990s recession. In general, they say, the alarmist publicity given to white-collar layoffs wasn't justified. "It's been overdone," says Henry Farber, a Princeton University economist and a leading expert on job tenure and mobility. "Long-term employment remains an important part of the labor market. The great American lifetime job is not a thing of the past."

While white-collar layoffs have indeed become more common in the 1990s, one reason is that white-collar jobs make up a much bigger share of the job market than ever before. Large layoffs have also become more conspicuous, in part because companies often tout cutbacks as a way to show they intend to operate leanly—a move that can boost stock prices. Also, as in all economic downturns, it was blue-collar workers, not white, who bore the brunt of the job and income loss during the last recession, and they have been the slowest to recover their losses.

EXCEPTIONS TO THE RULES

However, within this broad picture, 10 there are signs that particular groups of white-collar workers have indeed been hard-hit. David Neumark, a Michigan State University economist, says new data show "a pretty sharp decline" in long-term job retention among the most-tenured workers. Peter Cappelli, chairman of the department of management at the University of Pennsylvania's Wharton School, says this decline reflects continued restructuring during the recovery, deepening a trend toward "eliminating traditional job ladders" and squeezing older middle managers. "There has been a shift in the last three years in who's getting whacked, from the youngest to the oldest workers," he says. Late-middle-age males may be particularly vulnerable. "They're the people that women and baby boomers are replacing," says Erica Groshen, a labor economist with the Federal Reserve Bank of New York.

Older workers who lose jobs also have the hardest time finding new ones; only about half of over-55 workers displaced in 1993–1994 were re-employed by February 1996, the most recent date for which full statistics are available. Mr. Cappelli believes employers may be wary of hiring older, displaced managers because of a fear that "they're going to feel undercompensated and underused, a feeling that 'I used to run a division that's bigger than this company,' and that this may make the people around them uncomfortable." These findings reflect the experience of the 10 displaced managers from the Main Line. The three youngest, ages 39 to 44 at the time of their layoffs, have fared best. Two have full-time managerial jobs, and the third, Mr. Kane, is doing well as a consultant. All, though, say they are still making up for income lost during the early 1990s and expect layoffs to be a lasting feature of the white-collar landscape.

"I feel as if I'm at the cusp," says 44-year-old Phil Purdy, who has had three jobs in the past five years and now manages distribution for an auto-parts manufacturer. "In another few years, I'll be facing what the older guys have."

AGE AS AN ISSUE

The older guys, now ages 53 to 61, have mostly become part-time consultants, or bounced between interim jobs offering considerably less income and authority than they commanded before. One works as a consultant for the company that let him go. Another recently landed a full-time job, but asked that his name not be used in this article. "The fear factor looms large," he explains. Having answered about 1,000 job ads and gone to 90 job interviews over the past five years, he worries that exposure of his past would make him seem like damaged goods. "I don't want my employer to think, 'We hired this turkey when 89 others didn't want him.'"

Jerry Young wishes he were so lucky. The co-founder of Executives in Transition (which disbanded several years ago), he has become a living job application, churning out more than 500 resumes and cover letters a year. On a recent morning at his comfortable suburban home, he perches in his bedroom-cum-office, armed with a fax, printer and computer, and runs through his daily routine: checking newspaper ads, scanning Internet sites such as Jobtrak, updating letters to headhunters.

Though there is no shortage of list- 15 ings, he feels his chances are slim of landing anything commensurate with his skills and experience as a former vice president of RCA Global Communications. "There's just no market for people my age," says the 58-year-old.

Recently, he applied for a job that sounded perfect, as a vice president, international, for a telecommunications firm. He fired off his resume, listing his M.B.A. and military service, but without the dates of each. "When we talked on the phone, that was the first thing they asked—when did you graduate from Wharton," he says. He told them the truth: 1967. He doesn't expect to hear from them again. "There's lots of younger people out there with similar credentials," he says.

Mr. Young and the other men say they have run into the age problem time and again. "The stock reasons you hear are that older workers are burnt out, that companies will have to fund your retirement, that you'll overload their medical insurance," he says. He also suspects an unspoken discomfort with older men. "I don't think a 45-year-old CEO wants a father figure working under him."

Mr. Young also senses that the longer he is out of work, the harder it becomes to find a job. In his resume and job interviews, he doesn't dwell on his past eight years of occasional employment. "I try to gloss over it quickly and go to the meat of my career, back in the '80s," he says. Also, technology and terminology change; he is currently reading a book called "The Euro" to stay abreast of international trends. And he tries not to become bitter, though he admits, "I'm p——ed off that I can't contribute, that

my skills and energy are being wasted. I could get back in harness and work circles around those young guys."

CHANGING ROLES

Mr. Young and men like him have also had to deal with role reversals at home. Sally Young taught home economics for the first two years of their marriage, then spent decades raising three children and doing volunteer work. She dreamed of one day accompanying her husband on his many foreign trips. "Now was the time—I've got the empty nest," she says.

Instead, Ms. Young got a job when 20 her husband lost his, and the couple now relies on her salary and health benefits. She has found the work as a church fund-raiser fulfilling, but wishes that their holidays weren't limited mostly to visiting friends at their beach houses. "I get together regularly with 15 high-school girlfriends, a lot of whom have been through the same thing," she says. "We all look at each other and say, 'We never dreamed it would be this way.' But we've all made lemonade out of the lemons."

In one sense, the Youngs and others hit by white-collar layoffs have been fortunate. The strong economy has boosted their stock portfolios, and Mr. Young reckons his investments yielded more than $50,000 in paper profits last year. Added to the $30,000 or so Ms. Young earns, this has cushioned the family from financial free fall.

Mr. Young says this money, as well as pride, has prevented him from ever collecting unemployment benefits. But several other members of Executives in

Transition have done so. In general, they say, the stigma of unemployment weighs on them far less heavily than it did five years ago, when they and their wives spoke of feeling shunned by friends and neighbors, and of hiding in their homes because of their shame. "In retrospect, most of the stigma was self-induced," says Pete Wenzlick, now a consultant.

John Haley, who works with a Wayne counseling group called Career Crossroads, agrees. "People who lose their jobs don't melt down the way they did five years ago," he says. "Now, many of them have been through it two and three times, or it's the first time and they think, 'It's gotten everyone else — now it's finally got me.'"

The Main Line managers also have come to appreciate the positive aspects of their situation, especially time with their families. When the Youngs' two sons were growing up, Mr. Young was frequently away on business. But during their daughter's adolescence, he was able to attend her sports events and become involved in her studies. "She had Jerry, whereas the boys didn't," Sally Young says.

Bill Kane found the same with his ²⁵ teenage daughter, and decided after several years of job searching that he preferred working for himself to riding the 7:10 train into Philadelphia every morning. "In a corporation, you can't walk out of the office at two for a lacrosse game and come back later to work through the evening," he says, taking a break from his home-based consulting business to visit with his daughter, who is home from college for the summer.

Mr. Kane also enjoys the variety that comes with consulting. He works with several companies, both on-site and from home. "I'm not always doing the same thing in the same place every day," he says. Also, paradoxically, he feels that losing his bank job and going out on his own has prepared him for the next economic downturn. "Companies will eliminate bodies to look good on the books, but they'll still need to get the work done," he says. "They'll fill the need with contractors like me."

Many of the men have also stepped up their involvement with church and civic groups. And they all speak of becoming much more sensitized to the needs and suffering of others. As a hospital executive, Pete Wenzlick used to lay people off; even as a consultant, he still must recommend cutbacks. "But I do it differently now," he says, adding that he recently acted as a reference and helped locate a new job for someone whose position he eliminated.

Mr. Wenzlick has also taken three missionary trips with his church to help rebuild homes in hurricane-ravaged areas. Another member of the group, a self-described "conservative Republican," says that if he had won the lottery 10 years ago, he would have given a chunk of the money to his Ivy League alma mater. "Now I'd give a third of it to Habitat for Humanity or the United Negro College Fund," he says. "People who need a boost and are trying to help themselves."

Phil Purdy agrees. "I'm more tolerant than I was. I'm willing to accept that there are situations beyond people's control," he says. "People on welfare, for instance, I feel a lot of them really do try. If you'd asked me before, I probably would have said that they were lazy SOBs."

The men also have learned to see themselves differently, experiencing what Mr. Purdy calls a "values readjustment." Few are now willing to sacrifice everything at the altar of their jobs, as they once did, relocating at a moment's notice or taking assignments requiring 200 days of travel a year. Wives, children and elderly parents are a much more important part of the equation. So is mental balance.

"I'm a lot less material and I'm not so hard on myself," says Mr. Purdy, who has had problems with depression over the past five years. "I've come to realize that success isn't defined by what company you work for and what toys you have. It's who you are and the satisfaction you get from your life."

Some of that satisfaction comes from unexpected places. Mr. Young, for instance, now prides himself on being a "Mr. Mom" who shops, washes clothes, vacuums and cooks for his working wife. He reads voraciously and provided the "sweat equity" when he and his wife recently landscaped their garden.

But on a recent afternoon, his house cleaned and job letters sent, he can't help feeling jealous of his next-door neighbor, a retired lawyer who is heading for Cape Cod for the summer after spending much of the winter in Florida.

"That's not the retirement I see for myself," he says. "I've had my retirement already these past eight years. I'm ready to go back to work."

DOWNSIZING COMES BACK, BUT THE OUTCRY IS MUTED

Louis Uchitelle

Louis Uchitelle writes about labor and business economics for the New York Times, *in which this article appeared in December 1998. He also writes a biweekly column, "Business Scene," in which he assesses economic issues.*

While Tony Horwitz in the previous reading reports on late-career, middle-management job losses in Philadelphia, Uchitelle reports here on late-career job losses among blue-collar workers in their 40s in Indianapolis, Indiana. Rhoda Wright and Martie Hammer both lost their Thomson Consumer Electronics jobs when the company closed its Indiana television plant and moved the operation to Mexico. Margaret and Clifford Edens lost their long-term jobs at a Maytag stove plant when the company decided to move the operation to a nonunion factory in Tennessee. Uchitelle focuses on these blue-collar workers' efforts to find retraining and new jobs and on the lack of an outcry over their job losses. You will learn

that by 1998 communities and labor unions had accepted the fact that plant clos-
ings and widespread job losses were inevitable, a regrettable but understandable
feature of the restructured economy.

As you read, focus on how these unemployed workers sought new jobs and
what success they had. Notice also how their lives have changed.

INDIANAPOLIS—When Rhoda Wright learned that the television assembly plant where she had worked for 27 years would close, she did all the right things. She helped to counsel fellow workers through their shock. She used her $13,000 in severance to pay off a car loan. And once the plant shut in April, she enrolled as an accounting student—hoping to one day get back to her old wage of $10.60 an hour.

But for all her energy and determination, a bleakness creeps into Ms. Wright's story. Her unemployment insurance will run out by next December, six months before she graduates. She expects to land an accounting job quickly enough, even at age 49, but only at $8 an hour. "I don't have a clue anymore what our income is going to be," she said, "but we'll get by. We always have."

She has told her two grown daughters not to come to her for help any more. Her big concern is that her husband, Ronald, who is 53 and just back at work as a metal worker after suffering a mild stroke, will fall ill again. "I would probably have to quit school and take one of those $6-an-hour jobs," she said.

Ms. Wright is hardly alone in the difficult choices she must make after losing a job she had counted on to sustain her until retirement. Plant closings, layoffs and forced early retirements are ris-

ing sharply again. The cutbacks announced recently at Bankers Trust, Boeing and Johnson & Johnson, and threatened at Exxon and Mobil, are only the latest examples. But the outcries and conflict that characterized the waves of downsizing in the 1980's and early 1990's are largely gone now.

Rather than protest, unions are more 5 likely to help laid-off members make the transition to other jobs, often working in tandem with the very managers who did the laying off. For their part, corporate executives no longer call attention to downsizing as healthy for profits and stock prices. Much more often they express regrets, blame global forces beyond their control, fatten severance packages for workers and announce layoffs well in advance of the final day.

The downsizing is coming just when a strong job market, mainly in the service sector, offers new jobs more quickly than in the past, softening the blow considerably. Unemployment has fallen to 4.4 percent nationally and less than 3 percent in central Indiana. The layoffs are concentrated in manufacturing, both nationally (245,000 jobs have disappeared through layoffs and attrition since March) and here in central Indiana. More than three dozen companies have announced or carried out layoffs here in recent months.

"You would see a more militant and adversarial relationship come back if the unemployment rate were two or three percentage points higher than it is today," said Larry Gigerich, president of the Indianapolis Economic Development Corporation. "There are plenty of unfilled jobs, and although they are at lower pay, people feel they can take them and work back up to their old wage, or they feel that another job will soon open up like the one they lost. Such expectations are not necessarily realistic."

Certainly Ms. Wright is far from regaining her old wage, and so are most of her former colleagues at Thomson Consumer Electronics. Thomson gave 14 months' notice to 1,100 workers that its television plant in nearby Bloomington would be closed last April, and the operation moved to Mexico. Since then, only 100 have matched or bettered their old pay—at a General Electric Company plant in Bloomington that makes a popular double-door refrigerator and has been adding staff at $10 to $12 an hour. Thomson had paid $10.50 to $11 an hour.

Still, labor unions and workers seem more willing than in the past to accept, as beyond anyone's control, the reasons offered by corporate America for a plant closing or a layoff—the main reasons lately being the Asian crisis° and too much production capacity.°

"Let's be realistic," said George **10** Becker, president of the United Steel-workers of America. "If it is inevitable that a place is going to go down and there is nothing that can be done to save it, if there is no way to compete or there is no market for the product—if that is going to happen, we are going to negotiate with the company."

Federal subsidies, channeled through the states, also ease the pain, making layoffs seem more routine. The money goes not only for retraining but increasingly for counseling, often on the shop floor right after a layoff is announced. Some of the Federal money pays the wages of labor union staff members involved in retraining. But despite all the help, regaining the old wage rarely happens.

The largest group of former Thomson workers, more than 500, has taken early retirement, accepting lump-sum pension payments of $80,000 or less instead of the $90,000 or more they would have received at full retirement. Ms. Wright is in a group of 200 men and women who are either unemployed or going to school to qualify for new careers, according to the company and the union, the International Brotherhood of Electrical Workers. And finally there are 200 ex-Thomson workers who have found new jobs at lower pay.

Many in this group joined Cook Inc., a nonunion shop that makes medical catheters in Bloomington, and pays $6 to $8 an hour. But some, like Martie

---

°**the Asian crisis:** The severe economic downturn that began in 1997 in several large Asian nations, including Indonesia, Thailand, and Japan. °**production capacity:** The amount of space, resources, and equipment manufacturers devote to producing their products. In part because of the Asian crisis, some manufacturers no longer needed so much production capacity.

Figure 7.9
By the Numbers

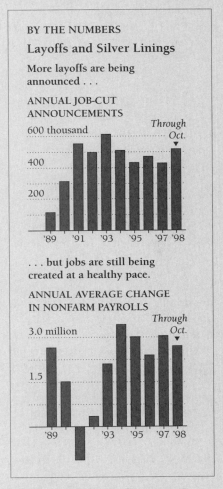

BY THE NUMBERS

Layoffs and Silver Linings

More layoffs are being announced . . .

ANNUAL JOB-CUT
ANNOUNCEMENTS

600 thousand   *Through Oct.* ▼

400

200

'89   '91   '93   '95   '97 '98

. . . but jobs are still being created at a healthy pace.

ANNUAL AVERAGE CHANGE
IN NONFARM PAYROLLS

3.0 million   *Through Oct.* ▼

1.5

'89   '93   '95   '97 '98

Sources: Challenger, Gray & Christmas Inc.; Bureau of Labor Statistics

Hammer, a 46-year-old divorced woman with no children, were more adventuresome.

Ms. Hammer, who drove a forklift at Thomson for 17 years, took a four-month course in truck driving, and now drives a tractor-trailer cross-country for the Celedon Corporation, one of numerous truckers here, all of which seem constantly short of drivers.

Her life has changed. Instead of 15 being home every evening—she owns a house on the White River near Bloomington—she is on the road for 10 days, sleeping in a bunk in her tractor cab, then at home for two days. That is a disruption, she says, to her social life. And her pay is less: Not quite $400 a week, compared with her Thomson wage of $424, excluding overtime, which in her case averaged 15 hours a week.

"I don't mind driving a truck," she said. "A lot of people would not do it, but I am trying to get back to where I was at Thomson. It takes away from your self-esteem until you find something as good, or better. You know there has to be something better."

Maybe. Thomson's ex-employees have been engaged in this odyssey to regain their old wages for only eight months. Six hundred former Maytag Corporation employees have been struggling for two years, with little more to show for it. Their Maytag jobs ended in December 1996, when the company closed a stove factory in Indianapolis and, to cut costs and improve efficiency, moved the operation to a nonunion Maytag stove factory in Tennessee.

"We had 400 of the 600 workers placed in jobs in less than a year; we were happy about that," said Mr. Gigerich, who worked with the Private Industry Council, a local group of union and corporate representatives that lent a hand. But today few of the former Maytag workers earn the $34,000 annually they averaged at Maytag.

The best paid, roughly a third of the old work force, earn about $25,000, mostly at the numerous machine tool shops in this area, Mr. Gigerich said. Another group found work at about $22,000 in warehouses and distribution centers, as forklift drivers or loading trucks. And a third group earns about $20,000 in retail stores or at the telephone customer service centers and data processing operations that have proliferated in this area.

In hindsight, the Maytag layoff— [20] announced in February 1996, nine months before the plant closed—was a turning point, the first significant example in greater Indianapolis of the softer approach to downsizing. A year earlier, the First Data Corporation, which employed 1,000 people at a telephone service center here, had closed the operation on short notice without first notifying the local government. Downsized workers told hardship stories in television interviews, and city officials were publicly critical.

The officials wanted less confrontation. And Maytag obliged. Apart from the nine-month lead time, Maytag sweetened the severance package beyond what the contract with the Sheet Metal Workers Union required. The company also piled on overtime in the final months to stockpile stoves and to give workers extra money to pay off debts and build up nest eggs— an opportunity most took. Finally, the company participated in a worker-management committee that supervised retraining and counseling. A $1 million Federal grant financed the endeavor.

"We were trying to tell that work force that you could not have done any-thing to prevent the move," said Thomas Schwartz, a Maytag spokesman. "That plant closing, and the way we worked with the city, and the employee group, that is as close to a model as I can come up with."

That still leaves Margaret Edens and her husband, Clifford, struggling. Both had worked at Maytag, she assembling stove counters at $12.50 an hour, he repairing damaged stoves at $13.13 an hour. Both lost their jobs. They finished up in a marathon of overtime and then, when the end came, they used some of the accumulated pay to finance a week's vacation in the Southwest—the Grand Canyon, Las Vegas, Nev., Monument Valley—before facing their new, diminished life.

Mrs. Edens, who is 44, is the sort of worker that corporate managers and union officials point to as ideal in a downsizing situation. She is among a minority, they say, with the self-discipline and focus to benefit from job training, and also among a minority with the emotional fortitude to overcome the trauma of losing a pay package she cannot easily replace, and yet get on with life.

After Maytag announced the clos- [25] ing, Mrs. Edens became a union representative on the transition committee. For a while, she drew a Federally subsidized salary as a case manager, counseling laid-off workers, including some from Maytag—work she loved. Now she is a part-time claims taker in the state employment office, earning $8.05 an hour, without benefits. Her goal is to work full time in the employment office, with benefits, although the pay, she says, will probably be less than what she earned at Maytag.

"We used to make money and our life style just rose," Mrs. Edens said. "Now when I get up, it is, 'How much do we have to earn to get by?' And that is $8 or $9 an hour for each of us just to maintain a middle-of-the-road life. We are just managing to do that."

Clifford Edens, also 44, reacted to the downsizing the way many workers do. He shunned job training or counseling, and did not accept, until months later, that he would probably never match his Maytag earnings and company-paid health insurance. "You work so long for a company, you lose touch with the job market," he said. He had entered the factory in 1972, right out of high school.

Mr. Edens had hoped to shift into social work, but without more schooling, he said, the pay was an "unrealis-tic" $7.50 an hour at best. He took a job at a Goodwill Industries factory, as a group leader at $9 an hour, helping disabled workers keep an assembly line going. But the work was too stressful and he soon left.

Finally, he learned from a friend of an opening at Flexalloy Inc., as an inspector of the giant bolts and other fasteners the company supplies for bridge and building construction. There was an on-the-job training requirement, and a Federal training grant helped for a while to pay Mr. Edens's starting wage of $9.25 an hour. That was in September of last year; he now earns just over $10, and pays $12 a week for health insurance.

"I am treated very well at this com- 30 pany," Mr. Edens said, allowing himself a little optimism. "There are positions there that pay $13 an hour or more that I could possibly attain."

MOST WORKERS FIND A SENSE OF SECURITY IN CORPORATE LIFE

Sanford M. Jacoby

Sanford Jacoby, a professor of management, history, and public policy at the University of California, Los Angeles, is a well-known scholar and commentator on the U.S. economy. Among his books are Employing Bureaucracy: Managers, Unions, and the Transformation of Work in American Industry, 1900–1945 *(1985) and* Modern Manors: Welfare Capitalism since the New Deal *(1997). This reading was published in 1998 as a column in the* Los Angeles Times.

Jacoby has some reservations about recent reports, like those of Barbara Rudolph, Tony Horwitz, and Louis Uchitelle, suggesting that job security is a thing of the past. Using statistics that differ from those in such reports, he argues that most employees are in long-term jobs with benefits. He readily acknowledges that employees must now live with less security and assume greater risks; however, he insists that "welfare capitalism"—that is, an economic system in which employers, rather than government, provide most of the secure jobs as well as the health and retirement benefits—is still alive and well.

As you read, try to understand why Jacoby believes that a high degree of job security still exists in the U.S. economy. Note the reasons why he thinks welfare capitalism will continue to be the dominant mode of employment.

Despite low unemployment rates, Americans remain anxious about job security. The latest figures show that mass layoffs are at the same level as in the 1993 recession, while the share of employees who say they are frequently concerned about layoffs has risen from 20% in 1990 to 43% this year. Accompanying the rise is continuing unease about the availability of "good" jobs: career-type positions that offer decent wages and benefits. Politicians are adept at tapping into this anxiety, as in 1996, when Patrick Buchanan, then running for the GOP presidential nomination, chided AT&T as "corporate butchers" for a plan to lay off 40,000 workers.

The notion that corporations have responsibilities to employees is hardly new or radical. Its roots lie deep in the American past—back a century or more—when employers first began systematically to provide stable jobs and benefits such as health and pension programs and company housing. The system was known as "welfare capitalism." To Americans concerned about the labor question of the early 20th century, welfare capitalism offered a distinctively American answer: The business corporation, rather than government or trade unions, would be the source of security in America's industrializing society. Challenged by the rise of mass unions and social insurance programs during the 1930s, welfare capitalism nevertheless proved resilient. Unions became partners in the administration of benefit programs, while Social Security became a complement to, not a substitute for, corporate benefit programs.

During the past 15 years, however, welfare capitalism has experienced its most critical test since the 1930s. Heightened competition, mergers and rapid technological change have caused layoffs throughout American industry. These layoffs were—and are—a shock to those who thought themselves immune from job loss. Middle-level managers found that the elimination of their jobs was often the chief goal of industrial restructuring. Furthering the sense of insecurity is the expansion of nonstandard jobs (part-time, temporary or contractual), which today account for about 20% of employment. Those in nonstandard jobs are far less likely to receive health and pension benefits. Even in standard jobs, research indicates benefit coverage has dropped sharply for less educated males.

Yet reports of welfare capitalism's demise are exaggerated. We are not moving to an economy made up only of short-term jobs and indifferent employers. True, the mix is shifting. But as economists often warn, don't confuse stocks (in this case, our endowment of jobs) and flows (the jobs being created or destroyed in the current period). The stocks usually dwarf the flows.

Take, for example, the data on 5 employee job tenure, a good gauge of long-term employment. The data show little change in job duration in the 1980s and only a moderate decline in long-term stability in the first half of the 1990s, primarily among older males. The share of men employed more than 10 years with the same employer fell from 50% in 1979 to 40% in 1996; for women, however, this share *increased* slightly, from 29% to 31%. Focusing on flows, one sees a modest, albeit unprecedented, drop in the prevalence of career jobs; focusing on stocks, one sees two-thirds of the labor force still employed in long-term jobs.

As for nonstandard employment, while it has grown since 1970, the increase has been small. Temporary help and day labor currently account for less than 3% of employment; regular part-time work comprises an additional 13%. Such jobs do not constitute a replacement for regular, full-time work.

Some industries — like Silicon Valley — have high employee turnover, but most of today's workers are not job hoppers. One survey this year found that the proportion of young workers who said they were very likely to leave their employer within the next year was the same as in 1977 (22%). About two-thirds of all employees say that they definitely will stay put for the coming year.

What about fringe benefits? The stock/flow distinction is relevant here as well. Employers — not government, unions or individuals — are still the linchpin of our health insurance system and still a major provider of old-age pensions. Sixty-nine percent of full-time workers receive employer-provided health insurance; for pension coverage, the corresponding figure is 63%. And while some employers are cutting benefits, others are adopting new ones, such as flextime for parents.

Rather than killing welfare capitalism, what employers are doing today is preserving its basic structure but shifting more risk to employees. Thus, career jobs still abound, but they no longer come with an iron-clad guarantee of permanence. Employers still insure the majority of U.S. employees but are asking them to shoulder more risk via defined-contribution pension plans° and higher deductibles on health insurance.° And a larger proportion of employee pay is now "at risk," that is, contingent on profit levels and stock prices.

Does this mean, then, that all risk 10 eventually will be shifted to employees and that employers no longer will provide career jobs and fringe benefits? The short answer is: no. To assume that current trends will continue without limit is a *reductio ad absurdum*° (just as it would have been absurd to predict in the 1940s

---

° **defined-contribution pension plans:** A pension plan to which the employee contributes a specific amount at each pay period. Some employers also contribute.   ° **deductibles on health insurance:** Amount of medical costs the insured must themselves pay before the insurer will begin to pay. ° *reductio ad absurdum:* An idea carried to an absurd extreme.

that all jobs would become career positions). That's because there are economic and political limits to the risk reallocation process currently underway.

One such limit is based on the economics of managing a work force. New workers have to be trained, which makes employee turnover costly. Employee skills are more important today than in the past, especially in fast-changing situations. Even after extensive layoffs, companies like AT&T and IBM have preserved career ladders and fringe benefits because there is plenty of evidence that these practices boost corporate performance.

Pundits claim that the future lies with sectors like Silicon Valley and Wall Street. Here, workers are younger and highly educated. They move easily from job to job, and some employers welcome such mobility because it keeps them abreast of competitors. Workers are relatively well paid and can afford funding their own health and pension plans.

But these workers are atypical, and the companies employing them are dissimilar from the firms that comprise the bulk of the U.S. economy. Today, most American companies are service providers of one sort or another. Their success depends less on technological breakthroughs than on customer attraction and retention. Experienced and satisfied employees are much better at retaining customers than fresh recruits.

Even high-technology companies are finding that employee turnover can be detrimental. Companies like Cisco Systems, a high-technology company, and SAS, a software giant, are throwbacks to the heyday of welfare capitalism. They offer exercise facilities, dining rooms with live music, even company doctors and massage therapists. To retain potentially mobile workers, they try to accommodate employees' career shifts via transfers within the company. As one SAS manager said, "At 5 p.m., 95% of our assets walk out the door. We have to have an environment that makes them want to walk back in the door the next morning."

Finally, there are political limits to 15 the risk shifting that employers can pursue. Among the advanced nations, the United States has the lowest unionization rate and the smallest share of health and retirement insurance funded by government. Corporate managers know—or may eventually discover—that if they let welfare capitalism wither, government and unions will seek to fill the gap. In fact, unions are more actively engaged in organizing than at any time since the 1970s, while politicians—from Republican Buchanan to Democratic House Minority Leader Richard Gephardt—are poised to revisit the issue of employer responsibility in next year's presidential campaign.°

Ironically, public concern over downsizing and other forms of risk shifting demonstrates that Americans retain their faith in welfare capitalism as an economic ideal. There still is widespread support for the notion that corporations should remain the keystone of economic security in American society.

°**next year's presidential campaign:** The campaign for the election in 2000.

SKILLED WORKERS WATCH THEIR JOBS MIGRATE OVERSEAS

Keith Bradsher

Keith Bradsher, Detroit bureau chief for the New York Times, *writes about transportation, economic policy, and telecommunications. In Detroit, the traditional home of America's automobile industry, Bradsher specializes in reporting on the global auto industry. In 1997 he won the George Polk Award for his stories on "the human and financial toll sport utility vehicles and light trucks take on the nation's roadways."*

A prominent, long-term feature of the new economy is the displacement of jobs abroad. More and more American corporations have moved all or part of their production outside the country, in order to increase their profits by paying lower wages to workers in other countries. Both low-skilled assembly-line work and high-skilled computer work have migrated. In this 1995 New York Times *report, Bradsher focuses primarily on the migration of jobs in computer programming and data processing. As examples of this practice, he cites three major corporations: Texas Instruments, Sea-Land Services, and Motorola.*

As you read, focus on what kinds of work are being shipped outside the country and the advantages that corporations claim such practices give them. Notice, too, what direct impact this feature of the new economy has had on skilled white-collar workers in the United States.

WASHINGTON, AUG. 27 – Texas Instruments is designing some of its more sophisticated computer chips in India. Motorola Inc. recently set up computer-programming and equipment-design centers in China, India, Singapore, Hong Kong, Taiwan and Australia, and it is looking for a site in South America.

And while big American banks already process some account statements overseas, large accounting firms and insurance companies are looking at ways to prepare American tax returns and handle American insurance claims in East Asia.

The day may yet arrive when millions of Americans will desert their offices for laptops in exotic lands. But corporate America has already made half of that vision a reality, many economists say. It is getting a lot of work done on foreign shores — but not by Americans. Instead, corporations are paying educated locals to do the same chores for a fraction of the cost.

The new tools of the information age were supposed to help the United States regain an edge in international competition. And while that has happened in many advanced-technology industries, the combination of powerful personal computers and high-capacity undersea telephone cables is also subjecting millions of white-collar Americans to the same global wage pressures that their blue-collar counterparts have long faced. As with steel and garment workers, the white-collar workers' positions and salaries increasingly depend on whether they can justify their higher pay with higher productivity.

The transfer of semi-skilled jobs 5 overseas is hardly new. American companies have long assembled computer circuit boards in Malaysia, for example, and Western financial-services concerns have done processing work in Singapore.

But consulting firms say the shift is taking place at an accelerating rate and involves ever-higher-paying jobs. Constant improvements in computers and communications, particularly modems, have made it easier and cheaper to move large quantities of computer data, even for complex engineering designs. And foreign workers are designing more advanced products, like chips for complex graphic and multimedia applications.

"There's a really strong parallel to the 1960's and 1970's when U.S. manufacturers sent everything offshore," said Thomas G. Watrous, the managing partner of the Andersen Consulting office in Manila. "The difference is it's being done electronically."

Such moves can mean real pain for some Americans. When Sea-Land Services Inc. asked Jessie B. Lindsay, a longtime computer programmer for the company, to sign form letters to Congress last winter supporting legislation to protect American shipping jobs from foreign competition, she loyally agreed.

But a week later, Sea-Land, a unit of the CSX Corporation, announced that it was shutting down her division in Elizabeth, N.J., laying off most of the 325 employees and subcontracting the work to programmers in India and the Philippines. Mrs. Lindsay was offered a job at least temporarily in Charlotte, N.C., to make sure the transition went smoothly, but quit because she had a baby and was reluctant to move.

"I felt betrayed," Mrs. Lindsay said. 10 Her family faced that situation twice last winter. Her husband, William F. Lindsay, also left his programming job at the American International Group when it, a large insurance company, brought programmers from India to his office and began training them to replace the American workers.

Many fear that the growing tendency of corporations to farm out tasks to developing countries is widening the gap even further between the rich and everybody else in American society by eliminating some categories of high-skill, high-wage jobs that make up the heart of the middle class. But the temptation to use cheap foreign labor is too great for companies that are desperate to stay competitive in an increasingly global marketplace.

India is fertile ground for these companies because it inherited a strong English-language school system from the days of British rule, and has emphasized mathematical education since then. Yet computer scientists trained at Indian universities come relatively cheap. Experienced programmers command salaries of $1,200 to $1,500 a month, compared with $4,000 to $6,000, or even $10,000 for stars, in the United States. The result has been explosive growth in the number of Indians working on computer programs, mainly for the American market, to nearly 75,000 today from several thousand in the early 1980's.

New jobs overseas do not necessarily mean the elimination of jobs in the United States, of course. Indeed, while Sea-Land laid off many of its programmers, Motorola and Texas Instruments are expanding in the United States as well as abroad and attribute their overseas moves in part to a scarcity of good engineers in the United States.

"Software applications are growing so quickly that we're nowhere near a finite number of jobs to be parceled out around the globe," Labor Secretary Robert B. Reich° said in an interview.

Some of the best-paid computer 15 jobs in the United States require writing original programs for a customer's precise needs, and these jobs tend to be staying, experts said.

But rapidly evolving computer technologies are turning skilled tasks into routine work that can easily be shipped overseas. Mainframe computing jobs like Mrs. Lindsay's are particularly vulnerable because many companies are changing over to networks of desktop computers, and many Asian programmers specialize in adapting software to run on different computers.

All of this keeps the pressure on the United States to maintain its technological edge over the rest of the world.

Mr. Reich contends that many high-technology jobs will inevitably remain in the United States because electronic mail and facsimile machines are no substitute for working side by side with customers and colleagues. "It's the rubbing of shoulders, the cup of coffee over a lunch counter, where the spark of innovation occurs," he said.

Still, for many tasks, companies like Sea-Land say they must spread their work to lower-cost countries to stay competitive. "Any service like this we would shop on a worldwide basis," said M. Clint Eisenhauer, a spokesman for Sea-Land.

The exodus of white-collar jobs to 20 developing countries troubles some economists. Even those who dismissed the warnings of politicians like Ross Perot° and Patrick J. Buchanan° that dismantling North American trade barriers would lead to a flight of blue-collar jobs to Mexico say the danger is all too real for skilled labor.

These economists argue that companies will often want to keep their factories in the United States to be close to good roads and railways that can supply their raw materials and deliver their goods to market. But, they add, the growing part of the economy based on ideas and information does not always need such physical proximity.

Prof. Jagdish Bhagwati of Columbia University, a critic of the notion that freer trade jeopardizes unskilled labor, for example, takes a different stance when it comes to skilled workers, particularly in the computer industry.

°**Robert B. Reich:** Secretary of labor (1993–96) during President Clinton's first term.   °**Ross Perot:** Unsuccessful Independent Party candidate for president in 1992 and 1996.   °**Patrick J. Buchanan:** An unsuccessful 1996 candidate for the Republican Party's nomination for president.

"You're definitely seeing an enormous integration of the markets, and therefore a drag on the real wages here of the semiskilled, of the computer programmers, of the skilled," he said.

Texas Instruments, for example, does not have to worry about infrastructure° for its computer-chip-designing operation in Bangalore, India. All it needs is a private satellite link. The system works so well that the company has announced plans to expand the Bangalore office by 40 percent, to 350 workers.

Rick Younts, the executive vice president for international operations at Motorola, said it was not just lower wages that made Asian sites so attractive. Engineers in the United States can work on a project during the day, then send it electronically for more work in Asia while they sleep. As a result, projects can be completed in up to 40 percent less time, said S. Remadorai, the deputy chief operating officer of Tata Consulting Services in Bombay.

Until recently, many such companies were reluctant to hire foreigners. "The arrogance that we used to have, that nobody could be as good as we were, except maybe a European, is all going away now," said Edith Holloman, the Washington representative of the American Engineering Association, a trade group based in Fort Worth.

To be sure, skilled American workers maintain many advantages over their foreign counterparts and also benefit from the upgrading abroad through increased demand for their own output.

For now, though, the increased foreign competition has set off a political backlash in the United States. The Software Professionals' Political Action Committee, a lobbying group in Austin, Tex., wants to limit immigration visas for computer programmers. Sea-Land, American International and other companies have brought foreign workers into the United States temporarily under such visas for training, before sending them back to do their jobs in their home countries.

But the overall direction of American immigration policy in recent years has been to encourage skilled workers to come to the United States and discourage unskilled workers.

And even if policy makers wanted to, it might well be impossible to build walls around the country. Clearly, Professor Bhagwati said, American companies will go wherever they can find the best deals. "This is relentless," he said.

°**infrastructure**: Buildings, equipment, parking lots, roads.

A 20-YEAR G.M. PARTS MIGRATION
TO MEXICO

Sam Dillon

Sam Dillon, Mexico City bureau chief of the New York Times, *has twice been part of a Pulitzer Prize–winning team of reporters: in 1987 at the* Miami Herald *for coverage of the Iran-Contra affair and in 1998 at the* New York Times *for reports on drug corruption in Mexico. He also has written* Commandos: The CIA and Nicaragua's Contra Rebels *(1991), which won the Overseas Press Club's 1991 Award for Best Book on Foreign Affairs.*

Writing in the New York Times *in 1998 at the time of a strike by the United Auto Workers (UAW) against General Motors Corporation (GM), Dillon reports on GM's shifting of production, especially for auto parts, from U.S. plants to plants in Mexico. These major changes at GM reflect the increasing numbers of U.S. manufacturers who are producing parts or complete products in Mexican factories, known as* maquiladoras, *which are owned by U.S. manufacturers. (*Twin Plant News *reports that, at the end of 1997, 2,624 maquiladoras employed one million Mexican workers.)*

The pay differences between Mexican and U.S. workers are striking—from as low as $8 to $180 or more for an eight-hour day. Since 1935 GM has been assembling cars in Mexico to sell to Mexican consumers, but only in 1978 did it begin producing parts to ship to its U.S. assembly plants.

As you read, pay attention to how GM justifies producing car parts in Mexico rather than in U.S. plants and what recourse U.S. workers have had in responding to the loss of their jobs.

MATAMOROS, MEXICO, JUNE 20—In one of General Motors' sprawling auto parts plants in a Matamoros industrial park just south of the Rio Grande, thousands of Mexican workers earn $1 to $2 an hour producing instrument panels and steering wheels for G.M. cars and trucks.

Until just a few years ago, United States workers earning close to $22 an hour at G.M.'s Delphi East factory in Flint, Mich., made the instrument panels. And those at a plant to the north in Saginaw produced the steering wheels.

G.M.'s shift of production from Flint and Saginaw to this border city facing Brownsville, Tex., was part of a sweeping 20-year transfer of its United States auto parts industry across the border. Since 1978, General Motors has built more than 50 parts factories in Mexico, which today employ 72,000 workers, making its parts subsidiary, Delphi Automotive Services, Mexico's largest private employer.

Other companies from the United States have, of course, also moved plants to Mexico. The Ford Motor

Company has 11 parts factories in Mexico; Chrysler has none.

The transfer of production to Mexico and other countries has become a focus of the United Automobile Workers' strike against G.M., which began at a stamping plant in Flint and at the Delphi East factory. U.A.W. officials in the United States have accused General Motors of "putting America last."

In Mexico, where the strike has idled 23,000 workers at two dozen Delphi plants, managers have told workers that the union is demanding that G.M. close its Mexican plants and return its parts production to the United States, said Juan Villafuerte Morales, a union officer representing workers at Delphi's Matamoros factories. The plants have been partly idled by the strike in Flint.

"Most of our workers understand that they're doing work that used to be done in United States factories because managers explain that to them on the plant floor," Mr. Villafuerte said. "And let me tell you, the jobs are very welcome here."

General Motors says that transferring production south has enabled it to cut costs in labor-intensive assembly production, compete more effectively against Ford, Chrysler and Japanese auto makers, and keep engineering and other operations in the United States.

The financial advantages of producing parts in Mexico are substantial, and some economists say that the North American Free Trade Agreement, which went into effect in January 1994, has only increased them. Many plants have no union, and those that do are represented by the Confederation of Mexican Workers, which is controlled by Mexico's ruling Institutional Revolutionary Party and works with the Government to avoid strikes. The union has kept the U.A.W. at arm's length.

Thousands of Mexican workers at G.M. and other United States-owned factories live in dirt-floor shacks in slums ringing the industrial parks where they work. Yet many say that they are delighted to have their jobs, which often start at Mexico's minimum wage of $3.40 a day but can pay experienced workers several times that. A Delphi spokesman said the company would in the next 18 months help 7,000 employees buy their own homes.

"It's a good job," said a 23-year-old woman who earns $1.36 an hour painting buttons on car radios at Deltronicos de Matamoros, a Delphi plant. The woman, who asked that her name not be used during an interview at her one-room wood-frame shed in a gritty, wind-blown Matamoros squatters' settlement, said the choking smell of solvents at her work station gave her headaches. "It's difficult work," she said. "But I'm glad to have it."

G.M. opened its first factory in Mexico in 1935, assembling trucks in the capital from parts imported from the United States. After a 1962 Mexican law required foreign auto makers to increase the local content of their vehicles, G.M. built three engine and vehicle plants in the 1960's and 70's. The new plants, like similar factories built by Ford and Chrysler, assembled vehicles for the Mexican market. In the decades since, G.M. has continued to assemble vehicles in Mexico.

But in the late 70's, in response to a 1965 law encouraging foreign manufacturers to produce goods here for export tax-free, General Motors changed strategy. "G.M. began to see Mexico as a supplier for its U.S. vehicle assembly plants, and in the 1980's built an entire parts industry here," said Arnulfo Arteaga, a Mexico City professor who studies the auto industry. "Now, Delphi's Mexican plants basically turn out parts once produced in the United States."

G.M. erected its first Mexican parts plant, to assemble wiring systems, in the large border city of Juárez in 1978.

"What is now Delphi Automotive 15 had run into unprecedented competition," said Michael J. Hissam, a spokesman at Delphi's Mexican headquarters in Juárez. "We embarked on a plan to reduce costs by focusing final assembly in Mexico while keeping our more capital-intensive engineering, tooling and prototyping activities in the U.S. Did we come to Mexico for lower labor costs? Yes. But we also found something else — excellent Mexican management and a dedicated Mexican work force."

Nicholas Lobaccaro, an auto industry analyst with Merrill Lynch, said General Motors had no choice but to seek lower-cost labor for parts production. "G.M. is not doing anything that their competitors and that independent auto suppliers aren't doing," Mr. Lobaccaro said, adding:

"There's been tremendous pressure on parts pricing. To compete in the global economy, you need labor to be paid commensurate with value added. And you can't pay $46 an hour to do wire harnesses."

Dozens of other G.M. parts plants would be built across northern Mexico in the years that followed. In Matamoros, four Delphi plants were built in an industrial park near the intersection of Ohio Street and Michigan Avenue.

One Delphi plant, Componentes Mecanicos, opened in 1980. About 10 years later, Delphi began shifting production of instrument panels to the factory from Delphi East in Flint, said Larry Mathews, a spokesman for Flint's U.A.W. Local 651, which is currently on strike.

"They just crated the equipment, 20 hoisted it onto a tractor-trailer, and sent it away to Mexico," Mr. Mathews said. "There's hardly anybody at this plant who hasn't seen machinery moving out in a crate with an address on it that says 'Mexico.'"

In the 1970's, Mr. Mathews added, the Delphi East plant had 13,000 workers; today, it has fewer than 6,000.

A 37-year-old worker at Componentes Mecanicos, who asked that his name be withheld, said in an interview outside his two-room Matamoros home that if he qualified for a weekly attendance bonus, he earned about $1.90 an hour. Newly hired workers receive $1.05 an hour, he said. His wife also works at a G.M. assembly plant in Matamoros, and by pooling salaries, the couple has managed to rise slightly above subsistence. They own a battered Ford pickup truck, and although their home has no indoor plumbing, they have equipped it with a television set and an electric fan. He coaches his three sons in a soccer league.

Next door to Componentes Mecanicos is the Deltronicos plant, built in 1979. In the mid-1980's, G.M. shifted much of its car radio production from its Delco plant in Kokomo, Ind., to Deltronicos, U.A.W. officials said. The work force at Kokomo has dropped to 4,800 from 11,000 in 1977, the union said. The Deltronicos plant employs 5,400 workers.

Across the street from Deltronicos is a Matamoros plant owned by the Trico Products Corporation of Buffalo, a unit of Tomkins P.L.C., which supplies windshield wipers to G.M. as well as Ford and Chrysler. The transfer of much of Trico's production to Mexico since 1987, which came despite entreaties from Buffalo city officials, has reduced Trico's Buffalo work force to 200 from 2,400, U.A.W. officials said.

Misaela Castro Margaro, who is 21, 25 earned $1.05 an hour fitting vinyl blades onto wiper assemblies at the Matamoros plant until her three-month contract expired earlier this month. She said the work was hard but she missed her job.

"I loved that plant," she said.

Figure 7.10

General Motors has four assembly plants and more than fifty parts factories in Mexico; its parts subsidiary, Delphi Automotive Services, is Mexico's largest private employer. There are eighteen Delphi plants in Juárez alone, six in Reynosa, five in Chihuahua and four in Matamoros.

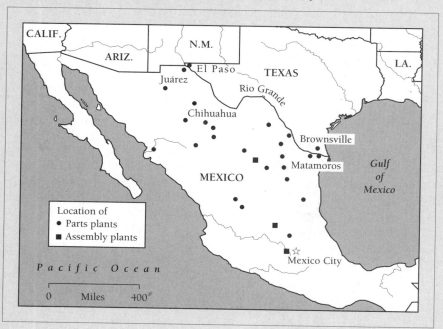

POLITICAL CARTOONS
ABOUT THE RESTRUCTURED ECONOMY

Political cartoons can reinforce your understanding of the restructured economy, both adding information and expressing a point of view on economic trends and controversies. Writers on the economy can assume that readers know little if anything about the wealth gap or contingent work. Cartoonists, however, must assume that you know something about the new economy and even about current debates over what it may mean for the future of work in America. Through stylized drawings and sharply tuned language, cartoonists suggest their central point, leaving much for readers to infer. Leading to laughs or groans of recognition, these inferences are part of the pleasure of reading cartoons.

The following three cartoons are typical of hundreds that have been published in the last several years relating to the new economy. Analyze them yourself and discuss them with your classmates. If one turns out to be relevant to the argument you develop about the consequences of the new economy, consider including it in your essay. Task 13 in the writer's notebook suggestions that follow these cartoons outlines a strategy for reading political cartoons critically.

Figure 7.11

Figure 7.12

Figure 7.13

Understanding the Restructured Economy

The following tasks are designed to help you think about the readings and identify and start to work up material you might use in your own essay. If you need help with tasks that require summarizing, see Appendix 1.

1. *Interview people from an earlier generation.* As you begin reading about the new economy, choose at least two people in their mid- to late forties or fifties whose occupation and standard of living you know something about. With a list of key questions to guide you, interview these two people in person, by phone, or online. Take notes in your notebook as you talk, including as many details as possible. Your goal is to discover how the person has been affected by economic changes of the sort you have now read about. Ask about the person's occupation, whether job prospects have improved for that occupation or not, and what future job prospects seem to be. Find out about how the person's jobs have changed over the years in terms of locations, working conditions, and wages. Ask the person to reflect on his or her work history and the economy in general. The readings may suggest further questions.

   Immediately after each interview take a few minutes to add notes that you were not able to write down during the rush of the conversation. (The more detailed and specific your notes, the more likely you can use information from the interview in your essay.) Then review all of your notes and write several sentences about your most surprising or significant discoveries.

2. *Make a list from Andrew Hacker's scenario.* In paragraphs 5–7, Hacker surveys what he calls "these new configurations," the same thing we mean in this chapter by "the restructured economy." Reread the paragraphs carefully. Then list some prominent features of the reconfigured or restructured economy, using your own words or those in the text. Then single out the feature that most surprised, pleased, troubled, or puzzled you and write a few sentences exploring your reaction.

3. *Summarize part of Lawrence R. Mishel, Jared Bernstein, and John Schmitt's report.* Some economists have criticized reports like this one for failing to take account of the fact that an individual's income nearly always grows from one decade to the next. Mishel et al. attempt to answer this criticism in paragraphs 21–26 and Table 7.5. Summarize these paragraphs. (In this chapter, choose "longer summary" in Appendix 1 as the model for summarizing.)

4. *Describe the information in one of Edward N. Wolff's graphics.* Look at Wolff's Figure 7.4, "Winners and Losers in the 1980s" and then write several sentences explaining the information it presents. Be sure that your explanation contrasts the percent of wealth growth to the percent of income growth.

5. *List key information in Janice Castro's report.* To gain a better understanding of contingent work, reread Castro's article, focusing on the advantages and disadvantages of contingent work for both workers and employers. For each group, create a list of advantages and one of disadvantages. Include the paragraph number of each item in your lists.

6. *Collect information on personal experiences with contingent work.* After reading the Castro article, describe a part-time or contingent full-time job you hold or have held, if any. Give specific details about this job: your age, your duties, working conditions, pay, people with whom you worked, and so forth. At the time you held

the job, what were the advantages and/or disadvantages for you personally? What was the ratio of part-time or contingent full-time jobs to permanent jobs where you worked? Alternatively, interview (in person or by phone) a business owner who employs or has employed contingent full-time workers. Find out his or her responses to specific issues raised in the Castro article. Take notes during the interview and then write a few sentences about what you learned. As another alternative, interview someone you know who has a contingent full-time job and would like to have a permanent full-time job. The Castro article will suggest questions you might ask. Take notes during the interview and then write a few sentences that present your interviewee's story. (The more detailed and specific your notes, the more likely you can use information from the interview in your essay.)

7. *List important information from Barbara Rudolph's reading.* Rudolph details the characteristics of job security as well as job insecurity. As you reread paragraphs 9–19, list in a word or phrase the main characteristics of job security. As you reread paragraphs 20–34, list the main characteristics of job insecurity. Then write a few sentences that capture the essence of the contrast.

8. *React to the story of an unemployed manager profiled by Tony Horwitz.* Reread paragraphs 14–22, 24, and 32–34, in which Horwitz profiles Jerry Young. Describe Mr. Young's story briefly and then write a few more sentences reacting to his case. Among the other older managers Horwitz profiles, does Mr. Young seem typical? Why do you think he wants to go back to work? Do you think he has correctly assessed the reasons why he has not been hired? Do you think his resentment is justified? What do you make of the adjustments he has made in his life?

9. *Summarize information in Louis Uchitelle's report.* Uchitelle profiles blue-collar workers to illustrate several general points about blue-collar job insecurity, primarily in paragraphs 4–11 and 17–22. Summarize the information in these paragraphs.

10. *Explain part of Sanford M. Jacoby's argument and react to it.* Jacoby argues that job security will remain an important goal of American businesses because economic and political limits prevent them from doing otherwise. Explain briefly what Jacoby means by economic limits (paragraphs 11–14) and political limits (paragraphs 15–16). Given what you have learned about job insecurity from the Rudolph, Horwitz, and Uchitelle readings, your personal experience, and the interviews you may have conducted, write a few sentences about what you find convincing and unconvincing in Jacoby's argument.

11. *List important facts from Keith Bradsher's report.* Reread Bradsher's essay to find all the reasons — technological, cultural, economic — that U.S. corporations are sending increasing amounts of their computer programming and data entry work to workers in other countries. List each reason in a word or brief phrase.

12. *Collect facts about Mexican workers from Sam Dillon's report.* To gain a deeper understanding of the lives of Mexican workers employed by U.S.-owned factories in Mexico, reread Dillon's report and list facts in these categories: wages (exact hourly wages for different jobs), living conditions, working conditions, and attitudes about work.

13. *Describe and interpret a political cartoon.* Write a page or so about one of the cartoons that precede this writer's notebook section. Describe its content, both

visual and written, and make inferences about the intended meaning and about the cartoonist's apparent purpose. For reading cartoons closely and critically, these questions should prove helpful:

- If the cartoon is presented in two or more panels, what story do they tell?
- If people are present, how are they alike and different? Look closely at their clothing, hairstyles, gestures, and facial expressions. Note how people's actions and appearance change from panel to panel.
- Who might the people represent or symbolize? Do any of the people sug- gest stereotypes?
- What kind of language does the cartoon include? Consider dialogue, titles, labels, dates, or any other use of language. Who talks most, least, not at all? Is the language in any way ironic?
- What is the scene or setting? What kind of space is represented, and how are the people drawn in relation to each other? What objects are present?
- What does the cartoonist seem to assume readers know about the subject or topic of the cartoon? What information is supplied?
- What social or political point of view is expressed by the cartoon? What seems to be the cartoonist's purpose?

UNDERSTANDING GENERATIONAL COMPETITION

There is a great deal of evidence—as well as concern—that younger genera- tions of Americans may be more seriously affected than older generations by the restructured economy. Therefore, in addition to the general background on the economy, you need to understand how your generation may be affected.

In speculating about the life opportunities of your generation, the concept of generations is useful because since World War II, which ended in 1945, dif- ferent generations have faced differing degrees of prosperity. You may already be familiar with some of these generational differences because of recent debates about reforming Social Security—debates arising in part because it is possible that the generation now entering old age will take a larger share of resources than the generations currently under forty. Similarly, the baby boomers born after World War II and up into the 1960s are a particularly large generation that is having a major effect on every American's economic prospects. After the year 2000, as the baby boomers reach retirement age, the percentage of Americans who are retired—and requiring Social Security, increased medical care, even expanded leisure activities—will be far higher than it was in the 1950s when people did not live so long and there were more young workers per older retiree.

The readings in this section introduce you to the current generations in the United States and describe the competition—and possible conflict— between your generation and the large baby-boom generation ahead of your own.

THE BABY BOOM — ENTERING MIDLIFE

Leon F. Bouvier and Carol J. De Vita

Leon Bouvier is retired from Tulane University School of Public Health, where he specialized in demography. His publications include two coauthored books: How Many Americans: Population, Immigration, and the Environment *(1996) and* Florida in the 21st Century: The Challenge of Population Growth *(1992). From 1988 to 1997, Carol J. De Vita was senior research demographer and director of publications for the Population Reference Bureau in Washington, D.C. Subsequently, she became senior research associate at the Urban Institute in Washington, D.C. She has two publications in the* Population Bulletin *series: "The United States at Mid Decade" (1996) and "New Realities of the American Family" (1992).*

Bouvier and De Vita offer data about the relative population size of recent generations. They also report on a theory that explains why a generation's size, relative to those generations ahead and behind it, influences the opportunities and general well-being of a generation's members. Turn ahead to Figure 7.14: U.S. Population Pyramids, 1960–2040, and locate your own generation. (Bouvier and De Vita use the terms cohort *and* generation *interchangeably.) Notice how the extraordinarily large baby-boom generation ahead of yours will dominate your generation almost until the end of your life. If you are among the late baby boomers returning to college or starting college in your late thirties or early forties, you will likely experience the same economic impact as will the generations behind you.*

As you read, try to understand how generational size influences the well-being of a generation's members. Begin thinking about how your generation's life chances will be influenced by its relationship to the baby-boom generation.

Some analysts, most notably economist Richard Easterlin, theorize that the relative size of one's generation (or birth cohort) is an important factor in influencing the life chances and personal well-being of individual members of a cohort.[1] According to Easterlin's theory, the size of a generation shapes the social and economic climate of a society and hence the life choices that each individual must make. Small generations precipitate (and benefit from) labor shortages, which tend to increase wages and create more social and economic opportunity. Large generations, in contrast, create labor surpluses and hence command lower wages, encounter more congestion on the career ladder, and may even generate more unemployment. In short, small generations are likely to face a climate of promising economic circumstances, while large generations may struggle with greater economic uncertainty. Within this context, small

---

[1] Richard A. Easterlin, *Birth and Fortune: The Impact of Numbers on Personal Welfare* (Chicago: University of Chicago Press, 2d ed., 1987).

generations, buoyed by optimism, are likely to marry early and produce large families. Large generations, tempered and cautious through experience, are likely to delay or forgo marriage and family commitments.

Easterlin's theory is based largely on the life experiences of the 1930s Depression cohort and the still unfolding experiences of the post–World War II baby-boom and baby-bust cohorts. For example, although the Depression hung over their early years, the 1930s cohort reaped the social and economic benefits of being smaller than the cohort that preceded it as well as the one that came after. They faced less competition in school, found jobs more readily, and advanced relatively quickly in their careers compared with the larger cohort that preceded them. Indeed, the 1930s cohort has been called the "good times" cohort because of the relative ease with which they established careers and prospered.[2]

On the other hand, because of its large size, the baby-boom cohort is thought to be less fortunate, even though the economic times have been much better. As economists John Katosh and Mathew Greenwald put it: "The baby boom's disproportionate size has distended° every social institution it has dealt with—usually to the generation's detriment."[3]

While the actual life experiences of the baby-boom generation are still somewhat limited, some researchers are finding that the baby-boom generation appears to be doing less well economically than their parents' generation at similar stages of life.[4] This finding challenges the long-held assumption that each generation of Americans will enjoy greater material well-being and an improved standard of living than its predecessor. But other analysts argue that while the baby-boom cohort may have gotten off to a slow start in establishing careers or forming families, the effect is merely temporary. They have delayed, not abandoned, entering specific phases of the life-cycle process. In the long run, it is argued, the baby boomers are likely to achieve as much success as previous generations.[5]

The real test of the cohort-size theory may well come with the maturing of   5 the baby-bust generation—the smaller cohort of individuals that follows behind the baby-boom generation.

According to Easterlin's theory, the small baby-bust generation (born primarily in the 1970s and roughly ages 11 to 20 in 1990) should find a more favorable social and economic environment than did the baby boomers. With fewer labor force entrants, employment opportunities for members of the baby-bust generation should flourish, wages should once again rise, and the material

---

° **distended:** Expanded or swollen.

[2] Carl L. Harter, "The 'Good Times' Cohort of the 1930s," *PRB Report* 3, no. 3 (Washington, DC: Population Reference Bureau, 1977).

[3] John P. Katosh and Mathew H. Greenwald, "From Boom to Bust," *Mortgage Banking* (October 1989): 21.

[4] Frank S. Levy and Richard C. Michel, *The Economic Future of American Families: Income and Wealth Trends* (Washington, DC: The Urban Institute Press, 1991).

[5] Louise B. Russell, *The Baby Boom Generation and the Economy* (Washington, DC: The Brookings Institution, 1982).

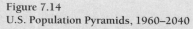

Figure 7.14
U.S. Population Pyramids, 1960–2040

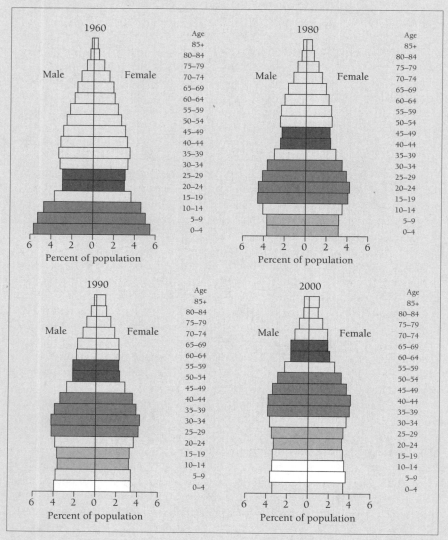

trappings of success may encourage the baby-bust generation to get married and start families at younger ages than their predecessors.

This is not to suggest any form of demographic determinism.° Some individuals always seem able to beat the odds and succeed under adverse circumstances, while others may fail to seize even the most attractive and favorable opportunity. Yet, being born a member of a large or a small cohort does, in part, alter one's chances of succeeding. Demographic factors, however, do not operate

Figure 7.14
U.S. Population Pyramids, 1960–2040 (*continued*)

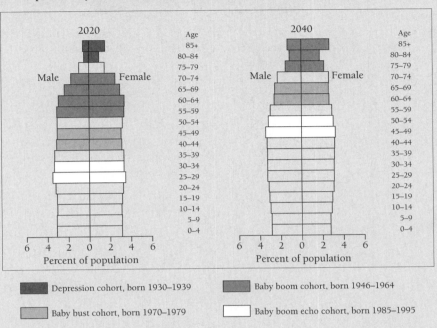

Depression cohort, born 1930–1939

Baby boom cohort, born 1946–1964

Baby bust cohort, born 1970–1979

Baby boom echo cohort, born 1985–1995

Source: U.S. Bureau of Census and PRB projections.

in a vacuum. Rapid economic, technological, and political changes affect our daily lives and interact with demographic trends to create barriers and opportunities to social and individual well-being. While demography is not destiny, it is a powerful influence in shaping the life chances of individuals and societies. The demographic importance of the baby boom is best seen through a series of population pyramids. Figure 7.14 traces the changing shape of the age structure of the United States from 1960 to 2040 as the baby boom ages. While the size of future generations cannot be predicted with complete accuracy because population projections necessarily stem from assumptions about future demographic behavior, particularly changes in fertility levels, the movement of existing generations through their life cycles can be clearly demonstrated.

In 1960, members of the 1930s Depression cohort were 20 to 29 years old. Their fewer numbers cause a narrow spot in the pyramids even into the 21st century. By 2000, this cohort will be ages 60 to 69. At all ages, it is smaller than either its predecessor or its successor.

The baby-boom cohort (born 1946–1964) stands out in all the pyramids,

---

°**demographic determinism:** The idea that the generation into which you are born determines your life opportunities absolutely.

even in old age! In 1960, it forms the base of the pyramid; by 1990, it extends across the broad middle section (ages 25 to 44); and by 2040, it represents the protruding bands of people age 75 and older. These pyramids vividly demonstrate the impact of this crowded generation as it passes through its life cycle.

In marked contrast is the baby-bust generation (born primarily in the 10 1970s). It is sharply defined by the pinched-in base of the 1980 pyramid. There were 7 million fewer births during the 1970s than during the 1950s. Throughout its life, this cohort will be overshadowed by its giant older relative—the baby-boom cohort—as well as the succeeding baby-boom echo.

The echo cohort—37 million in 1990—is considerably larger than its predecessor. However, it is only in 2020 that it catches up to the baby-boom cohort in size. By then, of course, mortality has begun to have an effect on the latter group.

REVOLUTION X: A SURVIVAL GUIDE FOR OUR GENERATION

Rob Nelson and Jon Cowan

Rob Nelson and Jon Cowan founded Lead…or Leave, an advocacy group concerned with political issues important to Generation X, or the Thirteenth Generation, those born between 1961 and 1981. They have written Revolution X: A Survival Guide for Our Generation *(1994), from which this reading was taken. Aiming at a wide readership, the authors adopt a newspaper style and format.*

Nelson and Cowan's Generation X includes Leon F. Bouvier and Carol J. De Vita's baby-bust generation. The two writers here focus on what they see as the inevitable backlash that the entitlement demands of the baby-boom generation will spark in younger generations. They describe the source of this generational conflict and the trends leading toward it. They argue that the tensions they describe are already apparent, and note that their organization, Lead…or Leave, seeks to influence Congress in passing legislation that will shift resources away from the baby boomers to the later, smaller generations.

As you read, look closely at statistics concerning the baby-boom generation's retirement entitlements. Consider whether you think a backlash by the later generations is inevitable.

A quiet crisis is brewing today in America.

It gets little notice in the media and is rarely discussed around the dinner table, but it will radically change all of our lives. That crisis is the baby boomers' retirement early next century.

For as the baby boomers (Americans born in the post–World War II boom between 1946 and 1960) age, their economic interests will directly clash with those of our generation and the generation behind us—their kids and grandkids.

As they grow gray, boomers will step right into the shoes of today's seniors, demanding more and more attention be paid to the largest conglomeration of elders America has ever seen: over 50 million highly organized boomer seniors demanding extensive health care and retirement services from the government.

If elderly boomers want the same kinds of benefits as today's seniors (and 5 most likely they will), that means higher and higher taxes on our generation and the generations that follow us.

And if today's politics are any indication, the boomers will have more than enough political power to win what they want—whatever the cost to those who come behind them.

With over 34 million members, the American Association of Retired Persons is already considered the most powerful lobby in the country—able to scare politicians of both parties into supporting virtually any policy it wants. The boomers' retirement will nearly double that power.

In addition, retired boomers will be better educated than today's seniors (the number of senior citizens with high school diplomas will double by 2020), which has historically meant a higher voting rate. They will be more affluent as well.

As a group of demographic experts warns in *Lifetrends,* the baby boomers, in an effort to get age-related benefits from the government, could "come on like a political juggernaut in the twenty-first century, ramming their pet programs through . . . Congress."

The problem: Who will pay for them?   10

THE SOURCE OF A GENERATIONAL SCHISM

Strapped by a $6 trillion (or much larger) debt and an ever-widening social gap, Washington will not be able to continue borrowing to finance the boomer retirement without dramatically raising our taxes.

"I think [the baby boomers] care more about just making money and materialistic things and how much they can get."
                                        —DENISE, 30-year-old benefits administrator

---

The U.S. Office of Management and Budget found that by the end of fiscal year 1991, the baby boomers had been promised $14 trillion more in federal benefits than they contributed in payroll taxes.

That's where the generational conflict will occur: Seniors expecting their benefit checks will be pitted against young families and struggling workers who will already be paying steep taxes and who won't want to pay more.

Everyone will be deserving—but only some of us will be able to get a bigger slice of a rapidly shrinking pie. So Washington will have to make a harsh choice:

- Sharply boost taxes for everyone under age 65 (the Social Security Administration projects that the cost of Social Security and Medicare could rise to between 38 and 53 percent of payroll in 2040);
- Slash spending on all other government programs to keep pumping money to seniors; or
- Cut benefits to baby boomers who've been paying into Social Security since their early 20s and are counting on their U.S. government retirement check.

In simplest terms, it comes down to this: Our generation, and to a larger 15 extent the younger generations behind us, will be forced to take another blow to our already declining living standards or cut off a deserving but unaffordable senior population. We will in effect have to choose between providing for our parents or our kids.

HEADING TOWARD A CONFLICT

No one wants to face this kind of intergenerational tension. It runs completely against the grain of family ties and social responsibility. As activists, neither of us has ever advocated starting a generational political war, and we have argued against those who do.

But unless America dramatically shifts our budget priorities over the next 10 to 15 years to create new policies that are fair to all generations, we will confront an unprecedented budget battle between the baby boomers and everyone born after 1960.

The signs pointing to such a battle are numerical, not rhetorical.... They are based on reliable demographic and economic forecasts, not on radical projections.

Three main trends drive us toward a generational conflict:

- As the baby boomers reach age 65, America will have the largest senior (and retirement) population in its history;
- At the same time, the ratio of workers supporting those retirees will be shrinking, with record numbers of illiterate and poorly trained adults inflicting a drag on the economy;
- As the financial costs of caring for the elderly spiral out of control, we will be forced to cut or shut down senior programs like Social Security and Medicare (as well as many other government services that benefit Americans of all ages), or else raise taxes dramatically.

"I don't see our generation as being really content. I think they're searching for something. I see a lot of people rejecting what their parents have had or have done."
— ELIZABETH, 25-year-old graduate student

The genesis of potential generational conflict is that simple. As Wall Street 20 banker Pete Peterson says, "When [our kids] understand the size of the bad check we are passing them, they could, amid ugly generational conflict, simply decide not to honor it at all."

If pushed to the edge economically, younger Americans, particularly people in their 20s and early 30s, would be the principal activists in this battle, taking to the streets and ballot boxes to demand immediate redress of their equity grievances. And the highly organized senior lobbies would hit back twice as hard.

Whether the youth of the 21st century will succeed in mobilizing enough political support to maintain generational equity is uncertain. But an economic battle between generations would be dangerously disruptive to America's social order and its economic stability.

At the state level, we've already seen how limited budget resources can force age groups to compete over spending cuts and tax increases.

In the early 1990s, taxpayers in Michigan and Wisconsin refused to pay higher property taxes to fund local schools. The conflicts led to school closings and shocking pictures of 10-year-olds in picket lines calling to have the doors to class reopened.

Social Security checks to people earning $100,000 a year are on average *twice* the size of the checks for those making less than $10,000.

Conflicts that lead to these school closings will only get more frequent, as 25 America's financial resources become ever more limited thanks to the strains of a crushing national debt. The middle-class squeeze will see millions of us working longer hours for less pay, and we will all be paying the enormous cleanup costs that will result from short-sighted social policies.

Add the financial burden of having 20 million more retirees in 2020 than we have today, and a backlash against the baby boomers doesn't seem that hard to imagine.

Let's take a closer look at the three trends that are leading America toward intergenerational chaos.

Trend #1: Rising Senior Population

Around 2010, tens of millions of baby boomers will be stepping off the employment treadmill and into their retirement slippers. Once in retirement, they will make up the largest block of elderly that America has ever seen — roughly 20 percent of our nation's population by the year 2030.

"The relevant question becomes: When and how are benefits . . . going to be scaled back?" asked one equity expert. "In a political crisis or gradually? Before or after we have sacrificed a generation?"

To put that in perspective, in 1950, 8 percent of the population was made up of senior citizens. Today the number is 13 percent. California has a projected

69 percent increase in elderly population by 2010—and that's *before* the baby boom retirement.

The number of people over 85 (who are four times more likely than younger seniors to require expensive long-term care) is going to triple or quadruple by 2030. Never before will America have aged so rapidly, and with such startling implications for our national budget and economic priorities.

Trend #2: Fewer Workers

If the only issue were the skyrocketing number of seniors, perhaps we'd be able to survive their massive retirement. But the ratio of workers to retirees is shrinking rapidly—and that's where the trouble lies.

Between 2010 and 2025, the number of working-age Americans (people 15–65) will increase by only 4.5 percent—or 9 million—while the elderly population (people 65 and over) is expected to grow by 22 million, a 55 percent increase. In the bigger picture, over the next 50 years America's elderly population will grow by 135 percent while our working-age population will grow by only 35 percent.

By the middle of the next century, there will be 1.2 million centenarians, up from 49,000 in 1994.

In 1900, workers outnumbered the elderly by a margin of 15 to 1, so there were more than enough workers whether families were supporting seniors at home, or whether the government was providing a benefit check.

By 1980, however, the margin had shrunk to just under six workers for every retiree. By 2010 it will be down to five to one; and by 2030, there will be only three workers for every senior, hardly a ratio that is sustainable over the long run.

Trend #3: An Explosion
in Federal Benefit Programs

In 1966, at the height of the Great Society, President Lyndon Johnson strong-armed Congress into passing a new tax on workers.

The tax was intended to finance a new health care program for the elderly called Medicare. Medicare was one of a series of government programs—like Social Security, farm aid, veterans' pensions—that were intended to provide a social safety net, lifting millions of Americans out of poverty.

These programs, called entitlements, now account for the fastest-growing portion of the federal budget. And unlike other items on the federal budget, entitlements aren't funded by annual government allocations. If you qualify, you get them. It's automatic.

Even under Reagan and Bush, two conservative presidents who attacked the so-called welfare state, benefits grew 54 percent (inflation adjusted) from 1981 to 1993.

Originally, federal entitlements made up a small and manageable portion of the budget: only 27 percent in 1960. But as benefits have become more generous over the last 30 years, we've seen an explosion in their growth; today they eat up almost 54 percent of all federal spending.

In 1960, we handed out nearly $25 billion in entitlements.   40

If the growth of benefits had been limited since 1960 to covering all new recipients *and* keeping pace with inflation, they would have been $176 billion in 1993. They were actually $807 billion—more than four times larger than necessary. One hundred seventy-six billion dollars versus $807 billion.

According to the Urban Institute, almost all retirees since 1940, whatever their income or family status, have received (or will receive) more than they paid into Social Security.

Why? Because politicians swayed by powerful lobbies° keep handing out more benefits than we can afford—and sticking the tab on their Congressional Express charge card (to be paid off down the line by all of us and our kids, tomorrow's workers).

In 1965, for example, when Medicare began, the U.S. government predicted a total cost of less than $10 billion by 1990. They were wrong. Way wrong.

The program had actually cost us $128 billion by 1993—and the price is still 45 rising. *For every dollar spent on Medicare, the U.S. goes 50 cents deeper into debt.*

Decades ago, as our economy was expanding briskly compared to those of the rest of the world, we could pay for such federal generosity. But today, with a debt crisis looming over us and a huge increase in the number of baby-boom retirees, we can no longer afford to sustain the explosive growth of entitlement programs.

Without fiscal restraint,° before the middle of the next century workers will be paying over half their salaries just to cover benefits to seniors.

The Social Security and Medicare boards of trustees have already warned that the Medicare trust fund will go bankrupt within the decade, or earlier. At that point, the government will have to raise our taxes dramatically to cover the benefit demand—or stop paying benefits to retirees.

We can close our eyes to the problem, or we can attempt to deal with it today, in a way that is fair to all generations and that protects those most in need of the government's helping hand. The costs of avoidance are frighteningly high for all of us.

THE COMING GENERATIONAL BACKLASH

If America does not begin to plan for demographic shifts ahead, a backlash 50 against the elderly might be unavoidable, where reasonable but difficult

---

°**lobbies:** Organized groups, like the American Association of Retired Persons, who contribute money to, and seek to influence, politicians.   °**fiscal restraint:** Holding back or reducing costs.

demands for change from younger workers could mean moving retired boomers closer to the edges of poverty.

Flashpoints in a boomer-buster conflict might include

- rationing of health care to the elderly;
- shutting off the entitlement spigot, even to the poor;
- eliminating all tax breaks that benefit older Americans;
- shifting unprecedented amounts of federal funding into schools and training and away from all senior programs; and
- massive political pressure for a steep payroll-tax cut.

Before we're driven to this point, we need to take strict measures now. Health care rationing, for example, sounds draconian° from today's vantage point, but it will be inevitable tomorrow without a dramatic restructuring of our economic priorities.

According to the Congressional Budget Office, health care costs will account for 18 percent of the U.S. economy by the year 2000, three times as much as in 1960.

With the very old as the fastest-growing segment of the country, experts estimate that a new 220-bed nursing home will have to open every day between 1987 and the year 2000 just to keep even with the demand—and this is long before the arrival of the baby boomers.

HOW MUCH CAN WE AFFORD?

Between 1960 and 1990, the elderly population roughly doubled, yet federal programs serving the elderly nearly quintupled. By 1999, Medicare spending could increase by 67 percent while Social Security spending could rise 36 percent.

The cost of helping to defray the health care expenses of the growing retiree 55 population will soon be enough to bankrupt many companies.

How will a company like the Bethlehem Steel Corporation—which has 21,000 working employees and 70,000 retirees—get by?

Instead of paying the higher taxes needed to finance the retirement health care of the baby boomers, younger workers would be forced to either form their own health care cooperatives (excluding seniors) or push the government to ration health care based on life expectancy.

Given the burst in the number of elderly, and the rising costs of their care, we must all face one tough question: Unless current trends are reversed, will we be able to take care of all our elderly—and still have the resources to defend America, invest in our children and our companies, and provide a reasonable living standard for coming generations?

°draconian: Severe or even cruel.

A WRITER'S NOTEBOOK
Understanding Generational Competition

The following tasks are designed to help you think about the readings and identify and start to work up material you might use in your own essay. If you need help with tasks that require annotating, outlining, or summarizing, see Appendix 1.

1. *Identify your generation and interview someone from an older generation.* Study Leon F. Bouvier and Carol J. De Vita's population pyramids and describe in a sentence or two which generation you belong to. Then choose someone you know well who belongs to an older generation and interview that person in person, by phone, or online in order to discover how his or her opportunities *at the same age* compare with yours. Take notes during the interview.

   For example, ask whether the person had more or fewer students in grade-school classrooms than you did. Has he or she faced more or less competition in school or in the workplace than you? Growing up, what were his or her assumptions about going to college, seeking employment, and so forth? If she went to college, what did her first year cost her? How did she see her chances for success and financial security? How did she imagine her life would unfold when she was your age?

   After the interview, add notes that you did not have time to make during the interview. Then write a few sentences explaining what you learned from this interview. Finally, write a few more sentences about how the opportunities and life chances of your generation seem to differ from those of the person you interviewed.

2. *Interview a retired person.* On the phone or in person, interview a retired person over sixty-five years old to learn what sources of financial support the person has and what other kinds of support the person relies on from local agencies, relatives, or friends. Take notes during the interview. Does the person receive payments from a private pension, from a tax-deferred retirement investment like an annuity or an Individual Retirement Account (IRA), or from Social Security? How many people are involved in giving support, including relatives, members of government and volunteer agencies, and paid help? How does the retired person feel about receiving support? (You might also interview one or two support providers about their feelings.)

   Immediately after the interview, note information and insights you did not have time to record during the interview. Then write a few sentences about the most important insights you gained from the interview.

3. *Summarize important information from the Rob Nelson and Jon Cowan reading.* To gain a fuller understanding of the three trends that seem to be leading toward generational conflict, summarize the information in paragraphs 28–49.

SURVEYING CONSEQUENCES
OF THE RESTRUCTURED ECONOMY

If you have completed the readings and tasks in the previous sections, you have a detailed understanding of the restructured economy and some sense of generational competition, and you can turn your attention to the likely consequences for you and your generation. Some of the previous readings suggest several consequences, some already apparent and some possible in the future. For example, Barbara Rudolph documents the already apparent job insecurity felt by many managers, and Keith Bradsher's and Sam Dillon's reports suggest that in the future even more businesses will move production to other countries where wages are relatively low. Consequently, you may already have begun to consider how the restructured economy could affect future opportunities. In this section, the readings are all concerned directly with what the restructured economy may mean for your generation: each suggests several possible consequences. The speculations in these readings—along with your own observations, experience, and interviews with others—will provide the basis for your essay speculating about the future work and life opportunities of your generation.

As you read, list the various speculations these writers make about changes in job opportunities, career paths, living standards, and quality of life in the years ahead. Identify the source of each consequence on your list by including the last name of the author and the number of the paragraph in which you found it. This will help you later locate the full argument for a particular consequence you may want to include in your essay.

Making this list may be the most important writing you do to prepare to plan and develop your essay. Work at it carefully, keeping in mind that there is no particular number of consequences you must find in each reading.

FUTURE WORK POLICIES MAY FOCUS ON TEENS, TRIMMING WORKLOADS

Sue Shellenbarger

Sue Shellenbarger has worked for the Wall Street Journal *since 1980, specializing in agriculture, commodities, and workplace issues. She writes the weekly "Work and Family" column for the* Journal *and from 1986 to 1989 hosted a radio show of the same name produced by the Wall Street Journal Radio Network. In 1999 she became a news editor for the* Journal. *She has won numerous awards, among them a 1998 Clarion Award, sponsored by the Association for Women in Communication, for her column "Work and Family."*

In this December 1998 column from the Journal, *Shellenbarger focuses on the connections between family life and work and the possibility—very real, as she sees it—that workplace routines and demands will need to become more flexible to accommodate workers with children. She speculates about a "parenting revival" and proposes that working parents in the future will be particularly concerned not to neglect their teenage children. Assuming that generations reflect different lifestyles and even values, she also speculates that while the baby-boom generation was willing to bend to the demands of the workplace, generations following the boomers may not be so pliant.*

As you read, consider the full range of speculations Shellenbarger offers and note the ways she thinks businesses may try to accommodate the demands of working parents.

If our future is evident anywhere, I think, it's along the fault line where the two great preoccupations of our lives—work and love…—collide. Amid the friction and stress along that fault, creativity and change bubble up.

What do current developments on the work-love front suggest about the future? A few forecasts:

Families will break the mold in their quest for better ways to blend work and child-rearing.

Tim Clark and his wife and business partner, Keiko Onodera, operate what I see as the family farm of the future. When this couple decided to have a baby, they bought a home in Portland, Ore., with a free-standing, 660-square-foot garage that they converted to an office for their Internet consulting business, TKAI Inc.

Networked workstations occupy house and office, and an intercom links the buildings to allow Mr. Clark and Ms. Onodera to talk easily to each other about work or their baby. They also employ two part-time baby sitters, enabling them to move back and forth between work and parenting, as needed. "If you want to enjoy a truly integrated home/work life, you'd best consider designing and creating it yourself," Mr. Clark says.

Three factors will fuel more innovations. First, after decades of growing reliance on wives' income, many families are hooked. Working wives contributed 23 percentage points of the 25% increase in family income, adjusted for inflation, since 1969, the Census Bureau says.

Second, technology is opening frontiers. This year's 7% growth in all forms of working at home, full time or part time, will likely continue for another year or two, predicts Tom Miller of Cyber Dialogue, an Internet consulting firm in New York. And third, parents will turn an increasingly keen eye on kids' developmental needs, amid a continuing parenting revival.

Concerns about parenting teens will reshape use of employer benefits and scheduling. As the vast baby boomlet generation moves through adolescence, teens will outnumber people in their 20s by 7%, and a generation of parents will "discover" teen problems anew.

Though parents have traditionally thought of working part time when children are small, Catherine Brillson temporarily switched to three days a week as a marketing manager when her daughter turned 14 and was changing schools. Sensing that her child needed a mother's help navigating adolescence, she says, she traded "two-fifths less money" for "100% more interaction. I was accessible when I was needed. I did not always have my eye on the clock."

The payoff: "an incredibly reinvigorating time" for mother and daughter. With her daughter thriving after 15 months, this Chicago mother will return to full-time work next week.

Programs providing after-school activities for teens will be hot. And "the perk du jour° may be college loans," says WEFA Group's Sandra Shaber.

"Work redesign" will be the new work-life buzzword. After several years of stressing flexible schedules, most big companies now have flexibility language on the books. But the policies lack impact, largely because Godzilla-size workloads keep employees from using them. "Workload is the issue, and it has become the greatest single obstacle to flexibility," says Paul Rupert, a flexibility consultant with WFD Inc., Boston.

Few employers will hire more people amid a likely economic slowdown, but many will give employees a fighting chance to work flexibly by redesigning work—putting tasks in priority, erasing nonessential duties and smoothing work flow. Citibank, Chevron and Warner-Lambert were among 10 employers that met last month with WFD consultants to air work-redesign efforts.

The work-life generation gap will widen. Differences between the work-life attitudes of baby boomers and everyone else will become more marked as Gen-Xers° take a bigger workplace role and the baby boomlet° enters the workforce.

While boomers were known for paying their career dues with long hours and other sacrifices, post-boomers° are more diverse. Some Gen-Xers still are willing to log killer hours in offices where "there's almost a cult around working around the clock," says Maury Hanigan, Hanigan Consulting Group, New York. But a second, polar-opposite group resists, hewing early toward nesting, family and community, she says.

In an e-mail, a post-boomer man writes me: "The tide is turning as the children of divorce and neglect recommit themselves to family."

Employers will adapt to this diversity by handing workers more control over their time. Paid-time-off banks, awarding days off for any purpose, will grow as much as 20% in 1999, says Carol Sladek, a Hewitt Associates work-life and time-use specialist. Sabbatical policies° will continue to grow at a brisk 10% to 15% annual clip.

Coming up behind Gen X, the baby boomlet will further rewrite the work-life recipe book, with technology as its tool. Children using the Internet rose 63% to 16 million in the past year, Cyber Dialogue says. This generation will further integrate work and home; a Drexel University study found 42% of teens see at least an 8-in-10 chance of working at home as adults.

How does it all add up? If you think the family dynamics of the workplace are in turmoil now, you ain't seen nothin' yet.

°**perk du jour:** Special privilege of the day.   °**Gen-Xers:** The generation of Americans born approximately between 1961 and 1981.   °**baby boomlet:** The generation of Americans born approximately between 1985 and 1995.   °**post-boomers:** Gen-Xers.   °**Sabbatical policies:** Policies that give employees paid time off to pursue a research project or acquire further education.

AMERICA'S ANXIOUS CLASS

Robert Reich

Robert Reich, for many years a professor of business and public policy at Harvard University, now teaches at Brandeis University. He pursued postgraduate work as a Fullbright Scholar at Oxford University and holds a law degree from Yale University. From 1993 to 1996, he was secretary of labor during the first Clinton administration. He is an influential lecturer and writer, and his books include The Next American Frontier *(1983),* The Power of Public Ideas *(1988), and* Preparing Ourselves for 21st-Century Capitalism *(1991).*

In this essay from New Perspective Quarterly, *written in 1995 during his term as secretary of labor, Reich argues that we are living in worrisome, even perilous, times because of economic restructuring. He speculates that the traditional middle class is "disintegrating." (By the year 2000, a middle-class family income was projected to be between $50,000 and $120,000.) Reich sees a way out, however: high-quality education and continuous on-the-job training to permit everyone a stake in economic growth.*

As you read, think about why Reich is worried and evaluate the basis for his concerns in light of what you have learned about the new economy and generational competition. Also consider his solution. Would it make the future brighter for your generation if it were implemented?

WASHINGTON—The American middle class is disintegrating and turning into three new groups: An underclass largely trapped in central cities and isolated from the growing economy; an overclass profitably positioned to ride the waves of change; and an anxious class, most of whom hold jobs but are justifiably uneasy about their own standing and fearful for their children's future.

What divides the over, the under and the anxious classes is both the quality of their formal educations and their capacity and opportunity to learn throughout their working lives. Skills have always been relevant to earnings, of course. But they have never been as important as they are today. Only 15 years ago, a male college graduate earned 49 percent more than a man with only a high school degree. That's a sizable difference, but it's a divide small enough for both men to occupy terrain each would call middle class. In 1992, a male college graduate out-earned his high school graduate counterpart by 83 percent—a difference so great that they no longer inhabit common territory or share common prospects. Women are divided along similar, though slightly less stark, lines.

Traditionally, membership in the American middle class included not only a job with a steadily increasing income, but a bundle of benefits that came with employment. But a gap has grown here as well. Employer-sponsored health coverage for workers with college degrees has declined only slightly, from 79 percent in 1979 to 76 percent in 1993. But for high school graduates, rates have fallen further: 68 percent to 60 percent over the same period. And rates for high school dropouts have plunged—from an already low 52 percent in 1979 to only 36 percent last year.

Retirement will only harden these divisions. Nearly two out of every three workers with college degrees get pension coverage on the job. More than three out of four high school dropouts do not.

But earnings and benefits don't tell ⁵ the complete story. Merely getting a job and holding on to it depend ever more on strong skills. In the 1970s, the average unemployment rate for people who had not completed high school was seven percent; by 1993 it had passed 12 percent. Job loss for high school graduates has followed a comparable trajectory. By contrast, the unemployment rate for workers with at least a college degree has remained around three percent. . . .

As they take hold in the neighborhoods and workplaces of America, these forces are ominous. Consider the physical separation they have already helped forge.

The overclass has moved to elite suburbs—occasionally into their own gated communities or residential compounds policed by their own security forces. The underclass finds itself quarantined in surroundings that are unspeakably bleak and often violent.

And the anxious class is trapped, too—not only by houses and apartments often too small for growing families, but also by the frenzy of effort it takes to preserve their standing, with many families needing two or three paychecks to deliver the living standard one job used to supply.

In other words, even as America's economic tide continues to rise, it no longer lifts all boats. Only a small portion of the American population benefited from the economic growth of the 1980s. The restructurings and capital investments launched during the 1980s and continuing through the 1990s have improved the productivity and competitiveness of American industry, but not the prospects of most Americans. And the people left behind have unleashed a wave of resentment and distrust—a wave buffeting government, business and other institutions that the anxious class believes has betrayed them.

This creates fertile soil for the dem- ¹⁰ agogues° and conspiracy theorists° who often emerge during anxious times. People in distress, people who fear their future, naturally cling to what they have and often resist any-

---

°**demagogues:** Leaders who attempt to gain power by exciting peoples' prejudices, distorting the truth, and promising sweeping change.   °**conspiracy theorists:** People who believe that secret organizations—possibly within the government—mastermind plans to take advantage of the general public.

thing that threatens it. People who feel abandoned—by a government that has let them slide or a company that has laid them off—respond to opportunists peddling simplistic explanations and sinister solutions. Why are you having trouble making ends meet? We're letting in too many immigrants. Why are you struggling to pay your bills? Affirmative action tilts things in favor of African-Americans and Hispanics. Why is your job at risk? Our trade policies have not been sufficiently protectionist.°

As a solution, we can't turn back the clock and return to the safe old world of routine mass production that dominated postwar America. Efforts to do so—say, by keeping foreign investment and goods outside our borders or by stifling technological advances—would not resurrect the old middle class. They would only inhibit the ability of every American to prosper amid change.

The real solution is to give all Americans a stake in economic growth, to ensure that everyone benefits from our newfound competitiveness. This economy will not be at full capacity until we tap the potential of all our citizens to be more productive.

Individuals and families shoulder much of the responsibility here, of course. Ultimately, they must face the realities of the new economy and ensure that they and their children have the basic intellectual tools to prosper in it. Government has a role, too. It can clear

away some of the obstacles—improving the quality of public education, setting skills standards and smoothing the transition from school to work and from job to job.

But individuals, however resourceful, and governments, however reinvented, can't build a new middle class on their own. Business has an indispensable role to play. Unless business joins in a compact to rebuild America's middle class—training and empowering ordinary workers to be productive and innovative—this task cannot succeed.

There are two good economic reasons for business to enlist: First, the members of America's imperiled middle class are key productive assets. Second, they form the majority of most companies' customers.

What should be the specific contents of this compact? I cannot predict the exact provisions. Obviously, one means of committing American business to workforce investment would be through a simple requirement that firms spend a small portion of their payrolls upgrading the skills of all employees. The Administration° is not advancing such an option as a formal policy proposal because we are not convinced it is the best way to achieve the goal of stepped-up investments in worker skills. Flat requirements like this can invite endless legal pirouettes, resulting in ever more intrusive regulation.

I hope American business and government can discover together a better

---

° **protectionist:** Protecting U.S. interests by making it harder to import goods from other countries.
° **The Administration:** The first Clinton administration (1993–97).

way—voluntary commitments to, and disclosure of, such workforce investments; cooperative agreements among firms in an industry to share the costs of basic-skill training; agreements between large firms and their smaller suppliers and customers to do so; employee education as an object of collective bargaining; awards or certifications for businesses that invest substantially in their workers; collaborations between high schools and companies to hire school-to-work apprentices; shifts in the tax code to create added incentives for workforce training.

These and other approaches—alone or in combination—may be more effective than a uniform requirement. But if we cannot develop a superior approach, it would certainly be better to embrace that method than to abandon the goal.

The centrifugal forces that are pulling America apart call for even greater resolve. Americans can build a new middle class and a new ladder into it for the underclass. But without the redoubled energies of American business, the sturdy middle class that was once our country's defining quality will continue its steady erosion.

THE END OF WORK

Jeremy Rifkin

A well-known author and lecturer, Jeremy Rifkin has written about several controversial issues of our time: workers' rights, human genetic research, biotechnology, and biological weapons. His books include Own Your Own Job *(1977),* Time Wars: The Primary Conflict in Human History *(1987),* Beyond Beef: The Rise and Fall of the Cattle Culture *(1992), and* The End of Work: The Decline of the Global Labor Force and the Dawn of the Post-Market Era *(1995).*

In this reading from The End of Work, *Rifkin explores the possibility—indeed, the need, as he sees it—of a shorter work week so that more people can be employed. After arguing that free time is the highest human value, Rifkin traces the gradual reduction of working hours in industrialized countries. He hopes to demonstrate that a shorter workweek is not just inevitable but a positive development, both socially and personally.*

As you read, consider the plausibility of this proposed consequence of the restructured economy. What seem to be its advantages? Who might resist it and why?

Nearly fifty years ago, at the dawn of the computer revolution, the philosopher and psychologist Herbert Marcuse made a prophetic observation—one that has come to haunt our society as we ponder the transition into the Information Age: "Automation threatens to render possible the reversal of the relation between free time and working time: the possibility of working time becoming marginal and free time becoming full time. The result would be a radical trans-valuation of values, and a mode of existence incompatible with the traditional culture. Advanced industrial society is in permanent mobilization against this possibility."[1] ...

Technological utopians° have long argued that science and technology, properly harnessed, would eventually free human beings from formal work. Nowhere is that view more widely held than among the champions and advocates of the information revolution.° Yoneji Masuda, one of the prime architects of Japan's computer revolution, envisions a future computopia where "free time" replaces "material accumulation"° as the critical value and overriding goal of society. Masuda agrees with Marcuse that the computer revolution opens the door to a radical reorientation of society away from regimented work and toward personal freedom for the first time in history. The Japanese vision-ary argues that while the Industrial Revolution° was primarily concerned with increasing material output, the information revolution's primary contribution will be the production of greater increments of free time, giving human beings the "freedom to determine voluntarily" the use of their own futures.

Masuda sees the transition from material values to time values as a turning point in the evolution of our species: "Time value is on a higher plane in human life than material values as the basic value of economic activity. This is because time value corresponds to the satisfaction of human and intellectual wants, whereas material values correspond to the satisfaction of physiological and material wants."[2]

In both industrial and developing nations there is a growing awareness that the global economy is heading toward an automated future. The information and communication technology revolutions virtually guarantee more produc-tion with less human labor. One way or another, more free time is the inevitable consequence of corporate reengineering and technology displacement. William Green, the former president of the AFL,° put the issue succinctly: "Free time

---

°**Technological utopians:** People who believe that technology—for example, computers, better transportation, medical advances—will enable us to live in a better world.   °**information revolu-tion:** The expanded use of computers and the Internet that allows more information to be processed and put to use.   °**material accumulation:** Accumulating goods such as cars, sports equipment, and CD players.   °**Industrial Revolution:** A revolution marked by power-driven machines put to many different uses for transportation and manufacturing, beginning in the eigh-teenth century in England.   °**AFL:** American Federation of Labor, a labor union organization.

[1]Marcuse, Herbert, *Eros and Civilization* (Frankfurt, Germany: Suhrkamp, 1979), preface.

[2]Masuda, Yoneji, *The Information Society as Post-Industrial Society* (Washington, D.C.: World Future Society, 1981), p. 74.

will come," the labor leader said. "The only choice is unemployment or leisure."[3]

Economic historians point out that in the case of the first two industrial rev-   5
olutions, the issue of rising unemployment versus greater leisure was eventually settled in favor of the latter, although not without a protracted struggle
between labor and management over the productivity and hours question.°
The dramatic productivity gains of the first stage of the Industrial Revolution in
the nineteenth century were followed by a reduction of work hours from eighty
to sixty hours a week. Similarly, in the twentieth century, as industrial
economies made the transition from steam technologies to oil and electric
technologies, the steady increases in productivity led to a further shortening of
the workweek from sixty hours to forty. Now, as we cross the divide into the
third stage of the Industrial Revolution and reap the productivity gains of the
computer and the new information and telecommunication technologies, a
growing number of observers are suggesting the inevitability of reducing work
hours once again to thirty and even twenty hours per week to bring labor
requirements in line with the new productive capacity of capital.°

Although in previous periods of history increases in productivity have
resulted in a steady reduction in the average number of hours worked, the
opposite has been the case in the four decades since the birth of the computer
revolution. Harvard economist Juliet Schor points out that American productivity has more than doubled since 1948, meaning that we can "now produce
our 1948 standard of living (measured in terms of marketed goods and services) in less than half the time it took in that year." Yet Americans are working
longer hours today than forty years ago at the outset of the information-
technology revolution. Over the past several decades, work time has increased
by 163 hours, or one month a year. More than 25 percent of all full-time workers put in forty-nine or more hours on the job each week. The amount of paid
vacation time and sick leave also declined over the past two decades. The average American worker now receives three and one-half fewer paid vacation and
sick days than he or she did in the early 1970s. With working hours now longer
than they were in the 1950s, Americans report that their leisure time has
declined by more than one-third. If current trends in work continue, by the end
of the century American workers will be spending as much time at their jobs as
they did back in the 1920s.[4]

°**productivity and hours question:** The conflict between employers seeking increased productivity
and workers reluctant to put in increased hours.   °**productive capacity of capital:** Capital, or
money, buys automated equipment to produce goods, reducing the need for human labor.

[3] *Society for the Reduction of Human Labor Newsletter,* Hunnicutt, Benjamin Kline, and
McGaughey, William, eds., Winter 1992–1993, vol. 3 #1, p. 14.

[4] Schor, Juliet, *The Overworked American: The Unexpected Decline of Leisure* (New York: Basic
Books, 1991), pp. 1, 2, 5, 29, 32.

The productivity revolution, then, has affected the amount of time worked in two ways. The introduction of labor- and time-saving technologies has allowed companies to eliminate workers en masse, creating a reserve army of unemployed workers with idle time on their hands rather than leisure time at their disposal. Those still holding on to a job are being forced to work longer hours, partially to compensate for reduced wages and benefits. Many companies prefer to employ a smaller workforce at longer hours rather than a larger one at shorter hours to save the costs of providing additional benefits, including health care and pensions. Even with the payment of time and a half for overtime, companies still pay out less than they would if they had to pay for benefit packages for a larger workforce.

Barry Jones, former Minister of Technology for the Australian government, raises a question that is in the minds of many: if, as virtually every economist agrees, it was beneficial to significantly reduce the number of hours of work in both the nineteenth and early twentieth centuries to accommodate the dramatic increases in technological productivity, why isn't it just as beneficial, from a societal perspective, to cut the number of hours by a like proportion to accommodate the dramatic rise in productivity coming out of the information and telecommunication revolution?[5] Former senator and presidential candidate Eugene McCarthy says that unless we shorten the workweek and more equitably distribute the available work, "we're going to end up having to let 20 to 30 million more people slip into the poverty class where they will have to be maintained with food stamps and subsidies."[6]

Today the demand for the shorter workweek is being actively promoted, once again, by a growing number of labor leaders and economists. With government less able or willing to intervene with tax-and-spend public-works projects, many see the shorter workweek as the only viable solution to technological displacement. Lynn Williams, past president of the United Steel Workers of America, says that, "We need to start thinking [now] about shorter hours...as a way to share in the improved productivity."[7] In 1993 Volkswagen, Europe's largest automaker, announced its intentions to adopt a four-day workweek to save 31,000 jobs that might otherwise have been lost to a combination of stiffening global competition and new work technologies and methods that had boosted productivity by 23 percent. The workers voted to support the management plan, making Volkswagen the first global corporation to move to a thirty-hour workweek. While take-home pay will be cut by 20 percent, lower taxes and a spreading of the traditional Christmas and holiday bonuses over the

------

[5] Jones, Barry, *Sleepers Wake! Technology and the Future of Work* (New York: Oxford University Press, 1982), ch. 9.

[6] Interview, March 18, 1994.

[7] Interview, April 8, 1994.

entire work year is expected to soften the impact.[8] Peter Schlilein, a spokesman for Volkswagen, said that both the company and the workers accepted the idea of a shorter workweek as an equitable alternative to mass permanent layoffs.[9]

THE DOWNSHIFTERS NEXT DOOR

Juliet B. Schor

Director of women's studies at Harvard University and professor of economics at Tillburg University, Juliet B. Schor has authored The Overworked American *(1992) and* Beyond an Economy of Work and Spend *(1997). In this excerpt from a chapter from her latest book,* The Overspent American *(1998), Schor reports on an already evolving consequence of the restructured economy: reacting against consumerism and materialism as well as the demands and pressures of the contemporary workplace, some middle-class workers have begun to downshift, voluntarily making the decision to live more simply on less money. Schor provides statistics from her surveys of many voluntary downshifters, and she profiles a couple and two individuals who have downshifted.*

As you read, try to understand the motives of these downshifters and what they have done to live comfortably while working less or relying on one income in the family. How do you react to the values and life decisions of these downshifters? Does it seem plausible to you that, as Schor suggests, the trend toward downshifting will continue to grow?

By the mid-1990s, consumerism was beginning to worry people. In surveys, 75 to 80 percent of the public was agreeing that the country had become too materialistic, even too greedy. They felt that Americans had become addicted to shopping, were spending wastefully, and had lost the values of thrift and prudence. They worried about how the ascendance of materialist values was affecting young people. Of course, we need to take these sentiments with a grain of salt. People often romanticize the past as a golden age of better values. And consumerism is an easy target when it's somebody else's disease. (These surveys show that people are more likely to attribute materialism to others than to themselves.) But that having been said, there's little doubt the nation's consumerist turn has generated considerable unease.

---

[8]"VW Opts for Four Day Week in Move to Cut Wage Costs," *Financial Times*, October 25, 1993, p. 1.

[9]Interview May 3, 1994.

For some, dissatisfaction with the work-and-spend culture has become palpable enough to spur them to action. They have begun "downshifting." In the years from 1990 through 1996, nearly one-fifth (19 percent) of all adult Americans made a voluntary lifestyle change, excluding a regularly scheduled retirement, that entailed earning less money. Just over half of these people, or 55 percent, consider their lifestyle change to be permanent. And nearly all of them (85 percent) are happy about the change they made. Surprisingly, given the popular perception, downshifters are no more likely to be women than men. And they are hardly wealthy; almost half made $35,000 or less before the change.

Another 12 percent of Americans were involuntarily downshifted, that is, through no choice of their own their incomes were reduced. They lost a job, had their hours reduced, or suffered a pay cut. But even among this group, one-quarter (24 percent) consider the change "a blessing in disguise." So just about one-fifth of the adult American population is happily living on less.

Why is this happening? Primarily because people have had it with demanding jobs and stressed-out lives. One-third of Americans say they always feel rushed, just over one-third say that their lives are out of control, two-thirds say they want more balance, and about 60 percent would like to simplify their lives. Downshifting is a response to these daily realities. The most common reason cited for downshifting, by a wide margin, is "wanting more time, less stress, and more balance in life." Downshifters also articulate the need to do something more meaningful with their lives and to spend more time with their children. They accomplish these goals by working less—much less. Before changing their lives, about half of all downshifters worked more than forty hours a week, and more than half of those worked in excess of fifty. Afterward, half (48 percent) logged in fewer than thirty hours. Of course, their incomes and spending were also reduced....

There are many historical antecedents to today's downshifters. David Shi's 5 *The Simple Life* is still probably the classic work on the recurring waves of people who have opted for intentionally simple living. What makes today's trend different is that downshifters are not dropping out of society, few are

Table 7.6
Voluntary Downshifters by Type of Downshift

Question: *Which of the following best describes the lifestyle change you made?*	
Changed to a lower-paying job	29%
Reduced work hours	12
Quit working outside the home	16
Changed careers and/or went back to school	17
Started own business	10
Reduced the number of jobs held	2
Refused a promotion	1
Other	12

Table 7.7
Hours Reductions among Voluntary Downshifters

Weekly Hours	Pre-Downshift	Post-Downshift
< 30	7%	48%
31–40	40	31
41–50	24	14
50+	28	7

Table 7.8
Demographic Characteristics of Voluntary Downshifters

SEX	Male	48%
	Female	52
EDUCATION LEVEL	Some high school	8
	High school diploma	21
	Some college	30
	Four-year college degree	25
	Postgraduate degree	14
CHILDREN UNDER 18	None	53
	One	17
	Two	20
	Three	8
	Four or more	3
RACIAL/ETHNIC RACKGROUND	White Caucasian	85
	African American	9
	Hispanic	4
	Asian	0
	Other	2
MARITAL STATUS	Married	54
	Single, never married	24
	Divorced, separated, or widowed	19
	Living with partner	3
AGE	18–19	3
	20–29	18
	30–39	34
	40–49	27
	50–64	15
	64+	4

Table 7.9
Primary Reason for Downshifting among Voluntary Downshifters

Wanted more time, less stress, and more balance in my life	31%
Wanted to spend more time caring for my children	18
No longer interested in material success	5
Succeeding in today's economy is too difficult	5
Wanted a more meaningful life	15
Wanted a less materialistic lifestyle	3
Other	23

Table 7.10
Pre-Downshift Incomes of Voluntary Downshifters

< $10,000	7%
$10,001–25,000	30
$25,001–35,000	18
$35,001–50,000	17
$50,001–75,000	7
$75,001–100,000	6
$100,000+	5
Don't know/refused	11

Table 7.11
Post-Downshift Attitudes among Voluntary Downshifters

I'm happy about the change, and I don't miss the extra income very much.	28%
I'm happy about the change, but I miss the extra income.	35
Losing the income was a real hardship, but I'm still happy about the change.	19
I'm unhappy about the change.	15

Table 7.12
Permanent versus Temporary Change among Voluntary Downshifters

Question: *Do you think your lifestyle change will be permanent or just temporary?*	
Permanent	55%
Temporary	44

living communally,° and most are not ideologically motivated.° They are smack in the middle of the American mainstream. But they are swimming against a long-standing current of "economic progress." ...

MAKING IT ON ONE INCOME: LOUISE AND JOHN MATTSON

Louise and John Mattson ... are what we might call "traditional" downshifters. Louise quit her job working with disabled children just before the birth of their son, [Adam], and she is planning to stay out of the labor market at least until their second child (on the way at the time of the interview) enters school. John is an engineer at a large company in Seattle. They are in their early thirties, both from middle-class families, both with college educations from the state university. They married young and live near where they grew up, in a middle-class but increasingly trendy neighborhood.

According to Louise, "I've always had in my mind that family is important, and that I would like to stay home with my children, [and that] knowing the people you raise and are married to, that brings a lot of satisfaction in life." She and her husband have no doubts about their decision, but what they anticipated would be "pretty easy" is not. "Not that it's been extremely difficult, but, my gosh, it's really kind of hard to make a one-income family work." John earns in the midforties. They bought a fixer-upper house a few years ago for $140,000 and have put at least another $20,000 into it, plus a tremendous amount of work. They have something under $10,000 in the bank and no consumer debt, and they put away the maximum amount each month into John's 401(k) plan. Louise drives a Ford Taurus wagon, which she considers the minimum she will accept for Adam in terms of safety. John has in "old tin box" for commuting. They watch their money, tracking the big expenditures on a spreadsheet. Louise is always looking for ways to save — reducing the grocery bills, buying children's clothes at garage sales, even doing her own diapers. If they eat out, it's for less than $25. Their only really extravagant expenditure, she feels, was their wedding ($10,000) and honeymoon ($2,500).

I ask them whether they feel concerned about "keeping up with the Joneses," who, in the 1990s, live on two incomes. John answers: "This keeping up with the Joneses has a lot of different angles to it. And one of them I guess I kind of use to make myself feel better is that we're raising Adam in a way that we don't see a lot of other people able to do at this point. And it's really important to us. We look at friends who are making other choices, and it's kind of like, well, we feel like we're doing better at this than you. I don't know, we're into different rewards." Louise concurs that "we do feel, I think, pretty smug"

°**communally:** Refers to a group in which everyone shares property, resources, and work equally.
°**ideologically motivated:** Motivated by shared ideas and vision of the future.

(hardly a word one would associate with two such nice people). "Although it hasn't been ideal the way I'd like it to be in terms of time, because of the remodel, I do feel there's a light at the end of the tunnel. You caught us in the 'we've arrived' mode." She talks about how good it feels not to be dropping Adam off at the baby-sitter's, about wanting to be with him rather than to escape. They relish the fact that he's well behaved and a joy to be around and believe it has to do with the choice they've made. They also note that social comparisons are easier in a neighborhood like theirs, which is homey, not ostentatious.

At the same time, they do feel deprived in some ways; more would definitely be better. John likes his occasional toys, and he's worried that he may have to give up more of those. This year he was pushing for a computer, partly for Adam, but they bought a new rug instead. John also shares the widespread middle-class fear of falling. "We're both middle-class. But [with] all the different things going on tax-wise, it's just very difficult to stay where we are. There's either a push to go up, by her getting another job, or kind of go down the drain. And we've got friends—I don't want to get into it, but they've been on welfare for five years now. And we live better than them, but we don't live a lot better than them. And they haven't earned a cent for five years." Falling is represented by losing the house, a prospect he concedes is unlikely.

Both Louise and John do have "high expectations of their financial future." 10 But they believe that growth in John's income is not the only source of more leeway. They want to continue to "learn to scale back better on financials and not keep upscaling our home and cars." For now, as they await their second child, they are cautiously optimistic. . . .

SUSAN ANDREWS: STRUGGLING ON $18,000

Susan Andrews's story, still in progress when we met, is more of a cautionary tale—about how difficult it can be to keep up a middle-class existence on a single income in a high-cost city such as Boston.

Susan is a registered nurse, thirty-two, and single. Some years ago, she gave up a job in clinical nursing at Massachusetts General Hospital, Harvard's flagship, where she'd been earning about $45,000 a year. Like many other clinical nurses, she'd burned out working more than fifty hours a week, including nights and holidays, and taking on extra responsibilities. She had lost *balance* in her life, a word that resonates with many downshifters, and one that Susan used repeatedly. Her bottom line is to regain that balance, with a job that provides meaning, challenges her intellectually, and has reasonable hours and stress levels. She has ruled out a return to clinical nursing. "My quote for the last year was, 'They could pay me $100,000, and I wouldn't be here.'"

After leaving MGH, Susan took a job with an insurance company, along with a 15 percent pay cut. When that office closed, she began working on a per diem° basis, but she hasn't found much work. The year we met she earned $18,000. "This is not acceptable. I had to question the little lunch maybe once every two weeks, and it's the most inexpensive little turkey sandwich I can get."

The bottom line is that $18,000 can't give her true balance. To find out what annual income would, she asks herself, "What is essential for me? What enhances me?" In the past, the answer has been to travel—"to take your adventure. Europe, $2,000 Caribbean vacations, exploring." As a single woman without much personal life, she found these jaunts essential. Now she can only afford day trips. Even chipping in with friends for a cottage last summer was too stressful—they didn't stay within her limited budget.

Travel aside, the bottom line for Susan is her growing inability to keep up a 15 middle-class lifestyle. Not luxuries, but basics. She comes from an upper-middle-class family. (The neighbors on either side of her parents' suburban home would probably "be considered millionaires.") She is keenly aware of what "society" expects from someone of her level. "I think a lot of the issues that I'm dealing with have to do with what society feels." Discussing the difficulties of keeping up her appearance, she notes that "in this society I find that important, and I struggle with not having the haircut and, you know, needing the contact lenses and not being able to afford the teeth cleaning. My hair's ridiculous now." She is also "embarrassed to be out and about" in "one level" of her wardrobe, describing it as too old and ratty.

She is upset about no longer being able to keep up her customary level of gift giving. "My brother and my sister have had a birthday, and I had a budget of $5–7 for the gift, and that is not acceptable to me. Being a caregiver, I like to give presents. Now I can't go to the card store and buy a $2 card. Christmas has always been a big, big budget thing for me. The people I used to give gifts to I gave cards. The ones I gave cards, they'll get 'Merry Christmas' from me. I feel reduced."

Coming to realize that she may never be a homeowner, Susan is frustrated by "society's" insistence that a person own to be a real part of a community. But in speaking of her relationship to the middle-class society of which she has always been a part, we had entered territory so painful she could no longer speak aloud. "What do you do when your whole peer group and all of society says, 'You're living on $18,000?'" Her voice becomes completely inaudible.

Susan Andrews is living proof of the power of class-based consumption norms. After two years of declining income, she found herself perilously close to the rock bottom of her middle-class world. Her emotional balance, sense of self, and belief in her ability to have a good life were all jeopardized by this experience. The pain, humiliation, and fear silenced her. Her situation became urgent, and despite her deep belief in what she was doing, she felt panic at

---

°per diem: Daily.

times. She had reached the limits of her downshift. Meaning, challenge, and reasonable levels of stress were essential in a job. But so too was a salary of at least $30,000 a year.

WHEN $18,000 FEELS LUXURIOUS: JEFF LUTZ

Susan Andrews saw only one way out of her difficulties. Earn more. Some Americans are pursuing another path. Want less. Live more simply. Slow down and get in touch with nature. A growing "voluntary simplicity" movement is rejecting the standard path of work and spend. This is a committed, self-conscious group of people who believe that spending less does not reduce their quality of life and may even raise it. Their experience is that *less* (spending) is *more* (time, meaning, peace of mind, financial security, ecological responsibility, physical health, friendship, appreciation of what they do spend). Seattle, long a laid-back, nature-oriented city, is home not only to Boeing and Microsoft but also to many of these individuals. I spent nearly a week there in the summer of 1996, meeting people who were living on less than $20,000 a year. Jeff Lutz was one of them.

After graduating from a small college back east, Jeff and his girlfriend Liza [20] moved to Seattle, where they inhabit a nice, spacious old house in a middle-class neighborhood. They share the place with one friend; their rent is $312 per person. Jeff is self-employed as a medical and legal interpreter and is putting a lot of effort into "growing" his business. Nicely dressed and groomed, he doesn't look too different from other twenty-five-year-old graduates of the prep school and college he attended. But he is. Living on about $10,000 a year, he says he has basically everything he wants and will be content to live at this level of material comfort for the rest of his life. Youthful naïveté? Perhaps. But maybe not.

Lutz grew up in Mexico. His mother, a writer and social activist, went to Mexico with her parents, refugees from Franco's civil war.° His father was a lawyer from New York. Family role models helped form his commitment to a frugal lifestyle. "My great-grandfather, who escaped czarist jail in Lithuania, lived in Mexico with one lightbulb and a record player...."

As a teenager, Lutz went to a private school in western Massachusetts. There he began to feel like "part of a herd being prodded along to do one thing after the next in semiconscious wakefulness. You go to elementary school, and then you go to junior high, and then you go to high school, and then you go to college in order to get a job, in order to compete with other people in higher salaries, in order to have more stuff. I saw really clearly in high school just

---

°**Franco's civil war:** Francisco Franco was a Fascist dictator who won the Spanish Civil War in the 1930s. He was opposed by many Europeans and Americans who preferred democracy or communism to fascism.

where it was leading." At that point, he made up his mind about two things. First, "I needed to find a way to not be in a nine-to-five-until-I-died treadmill. I had a vision of life being much, much more than spending most of my life in a job that was somebody else's agenda." Second, "I wanted to learn how human beings could live more lightly on the earth."

His experiences in Mexico motivated these sentiments. "I spent a week with some Mazotec Indians in the mountains. And some of these kids my age, one of them had a Washington Redskins jersey. I mean, Spanish is their second language; they spoke Mazoteca, and yet they were listening to Michael Jackson and they wanted to buy my sunglasses and they wanted to buy my watch. And they wanted me to bring more sunglasses and watches so that they could resell them to their friends. It was very clear that our culture was sort of surrounding other cultures through the media. I grew up watching *The Love Boat* dubbed in Spanish."

In college, he designed his own major in environmental studies. But unlike many young people who begin their work lives enthusiastically believing they can combine improving the world with making a good salary, Lutz never really considered that path. "The things I was interested in were pretty outside the box." Near the end of his college years, he came across an article by Joe Dominguez, the creator of a nine-step program of "financial independence." Dominguez's program, contained in his best-selling book (with collaborator Vicki Robin) *Your Money or Your Life,* promises freedom from the grind of the working world, not through getting rich but by downsizing desire. Dominguez and Robin believe Americans have been trained to equate more stuff with more happiness. But that is true only up to a point, a point they feel most of us have passed. Doing it their way, you don't need to save a million dollars to retire, but just one, two, or three hundred thousand.

The program involves meticulously tracking all spending. And not just 25 tracking it but scrutinizing it, by comparing the value of whatever you want to buy with the time it takes to earn the money for it. That calculation involves determining your real hourly wage, by taking into account all the hours you work and subtracting all job-related expenses, including the cost of your job wardrobe and takeout food because you're too tired to cook. Equipped with your real wage rate, you can figure out whether a new couch is worth three weeks of work, whether four nights in the Bahamas justify a month of earning, or whether you want to stick with the morning latte (even those half-hours add up). People who follow the program find that when they ask these questions, they spend less. Much less.

Jeff was getting close to financial independence, which entailed earning enough to spend between $800 and $1,200 per month, including health insurance. He says he does not feel materially deprived, and he is careful to point out that voluntary simplicity is not poverty. While he decided against the lattes, he does own a car and a computer, goes out to eat between one and three times a month, rents videos, has friends over for dinner, and buys his clothes both new and used. His furniture is an eclectic mix—nothing fancy, but nothing shabby either. He is convinced that "a higher standard of living will not make me happier. And I'm very clear internally. It's not a belief I picked up from somewhere." It's "something that I've gained an awareness about."

While most of the people I interviewed had a strong community orientation, there are aspects of this lifestyle that emphasize separateness, independence, and self-reliance. Couples often keep their finances separately. Simple-livers limit their spending by bartering their services and limiting shared restaurant meals and gifts.

Finally, simple-livers insist that although they might meet the government's criterion, they are not poor. This is true, but for reasons they sometimes do not recognize. Few Americans can thrive on $10,000 a year. Simple-livers can.... Some started with hefty bank accounts or homes of their own. Because they tend to be at least middle class and well educated, they are able to manage the world around them. They have social and personal confidence, know how to work the system, and have connections to powerful people and institutions. Unlike the traditional poor, they have *options*—including the option of jumping back into mainstream culture.

THE SECRET LIVES OF AMERICAN CITIZENS

Thomas Geoghegan

Thomas Geoghegan, a practicing attorney in Chicago, has published essays on politics and public policy in the New York Times, *the* Chicago Tribune, *the* New Republic, *and other publications. His first book,* Which Side Are You On? *(1991), was a finalist for the National Book Critics Circle Award. This reading, from Geoghegan's most recent book,* The Secret Lives of American Citizens: Pursuing the Promise of American Life *(1998), focuses on the present plight and future opportunities of poor teenagers.*

Geoghegan begins by reminding readers of the growing gap between rich and poor. He is personally troubled by this gap and believes that there are ways to reduce it, but he is highly skeptical of proposals to "send everyone to college." Instead, he believes that schools should teach the poor how to act collectively in their own best interests so that they can achieve "the promise of American life." Yet he is not hopeful, as his experience helping unemployed young people interview for jobs reveals.

Geoghegan's writing is conversational and reflective. He sometimes seems to be talking to himself or trying to engage the reader in a conversation. One reviewer describes his style of writing as "quirky, funny, accessible." Another contrasts it with the writing of "propagandists and professors." Several writers in this section are professors whose writing reflects the style of conventional public argument, which Geoghegan pointedly avoids.

As you read, think about how you would answer some of the many questions Geoghegan poses. Also consider what the future may be like for workers who go into the job market with only a high school education.

There's a Republican, conservative side to me. Every time I read an article on inequality, a little voice inside me says, "Oh well, that's not so bad." But the other day I met a man looking at the old census records of the city. "You know," he said, "it's amazing how big the gap in the city is now between rich and poor. I was looking at census numbers in the 1950s, 1960s. Even in the poorest wards, in the all-black ghettoes...they're still at sixty percent of the city's median income."

Now?

"Oh, it's twenty to thirty percent."

And I thought, "Well, that's not so bad." But I know it is bad. How can we be in the same city together?...

It's disturbing to walk around the city. What do I see people doing? Or to 5 walk in a factory, as I sometimes do. Poor people, no English, do they have skills, or do they need them?

But suppose we had the high-skill workers we always say we want. Suppose we set up our workplace more like Europe. What would happen to the profit margins?°

Do the elite really want people to have more skills? If they have more skills, who's going to park the cars? Or bus the tables? Or do all the things that I see people doing in my city?

I want to believe in public schools. It's not controversial, like unions, collective bargaining. We can change the income structure, and no one will raise a fuss.

What's wrong with this way of achieving the Promise of American Life? It's what Clinton wants to do. In every State of the Union, until now, there's a line or two somewhere, which implies grandly we'll send everyone to college.

How can there be a gap between high school and college graduates' incomes 10 if...well, if everyone goes to college?

Now I know Clinton doesn't mean this literally. But what would happen if we double the amount of college graduates?

°**profit margins:** The profits remaining for businesses and corporations after they pay their employees and the other costs involved in producing their products.

First, it's impossible to imagine. Even now, if the percent going to college remains constant, it's estimated that by 2015 the cost of college tuition will have doubled.

But isn't that like a tax on kids to let them get the same sub-Dilbert°–type jobs?

Second, there's a glut of B.A.s now, with one in five in noncollege jobs. That by itself is OK, as long as the supply of B.A.s stays fairly steady. What's more depressing is the kind of work we now call "college jobs."

To the BLS,° a "college job" is any job the boss wants a B.A. for and actually 15 fills with a B.A. By that technical standard, here is what we now call "college jobs" in the BLS studies: legal secretary, insurance claims adjuster, manager of Blockbuster, assistant manager of Blockbuster.

Will doubling the number of people bidding on these jobs change the way we live? . . .

It vaguely stirred in my head: . . . The purpose of education wasn't to skill kids up for the New World Economy, or to have seven careers. . . . No, wasn't it to get people to vote? That's what Dewey° wanted the schools to teach. Not to get ahead of the other kid, but for all the kids to act together. Dewey's still our master on how to teach kids to live in a democracy.

Indeed, it's the rest of the developed world that vindicates Dewey. He argued against "private collectivism," i.e., big private business. And "public collectivism," i.e., the government.

He and his disciples thought that we should teach our kids to act collectively, *outside* of the state: i.e., to form unions, to "vote" on our wages. It's a mistake that Dewey cared more about "how to think" than "what to think." It's true he didn't want kids to memorize the Great Books. But at least by the New Deal,° he and his disciples argued that we should teach our kids, in the schools, how to act collectively.

Some of his protégés even started a magazine, *The Social Frontier,* at Colum- 20 bia Teachers' College, and that's the message.

Don't trust business. Don't trust government. But act collectively as a group to keep an eye on both.

Dewey's disciples then would say that is the most crucial of all skills that schools need to teach kids.

The 26 million kids, sloshing around down there below the poverty line.

Dewey would say, I believe, that the schools should teach these kids how to . . . vote, the way Europeans do, and fend off those who drag their wages down.

°**Dilbert:** A cartoon-strip character who bumbles through the workplace.   °**BLS:** Bureau of Labor Statistics, an agency of the U.S. government.   °**Dewey:** John Dewey (1859–1952), American philosopher and educator.   °**New Deal:** President Franklin D. Roosevelt's name for his social program during the 1930s.

But what if democracy in Dewey's sense is only possible somewhere else? 25
Then the kids should learn to work long hours, and show up on time.

A friend of mine points out this is really all that many a business person
asks. "Just get them to *show up*."

...Just at least teach them the skills of getting on the El,° showing up, holding the broom.

That's what much of the welfare reform really consists of. Maybe if there is one
thing we should do as citizens in the Clinton era, it's to teach people to show up.

Fill out applications.

Hold the broom. 30

I was involved briefly with a volunteer group that simply worked with kids,
eighteen or nineteen years old, to get them jobs as movie ushers. And it's not so
easy to be an usher, or take the tickets. You have to teach the kid to show up.
Fill out the application. And above all, get through the interview.

I was supposed to help the kid get through the interview. That meant, I too
needed a mentor to tell me what to tell the kid.

"All these kids," my mentor said, "have gaps in their lives that have to be
explained. I mean, these are great kids. They're hardworking. They're in this
program, right? But they have to learn how to do an interview. So the interviewer says, 'I see you dropped out of school. Why?' Now what's the wrong
answer? The wrong answer is, 'I was pregnant.' The right answer is, 'I did a
foolish thing, but this has helped make me a more serious person. I went back
to school and now I have my G.E.D.'"

"OK," I said. "Right answer, wrong answer."

"Or they say to the kid, 'Why did you leave your last job?' The wrong answer 35
is, 'My boss was hitting on me.' The right answer is, 'I felt I needed a new challenge, I wanted to grow as a person.'"

"OK," I said. "I have this."

I looked around the room, and I was impressed how many of the business
people helping these kids were black.

I did this for a while. And all the time I hoped Dewey, wherever he was,
wouldn't be ashamed of me. If he ever did come back, I would tell him: "We're
never going to do in this country what you thought we'd do, raise the wages of
the kids generally. So at least let's teach them to park the cars."

So I sat there silent when I was told:

"Tell the kids not to ask about how much they'll make, or about benefits. At 40
least not the first interview."

I know that's wise. It bothers me, though.

And what's so wonderful is that there are volunteers. And the kids come in,
one by one, out of the 26 million who (this week at least) are in poverty. They
just want an adult to help.

°El: The elevated commuter train in Chicago.

They come here on their own, no one pushing them, with wild ideas of what a job will be like: dangerous fantastical ideas of what a paycheck can do. They'd do anything for a job. One of my mentors told me, "These kids are really, really serious."

THE END OF AFFLUENCE

Jeffrey Madrick

Jeffrey Madrick won an Emmy Award for his economics reporting with NBC News, where he worked from 1985 to 1993. He has been finance editor of Business Week *and a columnist for* Money *magazine and has written articles on the American economy for many other publications. His book,* The End of Affluence: The Causes and Consequences of America's Economic Dilemma *(1995), was praised as what "will be one of the best books on what's happening in the American economy in many years."*

In this reading from The End of Affluence, *Madrick identifies social and political changes that trouble him. Taking a more relentlessly gloomy view than any other writer in this section, he sees many Americans as angry, frightened, divided, intolerant, even bitter. He blames this on economic restructuring and argues that the public mood will not change until greater prosperity for all returns.*

As you read, try to understand why he feels so gloomy. Do his views seem reasonable in light of your reading and personal experience?

Increasingly insecure about our place in society and among our families, friends, and communities, and finding that working harder and longer doesn't make us better off, we have become understandably nostalgic for an era of fast economic growth when families seemed to be financially secure, government did not encumber our standard of living, and our financial expectations were usually met and often surpassed. As our old values have become increasingly undependable, many Americans have looked elsewhere for stable ground: personal fitness, psychotherapies of many kinds, exotic religions and new orthodoxies,° new strains of feminism, environmentalism, and, of course, "family values." The increasing popularity of third-party and independent political candidates is typical of this struggle to find answers to the unprecedented shift in our fortunes....

°**new orthodoxies:** New beliefs that quickly become conventional.

This frustration also accounts for our rising anger and divisiveness. Since at least the early 1980s, critics have called attention to a new separatism among ethnic and religious groups that extends from the suburbs and ghettos to high schools and college campuses. The degree of separatism has only increased. In 1994 suburban communities in Washington, Dallas, and elsewhere tried to ban churches that provide services to the poor, new immigrants, or other unwelcome groups. In Alabama a high school principal forbade interracial dating at the senior prom, and throughout the United States, African-American college students, denouncing integration in favor of empowerment, increasingly separated themselves from the rest of the student body. In the suburbs, segregation became a way of life. Ninety-five percent of blacks on Long Island, New York, for example, lived in only 5 percent of the census tracts. In a Florida county a religious organization demanded that schoolchildren be taught that American values are superior to all others, a reaction to the demands of various American ethnic groups for inclusion of their respective heritages in our public school curricula. The state of California voted to deny public services to illegal immigrants, including school for their children. Between Washington and local lawmakers, partisan animosity rose, as they found it increasingly difficult to satisfy their unhappy constituents by providing them with new programs. Political pundits blamed this on politics as usual; more likely, it was the result of slow growth.... Congress was almost unable to pass the widely popular but stripped-down crime bill in the summer of 1994 largely because there was not enough pork° to pass around to the warring constituencies. The new Speaker of the House, Newt Gingrich, suggested putting children of impoverished parents in orphanages and refusing benefits to unwed mothers, a trivial contribution at best to our fiscal balance,° but attractive to many frightened and angry voters.

Americans have often been in conflict before, of course. Today's public anxiety over national values and our common future recalls the unrest of the early 1800s as the United States was transforming itself from a traditional agrarian° economy to a largely mercantile° and industrial one that lifted incomes quickly and broadly. Strains brought about by this new commercial economy—emigration from farms to increasingly dense cities and the widespread creation of new wealth, which challenged the traditional agricultural hierarchy—produced a contentious social, political, and religious environment in which...the old Calvinism° gave way to the democratic Christianity of the Second Great Awakening,° in which anyone,

---

°**pork:** Government money allocated to benefit special interests, often of questionable merit.   °**fiscal balance:** A reference to the controversy over balancing the federal budget.   °**agrarian:** Based on agriculture.   °**mercantile:** Based on buying and selling products or trading them with other countries.   °**Calvinism:** A set of Protestant religious beliefs stressing strict morality and family life. Calvinists believed that only those whom God had elected could be saved.   °**Second Great Awakening:** In the nineteenth century, a period of religious revivals, formation of new religious denominations, and increasing religious tolerance.

not just a chosen elite, could be saved. From this same democratic fervor arose feminism and abolitionism,° labor unions, and temperance societies, as well as the political movements that eventually won universal suffrage for all white males, not simply men of property as provided in the Constitution.

These battles in behalf of greater opportunity were not easily won. The new movements, as well as the new churches, were often antagonistic toward one another. But the dislocations they caused were typical of the turmoil that usually accompanies rapid economic transformation, in this case the same rapid transformation that inspired our national optimism and the faith, soon broadcast around the world, that America was the land of opportunity for all.... [I]ncomes periodically fell but typically rose again within a matter of years. As markets grew and productivity increased, the economy in general began to expand more rapidly. Material well-being and prosperity validated the principles of equality and democracy. The Emancipation Proclamation° and the war that made it possible were rooted in the optimistic movements that emerged in the 1820s, culminating in Lincoln's claim that under God all men are created equal. (As for women, they would have to wait for the next century, although they were to win the right to vote in some western territories as early as the 1870s and 1880s.) Rapidly increasing prosperity ultimately fostered a national spirit of inclusion, tolerance, and compromise that enhanced the rights of the so-called common man as it would eventually those of blacks, new immigrants, and women, at least by the standards of the times, while it subdued the more pessimistic elements in our society. As we progressed materially we found common cultural and social ground to share. Prosperity was the foundation of our best convictions as a nation, for what equality of opportunity meant in a rising economy was that with a lot of hard work most Americans could live a decent life and expect better for their children.

The dislocations that we have experienced since the 1970s are also the results 5 of an economic transformation, marked this time by narrowing opportunity over two long decades. As our material expectations are disappointed our new social, political, and religious movements become increasingly exclusionary, intolerant, and uncompromising, for now equality of opportunity implies sharing scarce resources, not voluntarily but under the compulsion of the government and the labor markets. No wonder that politicians often invoke an imagined golden age of stable nuclear families, frontier individualism, and opportunity for all, free of government interference and high taxes. But if slow economic growth stimulates such compensating illusions, it also destroys them as one set of political promises after another is inevitably broken, leaving many of us increasingly bitter and anguished as we grope for solutions that can't be

---

°**abolitionism:** The movement to abolish, or end, slavery in the United States.   °**Emancipation Proclamation:** Issued by President Abraham Lincoln in 1863 at the height of the Civil War, it proclaimed the freedom of all slaves in the Confederate states.

found. This bitterness is likely to continue. Without increasing prosperity, Americans are losing the courage of the convictions they once shared. The idea of equality and the democratic values that accompany it are no longer as honored as they were when we were getting richer and could imagine prosperity for all. As personal resources decline and national prospects dim, we are losing our nerve as individuals. National paranoia° shows signs of revival. We seek scapegoats° and hide in illusions about our past. As many of us retreat to the safety of this imaginary past, we forget that the very forebears whom we invoke abandoned the exclusionary politics and social institutions of their own past as their economic environment improved.

A WRITER'S NOTEBOOK

Surveying Consequences of the Restructured Economy

The following tasks are designed to help you think about the readings and identify and start to work up material you might use in your own essay. If you need help with tasks that require summarizing, see Appendix 1.

1. *Review your list of consequences.* If you compiled a list of consequences relating to the restructured economy that the authors of the readings in this section presented, look it over now. Compare your list with those of your classmates and make it as complete as possible. This list will be the basis for your essay speculating about possible consequences of the restructured economy.

2. *React to Sue Shellenbarger's proposed consequences.* Select one consequence you consider likely and one you consider unlikely. Describe each one briefly and write a few sentences explaining why you evaluate it as you do.

3. *Speculate about Robert Reich's proposals.* In paragraphs 12–19 Reich speculates that the future may be brighter if individuals, government, and business work together "to give all Americans a stake in economic growth, to ensure that everyone benefits from our newfound competitiveness." Highlight or underline the specific contributions that individuals, government, and business must make. Then write a half-page or so speculating about the likelihood of any of these contributions being implemented in the near future so that your generation could benefit from them.

4. *Summarize and respond to part of Jeremy Rifkin's argument.* Summarize Rifkin's argument in paragraphs 7–9 for a shorter workweek. Then write a half-page or so speculating about this possibility for you personally and for your generation. Address these questions: Would you like to see it happen? How likely is it to become widespread? What advantages and disadvantages do you see in a shorter workweek?

5. *React to the statistics and one of the profiles in Juliet B. Schor's reading.* Select two or three sets of statistics about voluntary downshifters that surprised or inter-

---

°**paranoia:** Irrational distrust of others.   °**scapegoats:** Objects of blame, usually unjustified.

ested you and write a few sentences explaining your reaction. Also reread one of the three profiles of voluntary downshifters and comment on what motivated them to change and what effects it has had, what you find positive, and what you question.

6. *React to part of Thomas Geoghegan's argument.* Geoghegan argues that poor students need not go to college. Explain why he thinks they probably should not and what the schools should do for them instead. Then write a few more sentences reacting to this argument.

7. *Respond to Jeffrey Madrick's speculations.* In paragraph 5, bracket the final seven sentences of Madrick's speculations about the future. Highlight or underline the specific consequences he mentions. Then write a page or so responding to his views. Do you think members of your generation are losing their nerve, becoming bitter, looking for scapegoats? In developing your ideas, refer to your own experience, your interviews, or anything relevant that you remember from the readings.

Now it is your turn. What do you think about the future of your generation in light of the restructured economy? You are in a very favorable position to plan and write an essay on this issue. You command a large amount of material, including the readings in this chapter about the economy, about generational competition, and about consequences for your generation. If you have been doing the work suggested in the writer's notebook sections, you also have notes from interviews, observations, and personal experience, and you have probably benefited from class discussion and personal reflections on the readings.

This writing guide will help you

- plan, draft, revise, edit, and proofread an essay speculating about the consequences of the restructured economy
- try out certain kinds of sentences that are useful in speculating about the future
- work with sources — to gather current information and to cite sources that you draw on
- reflect on what you learned completing this assignment

PLANNING AND DRAFTING YOUR ESSAY

This section provides guidelines and examples to help you plan and draft a convincing essay about some likely consequences of the new economy for your generation. It will help you

- understand your readers and your writing situation
- select materials
- prepare a prospectus
- organize your essay
- devise a convincing argument
- cite sources

THE WRITING ASSIGNMENT   Write an essay speculating about the most likely consequences of the restructured economy for one economic group within your generation. In your essay, you will need to inform your readers about the basic features of the restructured economy and help them understand the sources of generational competition. Most important will be your argument that some possible consequences of the restructured economy are more likely than others. You will need to support your choice of consequences by citing the readings and, perhaps, interviews you may have conducted and your own experience. You should also help readers understand that consequences they might have thought likely may not be so likely after all.

Assume that you are writing this essay as an opinion piece to be published in a college newspaper or a magazine for college students.

Understanding Your Readers

Assume that your readers will be your peers: other students in colleges across America. Your purpose is to convince them to take your argument seriously. You can do so only if you demonstrate that you are well informed about the economy and its possible consequences for your generation and if you can devise a plausible argument for the consequences you think most likely. Since the restructuring of the economy and its possible consequences are of great importance to everyone's future, you can assume that they will be eager readers—if you can pull them into the essay and sustain their interest.

Except for a few upper-division students majoring in economics or political science, your readers almost certainly will know no more than you knew before you started reading about the economy. In your role as an expert, you can provide them with valuable information by sorting through the diverse consequences others have proposed and singling out the ones that seem most likely to you.

Your readers—college students across the country—are a surprisingly diverse group. They come from all social classes, although a high percentage are middle class. Twenty-eight percent are ethnic minorities or foreign students. Half are twenty-two years of age or older; a quarter are thirty or older. A slight majority are women. Almost half of all students attend community colleges. Eighty percent go to public colleges or universities. At the same time, your readers share the desire for a good job and a rewarding career after graduation. Focus on these shared values and goals, but at the same time keep the diversities in mind. The students in your writing course very likely represent the ethnic groups and economic levels among the student body. In your class discussions, you will get a good idea what your classmates knew about the economy before the course began and what diverse views they have about the consequences for your generation. This knowledge will help you anticipate how much your readers know and how they may react to your argument.

Perhaps the important thing to keep in mind is that you may not have especially good news to deliver to your readers. Compared to those in college in the 1950s and even in the 1970s, college students today have a relatively less certain future, as the readings suggest. Therefore, you will need to think carefully about how to interest your readers in news that they may find sobering and how to hold their attention while you speculate about what its consequences might be for them.

Selecting Materials

The readings and writing tasks in this chapter contributed to your understanding of the restructured economy. Now you can select from those resources materials to describe that economy and speculate about a few of its likely consequences.

List and Review Consequences.   If you prepared a list of consequences from the readings in "Surveying Consequences of the Restructured Economy," review your list to refresh your memory about what you discovered. To extend your list, look now for possible consequences mentioned in the following readings in "Understanding the Restructured Economy" and "Understanding Generational Competition": Andrew Hacker (paragraphs 9–13); Lawrence R. Mishel, Jared Bernstein, and John Schmitt (paragraph 26); Edward N. Wolff (paragraph 16); Janice Castro (paragraphs 23–24); Barbara Rudolph (paragraphs 26–34); Tony Horwitz (paragraphs 16–18, 24–34); Keith Bradsher (paragraphs 21, 28); Leon F. Bouvier and Carol J. De Vita (paragraphs 6–7); and Rob Nelson and Jon Cowan (paragraphs 50–58). Since you may decide to include some of these consequences in your essay, record the author and paragraph number of each one you add to your list for easy identification.

From your interviews, observations, reflections on your own experience, and class discussions, you may have discovered possible future consequences not mentioned in the readings. If so, include any that are relevant in your list.

This list of consequences will prepare you to plan the most important part of your essay—the argument you make to support the likelihood or plausibility of the consequences you find most convincing. It will give you an overview of all the consequences proposed in this chapter's readings, ensuring that you do not overlook any that may interest you and allowing you to connect related consequences. The list will also make it easy for you to identify consequences that challenge your own so that you can counterargue them.

Focus on One Income Group.   It would be quite difficult to speculate about the consequences of the restructured economy for an entire generation, for both men and women, working-class and upper-middle-class workers, high school dropouts and MDs or Ph.D.s, employees and employers, Southerners and Westerners, or recent immigrants and long-timers. Therefore, you can benefit greatly by focusing on one of the groups in the following widely recognized income-level categories:

- working poor (less than $18,000 a year)—fast-food preparers and servers, laborers working for roughly minimum wage
- lower-middle class ($18,000–$30,000 a year)—lower-level office workers, noncommissioned and telephone salespeople, security guards, managers of fast-food franchises
- middle class ($31,000–$60,000 a year)—teachers, nurses, social workers, police officers, skilled and union laborers, small-business owners, midlevel office workers, manufacturers' representatives

- upper-middle class ($60,000–$150,000 a year)—lawyers, medical doctors, engineers, architects, and other degreed professionals, medium-size business owners, upper-level managers and executives
- wealthy ($150,000 to millions of dollars a year plus earnings from stocks, bonds, property, and other investments)—corporate chief executive officers, investors, real estate developers, surgeons, large-business owners, media celebrities, professional athletes, people with inherited wealth

Choose one income group and speculate about the consequences for that group alone. (You could also focus on women or some ethnic group within one of these income categories.) You need not be a present or prospective member of the group you choose, and you need not assume your readers are primarily in the group.

Select Consequences.   Review your list of consequences to identify those concerned with *future possibilities*. These are the consequences that are highly speculative, that may or may not happen. Depending on your point of view, they are either likely or unlikely, but they are not certain. Put an "x" or an asterisk in the margin by each one of them.

The remaining unmarked consequences in your list can be considered *already apparent* consequences, the ones that do not invite speculation because they are already obvious to everyone who is informed about the restructured economy. They need not be debated. This list of *already apparent* consequences will be useful to you when you introduce the restructured economy to your readers.

Sometimes distinctions between consequences that are already apparent and those that are possible in the future are not easy to discern. Distinguishing between the two, however, ensures that your argument will be focused on possible future consequences. The following guidelines may help you distinguish between the two types of consequences suggested in the readings.

Start by considering a well-established *feature* of the new economy, such as flat or declining income for most employees. An *already apparent* consequence of this feature is that some people are working more hours. *Possible future* consequences are (1) that income disparity will decrease either because labor unions become reenergized or because politics turn progressive and new federal laws and programs lead to more equal distribution of income, or (2) that income will continue to decline and employees at the bottom will become increasingly frustrated, financially insecure, and politically alienated.

Do not spend too much time debating whether a consequence is already apparent or only a future possibility. Your goal is to create a comprehensive list of possible future consequences that will help you make choices when you draft your essay.

Finally, with your readers and the income group you are focusing on in mind, select at least three to five *possible future* consequences of interest to you, ones that you believe are likely and that seem particularly relevant to the work and life opportunities of the income group you have targeted.

Identify Key Readings and Interviews.   Identify two or three key readings and interviews you may have conducted that you now think will provide essential support for the consequences you have selected. Review these readings and interview notes to think about how you will make use of them to develop a convincing argument that each consequence is likely to become a reality in the short or long run for members of your selected income group.

Preparing a Prospectus

At this point, your instructor may want you to prepare a prospectus for your essay, to plot out some of its parts. Engineers, businesspeople, and other professionals write prospectuses for projects to win support and funding. In much the same way, a prospectus for an essay allows you to try out your argument for particular readers and to begin thinking seriously about how you will support it. Approach it as an informal writing task, a first draft of your still-tentative ideas.

Here are some guidelines for drafting a two- or three-page prospectus.

1. *Identify an income group.* Identify the income group you will focus on. Write two or three sentences explaining why you selected it.

2. *List possible future consequences.* From your list, choose three to five possible future consequences that seem to you likely for this income group. Then write a few sentences exploring how these consequences are related. Do they seem alike in certain ways or different? Does one lead to another? If you discover that two or three of them are much alike, you may want to combine them and then add to your list one or two different consequences. Other discoveries may lead you to reconsider your initial list of consequences. You need not start over with this task if you decide to add to or subtract from your initial list of consequences; instead, write informally about your changes of direction or additions.

3. *Try out a logical sequence for your proposed future consequences.* List the consequences you want to speculate about in the most logical, convincing sequence you can imagine for now.

4. *Identify one important reading and interview.* Which single reading and interview will be most important in supporting your speculations? Explain in two or three sentences why each one will be so important.

5. *Identify a consequence that challenges the consequences you believe to be most likely.* Identify one consequence from another reading that seems to challenge or question any of those you plan to argue for. Describe it briefly and write a few sentences explaining the challenge it poses and exploring how you might counterargue it. (To counterargue is to attempt to convince readers that this consequence is either not likely to affect the income group you focus on or not such a contradiction to your speculations as it might first appear to be.)

6. *Try to support one part of your argument.* Select one consequence and write a page or so supporting—arguing for—its likelihood with facts, statistics, examples, anecdotes, or quotations from the readings. Do not take time now to

consider the readings. Rely on your memory, notes, and perhaps a quick look at one key reading. Include relevant evidence from your experiences, observations, and interviews. Write quickly. Your purpose is merely to try out one small part of your argument in order to discover what you have to say before you plan your entire essay. You may want to begin directly like this: "One likely consequence of the new economy for members of the [income group you have chosen] of my generation is _____."

Organizing Your Essay

Readers familiar with writing that speculates about the consequences or effects of phenomena (like the restructured economy) expect the writer to present the subject clearly at the very beginning and to interest them in the subject, perhaps by demonstrating that it has relevance for their lives or that it poses questions or challenges that need to be thought through. They also look for the writer to identify the consequences he or she thinks most likely and to argue energetically in support of these consequences, relying on information from other writers and perhaps on personal experience, interviews, and other observations.

Many writers follow a simple two-part plan, first informing readers about the subject, then speculating about its consequences.

To develop your essay, you might expand this plan in the following way:

Presentation of the subject
—an engaging opening
—information about the subject
—a sampling of already apparent consequences

Argument and counterargument
—thesis and forecast
—arguments to support the likelihood of the possible future consequences, including anticipation of readers' likely objections or questions
—counterarguments to different possible consequences
—conclusion

A plan of this sort can serve you well as you organize your essay. Some parts may be accomplished in one paragraph, while others may require several paragraphs.

Following are some guidelines for implementing this plan.

Presenting the Subject.   In addition to describing the subject to readers, you also need to help them to see its larger social significance and its importance to them personally. You want to spark their interest and to provide adequate background for your argument.

WRITING AN ENGAGING OPENING.   Try to catch your readers' attention and get them to see the significance of the subject. You might try one of these approaches:

- Narrate a scenario, something that could have happened or might happen (as Hacker does in paragraph 1).

- Report a case or two based on interviews (as do Horwitz in paragraphs 1–4 and Louis Uchitelle in paragraphs 1–3).

- Give brief examples (as do Bradsher in paragraphs 1–2 and Sam Dillon in paragraphs 1–3).

- Report a troubling trend (as do Sanford Jacoby, Robert Reich, Juliet B. Schor, and Jeffrey Madrick in the opening paragraph of their readings).

- Declare a crisis (as do Mishel, Bernstein, and Schmitt in paragraphs 1–2; Wolff in paragraphs 1–4; and Nelson and Cowan in paragraphs 1–4).

- Feature a revealing quotation (as Jeremy Rifkin does in paragraph 1).

- Announce surprising facts or statistics (as do Janice Castro in paragraphs 1–2 and Geoghegan in paragraphs 1–4).

You may want to draft your opening after you have drafted the rest of the essay: knowing what you are going to say can make it easier to discover a way to connect it to readers' interests. Whatever opening you choose, keep in mind that you are writing for college students who are not experts about the new economy.

PROVIDING INFORMATION ABOUT THE SUBJECT. Your first obligation is to help your readers understand the nature of the restructured economy and of generational competition. Without a solid—though necessarily limited—understanding, they will be in no position to follow your speculations about the consequences for your generation. Here are several ways to provide that information:

- Present key statistics (as do Mishel, Bernstein, and Schmitt throughout their reading; Castro in paragraphs 4–5; and Bouvier and De Vita in paragraphs 8–11).

- Give examples (as do Jacoby in paragraph 11; Bradsher in paragraphs 12–13 and 23–24; and Dillon in paragraphs 11, 19, and 22–26).

- Provide definitions (as do Castro in paragraphs 4 and 15 and Wolff in paragraph 10).

- Detail cases (as do Bradsher in paragraphs 8–10; Horwitz in paragraphs 1–2 and 14–34; and Uchitelle in paragraphs 1–3, 14–16, and 23–30).

- Quote authorities (as Castro, Bradsher, Horwitz, and Uchitelle all do).

- Make generalizations or assertions (as do Rudolph in paragraphs 1 and 20–34 and Uchitelle in paragraphs 4–6 and 20–21).

- Mention causes (as do Castro in paragraphs 18–19 and Nelson and Cowan in paragraphs 27–45).

- Provide historical context (as do Rudolph in paragraphs 2–19; Jacoby in paragraphs 2–3; and Dillon in paragraphs 3–4 and 12–14).

Look closely at several of these illustrations to become familiar with strategies you may want to adopt to present information about the economy to your readers. Because you need to present the restructured economy efficiently and briefly, emphasize its main features and select a limited amount of revealing information.

PRESENTING A SAMPLE OF ALREADY APPARENT CONSEQUENCES.   In addition to information about the major features of the economy, you need to tell readers some of the ways the new economic arrangements have already changed the workplace and people's expectations about the future. From the following readings, you can select some already apparent consequences and observe how the writers present them: Hacker (paragraphs 6–7 and 10–12); Mishel, Bernstein, and Schmitt (paragraph 28); Wolff (paragraph 2); Castro (paragraphs 3–5); Rudolph (paragraphs 1 and 23–25); Bradsher (paragraphs 5–6, 11, and 16); Dillon (paragraphs 16–18); Reich (paragraphs 9–11); Schor (paragraphs 2–4); and Geoghegan (paragraphs 1–3).

Sequencing Your Argument and Counterargument.

Once you have oriented your readers to your subject and made them aware of its significance, you come to the heart of your essay—convincing them that certain future possible consequences of the restructured economy are plausible, even likely.

SEQUENCING CONSEQUENCES.   Your primary organizational task is to decide the order in which you will present these consequences. Which one should come first? Which one next? Which one last? There is no formula, but the following suggestions may be helpful.

You might begin with the consequence you think readers will find most plausible or for which you have the strongest support. Alternatively, to establish your authority, you could lead off with the consequence you plan to support primarily with your own work experiences or with interviews.

Another option is to group related consequences. For example, if two of your consequences concern changes in lifestyle, place one after the other. You might also begin by naming consequences that are likely to be noticed in the next few years and then go on to those likely to be noticed in later years. Some researchers who have studied the impact of arguments on readers recommend stating the most likely or significant consequence last because readers are more likely to remember what they read last.

The most important thing is that you come up with a logical progression so that each consequence prepares readers for the next one. Think also about transitions that will explicitly indicate how your consequences are related to each other. Let your tentative sequence guide your drafting, but be prepared to change it as you learn more about what kind of argument you can actually make.

CONSIDERING YOUR COUNTERARGUMENTS.   When you counterargue, you anticipate and respond to readers' questions and objections about your argument and show them that you are aware of consequences that challenge your own, that predict a different future from the one you envision. For example, if you speculate that women managers will find great advancement within the next twenty years, you might need to counterargue the speculation that as social separatism and divisiveness increase under the strain of the new economy, equality for women in the workplace will be seriously set back. In the next section, you will learn about strategies of counterargument. The question for now is where to position counterarguments within your step-by-step argument for consequences. Again, there are no formulas, but consider the following suggestions.

Perhaps the best location for counterarguing readers' likely questions or objections is at any point where you think they might occur to readers. This approach would lead you to respond to readers' questions or objections as you argue to support your proposed consequences. Examples of this approach can be seen in Nelson and Cowan (paragraphs 16–18) and Geoghegan (paragraphs 5–7), who poses questions he assumes that readers may have.

You will probably need to counterargue any consequences that challenge the ones you foresee either before or after you present your argument for the consequences you foresee. The advantage of admitting challenges first is that it shows you to be knowledgeable and fair minded and allows you to develop your speculations as a refutation of the challenges. Madrick (paragraphs 1–4) takes this approach. You can also put your refutation at the end of your speculations, but you then need to reiterate your own view of the future before closing. Nelson and Cowan take this approach (paragraphs 50–58), although instead of reiterating their own speculations, they close with a rhetorical question, which is a way to invite readers to reiterate the writers' views by answering the question as they would.

Closing Effectively.   Try to close your essay gracefully and memorably, perhaps even with a flourish. What are some of your options?

- Reiterate your main point, as Hacker, Jacoby, Nelson and Cowan, and Shellenbarger do.

- Summarize your argument, as Mishel, Bernstein, and Schmitt (paragraphs 27–28) and Schor (paragraphs 27–28) do.

- Frame your speculations by referring to something at the beginning, as Reich and Madrick do.

- Introduce a new possible consequence implied by the preceding argument, as Rudolph does (paragraphs 33–34).

- Quote an authority or person profiled, a popular strategy with this chapter's writers, including Castro, Horwitz, Uchitelle, Bradsher, Dillon, Rifkin, and Geoghegan (paragraphs 40 and 43).

You might decide to use one or more of these strategies for your conclusion — or something entirely different. Whatever you decide, take advantage of this opportunity to make a memorable final statement.

Developing Your Argument and Counterargument

This section will help you construct a thesis, argue to support the consequences you propose, and counterargue readers' likely questions or objections as well as consequences in the readings that challenge your own.

Constructing a Thesis.   A *thesis* is a clear assertion of your position, in this case your judgment about the future and your statement about the specific consequences that follow from that judgment. A strong and workable thesis requires a small set of key terms that identify your subject and the consequences you propose. These key terms should be repeated throughout the essay to help you stay focused on the consequences you are arguing for and to help readers follow your argument. Most theses also forecast the sequence in which the consequences will be presented, making your argument easier to follow and more memorable.

You need a tentative thesis now in order to start organizing and drafting your essay. Keep in mind, however, that you may revise — or even replace — your thesis several times during the writing process.

Although a thesis and forecast can be delivered in one sentence, they usually require several sentences. Here is an example from an essay by Charlotte Austin, who speculated about the future of the working poor. Early in her essay, as she presented a picture of the restructured economy, she introduced and cited Bouvier and De Vita, Reich, and Rifkin (and other readings) and then referred to them again at the beginning of her thesis statement:

```
Though Bouvier and De Vita, Reich, and Rifkin believe
the future can be bright for the working poor of my
generation, I believe the future looks grim for them. From
my reading and interviews, I believe that the working poor
will increasingly fall into the impoverished underclass,
bringing about frustration and anger. This anger, I am
afraid, will lead to dangerous levels of family crisis and
to larger social divisiveness. These consequences need not
occur, but I believe they will because jobs for the
working poor will be increasingly contingent, leading to
long periods of unemployment, and the public schools will
fail to educate children of the working poor to a level
that would let them climb into the middle class.
```

This ambitious thesis is grounded in the readings and in Austin's writer's notebook tasks. Notice first that it focuses on one income level and asserts a clear, if pessimistic, judgment about the future for the working poor. To justify this pessimism, Austin proposes six possible consequences of the restructured economy for this group:

- downward mobility into poverty or the underclass for many
- growing frustration and anger as a result

- more crisis within working-poor families
- increased social divisiveness between the working poor and classes above them
- more working time spent in contingent jobs, with subsequent periods of unemployment
- further failure of the schools to educate the children of the working poor

Austin grouped these consequences to reveal their logical relationships, which she made explicit as she developed her argument. The first four consequences — downward mobility, frustration and anger, family crises, and social divisiveness — compose a logical sequence, each resulting from the one before. The last two — contingent work and school failure — are the primary consequences that set into motion the other four. Instead of beginning with these primary causes, though, Austin began with social and psychological consequences, perhaps because she believed they would have more impact on readers. Austin's thesis forecasts this sequence: in her argument she begins with downward mobility and ends with school failure, just as she promises. Readers need this kind of forecast so they know what is coming and, therefore, can read with greater confidence and understanding.

Austin settled on her thesis only after class discussion of thesis drafts, a brief conference with her instructor, and frequent tinkering with key terms and sentence structure. She was prepared to devise a workable thesis only because she had command of the readings and had learned a great deal from her interviews. For example, she gained confidence to question Reich's proposal for school reform from interviews with her uncle, a retired urban high school principal.

This next thesis is from an essay by Wilson Ng.

```
The upper-middle-class members of my generation have a
bright future because most of us will be willing to
accept a realistic definition of success. We will have
historically low average incomes for our class during the
early and middle part of our careers, but later on, as the
baby boomers retire, more upper-level positions at higher
salaries will open up. During our careers we will see
the workweek shortened, and, as a result, we will have
more free time than previous generations had. A shorter
workweek will enable more of us to keep full-time jobs,
even though it may mean lower top salaries than in
previous generations. As a consequence, we will consume
less and be less materialistic than previous generations.
A few baby boomers have already voluntarily adopted a
lifestyle in keeping with this realistic definition of
success, and I am convinced that the vast majority of the
upper middle class of my generation will do so as well.
```

Ng is as optimistic as Austin is pessimistic. There is no mistaking his judgment and his reasons for making it. The economic consequences he thinks most likely for the upper middle class are

- low incomes early but higher incomes later
- shorter workweek and more free time
- less consumption and materialism

Robert Smith launched his essay with this thesis:

```
Many experts believe that the inequities of the new
economy can be corrected. They write about a rebuilt
middle class, improved education, flexible and shorter
work schedules, more self-reliance and creativity on
the part of workers, and voluntarily chosen simpler
lifestyles. My research has convinced me that none of
this is likely to happen. The future I see for the
middle class is one of working conditions that benefit
only corporations and bureaucracies--long hours,
contingent work, fewer benefits, lack of training, and
low top wages and limited opportunity for advancement.
During the most productive years of my generation,
the baby boomers will have the political clout to
demand more and more of the resources that might have
gone to us to support ourselves in our retirement.
The result will be a lower standard of living than
that of the middle class in three previous generations.
And there will be disillusionment and bitterness as
members of my generation watch certain highly skilled
professionals and corporate CEOs become richer and richer.
```

Smith's speculations center on four consequences:

- unfair working conditions
- demands of retiring baby boomers
- low standard of living
- disillusionment and bitterness

Smith's gloomy judgment is unmistakable, and he has singled out consequences that will enable him to defend this judgment with information from the readings. Smith's thesis shares an interesting feature with Austin's: it not only identifies consequences and forecasts their sequence, but also anticipates for readers at least part of the counterargument Smith must attempt. In the first sentence he lists experts' views that differ from his. To succeed with his argument, Smith must attempt to refute these views. Because he lists these views before identifying his own, readers would assume that he will attempt to refute them before he argues to support his own views.

EXAMPLES FROM THE READINGS. For further examples of thesis statements, examine the following readings: Reich (paragraphs 1 and 6); Schor (paragraph 1); Geoghegan (paragraphs 1–5); and Madrick (paragraph 1).

Arguing.   The heart of your essay and easily the most challenging section for you as a writer is the argument for the consequences you find most likely. You cannot simply list the consequences. That would leave in readers' minds too many questions:

- How did the writer select these consequences from among all those possible?
- Why does the writer expect these consequences to occur?
- What's the connection among these consequences?
- I wonder why the writer did not focus on some of the consequences that seem most likely to me?
- What gives this writer the authority to assert that these consequences are likely?
- Are these short-term or long-term consequences?
- Does anyone else think these consequences are likely?
- Why are these consequences presented in this order?

When you argue for consequences, you answer questions like these. You need not attempt to prove that you are right about the future and everyone else is wrong. You need only convince readers that the consequences you foresee *may* come about and that they should take your speculations seriously.

The first example comes from the essay by Charlotte Austin, whose thesis appears in the previous section. Austin believes that the working class has a bleak future and that one of the consequences for them is downward mobility. (In the student examples in this section, Austin and Wilson Ng rely on formal citation, following MLA style; Robert Smith relies on informal citation.)

```
Downward mobility will become a reality for more and more
of the working class in the years ahead. In my research,
not a writer I encountered held out hope that life could
get better for more than a few fortunate members of the
working class. Unfortunately for the working class,
manufacturing jobs paying $10 to $20 an hour have been
disappearing. As workers lose manufacturing jobs, they are
lucky to find jobs paying the same wage. For example,
Thomson Consumer Electronics closed an Indiana television
plant in 1998, and 1,100 workers lost their jobs. Seven
months later only 100 of these workers had found jobs that
payed as well as or better than their Thomson jobs
(Uchitelle 580). An employment expert in Indianapolis
described these workers' expectations of finding good-
paying jobs and maintaining their standard of living as
"not necessarily realistic" (Uchitelle 580). The Thomson
jobs were moved to new factories in Mexico, and other U.S.
companies have been moving American jobs to Mexico.
General Motors, for example, has built more than fifty
parts factories in Mexico since 1978. In these factories,
72,000 Mexican workers earn $1 to $2 an hour in jobs that
```

```
once paid U.S. workers $20 or more an hour (Dillon 591).
When manufacturing jobs move to other countries, workers
left behind must often take service jobs like house and
office cleaning and fast-food preparation, but these jobs
pay a couple with a child or two working full-time barely
enough to live above the poverty line. I believe this
trend will continue, ensuring a bleak future for more and
more members of the working class.
```

Austin effectively uses two basic strategies of supporting an argument: authorities and examples. She relies on two readings — those of Louis Uchitelle and Sam Dillon — to support her argument for this consequence. From Uchitelle, she borrows a quote by an authority and makes use of the example of the closing of the Thomson television factory. From Dillon, she selects one example of U.S. auto parts suppliers' plants in Mexico. Except for the quote from Uchitelle, she paraphrases information from the two reports.

Another example of arguing to support consequences comes from the essay by Wilson Ng, whose thesis appears in the previous section. Ng is optimistic about the future for upper-middle-class members of his generation. At the beginning of his argument, he speculates that even though incomes remain historically low during the early and middle periods of people's careers, they will end up as high as in previous generations. Here is that section of his argument:

```
No income level escapes the consequences of the
restructured American economy, not even the privileged
upper middle class. These men and women managers and
professionals in all parts of the country will see the
pattern of their careers unfold differently from the
pattern for previous generations. A fundamental difference
is that they will have to wait longer to achieve the high
incomes associated with their class. Demographers have
argued, "the small baby-bust generation [...] should find
a more favorable social and economic environment than
did the baby boomers. With fewer labor force entrants,
employment opportunities for members of the baby-bust
generation should flourish, wages should once again rise
[...]" (Bouvier and De Vita 602). I expect this
prediction to come true only for the upper middle class,
and for them not until their late forties and fifties. The
reason is that they will have to wait for aging baby
boomers to move out of the high-paying jobs. This reality
will force some hard choices on the upper middle class.
During the child-rearing years, many will not have the
income to support both children and a lifestyle that
includes travel, minimal luxuries, and a nice house in an
upscale neighborhood (Hacker 541).
        In addition to waiting for the baby boomers to clear
out, some members of my generation must deal with the
```

```
career-path uncertainties of contingent work. While
professional freelance consultants stand to lose least
from contingent work (Castro 562), they may need a long
time to make the connections and develop the skills to
make it on their own. Robert Schaen, a former corporate
employee who now runs his own small publishing business,
says, "People are going to have to create their own lives,
their own careers and their own successes.[...] You're
now in business for yourself" (Castro 566). Unlike
managers on a well-defined promotion track in a
corporation, upper-middle-class contingent workers will
have to create their own track. There will be more
uncertainty and more ups and downs, but for those who
persist and develop highly refined skills that are in
demand, the payoff should eventually arrive.
```

Ng speculates that members of the upper middle class in his generation will eventually prosper but only if they are patient. To convince his readers of the likelihood of this consequence, he must find a way to support the argument that success will come later for this income level than in previous generations. He does so by relying on two strategies: quoting authorities and pointing out contrasts (between present and past generations, early and late career possibilities, and conventional managers and contingent specialists). He makes effective use of three readings, quoting Bouvier and De Vita, paraphrasing Hacker, and paraphrasing Castro and quoting an authority she quotes.

EXAMPLES FROM THE READINGS. You can find further arguments for consequences in the readings by Shellenbarger, Reich (paragraphs 9–10 and 13–14), and Madrick (paragraphs 2 and 5).

Counterarguing. You should assume that some of your readers will object to or question your speculations and will be aware of consequences proposed by others that challenge your own. Anticipating these questions, objections, and challenges and addressing them directly in your essay is what is meant by counterargument. You may counterargue by acknowledging that you are aware of others' views, by conceding the value or wisdom of those views, or by refuting them.

Charlotte Austin's essay speculating about the bleak future of the working class provides a good example of counterargument. One of the consequences she foresees is the failure of the public schools to prepare working-class children to avoid falling into poverty and to move into the middle class. Aware that Robert Reich hopes that the public schools will do their part to prepare the poorest Americans to find work and support themselves, Austin refutes this expectation:

```
In spite of this record of failure by urban high schools,
where nearly all working-class and poor teenagers go to
school, some Americans continue to believe that urban high
```

schools can transform themselves in time to make a
difference in the lives of teenagers in our generation.
Robert Reich, President Clinton's first-term labor
secretary, writes about government's role in "improving
the quality of public education, setting skills standards
and smoothing the transition from school to work [...]"
(617). But government from local to federal has had a role
all along since the economy began to change in the early
1970s, and most people seem to think that the schools are
worse now than at the beginning of the restructuring. For
Reich's hopes to be realized, there would have to be major
immediate changes in the kind and amount of government
support for the schools. Unfortunately, it is very
unlikely that this can happen. Americans seem less willing
to spend money on education. City University of New York
political scientist Andrew Hacker points out that in the
1950s and 1960s "citizens willingly invested in education,
from kindergarten through graduate school, because they
wanted the forthcoming generation to be the best in the
world" (541). He concludes, however, that "today that
spirit is strangely lacking" (541). In the next decades,
as the children of our generation enter school, new
resources for schools are even more unlikely because of
the strains placed on the economy by aging baby boomers
(Nelson and Cowan 607).

Austin counterargues effectively and responsibly. First, she accurately represents Reich's views by quoting him. She then asserts emphatically that she
believes he is wrong to place any hopes in school reform and devises a careful
step-by-step argument to refute him.

Robert Smith, whose essay speculates that the middle class faces an
unpromising future, counterargues several hopeful consequences other writers have mentioned. One of these is Janice Castro's suggestion that middle-
class workers will have the opportunity to demonstrate greater self-reliance
and creativity. Here is Smith's counterargument:

Greater self-reliance and creativity is another promised
consequence of the new economy. Reporting in _Time_ magazine
in 1993, associate editor Janice Castro quotes a former
corporate executive: "People are going to have to create
their own lives, their own careers and their own
successes." The executive refers to highly skilled,
resourceful middle- and upper-middle-class people who want
to work as consultants or contingent employees. While most
working-class people in our generation will be employed
contingently during much of their working lives, I think it
is more likely that the middle class will have permanent
jobs in businesses and bureaucracies of all sizes. Some
will be employed contingently, but most, I think, will have

permanent jobs. Whether they have contingent or permanent
jobs, the question is whether their working conditions will
encourage self-reliance and creativity. I doubt that they
will, and support for my position comes from two prominent
writers. Robert Reich, a professor of business and public
policy at Harvard University and President Clinton's
secretary of labor during the first term, writes in a 1995
New Perspective Quarterly article that "individuals,
however resourceful, and governments, however reinvented,
can't build a new middle class on their own. Business has
an indispensable role to play." Reich recognizes that few
businesses are doing their part to support their most
resourceful workers, and Reich was never able to convince
Clinton or the Congress to put pressure on business or to
come up with government money for retraining programs and
on-the-job programs that would develop workers' self-
reliance and creativity. Editor and columnist Jeffrey
Madrick argues in his 1995 book The End of Affluence that
"without increasing prosperity, Americans are losing the
courage of the convictions they once shared. [. . .] As
personal resources decline and national prospects dim, we
are losing our nerve as individuals." Possibilities,
confidence, and courage all seem to me essential to self-
reliance and creativity. Without them, what hope does
the middle class have for professional development and
rewarding careers?

Smith's thoughtful, well-supported counterargument makes good use of the
readings, but he does more than just stitch them together. *Self-reliance* and *creativity* are his own terms, and he keeps them in focus all the way through the
paragraph. The relevance of his paraphrases and quotations from the readings
is always clear.

EXAMPLES FROM THE READINGS. You can find further examples of counterarguments in Reich (paragraphs 16–17) and Geoghegan (paragraphs 9–16).

SENTENCES FOR SPECULATING ABOUT CONSEQUENCES

Different writing situations require different kinds of sentences. Speculating
about consequences requires special kinds of clauses to express important
logical relationships, as well as frequent shifting among past-, present-, and
future-tense verbs.

You may want to review the material in this section now as a preview of
some special kinds of thinking and writing you will be engaged in as you draft
and revise your essay. You will find the definitions and examples here most

helpful, however, as you revise your essay. At that time, you will want to examine closely the logical relationships between all of your sentences and the shifts among various verb tenses. (You may also find it helpful to review "Sentences That Keep Readers on Track," page 208 in Chapter 3.)

Expressing Logical Relationships

Two kinds of adverbial clauses—conditional and causal—enable you to express logical relationships important to speculating about the future.

Conditional Clauses.   Adverbial clauses of condition begin with *if* or *unless*. They express a condition that must be fulfilled if something is to happen in the future:

> *If* current trends at work continue, by the end of the century American workers will be spending as much time at their jobs as they did back in the 1920s. (paragraph 6)
>
> —JEREMY RIFKIN
> "The End of Work"

In this example, the opening *if* clause establishes a condition (the continuation of current work trends) that must be fulfilled for longer working hours to become a reality—the speculation about the future. This relationship between current conditions that must be fulfilled and speculations about the future will be fundamentally important to your thinking and writing. All of the explicitly speculative readings in the chapter include clauses of condition. Here are further examples:

> *If* America does not begin to plan for demographic shifts ahead, a backlash against the elderly might be unavoidable [. . .]. (paragraph 50)
>
> —ROB NELSON AND JON COWAN
> "Revolution X: A Survival Guide
> for Our Generation"

> But *if* slow economic growth stimulates such compensating illusions, it also destroys them, as one set of political promises after another is inevitably broken [. . .]. (paragraph 5)
>
> —JEFFREY MADRICK
> "The End of Affluence"

> Even now, *if* the percent going to college remains constant, it's estimated that by 2015 the cost of college tuition will have doubled. (paragraph 12)
>
> —THOMAS GEOGHEGAN
> "The Secret Lives of American Citizens"

Occasionally conditional clauses can be introduced by *unless:*

> But *unless* America dramatically shifts our budget priorities over the next 10 to 15 years to create new policies that are fair to all generations, we will confront

an unprecedented budget battle between the baby boomers and everyone born after 1960. (paragraph 17)

> —ROB NELSON AND JON COWAN
> "Revolution X: A Survival Guide
> for Our Generation"

Conditional logic can also be set up by the prepositions *with* and *without:*

> *Without* fiscal restraint, before the middle of the next century workers will be paying over half their salaries just to cover benefits to seniors. (paragraph 47)
> —ROB NELSON AND JON COWAN
> "Revolution X: A Survival Guide
> for Our Generation"

You already speak and write conditional clauses. Therefore, you need not acquire any new grammatical knowledge to make wise use of these clauses in your essay. As you speculate about the future in your first draft and later as you revise, consider whether conditional clauses can help you realize your vision more precisely.

Causal Clauses.   Clauses of cause or reason usually begin with *as.* These clauses are important in writing that speculates about consequences because they suggest a possible cause of a future consequence, as in this example:

> *As* the underpinnings of mutual commitment crumble, time-honored notions of fairness are cast aside for millions of workers. (paragraph 10)
> —JANICE CASTRO
> "Disposable Workers"

The *as* clause here identifies a continuing phenomenon—gradually crumbling underpinnings of mutual commitment—that may cause or lead to something in the future—the casting aside of notions of fairness. The *as* clause grounds the writer's speculations about the future, connecting the present and the future logically and plausibly. Here are some more examples:

> *As* they take hold in the neighborhoods and workplaces of America, these forces are ominous. (paragraph 6)
> —ROBERT REICH
> "America's Anxious Class"

> *As* the vast baby boomlet generation moves through adolescence, teens will outnumber people in their 20s by 7%, and a generation of parents will "discover" teen problems anew. (paragraph 8)
> —SUE SHELLENBARGER
> "Future Work Policies May Focus
> on Teens, Trimming Workloads"

> *As* our old values have become increasingly undependable, many Americans have looked elsewhere for stable ground [...]. (paragraph 1)]
> —JEFFREY MADRICK
> "The End of Affluence"

Shifting among Past, Present, and Future Tenses

Speculating about consequences invites sentences about what may happen in the future, and since speculations are grounded in present trends and events or even anchored in past events, you will be constructing sentences that move back and forth among past, present, and future times. Grammatically speaking, you will be choosing among three different verb tenses—past, present, and future. In English, different *forms* of a verb indicate present (*search*) and past (*searched*), but there is no form for future actions or states. Instead, we create future-tense verbs by combining kinds of words called *modals*—*will, would, could*—with present-tense forms (*will search, could succeed*). Consider this speculative sentence with a future-tense verb:

> We *will* in effect *have* to choose between providing for our parents or our kids. (paragraph 15)

> —ROB NELSON AND JON COWAN
> "Revolution X: A Survival Guide
> for Our Generation"

You already use all of these verb tenses. Speculating about the future may nevertheless pose a challenge because you may find yourself shifting more frequently among the tenses than you are accustomed to doing in other writing situations. Consider this series of verbs in the last four sentences of Jeremy Rifkin's paragraph 6. Only enough of each sentence part is presented for you to see how quickly Rifkin must shift among past, present, and future tenses.

> *past:* the amount of paid vacation and sick leave also *declined*
>
> *present:* the average American worker now *receives* three and one-half fewer paid vacation and sick days
>
> *present:* working hours [*are*] now longer
>
> *past:* than they *were* in the 1950s
>
> *past:* leisure time *has declined* by more than one-third
>
> *present:* if current trends in work *continue*
>
> *future:* workers *will be spending* as much time
>
> *past:* as they *did* back in the 1920s

To arrive at the one clause that speculates about the future, Rifkin must offer a context of facts and examples about past and present working conditions. After offering the future-tense speculation, he returns to the past in the same sentence in order to make a comparison. In these eight parts of four sentences there are five shifts in tense. While shifts this frequent are not typical, they are not unusual.

For further examples of verb shifts, see Nelson and Cowan (paragraphs 44–48) and Shellenbarger (paragraph 18). When you revise your essay, check to be sure that your verbs point readers in the right direction to past and present conditions that may lead to future consequences.

CITING SOURCES

Since this chapter's readings contribute so much to your essay, you will frequently quote, paraphrase, or summarize them as you present the restructured economy and speculate about its consequences. When you use others' ideas in this way, you must cite them—that is, identify the source. You may do so informally or formally.

Informal Citation

Informal citation allows you to identify all of your sources within the text of your essay, without adding source notes or a list of works cited at the end of your essay. You identify the author, the publication, and perhaps the date of publication right in your own sentences. (You identify sources of your interviews in the same way.) You may want to add a phrase or a sentence describing the author to establish his or her authority. When using informal citation, you do not cite page numbers or identify sources in footnotes or in a works-cited list at the end of your essay.

Many of the readings, especially those originally published in newspapers or magazines, rely on informal citation. To see how writers use this citation style gracefully, look at these examples:

> David Neumark, a Michigan State University economist, says new data show "a pretty sharp decline" in long-term job retention among the most-tenured workers.
> —TONY HORWITZ
> "Some Who Lost Jobs in Early '90s
> Recession Find a Hard Road Back"

> According to the Congressional Budget Office, health care costs will account for 18 percent of the U.S. economy by the year 2000, three times as much as in 1960.
> —ROB NELSON AND JON COWAN
> "Revolution X: A Survival Guide
> for Our Generation"

Formal Citation

When you use formal citation, you follow a specific style used by a particular academic or professional group. Appendix 2 of this book outlines two of these styles, one from the Modern Language Association (MLA), which is favored by scholars in the humanities, and one from the American Psychological Association (APA), which is favored by scholars in psychology. Ask your instructor which you should follow.

If you are referring to one of the readings in this chapter, you can cite it as a work in an anthology or edited collection, using either the MLA or APA models in Appendix 2 and referring to the page numbers from *Writing the World*. If you cite an example from a book such as Jeffrey Madrick's, for instance, your in-text reference or works-cited item will list Madrick as the author of *The End of Affluence* and *Writing the World* as the anthology in which the Madrick reading appears. If you cite an example from an article, such as Sue Shellenbarger's "Future Work Policies May Focus on Teens, Trimming Workloads," you will list Shellenbarger as the author, "Future Work Policies May Focus on Teens, Trimming Workloads" as the title of article, and *Writing the World* as the anthology in which the Shellenbarger article appears.

Note: Writers usually do not document sources that provide commonly known facts, general background information, or common knowledge, but if you want to make use of some of the background material in this chapter's introductions or reading headnotes—material not written by Madrick, for instance, or the other authors in this chapter—then you have two choices. You can paraphrase the material without giving a citation if it appears to be common knowledge. Otherwise, you can cite Charles R. Cooper and Susan Peck MacDonald as authors of *Writing the World*, using the models for a work by two or more authors in Appendix 2.

EVALUATING AND REVISING

The following guidelines for revising will help you evaluate your own draft and provide useful advice to other student writers about theirs. As you read a draft, try to identify what has been done well and to come up with specific ways to improve the presentation of the subject and the argument. As you begin the revision process, focus on the big issues; save spelling and grammar for later.

Whether revising your own draft or helping classmates with theirs, you may need to refer to specific readings, so have them handy as you work. If you prepared a reading-by-reading list of possible future consequences of the restructured economy, this list should prove helpful now as you analyze a draft about this subject.

If you are reading someone else's draft, it is a good idea to write out your comments on a separate sheet of paper, perhaps following the headings used in this section.

Read to Get a General Impression

Even if you are reading your own draft, read it straight through without marking on it, as if you are encountering the essay for the first time in a magazine for college students. Then write three or four sentences summarizing your first impression. What aspect of the essay seems most successful? What is most interesting or surprising? What one major improvement would make the argument more convincing?

Read to Analyze the Draft More Closely

Next, number the paragraphs and mark the point at which the essay divides into two major parts: the presentation of the restructured economy and the argument supporting speculations about its consequences. Reread the draft, keeping in mind that the intended readers may not be very knowledgeable about the restructured economy. Ask yourself, What do these particular readers need to know? Write down what is good about the draft as well as specific ideas for revision.

The Opening.   What strategy does the writer adopt to engage and hold readers' attention? How does the writer connect to readers' knowledge and concerns? How successful do you think the opening will be with the intended readers? Reflect on all the openings in the readings and suggest ways to strengthen this opening or propose an alternative opening.

The Presentation of the Subject.   Consider how well the writer has presented to readers facts about economic restructuring. Do you think readers need more, or less, information about the economy? If less, suggest specific cuts. If more, suggest specific facts, examples, or cases. *Refer to specific readings.* Might the writer make better use of already apparent consequences and of the sources of generational competition?

Now look at both the opening and the part presenting information about the economy. Even if they are interesting, do they seem disconnected from the essay's argument or do they anticipate it well? Do they prepare readers for the particular thesis and speculations of this unique essay? Is it clear that the essay will focus on the *consequences* of the restructured economy for the writer's generation? Help the writer ensure that the opening and the background information engage and inform and also set readers up for the argument and lead directly to it.

The Thesis.   Find the thesis statement and give advice on strengthening and clarifying it, if necessary. Given what has come before in the essay, do you think the thesis will be immediately clear and meaningful to readers? Does it mention the writer's generation and identify one income level as the focus of the argument? Are the terms clear? Does the thesis claim too much? Too little? Does it forecast accurately the specific consequences the writer will attempt to support and their sequence in the argument? Suggest specific ways to revise the thesis.

The Argument Supporting the Consequences.   Bracket the part of the essay in which the writer takes up the consequences he or she argues will occur. Taking each consequence in turn, advise the writer on strengthening the argument for it. Ask yourself, What more might the writer do to convince readers that this consequence is likely to happen? From specific readings, suggest facts, examples, quotes, graphs, statistics, or cases that might make each consequence more convincing.

Be sure to tell the writer what seems to be working well in the argument.

The Counterargument.   Though they may be woven into the argument, carefully note in the margin each counterargument—those places in the argument in which the writer seems to be answering readers' questions, or conceding or refuting their objections, or conceding or refuting possible consequences that challenge the writer's predicted consequences.

Evaluate each of the writer's attempts to *answer* readers' questions or respond to their objections. For each, tell the writer whether the counterargument seems likely to be convincing to readers. Is it clearly informed by the writer's experience or by the readings? Is it thoughtful and authoritative? Does it avoid attacking the reader for daring to raise a question?

Then evaluate each of the writer's attempts to *concede* (accept, acknowledge the weight of) or *refute* (argue against) readers' objections to the consequences or support for them. Advise the writer on ways to strengthen each concession and refutation. What further support can be brought to bear from the readings or class discussions?

Before you leave this part of the counterargument, think as a skeptic might: try to identify several further questions and objections readers are likely to have. List any such questions, reservations, or objections and suggest specific ways to concede or refute them. This imaginative exercise can be one of your most important contributions.

Finally, turn to those places in which the writer has attempted to concede or refute consequences that call into question his or her own predictions. How might the writer strengthen the counterargument to each of these challenges? Rely on your own ideas and ideas from the readings and class discussions. List any consequences you can think of that some readers may believe to be more likely in the future, and help the writer concede or refute them.

The Cues to Keep Readers on Track.   Think about how well the essay is organized. Notice whether the argument has been accurately forecast. Evaluate whether the presentation of the restructured economy is easy to follow and the speculations about consequences arranged in a logical, step-by-step sequence. Alert the writer to any places where you felt confused, where the direction of the argument seemed unclear, or where there seemed to be gaps in the reasoning.

Suggest ways to make the organization easier to follow—for example, by giving readers cues and transitions to make the organization visible, combining paragraphs or creating new ones, eliminating unnecessary material to quicken the pace, relocating counterarguments, or resequencing the consequences.

The Closing.   Notice how the writer closes. Tell the writer what seems to be working well and suggest specific ways the closing might be made even more effective.

EDITING AND PROOFREADING

As you revise, you will be concerned primarily with strengthening your presentation of the subject and your argument. However, you will also want to clarify your sentences and tighten the connections among them. In particular, you will need to check to see that the logical relationships among your sentences are clear and that there are adequate cues to keep readers on track through your argument.

Examine the connections between all of your sentences. If you sense misdirection or a gap that would break a reader's momentum, try reorganizing one sentence or writing new material. Check to see whether you shift terms unnecessarily. Look for sentences that might be combined to better show relationships among ideas. Look as well for long or garbled sentences that might be broken up into two or three sentences.

As you work on your sentences, look for errors in spelling, capitalization, punctuation, usage, and grammar, consulting a writer's handbook for information about correcting any you find. Ask a friend or a classmate to read over your draft to help you spot errors.

Before you hand in your final revised essay, proofread it carefully and run it through a spellchecker, trying to make it error free.

REFLECTING ON WHAT YOU HAVE LEARNED

Once you have completed this chapter's reading and writing tasks, it is a good idea to think about what you have accomplished and learned. Doing so will help you consolidate your new knowledge and remember it longer.

As you worked your way through the chapter, you were actually engaged in two closely related types of learning: becoming informed about the restructured economy and speculating about its consequences. Integrating these two kinds of learning, then, has been your major achievement. Using the following questions as a starting point, write a page or so reflecting on this accomplishment.

- What was the most difficult part of coming to understand the restructured economy and its possible consequences? What was the most surprising?

- How have your views about the economy been confirmed or changed? What questions remain for you?

- What was most difficult for you in planning your essay? When you began drafting, what was your biggest surprise? Think of the most important revision you made in your completed draft. How did you come to make this revision?

- What advice would you give writers who are just starting an assignment to speculate about the future?

- What are you most pleased with in your essay? How would you revise it further if you had more time to work on it?

GATHERING ADDITIONAL INFORMATION

To supplement the readings in this chapter on the restructured economy and its consequences, you may want to do further research. For example, you might want to know more about the history of the economy's restructuring or to find out whether new speculations are being made about the future of your generation. Following are some suggestions that should help you find other sources on this subject.

Books

Books are good sources of information about complex subjects like the restructured economy because they provide an overview as well as specific details. In this chapter's section "Surveying Consequences of the Restructured Economy," all of the readings, with two exceptions, come from books.

You can locate books by searching your library's online catalog by subject or by author. The following terms will help you conduct a *subject* search:

United States—Economic conditions—1981–

United States—Social conditions—1980–

Economic forecasting—United States

United States—Politics and government—1993–

These subject headings, from the *Library of Congress Subject Headings Catalog,* describe the contents of books. The dates limit your search to books published, for example, between 1981 and the present. It is advisable to limit an initial follow-up search like this one to even more recent books, from 1997 or 1998 to the present, particularly if you are looking for the latest speculations about the consequences of the restructured economy and of generational competition.

You can also use the names of book authors represented in this chapter to see whether any have published new books on aspects of the economy or its consequences. An author search can be helpful in another way: In the online catalog, look up any book represented in this chapter and notice the subject headings that describe its contents. For example, if you were to look up Jeffrey Madrick's *The End of Affluence,* you would find which subject terms a book like his uses:

United States—Economic conditions

You can then use those subject words or headings to find related books.

Articles

Article-search strategies differ depending on whether the articles are written for a general or an expert readership. This chapter's reading by Andrew

Hacker, "Meet the Median Family," which appeared in *Time* magazine, is an example of an article written for a general readership. The reading by Leon F. Bouvier and Carol J. De Vita, "The Baby Boom—Entering Midlife," which appeared in *Population Bulletin,* a journal read by specialists in population trends, is an example of an article written for experts. In your search for further information about the restructured economy, you will want to rely on both kinds of articles. General articles are easy to understand and provide a good introduction to a subject, but they are necessarily superficial and may avoid difficult concepts. Articles written for experts, by contrast, may examine certain aspects of a subject more fully and provide detailed explanations of key concepts.

General Interest.   To find general-interest articles, use indexes like *Expanded Academic Index, InfoTrac,* or *Social Sciences Index,* which cover general-interest magazines and basic academic journals. In these indexes, the following search terms may be useful:

Cost and standard of living

Income distribution—Analysis

Wealth—Social aspects

Poverty—Social aspects

Distribution (Economics)

Middle classes—Economic aspects

Newspapers are another good source of general-interest information. Since they often focus on particular incidents, you may be able to find accounts of things like plant closings, downsizings, and new employment opportunities. Look in the *National Newspaper Index, NewsBank,* or other newspaper indexes using subject-search terms like these:

Downsizing (Management)—Demographic aspects

United States economic conditions—Public opinion

Unemployment—Statistics

Industrial productivity—Social aspects

Scholarly.   In order to find articles written for experts or scholars, use indexes like the *Journal of Economic Literature* (in spite of its title, it is an index, not a journal) and *Public Affairs Information Service* (PAIS). College and university libraries are most likely to have these indexes, as well as the journals covered by them and other databases.

Many of the search terms for books work in searches for articles written for experts. In addition, you could try terms like *income distribution* and *downsizing.* To narrow your search, combine subject headings—for example, use *downsizing and trends* to find sources on the future of downsizing and on possible consequences.

Statistics

It is hard to imagine writing about a subject like the economy without using statistics, which help us understand large-scale patterns and trends in such areas as average wages, consumer prices, costs of Social Security and Medicare, contingent employment, CEO salaries, and worker productivity. The statistics that economists rely on for their reports, arguments, and speculations are readily available in libraries and on the Internet.

An excellent source of statistics compiled and published by the federal government is the *Statistical Abstract of the United States,* which is also available on the World Wide Web at <http://www.census.gov/ftp/pub/statab/www/>. Other Web sources for statistics on the economy are the U.S. Bureau of the Census at <http://www.census.gov/> and the U.S. Department of Commerce at <http://www.doc.gov/>.

Many college and university libraries have government document departments staffed by librarians who can help you find statistics on all aspects of the economy and will also know about relevant special reports published occasionally by government agencies.

Cartoons

You can find books of political cartoons by using these Library of Congress Subject Headings:

American wit and humor, pictorial

Caricatures and cartoons, United States

Political cartoons

United States—Politics and government—1989–1998—caricatures and cartoons

The last item is a reminder that you can limit any subject search by adding dates and that the subheading "caricatures and cartoons" can sometimes be helpful.

Subject headings that will lead you to written political humor and satire as well as to cartoons include "Economics—humor" and "Political satire, American."

To find cartoons in journals, magazines, and newspapers, use the *Expanded Academic Index, InfoTrac,* and *Newspaper Index.* For a subject search of these indexes, add to any subject headings the subheading "Anecdotes, cartoons, satire, etc.," as in the following examples:

United States—Economic conditions—Anecdotes, cartoons, satire, etc.

Recessions—Anecdotes, cartoons, satire, etc.

You can also locate political cartoons on the World Wide Web. Here are two sites:

The Comics Hotlist
<http://www.uta.fi/yhteydet/sarjlite.html>

Daryl Cagles Professional Cartoonist Index
<http://www.inet1.com/Toons/true/art/ToonLinks.html>

FURTHER READINGS ON THE RESTRUCTURED ECONOMY

Bluestone, Barry, and Irving Bluestone. *Negotiating the Future: A Labor Perspective on American Business.* New York: Basic, 1992.

Finnegan, William. *Cold New World: Growing Up in a Harder Country.* New York: Random House, 1998.

Frank, Robert H., and Philip J. Cook. *The Winner-Take-All Society.* New York: Free Press, 1995.

Greider, William. *One World, Ready or Not: The Manic Logic of Global Capitalism.* New York: Simon & Schuster, 1997.

Hochschild, Arlie Russell. *The Time Bind: When Work Becomes Home and Home Becomes Work.* New York: Metropolitan, 1997.

Krugman, Paul. *Peddling Prosperity: Economic Sense and Nonsense in the Age of Diminished Expectations.* New York: Norton, 1994.

Luttwak, Edward. *Turbo-Capitalism: Winners and Losers in the Global Economy.* New York: HarperCollins, 1999.

Mishel, Lawrence R., Jared Bernstein, and John Schmitt. *The State of Working America, 1998–99.* New York: Cornell UP, 1999.

Rifkin, Jeremy. *The End of Work: The Decline of the Global Labor Force and the Dawn of the Post-Market Era.* New York: Putnam, 1995.

Samuelson, Robert J. *The Good Life and Its Discontents: The American Dream in the Age of Entitlement, 1945–1995.* New York: Times, 1995.

Sennett, Richard. *The Corrosion of Character: The Personal Consequences of Work in the New Capitalism.* New York: Norton, 1998.

Thurow, Lester C. *The Future of Capitalism.* New York: Morrow, 1996.

Wuthnow, Robert. *Poor Richard's Principle: Recovering the American Dream through the Moral Dimension of Work, Business, and Money.* Princeton: Princeton UP, 1997.

ADDITIONAL WRITING PROJECTS

Here are some additional writing projects on the restructured economy and its consequences that make use of the readings and ideas in this chapter.

Personal Experience Essay

Tell a story about your own work experience in the restructured economy. Focus on one memorable, significant event at work—preferably one that took place over a relatively short period of time—that illustrates a feature of the new economy you have learned about in this chapter's readings. For example, you may have been asked to work more overtime than you would prefer, or lost a job unexpectedly, or been assigned duties you had not been properly trained to carry out. You may have had a pleasant or an unpleasant contingent-work assignment, received an unexpected raise, or decided to work fewer hours in order to have more free time. Any event that reveals a special characteristic of work in the first years of the twenty-first century is a good subject for the essay. Disclose only those aspects you feel comfortable sharing with others.

Purpose and Readers.   Your purpose is to help your classmates see clearly what happened and understand what the experience was like for you. You also want to gain greater understanding of the event by writing about it in a thoughtful and observant way.

Resources to Draw On.   Your most important resource will be your memory. Because you will not be able to recall every important detail at once, make notes as frequently as you can over several days. The accumulating notes will jog your memory and help you discover other important details. List the other people who were directly involved in the event, their names, roles, personal qualities. Outline what happened chronologically—first, next, and so on. Write down what you did after the event: whom you talked to, what actions you took, and what other people did. Also note your feelings at the time of the event, soon after it occurred, and now. Models of this kind of personal experience essay can be found in Chapter 5 in the readings by Luis J. Rodriguez, Nathan McCall, and Rita Williams.

Tips for Writing a Successful Personal Experience Essay.   One way to begin is by describing the workplace and the job you held and presenting the context for the event: what led up to it, whether you were expecting it or were completely surprised, or whether similar events had previously occurred at your workplace. As you tell your story, try to use vivid descriptions and strong verbs to explain what the workplace was like, who was involved in the event, what was said, what you did, how people were acting, and what you felt at the time. Also try to re-create any conversations that were central to what happened. Unlike other essays, in which a personal experience might support a very small part of your argument, this essay consists primarily of personal experience. Consequently, it should be richly detailed and offer readers a memorable example of what the workplace is like. Finally, reflect on this experience from your present perspective. How does it look to you now? How has it influenced your feelings or beliefs? How has it changed your behavior?

Attach to your essay a page or so of explanation, showing your instructor the connections, as you see them, between the personal experience in your essay and what you have learned from the readings in this chapter.

Report on a New Phenomenon

Write a report on the new, restructured economy. Contrast it with the economy of the late 1940s to the early 1970s and describe its main features, including its already apparent consequences. Unlike in the main assignment of this chapter, you need not speculate about the consequences of the restructuring or take a position on whether the new economy has been a good thing for the country.

Purpose and Readers.   Your purpose is to demonstrate to readers that the restructured economy is a subject worth learning about and to inform them about this major transformation. Write your report for other college students who are aware that the economy and the workplace are changing but have little information about the forty-year restructuring that is still unfolding. (For more information about readers, see "Understanding Your Readers" on page 641.) So that readers will accept your authority to inform them about this complex subject, show them that you have a good understanding of it.

Resources to Draw On.   The readings in this chapter, particularly those in the section "Understanding the Restructured Economy," provide all the resources you need to write a successful essay. If you have time, you could gather more information on the economy, using the guidelines in "Gathering Additional Information" on page 665. For help planning and developing a report, see the Writer's Guide in Chapter 2. There the subject matter is different from yours here, but the principles of classifying and organizing information, planning the overall organization of a report, and developing a report still apply. If you have personal experience with any aspect of the new economy, include it in your report if it is relevant—it could add to your perceived authority.

Tips for Writing a Successful Report.   You might begin by announcing the subject and appealing to readers' interests. Make the subject seem worth learning about and of personal significance to them. You could open with a particularly memorable quote from a reading or even a set of such quotes. You could also begin by describing a particularly important or unexpected aspect of the restructured economy. Then tell readers what you plan to do and how you will go about it. Instead of reviewing what a series of writers say separately about the restructured economy, find a way to organize the information that will make it easy for readers to grasp the main features of the economy. You might want to draw upon several writers to explain a particular feature. Contrast key features of the current economy with key features of the economy between the late 1940s and the early 1970s. In fact, you might organize your report around a few such contrasts. Quote, paraphrase, and summarize the readings to present the information to readers. (Appendix 2 offers strategies for integrating quoted material into your report, and Appendix 1 provides guidelines for summarizing.)

Interview-Based Report

Write an essay in which you profile a person you know well as an example of one worker who has lived through all or most of the period in which the U.S. economy has been restructured. Choose a family member, relative, or neighbor in the Depression, baby-boom, or baby-bust generation.

Purpose and Readers.   Your purpose is to present this person to your readers and to help them understand how the new economy has affected him or her. You want to engage readers with the person's story and inform them about the main features of the new economy as it has affected the person you are profiling. Assume that your profile will be published in a magazine for college students and that most of your readers will not have much information about the new economy though they likely have worked at least part-time.

Resources to Draw On.   You will have two equally important resources to draw on: the readings in this chapter and your interviews with the person you are profiling. The readings will enable you to present the main features of the new economy to your readers; the interviews and your notes on them will enable you to tell this person's story as an example of one person who has lived through an important period in economic history. Interview the person on the phone or in person several times to get full information about schooling, employment history, career path, and life opportunities. Take notes during the interviews and supplement them as needed immediately following each interview. Readings in this chapter will suggest questions you can ask to learn whether the person's experience confirms or contradicts facts or speculations reported in the readings and whether it parallels or diverges from others' experiences. Several of the readings offer profiles that are shorter than the one you will write, but they nevertheless can suggest strategies to use in your profile. For example, see Horwitz's profile of Jerry Young (paragraphs 14–24); Uchitelle's profiles of Rhoda Wright (paragraphs 1–3), Martie Hammer (paragraphs 13–16), and Margaret and Clifford Edens (paragraphs 23–30); and Schor's profiles of Louise and John Mattson (paragraphs 6–10), Susan Andrews (paragraphs 11–18), and Jeff Lutz (paragraphs 19–26). Notice that these writers frequently let the persons profiled speak for themselves.

Tips for Writing a Successful Interview-Based Report.   You might begin by introducing the person briefly, focusing on an unusual or colorful part of the person's work history. Choose a part that best characterizes the person and anticipates the main point you want to make. Then you could describe the purpose of your project, introduce the person more formally, and explain briefly how you went about conducting the interviews. Next, you might want to briefly present the main features of the new economy so that readers will have an adequate context for following your career profile of the person. You will need to be very selective about the information you include because you want to get quickly to the profile. Present what you learned about the person from the interviews, with the information organized in a way that will make it easy for readers to follow. You could simply tell a story about the person's career, from beginning to end, highlighting those events that best reveal the ups and downs of the career. Or you might look for themes in the interview material, perhaps suggested by ideas in the readings, and organize your writing around these themes.

Research Report

Report on the economic history of a single occupation—such as nursing, teaching, accounting, dentistry, real estate sales, farming, counseling, public safety, the military, small-business ownership, business or corporate management, law—since 1950. This occupation may have experienced decline in numbers or average income or it may have fared well since 1973, the year usually given for the beginning of the current economic restructuring. In effect, you will be writing a brief economic history of one occupation or profession.

Purpose and Readers. Your purpose is to inform your readers about the status of one occupation from the post–World War II decades of rapid economic growth and shared prosperity to the decades of the 1970s–1990s, which saw slower growth and increasing disparities in income and wealth. Your readers are other college students with a specific interest in the occupation or profession you are writing about. Maybe they grew up in a household where an adult practiced the occupation, or they have worked part-time or interned in the occupation, or they are considering preparing themselves for this occupation, but they know little, if anything, about its economic history.

Resources to Draw On. Your primary resources at hand are the readings in two sections of this chapter: "Understanding the Restructured Economy" and "Understanding Generational Competition." You may also find helpful suggestions in the Writer's Guide in Chapter 2 (see particularly the sections on classifying and organizing your information, the first two sections under "Developing Your Report," and the section "Sentences for Reporting Information." Though the subject matter is different in Chapter 2, the writing principles and strategies are similar to those for reporting on the history of an occupation). Other resources essential to your success with this project are in the library or on the Internet, where you can research this occupation, relying at least in part on trade or professional journals read by those in the occupation you choose. Such journals are more likely to be concerned with working conditions, employment possibilities, pay, and benefits, which should be your focus. You might also interview people who have worked in the occupation for a long time.

Tips for Writing a Successful Research Report. The successful essay will inform readers about the economic ups and downs of one occupation or profession from about 1950 to the present. You might begin by briefly describing the current state of the occupation, including training required, the typical career path a person would follow over a lifetime, current working conditions, employment possibilities, and average income. Then present your information on the economic history of the occupation. To succeed, you will need to organize the information so that you can present it selectively and readers can understand it readily. You may want to make use of charts or graphs. Be sure that your presentation is organized to help readers understand the status of the occupation in the restructured economy.

APPENDIX 1

Strategies
for Close Reading
and Critical Thinking

Appendix 1 illustrates six strategies for close reading and critical thinking:

- **previewing:** gaining knowledge about a text before reading it for the first time
- **annotating:** recording your questions, insights, and responses on the pages of a text and looking for patterns in these annotations
- **outlining:** listing the main ideas of a text
- **summarizing:** presenting in a brief but coherent way the main ideas in a text
- **synthesizing:** bringing together for a particular purpose the information and ideas in one text or from several texts
- **evaluating arguments:** evaluating how convincing an argument is for its intended readers

Consider these the basic strategies for preparing to read an unfamiliar text, learning more about it after your first reading, and thinking about it more deeply, more critically. Except for previewing, these strategies require you to take action with your pencil or keyboard—to produce writing that can lead to deeper thinking as you reflect on what you have written and seek to clarify it. This writing may also contribute directly to your completion of the essay assignment in each chapter of *Writing the World:* always the writing will lead to a fuller understanding of readings, a key to your success on each assignment; and it may contribute some sentences to your essay. In every college course you take, the close-reading and critical-thinking strategies will be useful to you.

The four strategies that require writing—outlining, summarizing, synthesizing, and evaluating an argument—are introduced in the writer's notebook tasks following the Supreme Court cases in Chapter 3, "Taking a Position on a

Constitutional Issue." Should your class be assigned Chapter 3, you would have an opportunity to practice the four strategies, following the guidelines in this appendix, and then benefit from discussion of any problems you encounter. In addition, you may use the strategies in other writer's notebook tasks. Most of these tasks throughout the assignment chapters invite informal writing of many different kinds. Occasionally, however, when we believe that you can learn most about a reading by applying one of the formal strategies in this appendix, we invite you to do so by naming the strategy exactly as it is named here.

Before illustrating the strategies, we must define *close reading* and *critical thinking,* the key terms of this appendix.

DEFINITIONS OF CLOSE READING AND CRITICAL THINKING

Close Reading

Consider the difference between a first reading and subsequent readings. During a first reading, you assess the ease or difficulty of a reading. You speculate about the writer's purpose. You gather a few ideas and make connections to your own knowledge. You try to establish the main point. In contrast, when you return to a reading with a particular purpose in mind — to understand it better, tell someone about it, prove that you have read it, relate it to other readings, or write about it — you must read it more slowly and more carefully. This kind of reading is what is meant by *close reading.* It is the kind of reading required of you in *Writing the World.* Primarily, you need to read closely to find connections among readings and to write about them. You also need to read closely so you can talk productively with classmates about the readings.

Think of close readings as second, third, or subsequent readings. As you complete the writer's notebook tasks in a chapter, you will be giving parts of a reading at least a second close reading. As you plan your essay, you will be rereading closely the readings that have made the most important contributions to your thinking. As you draft your essay, you will be digging into key readings to select the materials that will directly support your argument and counterargument. When you revise your essay, you will return to certain readings to search out materials that will strengthen your argument. Throughout these close readings — close *re*readings, really — you may make good use of the strategies of annotating, outlining, summarizing, synthesizing, and evaluating an argument. You need not deploy them in the systematic way you would practice them in the Chapter 3 notebook tasks and in occasional other such tasks throughout the book, but your knowledge of them will make your close readings more searching, insightful, and productive. Your experience with these strategies will increase your confidence in approaching difficult new readings in other college courses.

Critical Thinking

Because your brain is designed for critical thinking, you think critically about your own personal experiences many times each day. For example, you may decide what advice to give a friend who has asked for your help, choose among several alternative routes as you drive to an unfamiliar destination, solve a problem or resolve a dispute at work, or closely compare the price and quality of competing brands before you make a purchase. You have also had experience thinking critically about written texts. In high school, for example, you may have written a library research report taking a position on an environmental or a health issue, an essay interpreting a short story, or an argument speculating about how American history might have taken a different course if a military or a political leader had made a different decision.

Clearly, critical thinking means more than criticizing or finding fault. In fact, critical thinking may lead you to praise or value something you have read. The word *critical* in the phrase *critical thinking* means to analyze or evaluate a text. In this sense, a critic (from a Greek word meaning "to discern or judge") is someone who expresses a reasoned evaluation of a text. Critical thinking, therefore, involves raising questions, making judgments, discovering connections, and drawing conclusions based on what you are learning from texts and on your previous knowledge and experience. It requires a stance that is open to challenging new ideas. It begins with close reading to understand new information and ideas so that your questions and conclusions are based on what a text actually offers rather than on what you might want it to offer or on what you believe that it does offer after only a first reading. Every assignment and activity in *Writing the World* is designed to foster this kind of close reading. The six strategies in this appendix make an important contribution because they increase your confidence that you understand a reading well enough to challenge the author, relate it to other readings, and enter into serious discussion with others about it — in other words, to think critically about the reading.

Illustrations of the strategies in this appendix are based on an argument taking a position on a current issue. College instructors consider reasoned argument one of the best examples of critical thinking. Many of your opportunities to make use of the strategies through the writer's notebook tasks involve readings that make arguments. Keep in mind, too, that all but one of the essay assignments in *Writing the World* are argument assignments: many of the readings make arguments, and you will write argument essays. Therefore, you will be continually engaged in the highly valued form of critical thinking known as *reasoned argument.*

A final note: Because critical thinking requires that you understand others' ideas and arguments well, it can be enhanced by strategies like outlining and summarizing. It requires more, however — a critical perspective or framework. Some instructors believe that students' primary goal in college should be to learn about many different critical perspectives. You come to college with certain perspectives that are related to your most deeply held values and beliefs. For example, you may have a political perspective—liberal, or conservative, or some other—that influences how you see the world, or you may have a certain religious perspective, such as Islamic moderate, Protestant fundamentalist, traditional Catholic, or secular humanist. These beliefs give you particular perspective on your reading, leading you to ask certain kinds of questions, reach certain kinds of conclusions, and so on. In college, you are able to learn about many other critical perspectives. This learning may confirm the perspectives you brought with you, or it may lead you to modify them or even to take up new perspectives. For example, in Chapter 4, "Evaluating Civic Stances," you can learn about three prominent civic or political perspectives: liberalism, conservatism, and libertarianism. What you learn may influence your political views; even more important, what you learn about any one of these perspectives will allow you to adopt it or try it out more searchingly as a perspective from which to think critically about political arguments. In Chapter 6, "Interpreting Popular Culture," you can learn how to interpret tabloid television from a social perspective derived from contemporary cultural studies. The important thing to keep in mind is that when you think critically about a reading, you must make use of some critical perspective, whether you are aware of it or not. It is best to make yourself aware of it; such an awareness inevitably involves knowledge of competing perspectives.

The following annotated reading illustrates the six strategies for close reading and critical thinking. It is a portion of the longer reading by Dionne in Chapter 4.

THEY ONLY *LOOK* DEAD: WHY PROGRESSIVES WILL DOMINATE THE NEXT POLITICAL ERA

E. J. Dionne Jr.

Those who believe in government's possibilities cannot 1 pretend that they share the new conservatism's view of the state. At the heart of the new conservatism is the belief that government action is not only essentially

oppressive = excessive exercise of power, weighing down or crushing

inefficient but also inherently oppressive. Democratic government, in this telling, has interests all its own that have nothing to do with what the voters want. What's especially important about this idea is that it ultimately sees no *fundamental* distinction between free government and dictatorship. The differences are only a matter of degree, not of kind: The more limited democratic government is, the better; the more active democratic government is, the more it begins to approach the evils of Nazism or communism. "Behind our New Deals and New Frontiers and Great Societies," writes [conservative] House majority leader Dick Armey, "you will find, *with a difference only in power and nerve,* the same sort of person who gave the world its Five Year Plans and Great Leaps Forward — the Soviet and Chinese counterparts." [Emphasis added.]

New Deal = Roosevelt
New Frontier = Kennedy
Great Society = Johnson

This is an extraordinary and radical claim, effectively equating Roosevelt, Kennedy and Johnson with Stalin and Mao. If the problem is stated like this, then there is only one choice: Preserving freedom means having government do as little as possible. A government that might levy taxes to provide health care coverage for all or pensions for the old is seen as marching the people down "the road to serfdom," in the evocative phrase of the libertarian economist Friedrich A. Hayek. Better, in this view, to have no health care and no pensions than to have the government embark on this terrible path. Environmental regulations are seen not as preserving streams and forests for future generations; they are viewed as ways of interfering with the free use of private property. Work safety regulations are no longer ways of providing employees with some protections against hazardous machines or conditions; they are seen as "interference in the right of contract."

who could oppose these government actions?

Rosenblatt also mentions those programs and the rights below in paras. 5, 6

This sort of thinking is now so common that it has been forgotten how radically different it is from the

tries to make conservatives seem radical and dangerous

tradition on which the United States was founded—a tradition to which contemporary liberals, moderates, conservatives and libertarians all trace their roots. As the political philosopher Stephen Holmes has argued, the entire project of freedom going back to America's founders rests [not on *weak* government, but rather on an *energetic* government,] government strong enough to protect individual rights. Free government is different in *kind* from (despotic) regimes because its fundamental purpose—to vindicate the rights of individuals—is different.

important contrast: not "big" govt. but "energetic" govt.

despotic = governments that have unlimited power and abuse it

Imagine on the one side a (dictatorship) that has no government-provided social security, health, welfare or pension systems of any type. It levies relatively low taxes which go almost entirely toward supporting large military and secret police forces that regularly jail or kill people because of their political views, religious beliefs—or for any other reason the regime decides. Then imagine a (democracy) with regular open elections and full freedoms of speech and religion. Imagine further that its government levies higher taxes than the dictatorship to support an extensive welfare state, generous old-age pensions and a government health system. The first country might technically have a "smaller government," but there is no doubt that it is *not* a free society. The second country would have a "bigger government," measured as a percentage of gross domestic product, yet there is no doubt that it *is* a free society. This point might seem obvious, but it is in fact

tries to undermine the idea that the size of govt. is the issue obscured by the presumptions that underlie the conservative anti-government talk now so popular. The size of government is an important issue, but it is not as important as — and should not be confused with — the *kind* of government a society has.

big govt. vs. kind of govt.

Because the anti-government (ideology) of the new conservatism views almost all forms of government intervention (beyond basic police protection) with suspicion, it misses entirely the fact that democratic governments can intervene in ways that *expand* individual liberty. At the extreme, it took a very strong national government (and very forceful intervention) to end slavery and literally free four million Americans from bondage. It's worth remembering that supporters of slavery saw abolitionists as "enemies of liberty" interfering with the "property rights" of slaveholders and imposing the federal government's wishes over "the rights of states." Similarly, it took a strong federal government to end segregation in the 1960s and vindicate the right of African-Americans to vote. Such actions were well within the liberal tradition of free government which, notes Stephen Holmes, accepted that there were occasions when "only a powerful centralized state could protect (individual rights) against local strongmen and religious majorities."

ideology: a system of ideas about human life and culture

liberty and rights (para. 3)

energetic govt. protects and expands these examples: end slavery, end segregation, and expand voting rights

In the current cacophony of anti-government sloganeering, it is forgotten that the ever-popular slogan "equality of opportunity" was made real only by extensive government efforts to offer (individuals opportunities)

are these the same?—seem to be closely related

to develop their *own* capacities. As Holmes points out, Adam Smith, the intellectual father of the free market, favored a publicly financed, compulsory system of elementary education. After World War II the government's investment in the college education of millions through the GI Bill simultaneously opened new opportunities for individuals and promoted an explosive period of general economic growth. As Holmes puts it: "Far from being a road to serfdom, government intervention was meant to enhance individual autonomy. Publicly financed schooling, as Mill wrote, is 'help toward doing without help.'" John Stuart Mill offers here a powerful counter to those who would insist that government intervention always and everywhere increases "dependency."

my grandfather went through college and graduate school on the GI Bill—money he earned pays some of my college bills

Government also fosters liberty by doing something so obvious that it is little noticed: It insists that certain things cannot be bought and sold. We do not, for example, believe that justice in the courts should be bought and sold. We presume that votes and public offices cannot be bought (even if expensive political campaigns raise questions about the depth of our commitment to this proposition). We now accept, though we once did not, that it is wrong for a wealthy person to buy his way out of the draft during a time of war. And, of course, we do not believe that human beings can be bought and sold.

how active govt. helps individuals

O.K., but what about govt. inefficiency (para. 2) which Dionne doesn't seem to deny? Govt. does waste money; some programs don't work. What about pork barrel spending?

But these do not exhaust the instances in which a free people might decide to limit the writ of money and the supremacy of the market. As the political philosopher Michael Walzer has argued, one of the central issues confronting democratic societies concerns which rights and privileges should not be put up for sale. As an abstract proposition, we reject the notion that a wealthy person should be able to buy extra years of life that a poor person cannot, since life itself ought not be bought and sold. Yet the availability of health care affects longevity, and by making health care a purely market transaction, we come close to selling life and death. This was the primary argument for Medicare and remains the central moral claim made by advocates of national health insurance. Similarly, we do not believe that children should be deprived of access to food, medicine or education just because their parents are poor. As Holmes puts it, "Why should children be hopelessly snared in a web of underprivilege into which they were born through no fault of their own?"

The current vogue for the superiority of markets over government carries the risk of obscuring the basic issue of what should be for sale in the first place. In a society characterized by growing economic inequality, the dangers of making the marketplace the sole arbiter of the basic elements of a decent life are especially large. Doing so could put many of the basics out of the reach of many people who "work hard and play by the rules." The interrelationship between the moral and economic crises can be seen most powerfully in families where the need to earn enough income forces both parents to spend increasing amounts of time outside the home. One of the great achievements of this century was "the family wage," which allowed the vast majority of workers to provide their families with both a decent living and the parental time to give their children a decent upbringing. The family wage was not simply a product of the marketplace. It was secured through a combination of economic growth, social legislation and unionization. If the marketplace becomes not simply the main arbiter of income, as it will inevitably be, but the *only* judge of living standards, then all social factors, including the need to strengthen families and improve the care given children, become entirely irrelevant in the world of work.

Two questions are frequently confused in the current 10 debate: whether marketplace *mechanisms* might be usefully invoked to solve certain problems, and whether the solution of the problems themselves should be left *entirely* to the market. This confusion afflicts Progressives and conservatives alike.

On the one hand, applying marketplace logic to government programs can be highly useful. One of the most telling criticisms of government is that it does not live by the disciplines of the market, and can thus—in theory at least—deliver services as shoddily as it chooses, with as large a bureaucracy as it wishes. This argument can become a parody of itself, denying that there are, in fact, good public schools, fine police forces, excellent public parks, great public libraries and the like. But the argument does point fairly to certain limits on the government's capacities.... There *are* instances when it is more efficient for government to give each citizen a voucher to purchase services in a competitive marketplace than to provide the services directly. The GI Bill, for example, did not prescribe where veterans would go to college. It let them choose and gave them the means to pay for the education of their choice. Clinton's housing secretary, Henry Cisneros, proposed scrapping federal subsidies for local public housing *agencies* and turning federal aid into housing vouchers that would go directly to poor people. If a given public housing project was so crime-infested and run-down that poor people would choose not to live in it, it could be closed and sold off. An abstract fear of marketplace logic should not impede experiments of this sort.

But supporting market-oriented solutions to problems is *not* the same as suggesting that the market itself, left to its own devices, will solve all problems. If the government had not given the education vouchers to the GIs, many of them would never have gone to college. The market can break down, recessions can throw people out of work, families can lose their health insurance, poor people can lack the money to buy food and shelter for their children. The answer to the most rabid free-market advocates is that the free market is a wonderful instrument that also creates problems and leaves others unsolved. To assert as a flat rule, as Representative Armey does, that "the market is rational and the government is dumb" is to assume that it is rational to accept problems created by unemployment, low wages, business cycles, pollution and simple human failings; and dumb to use government to try to lessen the human costs associated with them. Mr. Armey might believe that; most Americans do not.

The difference between this era's conservatives and the American Progressive tradition lies in the distinction between two phrases, "freedom from" and "freedom to." Free-market conservatives are very much alive to the importance of what the philosopher Isaiah Berlin called "negative liberty," defined as freedom *from* coercion by the state. American Progressives and liberals share this concern for negative liberty, which is why they accept with the conservatives the need for limited government. Historically, however, Progressives have been more alive to the promise of "positive liberty" and to free government's capacity for promoting it. To be the master of one's own fate—a fair definition of liberty—means not simply being free from overt coercion (though that is a precondition); it also involves being given the means to overcome various external forces that impinge on freedom of choice and self-sufficiency. It means being free *to* set one's course.

From the beginning, therefore, the Progressive project has involved the use of government to give men and women the tools needed for achieving positive liberty, beginning with free elementary and secondary education and moving in the Depression and postwar era to Social Security, unemployment compensation and access to college and to health insurance. (The Progressives, beginning with women's suffrage, were also at the forefront in expanding the realm of freedom for women.) . . .

In our era, conservatives have monopolized the con- 15 cept of liberty and given it a particular and largely negative definition. Progressives have been cast—and have sometimes foolishly cast themselves—as defenders of coercion and bureaucracy, of government for government's sake. The imperative for Progressives is to rediscover their own tradition as the party of liberty. In a free society *all* parties to the debate should be arguing about the best ways to enhance and advance human freedom. For Progressives, that is and always has been the central purpose of government.

PREVIEWING

When you preview a text, you attempt to gain knowledge about it before you read it the first time. Two or three minutes spent previewing a text like one of the relatively brief readings in *Writing the World* can make your first attempts to read it more focused and productive. If you take time to preview, you can know the beginning of an argument and its outcome, identify most of the key terms, glimpse a few turns in the argument, and track the overall plan and sequence.

For example, to preview the reading in Chapter 4 by E. J. Dionne Jr., "They Only *Look* Dead: Why Progressives Will Dominate the Next Political Era," first turn to the headnote that immediately precedes it. Anthologies of readings, like this book, often include such headnotes, which provide valuable information about the author and a brief orientation to the reading. From the headnote, you learn that E. J. Dionne Jr. is a prominent, prize-winning author who writes for one of the most influential daily newspapers in the United States, the *Washington Post*. These facts may lead you to respect his authority as a commentator on political matters. If you know, in addition, that the *Post* is a liberal-progressive newspaper, you will not be surprised that Dionne takes the position he does in the ongoing debate between conservatives and liberals. The headnote also provides information about the purpose and focus of the reading, relating it to other readings through key questions.

Next move to the text itself to attempt to get an overview. An overview begins with reflections on the title. The title of the Dionne reading implies an argument—an answer to the implied "why" question in the title—and it makes clear Dionne's position on whether progressivism is dead. Conservatives may be dominating politics in the 1990s, but Dionne believes that progressives will rise again soon, in the "next political era," a phrase that allows him to sidestep naming a particular year, presidential term, or even decade. From the title alone, you can anticipate that Dionne will argue to support his position—and perhaps also counterargue conservative positions.

After examining the headnote and the title, preview the text itself by reading the first and last paragraphs and the first sentences of the other paragraphs. The first paragraph focuses on conservative views Dionne will attempt to discredit; the last paragraph also criticizes conservatives while stating in a general way what progressives must do to shake their image as proponents of big government. First sentences of paragraphs introduce most of the key terms in Dionne's argument and show how the argument is organized, giving a reader an invaluable head start toward understanding on first reading what the text has to offer.

Guidelines for Previewing

Follow these steps to orient yourself to an unfamiliar reading:

OVERVIEW.   Consider the title carefully. What are its key terms? How might it help you anticipate the subject matter of the reading?

In a book, carefully read the introduction and examine the entire table of contents. Note the date of publication and any information about the authors. In a book-length collection of readings or in a textbook with readings like *Writing the World,* headnotes usually offer information about authors.

In a magazine, examine the statement of purpose, if there is one; skim editorials or editors' columns; and survey titles of articles to assess the intended readership and political slant. (Your college library offers two valuable references that identify the political slant of current periodicals: *Gale Directory of Publications and Broadcast Media* [1990] and *Magazines for Libraries* [1992].) A brief description of the author of an article may appear at the end of the article.

SKIM.   Skim the book chapter, magazine article, or journal report. First, read the opening and closing paragraphs. Then look at any headings and subheadings and at any graphics. Finally, read the first sentence of each paragraph or, if the reading is relatively long, the first sentence of several paragraphs, particularly those in the first and final paragraphs of subsections marked by headings.

IDENTIFY THE TYPE OF TEXT.   Try to identify the purpose of the text you will be reading. Does it, for example, aim to convince you of something, explain some subject to you, or present personal experiences and observations?

REFLECT ON PRIOR KNOWLEDGE.   Pause to reflect on what you already know about the subject of the reading.

ANNOTATING

When you annotate a text, you write directly onto the text. Pencil in hand, you circle unfamiliar words, underline a key word or phrase, connect two related ideas with a line, number sequentially a few related ideas, write a question or comment in the margin. Annotation encourages you to interact purposefully with a text and leave a record of your reading. Depending on your purpose, you might annotate lightly or heavily. Close readers often annotate in layers, adding annotations in subsequent readings of a text. Annotating can help you understand a text better and construct meanings for it.

Take a moment to examine the annotations to paragraphs 1–7 of the Dionne reading on pages 678–82. Consider these paragraphs an example of heavy annotation layered on while rereading and moving back and forth within the text to understand it better. You need not always aim to annotate this heavily.

MARKING THE TEXT.   Notice first the great variety of markings on the text itself. They include symbols (arrows, a star), circles, boxes, brackets, underlinings, and lines.

WRITING IN THE MARGINS.   Now look closely at the writing in the margins. These writings can be classified and located by paragraph as follows: definitions (paragraphs 1, 4, 5), questions (2, 6), connections to other readings (2), inferences (3), comments (3, 4, 5, 6), distinctions and contrasts (3, 4), lists (5), connections within the text (7), and challenges (7). As you annotate readings in this book, you will find yourself using these kinds of marginal annotations and more. Write whatever helps you construct meanings for the readings text and leaves a meaningful record of your insights for when you return to the readings during class discussion or as you are working on an essay.

USING A PENCIL VS. A HIGHLIGHTER.   You may have used a highlighter to annotate a text, but a pencil offers certain clear advantages. Readers who use highlighters usually mark too much of a text, covering it with large blocks of their favorite colors, or they attempt to mark sentences selectively but tend to do so before they have a full view of a text. Once you have marked a text with indelible yellow, orange, or green, you cannot erase it. Consequently, when you review a text for a test or for essay material, you tend to reread only those sentences or passages you marked prematurely. Moreover, the wide nib on most highlighters makes it nearly impossible to write words in the margins of a text.

For annotating, a pencil with an eraser is a much better choice. A pencil allows you to erase or draw a line through a marginal comment. You can erase an underlining. You can make use of a great variety of small symbols: letters, numbers, stars, dots, exclamation points, question marks, arrows. You can circle, box, or bracket a word, phrase, or passage. Perhaps most important, you can pack a lot of annotations into the margins of your texts: you can define unfamiliar words, challenge the text, ask questions, note how a passage could be useful in your essay, compare an idea to an idea in another text, and so on. You also can easily add further annotations when you reread an annotated text.

INVENTORYING ANNOTATIONS.   Annotations can sometimes reveal interesting patterns of meaning. To find possible patterns, inventory the annotations looking for repetitions, contrasts, relationships, and categories. To see these patterns, it is usually helpful to make lists. Here are two lists that resulted from inventorying the annotations on paragraphs 1–7 of the Dionne reading:

health care (paragraph 2)	individual rights (paragraphs 3, 5)
pensions (2)	individual liberty (5, 7)
environmental regulations (2)	individual opportunity (6)
work safety regulations (2)	individual autonomy (6)
GI Bill (6)	
compulsory, free education system (6)	

The goal of inventorying is to construct meanings that may not be apparent until items are pulled out of a text and listed. There is no formula for inventorying. Look for related items. Try different kinds of lists. The longer list includes every mention of beneficial government actions in the reading. One thing it reveals is Dionne's decision to appeal to the widest possible readership: the wide range of government actions includes every age group and the interests of people at every income level except perhaps the wealthy. The list encompasses health care, pensions, the environment, the workplace, higher education (the GI Bill), and elementary and secondary education. Looked at in a different way, the list enables you to think critically about what is missing. Are there any obvious omissions? Abortion rights and protections for gays in the military are examples of government action. Perhaps Dionne thought these were too controversial or appeal only to a limited readership. Federal bailouts for ailing corporations and yearly subsidies to the U.S. sugar industry are also examples of government action. Would Dionne consider these actions wasteful or necessary?

The shorter list collects Dionne's references to the individual. It suggests that Dionne is attempting to associate liberalism with certain values nearly all Americans support. Liberals stress rights. Conservatives favor opportunity. Libertarians foreground autonomy. You might notice that *responsibility*, a high-priority value for conservatives, is missing.

If you are assigned Chapter 4, "Evaluating Civic Stances," you will find that such inventories from several readings help you discover differences and similarities among conservatism, liberalism, and libertarianism.

Guidelines for Annotating

These guidelines will remind you of the many possibilities for marking a text to reflect your insights and reactions:

UNDERLINE.   Underline key words and phrases and words to define in the margin.

BRACKET.   Bracket important sentences and paragraphs.

CONNECT.   Draw lines or arrows to connect related words and ideas.

COMMENT.   Write comments in the margin. These can include definitions of unfamiliar words, questions, reactions, reflections, and connections to prior knowledge or to other readings.

LOOK FOR PATTERNS.   Review your annotations, looking for patterns. You might find that you have focused on certain ideas, contrasts, repetitions, images, or difficult concepts. Perhaps you have written more questions than comments or assertions. Maybe your comments reflect agreement or disagreement with the writer.

OUTLINING

An outline lists in sequence the main ideas or topics in a text. As a close-reading strategy, outlining helps you understand a text more fully. If you outline a text, you will not overlook any important ideas, and you will see clearly how all the important ideas are organized and connected to each other.

Outlining can be formal or informal. For close reading, informal outlining—sometimes called *scratch outlining*—is adequate. When you create a scratch outline, you write a phrase or a sentence for each topic captured in your outline. You rely on key words and phrases from the text but put them into your own phrases or sentences. Even though you scratch outline a reading just for yourself, you should do it with care so that when you refer to the reading later as you are planning, drafting, or revising your essay, the outline will still be meaningful and useful.

Outlining may seem limiting or too easy because it holds you so closely to the text. Done thoughtfully, however, it can be a challenge. You have to search out the topics, separating them from supporting or explanatory material. These topics may appear paragraph by paragraph in a text, but they may also double up in one paragraph or encompass two or three paragraphs. Though you must rely on key words and phrases from the text, you integrate them into your own new sentences, relying on some of your own language. You attempt to state each topic so that key language from the text suggests connections among the ideas in your outline. In all of these ways, scratch outlining is creative and interpretive.

You may want to number the items in your outline. In addition, when outlining readings in this book, indicate the paragraph number(s) of each item so that when you revisit a reading you have outlined while working on your essay, the outline will lead you quickly to sections of interest in the reading.

Here is a possible scratch outline of the Dionne reading. (The items are numbered to make it easy for you to follow the explanation after the outline.)

1. Some conservatives believe that an active democratic government oppresses its citizens. (paragraph 1)

2. All government actions are suspect, if not dangerous, some conservatives believe. (2)

3. Yet our government was founded on a tradition of government action to protect individual rights. (3)

4. It is not the size but the kind of government that is important. (4)

5. There are many instances in which our government has intervened to ensure individual liberties. (5)

6. The government has taken action to help individuals develop their own abilities and have greater opportunities. (6)

7. The government has taken action to prevent or reduce the influence of money in obtaining justice, swaying elections, avoiding the draft, and obtaining health care. (7, 8)

8. Too much enthusiasm for market solutions to social problems will harm many middle-class and poor families. (9)

9. While certain marketplace ideas can make government more efficient, government action is still needed to solve economic and social problems created by the marketplace. (10, 11, 12)

10. Progressives believe that government must guarantee freedom both to choose one's direction and to become self-sufficient. (13,14)

11. Progressives must resist conservatives' attempts to define them and offer a positive definition of liberty that emphasizes advancing human freedom. (15)

PARAGRAPH NUMBERS.   Following each item in the outline is the paragraph number or numbers on which the item is based. Notice that there are eleven items but fifteen paragraphs. Items 7, 9, and 10 encompass more than one paragraph.

COMPLETE SENTENCES.   Each item is stated as a complete sentence. A scratch outline does not require complete sentences — brief phrases will do — but complete sentences lead you to a fuller, and therefore more-likely-to-be-useful, statement of a topic.

TOPICS.   The first item captures the topic of paragraph 1. For content it relies on the first three sentences, particularly on the second sentence. The other sentences in paragraph 1 support this topic with contrasts, examples, and a quotation from a conservative.

KEY TERMS.   If you compare item 1 to paragraph 1, you will see that two key terms from the paragraph are brought into the item: *conservatives* and *active democratic government*. The outline writer translates the noun "oppressive" into the verb "oppresses" and supplies the remaining words. The writer also constructs the sentence, which is unlike any sentence in the paragraph.

CONNECTIONS.   If you skim the items, you will notice that certain terms are repeated: *conservatives, progressives, government, individuals, freedom, action, the market.* These repetitions in the outline make it more useful because they identify the parts of the reading in which the terms are centrally important.

Because outlining involves interpretation, there is no ideal outline for a given text. Your outline may not conform exactly to another reader's outline. Your goal is to produce an outline that is useful for you and that other readers would almost certainly agree reflects a careful, responsible reading of a text.

Guidelines for Outlining

Follow these steps to produce a scratch outline that reveals the sequence of main ideas in a reading:

IDENTIFY TOPICS OR MAIN POINTS.   Carefully reread the text, identifying each topic, point, or main idea. Assume that you will find a topic in each paragraph. As you learn more about the text, however, you may find that a relatively long paragraph offers more than one important topic or that two or more relatively short paragraphs offer only one important topic.

CONSTRUCT A TOPIC STATEMENT.   Relying on key language in a paragraph, but constructing a phrase or sentence of your own, state the topic of each paragraph. The topic may be stated or only implied. Exclude examples, illustrations, quotations, statistics, anecdotes, and all other kinds of explanatory or supporting material from your topic statement. Search out the one topic or point. You may need to annotate further as you work.

LIST THE TOPICS.   List the topics in sequence and indicate the paragraph number(s) after each topic.

REVISE OR REFOCUS AS NECESSARY.   As you develop your scratch outline, assume that you may need to revise or refocus earlier topic statements as you learn more about the text.

SUMMARIZING

A summary presents in a brief but coherent way the main ideas in a text. It focuses on a few main ideas, leaving examples and support behind. While summaries are always much shorter than the texts they summarize, they may vary widely in length for the same text, depending on the writer's purpose. A summary can be as short as two or three sentences or as long as two or three pages. Summaries provide balanced coverage of a text, giving no more weight to the end than to the beginning. They always take a neutral stance, avoiding any hint of agreement or disagreement with the ideas in a text. Summary writers rely on key words and phrases from the text, but they must weave these into their own sentences.

During your college years, you will write many summaries. Some will be informal, for your own learning; others will need to be formal, following guidelines and illustrations like those presented in this appendix. Summarizing will play an important role in all of the essay assignments you complete in this book because they are all based on texts.

Like outlining, summarizing holds you very closely to a text. It does not invite you to bring in personal knowledge about the subject of the text, nor does it permit you to include personal response or opinion. Consequently, summarizing may seem very constraining. What you gain from summarizing may make it worth your while to accept the constraints, however. A summary increases your understanding of a text and enables you to make it more your own by finding the words and sentences to present it concisely to others. It increases your credibility as a writer because it demonstrates to your readers that they can trust you to present other writers' material responsibly.

Brief Summary.   This first summary of the Dionne reading illustrates a very brief summary. Imagine it as two sentences in an essay in which the Dionne reading plays a minor role. Dionne needs to be brought in only to present typical liberal views or to support an argument that liberalism is to be preferred over conservatism or libertarianism (Chapter 4, "Evaluating Civic Stances)."

> Refuting conservatives' attacks on progressivism, Dionne argues that only an active government can protect individual rights and ensure opportunities for all citizens. He warns that conservatives' favored market solutions to social problems will harm many Americans.

In two sentences this summary attempts to present the most important of the main ideas in the Dionne reading. It relies on several key terms from the reading (*conservatives, progressivism, active government, individual rights, market solutions*), but most of the words and the sentence structures are the writer's. There are no sentences in the Dionne reading like these two.

Longer Summary.   Here is a longer summary, which includes ideas from most of the paragraphs in the Dionne reading. Before you read it, skim the outline in the previous section. This summary is based on the outline.

> In a recent book, <u>They Only Look Dead: Why Progressives Will Dominate the Next Political Era</u>, E. J. Dionne Jr.

attempts to refute conservatives' attacks on liberalism
and to affirm the importance of government programs
designed to protect individual citizens and increase their
opportunities. Dionne contends that conservatives believe
that an active government oppresses its citizens, creating
actual dangers for them by interfering with their
freedoms. Insisting that the kind--not the size--of
government is of greatest importance, Dionne claims that
the United States government was founded on a tradition of
government action to protect individual rights and ensure
individual liberties. Moreover, government has taken
action to help individuals develop their abilities and
enjoy greater opportunities. Government has prevented or
reduced the influence of money in obtaining justice,
swaying elections, avoiding the military draft, and
obtaining health care. Dionne goes on to warn against too
much reliance on marketplace solutions to social problems.
He maintains that liberals must resist conservatives'
attempts to define them and offer instead a positive
definition of liberty that emphasizes advancing human
freedom.

Imagine this paragraph in an essay evaluating civic stances (Chapter 4). It might appear toward the beginning, when the writer is trying to present each civic stance neutrally, with Dionne chosen as one representative of the liberal stance.

Features of Longer Summaries.   As in many summaries written for college courses, the longer summary begins by identifying its source. Throughout the summary, the writer observes an academic convention by referring to Dionne's writing in the present tense. Using various introductory phrases and transition words, the writer creates a coherent, readable text in its own right; it is not merely a list of main ideas, as in the outline. Finally, it includes a continuation phrase ("Dionne goes on to warn against[...]") that reminds readers that the summary continues. As in the brief summary, the writer relies on keywords and phrases from the reading but situates them in his own sentences. There are no sentences or long phrases brought into the summary from the reading, avoiding the accusation of plagiarism. (See Appendix 2 for information on plagiarism.) Note, too, that the writer does not quote from the reading.

Guidelines for Summarizing

These guidelines will help you summarize a text to capture briefly its main ideas.

OUTLINE.   Make a scratch outline of the text. (See the previous section in this appendix.)

CONSIDER CONNECTIONS OR LOGICAL RELATIONSHIPS. Before beginning to draft your summary, consider carefully the connections or logical relationships among the main ideas or topics in your scratch outline. You may have to reread parts of the text. On your scratch outline, make notes about connections.

SUMMARIZE. Write several sentences presenting the text's main ideas. You will need to rely on key words and phrases in the text but construct your own sentences. Include all of the text's main ideas and attempt to show clearly the connections among them. Ensure that your summary gives roughly equal weight to all parts of the text and takes a neutral stance.

REVISE FOR COHERENCE AND READABILITY. Because writing a coherent summary is such a challenge, your first attempt will inevitably require revising. Review the text and revise your summary as needed so that all the ideas are clearly expressed and all the connections among them well established. Your revised summary should be readable, coherent, even graceful.

SYNTHESIZING

Synthesizing involves selecting materials from one or more texts and then bringing them together for a particular purpose to create your own text. For example, if you write an essay to convince readers that your preference for one civic stance over another is reasonable (Chapter 4), in one part of your essay you might want to summarize different parts of a key reading and also quote from it to support your preference. In another part of your essay, you might want to summarize, paraphrase, and quote from three or four different readings. The creative challenge is to find the right materials and to weave them together with your interpretive comments into a readable new text designed to realize your purpose for writing it.

Because all of the essay assignments in *Writing the World* are based at least in part on texts you have read and discussed, synthesizing is fundamentally important to your work on the assignments. In *Writing the World* assignments, there are two basic occasions for synthesizing—explaining and arguing—which require quite different close-reading strategies.

Synthesizing to Explain. Synthesizing to write an explanation of some subject requires that you read to identify recurring topics in several texts. These topics then become the focus of your newly synthesized explanation. Explaining a subject by synthesizing information from several readings is central to the essay in Chapter 2, "Reporting Information." The essays in other chapters may also require you to synthesize from several readings in order to explain or introduce the subject of your essay to readers. For example, you might need to explain the debate on an issue to your readers before you announce your position on it, as in Chapter 3, "Taking a Position on a Constitutional Issue." In addition, some writer's notebook tasks in several chapters also ask you to try your hand at explaining or presenting a subject by selecting relevant materials from a reading.

Synthesizing to Support an Argument.   Synthesizing to write an argument requires you to read first to discover the full range of positions and arguments in the texts you have available and then, as you begin to plan an essay, to select from the readings relevant support for the argument you want to make. Supporting an argument by synthesizing materials from several readings is central to all of the assignment chapters. On these writing occasions, even though your personal experience and observations may play a role, the chapters' readings provide the primary support through the syntheses you create from them to support your argument. In the argument chapters, some writer's notebook tasks enable you to practice synthesizing materials from one or more readings.

Reading to synthesize material from diverse sources clearly requires a special kind of close reading: reading to select materials for a text of your own. It is also an excellent example of critical thinking. It engages all your powers of judgment, discrimination, and interpretation. As you read to select materials to construct a synthesis, you strive to make meaningful connections among sometimes widely scattered materials. You discover new relationships among materials and uncover connections to what you already knew about a subject before you started reading about it. You make countless decisions about what to select and what to exclude.

The following illustration of synthesizing is based on paragraphs 9–12 in the selection from the Dionne reading in Chapter 4. Pause to reread these paragraphs, in which Dionne focuses on the intense late-1990s political debate over whether markets are superior to government. By *markets* (and the closely related term *free market* and *marketplace*), Dionne means the private (nongovernmental) and lightly regulated selling and buying of goods and services. The market includes banks, manufacturers, railroads and trucking companies, car dealers and cafes, private schools, and us consumers when we go shopping.

In this illustration, a student attempts to support his preference for liberalism as a civic stance by synthesizing materials from Dionne's paragraphs 9–12:

```
Another reason I prefer liberalism is that liberals are
highly skeptical of conservatives' reliance on business
or market solutions to social problems. For example,
conservatives would like to replace workers' payments to
the federal Medicare program with payments into medical
savings accounts, which workers themselves would manage.
Liberals wisely oppose this change because they believe it
would privilege people in the higher income brackets and
deny adequate coverage to middle-class and poor people
with serious or long-term illnesses. E. J. Dionne Jr.,
author of They Only Look Dead: Why Progressives Will
```

Dominate the Next Political Era, expresses skepticism about conservatives' eagerness to replace government programs with free-market programs. Dionne warns: "In a society characterized by growing economic inequality, the dangers of making the marketplace the sole arbiter of the basic elements of a decent life are especially large" (260). He points out: "The market can break down, recessions can throw people out of work, families can lose their health insurance, poor people can lack the money to buy food and shelter for their children" (261). Dionne does acknowledge that strategies devised by businesses to operate more efficiently can improve government programs. He also recognizes that instead of setting up a government program, it can be more effective to give people a voucher for education or housing and let them spend it wherever they want. He uses the highly popular and effective GI Bill as an example. Veterans returning from World War II relied on the GI Bill to continue their college educations at colleges of their choice. Dionne seems especially skeptical about the consequences of relying solely on the marketplace to ensure working families a decent income and benefits. He argues: "If the marketplace becomes [...] the only judge of living standards, then all social factors, including the need to strengthen families and improve the care given children, become entirely irrelevant in the world of work" (260).

Collecting. Hoping to incorporate Dionne's skepticism about marketplace values into his argument, the student reread closely paragraphs 9–12, looking for relevant material that he might quote, paraphrase, or summarize. His general plan was to include Dionne's reason for valuing liberalism—liberals recognize that the market creates problems government must solve—among the reasons in his argument for preferring liberalism over conservatism and libertarianism. In the margins, he marked material that might be quoted, choosing sentences that accurately represented Dionne's views and that would likely be clear to readers. Knowing that liberals' skepticism about marketplace values would be only part of his argument, probably no more than a paragraph or two, he tried to collect only the most highly relevant sentences.

Selecting. Guided by his purpose, the student tentatively selected the materials that seemed most useful. He selected three sentences to quote, from paragraphs 9 and 12, and bracketed the GI Bill example in paragraphs 11 and 12. He also made brief notes about medical savings accounts, which he had learned about from talking to his uncle, who hoped to be able to offer them to the employees in his five auto parts stores.

Organizing. Next, the writer quickly made a scratch outline, creating a possible sequence or progression of these materials:

reason—liberals are skeptical about free-market programs

medical savings account example

Quote 1: dangers of relying on marketplace

Quote 2: market is unreliable

acknowledge that market strategies can sometimes help

GI Bill example

mention Dionne's concern about working families

Quote 3: irrelevance of family welfare to marketplace

The writer hoped this plan would allow him to support this part of his argument readably and convincingly.

Connecting. A successful synthesis must connect all of its materials into a readable, coherent, logical new text. The starting point is a first draft of the imagined synthesis. As in all first drafts, plans will inevitably change. Some materials may not fit, and new materials may need to be selected. The plan for sequencing the selections may need to be changed.

Notice how this student connects all the parts into a coherent text of his own. The paragraph opens with a clear signal that a new step in the argument begins here—a step that announces another reason why the writer prefers liberalism. This first sentence introduces the key terms: *skeptical* (the noun *skepticism* appears in subsequent sentences) and *market* (the synonyms *free market* and *marketplace* appear in subsequent sentences). The second sentence offers an example of a market solution to workers' need for medical insurance. The third sentence asserts the writer's and other liberals' position on medical savings accounts. These first three sentences derive from the writer's knowledge. The remaining sentences all come from the Dionne reading and, with one exception ("Veterans returning"), begin with "Dionne" or "he." Nearly every other sentence includes the key terms *skeptical* or *market* or their synonyms. The three quotes—introduced by the verbs "warns," "points out," and "argues"—are smoothly integrated into the paragraph. The writer carefully balances quotations from Dionne with brief summarizes of what he says. These and many other strategies are available to writers for creating a well-connected synthesis.

Guidelines for Synthesizing

ESTABLISH A PURPOSE. First, clarify your purpose. In the assignments in *Writing the World*, your purpose could be any of the following:

- to illustrate a category of information you have set up
- to introduce an issue, or a crisis, or a phenomenon to your readers
- to support your speculations about the causes of a social crisis
- to support your position on a question of constitutional importance
- to justify your preference for a particular civic stance
- to refute an argument that challenges your own

Keep your purpose clearly in mind as you search the readings for relevant material. You may have different purposes within the same essay: introducing an issue to your readers, arguing to support your position on the issue, counterarguing the most convincing arguments of those who take positions different from yours.

SELECT RELEVANT MATERIALS.   From an initial, tentative annotation of materials that may be useful for your purpose, select those materials that you think you will want to weave into your essay. Select promising quotations, as well as material you might want to summarize. You may select materials from the readings or your writer's notebook. Your selections must be relevant to your purpose and readers, as well as representative of the texts from which they come.

ORGANIZE THE MATERIALS.   As you begin to draft your essay, guided by a tentative essay outline, pause to make scratch outlines of each section to decide how you might arrange or sequence the varied materials that will go into each part of your essay. If the writing is going well, you may not need to outline every section, but then you may expect to do more revising.

SYNTHESIZE THE MATERIALS TO MAKE A TEXT OF YOUR OWN.   Write a draft in which you attempt to synthesize the materials into a readable, coherent text of your own. Expect to change your plans once you start drafting. You may find that some materials do not work or that you need to select more materials. Alternate between quoting and summarizing. Help your readers understand the significance of every quotation. Give them the impression that you are in charge of all the materials you are synthesizing. Demonstrate that you are sequencing and connecting the materials to suit your own purpose.

A draft is always something of an experiment. Invest enough in it to see what the possibilities are but not so much that you exhaust yourself trying to get it perfect. Try to push through to the end of one section and then step back to evaluate how it came out.

REVISE FOR COHERENCE AND READABILITY.   As you make progress through the different stages of an essay, spend only enough time revising each section to ensure that each synthesis you create is relatively logical and readable for your particular readers. When you have a complete first draft, then you can devote more time to making all the connections clear.

EVALUATING ARGUMENTS

When you evaluate an argument, you make judgments about how convincing it is for its intended readers. To carry out a comprehensive evaluation of an argument, you first learn what you can about the context of its publication and about its readers and purpose. You then read it closely to evaluate its credibility, emotional appeal, and logic. Because all but one of the assignment chapters in *Writing the World* focus on argument by immersing you in reading arguments and writing one yourself, evaluating arguments is central to your work. In these chapters, occasional writer's notebook tasks invite you to evaluate arguments you are reading. In class discussions of the readings, you will be constantly evaluating arguments, analyzing what makes readings more or less convincing for their intended readers. Equally important, as you sort out issues and settle on your own positions, you will be evaluating readings in terms of how they enable you to support an argument and anticipate readers' objections and questions.

In learning how to evaluate arguments more comprehensively and insightfully, you will be engaged in a highly regarded close-reading and critical-thinking activity. You must project yourself imaginatively into the role of intended reader of the argument, paying close attention to the organization, content, and language of the argument and making judgments about how convincing it is on the basis of what the text says and of what you infer about its assumptions about its readers.

Following is an illustration of an argument evaluation written by a student. Before you read it, take time to read the Dionne reading in this appendix. After the illustration, you will find commentary on the key features of the student's evaluation. Together, the illustration and the commentary prepare you to use the "Guidelines for Evaluating an Argument" at the end of this section.

Context

Situation. Dionne writes in the mid-1990s during Clinton's first term. The Republican conservatives had taken control of Congress after forty years of Democratic control and launched a political debate about reducing the size and role of government. Conservatives want to eliminate or privatize many government programs. They want to apply market mechanisms to other programs in order to make them more efficient. Liberals feel threatened and defensive. Dionne is a well-known liberal writer. He has years of experience as a Washington Post reporter and columnist interviewing political leaders, reading widely about politics, and writing about political affairs. He seems very well informed and seems to understand conservative as well as liberal ideas. Probably conservatives have to take him seriously, even though they disagree with him.

Readers and purpose. Dionne may hope that
conservatives read his book, but I'm sure his primary
readers are liberals. His purpose seems to be to encourage
them and to reassure them that they'll be back on top
soon. He wants to strengthen their determination to oppose
conservative policies.

Evaluation

Credibility. I believe that Dionne's argument would
be very convincing to his readers--other liberals like
himself. Dionne seems to respect his readers. He doesn't
talk down to them and seems to assume that they are
capable of following a careful argument based on sources
unfamiliar to them. Readers will trust him and find him
believable because of his wide reading and use of many
sources in his argument. He's not just some angry person
spouting uninformed and unformed ideas. He's not an
amateur at analyzing politics. His career has been
devoted to reading, talking, and writing about political
issues.

Emotional Appeal. Dionne relies on sources to present
conservative and liberal views and information about
government programs, but he also appeals directly to
his readers' emotions. He wants to get them stirred up
about conservative ideas and their attempts to overthrow
decades of liberal programs. He's not above using scare
tactics, as when he uses the word "radical" to refer to
conservatives' ideas. He may hope to outrage liberals by
showing that Representative Armey equates three liberal
Presidents--Roosevelt, Kennedy, and Johnson--with Stalin
and Mao. I think that Dionne goes too far in manipulating
his readers' emotions. All politicians accuse the
opposition of radicalism. It's just name-calling meant to
stir up anger rather than engage everybody in a cooler
evaluation of arguments and support on both sides. Also,
because I haven't read Armey, I can't tell whether the
comparison of Roosevelt and Stalin is representative of
Armey's writing. It does seem reckless to me for Armey to
make such a comparison, but Dionne may be setting up a
straw man. It seems to me Dionne should have let the facts
speak for themselves about the programs conservatives
promote and those they oppose.

Logic. Dionne's argument moves in a logical step-by-
step sequence. There don't seem to me to be any gaps. On
first reading, I found the marketplace section beginning
in paragraph 9 hard to follow, but, rereading to annotate,
I thought it was logically organized.

The support seems adequate in all stages of Dionne's argument. He sometimes give several examples, as in paragraphs 2, 5, and 13. In paragraph 2 he gives four examples of government-sponsored programs that conservatives like Armey are philosophically opposed to-- health care coverage, pensions, environmental regulations, and work safety regulations. Sometimes he develops an example in some detail, as in the GI Bill example in paragraphs 11 and 12. At no time did I feel I needed more support to understand a part of Dionne's argument. All of the support Dionne provides seems relevant. Dionne's argument seems internally consistent. I am not aware of any place where he contradicts himself.

Dionne's counterargument is especially convincing. You might say his basic strategy is counterargument. He begins by presenting conservative views and quoting conservatives. His strategy seems to be to make them look reckless, dangerous, and heartless. I have criticized him for playing on liberal fears, but I recognize that, given his purpose to energize liberals, his approach is very convincing. For his purpose and readers, he successfully refutes conservatives' views. He then argues that conservatives aren't even thinking correctly about government. What they see as big government is actually only energetic government protecting citizens' rights and freedoms and ensuring them certain opportunities--food, a school to go to, etc.--even if they are poor. While they worry about the size of government, they should instead focus on what kind of government we have. Instead of relying on market solutions to social problems, they should recognize that the market provides deserving people little protection. I do think that Dionne fails to counterargue an obvious conservative criticism of government--that it is inefficient and wasteful. Some liberals probably believe government is inefficient. He should have conceded this point and pointed to any examples he knows about of liberal members of Congress supporting proposals to reduce waste and reform or close inefficient programs.

Situating.   This student's evaluation illustrates how responsible evaluations begin with a full understanding of the context for the argument. Context includes the situation in which the argument was written and its intended readers and purpose. In the illustration, the writer begins by situating the Dionne reading historically. This material comes from the headnote to the reading in Chapter 4, from the writer's personal knowledge about the Republican takeover of Congress, and from the writer's inferences about the reading itself. With more time, the writer might have looked in the library or on the Internet for more information about Dionne and the *Washington Post*, searched for reviews of the book at the time it appeared, and examined accounts of liberals' dismay when the conservatives took over Congress.

Situating an argument is particularly important in writing an evaluation. It seems unlikely that Dionne would have written his book during the Kennedy or Johnson administrations, when liberals controlled Congress and the presidency. Instead, he wrote it at the end of several conservative presidencies, those of Richard Nixon, Ronald Reagan, and George Bush.

Inferring Readers and Purpose.   The writer then speculates about Dionne's readers and purpose. Sometimes authors identify their intended readers and assert their purpose. If not, the person writing the evaluation must infer the readers and purpose from the publication source and the reading itself. Such inferences are important because it is hardly fair to evaluate the likely impact of an argument on readers for whom it was not intended. Also, you must resist evaluating how convincing an argument is to you personally, especially if you are not among the intended readers. This requirement makes evaluating an argument a particular challenge intellectually. Notice that you cannot tell whether the student who wrote the evaluation is a conservative or a liberal. Instead of evaluating the Dionne reading from either perspective, she tries to imagine how convincing it would be to politically liberal readers. Of course, there are occasions when a writer for a liberal magazine would want to review a conservative's book unfavorably or a writer for, say, a Southern Baptist magazine would want to express reservations about a book by a secular humanist. You will find yourself in a similar position — evaluating from a particular perspective when you complete certain writer's notebook tasks and take a stance on the issues in this book's essay assignments. For this close-reading and critical-thinking strategy, however, we want you to practice evaluating an argument in terms of its context and its intended readers and purpose.

Evaluating.   With the context established, this writer began evaluating the reading. A comprehensive evaluation involves thinking critically about the writer's credibility, emotional appeals to readers, and the logic of the argument. Notice that under credibility she evaluates Dionne's authority to write about political subjects, his attitude toward his readers, and the trust they would likely have in him. Under emotional appeal, she evaluates how he appeals to his readers' emotions. All arguments appeal to readers' emotions because arguments engage divisive, unsettled, or worrisome aspects of our personal, social, civic, or political lives. The question is whether the appeal to emotions engages readers' legitimate feelings or attempts to incite their fears. The writer faults Dionne for trying to frighten or outrage his readers. Another evaluator might have praised Dionne's strategy of agitating his readers, given the urgency he clearly feels about overturning the conservative revolution.

Under logic, the writer evaluates whether the organization of Dionne's argument seems logical; whether the support for the argument is adequate, believable, and consistent; and whether the counterargument is convincing.

Notice that she uses examples from the argument to support her evaluation and sometimes refers to specific paragraphs by number.

Writing the Evaluation. As you read any argument, you continually evaluate it, resisting its appeal, cheering its clever counterarguments, or questioning its assumptions. When you write an evaluation, however, you do so to show someone else that you can carry out a comprehensive evaluation. Writing in your writer's notebook, you assure your instructor that you are learning how to evaluate arguments—and incidentally perhaps produce some material that you can use in your essay. Writing your essay, you impress your readers and strengthen your argument by evaluating various readings.

As a close-reading and critical-thinking activity, writing an evaluation of an argument can be informal, not constrained by the formal requirements of a summary or a synthesis. Your written evaluation must be comprehensive, however, following the outline indicated by the headings and subheadings in the illustration. (These points are detailed in the guidelines that follow.) Basically, you establish the context of the argument, and then you evaluate it. You create a text of your own, as in the illustration, but for the purpose of learning how to evaluate an argument and demonstrating that you know how to do so, not for the purpose of demonstrating your best writing. Only if you were to use part of an evaluation in one of your essays would you revise it with the care required to produce a successful summary or synthesis.

Guidelines for Evaluating an Argument

LEARN ABOUT THE SITUATION. The situation for an argument includes the publication source, the time of publication, and the author's reputation at the time of publication. In *Writing the World,* reading headnotes provide this information in brief. The reading itself, and perhaps other readings in the chapter, may provide further information about the historical and cultural context for the reading. When you evaluate a reading for a writer's notebook task, this information will allow you to present adequately the situation of the argument. When you evaluate one or more key readings in one of your essays, however, you may want to learn more about the source, times, and author by visiting the library or the Internet.

ESTABLISH READERS AND PURPOSE. Headnotes may occasionally provide information about readers and purpose, or a reading may identify or describe readers or purpose. You may be able to infer such information in a reading as you gain knowledge of an issue from other readings in a chapter, and you can speculate about what the writer seems to assume about readers' knowledge, attitudes, and beliefs.

Some readings, like newspaper reports, are aimed at a broad, general readership. Even in these cases, there may be a way for you to characterize readers more carefully in terms of educational level or knowledge of the subject or related subjects. A book may be aimed at a relatively narrow readership, hoping to influence its audience in a particular way. Try to reach as specific an understanding of readers as possible. You may or may not be among the intended readers, but you must evaluate the argument in terms of how convincing it is for its intended readers.

REREAD TO EVALUATE THE ARGUMENT. Reread the argument closely to evaluate its credibility, emotional appeal, and logic. As you read and annotate, try to answer the following questions:

Credibility

- What is the author's reputation? How does it establish his or her authority to make this argument for these particular readers?
- What attitude toward readers does the text reveal? Respectful, condescending, bullying, sarcastic, or some other?
- What sources does the author rely on, and does the handling of these sources enhance the author's credibility with readers?

Emotional Appeal

- What kinds of feelings does the argument seem designed to elicit from readers? Are these feelings likely to increase readers' concern or engagement without playing on their fears or prejudices?
- Does the argument take a cynical or manipulative approach to readers? Does it threaten or unduly flatter readers? Does it rely on loaded or slanted language?

Logic

- Consider whether each stage or step in the argument is logically related to previous steps and to the thesis. Where does the argument fail to signal these logical relationships, creating a gap or a misdirection in the logical sequence?
- How believable is the support for each stage of the argument? What support seems particularly believable, and what support might the intended readers resist or question?
- How adequate is the support for each stage of the argument? Where does the support seem particularly convincing because it is full and comprehensive? Where might the intended readers find the support inadequate?
- Considering the argument as a whole, do you notice any inconsistencies or contradictions between different parts of the argument?
- Where does the argument acknowledge opposing views? Do opposing views seem to be presented fairly and responsibly?
- Where does the argument attempt to concede or refute opposing views? Which concessions or refutations seem convincingly argued? Which ones might seem thin and unconvincing to the intended readers? Can you think of readers'

likely questions or objections not addressed by the argument? Does the argument attempt to gain the attention or even respect of readers who hold opposing views?

DRAFT THE EVALUATION.   If you draft an evaluation in response to a writer's notebook task, organize it under the headings Credibility, Emotional Appeal, and Logic. Though your evaluation must be comprehensive, answering most of the above questions, it can be informal, but it should be readable and show that you have read the argument closely and critically. If you evaluate an argument as part of an essay you write, you may want to do so selectively, perhaps focusing only on your high regard for a writer's credibility or on your dislike of a writer's manipulating readers' feelings. As part of an essay, your evaluation would need to meet high standards of coherence and logical development.

Support your judgments about the argument by referring to specific parts of it (use paragraph numbers) and by quoting from it.

APPENDIX 2

Researching
Issues and
Citing Sources

This appendix gives general strategies for finding print and electronic sources and citing them in your own text. The "Gathering Additional Information" sections of Chapters 2–7 will help you supplement the particular kinds of sources in those chapters. If you do seek out other sources to use in your essays, you may need the further information offered here.

FINDING SOURCES

Such a vast amount of print and electronic information is available that finding sources involves more than just knowing the physical layout of a library. It involves combining a smart *search strategy* with an understanding of the type of information you want. Finding statistics, for instance, requires a different search strategy from finding personal anecdotes or research studies, as you may have seen in Chapter 5. The following four steps will help you determine what type of information you need and how to go about finding it.

1. Deciding what types of information you need

2. Learning about types of sources

3. Searching for specific sources

4. Evaluating sources

DECIDING WHAT TYPES OF INFORMATION YOU NEED

Deciding what you need begins with a clear sense of the question you are addressing and the types of sources likely to be appropriate for answering that question.

Formulate a Research Question

Each chapter in this book poses a question. In Chapter 5, for example, the question is: What are the possible causes of violence by young men? This question identifies both the general topic—violence—and a more specific part of it—the *causes* of violence. If you are researching the specific issue in a chapter, then, this first step is done for you by the research question in the chapter title.

If you want to branch out further, or if you are working on one of the additional writing projects, you will probably need to formulate a different question. If, for instance, you want to research what people are proposing to do about violence, then your question should be about *solutions* or *proposals* for dealing with violence. These examples below show how a writer might arrive at a research question. Note that each question is much narrower than the general topic with which the writer started. Starting with a specific, limited question will make your research more productive and efficient.

General Topic Area	Limited Topic	Possible Research Question
Violence	By young men	What are some solutions to the problems of violence by young men?
Freedom of speech	Freedom of speech on the Internet	Should the government attempt to curtail freedom of speech on the Internet?
Hate speech	Hate speech on college campuses	What are some solutions to the problem of hate speech on campuses, other than legal solutions?
Gender and talk	Conversation problems in romantic relations	What is the main cause of communication problems between husbands and wives?

Determining Needed Information

Once you have a research question in mind, think about the *types* of information you will need to answer the question. Will you be looking for specific facts, original research studies, background information, news reports, and so on? Will you need current, up-to-date data or sources that examine a phe-nomenon well after it has occurred?

Types of Information.   Some of the types of information you might need are single facts, general information, or specialized information or research stud-ies, and each may involve a different search strategy.

Single facts will be necessary for answering questions like these:

- What was the murder rate in 1997 in metropolitan areas?
- What was the name of the most recent Supreme Court appointee?
- What was the average income for a family of four in 1990?

Single facts come from a wide and unpredictable variety of sources, includ-ing statistical abstracts, encyclopedias, almanacs, atlases, and dictionaries. To find such factual information, begin by asking a reference librarian to help.

General information is likely to be helpful when you are first orienting your-self to a particular area of study. Many reference sources provide overviews or introductions. General encyclopedias, for instance, offer articles on all fields of knowledge, and specialized subject encyclopedias give background in a par-ticular field. If you are lacking a basic understanding of a subject, which the writers you are reading assume you have, consulting a general source may help you raise your level of knowledge. In addition, the bibliography at the end of an encyclopedia article might help you find more specialized informa-tion. Keep in mind, however, that you should not rely on encyclopedias or other general information sources for the major part of an essay requiring original sources.

Following is a list of a few common general information sources, and your librarian can direct you to many others.

- *Dictionary of American History*
- *Dictionary of American Biography*
- *Encyclopedia of the American Constitution*
- *Encyclopedia of the American Judicial System*
- *Encyclopedia Britannica*
- *Encyclopedia of Crime and Justice*
- *Encyclopedia of Philosophy*
- *Encyclopedia of Psychology*

Specialized information or research studies are what you are most likely to use in the major part of an essay on causes of violence or effects of economic restructuring, for instance. This type of information is likely to zero in on some particular aspect of a topic, to have a narrow focus rather than a general one. If you were to look for information on economic restructuring, you would find specialized sources that discuss only export and trade issues, oth-ers that cover only the balance between work and leisure, others that deal solely with housing affordability, and so forth. For such specialized information, books, journal articles, and government documents are likely to be your best sources because they are most likely to contain research, informed speculation, and interpretation.

Contemporary vs. Retrospective Materials. *Contemporary* information is information published at or close to the time when an event or idea occurs. Typical contemporary sources are newspaper, magazine, and journal articles because of their rapid publication. *Retrospective* information, by contrast, is information that appears after an event or an idea occurs. Take the subject of economic restructuring. If you wanted to find current information on family income, trade or budget deficits, or housing affordability, you would want to consult recent statistical abstracts, government documents, or journal and magazine articles. If, on the other hand, you wanted to understand the historical context for the debate on campus hate speech, you would want retrospective information, and you might look for that retrospective information in books or in scholarly journal articles in history.

This distinction between retrospective and contemporary materials is largely a matter of common sense, but it has consequences you might not foresee: the tools for finding retrospective materials differ in important ways from those for finding contemporary materials, as discussed further below.

After formulating a question and deciding what types of information you need, it is time to look more closely at the types of sources.

LEARNING ABOUT TYPES OF SOURCES

Understanding how information is published and then organized will help you know where to look when you begin your research.

Types of Published Sources

Major types of published sources include books, journals, magazines, news articles, government documents, and Internet documents. A basic understanding of how they are published, their purpose, and their intended readers can save you time and make your search more efficient.

Books. Books are written for many different purposes and many different readers. Those written by scholars to inform other scholars may be highly technical and somewhat difficult to understand. They may, however, contain the specific research studies you need for a particular essay. Books written to entertain and enlighten—novels, short stories, biographies, autobiographies—are usually more accessible to the general reader and may be useful when you are looking for anecdotes or examples of firsthand experiences. If you are looking for very current information, books are not likely to be your best source because it takes at least a year (and often much longer) to get a writer's manuscript through the book-publishing process.

Magazine and Journal Articles.   Magazine and journal articles are published more quickly than books and, therefore, may be one of your best sources for very current information. The distinction between *magazines* and *journals* can be fuzzy, but, in general, *magazines* are more often intended for entertainment whereas *journals* usually have a serious academic purpose. Thus, you are more likely to find scholarly research in journals and current news or articles for the general reader in magazines. The distinction between magazines and journals matters when you are deciding where to look for information. Magazines and indexes for locating material in magazines are more likely to be found in public libraries, while journals and journal indexes are more likely to be found in college and university libraries.

Newspaper Articles.   Newspaper articles are likely to be even more current than magazine articles because major newspapers are published daily. Even within newspapers, different types of information serve different purposes and are current in different degrees. Facts in a story on the front page or the baseball scores in the sports section, for instance, may be less than a day old. Newspapers also carry feature articles on special topics that often include up-to-date statistics, summaries of research, and personal anecdotes. The editorial pages offer opinion pieces by a paper's editorial board and by nationally syndicated columnists, which may be useful when you need some opinions on current issues. All libraries offer a selection of major newspapers.

Government Documents.   Most government documents are publications of the federal government. The Department of Justice—including the Federal Bureau of Investigation (FBI)—the Department of Commerce, and the Department of Education publish vast amounts of material. Until recently, these documents were most likely to be found in large libraries designated as special depositories for government publications. Now, though, many government documents, including state and local publications, are available on the Internet. Government documents are an especially good source of statistics, such as on violence or the economy, and of information on legal and constitutional issues.

Internet Material.   The Internet contains all the types of publication sources listed above. Newspaper, magazine, and journal publishers now publish many articles and reports on the Web, as do government agencies. Reviews of books and reference works can also be found on the Web, along with many other kinds of material. Since so many types of sources are available on the Internet, it is important to evaluate carefully the sources you find, checking for sponsorship, posting dates, and so forth. A further discussion of evaluating sources appears later in this appendix.

How Sources Are Organized

The two major classification systems that libraries use—Library of Congress (in colleges and universities) or Dewey Decimal (often in public libraries)—are organized more or less by discipline. For instance, books on language have call numbers beginning with the letter P in the Library of Congress system while books on English literature begin with PR. You do not need to remember this information, since it is readily available in any library, but there are times when it may help to know the general principle. For instance, a search for gender differences in conversation may turn up material on the *language* aspects of conversational differences in the P's or on *sex role* differences classified in the H's, where books on sociology are shelved. If you want to restrict your search to *linguistic* aspects of sex role differences, material under the H's is likely to be less useful than the material under the P's.

This same principle occurs elsewhere because historical subjects may be taken up by sociologists, or philosophical subjects by political scientists. Just remember that the library classification systems have their origins in academic disciplines. You will then be able to understand why material relevant to a particular topic can come from different parts of the library or, just as important, why material from a different part of the library may be not quite relevant to your topic.

SEARCHING FOR SPECIFIC SOURCES

Once you know what information you want to find and the type of publication source most likely to contain that information, you need to find out what your library has to offer.

The Role of Libraries and Virtual Libraries

Different kinds of libraries serve differing needs. If you are at a research university, your library is likely to have a larger collection of research material than if you are at a small liberal arts college or a community college. A town or a city library may have more popular magazines, business sources, and works of current fiction than a research library, but it may not have a great deal of specialized research material, and it may offer few academic indexes. If your library does not have the material you need, a librarian can refer you to the right kind of library for your needs.

Now that so much material is available on the Internet, the problem of limited library collections is less important. In its place, however, comes another kind of problem: too much material that is not organized in any systematic way. When you use a library, you benefit from a lot of behind-the-scenes cataloging of information that has already been done for you, thus making your search strategy more efficient. For example, since libraries are organized by academic discipline, you can readily find books on the language of conversation in one location. But the Internet has not benefited from decades of librarians' work in categorizing information, and new technologies constantly change the way virtual information might be organized. Keep in mind, though, that what you learn about research in the library can be applied to research on the Internet as long as you are prepared to evaluate sources carefully and be creative in your search strategies. There are a number of search tools you can use.

Search Tools

Search tools are catalogs, indexes, abstracts, and databases that help you identify the titles and authors of books or articles on your topic. Once you have the titles or authors, you can try to locate the items in a library or online.

Catalogs. The card or online catalog in your library is the first place to look for a book by title, author, or subject heading. It may also be the first place to look for a magazine, journal, or newspaper article if you have access to an online catalog containing periodical indexes or abstracts. Here is a sample online catalog entry for a book:

Author:	Dionne, E. J.
Title:	They only look dead : why progressives will dominate the next political era / E.J. Dionne, Jr
Imprint:	New York : Simon & Schuster, c1996
Description:	352 p. ; 25 cm
CALL NO.:	JK271 .D56 1996
Subj-lcsh:	United States—Politics and government—1993–
	United States—Economic policy—1993–
	United States—Social policy—1993–
	Conservatism—United States
	Liberalism—United States
	Progressivism (United States politics)
Note(s):	Includes bibliographical references (p. 315–333) and index
ISBN:	0684807688

The call number tells you where in the library the book is shelved; the information listed under the heading "Subj-lcsh" tells which Library of Congress subject headings apply to the book; and the note about bibiographical references tells you that the book may refer you to other relevant sources. You can use this information to help you decide whether a source is relevant or not or to get tips for extending your search.

Indexes and Abstracts. An index is the tool most likely to help you find contemporary material. Indexes, along with abstracts and other databases, cover a limited number of magazine, journal, or newspaper issues and list each article by topic. Some indexes also list each article by author and title. Instead of randomly hunting through magazines for views on the economy, for example, you can use an index to save time and give you a list of articles to consider using.

Some indexes focus on a broad subject and some on a narrow subject, some on more general sources and some on more academic sources. Their information may appear in print form in your library, online, or on CD-ROM. Since the name of an index in its print version may differ slightly from its name online, ask your librarian which form is available and which name it goes by.

Indexes for finding *general* periodical material can usually be found in any library. Such indexes are intended for the general reader and list relatively nontechnical sources.

InfoTrac—An electronic index to general interest and basic academic periodicals. *InfoTrac* is likely to be called by different names in different libraries, so ask a librarian.

Reader's Guide—A print (or CD-ROM) index to nonscholarly and general interest magazines.

Here is a sample entry from the *Reader's Guide to Periodical Literature*.

TABLOID TELEVISION
Why relevance is obsolete [broadcast journalism covering tabloid topics] J. Greenfield. il *Time* v149 p64 F 10 '97

SPECIALIZED OR ACADEMIC INDEXES. These indexes may be found in college and university libraries. They are likely to lead you to articles with more scholarly, in-depth analysis or research. Following are some examples of specialized indexes.

Business Periodicals Index

Education Index

General Science Index

Modern Language Association Bibliography

Philosopher's Index

Public Affairs Information Service (PAIS)

Social Science Index

NEWSPAPER AND OTHER NEWS INDEXES. These indexes are available in most libraries. Newspaper indexes may be available in print, CD-ROM, or online. Indexes such as those listed here will help you track down current news articles and opinion pieces.

Editorials on File

Facts on File

Los Angeles Times Index

National Newspaper Index

Newsbank

New York Times Index

Wall Street Journal Index

ABSTRACTS. Abstracts list not just the titles and, perhaps, authors of articles, but also brief summaries of articles' contents, under subject headings. Like specialized indexes, abstracts are a good search tool for finding scholarly information. Many abstracts are available online or on CD-ROM, as well as in college libraries. Here are some examples:

Communication Abstracts

Criminal Justice Abstracts

Linguistics and Language Behavior Abstracts: LLBA

Psychological Abstracts (PsycLit Database)

Sociological Abstracts (Sociofile on CD-ROM)

Women Studies Abstracts

Search Terms

For an effective search in any of the tools just discussed, you need to know something about the different kinds of search terms. *Subject headings* are one kind of search term used by catalogers to group materials on the same topic, thus enabling library users to look up those headings in card or online catalogs to find related materials. Since different words might be used for the same topic, subject headings are very useful. In looking up information on violence by young people, for instance, you might wonder whether you should use the terms *adolescence, teenagers, youth, or violence.* Most libraries use the *Library of Congress Subject Headings* (LCSH). These are published in several volumes and are likely to be available near your library's card catalog or online terminals. Anyone looking for material on a subject like *violence,* then, can use the LCSH to discover the standardized terms used by the Library of Congress to catalog the material.

On the next page are the *violence* listings from the *Library of Congress Subject Headings.* As this sample suggests, the general term *violence* is likely to lead in all sorts of directions. If you were writing the essay assigned in Chapter 5, you would probably choose *Violent crimes* or *Violent deaths—Murder* as the best subject headings for your purpose. While the broad subject heading *violence* leads to more material than you would want, at other times a subject search may turn up far less material. There is no set rule for deciding when you are using too broad or too narrow a term. Your need to expand or narrow a search will depend on the nature of your topic.

Excerpts from the Library of Congress Subject Headings.

Violence   *(May Subd Geog)*
  *[HM281-HM283 (Social
    psychology)]*
  [RC569.5.V55 (Psychiatry)]
  BT Agressiveness
       (Psychology)
       Social psychology
  NT Children and violence
       Conjugal violence
       Dating violence
       Family violence
       Fighting (Psychology)
       Political violence
       Prison violence
       Road rage
       School violence
       Violent deaths
  —Environmental aspects
       (May Subd Geog)
  —Folklore
  UF Violence (in religion,
       folklore, etc.)
       [Former heading]
  —Forecasting
  UF Violence—Prediction
       [Former heading]
  —Moral and ethical aspects
       May Subd Geog)
  UF Violence—Moral and
       religious aspects
       [Former heading]
  —Moral and religious aspects
  USE Violence—Moral and
       ethical aspects
       Violence—Religious aspects
  —Prediction
  USE Violence—Forecasting
  —Press coverage
       (May Subd Geog)
  UF Violence in the press
       [Former heading]
  —Religious aspects
  UF Violence—Moral and
       religious aspects
       [Former heading]
       Violence (in religion,
       folklore, etc.)
       [Former heading]
  **——Baptists, [Catholic
       Church, etc.]**
  **——Buddhism, [Christianity,
       etc.]**
  —Research   *(May Subd Geog)*
  UF Violence research
       [Former heading]
Violence (in religion, folklore, etc.)
  USE Violence—Folklore
       Violence—Religious
       aspects
Violence (Law) *(May Subd Geog)*
  UF Force (Law)

  BT Law
  NT Assault and battery
       Robbery
Violence and children
  USE Children and violence
Violence chips
  USE V-chips
Violence in art
Violence in children *(May Subd
  Geog)*
       Here are entered works on chil-
       dren's violent behavior. Works on
       children's experiences with, concep-
       tions of, and reactions to violence
       are entered under Children and
       violence.
  BT Aggressiveness
       (Psychology) in
       children
       Child psychopathology
  RT Children and violence
Violence in hospitals *(May
  Subd Geog)*
  UF Hospital violence
  BT Hospitals
  NT Violence in psychiatric
       hospitals
Violence in literature *(Not
  Subd Geog)*
       Here are entered works on vio-
       lence as a theme in literature, includ-
       ing violence in drama from a literary
       point of view. Works on violence as
       presented upon the stage are entered
       under Violence in the theater.
Violence in mass media *(Not
  Subd Geog) [P96.V5]*
  BT Mass media
  —Law and legislation
       (May Subd Geog)
Violence in motion pictures
       [PN1995.9V5]
  UF Violence in moving-
       pictures *[Former
       heading]*
  BT Motion pictures
Violence in nursing homes *(May
  Subd Geog)*
  BT Nursing Homes
Violence in popular culture
       (May Subd Geog)
       Here are entered works that discuss
       the representation of violence in pop-
       ular culture.
  BT Popular culture
Violence in prisons
  USE Prison violence
Violence in psychiatric hospitals
       (May Subd Geog)
       [RC439.4]
       Here are entered works on violence
       by patients or mental health personnel
       in psychiatric hospitals.
  BT Psychiatric hospital care
       Psychiatric hospitals
       Violence in hospitals

Violence in rabbinical literature
  BT Rabbinical literature
Violence in schools
  USE School violence
Violence in sports *(May Subd
  Geog) [GV706.7]*
  UF Sports—Violence
       Sports violence
  BT Sports
  —Law and legislation *(May
       Subd Geog)*
Violence in television
  USE Violence on television
Violence in the Bible
       [BS1199.V56]
Violence in the press
  USE Violence—Press coverage
Violence in the theater *(May
  Subd Geog)*
       Here are entered works on vio-
       lence as presented upon the stage.
       Works on violence as a theme in liter-
       ature, including violence in drama
       from a literary point of view, are
       entered under Violence in literature.
  BT Theater
  NT Stage fighting
Violence in the workplace *(May
  Subd Geog) [HF5549.5.E43]*
  UF Workplace violence
  BT Employee crimes
       Work environment
Violence in traffic
  USE Road rage
Violence in women *(May Subd
  Geog)*
  UF Violent women
  BT Women
Violence on television *(Not Subd
  Geog) [PN1992.8.V55]*
  UF Television violence
       TV violence
       Violence in television
       [Former heading]
  BT Television
  —Law and legislation *(May
       Subd Geog)*
Violence research
  USE Violence—Research
Violent crimes *(May Subd Geog)*
  UF Crimes, Violent
       Crimes of violence
  BT Crime
  —Cross-cultural studies
Violent deaths *(May Subd Geog)*
  BT Death—Causes
       Mortality
       Violence
  NT Accidents
       Asphyxia
       Drowning
       Homicide
       Murder
       Suicide
Violent women
  USE Violence in women

Once you have located the relevant LCSH, you can look for books under those headings in your online or card catalog. However, the LCSH may not be what you need when looking for articles in journals or magazines. The LCSH list is only one collection of search terms. Indexes for finding materials in journals or magazines may have their own subject headings, which may be different from the LCSH. For that reason, you should check the subject headings in each index before trying to use a particular term.

The subject headings you choose for locating material on the Internet are likely to vary even more widely from the standardized LCSH list than terms used in indexes. In addition, some Internet search tools may not take similar terms into account when indexing various articles. An article on *adolescence,* then, might not turn up in a subject search for the term *youth* unless the word *youth* occurs in the article. Common sense and your ability to think about synonyms will be your best guide in using subject headings to search the Internet. The following section also provides some useful information on such searches.

The Internet

Many different search tools are available for searching the Internet, and there will be more by the time you read this. At the time of this writing, there were two types of search tools: *subject directories* and *text indexes.*

Subject Directories. A subject directory lists categories of information from which you can then find particular sites containing information, opinions, and so on. A subject directory is a good choice when you want to find what is available on a broad topic. Here are some commonly used subject directories:

The Argus Clearinghouse <http://www.clearinghouse.net>

Library of Congress World Wide Web Home Page <http://lcweb.loc.gov>

WWW Virtual Library <http://www.w3.org/vl>

Yahoo! <http://www.yahoo.com>

You can think of a subject directory as a list of lists. Take the popular Yahoo!, for example. If you wanted to use Yahoo! to search for information on violence, you could follow its topic and subtopic directories until you found a list of Web sources on violence. You might decide to start with the *Social Science* directory, then go to the subdirectory *Sociology,* and then to the subdirectories *Criminology* and *Criminal Justice.* At that point, you would see a screen similar to the one shown on the next page.

After studying the screen on *Criminal Justice,* you might decide to check the sites of the Department of Justice and the National Clearinghouse for Justice Information and Statistics, both of which would probably contain more material than you could use.

Searching the Web with a subject directory like Yahoo! is partly a matter of common sense, partly of trial and error, and partly of knowing how a particular

An example of a Yahoo! screen.

topic might be classified. If you know that crime is often classified as a part of the discipline of sociology, then you have some idea of where to begin a search on violence. But a subject directory like Yahoo! is likely to have such material listed under other topics and subtopics as well. You could find information on violence by following these pathways, too:

Society and Culture → *Crime* → *Criminal Justice*

Society and Culture → *Crime* → *Juvenile*

Society and Culture → Crime → *Statistics*

News and Media → *Television* → *TV Violence*

To help you deal with the profusion of possible subjects to search, another resource is the *keyword* search available through most subject directories. With Yahoo!, for instance, you can find material on violence by searching with the keywords *violence* or with pairs of keywords, like *violence* AND *adolescents*. Using pairs of keywords in a search enables you to zero in on a more specific topic. If nothing else, a keyword search in a subject directory may help you identify the names of other subject directories that may contain related information on your topic.

Text Indexes.   Unlike a subject directory, a text index is designed to search for keywords in texts: it scans articles, reports, and other documents, looking for the keywords in a particular search, so it is a good choice when you want to see which sites contain a particular name, word, or phrase. Following are some popular text indexes:

Alta Vista <http://altavista.digital.com>—indexes texts of more than thirty million Web pages

Deja Com <http://www.deja.com>—searches news groups

Excite <http://www.excite.com>

Hotbot <http://www.hotbot.com>

Infoseek Guide <http://infoseek.go.com>

Lycos <http://www.lycos.com>—indexes texts of about twenty million Web documents

If you use a *keyword* search in a text index like Alta Vista, you may find more *hits,* or items, than you can sift through. Most text indexes, however, offer ways to limit a search and will offer possible ways of exploring further.

EVALUATING SOURCES

Evaluating sources, an extremely important element of research, is something that can—and should—become a natural part of the ongoing research process. You can develop a sense about what types of information come from what types of sources and how reliable the different types of sources are. The following four aspects of a publication—either print or electronic—can give you clues as to whether it is appropriate for your purpose. For further help on evaluating sources, see the Bedford/St. Martin's Web site at <http://www.bedfordbooks.com/english_research/eval/page2.htm>.

AUTHOR.   For many purposes, it is important to know whether the author is an authority on the subject. If you are looking for research on the economy or causes of violence, for example, you are probably also looking for an author who has scholarly credentials, such as a university position. If you are looking for samples of opinion, however, you may be less concerned with scholarly credentials and more concerned with whether a writer is knowledgeable about an issue or represents the opinion you are looking for.

PUBLISHER.   For print sources, you may want to consider the publisher's reputation. For instance, a book on the speech code debate published by a major university press might be more worthwhile than a book published by a company you do not recognize. University presses and some commercial publishers publish scholarly work in a number of academic areas. Some of these companies specialize in one or two disciplines and have earned good reputations in those disciplines over the years. Knowing about such companies may help you evaluate specific works.

Similarly, knowing the publisher of a journal or a magazine may help you evaluate a particular essay or report. An article on violence that appears in a magazine for the general public, for instance, may not contain the same kind of scholarly facts and opinions as a journal intended for academic readers. Facts from newspapers, too, should be checked for accuracy, since some have solid reputations for accurate reporting and others do not.

The same principles apply to electronic publishing. Some electronic publishing is done by individuals or organizations with highly credible reputations, but it is also easy for any person or group to publish opinions on the Web — with no fact checking, no screening for bias, and no credentials backing up the opinions. For this reason, you need to evaluate carefully all electronically published material. You can get some hints about what kind of group is sponsoring a Web site by checking its domain name. For instance, the FBI's Web site is located at <http://www.fbi.gov>. The *.gov* suffix indicates that it is a government site. Other common suffixes are *.com* for commercially sponsored sites, *.edu* for educationally sponsored sites, and *.org* for noncommercial or nonprofit sites. These suffixes can help you decide on how reliable an electronic site might be.

DATE OF PUBLICATION.   Date of publication is also important in evaluating the usefulness of a source. If you are interested in contemporary information, older sources may not be appropriate. Conversely, if you are interested in retrospective information, contemporary publications may not be helpful. If you are looking for recent facts or recent research, a general rule of thumb is to start with the most recent publications and work backward.

READERS AND PURPOSE.   Another clue you can use to evaluate a source is to consider the readers at whom it is aimed and its overall purpose. If a magazine or a TV show is intended to entertain the general public, then its facts and theories may be less reliable than a journal or a book that aims to inform interested readers about its research. Some publications may be biased because they are aimed at an audience that holds a particular set of opinions. For instance, a Web site that tries to appeal to readers in favor of either gun ownership or gun control will probably have a bias that you will want to take into account. Sometimes you can detect what sort of bias a Web site may have by noting the links it provides to further sites.

Your own common sense, some critical thinking, and these four clues should help you evaluate the usefulness and reliability of the sources you consider using.

DOCUMENTING SOURCES

Whenever you cite essays by other writers, as you do in the assigned essays in this book, you need to *document* your sources. Your *sources* are anything not your own—whether from books, journals, magazines, newspapers, or Internet material. If you find material that is common knowledge—such as facts that are available from many sources—you can assume that the material is commonly owned and does not require documentation. Sources that need to be documented include ideas, facts, or arguments coming from other people's work; ideas expressed to you orally in interviews or conversations; and facts and opinions found in electronic sources. The principle behind documenting sources is simple: you must acknowledge any idea or statement that comes from another person to give credit to that person.

Though the principle is simple, putting it into practice requires knowing how to quote, paraphrase, summarize, and refer to sources within the text of your essay, as well as how to list sources at the end of the essay. The following sections offer advice in all of these areas, including specific requirements for the style of the Modern Language Association (MLA) and that of the American Psychological Association (APA). For help with citing readings from this book, see "Citing Sources in *Writing the World*" at the end of this appendix.

CITING YOUR SOURCES

Once you have decided to use a source, you still must decide whether to paraphrase, summarize, or quote the source directly.

Quoting

When you quote a source, you use another writer's *exact* words in your own text. Quoting is most likely to be useful when the quotation is brief and the author's own words are particularly memorable. A good quotation may lend authority to a point of your own or provide evidence of someone's distinctive point of view. Regardless of your purpose, it is important to quote accurately.

In many instances, you will want to introduce a quote with a *signal phrase* of your own, such as these:

```
Dr. David Popenoe argues that "[ . . . ]"

As Deborah Tannen emphasizes, "[ . . . ]"

Isabel Wilkerson writes, "[ . . . ]"
```

The basic format, as in these three examples, may also be varied by placing the quotation at the beginning of the sentence, followed by information about the person being quoted. Here is one way that journalist Isabel Wilkerson (326) introduces information about an expert she quotes:

"We've been able to salvage people who otherwise would have been killed," said Dr. Robert McAfee, president-elect of the American Medical Association, who plans to focus his tenure on efforts against violence.

Signal phrases are discussed in more detail later in this section.

If quotations are longer than four lines (when you are using MLA style) or forty words (when you are using APA style), then they should be set off from the text by being indented from the left margin. The MLA requires that you indent such quotations ten spaces from the left; the APA requires a five-to-seven-space indentation. Indented quotations do not require quotation marks surrounding them unless you are quoting someone who is quoting someone else, as in dialogue in a short story. Anything you quote should appear exactly as it did in the original source—with two exceptions. First, you may occasionally want to shorten a quotation. This can be done by using a bracketed *ellipsis*—three periods with spaces in between—to indicate that something has been omitted from the original. When you omit a full sentence or more in the middle of a quotation, use a period before the bracketed ellipsis; if you omit the same at the end of the quotation, place the period after the brackets. Following are examples of how a sentence from E. J. Dionne Jr. might be shortened by using ellipses:

```
Dionne (260) quotes Holmes as saying, "Why should children
be hopelessly snared in a web of underprivilege [...]
through no fault of their own?"

Dionne (260) writes that "the current vogue for the
superiority of markets over government carries the risk
[...] of making the marketplace the sole arbiter of the
basic elements of a decent life [...]."
```

Second, you may sometimes need to change a word (a verb form or a pronoun) to make a quoted passage fit smoothly and grammatically into your own sentence or add a few words to clarify information. To do so, you can use *brackets,* square parentheses, to indicate what you have inserted or changed.

```
"Participation in serious violent offending behavior
(aggravated assault, forcible rape, and robbery) increases
[for all males] from ages 11 and 12 to ages 15 and 16,
then declines dramatically with advancing age" (Blumstein
18, quoted in Wilson 22).
```

Paraphrasing, Summarizing, and Avoiding Plagiarism

Paraphrasing is putting an author's ideas into your own words, usually in the order in which they were presented, whereas summarizing is putting a passage or idea into your own words in a significantly shorter version than the original.

Following, for instance, is a two-sentence summary of the reading from E. J. Dionne Jr.'s *They Only Look Dead* that you have seen in Chapter 4 and Appendix 1:

> After refuting conservatives' attacks on progressivism,
> Dionne argues that only an active government can protect
> individual rights and ensure opportunities for all
> citizens. He warns that conservatives' favored market
> solutions to social problems will harm many Americans.

A paraphrase allows you to note details of an original passage without quoting it, while a summary allows you to shorten a long passage and record only its main points. In both cases, though, you must still take care to acknowledge the source you are paraphrasing or summarizing. (See Appendix 1 for more detailed guidelines on writing summaries.)

In summarizing or paraphrasing, you must also be careful to avoid unintentional plagiarism. *Plagiarism* is using another person's words or ideas without acknowledging their authorship. To avoid plagiarism, you must, first, provide appropriate citations for all sources that you use. Second, you must acknowledge any language that you take more or less directly from your sources. If you take phrases or sentence structure directly from your sources without citing them, you may be guilty of plagiarism.

Here is a passage from a reading in Chapter 3 and an example of unacceptable paraphrase:

Original passage

Although the intentional infliction of emotional distress by communicative behavior has long been recognized in the common law as a tort—a wrong—for which one can be sued, the traditional interpretation of that tort by English and American courts was that the victim could win such a suit only when the stimulus had been followed by palpable injury, such as a heart attack or a physiological nervous breakdown (Haiman 30).

Unacceptable paraphrase

> Intentionally inflicting emotional distress by
> communication had long been recognized as wrong by the
> common law only if the wrong was followed by palpable
> injury (Haiman 30).

This paraphrase is unacceptable because it is too close to the language and structure of Haiman's original and does not acknowledge that much of Haiman's language is being used. (In addition, it does not clearly explain the point Haiman is making.)

Acceptable paraphrase

> Franklyn S. Haiman argues that common law traditionally
> penalized "communicative behavior" if it created signif-
> icant injury in the person at whom it was directed (30).

The acceptable paraphrase does not follow closely the wording of the source, and when the writer does use Haiman's own term—*communicative behavior*—she correctly surrounds it in quotation marks.

Integrating Source Materials into Your Own Text

Whether you are summarizing, paraphrasing, or quoting directly, you need to integrate source material smoothly, making it clear what the material contributes to your own essay. As noted earlier, a key device for aiding such integration is the *signal phrase*. Here are some examples of signal phrases used effectively:

```
As media scholar Todd Gitlin has argued, [...].

Government should [...], writes liberal columnist E. J.
Dionne.
```

As the preceding examples suggest, signal phrases are helpful whether you are introducing a direct quotation or presenting a writer's point of view in your own words. Signal phrases often establish a writer's credentials, as well as his or her bias or political beliefs; you may use them at the beginning, middle, or end of your own sentences.

The following verbs are often used in signal phrases. Note that some of them are effective for signaling that a writer is arguing (*insists, asserts, believes*) whereas others are helpful for more matter-of-fact reporting (*explains, notes, observes*).

acknowledges	implies
argues	insists
asserts	interprets
believes	notes
claims	objects
comments	observes
concludes	points out
criticizes	replies
declares	reports
disagrees	responds
discusses	says
emphasizes	states
explains	suggests
expresses	thinks
illustrates	writes

As you will see in the next section, signal phrases also help you to properly document your sources. A variety of different documentation styles are used by academics in disciplines ranging from literature to biology. The citations for readings in this book use MLA style, devised by the Modern Language Association for literature instructors. The rest of this appendix offers detailed information about using MLA or APA style within your essay.

DOCUMENTING SOURCES IN MLA STYLE

In MLA style, citations are included in an essay through a combination of *signal phrases* and *parenthetical references,* and complete sources appear in a list of *works cited* at the end of the essay. For further details about MLA style, consult the most recent edition of the *MLA Handbook for Writers of Research Papers.*

Citing Sources in Your Essay

If you mention the author's name in a signal phrase, include only the page number(s) you refer to in parentheses.

```
Deborah Tannen reports that women are often stereotyped as
talking more than men (74-75).
```

Note that a writer using pages 74–75 of Tannen's *You Just Don't Understand* directly will cite pages 74 and 75 in the parenthetical reference. However, if you are citing Tannen using the reading by her in *Writing the World,* you will still mention Tannen in your signal phrase (or in the parenthetical reference if there is no signal phrase), but the pages you refer to will be the appropriate pages in *Writing the World.* For further help, see pages 736–37.

If you do not use a signal phrase to name the author, include the author's last name and the page number in parentheses. Use no punctuation between the author's name and the page number and place the end period after the parentheses.

```
Some researchers have suggested that the baby-boom generation
[...] (Smith 43).
```

If you are citing a source by two or three authors, include all of the names either in a signal phrase or in parentheses.

```
Nelson and Cowan argue that an economic battle between
generations would be "dangerously disruptive" (59).
```

```
Some Midwest taxpayers in the 1990s refused to raise property
taxes to pay for education (Nelson and Cowan 59-60).
```

If you are citing more than one work by a particular author, include a shortened version of the title in parentheses or the complete title in a phrase.

```
Deborah Tannen reports that women [...] (You Just Don't
Understand 10).
```

If you quote material that is not taken from the original source, name the original author in your text and acknowledge in parentheses—by author(s) and page—the source of the quote, using the abbreviation *qtd. in.*

```
Pete Peterson, a Wall Street banker, says, "When [our
kids] understand the size of the bad check we are passing
them, they could [...] simply decide not to honor it at
all" (qtd. in Nelson and Cowan 607).
```

Preparing a List of Works Cited

A list of works cited appears at the end of an essay using MLA style. This list gives full publication information for each source and is organized alphabetically by the last name of the author. It should start on a new page. Leave a one-inch margin at the top of the page, and then center the heading "Works Cited." Do not indent the first line of each entry but do indent subsequent lines five spaces (or one-half inch). The MLA recommends the following formats for books and articles. For help on including *Writing the World* in your work-cited list, see pages 736–37.

Books

Book entries include the following information:

- **Author:** last name first, followed by a comma, and then the first name, followed by a period.
- **Title:** underlined, with all major words capitalized, and the full title followed by a period.
- **Publication information:** the city of publication followed by a colon, a short form of the publisher's name followed by a comma, the year of publication, and then a period.

A BOOK BY A SINGLE AUTHOR
```
Elgin, Suzette Haden. Genderspeak: Men, Women, and the
     Gentle Art of Verbal Self-Defense. New York: Wiley,
     1993.
```

TWO OR MORE BOOKS BY THE SAME AUTHOR.   Arrange entries alphabetically by title. After the first entry, use three hyphens instead of the author's name.

```
Boaz, David. Libertarianism: A Primer. New York: Free P,
     1997.

---, ed. The Libertarian Reader: Classic and
     Contemporary Readings from Lao-tzu to Milton
     Friedman. New York: Free P, 1997.
```

A BOOK BY TWO OR THREE AUTHORS.   After the first author, list subsequent authors' names in natural order.

> Frank, Robert H., and Philip J. Cook. <u>The Winner-Take-</u>
> <u>All Society</u>. New York: Free P, 1995.

AN ANTHOLOGY OR COMPILATION
> Newburn, Tim, and Elizabeth A. Stanko, eds. <u>Just Boys</u>
> <u>Doing Business? Men, Masculinities, and Crime</u>.
> London: Routledge, 1994.

A BOOK BY A CORPORATE AUTHOR
> American Civil Liberties Union. <u>Our Endangered Rights:</u>
> <u>The ACLU Report on Civil Liberties</u>. Ed. Norman
> Dorsen. New York: Pantheon, 1984.

A WORK IN AN ANTHOLOGY.   Start with the author(s) and the title of the selection, followed by the title of the book and its editor(s). List the selection's inclusive page numbers at the end of the entry.

> Henley, Nancy M., and Cheris Kramarae. "Gender, Power,
> and Miscommunication." <u>"Miscommunication" and</u>
> <u>Problematic Talk</u>. Ed. Nikolas Coupland, Howard
> Giles, and John M. Wiemann. Newbury Park: Sage,
> 1991. 18-43.

AN ARTICLE IN A REFERENCE BOOK
> Strasser, Michael W. "Liberalism." <u>Encyclopedia of</u>
> <u>Philosophy</u>. Ed. Paul Edwards. Vol. 4. New York:
> Macmillan, 1972.

AN EDITION OTHER THAN THE FIRST
> Kirk, Russell. <u>The Conservative Mind from Burke to</u>
> <u>Eliot</u>. 7th ed. Washington: Regnery, 1995.

A GOVERNMENT PUBLICATION. If no author is known, begin with the government's name, and then add the department or agency and any subdivision. For the U.S. government, the Government Printing Office (GPO) is usually the publisher.

> United States. Dept. of Justice. Office of Juvenile
> Justice and Delinquency Prevention. <u>Juvenile</u>
> <u>Offenders and Victims: 1996 Update on Violence</u>.
> Washington: GPO, 1996.

THE PUBLISHED PROCEEDINGS OF A CONFERENCE
> Hall, Kira, Mary Bucholtz, and Birch Moonwomon, eds.
> <u>Locating Power: Proceedings of the Second Berkeley</u>

<u>Women and Language Conference, April 4-5, 1992,</u>
<u>Berkeley, California</u>. Vols. 1 and 2. Berkeley:
Berkeley Women and Language Group, 1992.

Periodicals

A periodical is a publication that appears daily, weekly, monthly, or at other fixed intervals. Periodical entries include the following information:

- **Author:** last name first, followed by a comma, and then the first name, followed by a period.
- **Article title:** enclosed in quotation marks with all major words capitalized and followed by a period within the closing quotation marks.
- **Publication information:** the periodical title (underlined); followed by the volume number and, in some instances, the issue number, followed by the publication date. For journals, the year is in parentheses, followed by a colon and inclusive page numbers. For newspapers and magazines, the month or the day and the month appear before the year, and no parentheses are used. In MLA style, the month (except May, June, and July) is abbreviated.

AN ARTICLE IN A JOURNAL PAGINATED BY VOLUME.   Put the volume number after the journal title.

> Houston, Marsha, and Cheris Kramarae. "Speaking from
> Silence: Methods of Silencing and Resistance."
> <u>Discourse & Society</u> 2 (1991): 387-99.

AN ARTICLE IN A JOURNAL PAGINATED BY ISSUE.   Put a period after the volume number and add the issue number.

> McMasters, Paul. "Free Speech versus Civil Discourse:
> Where Do We Go from Here?" <u>Academe</u> 80.1 (1994): 8-13.

AN ARTICLE IN A MONTHLY MAGAZINE. Put the month(s) before the year and a colon before the page number(s).

> Straight, Susan. "The Gun in the Closet: The Arms Race
> Comes to Riverside, California." <u>Harper's</u> July
> 1994: 72+.

AN ARTICLE IN A WEEKLY MAGAZINE.   Add the date—in the order of day, month, year—using spaces between the elements.

> Shapiro, Bruce. "How the War on Crime Imprisons
> America." <u>Nation</u> 22 Apr. 1996: 14-21.

AN ARTICLE IN A NEWSPAPER.   Use a plus sign after the article's first page if the article does not appear on continuous pages.

McFadden, Robert D. "Two Youths Held in New Jersey in
Thrill-Killings of 2 Pizza Men." New York Times 22
Apr. 1997: A1+.

A LETTER TO THE EDITOR

Chapin, Daniel. Letter. "E-Mail Case Not Protected
Speech." Los Angeles Times 27 July 1997: B7.

A REVIEW.   Follow the author and title of the review with *Rev. of* and the title
and author of the work reviewed.

Dallek, Matthew. "The Conservative 1960s." Rev. of
Turning Right in the Sixties: The Conservative
Capture of the GOP, by Mary C. Brennan. Atlantic
Monthly Dec. 1995: 130-35.

A CARTOON.

Wilkinson, Signe. Cartoon. Los Angeles Times 17 Jan.
1997: B9.

Electronic Sources

The basic entry for Internet sources includes the following information:

- **Author:** last name first, with email address in angle brackets if it is given.
- **Title:** in quotation marks and followed by a period inside the closing quotation marks.
- **Publication information:** the date of publication, if available, followed by the address in angle brackets, and the date of access in parentheses, followed by a period.

WORLD WIDE WEB ADDRESSES.   Follow the author's name (if known) with the title of the document in quotation marks and the title of the complete work underlined. Include the date of publication, the date of access if known, and the address or URL (uniform resource locator) in angle brackets.

U.S. Department of Justice. "Criminal Offenders
Statistics." Bureau of Justice Statistics. 28 Apr.
1997 <http://www.ojp.usdoj.gov/bjs/crimoff.htm>

A MAILING LIST, NEWSGROUP, OR EMAIL CITATION.   Begin with the author's name, followed by the subject line in quotations, the date of the posting, the name of the forum, the date of access and, in angle brackets, the online address of the list's Internet site. If no Internet site is known, give the email address of the list's moderator or supervisor.

Chesler, David S. "Re: The Nanny President and Seat
Belts." Online posting. 18 Apr. 1997. Regulation

> Discussion Group. 21 July 1997
> <ne.politics,alt.politics.clinton.alt.politics.
> democrats.d,a>

SYNCHRONOUS COMMUNICATION. Begin with the name of the speaker(s) if known or the name of the site, followed by the title of the event in quotation marks, the date of the event, the forum for the communication, the date of access, and finally the URL in angle brackets.

> Smith, John. Online Seminar Discussion on Netiquette
> "Being Polite on the Net." LambdaMOO. 28 May 1996.
> <telnet://lambda.parc.xerox.edu:8888>.

Other Sources

A TELEVISION OR RADIO PROGRAM. List the title of the episode or segment, if appropriate, followed by the title of the program underlined, with writers, directors, or actors named as necessary. Then identify the network, followed by the local station and city and the broadcast date.

> "UFOs." Hard Copy. NBC. KNBC, Los Angeles. 14 Apr. 1998.

A PUBLISHED INTERVIEW. List the person interviewed, then the title of the interview in quotation marks, followed by the name of the interviewer and information about source and date of publication.

> Wilson, William Julius. "A Leading Scholar of Urban
> Poverty Has a Prescription for the Ghetto: Jobs." By
> Gerald Early. Mother Jones. Sept.-Oct. 1996. 20+.

A PERSONAL INTERVIEW. Give the name of the person interviewed, the kind of interview (personal interview, telephone interview), and the date.

> Lin, Julie. Personal interview. 2 Feb. 1998.

DOCUMENTING SOURCES IN APA STYLE

APA style is recommended by the American Psychological Association and is used in many of the social sciences. As in MLA style, in-text citations are included through a combination of signal phrases and parenthetical references, and complete sources appear in a list of *references* at the end of the essay. Note that APA citation conventions differ somewhat from those of MLA style. For further information on APA style, consult the most recent edition of the *Publication Manual of the American Psychological Association.*

Citing Sources in Your Essay

If you mention the author's name in a signal phrase, the year of publication appears in parentheses following the author's name.

```
Deborah Tannen (1990) argued that women tend to...
```

If you do not identify the author in a signal phrase, include the author's last name and the year of publication in parentheses. Insert a comma between the author's name and the year of publication and place the end period after the parentheses. When the material cited is a quotation, include the page number after the date.

```
Conversation, for women, tends to be "a language of
rapport: a way of establishing connections and negotiating
relationships" (Tannen, 1991, p. 77).
```

When citing a work by two to five authors, use all authors' last names the first time you mention them in the text, using *and* in a signal phrase but an ampersand (&) when the reference is in parentheses. If there are three or more authors, use *et al.* after the first mention in the text. If there are six or more authors, always use the first author's last name and *et al.* whenever you cite the work.

```
Delgado and Yun (1994) challenged four of the common
arguments....

Matsuda, Lawrence, Delgado, and Crenshaw (1993) emphasized
the harmful effect of "words that wound."... Furthermore,
Matsuda et al. emphasized....

Recently, critical race theory has suggested that hate
speech is harmful (Matsuda, Lawrence, Delgado, & Crenshaw,
1993).
```

When referring to material that is not taken from the original source, name the original author in your text and acknowledge in parentheses — by author, date, and page — the source in which the material is cited.

```
As Alfred Blumstein has found,...(as cited in Wilson,
1996, p. 359).
```

When referring to two or more sources within the same parentheses, list the authors' last names in alphabetical order, separated by semicolons.

```
Recent writers who have suggested that women talk
differently from men (Gray, 1992; Tannen, 1991) have been
criticized by some feminists.
```

Preparing a List of References

An alphabetized reference list at the end of an essay gives complete publication information for the sources cited. The reference list should start on a new page. Leave a one-inch margin at the top of the page, and then center the heading "References." Do not indent the first line of each entry but do indent subsequent lines five spaces (or one-half inch).

AUTHOR: Last name(s) first, followed by a comma. Use initials for first and middle names, followed by a period.

PUBLICATION DATE: This information appears in parentheses immediately following the author(s) name(s). For books, use year only; for periodicals, also include month or month and day. In APA style, all months are spelled out in full.

TITLE: Underline titles and subtitles of books and names of periodicals. Do not enclose titles of articles in quotation marks. Capitalize only the first word of a book's or an article's title and subtitle and all proper names but capitalize all major words of a periodical title.

PUBLICATION INFORMATION: For a book, list city of publication, followed by a colon and publisher's name. For a periodical, give the periodical title, underlined and followed by a comma; the volume number and, in some instances, the issue number, both underlined and followed by a comma. For periodicals, inclusive page numbers follow publication information, separated by a comma. For articles or chapters in books, page numbers—preceded by "p." for a single page and "pp." for multiple pages—appear in parentheses before publication information, separated from the latter by a period.

If you list two or more works by the same author published in the same year, arrange the entries alphabetically by title and add the letters *a, b, c,* and so on to the year of publication in parentheses.

    Goodwin, M. H. (1990a).

    Goodwin, M. H. (1990b).

Books

A BOOK BY A SINGLE AUTHOR

    Matsuda, M. J. (1996). Where is your body? and other
        essays on race and gender. Boston: Beacon.

TWO OR MORE BOOKS BY THE SAME AUTHOR. Arrange the entries in order of publication, with the earliest publications first.

    Dionne, E. J. (1991). Why Americans hate politics. New
        York: Simon & Schuster.

    Dionne, E. J. (1996). They only look dead: Why
        progressives will dominate the next political era.
        New York: Simon & Schuster.

A BOOK BY TWO OR MORE AUTHORS.   Invert all authors' names, use commas to separate authors, and use an ampersand (&) instead of the word *and* before the last author. For an edited book, give the editors' names in the author position, followed by *Ed.* or *Eds.* in parentheses after the last editor's name.

> Crane, E. H., & Boaz, D. (Eds.). (1989). An American vision: Policies for the '90s. Washington, DC: Cato Institute.

A WORK IN AN EDITED COLLECTION

> Newman, K. S. (1991). "Uncertain seas." In A. Wolfe (Ed.), America at century's end (pp. 122-125). Berkeley: University of California Press.

AN ANTHOLOGY OR COMPILATION

> Bucholtz, M., Liang, A. C., Sutton, L. A., & Hines, C. (1994). Cultural performances: Proceedings of the Third Berkeley Women and Language Conference. Berkeley, CA: Berkeley Women and Language Group.

AN ENCYCLOPEDIA OR DICTIONARY

> Furet, F., & Ozouf, M. (1989). "Rights of Man." A critical dictionary of the French revolution (A. Goldhammer, Trans.). (pp. 818-828). Cambridge, MA: Harvard University Press. (Original work published 1988)

AN EDITION OTHER THAN THE FIRST

> McElroy, W. (Ed.). (1991). Freedom, feminism, and the state: An overview of individualist feminism (2nd ed.). New York: Holmes & Meier.

Periodicals

AN ARTICLE IN A JOURNAL PAGINATED BY VOLUME

> Delgado, R., & Yun, D. H. (1994). Pressure valves and bloodied chickens: Paternalistic objections to hate speech regulation. California Law Review, 82, 871-892.

AN ARTICLE IN A JOURNAL PAGINATED BY ISSUE

> Sharpe, Myron E. (1999). Mismanaging companies. Journal of Organizational Behavior, 59(3), 129-136.

AN ARTICLE IN A MAGAZINE

> Straight, S. (1994, July 10). The gun in the closet: The arms race comes to Riverside, California. Harper's, 72-83.

AN ARTICLE IN A DAILY NEWSPAPER

> Goldberg, C. (1997, February 3). Family killings jolt a tranquil town. The New York Times, p. A8.

AN EDITORIAL OR LETTER TO THE EDITOR

> Kitsikopoulos, H. (1996, August). Working hard, hardly working [Letter to the editor]. Harper's, 4.

A REVIEW

> Dalleck, M. (1995). [Review of the book Turning right in the sixties: The conservative capture of the GOP]. Atlantic Monthly, 276, 130-135.

Electronic Sources.   As of this writing, the American Psychological Association has changed some of the recommendations given in their *Publication Manual* for citing electronic sources. For APA's latest guidelines on citing electronic sources, visit <http://www.apa.org/journals/webref.html>.

Other Sources

A TELEVISION OR RADIO PROGRAM

> Harrison, Mimi (Producer). (1998). Hard copy. Los Angeles: KNBC.

CITING SOURCES IN *WRITING THE WORLD*

As you develop the essays for assignments in this book, you will need to cite the readings, your primary source of research materials. You may also want to cite materials in the book's introductions and readings headnotes. This section demonstrates how to create an in-text citation and a list of works cited for these two situations.

Citing Readings in *Writing the World*

If readings in this book supply all the sources for your essay, you will cite these sources as works in an anthology or edited collection. There are two parts to citing a work from an anthology or any other kind of publication: (1) a very brief citation within your essay, called an in-text citation; and (2) a full citation of the source in a list of works cited at the end of your essay. Here is an example of *in-text citation* of the reading in Chapter 6 by Graham Knight:

> The most important features of tabloid journalism are its "substantive emphasis on coverage of events and issues concerning moral disorder" and "a stylistic emphasis on the subjective in news coverage" (Knight 479).

Following MLA guidelines here, the student cites Knight as the source of the quotation and indicates the page number in this anthology, that is, *Writing the World,* from which the quotation is taken.

For every in-text citation, there has to be a corresponding item in the *list of works cited* at the end of the essay. To create this correspondence for the in-text citation in the previous paragraph, the student, still following MLA guidelines, constructs this item for the list of works cited:

> Knight, Graham. "The Reality Effects of Tabloid
>   Television News." Writing the World. Eds. Charles
>   R. Cooper and Susan Peck MacDonald. New York:
>   Bedford/St. Martin's, 2000. 478-83.

The page numbers indicate the page range of the Knight essay in this anthology. You can find another example of this type of list-of-works-cited entry under "A Work in an Anthology" in the "Books" section of the MLA guidelines or under "A Work in an Edited Collection" in the "Books" section of the APA guidelines earlier in this appendix.

Citing Materials Written by the Authors of *Writing the World*

If you want to use information from this book's introductions or readings headnotes, do not cite facts about authors, titles, or information that most readers would consider common knowledge. You should, however, document any explanations or interpretations that you make use of in your essay, whether you paraphrase, summarize, or quote them. Here is an example of an in-text citation from a student essay:

> Cooper and MacDonald define families with a relatively high
> standard of living as those who "own a home; drive a late-
> model car or two; contribute to children's college
> expenses; take vacations; have job security, a retirement
> plan, adequate health coverage; and may, in addition, have
> some savings" (534).

The student names Cooper and MacDonald as the authors of the quotation and indicates the page number in this book where the quoted material appears.

For the in-text citation, the student—here following MLA style—creates this item in the list of works cited at the end of the essay:

> Cooper, Charles R. and Susan Peck MacDonald. Writing the
>   World. New York: Bedford/St. Martin's, 2000.

Earlier in this appendix, you can find further examples of this list-of-works-cited item under "A Book by Two or Three Authors" in the "Books" section of the MLA guidelines or under "A Book by Two or More Authors" in the "Books" section of the APA guidelines.

Acknowledgments (*continued from copyright page*)

David Boaz. "The Coming Libertarian Age" from Chapter 1, pp. 2–9, 16–19, in *Libertarianism: A Primer* by David Boaz. Copyright © 1997 by David Boaz. Abridged with the permission of the Free Press, a Division of Simon & Schuster.

Leon F. Bouvier and Carol J. De Vita. "The Baby Boom—Entering Midlife." Originally titled "Generational Size and Well-Being" by Leon F. Bouvier and Carol J. De Vita from *Population Bulletin* 6, November 1991, pp. 10–11. Reprinted by permission of Population Reference Bureau, Washington, D.C.

Krista Bradford. "The Big Sleaze." From *Rolling Stone*, February 18, 1993. Copyright © 1993 Straight Arrow Publishers, Inc. Reprinted by permission. All rights reserved.

Keith Bradshaw. "Skilled Workers Watch Their Jobs Migrate Overseas" from *The New York Times*, February 28, 1995, A1, C6. Copyright © 1995 by The New York Times Company. Reprinted by permission.

Sam Brownback. "A New Contract With America." From *Policy Review*, March/April 1996, pp. 16–20. © 1996 Policy Review. Reprinted by permission of The Heritage Foundation.

Carl M. Cannon. "Honey, I Warped the Kids: The Argument for Eliminating Movie and TV Violence." © 1994 Foundation for National Progress. Reprinted with permission from *Mother Jones* magazine.

Janice Castro. "Disposable Workers." *Time*, March, 29, 1993. © 1993 Time, Inc. Reprinted by permission.

Richard Delgado and David H. Yun. "Pressure Valves and Bloodied Chickens: Paternalistic Objections to Hate Speech Regulation." From *California Law Review* 82 (1994): 871–92. Reprinted by permission of the author and the University of California Press Law Journals.

Sam Dillon. "A 20-Year G.M. Parts Migration to Mexico" from *The New York Times*, June 24, 1998, p. c1+. Copyright © 1998 by The New York Times Company. Reprinted by permission.

E. J. Dionne, Jr. Excerpts from *They Only Look Dead: Why Progressives Will Dominate the Next Political Era*, pp. 286–299. Copyright © 1996 by E. J. Dionne, Jr. Reprinted with the permission of Simon & Schuster.

Timothy Egan. "From Adolescent Angst to Shooting Up Schools" from *The New York Times*, June 14, 1998, A1+. Copyright © 1998 by The New York Times Company. Reprinted by permission.

Jib Fowls. Excerpt from *Why Viewers Watch Television* by Jib Fowls, pp. 239–248. Copyright © 1992 by Sage Publications. Reprinted by permission of Sage Publications, Inc.

Ralph Frammolino. "Suit Forces U.C. Riverside to Rescind Fraternity Penalty." Originally titled "University of California, Riverside, Forced to Drop Punishment of Fraternity for T-Shirts Caricaturing Mexicans" by Ralph Frammolino. From the *Los Angeles Times*, November 11, 1993. Copyright © 1993 Los Angeles Times. Reprinted by permission.

Milton Friedman. Excerpt from pp. 199–201 in *Capitalism and Freedom*. © 1962 by Milton Friedman. Reprinted by permission of The University of Chicago Press.

Henry Louis Gates, Jr. "Let Them Talk." Originally published in *The New Republic*. Copyright © 1993 by Henry Louis Gates, Jr. Reprinted with permission of author.

Susan B. Gellman. Excerpt from *Sticks and Stones Can Put You in Jail, but Can Words Increase Your Sentence?* Originally published in 39 UCLAL. Rev. 333. Copyright © 1991 The Regents of the University of California. All rights reserved. Reprinted by permission of Susan B. Gellman and the University of California Law Review.

Thomas Geoghegan. Excerpt from *The Secret Lives of Citizens* by Thomas Geoghegan. Copyright © 1998 by Thomas Geoghegan. Reprinted by permission of Pantheon Books, a division of Random House, Inc.

Todd Gitlin. "The Symbolic Crusade against Media Violence Is a Confession of Despair." Originally titled "Imagebusters: The Hollow Crusade Against TV Violence." *The American Prospect*, No. 16, Winter 1994, pp. 42–49. Reprinted with permission of the author and The American Prospect.

Elizabeth Gleik. "Tower of Psychobabble." *Time*, June 16, 1997, p. 68+. © 1997 Time, Inc. Reprinted by permission.

John Gottman. "The Two Marriages: His and Hers" from *Why Marriages Succeed or Fail* by John Gottman, Ph.D., pp. 173–201. Copyright © 1994 by John Gottman. Reprinted with the permission of Simon & Schuster, Inc.

John Gray. Excerpt from *Men Are from Mars, Women Are from Venus* by John Gray. Copyright © 1992 by John Gray. Reprinted by permission of HarperCollins Publishers, Inc.

Andrew Hacker. "Meet the Median Family." *Time*, January 29, 1996. © 1996 Time, Inc. Reprinted by permission.

Franklyn S. Haiman. Excerpt from Chapter 4: "Hate Speech," pp. 26–34. Originally published in *Speech Acts and the First Amendment* by Franklyn S. Haiman. Copyright © 1991 by The Board of Trustees, Southern Illinois University. Reprinted by permission of the publisher.

Amy Harmon. "Caltech Student's Expulsion over E-Mail Contents Raises Concerns." *Los Angeles Times*, November 15, 1995, D1, D6–7. Copyright © 1995 Los Angeles Times. Reprinted by permission.

Michael de Courcy Hinds. "A Campus Case: Speech or Harassment?" *The New York Times,* May 15, 1993, 6. Copyright © 1993 by The New York Times Company. Reprinted by permission.

Tony Horwitz. "Some Who Lost Jobs in Early '90s Recession Find a Hard Road Back" from *The Wall Street Journal,* June 26, 1998, p.A1+. © 1998 Dow Jones and Company, Inc. Republished by permission of Dow Jones, Inc. via Copyright Clearance Center, Inc. All rights reserved worldwide.

Frank Houston. "TV Tabs' New Tone." *Columbia Journalism Review,* January/February 1996. © 1996 by Columbia Journalism Review. Reprinted by permission.

Sanford M. Jacoby. "Most Workers Find a Sense of Security in Corporate Life" from *The Los Angeles Times,* September 7, 1998, p. B1+. Copyright © 1998 by Sanford M. Jacoby. Reprinted by permission of the author.

Jacqueline R. Kasun. "Condom Nation: Government Sex Education Promotes Teen Pregnancy." From *Policy Review,* Spring 1994, pp. 79, 81–82. © 1994 Policy Review. Reprinted by permission of The Heritage Foundation.

Russell Kirk. "Who Are the Conservatives?" from *A Program for Conservatives* by Russell Kirk. Copyright © 1954 by Regnery Gateway. All rights reserved. Reprinted by special permission of Regnery Publishing, Inc., Washington, D.C.

Graham Knight. "The Reality Effects of Tabloid Television." From *Communication for and Against Democracy* by Marc Raboy and Peter A. Bruck, eds., pp. 111–129. Copyright © 1989 Marc Raboy and Peter A. Bruck. Reprinted by permission of Black Rose Books, Montreal, Quebec.

Andrew Lam. "Love, Money, Prison, Sin, Revenge." *Los Angeles Times* magazine, March 13, 1994, pp. 24–30. Copyright © 1994 by Andrew Lam. Reprinted by permission of the author.

Charles R. Lawrence III. "If He Hollers Let Him Go: Regulating Racist Speech on Campus." Excerpted from *Duke Law Journal,* 431 (1990): 431–83. Reprinted by permission of the author.

Robert Lichter, Linda S. Lichter and Stanley Rothman. Excerpt from *Prime Time: How TV Portrays American Culture,* pp. 404, 410–420. Copyright © 1994 by Linda S. Lichter and Stanley Rothman. Reprinted by permission of Regnery Publishing, Inc.

Kristin Luker. Excerpt from *Dubious Conceptions: The Politics of Teenage Pregnancy* by Kristin Luker, pp. 180–190. Copyright © 1996 by the President and Fellows of Harvard College. Reprinted by permission of the publisher, Harvard University Press.

Nathan McCall. "Falling." From *Makes Me Wanna Holler* by Nathan McCall. Copyright © 1994 by Nathan McCall. Reprinted by permission of Random House, Inc.

Michael W. McConnell. "America's First 'Hate' Speech Regulation." From *Constitutional Commentary 9* (1992): 17–23. Reprinted with permission of Constitutional Commentary.

Paul McMasters. "Free Speech versus Civil Discourse." From *Academe: Bulletin of the AAUP,* Vol. 80, No. 1, January/February 1994, pp. 8–13. Reprinted with permission of the author and Academe.

Jeffrey Madrick. Excerpt from *The End of Affluence* by Jeffrey Madrick. Copyright © 1995 by Jeffrey Madrick. Reprinted by permission of Random House, Inc.

Myron Magnet. Excerpt from *The Dream and the Nightmare: The Sixties Legacy to the Underclass* by Myron Magnet. Copyright © 1993 by Myron Magnet. Reprinted by permission of William Morrow & Company, Inc.

Mike A. Males. Excerpt from *The Scapegoat Generation: America's War on Adolescents* by Mike A. Males, pp. 101–121. Copyright © 1996 by Mike A. Males. Reprinted with the permission of Common Courage Press.

Mari J. Matsuda. "Assaultive Speech and Academic Freedom." From *Where Is Your Body? And Other Essays of Race and Gender* by Mari J. Matsuda. Copyright © 1996 by Mari J. Masuda. Reprinted by permission of the author. *We Won't Go Back: Making the Case for Affirmative Action* by Mari J. Matsuda and Charles Lawrence III was published in 1997.

Lawrence R. Mischel, Jared Bernstein, and John Schmitt. Excerpt from *The State of Working America 1998–1999* by Lawrence R. Mischel, Jared Bernstein, and John Schmitt, eds. Copyright © 1999 Cornell University Press. Used by permission of the publisher.

Rob Nelson and Jon Cowan. Excerpt from *Revolution X: A Survival Guide for Our Generation* by Rob Nelson and Jon Cowan. Copyright 1994 by Rob Nelson and Jon Cowan. Used by permission of Viking Penguin, a division of Penguin Books USA Inc.

Susan Page. "Essential Traits of Couples Who Thrive" from *Now That I'm Married, Why Isn't Everything Perfect* by Susan Page. Copyright © 1994 by Susan Page. Reprinted by permission of Little, Brown & Company, Inc.

Katha Pollitt. "Are Women Morally Superior to Men?" Excerpted from *The Nation*, 28 December 1992, pp. 799–807. Reprinted by permission.

David Popenoe. "Life Without Father: America's Greatest Social Catastrophe." From *Policy Review*, Winter 1990, pp. 40–45. © 1990 Policy Review. Reprinted by permission of The Heritage Foundation.

Robert Reich. "America's Anxious Class." From *New Perspectives Quarterly*, Winter 1995, pp. 28–30. Reprinted by permission of Blackwell Publishers.

Jeremy Rifkin. Excerpt from *The End of Work*. Copyright © 1995 by Jeremy Rifkin. Reprinted by permission of Jeremy P. Tarcher, Inc. a division of The Putnam Publishing Group.

Max Robins. "Here Comes the News Punks." From *Channels*, September 1988, pp. 39–43. Reprinted by permission.

Luis J. Rodriguez. Excerpt from *Always Running/La Vida Loca: Gang Days in L.A.* by Luis J. Rodriguez (Curbstone Press, 1993). Reprinted with permission of Curbstone Press.

Roger Rosenblatt. "The Triumph of Liberalism." *The New York Times* magazine, January 14, 1996, pp. 33–35. Copyright © 1996 by The New York Times Company. Reprinted by permission.

Barbara Rudolph. Excerpt from *Disconnected: How Six People from AT & T Discovered the New Meaning of Work in a Downsized Corporate America* by Barbara Rudolph. Copyright © 1998 by Barbara Rudolph. Reprinted with the permission of The Free Press, a Division of Simon & Schuster, Inc.

Andrea Sachs. "Tabloid TV with a Latin Accent." © 1993 by Columbia Journalism Review. Reprinted from *Columbia Journalism Review*, May/June 1993.

Juliet Schor. "The Downshifters Next Door" from *The Overspent American* by Juliet Schor. Copyright © 1998 by Juliet Schor. Reprinted by permission of Basic Books, a member of Perseus Books, L.L.C.

Sue Shellenbarger. "Future Work Policies May Focus on Teens, Trimming Workloads." From *The Wall Street Journal*, December 30, 1998, p.B1+. Republished by permission of Dow Jones, Inc. via Copyright Clearance Center, Inc. © 1998 Dow Jones & Company, Inc. All rights reserved worldwide.

Timothy Shiell. Excerpt from Chapter 7 in *Campus Hate Speech on Trial* by Timothy Shiell, pp. 153–163. Copyright © 1998 by Timothy Shiell. Reprinted by permission of the University Press of Kansas.

Thomas Sowell. Excerpt from *The Vision of the Anointed: Self-Congratulation as a Basis for Social Policy*. Copyright © 1995 by Thomas Sowell. Reprinted by permission of Basic Books, a division of HarperCollins Publishers, Inc.

Steven D. Stark. "Glued to the Set" from *Entertainment Tonight and the Expansion of the Tabloid Celebrity Culture*, pp. 249–253 in *Glued to the Set: The 60 Television Shows and Events That Made Us Who We Are Today* by Steven D. Stark. Copyright © 1997 by Steven D. Stark. Reprinted with the permission of The Free Press, a Division of Simon & Schuster, Inc.

Susan Straight. "The Gun in the Closet." Copyright © 1994 by *Harper's Magazine*. All rights reserved. Reproduced from the July issue by special permission.

Deborah Tannen. "Put Down That Paper and Talk to Me!" Excerpt from *You Just Don't Understand* by Deborah Tannen. Copyright © 1990 by Deborah Tannen. Reprinted by permission of William Morrow & Company, Inc.

Senta Troemel-Ploetz. "Selling the Apolitical." Excerpted from *Discourse & Society* 2.4 (1991): 489–502. Reprinted by permission of Sage Publications, Ltd.

Louis Uchitelle. "Downsizing Comes Back, but the Outcry Is Muted" from *The New York Times,* December 7, 1998, A1+ (with graphics). Copyright © 1998 by The New York Times Company. Reprinted by permission.

Samuel Walker. "The Campus Speech Codes in the Federal Courts." Reprinted from *Hate Speech: The History of An American Controversy* by Samuel Walker. © by the University of Nebraska Press. Reprinted by permission of the University of Nebraska Press.

Philip Weiss. "Bad Rap for TV Tales." Reprinted from *Columbia Journalism Review,* May/June 1989. © 1989 by Columbia Journalism Review. Reprinted with permission of the author and Columbia Journalism Review. Philip Weiss is a columnist for *The New York Observer* and a novelist.

Isabel Wilkerson. "Two Boys, a Debt, a Gun, a Victim: The Face of Violence." *The New York Times,* May 16, 1994. Copyright © 1994 by The New York Times Company. Reprinted by permission.

Rita Williams. "The Streets of Los Angeles." From *Utne Reader,* March/April 1993, pp. 60–61. Excerpted from *LA Weekly,* December 6, 1991. Reprinted by permission.

William Julius Wilson. Excerpt from *When Work Disappears.* Copyright © 1996 by William Julius Wilson. Reprinted by permission of Alfred A. Knopf Inc.

Edward N. Wolff. "How the Pie Is Sliced: America's Growing Concentration of Wealth" from *The American Prospect,* Summer 1995: 58–64. Copyright © 1995 The American Prospect, P.O. Box 383080, Cambridge, MA 02138.

Illustrations

Cover
©Karl Petzke 1994.

Chapter 5
© Anchorage Daily News: Evan Ramsey, February 1997.

© AP/Wide World Photos: Barry Loukaitis, August 25, 1997; Mitchell Johnson, March 27, 1998, "Will We Ever Learn?" photo of flower memorial, Thurston High School, Springfield, Oregon, May 21, 1998; Kipland Kinkel, May 22, 1998; Luke Woodham, June 5, 1998.

© 1998 The Courier-Journal: Michael Carneal, December 17, 1998.

© Michael Ramirez/Copley News Service: "Why?" Reprinted in the *Los Angeles Times,* Tuesday, March 31, 1998, B9.

Chapter 7
"The American Dream" cartoon by Scott Bateman. © Batetoon@aol.com. From *Z Magazine,* July/August 1996, p. 16. Reprinted by permission of Scott Bateman.

"Warning Labels Illustration" cartoon by Henry Payne. From *Reason* Magazine, January 1997. © 1999 by the Reason Foundation, 3415 S. Sepulveda Blvd, Suite 400, Los Angeles, CA 90034. Reprinted with permission.

"Investors are making more . . ." cartoon by Joel Pett. From the *Los Angeles Times,* February 24, 1997, p. B5. Reprinted with special permission of North American Syndicate.

"RALL" cartoon. © 1998 Ted Rall. Reprinted with permission of Universal Press Syndicate. All rights reserved.

"Now remember, you no longer . . ." cartoon by Harley L. Schwadron. From *National Review,* May 6, 1996. © 1996 Harry L. Schwadron. Reprinted by permission.

"TOLES" cartoon. © 1997 The Buffalo News. Reprinted with permission of Universal Press Syndicate. All rights reserved.

"Good News Sir" cartoon. © Signe Wilkinson/Cartoonists & Writers Syndicate. Reprinted in the *Philadelphia Daily News.*

"Trickle Down Economics" cartoon by Matthew Wuerker. © Matthew Wuerker. From *Chaos or Community* by Holly Sklar. Published by South End Press (1995), p. 5. Reprinted by permission of Matthew Wuerker.

Index